How to Do Just About Anything

Solve **Problems**, Save **Money**, Have **Fun**

Reader's Digest

PUBLISHED BY THE READER'S DIGEST ASSOCIATION, INC.
MONTREAL · NEW YORK

boil an egg, bandage a leg, pack a suitcase ...
As it says on the cover, **this book will show you how to do just about anything.** And we mean *anything:* 1,001 things to help you handle an emergency, improve your home and garden, cook basics (plus yummy extras), do repairs, play games—do surprising things you never realized you wanted to do. It's all here: the fun and the need-to-know, the modern and the traditional, the easy and the challenging—in clear words and helpful pictures. Dive into this ocean of information and discover how to ...

... drop an **anchor** ▪ identify **animal tracks** ▪ get rid of **aphids** ▪ set up an **aquarium** ▪ win an **argument** ▪ prepare an **artichoke** ▪ survive an **avalanche** ▪ make a **balloon animal** ▪ trim a **beard** ▪ choose **beef** cuts ▪ pour a **beer** ▪ make **blinis** ▪ build a **bonfire** ▪ tie a **bow tie** ▪ bake **bread** ▪ play **bridge** ▪ soothe **burns** ▪ sew on a **button** ▪ keep **cacti** alive ▪ decorate a **cake** ▪ back up a **camper** ▪ **carve** meat ▪ uncork **champagne** ▪ play **chess** ▪ use **chopsticks** ▪ open a **coconut** ▪ **complain** effectively ▪ make **compost** ▪ give **CPR** ▪ dress a **crab** ▪ relieve **cramps** ▪ follow **cricket** ▪ learn to **crochet** ▪ win at **croquet** ▪ do **cross-stitch** ▪ work out cryptic **crosswords** ▪ use **crutches** ▪ cook **curry** ▪ bandage a **cut** ▪ weave a **daisy chain** ▪ **darn** a sock ▪ impress your **date** ▪ groom a **dog** ▪ **draw** a face ▪ interpret **dreams** ▪ build a **drystone** wall ▪ **dye** clothes ▪ calculate the date of **Easter** ▪ use **eBay** ▪ observe an **eclipse** safely ▪ separate an **egg** ■ do **embroidery** ■ **exfoliate** skin ■ shape **eyebrows** ■ **face-paint** a child ■ draw up a **family tree** ■ fly a **flag** ■ get a **flight** upgrade ■ follow **football** ■ apply **foundation** ■ throw a **Frisbee** ■ thaw out **frozen pipes** ■ make **fudge** ■ cut **fuel consumption** ■ make **garnishes** ■ deal with a **gas leak** ■ look after **goldfish** ■ understand **golf** ■ make great **gravy** ■ create **greeting cards** ■ tune a **guitar** ■ clear **gutters** ■ cure a **hangover** ■ make a paper **hat** ■ deal with a **heart attack** ■ perform the **Heimlich maneuver** ■ stop **hiccups** ■ walk in **high heels** ■ play **hopscotch** ■ ride a **horse** ■ protect your **identity** ■ soothe **indigestion** ■ make your mark in an **interview** ■ send an **invitation** ■ unfreeze an **iPod** ■ make **jam** ■ remove lids from **jars** ■ beat **jet lag** ■ do the **jive** ■ tell a **joke** ■ master **judo** moves ■ learn to **juggle** ■ prepare **kebabs** ■ fly a **kite** ■ get **knitting** ■ sharpen **knives** ■ tie **knots** ■ choose **lamb** cuts ■ install a **lawn** ■ compose a **limerick** ■ apply **lipstick** ■ design a **logo** ■ perform **magic tricks** ■ peel a **mango** ■ play **marbles** ■ make great **mashed potatoes** ■ give a **massage** ■ choose a **mattress** ■ chair a **meeting** ■ treat **migraines** ■ win at **Monopoly** ■ create a **mosaic** ■ grow **mustard and watercress** ■ paint **nails** ■ remember **names** ■ fold a **napkin** ■ thread a **needle** ■ stop a

nosebleed ▪ make an **omelet** ▪ appreciate **opera** ▪ care for **orchids** ▪ open an **oyster** ▪ fold a **paper plane** ▪ **park** a car ▪ choose a **password** ▪ lay garden **paving** ▪ take good **photos** ▪ play a **piano** tune ▪ learn **Pilates** ▪ create a **podcast** ▪ play **poker** ▪ choose **pork** cuts ▪ grow **potatoes** ▪ make a **presentation** ▪ take a **pulse** ▪ carve a **pumpkin** ▪ get out of **quicksand** ▪ dance the **quickstep** ▪ **quilt** a cover ▪ host a **quiz night** ▪ handle a **rabbit** ▪ cook perfect **rice** ▪ build a **rocket** ▪ read **Roman numerals** ▪ climb a **rope ladder** ▪ grow **roses** ▪ place **roulette** bets ▪ **row** a boat ▪ build a **sand castle** ▪ rescue **sauces** ▪ win at **Scrabble** ▪ learn **semaphore** ▪ build a **shelter** ▪ fold a **shirt** ▪ lace **shoes** ▪ prune **shrubs** ▪ **skip** rocks ▪ get a good night's **sleep** ▪ improvise a **sling** ▪ stop **smoking** ▪ build a **snowman** ▪ dig **soil** ▪ bake a **soufflé** ▪ remove **stains** ▪ cook the perfect **steak** ▪ combat **stress** ▪ pack a **suitcase** ▪ set a **table** ▪ do the **tango** ▪ make a great cup of **tea** ▪ understand **teenagers** ▪ grow **tomatoes** ▪ sharpen **tools** ▪ learn to **type** ▪ repair an **umbrella** ▪ digitize old **videos** ▪ grow **vines** ▪ know your **vitamins** ▪ conserve **water** ▪ paint a **watercolor** ▪ build a **website** ▪ control **weeds** ▪ store **wine** ▪ **wrap** up a gift ▪ try the **xylophone** ▪ learn **yoga** positions ▪ perform **yo-yo** tricks ▪ make a **Yorkshire** pudding ▪ upload a video to **YouTube** ▪ repair a faulty **zipper** ▪ recognize signs of the **zodiac** ... plus hundreds and hundreds of other essential (and less than essential) skills and solutions, old and new.

CONTENTS

A-Z of just about anything

A

make Address labels on your computer

Address labels are a great time-saver if you have to send letters out to lots of people—for a charity drive, say, or if you're doing your Christmas cards. Using Microsoft software, all the work is done via a blank Word document. Open the Project Gallery, click on "**New**,"then select "**Labels.**" Click on "**Mailing Label Wizard.**" Follow the instructions to create a list of addresses for printing.

The labels themselves come in many sizes, each with its own code number. Word lists the most commonly used brands and sizes; when you select the corresponding code, your document will automatically be formatted to fit.

build Aerobic exercise into your life

Regular, energetic exercise will make you stronger, leaner, fitter and healthier. Not only that, but it can boost your self-confidence and even help stave off depression.

30-minute workout Always allow at least two hours after a heavy meal before exercising, and start and finish with five to ten minutes of gentle stretching (see stretching exercises, below) to prepare your muscles and joints. Wear appropriate clothing and invest in a pair of sneakers with good tread and cushioning. A park or other public space with stairs or a slope is ideal for a simple half-hour workout in five-minute segments (below).

START AND FINISH Stretch gently, focusing on your leg muscles to avoid injury. Stretch gently and progressively, leaning into the stretch as you find it more comfortable—don't bounce. Stretch more deeply after your workout than at the start.

calf stretch   groin stretch

hamstring stretch

1 **Walk briskly,** gradually increasing the pace and starting to use your arms.

2 **Power-walk** at a fast pace, pumping your arms like pistons.

3 **On the spot,** do jumping jacks or skip with a rope.

4 **Jog or power-walk,** remembering to breathe deeply and evenly.

5 **Run or jog** up a flight of stairs or up a slope.

6 **Walk leisurely** to cool down, shaking out your arms and shoulders.

Find your routine You don't need to join a gym to do aerobic exercise. Any brisk exercise will do the job, as long as it demands extra work from your heart and lungs. Aerobic training exercises the body's large muscles in the limbs, buttocks and chest. You should feel warm, perspire and breathe heavily, but still be able to hold a conversation on the move.

Choose exercises you enjoy. Swim, cycle and even dance to get your blood pumping. Badminton, tennis, squash, rowing, hiking with a backpack—all are aerobic. Vary your routine (walking one day and swimming the next, for example) to focus alternately on the lower and upper body. Just 20 minutes of high-intensity exercise three times a week, or a moderate 30-minute workout five times a week, can make a real difference to your fitness. Or try interval training; alternating short bursts of intense exercise with long, more gentle periods. For example, walk or jog for 90 seconds, then sprint for 30. It's super-effective and fun.

---

get the measure of Alcohol

The idea that "a drink"—a glass of wine, pint of beer or nip of scotch —equates to a standard drink is a misconception. In fact, it is easy to underestimate how much you're drinking, because bars and restaurants often serve drinks that exceed the standard sizes. For example, a standard beer in the United States and Canada is 12 fl. oz (350 mL). But a pint of beer in many restaurants or bars is 16 fl. oz (480 mL) in the US, or 20 imperial fl. oz (570 mL) in Canada. And many establishments offer doubles of hard liquor. That's something to remember next time you go for drinks.

Most American states, as well as the Canadian federal government, have set the legal blood alcohol limit at 0.08%. This is the point at which it is illegal to drive a car, though the effects of intoxication can appear as low as 0.02%. (Some states and provinces have their own different regulations.) How many drinks it takes to reach 0.08% depends on your size and weight.

> In North America, moderate drinking is defined as up to one serving per day for a woman, and up to two per day for men. In Canada, the standard drink includes 13.6 g of pure alcohol, while in the US, the standard drink has 14 g.
>
> | Drink | Volume | ABV%* |
> |---|---|---|
> | WINE | 5 fl. oz (150 mL) | 12–13 |
> | BEER | 12 fl. oz (350 mL) | 4–9 |
> | SPIRITS | 1.5 fl. oz (45 mL) | 40 + |

* alcohol by volume

get through Airport check-in quickly

Follow these tips to beat the lineups and speed your way from the check-in desk to the departure gate.

Before you leave home, check in online if you can. Most airlines allow this during the 24 hours before departure; some even let you print out your boarding pass.

As soon as you reach the airport, go to a self-service kiosk (if there is one) and pick up your boarding pass if need be. Lines are usually shorter than at the check-in desk.

Travel with carry-on luggage only to avoid the lineup at baggage check-in. Be sure that your bag is small enough; the International Air Transport Association specifies a maximum of 22 x 18 x 10 in. (56 x 45 x 25 cm), including handles, wheels and pockets, but check your airline's own specific rules. Make sure you're aware of and follow any restrictions on objects or liquids that aren't allowed in the cabin.

When you get to security, empty your pockets of all metal objects and put them in your bag or jacket before you reach the scanner. If you have a laptop or camera, take it out of its bag so it can be seen.

deal with an
Allergy emergency

Someone has been stung by a bee or eaten a peanut, triggering an extreme allergic reation (anaphylaxis). They may struggle to breathe, be unable to speak or swallow, have a swollen face or limb, show a rapidly spreading flush or rash (hives), feel a tight chest or weakness, or even collapse into unconsciousness. What can you do to help them?

Quick action
- Call 911; tell the operator what's happening.
- Have the victim sit down, upright.
- Does the person carry an autoinjector of adrenaline, such as an EpiPen? If so, find it and use it.
- If the person was stung by a bee and you can see the stinger, remove it at once (*see* BEE STING).
- If the victim becomes very pale and their pulse falters, lie them down with their knees raised above heart level. If they become unconscious and you can't perform cardiopulmonary resuscitation (*see* CPR), call for someone who can.

drop and set an Anchor

Don't be tempted to simply throw your anchor over the side of the boat and drop all the anchor chain at once—it might get tangled in the scope (the anchor line) or anchor. Then it won't catch properly on the bottom.

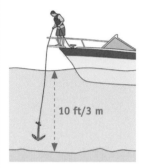

10 ft/3 m

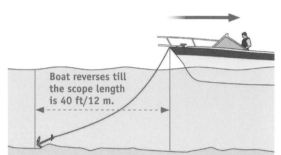

Boat reverses till the scope length is 40 ft/12 m.

1 Approach where you want to anchor, facing into the wind. Estimate the depth of the water, such as 10 ft (3 m), then pay out a length of scope equivalent to four times the depth for a chain anchor line; six times for a rope-and-chain combination. Secure the scope on the deck cleat.

2 Reverse slowly or let the boat drift until you feel the anchor bite, then set it in place with a short burst of astern power. Allow a longer scope if the water is rough. Check that the scope is securely tied and hoist your anchor ball (where required) or use an anchor light to indicate that you are at anchor.

eliminate Animal odors

Get rid of the smells associated with having a dog or cat.

To control a pervasive odor associated with a dog or cat, establish a permanent sleeping place for it, and wash the bedding regularly. Wherever your pet has slept on a carpet, scatter baking soda or carpet deodorizer, then vacuum. It also helps to keep your pet well-groomed.

Abnormal body odors If your dog or cat has an extra-strong odor even after grooming, consult a veterinarian. Your pet may have a skin disorder known as seborrhea, an ear infection or, for a dog, even impacted anal glands. Seborrhea can be controlled with a medicated shampoo. Signs of a glandular problem include biting and licking abnormally at the rear end or scooting along on it. This and ear infections require special treatment.

An older animal may have halitosis from deposits on its teeth. Prevention is the best cure; give a dog a rawhide bone, and give your cat dry food occasionally, if you usually feed it canned. You can also brush animals' teeth with baking soda and either a soft brush or a gauze square on your fingertip.

Animal mess? Immediately scoop it up and blot the area with paper towels. Neutralize the stain with vinegar or lemon juice, then scrub the area with soap and water to remove the odor.

identify Animal tracks

Wild animals leave a "signature" behind them in sand, snow, wet soil or parched earth, as they walk, run, hop, scuttle and slither, and each one can be read when you know how. When studying an animal trail, think about what species are native to the terrain. In your own backyard, that might be a fox, raccoon, coyote or tomcat on the prowl, while streams, forests, deserts, swamps, prairie, jungle, marsh and mountain will all yield different clues.

Within most landscapes there are wildlife hotspots in which many species congregate—near water, for example, or under a hedge. These provide rich pickings for the tracker, whether they are spotting out of curiosity or looking for signs that there are dangerous predators nearby.

DOGS, foxes and other canines leave triangular claw marks.

CATS retract their claws when on the move.

Close to home, look for dog or cat prints. Dogs and cats walk on tiptoes, so only the central pad and the four toes leave an imprint. Many dog prints are mistaken for big cats, but dogs tend to zigzag while cats walk in a straight line. A fox track is like a dog's, but more compact, with the outer digits curving inward. And while a dog will romp through mud, a fox will pick its way around the wet and dirt.

Hooved animals—horses, deer, sheep, cows and moose—also "tiptoe." Most recognizable is the print of a solid-hoofed horse, with its rounded fore hoof and more pointed hind. Cattle, like deer, are cloven-hoofed.

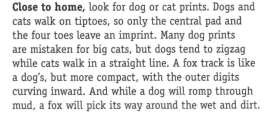
DEER are cloven-hooved and leave a distinctive print, like a heart split in two.

HORSE prints are deepest at the toe. They have heel bulbs and a triangular "frog" in the center of the sole.

A small print with four toes at the fore and five on the hind foot tells you that a rodent has passed by—a mouse, rat, chipmunk or squirrel, for example.

SQUIRREL

Rabbits' and hares' hind legs leave long, exaggerated prints, which, because of their leapfrog gait, appear ahead of the front paws.

RABBIT

Count five toes on both front and (smaller) back feet, and you're on the trail of a raccoon (the prints look like tiny human hand and footprints), weasel, badger, otter, skunk, beaver, opossum or even a bear. Unusually, an otter pad is almost round.

BADGERS have a large, kidney-shaped pad and visible claw marks.

BEAR prints are big, with significantly larger hind feet, and follow a drunken zigzag.

---

deal with Ants

If you find ants in your house, first follow the trail back to see if you can locate their nest. It's probably outside somewhere in soft or sandy soil, possibly under some slabs.

Apply ant killer to any large or busy holes. Boiling water poured repeatedly on the nest may also help to eliminate it.

Indoors, wipe up any ants you see with a soapy cloth; this will destroy the odour trails. Make sure your floors and surfaces are free of crumbs and other food debris.

Follow the ants back to their entry point into your house and seal it.

---

get rid of Aphids

Aphid infestations, which include greenfly and blackfly, build up quickly, so treat them fast.

If you garden organically, treat with pyrethrum insecticide, or try sprinkling leaves with wood ash or talc and hose them down the next day. You could also plant "decoys" such as nasturtiums nearby, and plenty of flowers to attract ladybugs—aphids' natural predators.

The best synthetic treatments include deltamethrin and lambda-cyhalothrin—look for them in the ingredients list of pesticides at the garden store. Thiacloprid is even more effective as it works systemically—that is, it spreads from where you spray it through the whole plant.

Always be careful when applying chemical treatments and follow the instructions to the letter. Treat the undersides of leaves, where aphids cluster most densely.

correctly use an
Apostrophe

In written English, the apostrophe does two different but equally important jobs.

Missing letters An apostrophe can indicate that a word is a contracted form of a longer word or phrase. *Don't* is short for *do not*.

Possession An apostrophe with an s indicates ownership—*the cat's whiskers*. The word *its* doesn't have an apostrophe in this case (*the cat twitched its whiskers*), though it does when *it's* is short for *it is*.

Plurals An apostrophe s is never used to denote plural nouns. If a noun is both plural and possessive then the apostrophe comes after the s—*both boys' bedroom*.

---

recognize the signs of
Appendicitis

If someone complains of severe abdominal pain, generally starting in the center and moving to the lower-right side, often accompanied by nausea or a raised temperature, it could be a sign that the appendix —a small pouch attached to the large intestine—is inflamed.

Quick action
■ Make the person as comfortable as you can and offer a hot-water bottle to hold on the stomach. Give them a bucket if they are feeling nauseous.
■ Give no food, drink or medication, in case they need an anesthetic.
■ If the pain persists or gets worse, or the person develops a high temperature, vomits or appears obviously ill, call 911.

create Appliqué embellishments

Appliqué adds a personal touch to clothes and home furnishings. Devise your own patterns, trace simple shapes or use stencils.

YOU WILL NEED **Fabric scraps (iron flat before you begin), template paper, tailor's chalk, medium-sized dressmaking scissors, embroidery scissors, needle, tacking cotton, thread, fusible web (for no-sew method), iron**

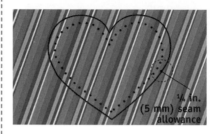

¼ in. (5 mm) seam allowance

1 Pin template to the correct side of appliqué fabric and chalk a dotted line around it. Remove the template and mark a ¼ in. (5 mm) seam allowance outside of the dotted line. Use dressmaking scissors to cut out shape.

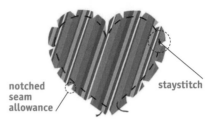

notched seam allowance

staystitch

2 Staystitch (*see* SEWING) just outside the inner seam line (dotted line) using ⅛ in. (2 mm) stitches. Use embroidery scissors to snip V-shaped cuts into the seam allowance around curves and corners to make it easier to fold.

REVERSE SIDE

Use tacking stitches to hold seam allowance.

3 Fold seam allowance back onto the wrong side along the seam line. Tack the folded edges as you go (*see* TACK).

tacking

slipstitch

4 Pin shape to background fabric and secure with large tacking stitches. Secure round the edges with slipstitch (*see* SEWING). Remove the tacking.

No-sew method

1 Cut out a template without seam allowance. Place wrong side of fabric onto melting side of fusible web and iron together. Cut out the shape, iron gently (paper side up). Peel off the paper.

2 Iron the appliqué (preferably over a damp cloth or from the wrong side) to fix in place. Stitch a zigzag or embroidery stitch around the edges for decoration and to prevent fraying.

win an Argument

In personal disagreements, as in war, an all-out assault is rarely the winning strategy. Keep calm: If you lose your cool, you've lost the argument.

■ Avoid statements that are totally dismissive, like *That's crap!* or *How dare you say that to me?* Instead, use words that invite the other party to let you have your say, such as *I think you might have misunderstood what I said* or *Can I just explain why I did that?*
■ However tempting it may be, don't resurrect old conflicts, and never make things personal. *You've never liked me, and you're just saying that because you're jealous.* Stick to the matter at hand and the relevant facts.

prepare an Artichoke

YOU WILL NEED **Large sharp knife, scissors, spoon, large stainless steel pan of boiling salted water, heatproof plate**

3 Plunge the artichokes into boiling water, using the overproof plate to keep them submerged.

4 Simmer for 20–30 minutes, or until a central leaf can be pulled out easily.

5 Drain upside down so that the water runs out and allow the artichoke to cool a little.

1 Break the stalk and pull off any tough fibers. Then trim the base to allow the artichoke to sit flat.

2 Trim the spiny ends of the leaves with scissors, then use the knife to cut off the pointed top.

8 Replace the central leaf cone upside down in the center, if you wish.

To serve
Globe artichokes make a simple but impressive starter. They are tastiest served hot, with plain or herb butter, or cold with a vinaigrette or mayonnaise. The dressings can be spooned into the center or set on the side for dipping the leaves one by one.

6 Grasp the central cone and twist quickly to pull it out. Set the cone to one side.

7 Scoop out the fibrous "choke" with the spoon, making sure it's all removed.

set up a freshwater Aquarium

YOU WILL NEED **Tank, gravel and rocks, water, dechlorinator, filter, lighting, water-testing kit**

Clean the tank Use warm water and no detergent. Wash gravel and rocks under the tap until the water runs clear. Position the tank where it will not be in direct sunlight.

Set it up Put in a few inches (5–7 cm) of gravel for plants to take root in. Fill it three-quarters full with dechlorinated water (treated with a water conditioner) and arrange plants and rocks in groups to make hideaway nooks. Install a filter where no plants will obstruct it. Top up with more dechlorinated water or leave for 24 hours to dechlorinate. Sct up the lighting and adjust the filter for a steady flow of bubbles.

Chemical balance Put your tank through a fishless cycle. It will grow bacteria that remove the toxins created by fish metabolism, turning harmful ammonia into less toxic nitrites, then to much less toxic nitrates. Keep testing the water for ammonia and nitrites. Ammonia levels will rise, then fall as nitrites increase. When you get a zero reading for both, replace half to three-quarters of the water to reduce excess nitrates.

Time for the fish Introduce just a couple of fish at first. Float the bag they came in for 15 minutes, then gently release them into the tank.

recognize
Architectural styles
see pages 12–13

A

recognize Architectural styles

Buildings have changed a lot in appearance over the centuries, thanks to engineering progress, social demands and changing fashion. Here's a guide to recognizing some of the most significant styles.

New and used A building's look isn't always a reliable guide to its age —architectural styles, like fashions in clothing, are subject to revival. Part of the interest lies in identifying the styles that have influenced a later building; the White House in Washington, DC, for example, borrows heavily from the classical era, while Canada's parliament buildings are a Gothic flight of fancy.

CLASSICAL AND RENAISSANCE
The architecture of ancient Greece and Rome was characterized by distinct "orders," most recognizable by their style of column (below left). In the Renaissance age, architects and other artists strove to revive Greek and Roman principles. There was a new interest in classical proportions, and the five orders were reintroduced. These classical ideas were also applied to new, technically innovative features such as the tall dome (unknown to the Greeks), and architects such as Andrea Palladio (1508–1580) took the idea of a columned classical temple and turned it into a façade. Both ideas were copied by Christopher Wren (1632–1723) at St Paul's Cathedral in London.

COMPOSITE (5) The Romans combined Ionic scrolling with Corinthian acanthus leaves to create a new ornate style.

TUSCAN (1) columns, introduced by the Romans, resemble the Greek Doric but are even simpler in style, with an unfluted shaft.

DORIC (2) columns have a simple head or "capital." On the long frieze above the columns are oblong blocks with vertical grooves (triglyphs).

IONIC (3) can be recognized by the scrolling on the capital, like a blanket rolled up from both ends

CORINTHIAN (4) columns have capitals that are carved to represent the bushy appearance of the acanthus plant.

1　2　3　4　5

ROMANESQUE AND GOTHIC Architecture in the Middle Ages (the period between the end of the Roman Empire and the Renaissance) is best assessed by looking at windows. If a cathedral, for example, has small windows with a rounded top, set in thick walls—a continuation from Roman architecture—it's built in the Romanesque style. Such windows were the first experiments in getting light into heavy buildings without compromising their structural integrity.

Romanesque leads seamlessly into Gothic. The earliest true Gothic windows are pointed at the top like the prow of a ship. This simple shape was later elaborated upon to create large windows that incorporate tracery of great complexity and beauty—like delicate lace wrought in stone and glass. This same airy delicacy is found in other aspects of High Gothic buildings: high roofs and elegant buttresses, like external ribs—as if the building had been pared back to its skeleton.

Gothic forms returned in the 18th and 19th centuries, particularly in public buildings such as museums and churches. This neo-Gothic style began in Britain and spread across the world.

ROMANESQUE: Old Cathedral, Salamanca, Spain

NEO-GOTHIC: Pitt Rivers Museum, Oxford

HIGH GOTHIC: Amiens Cathedral, France

BAROQUE AND ROCOCO The simple classical lines of Renaissance architecture gradually gave way to a style that was more theatrical, sumptuous and decorative. This style is known as baroque, and culminated in the frivolous and light-hearted rococo style. The first buildings in the baroque style were commissioned by the Catholic Church in late 16th-century Italy, but the style gradually traveled throughout Europe and was used in secular as well as religious buildings, including the great Palace of Versailles outside Paris. The Frauenkirche in Dresden, Germany (left), is a fine example of the late baroque period. It was built in 1726, destroyed by Allied bombing in 1945, rebuilt and reopened in 2005.

ART NOUVEAU: Elaborate doorway, Spain

ART NOUVEAU Architecture in the art nouveau style came to the fore around the turn of the 20th century. Its most noticeable feature is a playful obsession with stylized plant forms, both inside and outside a building. It might take the form of a wrought-iron balcony made to look like tangled ivy, or a sinuous staircase and balustrade, lettering that's curled like roots or fronds, or walls with organic curves, as if they had grown out of the earth rather than been built to a plan. The Spanish architect Antoni Gaudí (1852-1926) filled Barcelona with such buildings, including his unfinished cathedral, the Sagrada Familia.

ART DECO: Miami Beach, USA

ART DECO The art deco style, which originated in the 1920s directly after art nouveau, is a kind of opposite. Its defining characteristics are streamlined, mechanical shapes and strictly geometric patterns (think of New York's Empire State Building). Art deco buildings also feature unashamedly industrial materials, such as gleaming chrome, polished enamel and expanses of glass.

prepare and cook
Asparagus

Preparation Cut or break off any woody ends—they'll snap when you bend the spears. For white or thick-stemmed green asparagus, scrape off the skin with a small sharp knife, working downward from the tip.

Cooking Stand spears upright in an asparagus steamer and cook for 10-15 minutes in enough salted water to come halfway up their length; the stems will boil while the tips steam. Asparagus can be boiled or microwaved, but take care not to overcook it.

■ If you don't have an asparagus steamer, tie spears into a bundle and stand in a deep saucepan. Wedge them upright with new potatoes. Make a dome of foil over the top of the pan to seal it.

prevent
Athlete's foot

Wash feet daily and dry well, particularly between the toes—this is a fungal infection that thrives in damp conditions. Use foot or talcum powder to reduce perspiration.

Put on clean socks (cotton is best), tights or pantyhose twice a day and only when your feet are dry.

In changing rooms or showers, wear plastic shoes or flip-flops.

If you get athlete's foot, treat it with an over-the-counter remedy from your pharmacy. Apply to the rash and 2 in. (5 cm) around it. Continue for a week or two after symptoms have disappeared. In severe cases, consult a doctor.

deal with an Asthma attack

Asthma can be alarming to witness, but if you keep your cool you can help a sufferer get through it—and you might even save a life.

Quick action
If a person you're with becomes breathless, wheezy and distressed, keep calm and follow this procedure.

■ In calm tones, ask if they are having a panic attack, or have been diagnosed with asthma.
■ If they are asthmatic, encourage them to sit up, leaning slightly forward with a straight back, and to take slow, steady breaths.
■ Ask if they have an inhaler. Help them to take two to four puffs, talking them through what you're doing, and preparing them to take the medication down into their lungs. Wait a few minutes before offering them any more puffs from the inhaler.

■ It could be ten minutes before the medication takes effect. If, after that time, there's no improvement or if the patient is turning blue, call 911. Stay with the person, remain calm and continue to offer support.
■ Even if the inhaler has not appeared to work so far, continue to give puffs at two- to five-minute intervals. This should prevent a worsening of symptoms, speed the process of control and impart a comforting sense that something is being done.
■ If the sufferer has no inhaler, ask if anybody present has one. If not, or if this is a first attack, call 911 right away. A cup of strong coffee has been shown to help as an emergency measure.

survive an Avalanche

If you're going to an avalanche zone, consider renting or buying an avalanche transceiver (available online). Worn inside your clothing, it transmits a signal that can be tracked.

■ When you first realize you're in an avalanche, shout as loud as you can to let others know you're in trouble. Try anything, like running or rolling, to get off the moving snow. If this doesn't work, brace for impact.
■ When the avalanche hits, fight to stay at the surface—"swimming" motions sometimes help. As the

As soon as you stop moving, tuck your head into the crook of your arm to create an air pocket in the snow.

Try "swimming" to stay near the surface as you're carried along.

drift slows, before the snow hardens, put your face in the crook of your arm to make an air pocket.
■ Stay calm and control your breathing to conserve oxygen while you wait for help. Shout only if you hear someone close by.

keep a safe Backup on your computer

■ Windows PCs and Macs both come with automatic backup features. On the Mac, you simply set a time and a destination disk. On the Windows side, You can specify variables such as which files you want to back up, where you want to store the files and how often you want to run the program.

To set up in Windows, click on **Start**, type "backup" in the **Search** box, and click on **Backup and Restore**. Then follow the steps outlined on-screen.
■ It's even safer to back up to a separate device, such as an external hard drive. That way, you don't lose your files if your computer gets lost or broken beyond repair. Hard drives are available for both Macs and PCs.
■ For a small monthly fee, you can back up your files to a secure online server, also known as storing it in "the cloud" (google "online backup").
■ A crude way to make backups is simply to drag and copy all vital files to a new folder on an external hard disk (include the date of the backup in the folder's name). Just remember: Any backup is better than none at all.

---

pack a Backpack

When you pack a backpack for a hike or camping trip, you should have two aims in mind: allow easy access to the stuff you need frequently or urgently, and make sure the load isn't hard to carry.

Nothing should protrude from your bag into your back. The corner of a badly packed book will soon become excruciating on a long trek. Keep the weight evenly balanced—don't carry a huge water bottle in a side pocket. If you'll be on flat terrain, stash the weight near the top, so you can easily shift it over your center of gravity by leaning slightly forward.

Make sure that things that belong together—such as a hat and gloves—stay together in your backpack. Clothes should be wrapped tightly inside a heavy-duty garbage bag, like the ones used for rubble on building sites.

Remove any excess packaging from your food supplies before you pack them.

If you're going on an overnight trek, put the things that you need at the end of the day—your tent and your sleeping bag—at the bottom of your backpack.

Rain gear, snacks and first-aid kit should be near the top or in one of the side pockets.

Keep the heaviest items in your pack close to your spine.

■ Light
■ Heavy
■ Medium

master the rules of Backgammon

This game for two is played on a board divided into 24 points, with a six point "home" section for each player and a middle bar. Each player has 15 pieces (initial set up, below) that are moved from point to point on the roll of two dice.

black moves clockwise
white moves counterclockwise

white point 12
black point 13

white point 1
black point 24

white point 13
black point 12

white point 24
black point 1

The object is to move all 15 pieces to your home, then "bear them off" by rolling the number of the point on which a piece resides.
■ The dice scores can be used to move two separate pieces, or combined to move one.
■ Two identical scores are doubled to allow four moves, separately or in any combination.
■ A point occupied by two or more pieces of the same color is blocked to the other player.
■ If your opponent lands on a point occupied by only one of your pieces, your stone is moved to the bar. To re-enter it, use a later die roll to move the piece to whichever point in your opponent's home is indicated.

banish
Bad breath

- For a quick fix, swish water around your mouth, spit it out and drink a glassful.
- Fresh parsley, cardamom and fennel seeds also sweeten breath, but oral hygiene is key.
- Brush your teeth for a minimum of two minutes at least twice a day, with a small, soft toothbrush and unsing a separate toothbrush or scraper for your tongue. Floss daily and see your dentist every six months.

---

deliver
Bad news

It's never easy to deal a verbal body blow, but sensitivity helps. Choose somewhere quiet and private.

Sit eye-to-eye with a person and give them a gentle warning to brace them. *"I'm sorry to have to tell you," "I just heard from the hospital," "You know that John hasn't been well..."*

Empathize with their reaction. *"I know this is hurtful," "I realize this is a terrible shock..."*

Let them cry if they want to, let them say what they want and listen to them.

Offer any help you're willing to give—and deliver on your promise, if it's accepted.

---

look after a
Baby
see pages 18–19

---

learn the basics of Badminton

This indoor court game is played by two or four people with rackets and a light feathered projectile called a shuttlecock. The speed of the shuttlecock and its swift deceleration give the game its character.

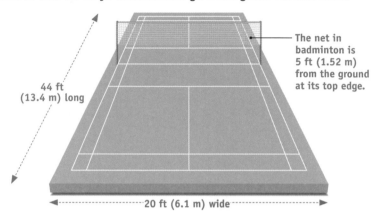

44 ft (13.4 m) long

The net in badminton is 5 ft (1.52 m) from the ground at its top edge.

20 ft (6.1 m) wide

Play begins with the server hitting the shuttlecock diagonally over the net toward the receiver. The players or pairs then take turns to hit the shuttlecock back over the net.

A point is won by grounding the shuttlecock within the court on your opponent's side of the net, or by forcing your opponent to hit the shuttlecock into the net or out of the court entirely. The winner of the rally becomes the server for the next point.

To win a game, a player or pair must reach 21 points. If the score ties as 20, the game continues until either a two-point lead is established or one side reaches 30 points. Matches are generally the best of three games.

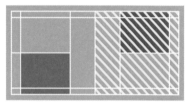

doubles

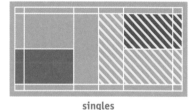

singles

- Server area on an even score
- Area that server can serve into
- Area of play after service

---

cook the perfect Baked potato

To enjoy that delicious combination of snowy white flesh encased in a crispy skin, choose good-sized potatoes of a variety such as Russett, Goldrush or Long White with a fluffy but firm texture. Scrub, wash, dry and prick all over with a fork, then rub with a little olive oil, followed by some sea salt if desired. Heat the oven to 400°F (200°C), place the potatoes directly on the rack and cook for 1¼–1½ hours, or until the outside is crisp and brown and the potato gives a little when squeezed. Split open and serve with anything you like; butter, sour cream and chives, chili or cheese are delicious choices.

make a Balloon animal

In the world of balloon twisting, the puppy dog is the lowest form of life (with the possible exception of the balloon worm), so it's the easiest for a beginner to make.

YOU WILL NEED Modeling balloons (regular length and thickness, known as 260s). Optional: balloon or bicycle pump

1 Blow up your balloon halfway and tie off.

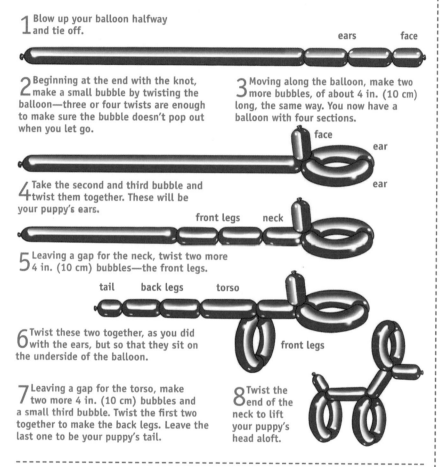

2 Beginning at the end with the knot, make a small bubble by twisting the balloon—three or four twists are enough to make sure the bubble doesn't pop out when you let go.

3 Moving along the balloon, make two more bubbles, of about 4 in. (10 cm) long, the same way. You now have a balloon with four sections.

4 Take the second and third bubble and twist them together. These will be your puppy's ears.

5 Leaving a gap for the neck, twist two more 4 in. (10 cm) bubbles—the front legs.

6 Twist these two together, as you did with the ears, but so that they sit on the underside of the balloon.

7 Leaving a gap for the torso, make two more 4 in. (10 cm) bubbles and a small third bubble. Twist the first two together to make the back legs. Leave the last one to be your puppy's tail.

8 Twist the end of the neck to lift your puppy's head aloft.

---

throw and catch a Ball

To throw a ball hard, run six or seven paces and turn your upper body away from the target as your throwing arm swings back. As your arm comes forward, twist your body with it so that all your weight and momentum is behind the throw.

To maximize your chance of catching a ball that's heading your way, you should cup your hands, with fingers splayed and pointing slightly toward the ground. Watch the ball approach; keep the hands relaxed or else the ball will bounce out of your palms. Give with the ball as it enters your grasp, and close your fingers firmly around it.

appreciate Ballet

Ballet is pure poetry in motion, a means of using dance as narrative and to express powerful emotions. It helps to have a little background understanding to get the most out of it.

Know the plot For your first ballet, choose one that tells a popular tale—*The Sleeping Beauty*, say, or *Cinderella*—so you can follow the story. Buy a CD and listen to the music to enjoy the thrill of anticipation beforehand—and to recognize it on the night.

Learn about the dancers Read up about the people who'll be dancing for you—especially the principals—to understand the hard work and devotion that lies behind each of their performances.

Recognize the moves Learn about the complex and beautiful moves from which classical ballet is wrought. Look out first for the slow, enfolding movements of *adagio*, which might include a graceful *arabesque* (one leg supports the body while the other extends behind) or a *fondu* (a slow melting movement in which the supporting leg bends at the knee).

Then there's the speed and spirit of *allegro*—featuring dramatic steps of elevation such as *entrechat* (a jump into the air accompanied by a rapid crisscrossing of the feet) and *grand jeté* (a full leg splits in mid-air).

Enjoy the story Most importantly, allow yourself to appreciate the narrative flow of the ballet, as the story is played out with extraordinary skill and athleticism by the dancers.

look after a Baby

*Whether you're a new parent or a grandparent with a small baby
for the first time since you had your own children,
here are some hints to help you to enjoy your time together.*

Keep it simple Concentrate on meeting a baby's
basic needs: food, comfort, sleep and staying clean and
dry. Anything beyond that is a bonus for you both. Be
alert to dangers you wouldn't normally consider—even
young babies can reach things that are small enough to
swallow, or touch electrical switches or outlets.

WHY IS THE BABY CRYING?

Is the baby hungry, wet, soiled or
tired? Do they have gas? If none
of these are the problem, try a
change of scenery. Go out for a
stroll, put the baby in a sling and
carry them as you move around
the house—or take time to play.

A routine can help to make sense
of your baby's needs, even if you
are feeding on demand. At around
six months old, many babies and
mothers follow a schedule similar
to this.

6-7:00	Wake up, morning milk and breakfast.
9:00	Nap for up to 1 hour.
10-11:00	Mid-morning milk and snack.
12:00	Lunch followed by long nap.
2:30	Wake from nap, afternoon milk.
4:00	Short afternoon nap.
6:00	Supper, then bath and bedtime milk.
7:00	Bed.
10:00	Some babies may still wake for a late-night feeding.

SLEEP TIME FOR BABY Whether it's baby's bedtime, or they just need a nap,
it's important that the conditions are right for a safe and peaceful slumber. A
crib or bassinet is the safest place for a small baby, so long as you follow the
guidelines below. Avoid the temptation to doze off with a baby on a bed, sofa
or armchair, as they may overheat or even be smothered.

1 Make sure that a baby doesn't
get too hot or too cold—make
their room comfortable for an adult
who is lightly dressed.

2 Dress a baby in a light sleeper,
place them on a firm, clean
mattress covered in a single, fitted sheet and lay them on their
back. Keep toys and dolls out.

3 If you need to cover a baby, use a
lightweight blanket, not a duvet or
quilt. Never use pillows, and keep the
head uncovered. Place the baby's feet
close to the foot of the crib so they
can't wriggle under the cover, which
should reach no higher than their
chest and be tucked in securely under
the sides and end of the mattress.

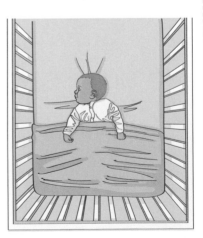

FEEDING Choose a calm place, without too many distractions for the baby.

Sterilizing a bottle Wash, rinse and sterilize bottle and nipple before use. Use one of the following sterilizing methods.
- Use a plug-in steam sterilizer or one for the microwave.
- Boil in water for ten minutes. Bottles must be fully submerged with no air bubbles inside. Cover the pan and leave the bottles in the water until you need one.
- Dissolve a sterilizing tablet or mix concentrate in a tub of cold water. Submerge the bottles and leave for at least 30 minutes. Rinse with cool, boiled water before use.

Mixing up a bottle of formula
Allow time for boiled water to cool or make bottles of water in advance, ready to add the powder.

1 Wash your hands. Boil a kettle of fresh water (filled from the cold tap), not water that has already been boiled, as minerals within it will be more concentrated. Let the water cool before measuring into the bottle.

2 Add scoops of formula to the water. Follow instructions on the package, filling and leveling the scoop for accurate measurements. Shake well to combine. Use within 1 hour and discard any leftovers.

To warm a bottle, stand it in hot water. Never use a microwave, as this can leave dangerous hot spots in the milk, even after a shake. Keep shaking and checking the milk until it's at a comfortable temperature. Never give milk to a baby without checking that it isn't too hot.

DIAPER CHANGING Always change a dirty diaper promptly. Get into the habit of changing wet diapers before or after each feeding, to ensure that they are changed frequently enough to avoid diaper rash.

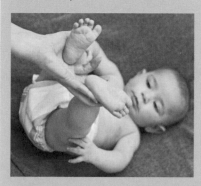

YOU WILL NEED **Changing mat, disposable plastic bag for dirty diapers, baby wipes or cotton cloths and warm water, possibly a towel, clean diaper, diaper rash cream (if necessary)**

BATHTIME Bathe a baby at a time when you're both relaxed.

1 Run about 4 in. (10 cm) water at a comfortable temperature. Soap or lotion isn't needed, but can be used if a baby is more than six weeks old.

2 Undress a baby except for their diaper and wrap them in a towel while you wash the face, ears and neck with warm water and a soft cloth.

3 Remove the diaper and clean the baby's bottom.

4 Put your arm around the baby's back, holding the arm that's farther from you. Use your other hand to support the legs and buttocks as you sit the baby in the bath.

Choose a warm, safe and comfortable place: a table, the bed or on the floor. Use a changing mat to cushion the surface and keep it clean.

1 Wash hands and gather everything you will need. Never leave a baby unattended on a table while you turn to reach for something.

2 Remove the dirty diaper and place it in a disposable plastic bag. Clean the baby's bottom with a baby wipe or soft cloth dipped in water. Use a fresh one for each wipe. Always wipe a girl from front to back and clean thoroughly around a boy's testicles. Don't try to pull back a boy's foreskin, as you could damage it or cause pain.

3 Pat dry with a towel if necessary, and apply cream to any areas that look red or sore. Then put on the fresh diaper, wash your hands to clean away germs and dress the baby.

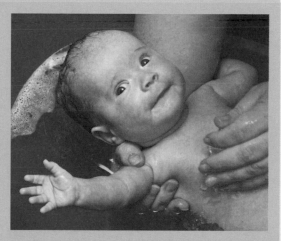

5 Keep your arm around the head and shoulders as you wash the body, rolling the baby onto their chest as you wash the back.

6 Lift the baby out, using both hands to support the body and buttocks then wrap in a soft towel and dry carefully, with attention to the skin folds.

B

light a charcoal
Barbecue

Don't mar a beautiful summer's day in the backyard fighting a losing battle with charcoal that refuses to light.

■ Set up in a sheltered corner and, instead of using smelly lighter fuels, try laying scraps of lightweight cardboard (torn-up cereal boxes, for example) under and poking through the charcoal, where you can light them.

■ A squeezable empty plastic bottle will do the job of bellows to fan the flames until they take hold.

■ A charcoal chimney—a metal cylinder with holes around the base, which you place on the grill—is a smart buy for easy lighting. Crumple some newspaper and push it loosely in, top up with charcoal then light the paper. In 20 minutes you can decant glowing coals onto the grill.

■ Start cooking when the coals are covered with fine, pale ash.

apply a Bandage

Bandage selection is vital. You need to be aware of the different uses of various types of wrap, and make your choice accordingly.

The key points When applying a bandage:
■ Make sure the person is comfortable and tell them what you're doing.
■ Work from the side of the affected part, not reaching across the person.
■ If you're bandaging an arm or leg, leave fingers and toes exposed so you can tell if it's interfering with circulation. If fingers or toes are really cold, with a bluish tinge to the nail beds, or the patient complains of tingling, you need to loosen the wrap.
■ A bandage should be applied firmly, not tightly. Remember that the affected part may swell after being bandaged, so the wrap may need to be loosened or retied.
■ Elbows and knees should be bound in a slightly bent position, and should be kept that way once the bandages are on.
■ Always keep bandages clean and dry.

Roller bandages These are long strips of cotton, gauze or elasticized fabric or linen, and are used to secure dressings and support injured limbs. There are three types of roller bandage.
■ Bandages made of open-weave material, which allow air to get through but don't put pressure on wounds and don't support joints.
■ Elasticized bandages, which mold to the contours of the body and are used to secure dressings and support soft-tissue injuries, such as sprains.
■ Bandages made of crepe, which are used to support injured joints.

The two most common bandaging techniques for roller bandages are the spiral and the figure eight.

Spiral technique The spiral is used to wrap cylindrical parts of the body, such as the lower leg and forearm.

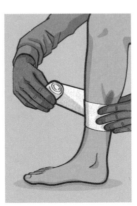  

1 Start below the wound and apply one or two firm turns directly around the limb.

2 Wind the bandage around and around in a spiral, with each turn overlapping the last by a half to three-quarters.

3 Make a straight turn and fix the end with a safety pin, a pair of bandage clips or tape.

Figure-eight technique This method is used to apply bandages to large joints such as elbows and knees—usually to hold a dressing in place on a wound or to support a sprain or strain.

1 Flex the joint slightly. Place the end on the inside of the joint and, working away from the body, make two straight turns to hold it in place.

2 Make alternate figure eight turns above and below the joint, each turn to overlap the previous one by about two-thirds.

3 Extend the bandage fairly far on each side of the joint. Make a last straight full turn over the preceding one, fold in the end and fix with a safety pin, a pair of bandage clips or tape.

Tubular bandages These are seamless tubes of fabric, which come in different sizes and types for different parts of the body. Elasticized ones can be used to support joints such as the ankle. Ones made of gauze are used to hold dressings on fingers or toes. Smaller tubular bandages are best put on using a specially designed applicator (right).

Triangular bandages These are large bandages that come folded in a triangle shape. They can be used as large dressings, slings to support a limb (*see* SLING) or a way to secure a dressing in place. You can also use a household item, such as a scarf, to make a triangular bandage.

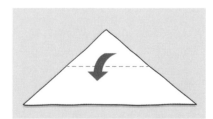 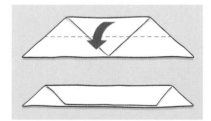

1 Before using a triangular bandage as a dressing—or to secure a dressing— fold it so that the point of the triangle touches the middle of the long edge.

2 Then fold it in half again in the same direction to make a broad strip. You can now use the spiral technique to secure the strip in place.

understand
Baseball

Everybody knows about baseball, right? Well, not really. For instance, did you know that America's national pastime evolved from the old English bat-and-ball game called rounders (*see* ROUNDERS)?

Baseball is played on a field with a large diamond. Home plate is on one corner and a base is on each of the others, known as "first," "second" and "third." Two teams of nine players take turns at bat and in the field.

- A pitcher in the center of the diamond throws the ball to the batter standing on home plate.
- The batter tries to hit the ball and run as far around the diamond as he can before the ball is fielded.
- The batter is "out" if the ball is caught before it hits the ground or if it's caught by the fielder on the base to which the batter is running before he or she can get there.
- Batters can choose to wait at first, second or third base if they cannot make it to the next base before the ball is fielded.
- A second batter then comes up to face the pitcher. Previous batters waiting on any base can continue their run if the new player at the plate hits the ball.
- A batter who makes it all the way around the diamond and back to home plate scores a point, and the team with the most points after nine innings wins.

Baseball uses skill and strategy. Fielders must be well-positioned, the pitcher tries to make the batter miss and the batter must hit the ball in a way that maximizes their opportunity to run.

B

reseal a Bath

There are various ways to seal a bath or shower. The one that looks best and works for most bathrooms involves squirting sealant from a gun. For this applicator method, you need a cartridge of silicone sealant and the gun applicator.

1 First, make sure all surfaces are clean and dry, and that you've removed all the old sealant. This is best done with a flexible razor blade and, if necessary, silicone sealant remover, also sold in cartridges. Then run a strip of masking tape along the wall and the rim of the bath or shower, to make a gap that corresponds to the space where you want the sealant to go.

2 Apply the sealant carefully, according to the instructions on the tube. The goal is to lay a straight, consistent bead along the middle of the gap.

3 Wet a finger and run it along the line of sealant or use a special tool to smooth it into the gap and create a neat, concave join between the wall and the rim of the bath or shower.

4 Remove the masking tape right away, while the sealant is still wet, to make a straight edge. Any sealant that has ended up in an unwanted area can be removed with a razor blade—but wait until it's completely dry.

follow a game of Basketball

This sport, invented by Canadian Dr. James Naismith, is an all-action game in which two teams of five battle it out to get the ball through each others' hoops.

The aim of basketball is to score points by throwing the ball into the opposing team's basket. Two or three points are awarded for a basket, depending on the distance from which the shot was taken. Games are played on a court that's just 94 ft (29 m) long—traversable in a few seconds. So points can be scored moments apart at opposing ends, and often are. The swift and constant scoring is part of the game's appeal.

Rules The design of the court tends to make the game fast-moving, and so do the rules. The game is based on five enduring principles: a light ball that's easy to bounce and throw; a goal (originally a half-bushel peach basket) fixed above head height (one reason why taller players have an advantage); no running while holding the ball (players must bounce it, or "dribble," while running); no interfering with opposing players when they shoot the ball; no body contact. In addition to these rules, the modern game has regulations stating that a team gaining possession must take it into the opposing half court within ten seconds, and shoot within 30. It all adds up to an end-to-end battle of the behemoths.

stay safe in the Bathroom

Between the water and the hard surfaces, the bathroom can be a danger zone. Follow these simple tips to avoid accidents and injury.

Water safety Slipping is the most likely hazard when your feet or the floor are wet, so always take care when getting into or out of the bath.
■ Use a bathmat if your floor has a hard surface that could be slippery.
■ Consider using a rubber suction mat or non-skid patches inside the bath if yours doesn't have a built-in non-slip area.
■ Use the bath's handrails, if it has them, to help you when getting out.

Children in the bathroom Never allow young children to play in the bathroom—it's neither safe nor hygienic.
■ If you have an older tub with separate taps for hot and cold water, always run the cold into the bath before the hot, in case a child climbs or falls in before the bath is ready. This ensures that they will not get scalded by too-hot water.
■ Where practical, replace an older two-tap system with a single mixer faucet or a newer thermostatic mixer, so there's never scalding water running.
■ Always store medicines and cleaning products in a locked cupboard.
■ Remove the bathroom door lock, or move it out of your child's reach.

Electrical safety Only use electrical equipment designed for use in a bathroom, and plug only into special shaver sockets. Never try to do your own wiring in a bathroom.

make Batteries last

It's frustrating when a battery dies while you're using something or trying to turn it on. And if your flashlight's batteries are dead just when you need it, it can even compromise your safety. There are things you can do to maximize battery life and avoid disappointment or inconvenience.

- Always buy your batteries from stores that have a high turnover, to ensure that they have been recently manufactured.
- Don't be tempted to buy a bulk pack of batteries to keep in storage—they can degrade over time. Just keep a few of each type and replace your spares as you use them.
- If you have a battery-operated device (a camera, for example) that you don't plan to use for awhile, take the batteries out and store them in a ziplock plastic bag in a dry place at room temperature until you need to use them.
- If you have a device that runs both on batteries and electricity, take the batteries out and store them, as above, while you're using the wall plug.
- Don't let batteries touch anything metal while they are in storage, as this can drain their power.
- Don't keep any battery-operated devices in places that are too warm, as this will reduce performance.
- Never mix new and used batteries or different types of batteries.
- If you use rechargeable batteries, don't mix different mAh (milliampere-hour) ratings, which indicates how long the battery will last on one charge.

---

create a simple Beaded necklace

Mastering beadwork is a great way of restringing old beads into attractive modern pieces. Bead shops or websites will sell everything you need.

YOU WILL NEED **Beads, piece of folded card stock, thread (the thickest that will fit, folded twice, through the beads), beeswax, a clasp for fastening, beading needle, tweezers or small pliers. Optional: glue**

Preparing beads and thread Decide how long the necklace will be, allowing at least 15 in. (38 cm) for a choker. If you're using large or oddly shaped beads, leave 5 in. (13 cm) free at the back of the neck for comfort. Cut a piece of thread six times the intended length of the necklace, rub it in beeswax and then double it over.

Assemble your chosen beads in order in the groove of a piece of folded card stock.

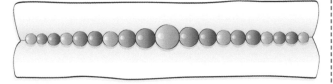

continued on next page →

sink those Battleships

In this pencil-and-paper game of guesswork and deduction for two players, you're admiral of a fleet comprised of a battleship, two cruisers, three destroyers and four submarines. Your opponent commands an identical fleet.

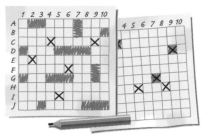

NUMBER OF SQUARES: battleship = 4, cruiser = 3, destroyer = 2, submarine = 1

How to play Each player draws up two "ocean grids," marked with the numbers 1 to 10 along the top and letters A to J down the side. Screen one of your grids from your enemy and position your ships by shading the correct number of adjacent squares in straight lines horizontally or vertically, wherever you choose.

Take turns to call out coordinates —for example, G9. If this square is occupied by part of a ship, you score a hit; if it isn't, that's a miss. Use your other grid to record your results and map the formation of your opponent's fleet. When all of a vessel's squares are hit, it has sunk, and its admiral must reveal what kind of vessel it was. The winner is the first player to sink their opponent's entire fleet.

Strategy Space your ships well apart, as randomly as possible; avoid predictable patterns of play; if you score a hit, target the surrounding squares.

trim Beards and mustaches

The easiest way to neaten your beard is to use an electric trimmer. The adjustable attachment on the head of the trimmer allows you to cut your beard to a uniform length. If you use a razor, make sure it's sharp. For mustaches in particular, it's also worth investing in a pair of professional barber scissors.

For beards, pay close attention to the edges of your chosen beard style. Make sure they are sharp and that the end result is symmetrical. Shave daily to maintain definition.

For mustaches, dampen the hair slightly and comb it downward with a fine-toothed comb. Use scissors to clip carefully and conservatively from the middle to the edge on each side in turn.

Beard styles A beard is a separate entity from a mustache or sideburns, but can be combined with either or both to create a range of styles. A goatee, for example, is a beard formed only with hair grown on the chin, while a Van Dyke (pictured) is a goatee joined to a mustache. When choosing a style, consider the shape and contours of your face, and the natural growth pattern of your facial hair.

continued from page 23

Threading the necklace

1 Thread on one bead (A). Pass one end of the doubled thread through the ring of the clasp then back through the bead.

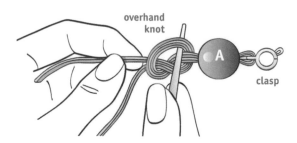

2 Make an overhand knot close to the bead and insert the threading needle into its main loop. Use the needle to guide the knot toward the bead, tightening as you remove it. Use the tweezers to hold the knot and pull the thread to compress the knot further. Leave just enough thread to pass through another bead and make another overhand knot.

3 Feed this shorter length of thread through the second bead (B) and tie a second overhand knot (as above). Cut the remainder of the short length of thread at this point, leaving only the doubled thread for further beads and knotting. You can also add a dab of glue to the knots to make them more secure.

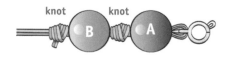

4 Keep threading beads, with an overhand knot between each and using the needle to tighten knots and beads.

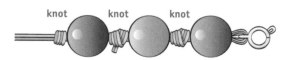

5 Continue until all the beads are in place except for the final two. Repeat steps 1, 2 and 3 with these beads and the other half of the clasp. Leave enough doubled thread at this end to pass back through the final beads and make the two knots. Cut off any spare thread, as before, at the final knot. **To leave some bare thread** at the back of the neck, you need to tie a knot an appropriate distance away from the clasp on both sides before threading the first bead.

---

choose Beef cuts

There are dozens of cuts of beef to choose from. The key to success is selecting the right cut for the right dish.

■ The best cuts of beef tend to come from the parts of the animal that move the least—the hindquarter, ribs and forequarter. The toughest, which need long, slow cooking, are the lower legs, shoulders, flank, neck and tail.
■ To be at its best, beef needs to be aged on the bone for three to four weeks. Inadequately aged beef will be bright red and shiny.
■ Some fat—which melts during cooking—is essential for a tender result.
■ Angus is the breed to select for superior quality. Hereford, Brahman, Brangus, Shorthorn, Longhorn and Beefmaster are also good.
■ Organic beef comes from cattle that weren't treated with antibiotics or hormones, and were fed only with organically certified grains and grasses.

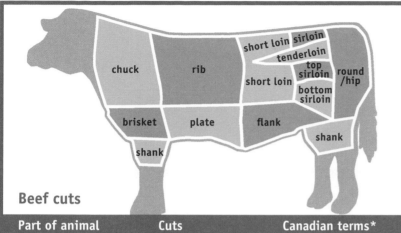

Beef cuts

Part of animal	Cuts	Canadian terms*
CHUCK	Shoulder Pot Roast Shoulder Steak Blade Steak Short Ribs 7-Bone Roast	
BRISKET	Point Half Brisket Flat Half Brisket	Brisket Point Flat & Rolled Brisket
SHANK	Shank Cross Cut	Shank Steak
RIB	Prime Rib Rib-Eye Rib Roast Back Ribs Short Ribs	
PLATE	Skirt Steak	Short Ribs
SIRLOIN		
SHORT LOIN	T-Bone Steak Top Loin Steak Strip Loin Tenderloin Porterhouse Steak	Wing Steak
FLANK	Flank Steak	
ROUND/HIP (CANADA)	Heel of Round Rump Roast Round Tip (Sirloin Tip) Top Round Bottom Round Eye of Round	Inside Round Outside Round
		*where different

make a
Bed with sheets

Using high-quality sheets, freshly laundered, adds a touch of luxury to your bedtime.

First, cover your mattress, ideally with a purpose-made cover (*see* MATTRESS).

If not using a fitted bottom sheet, place the straight bottom sheet right side up with equal amounts of fabric hanging over the sides and with at least 12 in. (30 cm) hanging over the foot.
- Tuck the bottom end firmly and neatly under the mattress from corner to corner. Do the same at the other end of the bed.
- Standing at the foot of the bed, take hold of the sheet overhanging one side of the bed at a point 16 in. (40 cm) along its edge away from the foot.
- Use a finger on your other hand to press on the top corner of the mattress while pulling the edge of the sheet directly upward. Then tuck in the small section of sheet still hanging beneath the level of the mattress nearest to the corner.
- Place your finger back on the top corner of the mattress and lower the sheet back over the side of the bed. The sheet should now appear to drop at an angle of 45 degrees from the top corner of the mattress.
- Tuck in the remaining fabric at the side of the bed and repeat for the remaining corners.

Add the top sheet so that, when folded back, its decorative edge is displayed, followed by blankets. Add pillows (see PILLOWS), with double covers: one utilitarian, the other chosen to match your bed linen. Allow two per sleeper. Cover with a bedspread tucked under the pillow.

B

make Beef stock

MAKES 8 CUPS

1 tbsp canola oil
½ lb (125 g) stewing beef
1 onion, quartered
1 carrot, chopped
1 stick celery, chopped
8 cups water
2 bay leaves
2 sprigs each parsley and thyme
10 black peppercorns
½ tsp salt

Put oil in a large heavy-bottomed pan and brown the beef over high heat. Remove meat and set aside. Lower the heat, then cook the vegetables. Add water and bring to a boil. Add the beef, skim off any scum, add the remaining ingredients and simmer for two hours. Strain, cool and skim off fat.

cope with a
Bee sting

Bees can turn on us if we frighten them or get too close to their hive. The barbed lance of the bee's stinger is torn off in the act of stinging. If it remains stuck in the victim, muscle works the stinger's venom-filled sac deeper into the flesh, increasing the venom injected. A bee sting is fatal to the bee, and occasionally to the victim (*see* ALLERGY EMERGENCY), though usually it's merely painful.

If stung, scrape the stinger out using a sideways movement with your fingernail or other hard edge, such as a credit card. Never pull it out with tweezers, as this squeezes more poison into the skin. Minimize swelling with an antihistamine and rub with ice to quell the itch.

pour the perfect Beer

Beer is best enjoyed when poured in a glass. The foamy head releases the beer's aroma of hops and retains its bitter taste.

Tilt a clean glass at 45-degree angle, and begin to pour so that the beer strikes the inside of the glass at the middle of the slope. Keep the flow steady and even.

When the glass is half full, bring it upright and continue to pour into the center of the glass. This will produce the foamy head, which should end up being about a finger's width for most beers.

deal with a swarm of Bees

It's an unnerving sight, but a swarm of bees isn't usually a risk. Left alone, a swarm is harmless, but if you see one in your garden, keep away and warn others to do the same. If the bees remain, contact a beekeeper to move them to a new home. Beware of using noisy garden machinery close to a swarm—it will antagonize them. In the unlikely event that the swarm chases you, stay calm and move out of the way slowly into the shade of a shed or tree. Don't swat at the bees; they will soon lose interest and leave you alone.

play Bingo at home

Bingo is a game of chance in which players hope to match a series of randomly selected numbers with those printed on their game card.

Getting started You need a set of 75 or 90 numbered bingo balls and some bingo cards, each of which is made up of a grid of randomly selected numbers. One person is the caller, blindly picking one ball at a time out of a bag and calling out its letter and number. When a number is called out, each player looks to find and mark off a match for it on their card. Usually, a player wins when he or she marks off all the numbers on one row of column of their grid (celebrating with a shout of "Bingo!"). To raise the stakes a little, players can pitch an agreed-upon sum of money into a pot at the beginning of each round, which the winner can claim as their prize.

If no one wants to be caller, there are websites that do the job for you—though with less panache. Most of these sites also allow you to download and print bingo cards for free. Google "online bingo caller."

build a Birdhouse

YOU WILL NEED **Plank of rough-hewn cedar or untreated ¼ in. (5 mm) outdoor plywood (sawn as shown below), drill, nails, hammer, brass hinge, latch**

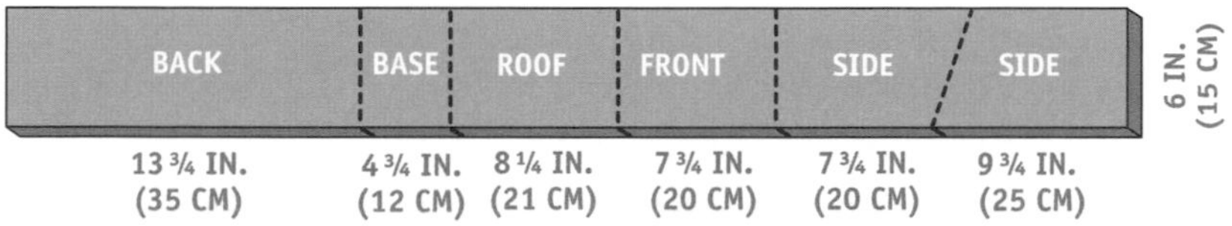
BACK
BASE
ROOF
FRONT
SIDE
SIDE
6 IN. (15 CM)
13 ¾ IN. (35 CM)
4 ¾ IN. (12 CM)
8 ¼ IN. (21 CM)
7 ¾ IN. (20 CM)
7 ¾ IN. (20 CM)
9 ¾ IN. (25 CM)

1 Drill a few ⅓ in. (8 mm) drainage holes in the base piece.

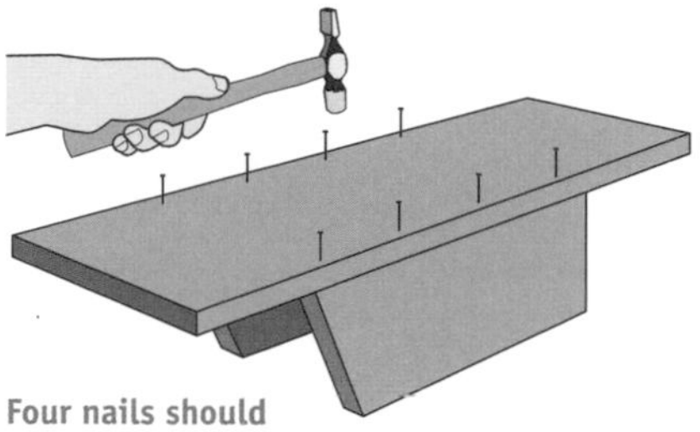

Four nails should suffice to join each side to the back.

Line the nails up centrally with the section beneath.

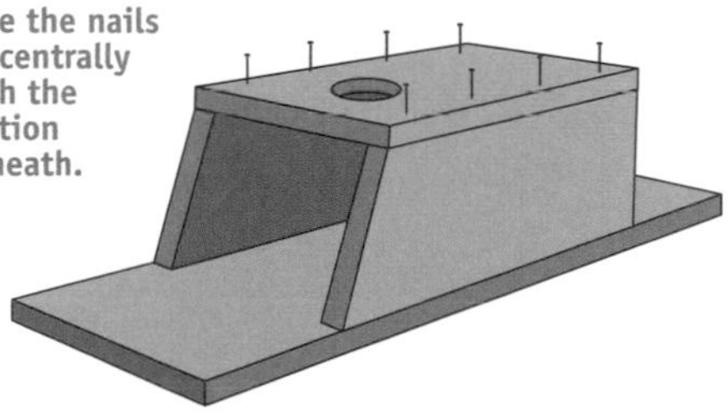

2 Nail the sides to the base, and the back section to the sides.

3 Before you attach the front section, use a space drill bit to create an entrance hole (see table below). The bottom of the hole must be positioned at least 5 in. (13 cm) from the floor of the box, so young birds cannot fall out.

A hinged lid allows you to open the box to clean it in autumn.

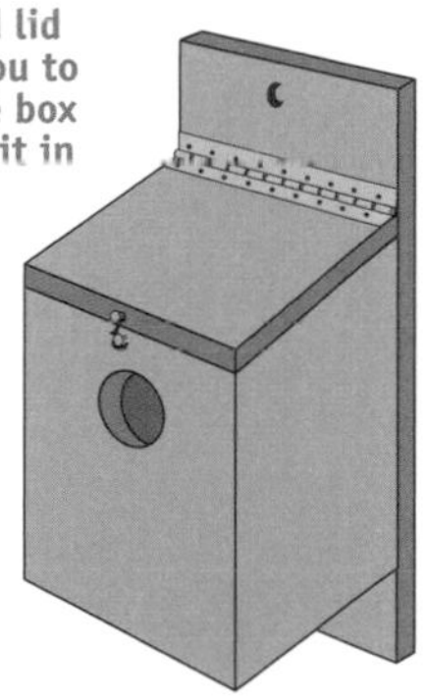

4 Nail on the front section, then attach the lid with a brass hinge, or a strip of inner tubing. Install a latch on the front of the lid. The inside wall below the entrance hole should be rough, to help young birds clamber up and out.

5 Fix your box using a nylon bolt or wire. A piece of hose around the wire will prevent damage to the tree. The box should face the northeast, and be tilted down to protect from direct sun and rain. Place the box high enough to escape the attention of cats.

The diameter of the entrance hole that you make depends on the kind of birds you want to attract.

Chickadee	**1⅛ in. (2.75 cm)**
Eastern bluebird	**1½ in. (3.5 cm)**
House finch	**2 in. (5 cm)**
House wren	**1¼ in. (3 cm)**
Swallow	**1½ in. (3.5 cm)**

An open front entrance is more suitable than a round hole for some birds. Here, what matters is the distance of the opening from the bottom of the birdhouse.

Bluejays	**8 in. (20 cm)**
Robins	**4 in. (10 cm)**
Wrens	**5½ in. (14 cm)**

get the knack of Blackjack

Fortunes are won and lost at this card game—but you can play at home, just for fun.

Casino rules for blackjack vary. This is a simple version to be played with friends and family. However many players are at the table, blackjack is fundamentally a two-person game—you against the dealer, with the aim of gaining a hand totaling closer to 21, without going over ("busting").

Scoring Number cards are face value. Aces can be one or 11. Face cards (jack, queen, king) score ten.

Rules Each player is dealt two cards, facedown. The dealer has one card faceup, the other facedown.

- If you're dealt an ace and a ten or face card, you have a "natural blackjack," an instant win—unless the dealer also has a natural, in which case there is a tie or "push" between you and the dealer while all the other players lose.
- If nobody has a natural, each player in turn has the option to be dealt another card ("hit"), stay with the cards they have ("hold") or surrender if they bust.
- When all players have chosen to hold or surrender, the dealer reveals their facedown card. If they have a total of 16 or less, they must hit, and as soon as they have 17 or more, they must hold. If the dealer busts, all players still in the game win. Otherwise, players with higher point totals than the dealer win.

maintain your
Bicycle
see pages 28–29

B

maintain your Bicycle

Your bicycle is a piece of machinery that needs to be looked after. Even if you don't ride often, there are some basic maintenance tasks you should carry out regularly, and you'll inevitably have to do repairs and replace worn parts from time to time.

Stay safe It's crucial that all the working parts of your bike are kept in good order to minimize the chances of your brakes failing, tires slipping or steering letting you down. Fortunately, most maintenance is simple enough that you can teach kids to look after their own bikes.

TIGHTEN THE HEADSET (A)

If your handlebars are loose, you need to tighten the top bearing in the headset. On most modern bikes with an A-head system, this is done by adjusting the top cap (sometimes under a dust cover) with an Allen key.

■ Loosen the stem bolts and tighten the top cap until it's no longer loose, then retighten the stem bolts. On older bicycles and some children's bikes, you'll need wrenches to make the adjustment.

■ Loosen the headset locknut a little, then tighten the upper bearing cup until no play is felt in the handlebars.

■ Retighten the locknut and hold it securely with a wrench. Then, using a second wrench, unscrew the bearing cup until it tightens against the locknut.

tightening an A-head system

ADJUST THE BRAKES (B)

The brake pads should be positioned so that they are close to the wheel rims—but they shouldn't touch until the lever is applied, or the pads will wear down and you'll find it harder to ride. Minor adjustments can usually be made using the barrel adjuster at the end of the cable, either at the lever or brake mechanism.

■ To tighten the cable further, use an Allen wrench to loosen the pinch bolt. Pull the cable until you're happy with the adjustment, and hold it while you retighten the bolt.

barrel adjuster

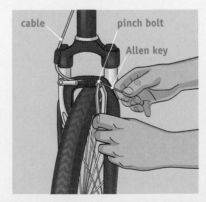

cable   pinch bolt

Allen key

BIKE MAINTENANCE CHECKLIST

A rickety bike is hard to pedal and unsafe to use. Brakes and tires are the main safety points to check, but every part of your bike must be working well for you to really enjoy your ride.

Before each ride Check your tire pressure, make sure brakes and cables are working well, and that any quick-release levers on the wheels or saddle are screwed tight.

After each ride Check tires for any sharp stones or glass. Make sure you don't have a leak and clean off any mud.

Once a month Inspect the chain, looking for wear, overly tight links or looseness. Lubricate the chain (see below). Check and lubricate brake levers, all cables and the derailleur gear mechanism. Look for wear on tires. Check and tighten all bolts, particularly on the stem post, headset and cable mounts.

Every six months Inspect the bike thoroughly. Look for any damage on the frame or signs of rust. Check the seat post, handlebar stem, handlebars, chainrings, brake calipers and levers, and make sure that all bearings (in the headset, hubs and pedals) are running smoothly.

MAINTAIN THE CHAIN (D)

Oil your chain once a month with bicycle oil. This is best done when the chain is clean. Remove it using a chain tool, and soak in mineral spirits, or use a cleaner that fits directly onto the chain. Chain cleaners are expensive and not as effective as a long soak, but they are quick and easy to use.

ADJUST THE GEARS (C)

Most modern road bikes have indexed derailleur gears that shift the chain to the next sprocket as you adjust the gear lever. Sometimes the mechanism gets out of sync and the gears fail to engage correctly. The most common cause of this is a maladjusted cable, which just takes a roadside adjustment to fix.

barrel adjuster

- The cable can be tightened or loosened using the barrel adjuster located at the point where the cable enters the rear derailleur.
- If the derailleur isn't moving the chain far enough to engage the sprocket, turn counterclockwise.
- If it's overshooting, turn the adjuster clockwise.
- Test the gears after each adjustment and keep tweaking until they change smoothly.
- If adjustments don't help, you may need a professional repair.

deal with Bleeding

Profuse bleeding can be fatal, so you need to act swiftly.

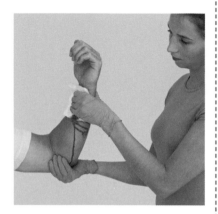

Call 911 as soon as possible and be prepared to treat the victim for shock (*see* SHOCK).

Check the wound to see if there's an object embedded in it. Wear clean disposable gloves, if available.

If there's no object embedded:
- Press a gauze pad firmly against the wound.
- If the wound is on an arm or leg, raise the limb above the head if possible—or above the level of the heart, if not—to slow blood flow to it. Be careful if you think a bone might be broken.
- To minimize shock, lay the victim on their back.
- Secure the dressing with a bandage (*see* BANDAGE).
- If blood seeps through, apply a second dressing and bandage.

If there's an object embedded.
- Apply pressure on either side of it.
- Raise the affected limb.
- Lay the victim down.
- Cover the wound and object with a dressing, without applying pressure. Build up padding around the object until the padding is higher than the object, then bandage over the object without pressing on it.

measure a window for Blinds

A well-fitted venetian or roller blind blocks out light without taking up wall space on either side of the window, like curtains do.

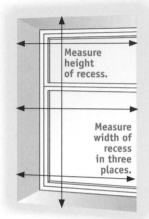

Measure height of recess.

Measure width of recess in three places.

Inside-mount blinds If your window has a deep recess, the blind can be fitted inside. Measure the width of the recess in three places, so you know its narrowest point. Measure the height in the same way. When you buy your blind or have it made, it should be the exact width of the narrowest point, so that it can be closed without obstruction, but cuts out light with maximum efficiency.

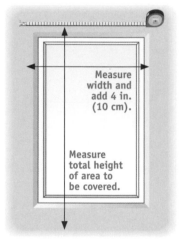

Measure width and add 4 in. (10 cm).

Measure total height of area to be covered.

Outside-mount blinds If there's no recess on your windows, measure the width in the same way and add 4 in. (10 cm), so that the blind is 2 in. (5 cm) wider than the window on both sides. Remember that the blind will need to be positioned 2 in. (5 cm) above the window, too. If the window has wide moldings, it will look better if you can tailor the blind to the exact dimensions of the moldings.

install roller Blinds

Before you begin, measure the window to determine what width your blinds need to be in order to fit properly (see above).

YOU WILL NEED **Measuring tape, junior hacksaw, long metal ruler, light pencil, scissors or utility knife, level, drill, wall plugs, screws, screwdriver**

Cutting a blind to fit Once you have established the required width of the blind, subtract the thickness of the brackets at either end to calculate how wide the roller needs to be.
- Fully unwind the fabric and peel it away from the roller at one end. Remember that if the blind has a symmetrical pattern or shaped bottom edge, you may need to cut an equal amount off each side. Use a hacksaw to cut through the metal tube.
- Use a long metal ruler and pencil to lightly mark a cutting line along the

full length of the fabric, about ¹⁄₁₆ in. (1.5 mm) in from the cut edge of the tube. Trim off the unwanted material with scissors.

■ Use the hacksaw to cut the bar at the bottom edge of the blind, replacing the end cap when you're done. Then re-roll the blind, tightly and evenly, back onto the roller—you may need help doing this.

1 Using a level as your guide, pencil a straight line across the wall or molding surfaces on which you want the blind to sit.

2 Hold the blind precisely in place while you mark the screw hole positions for the brackets, either in the top of a recess, on the face of a wall or window frame, or from the ceiling if it's low. You may need help doing this.

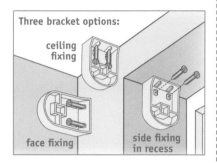
Three bracket options:
ceiling fixing
face fixing
side fixing in recess

3 Drill the screw holes and insert anchors into them, if necessary (you don't need anchors if you're drilling into wood).

4 Install the brackets, making sure that you place the bracket so that the scrolling cord falls on the side where you want it.

5 Slide the blind into the brackets as per the manufacturer's instructions (this may mean removing the plastic covers on the brackets, and replacing them once everything is functioning smoothly).

play Blindman's bluff

This game dates back 2,000 years to ancient Greece, and versions of it are played around the world, from Nigeria to Papua New Guinea. One player is blindfolded, then spun around until dizzy and disoriented. The other players dodge, dance and duck around him as he gropes and tries to catch them. When he catches someone, he has to guess who he caught. If he guesses right, the captive must put the blindfold on. If he guesses wrong, the captive is released. A favorite at kids' birthday parties, the game was once popular among adults, too.

treat Blisters

Blisters are raised areas of skin or mucous membranes under which fluids have accumulated. Never pop them! A blister caused by an infection will be teeming with bacteria or viruses, which could then spread. A blister with a noninfectious cause, such as a burn or sunburn, serves to protect underlying tissue, and reduces discomfort and the risk of infection.

If a blister bursts, expose it to the air in hygienic surroundings. Dress it if there's a risk of dirt getting in. See a doctor if it becomes inflamed, or if you suddenly develop widespread blisters, which suggest an underlying disease.

make Blinis

Authentic Russian blinis are best served with caviar, sour cream, onions and lemon. They are also excellent with smoked salmon and cream cheese.

MAKES ABOUT 30

2½ cups all-purpose flour
2 tsp instant yeast
pinch of salt
1 tbsp sugar
2 large eggs, separated
1¼ cups milk
1½ cups very warm water
1 tbsp unsalted butter
canola oil for frying

1 Sift the flour into a bowl, then mix in the yeast, salt and sugar. Make a well in the center.

2 Beat the egg yolks with the milk and water. Melt the butter and add it in, then pour half the liquid mixture into the well. Gradually beat in the flour to make a smooth batter, adding the remaining liquid in stages. Cover with a clean cloth and leave in a warm place until doubled in volume.

3 Whisk the egg whites to soft peaks and fold into the batter.

4 Heat the oven to 250°F (120°C). Heat a little oil in a heavy frying pan over high heat.

5 Spoon in enough batter to make blinis about 4 in. (10 cm) wide. Cook for about 1 minute per side until golden brown. Keep hot on a wire rack in the oven until all batter is used. During cooking, stir the remaining batter occasionally.

ATTRACTING BLOG READERS

■ Your blog is part of a much wider conversation. Read and leave comments on other people's blogs, websites and Twitter feeds, and they will be more likely to do the same with yours.

■ Contact authors of similar blogs to suggest linking to each other's sites.

■ Use other forms of media, such as Twitter, to alert readers to a new blog entry.

■ Above all, make your blog interesting and write regularly so readers will have a reason to visit frequently.

transfer files via
Bluetooth

Transferring data between electronic devices is easy using Bluetooth technology. You can use it to send pictures or documents over short distances—from your phone to another phone or computer, say—without having to connect the devices with a cable or use email.

For the system to work, both devices need to have Bluetooth turned on. Do this, and the devices will "discover" each other—that is, notice the presence of another Bluetooth-enabled device. Then it's a question of following the prompts and instructions of your own phone or computer—the exact procedure varies from one device to the next.

start your own Blog

A blog—short for "weblog"—is a kind of online diary that anyone can read. It's one of the many ways that you can use the internet to air your views and initiate a conversation with like-minded people.

Plan the content A blog can be personal, newsy, rambling or tightly focused on one topic, such as the environment, local politics or parenting. Decide on a theme, come up with an engaging title that reflects the theme and gather some ideas. Write some material before you go live—that way, you'll already have a direction and tone of voice when you make your debut.

Create your blog There are many free websites that host blogs and can give you the support you require to set one up. Google "free blog" to find one. Once you have registered, you can follow a few easy steps to design your blog, adding pictures, links and, above all, a way for readers to leave comments so that the conversation can continue.

use a home Blood pressure monitor

Most large pharmacies sell blood pressure monitors. Ask for one with a cuff that fits your arm.

A reading of 110/70 is ideal.

Wear a loose-fitting or short-sleeved shirt. Sit quietly for five minutes, with your arm resting on the table and feet flat on the floor. Then, with your arm (always use the same one) bared, relaxed and supported, wrap the cuff around the upper arm, level with your heart.

Stay still and silent as you take your reading. Repeat once or twice, at two-minute intervals, and take an average.
■ Ideally the average reading should be between 90/60 and 130/85.
■ If it's between 130/85 and 140/90 ("high normal"), or, more urgently, above 140/90 ("high"), you should make diet and lifestyle changes to reduce your risk of stroke.

Keep a record of your readings and see your doctor if your blood pressure is consistently high.

BLOOD PRESSURE TABLE

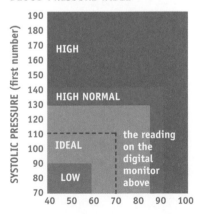

HIGH

HIGH NORMAL

IDEAL — the reading on the digital monitor above

LOW

SYSTOLIC PRESSURE (first number): 70 80 90 100 110 120 130 140 150 160 170 180 190

DIASTOLIC PRESSURE (second number): 40 50 60 70 80 90 100

read Body language

However hard we try to disguise our moods and motives, the way in which we hold and move our bodies speaks volumes about us.

We constantly telegraph unspoken messages about ourselves to one another, and learning to read those messages helps us to navigate the minefield of human interactions.

One of the most treacherous examples of body language is the blush or flush; it could mean arousal, attraction, embarrassment or anger. That, and yawning—sorry, are we boring you?

A nod of the head is a gesture of approval—but persistent bobbing of the head is a giveaway of nervousness or anxiety.

Open hands speak of sincerity and a willingness to help. Clenched fists are a sign of tension or anger.

When we like or agree with someone, we lean toward them. Leaning away, with folded arms, signals dislike or disagreement.

A sudden folding of the arms signals discomfort, defensiveness or a determination to resist.

Arms behind the back signals "stay back!"—it's an indication of anger, frustration or apprehension.

An inadvertently displayed thumbs-up or the turning up of a toe signals a positive thought or response.

Touching at the throat betrays doubt or insecurity.

calculate your Body mass index (BMI)

You can measure your BMI to see whether your weight is healthy for your height. Doctors consider it a useful indicator of overall health. Being underweight is linked with health problems like anemia and osteoporosis; being overweight increases your risk of heart disease, strokes and type 2 diabetes.

> There are two ways to calculate BMI. Here's how it works in both:
>
> **Imperial** If you are 5'3" (or 63") tall and weigh 140 lb, this is the calculation:
>
> $$\frac{(140 \times 703)}{63^2} \quad \frac{\text{weight} \times 703}{\text{height in inches}^2}$$
>
> 98,420 ÷ 3,969 = a BMI of 24.8
>
> **Metric** For someone 1.6 m tall who weighs 65 kg:
>
> **1.6 x 1.6 = 2.56**
> **65 ÷ 2.56 = a BMI of 25.4**

Analysis A BMI between 18.5 and 24.9 is ideal. Lower than 18.5 is considered underweight, and 25 or higher is deemed overweight. If your BMI is too low or too high, you should consider talking to your doctor about ways to bring yourself within the ideal range.

Accuracy BMI can also be deceptive. Muscle weighs more than fat, so exceptionally muscular people, such as weight trainers and athletes, may have a high BMI but still be a healthy weight. If you're in doubt, ask your doctor.

build a safe
Bonfire

Whether you're celebrating a special occasion or you live in an area where it's legal to burn garden waste, it's important to construct your fire safely and sensibly. Light your bonfire when it is least likely to affect neighbors—not on a warm, sunny day.

Safety first
- Let your neighbors know before you light your fire.
- Make sure that someone is supervising the fire at all times, and that children and animals are kept at a safe distance.
- Place the fire away from buildings, sheds, fences and overhanging trees.
- Use only dry wood. Damp material, green leaves and branches from live trees will produce clouds of unpleasant smoke.
- Don't burn household waste, especially rubber, plastics or painted materials.
- Keep a bucket of water nearby.

To build a fire
- Start with a heap of kindling (newspapers, small twigs, pine cones) that will burn quickly.
- Place a log or some wood prunings at either side, and then two logs across the top to make a platform.
- Build up the pyre with more branches, brambles, logs and other woody material in this crisscross manner, tapering toward the top.
- Fill any big gaps with more kindling or smaller twigs and branches. Light with a burning newspaper: Never use gas to get the fire going.

Boil an egg perfectly

Perfection in a soft-boiled egg is a firm but tender white and runny yolk, with no cracks in the shell to allow the white to seep out.

Use fresh eggs and make sure they are at room temperature to reduce the chances of them cracking during cooking.

Take a pin and make a prick in the shell at the round end (where the air pocket is). Then use a tablespoon to submerge the eggs in simmering water so that they are about ⅓ in. (less than 1 cm) below the surface. Use a small pan, to stop the eggs from banging together too hard during cooking.

Simmer for 3 minutes for very soft-boiled, 4 minutes for a set white and 6 minutes for an *oeuf mollet* (with a soft but not runny yolk).

If the shell cracks in the pan, add a dash of vinegar or lemon juice to the water. This makes any egg white that escapes set quickly, which helps to seal any cracks.

---

make the best Bolognese sauce

SERVES 4-6

1 tbsp olive oil
1 onion, finely chopped
1 carrot, finely chopped
1 garlic clove, minced
¼ lb (100 g) chicken livers, trimmed and chopped
1 lb (500 g) lean ground beef
¼ lb (100 g) mushrooms, thinly sliced
2 tbsp all-purpose flour
15 oz (540 mL) can chopped tomatoes
salt and freshly ground black pepper
1 bay leaf
½ tsp dried marjoram or oregano
2 tbsp tomato paste
½ cup red wine
1¼ cup beef stock (from cube, concentrate or homemade)

- Heat the oil in a heavy-bottomed saucepan and add the onion and carrot. Cover and cook gently for about 5 minutes, until the onion is tender.
- Add the garlic, chicken livers and beef, stirring until thoroughly browned. Add the mushrooms and fry for a few minutes.
- Stir in the flour followed by the tomatoes, seasonings and tomato paste. Add the red wine and stock and bring to a boil.
- Lower the heat, cover and simmer for 45–60 minutes. If the sauce is too liquid, remove the lid and raise the heat for the last 15 minutes, stirring occasionally.
- Remove the bay leaf before serving with spaghetti or tagliatelli. Alternatively, use with lasagne.

cover a Book

A simple protective cover for a book can be made from sturdy paper, such as wallpaper or a plain brown paper bag.

YOU WILL NEED **Paper, ruler, scissors, clear adhesive tape**

1 Measure and cut a piece of paper or plastic 2 in. (5 cm) larger all around than the open book. Center the book on the paper, with each cover face down. Cut diagonally across the paper at each of the four corners. Leave a little beyond each corner for overlap.

2 Make a diagonal cut in the paper at the top of the book tapering into the top left-hand corner of the spine. Then do the same toward the top right-hand corner. Repeat at the bottom to leave two flaps of paper, which you can cut off (at left) or tuck inside the spine.

Hold the pages of the book away from the cover while you tape the paper in place.

3 Fold the side flaps in, followed by the top and bottom flaps to create a seamless border. Secure each edge with tape.

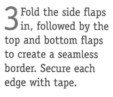

grow and care for Bonsai trees

The Chinese first grew miniature trees more than 1,000 years ago, an art later developed by Japanese monks. Almost any tree or shrub can be grown in this way.

To create an outdoor bonsai you can buy a starter seed kit or choose a tree seedling with a shape that you find interesting.

How to grow Pot the tree and leave it to establish itself for a year. The following spring, remove it, prune off any thick roots and pinch off all vigorously growing shoots. Repeat the process in the second year. In the third year, trim the roots by up to a third to fit a store-bought bonsai tray and continually pinch off unwanted shoots. Then spiral plastic-coated wire around branches to create twisted shapes. Bear in mind that deciduous trees such as maples are most pliable in spring, whereas evergreens such as pine and juniper are best shaped in autumn.

To protect your bonsai place it in a sheltered spot outdoors. If frost is forecast, wrap it in bubble wrap.

Indoor bonsai are tropical species best bought ready-grown from a specialist and kept permanently in a place away from direct sunlight. Look for one with evenly spread roots and an elegant shape. When the weather is mild, they will also appreciate a little fresh air from an open window.

B

escape Bores

It's relatively easy to get away from a bore at a party where you are standing up and mobile (escape is impossible at a sit-down dinner).

If you have been pinned to the wall by someone going on and on about their greenhouse, do anything to get a third person involved.

Catch the eye of an acquaintance and beckon urgently, as if you're enjoying an unmissable anecdote.

As soon as your friend arrives, drain your glass, mutter "Excuse me while I get a refill," and slip away without a backward glance.

You'll be free, and the bore will happily begin the story all over again with their new victim.

clean Bottles

For the outside of a bottle, warm water and dish soap are all that's needed. Always avoid using a scouring pad on antique glass.

For the inside If there's hardened residue, fill with warm water and dish soap and let soak for several hours before cleaning with a bottle brush.

For really stubborn dirt, put a tablespoon of dry rice or crushed eggshells into the bottle. Fill with water and add a denture-cleaning tablet. Let it dissolve, then cover the bottle and shake well.

For a tough white crust, try filling the bottle with white vinegar and leaving it for 24 hours. Then rinse out and wash the bottle as above.

Understand
Tenpin bowling
see page 328

play Boules

The French term boules *refers to a number of related games that involve two teams trying to place a ball or balls closest to a target.*

The most popular form of boules is the Provençal version, *pétanque*. It can be a contest between two players, or teams of two or three. It's usually played on a hard gravel surface.

The game begins when a player from one side, standing inside a throwing circle, throws the small jack (or *cochonnet*) some distance away. A player from the same team then tries to throw one of their steel balls (underhand) so it lands close to the *cochonnet*. A player from the opposing team then tries to place a ball closer still. The team with the closest ball is said to be "holding the point"; the team that is not "holding" continues to throw until they are closest to the *cochonnet*. Then it's the other team's turn again.

Once all balls have been thrown, the round ends. The team holding at the end wins one point for each ball closer to the *cochonnet* than the opponents' nearest. More rounds ensue, and the first team to reach 13 points wins.

tie a Bow tie

It takes practice to tie a bow tie. But once you've mastered it, it's no harder than tying a shoelace.

1. Drape the bow tie around your collar, so that end A is about 2¾ in. (7 cm) longer than end B. Cross A over B and feed through the gap at your neck to create a base knot.

2. Hold A out of the way. With your other hand, fold end B so it forms a bow centered over the base knot—here with the folded end to your left.

3. Drop end A so it hangs over the narrow part of the bow.

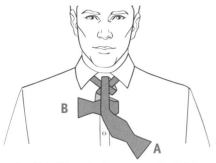

4 Still holding the bow at B, take hold of end A with your other hand.

5 Double end A on itself to form another bow and take the folded end up and behind B. Carefully feed A through the loop of the knot at your neck. You should now have a folded end and a loose end on each side of the knot at your neck.

6 Pull on the folded ends to tighten the new knot you created, and adjust so that all ends are of an even length.

Brainstorm a new idea

Generating ideas at work goes best when the participants can spark off each other, so get at least half a dozen lively people involved, if you can. Brainstorms are like parties; they often start slowly and may need something to break the ice. So make it fun; give everyone a glass of wine, or treat them to lunch. Use visual aids; if you're looking for new product ideas, have some good or bad products there on the table as conversation pieces. Scrupulously write down every idea that comes up on a whiteboard for all to see. And allow no negative criticism of any idea during the session.

clean Brass

Before cleaning brass, make sure you know whether it's protected with a lacquer coating if it's "raw."

To clean lacquered brass Apply a mixture of warm water and dish soap with a soft cloth or sponge. Rinse with clean water, dry thoroughly and buff with a soft cloth, chamois or old T-shirt.

To clean raw brass Use a soft cloth to apply a sparing amount of commercial metal polish, following the manufacturer's instructions.

To remove green corrosion Soak for several hours in washing soda, rubbing occasionally with an old cloth. Use an old toothbrush to get into crevices. Alternatively, rub with a cut lemon dipped in salt. Rinse well and dry.

B

measure up for a Bra

Four in five women wear the wrong size of bra, affecting shape and posture. Determine the ideal size for you, and you'll cut a better figure.

1 Wearing the best-fitting of your current bras, measure just under your breasts (A) with a tape measure with inches on it, keeping it taut but not tugging. If the measurement is an even number of inches, add 4 in. If odd, you should add 5 in. This gives you your band size.

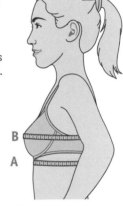

2 Now take the measure of the fullest part of your breasts (B), with the tape completely straight, flat against your back and drawn firmly, but not tightly, around your chest.

3 To find out your cup size, subtract the second measure from the first:
- "A" cup if there's no difference
- "B" if the difference is 1 in. (2.5 cm)
- "C" if the difference is 2 in. (5 cm)
- "D" if the difference is 3 in. (7.5 cm)
- "DD" if the difference is 4 in. (10 cm)

and so on through the cup sizes.

golden rules

BUYING A BRA
- **Always try before you buy.**
- **A new bra should be a good fit on the loosest hooks. As it slackens with wear, you can tighten them.**
- **If a bra leaves red marks on your skin, it's too tight.**

B

BREAD MAKING TIPS

■ Use a mixer with a dough hook (three minutes on low speed) or mix bread ingredients in an ordinary food processor—the ball produced won't require as much kneading.

■ Whole-wheat flour has less gluten than white flour, so it requires less kneading.

■ Speed up the rising process by using a microwave. After kneading, put the dough in an ungreased bowl and cover with lightly oiled plastic wrap. Heat on high for ten seconds, then let the bowl stand for 20 minutes in the microwave or other warm place. If the dough has not doubled in size, heat on high for another ten seconds, then let stand for another ten minutes.

bake your own Bread

There's nothing quite like the smell—or taste—of home-baked bread. As well as choosing from a wide range of flours, you can add seeds, nuts, raisins, sundried tomatoes, herbs or other flavorings.

TO MAKE TWO LARGE LOAVES

½ oz (15 g) fresh yeast, 2 tsp
    dried yeast plus 1 tsp sugar
    or 1 package self-rising yeast
2 cups lukewarm water
6 cups white bread flour
    (plus extra if needed)
1 tbsp salt
canola oil for greasing
beaten egg for glazing

YOU WILL NEED Small bowl for yeast mixture, two large mixing bowls (one warmed), fork, plastic wrap, two 1 lb (500 g) loaf pans, two plastic bags large enough to fit a loaf pan, pastry brush for glazing

VARIATIONS

Use half-and-half white and whole-wheat flour, or choose spelt or rye flour

1 Dissolve fresh yeast in the water and mash well with a fork. For dried yeast, dissolve sugar in the lukewarm water, sprinkle the yeast on top and let sit for 10 minutes until frothy. Stir well.

2 Sift the flour with the salt into a large warmed mixing bowl; pour in the yeast mixture or add the instant yeast. Mix with your hands, drawing in flour little by little to make a dough ball. Add flour if the dough is sticky.

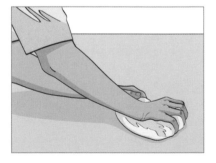

3 Turn onto a floured surface and knead for 10 minutes, flouring your hands as necessary. Work rhythmically, pushing the dough away from you, folding it back over and giving it a quarter turn each time, or knead in a mixer (see sidebar, top left). Knead until smooth and elastic, with a slightly blistery surface.

4 Lightly grease a clean bowl, add the dough and cover with lightly oiled plastic wrap. Leave in a warm place for 1½–2 hours, or until doubled in volume. Punch down with your fist to knock out the air in the dough, then take it out of the bowl and knead another minute.

5 Grease the loaf pans. Divide the dough into two portions and form each into a loaf shape to fit the pan. Pour a little oil into each bag, rub it around to coat the inside, then put a pan inside. Seal the bags' openings and let rise for about 40 minutes at room temperature.

6 Heat the oven to 450°F (230°C). Remove pans from bags. Brush the dough with egg glaze. Bake 35 minutes.

7 When the bread is done, the loaves should have shrunk from the sides of the pans and sound hollow when tapped on the base. Cook for a few more minutes if necessary. Remove from pans and place on a wire rack to cool.

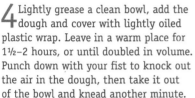

use up stale Bread

Stale bread has all kinds of uses. Try these simple suggestions to turn your leftovers into something delicious, or whizz them into breadcrumbs in a food processor and keep a bag in the freezer.

Slices without crusts Dip in egg and milk, then fry for French toast. Layer buttered slices in a dish with golden raisins and lemon zest, top with vanilla custard and bake to make a British-style bread and butter pudding.

Cubes Fry or bake in the oven, drizzled with olive oil, to make croutons. Add to tomato soup to create the Italian *pappa al pomodora*, or to any vegetable soup to thicken it.

Breadcrumbs Mix with onions and herbs to make stuffing; fruit and nuts, such as dried apricots and almonds, can also be added. Mix with chopped herbs and use to top shepherd's pie or other savory dishes as an alternative to potato. Use, following flour and beaten egg, to coat food before frying. Mix with sugar and lemon zest, then layer with apples, dot generously with butter and bake in the oven for an apple charlotte.

examine your Breasts

Examine your breasts monthly, just after your period. Get to know what feels normal for you so you'll recognize any changes. See your doctor if you notice any nipple discharge, a new lump or tenderness that lasts more than a month. Find a comfortable position, either lying down or standing up.

1 Raise your arm and use your fingertips to feel the breast tissue extending into the armpit. Remember to do both sides.

2 With the flat of your fingers, thoroughly examine the upper, outer quarter of the breast.

3 Examine the rest of the outer half, working towards the nipple. Then press the inner half of the breast against your ribs.

B

maximize
Broadband speed

Even if you're only browsing the internet, a slow connection speed makes pages frustratingly slow to open and navigate. Watching or streaming video, or making online phone calls, will be stuttery or even impossible.

■ One of the most effective things you can do to increase your connection speed is upgrade your router—some providers will send you a new one for free. Older routers can handle a maximum of 54 megabits per second (Mbps) or less, while the latest ones have a maximum of more than 200 Mbps.
■ Wireless broadband works best when the computer is in the same room as the router—solid walls and furniture muffle the signal.
■ Keep your browser software up to date, and empty caches (blocks of memory) regularly.
■ Consider changing your broadband provider. A different one may deliver much better speeds.

✴ golden rules

master the basics of Bridge

Bridge is perhaps the most complex and sophisticated member of the whist family. But the aim is simple; score points by winning tricks.

"Contract" bridge is played by two teams of two. The partners face each other across the table, and are known as north-south pairings and east-west pairings. A standard pack of 52 cards is dealt out to the four players.

How it begins Players conduct an auction, bidding in turn for the "contract." If a player bids *one diamond*, they undertake to win seven of the 13 tricks (*one* more than half the available tricks), with *diamonds* as trumps. The next player can then bid higher in terms of the number of tricks or the trump suit; ranked in descending order, they are spades, hearts, diamonds then clubs. If you have a strong hand spread over several suits, you can bid to play without a trump suit: a *no-trump* bid. *No-trump* beats all suits. A player wins the contract, say *four clubs*, when nobody outbids them. This "declarer" is committed to winning ten tricks (four more than half), with clubs as trumps.

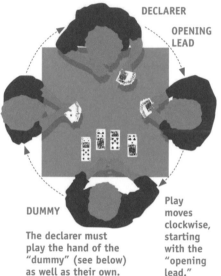

The winning bidder becomes the "declarer" for the hand.

DECLARER

OPENING LEAD

DUMMY

The declarer must play the hand of the "dummy" (see below) as well as their own.

Play moves clockwise, starting with the "opening lead."

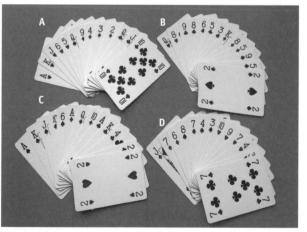

Hand A has six likely trick-winning cards (in hearts and clubs) and four diamonds; with diamonds as trumps, it might win eight tricks, so the player could bid "two diamond." Hand C has nine high-value cards (21 potential points) and would probably win the contract with a bid of "three notrump." With fewer strong cards, players B and D would be wise to "pass" and not make a bid.

The game continues The player to the left of the declarer, the "opening lead," lays a card. The declarer's partner (the "dummy") then lays all their cards face up on the table, sorted into suits, and takes no further part in the round; the declarer plays for them. Each trick is played the same as in whist (*see* WHIST): Every player must follow suit if they can, and the highest card wins the trick. Once all 13 tricks have been played, points are awarded for every one over six—to the declarer's team if their contract has been met, or to the opposing pair, if not.

Those are the mechanics of the game. But, as with chess, the skill in bridge lies in the ability to compute all the options during the auction, then in trick play, and to exploit the weaknesses of the opposing pair. In bridge, as in life, it's not so much the hand you're dealt, but how you play it.

help someone with a Broken bone

When someone takes a nasty spill, your first question should always be, "Is anything broken?" Pause to consider this before rushing to help them up to make sure you don't inadvertently make any injury worse.

What to look for
■ Look for outward signs of a fracture: visible swelling, bruising or discoloration of the skin around a joint; or an arm, leg or other body part that's at an unnatural angle—for instance, a leg turned outward.
■ There may be an obvious injury: Perhaps the victim can't put weight on one leg, bend an arm or move his or her fingers.
■ The victim may feel faint or dizzy and nauseous with pain, or complain of a grinding sensation in the bone. If there's any suspicion of a broken leg, do not encourage the person to try to walk.

What, and what not, to do
■ Avoid all unnecessary movement, as broken bone ends can do damage to surrounding blood vessels and nerves. Be alert to the dangers of shock (see SHOCK). Put a coat or a blanket around the victim to keep him or her warm, but don't offer a hot drink in case he or she needs an anesthetic later.
■ If there's a wound, cover it with a dressing and bandage (see BANDAGE) to keep it clean.
■ If a bone is poking out, lightly cover it with gauze.
■ Don't try to make a splint or support. Call an ambulance if the victim cannot move.

heal a Broken heart

When the one you lived for rejects you, it's tempting to wallow in pity or stew in a fury. But it's really time to live for yourself. Beware of falling for someone new on the rebound—learn to love yourself again first.

Draw support from friends and loved ones and make an effort to make yourself feel good. Eat well, get dressed up—even for a shopping trip—and hold your head high (literally—it works).

Get exercise Walking or dancing will boost mood-enhancing endorphins and your self-image. Fill your weekends with activities you enjoy.

Make a list of all that's good about you and all that's bad about your ex. Remind yourself of your own worth and try to avoid romanticizing the past.

treat Bruises

Bruising is caused when damaged blood vessels, especially tiny capillaries, bleed within the tissues.

■ To treat a bruise or black eye, apply a cold compress for 10–20 minutes at a time, every two to three hours.
■ Don't put ice directly on your skin. Make an ice pack using a bag of frozen peas or put ice cubes in a freezer bag, then wrap in a tea towel before applying.
■ Minor bruising is painful and unsightly, but nothing to worry about. Severe bruising can suggest more serious underlying damage, be accompanied by shock (see SHOCK) and require medical attention.
■ If you bruise easily or inexplicably, see your doctor.

disguise Bruises

You fell down or walked into a door and bruised your face. There's no way around it—you look terrible.

What to do? If ordinary makeup is not up to the job, take a tip from plastic surgeons and use camouflage cosmetics. Try a concealer, which is thicker and more opaque than regular foundation, or a color corrector—choose a lavender tint to hide bruising and green for redness. Both of these are applied under foundation and can be just as effective on men.

In the case of a black eye, apply concealer or corrector to both eyes, so they won't look too different. Concentrate on darkening the lashes with mascara (see EYES) and lightening the eyelids to draw attention away from the bruised area.

draw up a Budget

Successful budgeting depends on having complete and precise details of all your income and expenditures.

- Gather bank statements, investment accounts, utility bills, receipts and pay slips for the last 12 months, or as long as possible.
- Make lists on paper or, better still, in a computer spreadsheet program like Excel (*see* SPREADSHEET). Record all expenses under "fixed" (such as rent, mortgage and insurance) and "variable" (weekly groceries, gas, gifts, entertainment, vacations, emergencies).
- Categorize expenses as much as possible to help you highlight areas where you could cut back.
- Total everything coming in and going out.

If your expenses are higher than your income, go through your lists of variable expenses to see which can be eliminated or reduced. Cut down on take-out meals, use the car less or shop more economically, for example. Next, examine your fixed expenses and make sure you have the best possible deal for your utilities and mortgage.

Set yourself limits on expenditures. Deduct the fixed expenses from your income, then allocate a monthly proportion of the remainder to each of your expense categories. Be sure to keep a fund for emergencies and unexpected expenses and always prioritize the essentials, such as food and payments on any outstanding debts. Try to put some money into savings each month too.

Keep records of what you spend throughout the month so you always know that you're within your budget.

bake the best Brownies

The ideal brownies are crisp on the outside and soft inside. They go great with ice cream, chocolate sauce or raspberries.

YOU WILL NEED **Two mixing bowls, pot of water, whisk, 8 in. (20 cm) square cake pan greased and lined with parchment paper**

TO MAKE 20-24 BROWNIES

½ **cup unsalted butter**
7 **squares semi-sweet baking chocolate**
2 **eggs**
1 **cup superfine sugar**
1 **tsp vanilla extract**
½ **cup all-purpose flour**
2 **tbsp cocoa powder**
1 **cup walnuts, roughly chopped**

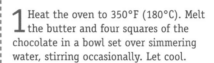

1 Heat the oven to 350°F (180°C). Melt the butter and four squares of the chocolate in a bowl set over simmering water, stirring occasionally. Let cool.

2 Whisk the eggs, gradually add the sugar and continue until the mixture is thick, foamy and leaves a ribbon-like trail when you lift out the whisk. Add the vanilla and the chocolate mixture and blend thoroughly. Sift in the flour and cocoa powder and add the nuts and remaining chocolate, chopped into small chunks. Fold it all in.

3 Pour into the prepared pan, spread evenly and bake for 30 minutes; the brownies should still have some "give." Cool in the pan for 10 minutes, then remove paper and cut into squares.

plant Bulbs for color

Carefully chosen, bulb plants will provide color in the garden in every season. Many spring bulbs will spread naturally in a lawn, but they are also ideal for borders and containers.

Planting bulbs in a border

1 Dig a planting hole large enough for a clump of bulbs, or use a slim trowel to make individual holes for each bulb. When planting a cluster of bulbs together—this will give the best show— make sure that they are spaced at least their own width apart. Give more space to species that will multiply, such as hyacinth and crocus. For a natural effect, plant in informal groups rather than symmetrical patterns or rows.

2 Scatter bonemeal in the base of the hole to give bulbs a good start—fork it in and water the soil. Incorporate some sand if your soil is heavy.

3 Gently cover the bulbs with soil, taking care not to knock them over. Firm the surface with the back of a rake and mark the area, so you don't dig up the bulbs by accident.

In lawns Drop handfuls of bulbs from waist height, then plant them where they land using a slim trowel or a cylindrical bulb planter. Or cut the outline of a large *H* with a spade and peel away the grass. Fork in bone meal if desired, then plant bulbs firmly before replacing the grass.

In pots Pack a large pot with bulbs for a stunning display—a single variety is most striking. Use potting soil plus a few handfuls of coarse sand to improve drainage. For a dense, long show of blooms, stagger bulbs in two or three layers, 2 in. (5 cm) apart in a pot at least 1 ft (30 cm) deep.

Planting depths for bulbs

As a rough guide, estimate the height of the bulb from tip to base, then cover it with twice that depth of soil, or three times the depth on light soils. The exceptions to this rule are lilies, which need a depth of three or four times their bulb height.

1 Glory-of-the-snow
2 Spring crocus
3 Cyclamen coum
4 Hyacinth
5 Grape hyacinth (Muscari)
6 Daffodil
7 Siberian squill
8 Tulip
9 Allium (large)
10 Daylily

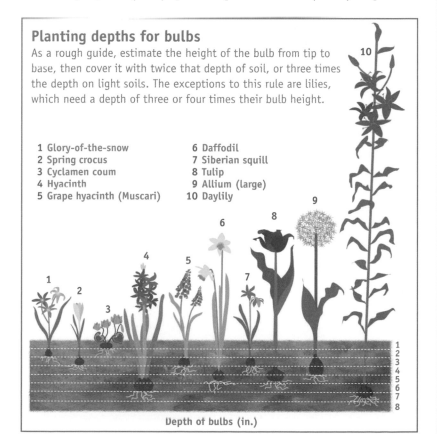

Depth of bulbs (in.)

get the better of Bullies

Bullying can happen anywhere—in school, work or cyberspace— and it ranges from name-calling to intimidation and violence. Bullies are generally weak, jealous characters and, in most cases, will stop if you don't give them the satisfaction of a reaction. But persistent bullying can be a matter for the police.

Physical bullying If you're subjected to physical assault or fear you're in real danger, report this to the police, or someone with authority: your human resources (HR) team or union representative if it happens at work, or a teacher if it's happening to a child at school.

Psychological bullying Your best weapon against people who try to undermine you is mental strength. Refuse to be riled by insults and negative comments. In the workplace, poor management can become bullying. Try to stay objective, keep notes of specific incidents and present a clear case to HR or a more senior manager. Most employers have a bullying policy.

Online bullying Try to avoid opening abusive emails or block the sender from your account, and stay away from social networking sites if this is where the bully contacts you. Never give others access to your Facebook or other networking site account, where they could post embarrassing or upsetting messages in your name, and always set privacy settings as high as possible, particularly for a child or young person's account. If you're being routinely bullied, save or print out any evidence—even anonymous posts can be traced by the police.

relieve the pain
of Bunions

A bunion is a harmless swelling of the joint at the base of the big toe resulting from bone overgrowth. It's a common problem for middle-aged women, who have, perhaps for too long, squeezed their feet into too-tight, high-heeled shoes. Heredity is also a factor.

Choose broad, flat or low-heeled footwear that doesn't crowd your toes. Bunion pads from the drugstore help to stop shoes rubbing.

An ice pack (*see* BRUISES) can help relieve pain and reduce swelling. Or try soaking your feet in a hot footbath laced with Epsom salts.

Complications of bunions include stiffness in the toe joints, pain under the ball of the foot, swelling or deformities such as "hammer" toes, discomfort when wearing shoes, difficulty walking and corns or calluses developing over the lump.

Bunions also increase the risk of osteoarthritis in the affected joint. Your doctor may refer you to be fitted with orthoses—devices such as bunion splints to realign the bones, and specially shaped insoles to relieve pressure.

If you are in severe pain, surgery may be a consideration.

Well-fitting shoes are absolutely vital for children and young people. Fashionable or not, sensible shoes will prevent the early onset of foot pain that could last a lifetime.

secure your home against Burglars

Burglars like easy targets, so make sure your home is a difficult proposition for opportunistic criminals. You want them to take one look and decide it's not worth the risk.

If you do nothing else, secure all points of entry to your home. Fit visible locks to all your windows. Most burglars will think better of it right away if they will have to break a window to get inside: They want access that's swift and silent.

A BURGLAR ALARM (1) is an effective deterrent. Some can be linked directly to the police or your cell phone. Don't choose an easy-to-guess deactivation code, like "0000."

USE TIMERS (2) that turn some lights on for a few hours each evening, or even automated curtain closers. Consider fitting outside security lights that come on as anyone approaches your house.

SIDE ENTRANCE (3) If there's a side entrance or a pathway to the back of the house, make sure it has a lockable gate so nobody can get into your backyard.

VISIBLITY (4) Make sure your front door and windows are visible from the street—trim high hedges, and remove bushes that grow close to your windows and provide cover.

DEADBOLT (5) Have a deadbolt fitted to your front door.

SPARE KEY (6) Never hide a spare door key under a mat or potted plant—any burglar will know where to look.

GARAGE DOORS (7) are often easier to force than house doors. Fit additional locks or a barrier to prevent a garage door from opening. Always lock any connecting door with the house and bolt it from the inside. If a burglar gets into the garage, they can work unseen at the inside door.

OCCUPIED Create the impression that your home is occupied even when it isn't. Cancel newspaper deliveries when you're away and get a trusted neighbor to collect your mail.

make clarified Butter

Brown butter (*beurre noisette*) is served with fish and vegetables. Heat ½ cup butter until golden brown. Remove the pan from heat and add 1–3 teaspoons of lemon juice. Use immediately.

Black butter (*beurre noir*), a classic accompaniment to poached fish, is heated until dark brown. Timing is crucial: It must be removed from the heat before it burns. When cooked, add 2 tablespoons drained capers. Use at once.

Clarified butter, or ghee, is used for sautéing and in Indian cooking. Melt a pat of butter in a small saucepan over very low heat and skim the froth from the surface. Pour slowly into a bowl, leaving behind the milky sediment. Or refrigerate until solid, then separate, discarding the sediment.

----

sew on a Button

Most buttons are sew-through, with two or four holes. On a shirt or blouse you can sew a button on flat; on thicker fabrics you may need the button to sit away a little by creating a thread shank (see below).

Four-hole shirt button

1 Anchor the thread on the reverse of the material with a knot and a few small stitches. Push the needle through to the front and thread on the button.

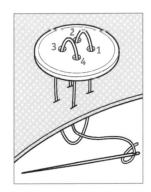

2 Take the needle down through a second hole, up through the third and down through the fourth, and continue to make about six stitches in each. You can also attach the button using the cross method: up through 1, down through 3, up through 2 and down through 4, starting again with 1. At the back of the fabric, make a few stitches through the thread to finish off, tie a small knot and snip off the excess thread.

Four-hole coat button with shank

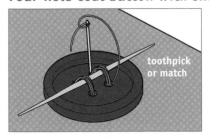
toothpick or match

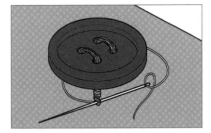

1 Anchor the thread and thread on the button (above, left). As you sew, loop the stiches over a toothpick or match to create some slack for the shank.

2 Before you finish off at the back, remove the stick, pull the button away from the fabric and wind the thread firmly around the stitches between the button and coat to make a shank. Make one stitch into the shank to secure it (above, right), then push the needle through the fabric and fasten the thread at the back.

treat Burns and scalds

A burn requires immediate action to limit skin damage.

Quick action

Stop the burning process— immediately douse the burn with cold water, if possible by holding the burned part under cold running water for at least ten minutes, even if the pain stops. If a tap is not available, any cold fluid, such as milk, will do.

Seek medical advice or call an ambulance if any of the following applies, or if you're in any doubt about the severity of the burn:
- Burns are severe, deep or larger than the size of the victim's hand.
- Burns were caused by chemicals or electricity.
- The victim is in shock (*see* SHOCK), in already poor health or shows signs of exhaustion—or is under five, over 60 or pregnant.

Remove clothing and jewelry around the burned area but don't pull any material stuck to the skin. After ten to 20 minutes cooling with water, allow the area to dry then cover with a clean, lint-free material, such as plastic wrap or a plastic bag.

Wrap a blanket around the person —avoiding the affected area—to guard against a dangerous drop in body temperature.

Superficial burns and scalds affecting only the surface of the skin may not need medical attention and should heal naturally.
- Keep the burn clean, don't apply cream and don't be tempted to pop blisters (*see* BLISTERS).

C

grow and care for Cacti

Success with growing cacti depends on imitating the conditions from which they originate as much as possible.

Desert cacti Good varieties include *Cereus*, *Opuntia* and *Mammillaria*. For flowers, try *Parodia* and *Rebutia*.
■ A cold greenhouse is ideal, though the cacti will thrive indoors on sunny windowsills in winter.
■ Use a good-quality commercial cactus soil and water regularly between May and September, allowing the top 6 in. (15 mm) of soil to dry out between waterings.
■ Water just enough to prevent roots from drying from December to February; increase watering gradually throughout March.

Jungle cacti These include the Easter cactus (*Rhipsalidopsis gaertneri*) and Christmas cactus (*Schlumbergera x buckleyi*).
■ Keep them out of direct sunlight at all times, provide a humid atmosphere and a temperature no lower than 50°F (10°C).
■ Pot as for desert cacti, including 30 percent leaf mold compost.
■ Keep moist in winter but allow cacti to dry out after flowering.

✳ golden rules

BOOSTING TIPS FOR CACTI
■ Water cacti with rainwater or cold, boiled water to maximize their nutrient uptake. Never overwater or they will rot.
■ If light is one-sided, turn cacti regularly to prevent distorted growth.

try your hand at Calligraphy

Expressive, flowing handwriting in colored ink will lend style and distinction to greeting cards and invitations.

The word calligraphy means "beautiful handwriting," but think of it more as drawing —one perfect character at a time.

Finding a template Select and download one of the calligraphy alphabets available free online. Choose either a forward-slanting or vertical alphabet. Don't mix styles or you'll lose the essential harmony that distinguishes calligraphy from individualized handwriting. Uniformity of size and style are more important than fancy flourishes, so practice copying letters over and over until you're confident enough to start writing freehand and creating your own work.

Pens A dip pen with a complete set of nibs is the choice of professionals, but cartridge calligraphy pens or calligraphy markers are less messy options for beginners. Doodle with your pens to get familiar with the nibs before you start work.

Paper and ink For the best results, use calligraphy paper of at least 90 gsm (24 lb) and water-based, colored calligraphy inks. You'll need a variety of each—sepia ink on cream paper will give a historic look; black or blue on white looks classic and formal.

Your workspace Work on a slanted surface, such as a board propped up with a block of wood or a thick book. Use a piece of paper under your free hand to secure the sheet you're working on.

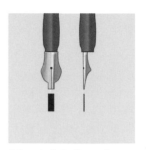

A broad, flat nib creates the distinctive thick and thin lines of calligraphy: thick when moving down, and thin when writing across the page.

Always keep the angle of the nib the same, usually pointing diagonally away from you to the left. Use a light pressure and lead the nib over the paper—don't push it or lean too hard.

Perfect the individual strokes that build up into complete letters. Practice writing perfectly regular, parallel lines in all directions, then build on these to add curves.

■ Some templates break down all the strokes that make up each letter. Draw faint guidelines to help you to keep letters regular.

■ Arrows indicate how to move your nib, in this case down from the midpoint and up to the top. Lift the nib at the end of the stroke.

■ Complete the ascender, or top of the *f*, with a second curving stroke, then add the crossbar at the midpoint, or x-height.

cut down on Calories

By making simple, smart food choices you can reduce your energy intake, eat satisfying portions and maintain a healthy weight—for life.

■ First and foremost, eat plenty of fiber in the form of whole grains, lentils, nuts and seeds, as well as the fruit and vegetables that should form the bulk of your meals. Obesity is clearly linked to low fiber intake, and just a small extra amount each day can make a difference.

■ Stop eating sweetened breakfast cereals, croissants and pastries; and white bread, pasta and rice. Switch to fiber-rich bran flakes, whole-wheat bread and pasta, and brown rice, which will keep you feeling full for longer.

■ Choose poultry or fish over fatty, additive-laden sausages and burgers. Use extra-lean ground beef and the leanest cuts of meat.

■ Bake, broil, poach or steam your food rather than frying it. Instead of french fries try a baked sweet potato.

■ Go for low-fat cheese and skim milk. Stop buying sugary, full-fat yogurt. Switch to low-fat plain yogurt and eat it with plenty of fruit.

■ Instead of eating a whole chocolate bar, try a couple of squares of dark chocolate that's high in cocoa solids to get your chocolate fix.

■ Swap fatty, salty, packaged snack foods for an apple, small bunch of grapes, some dried apricots or handful of unsalted nuts.

■ Switch from sugary soft drinks to mineral water or fruit juice.

conjure up party Canapés

These one or two-bite savory appetizers, served with cocktails or pre-dinner drinks, look good and are easy to eat—perfect for a party.

The best way to think of canapés is as bases with toppings. Allow ten canapés per person as an appetizer, and at least 20 for a cocktail party.

tomato and basil bruschetta

salami and cheese inside a tart shell

shrimp salad on a savory cracker

The bases
■ Bread (rye, whole-wheat or sourdough triangles, pita pieces or thin slices of baguette), with crusts removed as necessary. It can be toasted or heated in the oven.
■ Savory crackers or pancakes (*see* BLINIS *and* PANCAKES).

■ Pastry crusts (pie or puff).
■ For low-carbohydrate alternatives, use hollowed-out cherry tomatoes, sticks of celery or red pepper, crisp lettuce or endive leaves, or fruit, such as dried apricots.

continued on page 50 →

build a Campfire

YOU WILL NEED Tinder (dry twigs, paper, pine needles), kindling (small, short sticks), firewood (dead branches or dry logs)

1 Clear a space of all combustible material. If the ground is wet, use dry wood as a platform. Have a bucket of water at hand in case the fire spreads.

2 Place a handful of tinder at the center of your firepit. Make a "box" around it with kindling: Build up a teepee or cone shape for cooking, and a pyramid (constructed like a log cabin) if your fire is for warmth.

3 Place firewood around the outside of the box, so that the flames spread from the tinder to the kindling to the firewood. Light from the side that's sheltered from the wind.

find the right Campsite

Don't wait until it's dark to find a place to pitch your tent (*see* TENT). Look for a spot in daylight, so you can see the lay of the land. Choose a place that's out of the wind but not directly under trees. Long grass indicates that the ground is damp, and stagnant water will attract biting insects. The best kind of campsite is a place that's flat (and comfortable to sleep on), level, reasonably free of undergrowth and rocks, and well-drained. When you put up your tent, put the back or the narrowest side facing into the wind—never the entrance.

decorate a
Cake
see pages 48-49

C

decorate a Cake

Adding decoration to a cake need not be difficult and can give a professional look to everything from a simple sponge cake to cupcakes or a decorated cake for a special family celebration.

Types of frosting
Frosting, or icing, is always effective—and tasty. Glaze, buttercream and chocolate are best for soft cakes. Royal and ready-made fondant are best for firmer cakes, like fruitcake. To decorate, you can use fresh flowers, ribbons and candles, or some of the following suggestions.

GLAZE To cover the top and sides of a 7 in. (18 cm) round cake or about 15 cupcakes.

1⅓ cup (320 mL) icing (confectioner's) sugar
2–3 tbsp hot water

Sift the sugar into a bowl, add the water a little at a time then add any flavorings. To cover the top and sides of a cake, the glaze should coat the back of a spoon but flow easily. For cupcakes, it should be a little stiffer. Leave the iced cake to set for at least an hour.

HOW TO GET A SMOOTH FINISH

Pour the icing so that it drips down the sides of the cake and use a palette knife to smooth the top and sides.

CHOCOLATE GLAZE To cover the top and sides of a 9 in. (23 cm) round cake or about 15 cupcakes.

12 squares semisweet chocolate, in pieces
⅔ cup unsalted butter
⅓ cup apricot jam, strained and warmed

Melt the chocolate in a bowl over nearly simmering water. Add the butter and stir until melted. Brush the cake with the apricot glaze. Apply the chocolate glaze to the cake and leave to set for at least 4 hours.

ROYAL ICING To cover the top and sides of a 9 in. (23 cm) round cake with two thin layers.

7 cups icing (confectioner's) sugar
4 egg whites
2 tsp lemon juice
2 tsp glycerine (omit for a tiered cake—it makes icing too soft)

Sift the sugar and beat the egg whites until frothy, then add half the sugar a tablespoon at a time. Beat well for 5–10 minutes, until fluffy. Gradually add the lemon juice, glycerine and remaining icing (confectioner's) sugar, beating until it stands in peaks and loses its shine. Cover with a damp cloth and let stand for 2 hours. After icing the cake let it set for 4 hours before applying another layer. After the last layer, wait for 24 hours before adding decorations.

BUTTERCREAM To fill center and cover the top of an 8 in. (20 cm) round cake or about 15 cupcakes.

½ cup unsalted butter, softened
2 cups icing (confectioner's) sugar, sifted
1-2 tbsp milk and/or flavoring

For flavorings, swap the milk for:

1½ tsp instant coffee powder or strong black coffee
1 tbsp lemon juice and grated zest of half a lemon
2 tbsp orange juice and grated zest of half an orange
1½ squares melted semi-sweet baking chocolate

Use a wooden spoon to cream the butter until soft. Gradually beat in the icing (confectioner's) sugar with the flavorings, adding milk if necessary to make a smooth but stiff mixture.

buttercream

stenciled

fondant

chocolate leaves

sugared flowers

Simple decorations
As well as store-bought decorations, such as silver balls and sprinkles, there are easy ways to create a great finish.

Stencil Use a stencil to create patterns by dusting with icing (confectioner's) sugar or cocoa.

Sugared leaves, petals and flowers Brush leaves of sage, rose petals or whole violets with beaten egg white then dip in superfine sugar. Put on a rack and leave at room temperature to set.

Crunchy lemon top Mix the juice of a lemon with ½ cup superfine sugar. Pour onto a cake as soon as it's out of the oven. When cold, add strips of lemon zest.

Feathered frosting Drag a pointed knife across the frosting. Or pipe a spiral onto the cake and make lines from the center outward for a marbled effect.

Fondant Buy it ready-made and simply roll it out for use as a cake topping. Alternatively, shape it to make all kinds of novelty cake decorations, such as flowers or faces.

Peaks Use a knife to dab blobs of royal icing onto a Christmas cake, then lift the knife sharply to shape it into peaks.

Chocolate curls Using chocolate at room temperature, scrape a vegetable peeler over the flat side of the bar.

Chocolate shapes Spread melted chocolate onto parchment paper and cut into shapes with a knife or cutter. Or brush melted chocolate onto leaves (bay, for example), allow to set, then peel leaves off.

feathered

HOW TO PIPE FROSTING

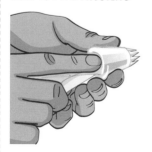

1 Fit a small round nozzle into the end of a piping bag. Twist and tuck the nozzle into the bag to stop any frosting from leaking.

2 Make a collar by folding the bag over your hand. Add the frosting with a spatula. Twist the top of the bag when full, expelling any air.

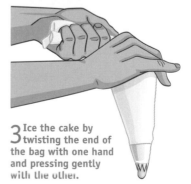

3 Ice the cake by twisting the end of the bag with one hand and pressing gently with the other.

prime and stretch a
Canvas

YOU WILL NEED Wooden frame, canvas 2 in. (5 cm) larger all around than the frame, pinking shears, staple gun, gesso primer, brush. Optional: canvas pliers.

1 Lay your frame, beveled edge down on the canvas, aligned with the weave. Cut to fit with pinking shears, allowing 2 in. (5 cm) overlap per side.

2 Fold canvas along one long side and fire in a staple at the midpoint. Rotate the frame 180°, draw the canvas firmly toward you (you can use canvas-stretching pliers), hold it taut with one hand and fire a staple opposite the first.

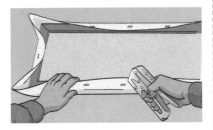

3 Repeat with the two shorter sides. Then staple 3 in. (8 cm) to the right and left of the center staple on all sides —grab, pull and staple each time. Repeat as necessary, rotating frame and canvas until it's taut all over.

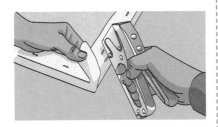

4 At the corners, tightly fold, tuck and staple to hold the canvas firm.

5 Apply gesso primer, suitable for acrylic or oils, to the canvas and allow to dry before starting to paint. For a smooth surface, dilute the gesso with a little water and apply two or more coats.

continued from page 47

Toppings and fillings
- Smoked salmon or gravlax with dill and a squeeze of lemon
- Mayonnaise
- Cream cheese: plain or with herbs and/or garlic, or with smoked salmon roe
- Olive tapenade (best toasted)
- Cold roast beef and horseradish
- Pâté (liver, eggplant or smoked mackerel, salmon or trout)

Choose from the suggested lists of bases and toppings, or mix and match your own combinations. Alternatively, spread thin slices of bread (crusts removed) with fillings such as cream cheese or smoked salmon pâté, add stuffed olives and roll up tightly. Cut into mini rolls or wheels. Don't prepare cold canapés more than an hour or so before.

Hot canapés
- "Devils on horseback" (left) are a classic: Wrap pitted prunes in a half-slice of bacon. Secure with a toothpick. Brush with olive oil and bake at 400°F (200°C) for 10 minutes or until crisp.
- Or serve sausages cooked in the oven with mustard and rosemary, hot mini meatballs or mini quiches.

understand the basics of Canasta

This classic card game is usually played by four players in two pairs, with two decks, including jokers, shuffled together.

There are many intricate variations on the detailed rules of canasta, so find one version in a book or online that you and your colleagues agree on—and stick to it. Variations aside, the aim of the game is to score the highest number of "melds" (three or more cards of the same rank, regardless of suit), including "canastas" (melds of seven or more cards).

- Start by dealing 11 cards to each player. The remaining pile is the "stock," placed face down on the table. The top stock card is flipped face up and begins the "discard" pile. The essence of the game is to pick up a card from the "stock" and discard one card from your hand at each turn, to acquire melds to lay down on the table.
- Points scored for the various cards range from 100 for a red 3 (a "bonus" card), through 50 for a joker, to 5 for a black 3. Jokers and 2s are "wild" cards that can be added to any meld. The cards in your hands count against you if you're left holding them when your opponents go out.
- When using wild cards, lay down jokers before 2s.
- Try to memorize the cards in the discard pile—they could come back into play, and it's worth being prepared for that moment.

make homemade Candles

All the materials for candle-making can be bought from craft stores. At home, it's easiest to create candles by rolling or dipping.

To make rolled candles

YOU WILL NEED Sheets of honeycomb beeswax, hairdryer, piece of wick at least 1 in. (2.5 cm) longer than the finished candle will be, utility knife, metal ruler, scissors, butter knife

1 Warm the beeswax until it's pliable. Use a blowdryer on a low setting or heat the wax on a radiator.

2 Lay the wick along one edge of the wax sheet and roll it tightly and evenly, as thick as desired.

3 Use the ruler and utility knife to cut away any excess wax, and use scissors to trim the wick. Wrap a piece of wax around the wick to prime it.

4 Smooth the seam with a butter knife warmed in hot water. Slide it back and forth to seal the join and leave a smooth finish.

For the dipping method

YOU WILL NEED Stearin powder, paraffin wax, wax dye disk, saucepans, sugar thermometer, wick, scissors

1 Pour 1½ oz (40 g) stearin powder into a saucepan deep enough to accommodate the length the wick. Place the pan inside a larger pan of water and boil until the stearin melts.

2 Add a quarter of a disk of wax dye and 14 oz (400 g) paraffin wax and heat to 175°F (80°C), stirring continuously.

3 Dip the wick in the wax, lift out, then pull taut and hold until the wax has set. Repeat until you have the required diameter, then trim wick.

---

act after a
Car accident

If you have a car accident, there are certain things you should do to make the scene safe and ensure that the circumstances are completely and accurately recorded.

Securing safety

■ First, check to see if anyone is hurt. If someone is bleeding profusely, unconscious or in serious pain, call 911 right away.

■ Make the scene safe, if possible, without endangering yourself. Put warning triangles 100 ft (30 m) ahead and beside the scene—farther if it's on a curve or hill. Place a third triangle about 10 ft (3 m) behind the accident.

■ Move the damaged cars off the road if it's safe to do so, but don't move anyone who is badly hurt.

Getting information

■ Gather and record any details that you may need later for legal or insurance purposes.

■ Take the names, addresses and registration numbers of any other drivers involved in the accident, and also of any witnesses. In some countries it's a legal requirement for drivers to swap insurance details.

■ Make a sketch or take a photo of the scene and any details of the location that may have contributed to the accident: If there was construction, was it adequately lit? Was there a pothole, or a car parked on a blind corner, that caused one of the drivers to swerve?

■ Never admit liability at the scene of the accident even if you feel it was your fault: Let the insurance companies deal with that.

C

unfreeze a Car lock

■ If you are at home, soak a cloth in warm water and apply it to the lock, or warm the lock with a hair dryer.

■ Away from home or in extreme cold, heat the door key gently with a lighter and insert into the lock to defrost it from within.

■ If no other options are available, place your hand over the lock for a minute or two—the heat of your palm may do the trick. Don't do this with bare hands, though, as you could risk freezing your hand to the door. Try it while wearing a glove or with a piece of material between you and the cold metal.

■ Bear in mind that if the lock is frozen, then the doors may be too. So don't yank the door open or force the passenger door from the inside—you may damage the seal.

play
Car games *on*
long trips
see pages 58-59

back up a Camper

Driving forward with a camper or trailer is a breeze, but reversing to turn around or maneuver into a space requires a little know-how and practice. In time, though, it will become second nature.

1 Go very slowly. Begin by turning the steering wheel slightly in the "wrong" direction—opposite to the way you actually want to turn.

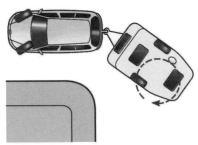

2 As soon as the camper starts to turn, begin to straighten out while reversing; you should feel as though your car is following the camper.

3 Carry on past the neutral point of the steering wheel and begin to steer the other way, following the camper.

4 Increase the lock to bring the car around the corner, just as you would without a camper.

5 Start straightening out. Use your side mirrors; if more of the camper appears in the mirror, steer towards that mirror.

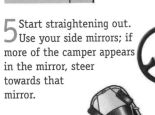

6 Continue straightening out until the car is fully in line with the camper and the maneuver is complete.

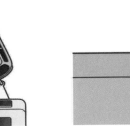

Car cleaning inside and out

A regular cleaning routine will make your car look good, and help to protect it from corrosion and other damage. It can even help to maintain a car's resale value.

Cleaning the interior
■ Remove the mat. Vacuum them if they are made of carpet or wash with an all-purpose cleaner if rubber. Let dry.
■ Carefully vacuum the upholstery and the carpets, using the crevice attachment to clean deep into the gaps.
■ Use soap and water to wash the doorjambs, and use a cotton swab to unplug the drainage holes on the bottom of the door, if necessary.
■ Clean the inside of the windshield with a 1:8 solution of white vinegar and water. Spray it on, then wipe dry with a soft cloth.
■ Wipe the dashboard and interior panels with a duster and diluted household cleaner.

Cleaning the exterior
■ First rinse the car gently from the roof down using a garden hose or by pouring clean water from a bucket.
■ In a bucket, mix non-detergent car cleaner (never dish soap) with warm water.
■ Wash one section at a time, using an old 100 percent cotton towel or chamois. Soap, rinse, dry—and move on.
■ Use a different bucket and rag to wash the wheels. Grit and rocks collect here and you could inadvertently transfer some onto your cloth and scratch the car's paint as you wash it.
■ Clean the outside of the windows the same way as you did the inside; with a solution of water and white vinegar.
■ Wax your car twice a year to protect the finish.

touch up Car paint scratches

Scratches should be repaired right away to prevent rust and corrosion from attacking any metal that's left bare.

A light scratch that hasn't exposed the metalwork can be repaired using a scratch remover. First, wash the car and let it dry. Apply the remover using a clean, damp cloth. Rub it onto the bodywork using a light circular motion over an area wider than the immediate damage.

Deeper scratches may need touching up with paint, which can be applied with a small paintbrush or spray can. If you use a spray can, apply several light coats, 15 minutes apart, rather than one heavy application that's likely to run. Allow the new paint to harden for a week, then blend it into the surrounding paint as above.

reduce your Carbon footprint

Chances are your carbon footprint is too big. But there are easy ways to make it smaller.

The term "carbon footprint" is a measure of the total greenhouse gases that a person or organization produces, usually given in terms of tons of carbon dioxide equivalent. A carbon footprint is complicated to calculate, but there are websites that estimate your footprint through an online questionnaire.

Easy ways to cut back Most simply, this means using less fuel and electricity in your daily life.
■ Insulate your house well, especially your roof, to cut down on energy used for heating.
■ Turn your heating down a notch or two—you'll hardly notice.
■ Boil only as much water as you need in your kettle—don't overfill.
■ Wash clothes in warm rather than hot water—they will still get clean.
■ Recycle as much as you can— this requires far less energy than creating products from scratch.
■ Cycle as much as you can, too. Ride a bike (or walk) whenever possible rather than taking the car.
■ Vacation close to home rather than fly. Trains are ten times more carbon-efficient than airplanes.

Food impact Small changes to eating habits can make a big difference.
■ Avoid buying fruit and vegetables that have been imported. Eat seasonal food produced locally to reduce your carbon footprint.
■ Eat less meat and dairy foods, because flatulent methane emissions from livestock are one of the main contributors to greenhouse gases.

C

get stains out of a Carpet

The table below shows the best way to remove a selection of common spills and stains, but there are some general principles in carpet cleaning that can also help.

Move fast The longer a stain sits, the harder it is to get it out without leaving traces behind.

Don't scrub You risk rubbing the stain in deeper and spreading it over a wider area. Instead, blot liquid spills with a cloth or paper towel to remove as much of the stain as possible. Work inward, so that the stain remains contained. Don't add more liquid; you'll make the job harder for yourself.

Soak it up To lift a wet stain from a carpet, the best strategy is sometimes to place a layer of clean white rags or paper towels, ⅓ in. (1 cm) thick, over the spill, weigh them down with a heavy object and leave overnight, so that the liquid is absorbed up and out.

Dry-clean grease Dry-cleaning solvent is the best way to lift greasy stains. You can buy it at most hardware stores.

Finish with a wash A wash with carpet shampoo is a good final step in any carpet cleaning job. Apply it with a cloth, using just enough to moisten the area. Use a clean cloth to help soak up the stain.

Stain	Treatment
BLOOD	Sponge with cold water, blotting with a towel as you go.
CANDLE WAX	Let the wax harden, then scrape off as much as you can. Cover the residue with blotting paper, brown paper or paper towel, and press with the tip of a barely warm iron. The wax will melt and be drawn into the absorbent paper. Don't let the iron scorch the carpet.
CHEWING GUM	Place a bag of ice cubes on the chewing gum to freeze it. You can then break the gum with a small hammer and lift off the pieces. Rub any residue with denatured alcohol on a soft cloth.
INK	Ink from a ballpoint pen should be dabbed with a cotton swab that has been dipped in denatured alcohol. Ink from a fountain pen should be thoroughly blotted and sponged with cold water before using a suitable stain remover for ink. Some felt-tip pens are water-based, and ink marks from these should be treated with carpet shampoo; if the felt-tip is alcohol-based, treat the marks with denatured alcohol.
MUD	Allow the mud to dry completely, then brush it out. Vacuum and use carpet shampoo on any residual stain.
TEA AND COFFEE	Blot thoroughly, and treat with a carpet shampoo. Use a dry-cleaning solvent on any stubborn stains.
URINE	Blot with paper tissues, and treat with carpet shampoo to which white vinegar has been added (¼ cup of vinegar for 2 cups of shampoo). Use a pet-stain remover to eradicate any smell.
VOMIT	Scrape up any deposits, taking care not to spread them over a wider area. Blot thoroughly with paper towel. Treat with a carpet shampoo and a little disinfectant to remove any unpleasant odor.
WINE	Blot fresh spills dry, then use carpet shampoo. Don't put white wine on red wine spills or cover with salt.

Carve meat perfectly

All roasts served hot will be more tender and easier to carve if the meat is covered in foil and left in warm place to "relax" for at least 15 minutes and up to half an hour before carving.

Boneless cuts are the easiest to carve, such as a rolled beef rump or sirloin, or a boned and rolled leg of lamb. As a rule, meat is best cut across the grain. Before you start, make sure that your knife is sharp and your board isn't going to slip (put it on top of a dish towel if necessary).

YOU WILL NEED Sharp carving knife, two-pronged carving fork, carving board, small sharp knife, warmed serving platter

Beef standing rib roast For a large roast, turn onto one side and make 2 in. (5 cm) cuts across ribs. Lay the roast rib side down and carve several slices. Place them on a warm platter then turn the rib back on its side and repeat. For a smaller cut, cut the meat away from the ribs all at once and carve it into slices.

Bone-in beef sirloin Use a small knife to loosen the meat from the bone. Carve down to the bone in thin slices, turn the meat over, remove bone and finish carving.

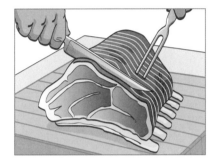

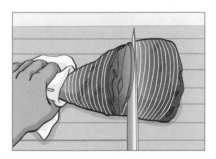

Leg of lamb or pork Place the leg meaty side up on the board. For pork, remove the rind and put to one side. Cut a shallow V from the middle then carve slices downward from both sides, widening the V. Turn the leg over and cut slices across the underside.

Shoulder of lamb Place roast with fat side uppermost. Cut a long slice about ½ in. (1 cm) thick from the center on the side opposite the bone, right down to the bone. Keep carving slices to widen the first cut then take horizontal slices from the top, over the central bone. Carve horizontal slices from the underside.

continued on next page →

lay a foam-backed Carpet

Foam-backed carpets are much easier to lay yourself than jute-backed ones, which need underlay and gripper strips around the edge. Don't put carpet down on uneven boards. It will look bad and wear out quickly. If necessary, cover the floor with hardboard to give an entirely smooth surface.

YOU WILL NEED Sheets of newspaper or a roll of paper underlay, double-sided carpet tape, carpet, bolster chisel, utility knife

1 Lay newspaper or carpet paper over the floor to prevent the foam backing from sticking to the wood beneath.

2 Fix double-sided carpet tape all around the perimeter of the room, but don't peel off the backing yet. Place the carpet loosely in position so that the pile runs away from the main window (it should feel smooth when you run your hand across it, starting at the light source). Trim off the excess but leave at least 1 in. (2.5 cm) on all sides.

3 Position the carpet in the correct position and make sure it's smooth and flat. Lift the edges and remove the backing from the carpet tape. Work around the room, pressing the carpet firmly into place. Use a clean bolster chisel to tamp the carpet well into the join between floor and baseboard.

4 Cut carefully around obstacles, such as radiator pipes, and awkward shapes, such as the door frame. Trim off the excess around the edges with a utility knife, taking great care not to cut off too much. Hold the point of the blade to the baseboard, with the handle angled away from the wall. Go around the perimeter checking that all the edges are firmly stuck down.

digitize your old
Cassette tapes

It's possible to digitize tapes using a working tapedeck, a cable that connects the deck to the line-in jack of your computer (ask at an electronics store) and a piece of software to help you control the process. There are many freely downloadable programs you can use—Audacity is one of the best.

Alternatively, you can buy tape players and record turntables that are designed specifically for the purpose of digitizing these obsolescent media, and that come with the necessary software. Clean the heads of your tapedeck before you begin so that the digital version of your tapes sounds as good as possible.

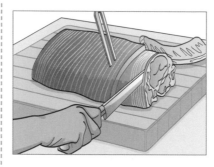

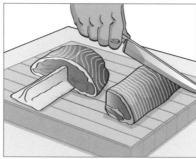

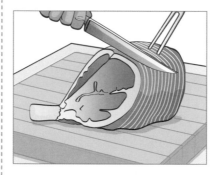

continued from page 55

Pork loin Use a small knife to cut between the backbone (that runs along the roast) and the meat. Then use the carving knife to remove the bone, cutting between the meat and ribs. Remove any pork crackling. Slice the meat, finding the natural divisions between the bones, and cut up the crackling.

Bone-in lamb whole loin The whole loin is essentially a double loin roast, including the tenderloin. Make a vertical cut across the roast away from the thicker end. Make a long cut down the length of the roast directly over the backbone then cut long thin slices parallel to the backbone. Repeat for the other side. Once you have removed all the meat this way, turn the roast over, remove the tenderloin from both sides. Alternatively, remove the loins from the backbone for carving.

Ham on the bone Make a cut down to the bone just above the knuckle. Cut slices at an angle toward the knuckle.

⭐ golden rules
SUCCESS WITH CARVING
- Always sharpen your knife before you start.
- A chopping board with spikes will help to hold the bird or meat steady while you work.
- Keep a warmed platter on the side to hold the meat as you carve it. This will help to keep it warm.
- With a small bird, remove the whole breast and slice it once it's off the carcass.

Carve poultry perfectly

Small birds can simply be cut into halves or quarters for serving, but larger ones need more expert treatment to separate drumsticks, thighs and wings, and to carve neat slices of meat. Aim to give each person some white breast meat and some dark meat.

YOU WILL NEED Sharp carving knife, two-pronged carving fork, carving board, large warmed serving dish

Removing the wishbone All poultry will be easier to carve if the wishbone is removed before cooking. Put the bird breast side up on a chopping board; pull back the skin from the neck and breast until you find the V-shaped wishbone. Expose the bone fully and cut around it with a small, sharp knife until you can pry it away. If the wishbone wasn't taken out before cooking, you can use a similar procedure on a cooked bird before carving.

Carving poultry Follow these steps whether you're carving a chicken, duck, goose or small turkey. Place the bird on its side, lift the leg up with the fork and cut under the thigh. Cut through the joint to separate the drumstick from the thigh. Slice through the breast halfway across the shoulder (below right) and cut away the shoulder, wing and a strip of breast. Carve the rest of the breast into slices, starting at the wing end—or, if it's small, cut it away in one piece and serve whole or carve on the board.

Carving turkey A large turkey (bigger than 10 lb/4.5 kg) is unwieldy for moving and turning on the board, as you do when carving a chicken (above), so place it firmly on the board and carve it in one position.

1 Remove any string that's trussing the bird together. Cut between the body and the thigh on each side, cutting all around the leg and through the sinews that are holding it in place.

2 Separate the legs from the body and carve on another board or on the side of your main board. Cut at an angle parallel with the bone (right) to make small slices of dark leg meat.

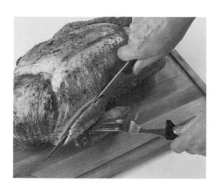

3 Cut through the breast and down into and through the shoulder joints to remove the wings.

4 Carve thin slices of breast meat, using the back of your fork to support the slices. Try not to make holes in the meat with the fork prongs.

deal with
Caterpillars

A sudden infestation of caterpillars will chew plants to bits in a matter of days. For the unsqueamish, the best solution is to remove them by hand and kill them in a strong solution of salt water. As you do so, rub off clusters of eggs on leaf undersides before they can hatch into a second generation.

Insecticide You can use a general insecticide to kill caterpillars (follow the instructions carefully) if you live in an area that allows chemical insecticide use, but the best organic treatment is a spray containing the microorganism *Bacillus thuringiensis*, which attacks caterpillars but won't harm other insects. It can be obtained from garden stores.

Prevention You can keep caterpillars off your plants by spotting and destroying eggs before they hatch, covering plants with fine netting to prevent adult butterflies from reaching the plant to lay their eggs, and encouraging plenty of birds to come into your garden to prey on the pesky insects.

C

play Car games on long trips

Keeping the kids happy on a long trip is tough—very tough. "I spy," counting colors or types of car, spelling or number challenges: These are all reliable distractions—for a while. When you have exhausted your usual games, try some of these suggestions to pass the time.

Be prepared There are things you can do before your trip to smooth the ride: buy puzzle books, make a CD of favorite music (songs that the adults can live with, too), pack a selection of snacks and treats, and plan a few games for the journey.

THREE FOR A PIG
A game for two children sitting in the back of a car, traveling through the countryside.

■ Each player looks out of the window on their own side of the road.
■ The aim is to amass points by spotting various animals in fields on your own side.
■ A pig or sheep scores three points, cows one each (make a fair guess if you spot a herd of them), other animals one each.
■ There are no points awarded for birds or humans.
■ Horses earn a player minus ten points, but you cannot go below zero.

■ Ten points are awarded for a cat or dog looking out of a house or car window.
■ The first player to reach 50 points wins. Players and their parents may invent their own house rules—awarding points for men with beards, for example, or haystacks—but appoint a judge to mediate arguments.

YES OR NO
An endlessly enjoyable old favorite for the whole family to play.

■ One designated person is forbidden to use the words "yes" and "no." Everyone else asks them questions to trick them into saying the banned words.
■ The trick is to get the player talking about something they are interested in—say, football—then sneak in a leading question such as, "But Green Bay won the 2011 Super Bowl, didn't they?"

KEEP THE BEAT
A singing game that anyone can play. Put a familiar song on the car's stereo.

■ One player sings along to the song. Without warning the driver or front passenger turns off the sound for a few seconds, but the person singing has to carry on.
■ If the singer is still in time with the music when the sound is turned back up, they pass.
■ Take turns until only one person is left in the game.

ROADWAY BINGO

This is a game that can be played in more than one way for all the family to enjoy during the journey.

In its simplest version, each player picks a color, and the first person to see ten cars of that color shouts "Bingo!" and wins the game.

Here is the more complex version, which involves a little preparation.

■ Before your journey, the bingomaster makes a list of ten objects for each young passenger. The lists consist of ten sights you might see along the way. Each person's list is different (though some overlap is allowed) and, if the bingo master is clever, will be tailored to the age and ability of the players. It might even take account of specific things or landmarks that are known to be on the route.

■ The first person to tick off all the objects on their list is the winner.

■ Here are some suggestions for things that might be on the lists: a cat, a street named after a person, an ambulance, a police car, a cow, a person wearing a hat, a car with licence plates from a different state or province, an airplane, a car with two children in the back (not your own), a camper, a windmill, a sign showing the town you are headed for (or other likely destination), a delivery truck, a house with a green roof, a neon sign on a building, a bridge, a motorcycle with two people on it...

FIZZ BUZZ

This number-based game for children of about six and up can be a challenge for adults too.

■ You take turns to count upward, remembering to say "fizz" before any multiple of three, and "buzz" before any multiple of five: "one, two, fizz, three, four, buzz, five, fizz, six, seven eight, fizz, nine ..." and so on. Or you can count one number each, moving around the car in turn.

■ Before multiples of both, such as 15, you say "fizz buzz."

■ The winner is the player who counts highest.

ALPHABETICAL SHOPPING LIST

Take turns to compile a shopping list using words starting with consecutive letters of the alphabet.

■ The first person says: "I went to the store and I bought apples." The next says: "I went to the store and I bought apples and bananas."

■ Each subsequent player has to recite the whole list from the beginning without making a mistake. It gets harder as the game goes on, but that is the challenge. The shopping list can be as surreal as you like: aardvark, bicycle, crab, dice ...

CIRCLE OF LIFE

Quick thinking is part of the challenge of this tricky word game. Ponder too long, and you're out!

The driver thinks of an animal—say, a wombat. The next person has to think of an animal that starts with the same letter as the last letter of the previous animal —so "wombat" might be followed by "turtle." The next person has to think of an animal that begins with the last letter of that animal ("emu"), and so on.

■ If you get stuck for more than 10 seconds, you're out.

■ The winner is the last person left in the game.

■ You can also play this game with any number of other categories: boy and girl names, towns, household objects, countries ...

house-train Cats

Cats are naturally clean creatures, so house-training a kitten isn't normally a difficult job.

- Put a layer of clumping litter in a tray, or use sand if your cat will eventually use the outdoors. For two cats, provide at least two trays.
- Place the tray in a quiet corner, away from food and water bowls.
- If the kitten does its business on the floor, transfer the solid matter to the tray. Don't be angry or react at all.
- Clean the tray once a week, using only hot water and detergent.
- If your cat has an accident, wash the area with a ten percent solution of laundry detergent with enzymes, spray with rubbing alcohol and scrub again.

groom Cats

Long-haired cats must be brushed and combed every day to avoid matted, tangled fur and skin problems that can result from a neglected coat. Start grooming often from a young age. Fur balls can build up in the stomach of all cats, so even a short-haired cat will benefit from grooming.

- Set aside a grooming area, with hygiene in mind—not the kitchen counter—and lay down a towel.
- Talking gently all the time, fluff the cat's coat with your hand then lightly brush from roots to tip in the direction of growth. Work in sections to get rid of mats or tangles, before moving on to a wide-tooth comb, then a fine-tooth comb.
- If the teeth of a comb snag in the fur, go back to the previous tool.
- When you have finished, praise your cat and offer them a treat.

have fun with Cat's cradle

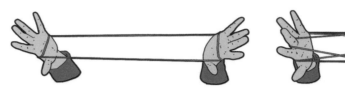

1 Slip your hands through a loop of string about 32 in. (80 cm) long and pull them apart. Wind the string once around each of your palms.

2 Slip one middle finger through the loop on the opposite palm and pull your hands apart. Repeat with the other hand to form the "cat's cradle."

 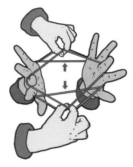 

3 You need another player to join you at this point. Your playmate pinches the crisscrosses in the string.

4 They should then pull the strings outward, then down and back under the straight sides of your cat's cradle, coming up through the center.

5 The second player lifts the string off your hands and pulls their own fingers and hands apart to create a new shape—the "soldier's bed."

give pills to Cats

Some cats happily take medication. Others think you're out to poison them, so giving them pills requires patience and determination.

- To try the easy way, buy pill pockets (available from vets), which many cats love. If that fails, wrap your cat in a towel and sit on the floor with them between your legs. Calmly wrap your dominant hand around the

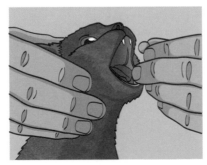

head so your fingers are under the cheekbone. Tip the head back; the lower jaw should slacken.
- Use your middle finger to ease the jaw down, and place the pill near the back of the tongue.
- Release the head and stroke the cat's throat to encourage it to swallow. Watch in case the cat spits the pill out.

look after your CDs and DVDs

For high-quality sound and pictures, CDs and DVDs are a vast improvement on their tape-based predecessors, but they are easily damaged if you don't look after them well.

Stop skipping Dust and dirt will make CDs and DVDs prone to skipping or freezing. The simplest way to clean a grubby disk is to place it in a bowl of warm water with a few drops of dish soap for a minute or two. Rinse the disk, then allow it to dry upright, like a plate in a rack. Never scrub with a wet cloth or apply any kind of pressure to the playing surface (the shiny side, without the label), and steer clear of unusual cleaning agents such as toothpaste or banana; these are often recommended, but are (at best) experimental. Blu-ray discs are more damage-resistant than CDs or DVDs.

Getting scratches out The surface of a disk consists of several layers. The outermost layer is a protective plastic film; a scratch that penetrates to the data layer beneath is irreparable, but shallow scratches can be "polished out" using a soft cloth and disk-cleaning fluid. Rub gently, and always from the center of the disk outward; polishing around the disk in a circle is likely to cause more damage. A lateral scratch—one that follows the groove—is likely to be more damaging than a radial scratch.

paint a Ceiling

Ceilings are best painted with a roller on a long handle to avoid using trestle platforms or moving a stepladder around the room.

There are specific ceiling paints available, but you can use any latex paint, poured into a paint tray. Cover the floor and furniture and wear overalls and safety glasses to protect against splatters. Rollers cannot paint right up to the edges, so "cut in" with a paintbrush first. Always paint the ceiling before you decorate the walls.

Cutting in With a 1½ in. (3.5 cm) brush, paint the corners, a strip around the edges that just reaches the top of the wall. This will leave a neat finish.

Order of work Paint the ceiling in strips, starting at the window—the reflecting light will make it easier to see where you've already been.

serve Caviar

Whether it's the real thing—sturgeon eggs, lightly salted—or salmon caviar, known as red caviar or keta, caviar is best served cold.

Because the eggs are extremely fragile, they need careful handling. The traditional way of serving is to set the can in a bowl of ice and to open it at the last minute. The aim is to minimize contact with the air, which will spoil the flavor.

Caviar needs no fancy treatment—it's special enough already. Serve it with triangles of hot toast and unsalted butter or on blinis (*see* BLINIS) with sour cream as an optional extra.

Champagne or vodka shots on ice are the traditional liquid accompaniments.

burn a CD

The most common reason for copying to a CD is to create a personalized music compilation for the car. This can be done using a music program such as iTunes or Windows Media Player, which allow you to create a playlist and burn it to a CD.

Archiving digital files CDs are a good medium for storing sets of files that you won't want to modify later—for example, scans of old family photos. The program that allows you to do this will launch automatically when you insert a blank CD in your computer's disk drive. Drag and drop the files you want into the appropriate window or folder, then follow the instructions to save them to the disk.

operate a
Chainsaw safely

A chainsaw is a highly effective and time-saving tool, but it's also one of the most potentially dangerous pieces of equipment you could use. You must take precautions to ensure your safety. When in doubt, ask for advice and instructions when you rent the saw.

■ Wear a helmet, eye protection such as a pair of safety glasses, steel-toed boots and upper body and lower limb protection.
■ The greatest hazard you'll encounter when using a chainsaw is "kickback." If the top of the saw tip encounters an obstacle that suddenly stops the the blade, the chainsaw will jerk back forcefully toward you, the operator.

kickback danger zone

■ To minimize the possibility of a kickback injury, you should grip the front handle with your thumb curled around it.
■ Concentrate, so that you always keep the kickback danger zone free of impediments.
■ Never cut anything with one hand, or use the saw above shoulder height.
■ Don't put the saw into tight spaces, where it might catch on small branches.
■ Keep children far away.

dance the Cha-cha

This dance of Cuban origin is sassy, fun and easy to learn
—a great party favorite suited to many music genres.

"Smooth Operator," "Light My Fire," "What a Difference a Day Makes" ... If you're already humming along, you're in the mood to cha-cha-cha. This dance's flirtatious nature is expressed in the footwork and "Cuban motion"—the swivel of your hips.

Five steps are taken to four beats: for instance, step, step, cha-cha-cha, with the first two cha-chas danced quickly on the third beat. Think slow, slow, quick, quick, slow. The example below shows the man's steps—the woman's steps are the mirror image of these.

Step, step, cha-cha-cha

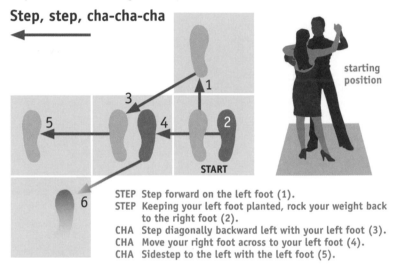

starting position

STEP Step forward on the left foot (1).
STEP Keeping your left foot planted, rock your weight back to the right foot (2).
CHA Step diagonally backward left with your left foot (3).
CHA Move your right foot across to your left foot (4).
CHA Sidestep to the left with the left foot (5).

Step, step, cha-cha-cha

FINISH

Posture and movement
■ Hold your head high and don't look down at your feet.
■ Take short, smooth, decisive steps and transfer your weight completely with each one.
■ Don't force the swivel of your hips; master the footwork, enjoy the music and let the hip movement follow.

STEP Step backward on the right foot (6).
STEP Keeping your right foot planted, rock your weight back to the left foot (7).
CHA Step diagonally forward right with your right foot (8).
CHA Move your left foot to your right foot (9).
CHA Shift your weight to the right foot (10).

fix an old Chair

The spindles or rails of old wooden chairs can easily come loose or get detached. Here's how to fit them back snugly and glue them tight, and how to cure a chair that wobbles.

YOU WILL NEED **Wood glue, cord, thick cardboard, length of wood, wooden wedge, hammer, wooden block, sandpaper, slivers of plywood, utility knife. Optional: varnish.**

Repair a loose rail

1 Sometimes all you need to do is glue the rail back, using wood glue as directed on the package. Then you must clamp the chair in position for at least 12 hours.

2 To do this, wrap a double length of cord around the chair, having placed protective pieces of thick cardboard between the cord and the chair legs. Insert a length of wood through the cords at the front, and twist to tighten like a tourniquet. This holds everything in position. Jam the wood against the rail to keep the cord from untwisting.

Fix a shrunken rail

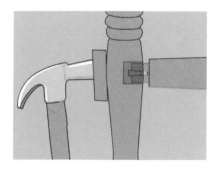

1 Sometimes the rail has shrunk in diameter, so it's too loose to glue. If so, saw a slot in the end of the rail, no deeper than the hole it goes in. Insert a wooden wedge cut to the length of the slot, but don't push it all the way in.

2 Apply wood glue, then insert the rail into its hole. Hammer the leg onto the rail, using a wooden block to prevent damage to the chairleg. The wedge will force the rail end open and make it fit tight.

Fix a wobbly chair

If one of the legs is too long, it's probably only by a little bit. Take some sandpaper and carefully sand off some of the leg end. Keep testing it on a smooth, hard, level surface until it stops wobbling.

If one of the chair legs is too short, try experimenting with a series of thin wooden shims.
- Build them up one by one until the chair stops wobbling. Test it on a hard, smooth, level surface.
- Glue the appropriate number of slivers to the leg end and to each other and allow them to dry. Trim off excess wood with a utility knife and smooth the end with sandpaper. Stain or varnish as necessary.

keep the fizz in Champagne

Champagne is all about its sparkle. You *can* drink flat champagne—it hasn't gone "bad" and it won't make you tipsy so quickly—but it will lack its very essence. Serve champagne in tall flutes to enhance the bubbles; they dissipate rapidly in a shallow coupe. It's a myth that a teaspoon dropped into the neck of the bottle preserves the fizz. There are two tried and tested ways to stop champagne going flat: Use a champagne saver—like a cork, but with a clamping mechanism to seal the bottle—or drink it! Alternatively, buy a half-bottle.

uncork Champagne

Ensure that the bottle is thoroughly chilled or it will foam too much and spill when the cork is released. Place the champagne in a bucket filled half with ice, half water, for 20–30 minutes, or refrigerate for three to four hours maximum.

- Have the flutes ready to receive the first gush.
- Strip off the foil and loosen the wire cage while covering the cork with your thumb in case it blows.
- Drape a linen napkin or dish towel over the top of the bottle and tilt it so that it points away from you and out of harm's way (you don't want any black eyes or breakage).
- Grip the cork and gently twist the bottle to ease the cork out.
- As the foam subsides, pour about two fingers into each glass, then top up to two-thirds.

dance the
Charleston

This can be danced solo, side by side or opposite a partner, or together in a ballroom position. Put on some fun 1920s music ("Ain't She Sweet," "Yes, Sir, That's My Baby"...), and feel the beat!

Practice the elementary footwork
■ You can either start right foot forward or left foot back.
■ Tap your right toe forward then step back on the right foot.
■ Tap your left foot behind then step forward. Repeat the cycle.
■ As you step and tap, turn your toes and knees in and then out to exaggerate the swing.

Get the arms moving
■ Keep your arms straight down with the palms of your hands facing the floor. Alternatively, bend your arms at right angles and point your fingers to the ceiling.
■ Swing your left arm back and right arm forward as you step back with your right foot, then reverse as you tap back with the left, like swinging your arms as you walk.
■ Move your arms or hands in circles as you gain confidence.

clean a Chandelier

The two-glove method is the best way to clean a chandelier without taking it down. Before you start, be sure to turn off the lights and remove the bulbs.

■ Put on two white cotton gloves (available from hardware or craft stores) and dampen one with glass cleaner. Massage each individual crystal with the damp glove, then wipe it with the dry glove.
■ If your chandelier is really dirty, you'll have to take down the crystals and wash them in a bowl half-filled with warm water with a drop of dish soap and 2 tbsp of white vinegar. Rinse each crystal under running water, and dry with a soft cloth.

play Charades

Two teams take turns to pick an opposition player to act out a phrase, book title, song or TV show (*Gone with the Wind* or *Desperate Housewives*, for example), supplied by a referee. The actor may not speak or point, but may use gestures and movements to mime either the whole phrase or title, or break it down into words and syllables. By holding up fingers the actor is allowed to reveal the number of words and which word is being acted out. The first team to guess the correct answer wins. Extra points can be awarded for how quickly the answer is given, with the referee acting as timekeeper.

make a baked Cheesecake

SERVES 6–8

FOR THE BASE

½ cup unsalted butter, plus a little for greasing
1 cup crushed graham crackers
¼ cup superfine sugar

FOR THE FILLING

3 eggs, separated
¼ cup superfine sugar
1 lb (500 g) cream cheese
2 tbsp cornstarch
2 tsp finely grated lemon zest
1 tsp vanilla extract
¾ cup Greek yogurt

1 Heat the oven to 350°F (180°C). Lightly grease an 8 in. (20 cm) springform cake pan, line with parchment paper and place it on a baking sheet.

2 Crush the graham crackers in a food processor or by putting them in a bag and pressing them with a rolling pin until they resemble fine crumbs. Mix with the sugar and melted butter and process for another 30 seconds, or mix thoroughly to combine. Press into the base of the prepared pan. Refrigerate for a minimum of 30 minutes.

3 Beat the egg yolks until smooth. Add the sugar and beat until light and fluffy. Gradually add the cream cheese, followed by remaining ingredients except the egg whites.

4 Beat the egg whites until stiff then fold into the mixture. Pour into the pan and bake for 10 minutes. Lower the heat to 300°F (150°C) and cook for another hour, or until almost set. If it appears to be over-browning, cover with foil. Cool thoroughly in the pan before unmolding. Top with fresh fruit.

master Chess basics

The game of chess is a tactical skirmish waged on a 64-square battlefield, in which the goal is to capture the opposition's king.

King · Queen · Bishop · Bishop · Knight · Knight · Rook · Rook · Knight

8 pawns

Set the board up with a white square in each player's right-hand corner. Center the king and queen on the back row—black queen on a black square, white on white. On either side place a bishop, then a knight, with the rooks (castles) in the corner. Line up the pawns in front.

How the pieces move

 PAWNS can move only forward (one or two squares with the first move, one thereafter), except to capture, when they move one square diagonally.

KNIGHTS move in an L shape, one or two squares vertically or horizontally, then two or one at right angles.

 ROOKS can move back or forth in straight lines over any number of unoccupied squares vertically or horizontally.

 BISHOPS can move back or forth in straight diagonal lines over any number of unoccupied squares.

 QUEENS can move back or forth in straight lines in any direction and over any number of unoccupied squares.

 KINGS can move one square in any direction—but not to a square menaced by an opposing piece. A king can therefore not attack a king.

White starts by moving either a pawn or knight (the only ranking piece that can pass over occupied squares, to land on an empty one or to capture a square). The players then take turns moving, picking off each other's pieces by landing on squares they occupy while trying not to put their own pieces in jeopardy.

The aim is to put the square occupied by your opponent's king under direct threat of being captured by your next move (putting the king "in check"). If you can target the king in such a way that your opponent can neither move him away from the threatened square, block the line of attack or capture the attacking piece, you have achieved "checkmate" and win the game. A draw, when a win for either player is deemed by both to be either impossible or unlikely, is called a "stalemate."

remove stubborn Chewing gum

The trick for getting rid of chewing gum is to act promptly.

Try cold For a carpet, scrape off as much of the gum as possible, then apply ice cubes in a plastic bag. Scrape some more, repeating as necessary. For clothes, seal in a plastic bag and deep freeze until stiff; scrape carefully.

Try heat Blast the gum on the carpet with a blowdryer for two minutes, then put a clear plastic bag over your hand and lift it off.

Try blotting Put one teaspoon of mild detergent in ⅔ cup of water and blot. Or apply a dry-cleaning solution.

Try oil For chewing gum in hair, work in olive oil to soften the gum before pulling it out with a piece of paper towel. Shampoo and rinse.

golden rules

CHESS TACTICS

- Gain control of the center of the board to optimize your access to other squares.
- Don't underestimate pawns. They can form powerful blockades and take more "valuable" pieces—and if one makes it to the back line, it's "promoted" to a ranking piece.
- When there are no pieces between a king and one of his rooks (and neither piece has yet moved), a king can "castle" —that is, move two squares toward the rook, which then moves to the space directly to the other side of the king.

make comforting
Chicken soup

As with any great soup, the best results begin with a good stock.

TO MAKE 2 QT/L OF STOCK

2 lb (1 kg) chicken bones, wings and giblets (except liver), washed
4 cups water
1 large onion, peeled and quartered
4 carrots, peeled and chopped
2 cloves garlic
1 large stick celery, chopped
bouquet garni
6 black peppercorns

1 Put the chicken ingredients into a large saucepan and bring slowly to a boil. Skim off any scum.

2 Add the remaining ingredients, cover and simmer for 3 hours, removing any further scum. Strain, cool and chill. Remove any fat from the surface.

SOUP FOR 4

2 tbsp olive oil
½ lb (225 g) uncooked skinless boneless chicken breast, cubed
4 cups chicken stock (see above)
2 carrots, peeled and diced
2 sticks celery, diced
1 medium onion, chopped
3 tbsp parsley, chopped
½ cup long-grain rice
salt and freshly ground black pepper

1 Heat the oil in a large saucepan. Add the chicken and brown lightly.

2 Add the stock, carrots, celery, onion, 2 tbsp parsley and the rice. Season with salt and pepper. Bring to a boil then simmer, covered, for about 20 minutes or until the rice is tender. Check and adjust the seasoning.

3 Serve in warmed soup bowls with the remaining parsley sprinkled on top.

joint a Chicken

YOU WILL NEED Chopping board, sharp knife, poultry shears or strong scissors

The trick when jointing is to be aware of the bird's anatomy and work with it. Dark meat cooks more slowly than light, so legs and thighs are best cut into smaller pieces than the breast meat. For an uncooked bird weighing 3 lb (1.5 kg) or less, six pieces (steps 1–4) should be sufficient. For larger birds, make eight pieces by dividing the breasts (step 5) or continue to make ten pieces by dividing the legs into thighs and drumsticks (step 6). Poultry shears or scissors aren't essential, but make the job a lot easier.

1 Place the chicken breast side up on a chopping board. Gently pull one leg out from the body, then cut through the skin between the body and leg. Bend the leg until it pops out of the socket. Cut through the flesh under the joint. Repeat with the other leg.

2 Use shears or a knife to cut off the wing pinions (ends) and discard. To separate the wings from the body, begin by making a deep cut in the breast, near the inside of each wing, angling the knife diagonally. Cut down into the meat to expose the bones.

3 To free the wings from the carcass, cut through the flesh and bone between the ball-and-socket joints with poultry shears or strong kitchen scissors. Carefully check for and remove any remaining bone splinters.

4 To remove the breast meat, use shears or scissors to cut through the thin rib cage on either side of the backbone. Discard the backbone or keep and use for soup stock (see left).

5 Divide the breast in two, carefully cutting crosswise or lengthwise through the flesh using a knife, and then through the bones and cartilage with shears or scissors.

6 Cut the legs in half through the joint between thigh and drumstick.

7 Remove the skin if you wish and trim excess fat or bone from all pieces.

keep Chickens for their eggs

Fresh eggs taste far better than anything the supermarket can offer. Chickens are fun and easy to keep, and take up little space—just make sure backyard chickens are legal in your municipality.

YOU WILL NEED **Chickens, henhouse, wood shavings for bedding, straw, food, grit and water containers, nest box, fencing**

Housing Provide a weatherproof, roomy henhouse with easy-to-clean surfaces, a secure door, roosting bars and at least one nest box for every three birds. Temperatures shouldn't be too extreme: Egg production decreases in very cold or very warm weather. A run outside the henhouse is essential—allow at least 11 sq ft (1 m²) per bird. Chickens that roam outside could have a wing clipped to stop them from straying, and must be fenced in for safety against foxes, cats or other predators. Sink the fence at least 8 in. (20 cm) below the surface to keep foxes from digging their way in.

Cleaning Once a week clean the house: Renew the straw and scrub the nest boxes and perches. Always wash your hands before and after handling birds.

Food Buy dry pellets or a mash to mix with water; 1–3½ oz (30–100 g) a day per bird is usually enough, but it depends on the weather, time of year, whether the hen is laying and how much free range she has. Hang grass or leafy vegetables in a string bag in the run, provide flint grit to aid digestion and soluble grit, usually oyster shells, to supply calcium. Daily fresh water is essential.

Laying Provide dark nest boxes with a deep bed of wood shavings, comfortable enough to accommodate a bird for up to two hours while she lays. Grit nearby will also help. Most hens lay in the morning after feeding.

Rhode Island Red

Issues Egg production drops in fall and winter. In late spring and early summer, remove eggs as soon as possible to stop the chickens from trying to hatch them. Consult your vet for health problems, and for more information google "poultry forums."

help with an emergency Childbirth

When a woman goes into early labor, call for medical help, then offer calm, practical assistance.

Get prepared
■ Help the mother into a position she finds comfortable. Put clean towels under her and supply pillows.
■ Scrub your hands and nails well.

During the birth
■ When you glimpse the baby's head, urge the mother to stop pushing and instead to pant.
■ Gently support the head as it emerges, but do not pull. Remove any membrane from the face.
■ If the cord is looped around the neck, slip it over the head.
■ With the next contraction, the shoulders will appear one at a time. Expect the baby's head to rotate slightly as its shoulders turn. Support the baby's body but don't pull or manipulate it.

After the birth
■ The baby will be slippery. Lay it carefully on the mother's abdomen, face down, so that mucus can drain from mouth and nose.
■ Check that the baby is breathing, then cover with a towel or blanket.
■ If the baby doesn't breathe within 30 seconds, gently rub its back or the soles of the feet. Wipe any fluids from mouth and nose. If this doesn't work, perform mouth-to-mouth: Seal your mouth over the baby's mouth and nose and give two to five very gentle puffs.
■ Wait for the placenta to be expelled, and leave it attached.
■ Don't cut the cord. The midwife or paramedic will do this.
■ There will probably be some blood, so provide warm water and towels, and a sanitary napkin if available.

C

clean and repair
China

Keep small or delicate china ornaments in a cabinet so they don't collect dust.

Cleaning For ornaments, use a long-haired soft-bristled makeup brush dipped in warm water containing a drop or two of dish soap.
■ Rinse ornaments using a brush dipped in clean water, and leave to dry on an absorbent paper towel.
■ Always wash fine dishes by hand. To prevent chipping, line the sink with a rubber mat or towel, and wash cutlery separately.

Repair Fix breaks with a two-part epoxy adhesive, which allows time to reposition the pieces if necessary, and is waterproof.

■ To position an awkwardly shaped item for gluing, place it in a box of sand, with the broken surface protruding. Apply adhesive to both pieces and carefully press together.
■ A newly glued cup handle can be taped in place with gummed paper, which shrinks as it dries, putting pressure on the join. Repairs to handles, however, are unlikely to be strong enough to withstand normal use.

make an authentic Chili con carne

Chili, one of the best warming comfort foods, is believed to have been "invented" in the 18th century by immigrants to Texas from the Spanish Canary Islands.

SERVES 6-8

⅓ lb (175 g) dried red kidney beans or 2 x 14 oz (398 mL) cans, drained
2 tbsp olive oil
1 large onion, chopped
2 cloves garlic, minced
1 large red chili pepper, seeded and chopped
1 red pepper, seeded and diced

1½ lb (750 g) lean ground beef
2 tsp chili powder
½ cup red wine
14 oz (540 mL) can chopped tomatoes
2 cups beef stock
4 tbsp tomato paste
salt and black pepper

1 If using dried kidney beans, soak for 12 hours or overnight in cold water. Drain, cover with fresh cold water and bring to a boil. Boil hard for 10 minutes to remove any toxins, then reduce the heat and simmer for 30 minutes. Drain.

2 Heat the oil in a large ovenproof casserole dish. Add the onion, garlic, chili and pepper and cook over low heat for 5 minutes.

3 Add the ground beef and cook, stirring, until browned. Stir in the chili powder and red wine and cook for 3 minutes, then add the tomatoes, stock and tomato paste. Mix well.

4 Add the partially cooked beans. Bring to a boil, then reduce the heat and simmer for 1½ hours, stirring occasionally, until the beans are completely tender. If using canned beans, add them for the last 30 minutes of cooking time.

5 Add salt and pepper to taste (don't salt the beans until they are cooked or the skins will become tough). Serve with rice and sour cream or guacamole. A green salad also makes a good accompaniment.

play Chinese checkers

This game for two to six players is played with colored marbles on a star-shaped board. The object is to move all your pieces from one of the six star points to the opposite before an opponent does the same.

■ Each player positions ten pieces of a single color (15 for a two-player game) in a point.
■ Players then take turns moving. When it's your turn, move one piece in any direction onto an adjacent hole, or you can jump an adjacent piece, be it your own or an opponent's, so as to place the piece in a more advantageous position.
Do not remove jumped pieces from the board.
■ When several marbles alternate with open holes in a line, you can jump them all.

make potato Chips

Double-frying and cutting potatoes into even-sized pieces will help you to make deliciously tender and crispy chips.

YOU WILL NEED 4 large potatoes, mandoline, canola oil, deep fryer, sea salt

1 Use the mandoline to slice the potatoes paper-thin, placing the slices into a bowl of ice water as you go. Let the potato slices sit in the bowl for an hour. Drain.

2 Heat the oil in the deep fryer to about 400°F (200°C). Place the potato slices in the oil in small batches until they turn golden. Let the potato slices drain on paper towels. Repeat until all the potato slices are cooked and drained.

3 Put the chips into one large bowl or four small bowls. Dust lightly with sea salt or other rock salt.

bake a great Chocolate cake

MAKES 8–12 SLICES

1²⁄₃ **cups brown sugar**
¼ **cup cocoa powder**
2 **tbsp water**
½ **cup butter, softened**
2 **large eggs, separated**
2 **cups self-rising flour**
½ **tsp baking soda**
½ **tsp salt**
²⁄₃ **cup sour cream**

FOR THE FILLING AND TOPPING

2 **squares sweet baking chocolate**
1 **tbsp instant coffee powder**
¼ **cup butter, softened**
²⁄₃ **cup icing (confectioner's) sugar, plus extra for dusting**

For the cake

1 Grease and line two 7 in (18 cm) round cake pans, or one tall one (springform is ideal), with parchment paper. Heat the oven to 350°F (180°C).

2 Put ⅓ cup sugar into a saucepan with the cocoa powder and water. Bring to a boil and simmer, stirring, until smooth. Let cool.

3 Cream the butter with the remaining sugar until fluffy. Beat in the egg yolks. Stir in the cocoa mixture followed by large spoonfuls of the remaining dry ingredients interspersed with helpings of sour cream. Beat the egg whites until stiff and fold in.

4 Pour into the prepared pan or pans and cook for 1–1¼ hours, or until a skewer inserted in the middle comes out clean. Let cool in the pan or pans for 5 minutes then remove, peel off parchment paper and let cool completely on a wire rack.

For the filling and topping

1 Melt the chocolate over hot water (see right) and mix in the instant coffee until smooth. Let cool.

2 Beat the butter until soft and creamy. Sift in the icing (confectioner's) sugar and add the chocolate mixture. Mix well.

3 Cut the cake in half horizontally, spread the filling, then replace the top half. Dust with sifted icing sugar then use the tip of a sharp knife to draw a lattice pattern.

melt Chocolate

Chocolate needs to be melted carefully or it will go grainy, or "seize."

1 Break chocolate into small squares or chop into fine pieces. Put into an ovenproof bowl.

2 Fill a saucepan one-third full of water and bring to a boil. Remove from the heat.

3 Place the bowl over the pan, making sure that the base doesn't touch the water. Let stand, stirring the chocolate occasionally, until smooth.

You can also melt chocolate in the microwave. Break it into small pieces and heat for 30 seconds, stir, then continue in five- to ten-second bursts, checking and stirring, until completely melted. Use a high setting for small amounts of dark chocolate, medium for more than 8 oz (250 g), and low or medium for milk or white chocolate.

help a
Choking person

If someone is gasping, turning blue and can't speak, there's probably a blockage. If there's another person present, ask them to call 911 while you help the victim.

Quick action
For an adult or child

■ Remove any food or false teeth from the mouth, but don't explore the mouth with your finger.
■ Encourage the person to cough to clear the blockage. Next, bend them over forward and slap between the shoulder blades three or four times with the heel of your hand, hard enough to induce a cough.
■ As a last resort, and only if you're sure someone is choking, perform abdominal thrusts (see HEIMLICH MANEUVER).

For a baby

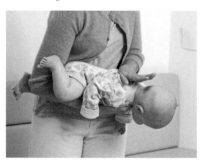

■ Lay the baby facedown along your forearm, supporting their head. Using the heel of your other hand, give five sharp blows gently but firmly between the shoulder blades. Sit down and support a larger baby across your thigh.
■ If this doesn't work, roll the baby over. Place two fingers a finger's breadth below the nipple line and press sharply inward and upward up to five times.

eat with
Chopsticks

Chopsticks work like levers and as an extension of the fingers. Don't worry about table manners, and lift the bowl close to your mouth to avoid spills.

The upper stick is pinched between thumb and forefinger, and rests against the middle finger.

The lower stick rests against the third finger, with the thicker end in the crook between thumb and forefinger.

For effective use, the two ends must meet evenly, with the sticks operating in the same plane.

The lower is held rigid while the upper moves against it to pick up food.

mix up a
Chutney

Chutney is named from the Hindu word chatni, *meaning "hot spiced relish." It needs to be cooked until it has the consistency of jam.*

Chutney is essentially a sweet-and-sour mixture of fruit and vegetables cooked with vinegar, sugar and spices. You'll need about 6½ lb (3 kg) fruit and/or vegetables, and 1 cup sugar to every 2 cups of vinegar, for a "keeping" chutney.

Good chutneys involve mixtures such as squash and tomato; beets and apple; pear, apple and golden raisins; dried apricots and sultanas; and blackberry and apple. Onions and garlic provide flavor, with spices such as cinnamon, cloves, cardamom, nutmeg and mace adding something more subtle. For a hotter chutney, use paprika, chili, ginger, garam masala or curry paste. Brown sugar is best for chutney. Vinegar can be malt, cider or wine, but should contain at least 5 percent acetic acid.

Apple and tomato chutney

MAKES ABOUT 4 LB (2 KG)

4 lb (2 kg) tart apples, peeled, cored and sliced
4 lb (2 kg) ripe tomatoes, peeled, seeded and coarsely chopped
4 onions, sliced
4¼ cups cider vinegar
2 cups dark brown sugar
2 tbsp salt
1 tbsp ground ginger
2 tsp whole peppercorns

YOU WILL NEED **Preserving pan or large heavy-bottomed saucepan, wooden spoon, glass jars with vinegar-proof lids (plastic, coated metal or glass)**

1 Combine all ingredients in a large preserving pan. Heat gently until the sugar has dissolved, then bring to a boil.

2 Simmer, stirring often, for about 1½–2 hours until the mixture is thick and pulpy, with no excess liquid.

3 Pour into sterilized jars and seal. Store in a cool, dark place, ideally for at least six months before eating.

■ Don't undercook chutney.
■ Use jars sterilized in boiling water with corrosion-proof lids.
■ Fill jars generously to within ½ in. (1.25 cm) of the rim, and put lids on while the chutney is still hot.

---

prune Climbing plants

Most climbers are easy to prune and need cutting back only to repair winter damage—though some need special attention.

As well as pruning to keep them in shape, climbers often need cutting back to prevent them from obscuring doors and windows. Those that cling can do structural damage if left unpruned (*see also* ROSES).

Wisteria Prune shoots back to about six flower buds in midsummer, then prune again, back to about three buds, in midwinter.

Self-clinging climbers Remove unwanted growth as necessary from climbers such as ivy and Virginia creeper, ideally in spring.

Twining forms Cut back climbers such as honeysuckle, passion flower and hydrangea between late autumn and early spring, or after flowering if really vigorous or straggly.

Herbaceous climbers Cut climbers such as hops and perennial sweet peas to ground level in late autumn.

Winter jasmine Thin out unwanted growth in late spring after flowering. Cut out dense tangled growth or unwanted long shoots at any time of year.

Clematis Pruning depends on variety and flowering time. When in doubt, treat as mid-season type.
■ Cut back early flowering varieties immediately after flowering to remove old growth and encourage new flowering stems—but only once plants are well established. Don't cut back to more than about 3 ft (1 m) in height, or plants won't flower the following year.
■ Once mid-season flowering varieties are well established, prune gently in early spring, removing only dead or damaged growth for flowers high up on stems. Prune a mature plant lower down in the same season (to about 5 ft/1.5 m) for flowers at head height. Cut to just above a pair of buds.

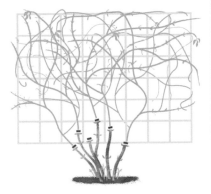

■ For varieties that flower late in the season (from midsummer onward), prune right back in early spring to about 1 ft (30 cm) from the ground, and to a pair of buds, before leaves are fully opened (see above).

---

support Climbing plants

Climbers look their best when properly trained and supported. As well as conventional solutions, a tree can make a perfect support for a vigorous climber.

However they are supported, climbers need to be tied on securely but loosely, using soft garden string or raffia (wire will damage stems rocked by the wind). Ideally, tie in shoots while they are young, flexible and easiest to manipulate. Twining climbers such as honeysuckle will need tying in only to keep them tidy.

Wires Horizontal wires placed about 1½ ft (45 cm) apart (with the bottom one 1½ ft/45 cm from the ground) and anchored to a wall at 6½ ft (2 m) intervals with "vine eyes" are ideal. Or, position one wire vertically up from the ground with a diagonal wire on each side to make a large V about 6½ ft (2 m) wide at the top. Make sure anchor points are strong and that the wire is thick enough to support a large plant.

Trellis Attach trellis panels to a wall leaving at least ½ in. (1 cm) space between them for air to circulate and to allow for tying in. Trellis panels can be mounted on wooden poles before being attached to a wall with long screws.

C

find and use
Clip art

Clip art graphics are a good way of livening up the documents you make on your computer. They are small images, often in a cartoon style, and thousands are available online for free. You can easily add a picture of a party hat to a birthday invitation or a drawing of praying hands to a church newsletter.

If you're working in Word, you can use images that have been installed on your computer as part of the Microsoft software.
■ Go to the **Insert** tab. In the Picture group, click on **Clip Art**. From here you can browse images, or search by keyword.
■ In the Clip Art window you can search in Microsoft's online library of images. This will take you to a website containing thousands of free drawings and photos. There are many other websites with similar free images.

Once you have chosen your image, you use the **Insert** command to drop it into your document. You can now manipulate the image as you wish: add borders, wrap text around it, change its color, make it fainter so you can run text over top of it. You can explore these and many other possibilities using the **Picture** options under the **Format** tab.

Climb a tree safely

First, take a good look at your tree to be sure that there are plenty of branches you can use for suppport. Never climb wet trees—they're slippery.

■ Wear shoes with a good grip.
■ Stick to the three-point rule: Keep both feet and one hand, or both hands and one foot, on the tree to support you at all times.
■ Stand only on upwardly slanting branches, as close to the trunk as you can.
■ If a branch looks dead, or too thin to hold your weight, avoid it.
■ Retrace your steps slowly and carefully as you come back down, making sure that your foot is secure before putting your weight on it.

iron Clothes correctly

Before ironing to remove wrinkles, check labels for symbols indicating iron temperatures. When in doubt, begin with a cool iron and increase the heat gradually. Some fabrics need to be covered with a cloth and gently pressed with an iron to avoid scorching or to prevent the fabric from becoming shiny. Pressing sharpens pleats, creases and lapels, and neatens the shape of the garment.

Ironing Use a steady back-and-forth motion and work methodically to avoid wrinkling sections that have already been ironed. If you don't have a steam iron, dampen badly creased areas using a spray bottle of clean water. Make sure you have a well-padded ironing board to get the best results. *See also* SHIRT.

Symbol	Fabric	Steam use
COOL IRON	Acrylic, nylon, polyester	Minimal or no steam
WARM IRON	Polyester blends, wool, silk	Moderate steam
HOT IRON	Cotton, linen, viscose	Maximum steam
DON'T IRON	Some synthetics	

Pressing To press a garment or iron delicate fabrics, use a pressing cloth, such as a dish towel. Apply light pressure, especially on pockets and seams, lifting the iron quickly as you go. Most items are best pressed inside out.

Tailored and lined jackets and pants Press over a just-damp cloth.

Silk Use a dry pressing cloth. Place silk ties front-down on a towel.

Wool and embroidered garments Place on a folded towel and press using a damp pressing cloth.

get Clothes clean

Following the care labels and interpreting symbols correctly are the surest ways of getting a good result with both washing and dry cleaning. It also helps to know how to solve common problems.

The numbers in the chart below refer to the water temperature (Fahrenheit), while the bars beneath the bowl show the strength of the washing cycle and the extent to which the machine should be filled. One bar means a "mild" wash with the machine drum no more than two-thirds full, two bars means a "very mild" one with the drum no more than one-third full. Reducing or omitting spinning is good for fabrics that crease easily. If the washing is too wet to take out, a second slow spin is better than one fast spin.

Washing symbols and fabric	Tips and variations
95 ▪ WHITE COTTON ▪ LINEN WITHOUT SPECIAL FINISH	For white sheets and towels. Normal rinse, can be fully spun. Use to kill germs, such as in washable diapers.
60 ▪ COLORFAST COTTON AND SOME POLYESTERS	Lower temperature prevents color from running. Spin fully.
60 ▪ NON-COLORFAST COTTONS AND POLYESTERS	Use "mild" setting for easy-care fabrics and reduce or omit spinning.
40 ▪ COTTONS AND VISCOSE AND OTHER SYNTHETICS ▪ WOOL	Can be fully spun.
40 ▪ NON-COLORFAST COTTONS	Use "mild" setting for viscose and synthetics, such as nylon, and reduce spinning.
40 ▪ DELICATE SYNTHETICS LIKE NYLON ▪ MODAL ▪ WOOL	Use "very mild" setting for machine washable wool. Reduce or omit spin on "very mild" setting.
▪ WOOL ▪ SILK ▪ CASHMERE ▪ DELICATE FABRICS ▪ ITEMS WITH DELICATE DECORATION	Hand wash in mild water (maximum 104°F/40°C). Rinse well, don't rub or wring. Can be spun if crease-resistant.
▪ WOOLS ▪ CASHMERE ▪ ANGORAS ▪ LEATHER ▪ SUEDE ▪ MOST TAILORED GARMENTS	Don't wash.

Common problems solved

Gray whites
▪ Insufficient detergent. Add more detergent, lemon juice or store-bought whitener.
▪ Water too cool. Rewash in hottest water safe for fabric.

Whites turn colored
▪ Incorrect sorting. Soak in color-remover and rewash. Soak colored garments in 1:16 water and vinegar solution to fix color.

Creasing and wrinkling
▪ Incorrect cycle. Reduce temperature and/or spin cycle.
▪ Overloaded machine or clothes left in for too long.

Fluff on garments
▪ Lint producers (such as towels) washed with lint receivers (corduroy). Sort washing better. Remove fluff with packing tape.
▪ Tissues left in pockets. Shake and brush off when dry.
▪ Clogged filter. Unblock, then run machine empty for one cycle.

Drying and dry cleaning
Check carefully before you tumble dry—even some cottons can shrink in a hot dryer.

Symbol and instruction	
	MAY BE TUMBLE DRIED
	TUMBLE DRY WITH CAUTION, REDUCE HEAT AND LENGTH OF CYCLE
	DON'T TUMBLE DRY
	DON'T DRY CLEAN OR USE STAIN REMOVERS
	DRY CLEAN PROFESSIONALLY

get rid of
Cockroaches

Act right away if you see a cockroach in your home. They are unsanitary, produce an unpleasant smell and breed incredibly fast.

■ You're most likely to find cockroaches in the kitchen by turning on a light at night. They will scurry back into hiding.

■ You may also see empty egg cases or skins, a dust of droppings or brown smears where walls and floor meet, where the cockroaches tend to run.

■ Keep your food areas scrupulously clean, empty the garbage and don't leave pet dishes on the floor once the food has been eaten.

■ Seal any cracks that might provide hiding places—and pour bleach down the drain if you suspect that's where the bugs are coming from.

■ Use a specific cockroach insecticide (available online or in hardware stores) to eradicate the infestation or, if all else fails, call a professional pest-control company.

Clothing sizes around the world

Numbers used for clothing sizing follow definite patterns but are far from universal, and can be unreliable because of variations between manufacturers, labeling and types of clothing. These handy charts are a good guide, but can never substitute for trying garments on in person.

WOMEN'S DRESSES										
USA, Canada	2	4	6	8	10	12	14	16	18	20	22
UK, Australia	4	6	8	10	12	14	16	18	20	22	24
Germany, Scandinavia	30	32	34	36	38	40	42	44	46	48	50
France, Spain, Portugal	32	34	36	38	40	42	44	46	48	50	52
Italy	36	38	40	42	44	46	48	50	52	54	56

MEN'S SUITS AND JACKETS									
USA, UK, Canada	36	38	40	41	42	44	46	47	49
Australia, Europe	46	48	51	52	54	56	59	60	62

MEN'S SHIRTS (BY COLLAR SIZE)									
USA, UK, Canada	14½	15	15½	16	16½	17	17½	18	18½
Australia, Europe	37	38	39	41	42	43	44	45	46

store your Clothes

Taking care about how you store your clothes will help them last longer and look better, as well as making it easier for you to find what you want.

■ Use strong wooden or padded hangers. Store skirts on hangers with slots for loops (sew loops inside, if necessary) or clips attached, which also work for pants. If space is at a premium, sew loops inside the waists of long dresses and hitch them up to prevent trailing. Avoid wire hangers—they can pull clothes out of shape and may even leave rust marks.

■ Hang ties over coat hangers or on special tie racks.

■ Stick rows of hooks inside a closet door for hanging belts.

■ In drawers, fold garments neatly. Store socks in matching pairs.

■ Store delicate fabrics, such as very fine wool or silk, folded between sheets of tissue paper. Roll linen to prevent it from creasing.

■ Keep leather or suede in a cool, well-ventilated closet, and in garment bags if worn infrequently.

■ Avoid damage from moths by keeping clothes clean, especially wool, and storing them in sealed plastic bags (*see* MOTHS).

■ Vacuum-seal bags will save space, but clothes will need pressing before use.

■ Clean clothes before storing between seasons but don't use fabric conditioner, which can encourage mold.

make a Cold frame

A cold frame is a box used to cover and protect plants from cold weather. One can be improvised using a large Styrofoam box covered with a sheet of thick polyethylene held on with packing tape, but a purpose-made frame isn't hard to build. You can use old window frames or new wood, or even pile up bricks to make the sides. A sheet of acrylic is a much safer alternative to glass for the top.

YOU WILL NEED ¾ in. (2 cm) exterior-grade plywood for front, back and side panels, preservative-treated sawn softwood planks for frame and top, saw, chisel, wood glue, 1½ and ¾ in. screws, screwdriver, 4 flat corner braces for top frame, clear acrylic (cut to size), glazing supports, silicone sealant, quarter-round, nails, hinges

BACK PANEL

FRONT PANEL

LEFT SIDE PANEL

RIGHT SIDE PANEL

1 Calculate, buy and cut the materials you need. A generous frame will be about 4 ft (1.2 m) wide and 3 ft (90 cm) from front to back, with a front wall 10 in. (25 cm) high and a back wall 14 in. (35 cm) high. All the plywood can be cut from two 4 ft x 2 ft (120 cm x 60 cm) sheets.

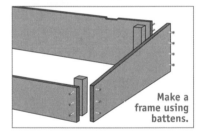

Make a frame using battens.

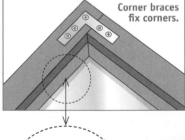

Corner braces fix corners.

2 Glue and screw corner pieces of plank to the front and back panels, then attach the sides. Cut recesses for at least two strong hinges at the back.

3 Glue and join wood for the top pieces using flat corner braces to make a frame for the acrylic. Then attach wood strips, glued and nailed into place, to hold the acrylic. Bed the plastic on silicone sealant, then finish with lengths of quarter-round, glued and nailed in place. Attach the top to the base with hinges (using the smaller screws) so it opens easily for ventilation. It can be propped open with a strip of wood. Site the frame facing south, protected from wind.

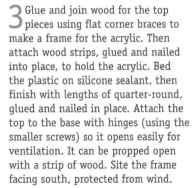

quarter-round

acrylic

silicone

frame

glazing support

open a
Coconut

As well as providing flesh to be used for cooking, coconut halves can be hung in the garden as bird food.

YOU WILL NEED **Small screwdriver, sieve, piece of cheesecloth, bowl, dish towel, hammer, sharp knife**

1 Use the screwdriver to pierce each of the three dark, circular "eyes"— the weak spots at one end of the nut.

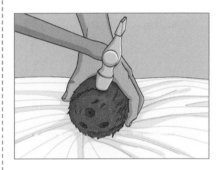

2 Drain off the liquid through a cheesecloth-lined sieve, then lay the coconut on the dish towel and tap it with the hammer, about a third of the way down from the eyes, while turning it slowly with the other hand.

3 Continue until it breaks into two, then cut out the white coconut "meat" with a sharp knife.

make classic
Cocktails
see pages 76-77

make classic Cocktails

Wow your guests by mixing them up some classic cocktails. These sophisticated, colorful drinks, blending alcoholic and nonalcoholic ingredients, date back to the early 19th century. Stock your liquor cabinet with a few essentials and become a mixologist.

Know your spirits Most classic cocktails are based on one of six spirits: gin, vodka, brandy, rum, tequila and whiskey. You'll also need a range of liqueurs and mixers—and plenty of ice.

Practice makes perfect

Cocktail-mixing is a genuine craft, and it takes practice measuring, balancing and mixing to concoct the perfect Bloody Mary or piña colada. The good news is that even your experiments, mistakes and disasters are likely to be deliciously drinkable.

YOU WILL NEED
- **Measuring cup**
- **Bar strainer**
- **Lemon squeezer**
- **Long-handled bar spoon**
- **Blender (for crushing ice)**
- **Muddler (for crushing sugar and herbs)**
- **Jigger (or shot glass)**
- **Set of measuring spoons**
- **Cocktail shaker with built-in strainer**

NONALCOHOLIC COCKTAILS Some classic cocktails can be made alcohol-free, such as the Virgin Mary variation on a Bloody Mary. Experiment with your own combinations of fruit juices, bitters, grenadine, cream, milk or coconut and nobody will miss the alcohol.

Choose the right glass

A martini will always look best in a martini glass. The shot glass is ideal for short, purely alcoholic cocktails, or "shots," usually consumed in one gulp. A margarita glass is used for the drink of the same name. A juice-based cocktail, such as a Bloody Mary, fits the highball, while the lowball, also called an "old fashioned," is good for simple, often whiskey-based mixtures that can be stirred, not shaken. The poco grande is the perfect shape and size to hold big, fruity cocktails like the piña colada.

shot glass

margarita glass

martini glass

highball glass

lowball glass

poco

MARTINI One of the earliest recorded cocktails, the martini is known the world over as James Bond's drink of choice—he prefers it shaken, of course, not stirred, and with a little vodka added. Vary the ingredients to your taste, using dry or sweet vermouth. A dirty martini is a modern twist, made cloudy by adding two tablespoons of brine from the olive jar.

1½ oz (45 mL) gin
½ oz (15 mL) dry vermouth
olives
orange or Angostura bitters (optional)

Pour the ingredients into a shaker filled with ice cubes. Stir for 30 seconds. Strain into a chilled cocktail glass. Add a dash of orange or Angostura bitters, if desired. Garnish with olives.

MOJITO A Cuban cocktail that was a favorite tipple of Ernest Hemingway's.

1½ oz (45 mL) rum
1 tsp superfine sugar
1 oz (30 mL) lime juice
8–10 mint leaves
1 lime
dash of soda water

Put the sugar and lime juice in a lowball glass. Add the mint leaves. Muddle, or crush, the leaves and sugar with a muddler or with the back of a spoon. Pour in the rum. Add four or five ice cubes and some lime slices. Top with soda water, and stir.

MARGARITA The most famous tequila-based cocktail makes for a perfect summer aperitif.

1½ oz (45 mL) tequila
1 oz (30 mL) Cointreau
½ oz (15 mL) lime juice
1 lime
fine sea salt

Rub the wedge of lime around the rim of a margarita glass or a martini glass. Dip the glass into a saucer of salt, coating the whole rim. Fill a shaker with ice. Pour in the tequila, Cointreau and lime juice and shake well. Strain and add a twist of lime.

PIÑA COLADA To make this punchy, fruity cocktail extra fun to drink, serve it in the hollowed-out shell of a pineapple.

generous bowl of crushed ice
3 oz (75 mL) white rum
2 oz (45 mL) coconut cream
4 oz (75 mL) pineapple juice
pineapple, for garnish

Put the crushed ice into a blender. Pour in the rum, coconut cream and pineapple juice. Add the pineapple chunks. Blend until smooth. Pour straight into a tall goblet (poco glass) or into a pineapple shell. Top with pieces of fruit, if you wish.

SIDECAR A delicious combination of sweetness, sourness and alcoholic punch.

1½ oz (45 mL) brandy
1 oz (30 mL) Cointreau
1 oz (30 mL) lemon juice
twist of lemon peel (optional)

Fill a shaker with ice. Add the brandy, Cointreau and lemon juice. Shake well, then strain into a lowball glass, partly filled with cracked ice. Decorate with the twist of lemon, if you wish.

BLOODY MARY The archetypal hangover cure cocktail.

1 oz (30 mL) vodka
3 oz (100 mL) tomato juice
½ oz (15 mL) lemon juice
2 dashes Worcestershire sauce
2–3 drops Tabasco sauce
black pepper
celery stick
twist of lemon or lime

Fill a shaker with ice cubes. Add the vodka, juices, Worcestershire sauce and Tabasco. Shake, then strain into a highball filled with more ice cubes. Garnish with a little black pepper, the stick of celery and twist of lemon or lime.

MANHATTAN Some people like dry vermouth in their Manhattan; others prefer sweet. Either way, the cherry is essential.

1½ oz (45 mL) whiskey
1 oz (30 mL) vermouth
2 or 3 drops of Angostura bitters
maraschino cherry, on its stem

Half-fill a tall glass with ice cubes. Pour in the whiskey and vermouth, add the bitters and stir well to chill. Strain into a well-chilled martini glass, and drop in the cherry.

get rid of
Cold sores

A tingling sensation near your lips or nostrils may mean a cold sore is coming. Act fast with over-the-counter remedies to stop it.

■ Antiviral cream applied as soon as the tingling starts will speed the healing process.
■ Patches that contain hydrocolloid gel aid healing and hide the sore.
■ Cold sores are infectious, so avoid kissing and oral sex, and don't share cups, lipstick, towels or washcloths until a complete scab forms.
■ They are caused by the herpes simplex virus HSV-1, last for eight to ten days and will often recur, especially when you're run down.

alleviate symptoms of
Colds

Pharmacy shelves sag under treatments meant to soothe sore throats and unblock noses, but there's little evidence to suggest than any work better than these simple tips.

■ Gargle with saltwater to relieve a sore throat.
■ Drink plenty of liquids.
■ Try inhaling steam from hot water laced with menthol, eucalyptus or pine oil to clear blocked airways.
■ Use vapor rubs to soothe symptoms in babies and children.
■ There have been studies of black elderberry (*Sambucus nigra*) that suggest it may lessen the symptoms and shorten the duration of a cold. Zinc supplements taken at the onset of symptoms may also help. Look for both in health food stores.

relieve your baby's Colic

Colic is most common in babies between two weeks and four months old, after which it usually passes. Telltale signs include persistent and fractious crying for several hours at a particular time of day, passing gas and a flushed face.

Soothing solutions
There's no guaranteed cure, but there are things you can do for your baby that may help to lessen or avoid any pain and soothe the crying.
■ Ask your doctor to check your breastfeeding technique, as too much foremilk can be a cause.
■ When breastfeeding, try not to change sides too quickly or cut feeds short.
■ If you're bottle feeding, ensure the hole in the nipple is the right size; the milk should flow out at a drop a second without being shaken.
■ Avoid caffeine and spicy food if you're breastfeeding.
■ Rocking, carrying, heat, massage or white noise can also calm the crying.

Try different approaches Your doctor or pharmacist may recommend adding drops that release trapped air in the digestive system to the baby's milk, or lactase drops that help to break down the protein lactose, which may cause digestive problems. Try each thing for one week. Persist if effective, or try something else. Lactose intolerance could be the cause. If breastfeeding, try avoiding dairy products in your diet, or try a hypoallergenic milk formula. See your doctor for more advice if this seems effective.

make a Collage

You don't need to be Picasso to create a successful collage. You just need the eye of a magpie, a wealth of scraps and imagination.

YOU WILL NEED **Plywood base, acrylic primer, sheet of paper or canvas, scissors, scraps to stick on, white glue or wallpaper paste for the paper or canvas, glue for the items you want to stick on, spray varnish (available at craft and hardware stores)**

Build a collection of images cut from magazines, greeting cards or postcards, as well as bright foil wrappers, scrunched tissue paper—anything that pleases you or has special significance. For a simple collage, you can work with just paper, but a more ambitious piece might include buttons, shells, beads, scraps of fabric, trinkets, ribbons or anything with meaning to you.

1 Prepare the plywood by painting one side with acrylic primer. Let it dry for about 30 minutes, cover it with glue and stick the paper or canvas to it. Don't worry about wrinkles and creases; they will add to the effect. Let dry.

2 Lay your paper cuttings beside the prepared surface and arrange any objects on top of them. Move things around and experiment. When you're satisfied with the effect, glue everything in place on the prepared surface.

3 Once all the glue is dry, apply a coat of acrylic varnish to give the finished work a sheen and protective coating.

test for Color blindness

Complete color blindness—where someone sees only in shades of gray—is rare. The most common color vision deficiency is red-green, which can cause sufferers to confuse shades of red, brown, green, purple and other colors with elements of red or green in them. More rare is a blue-yellow deficiency. Pseudoisochromatic plates—like these below—are often used as tests. There may be numbers within the dots or lines to trace.

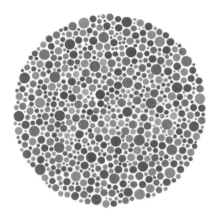 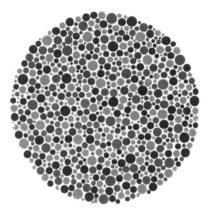

For instance, if you cannot see the figures 74 and 42 in the circles above, you may have a deficiency. There are many more online tests you can take and other types of tests, too. If these lead you to suspect that you or a child has a color deficiency, it's best to consult an eye doctor.

There's no way to correct color blindness, but it's rarely an impediment—although it may rule out some career choices, such as being an electrician or pilot, where any mistakes interpreting colored dials, cables or warning lights could be dangerous, even life-threatening.

Complain effectively

If you want to complain about a purchase or a service, be prompt. Any delay weakens your argument, and may affect your case.

■ The first step is to go back to the store or provider and politely explain to the manager why you're dissatisfied. Take note of their name.
■ If you're returning a purchase, remember to take your proof of purchase.
■ Know what you want: Is it a replacement, repair or refund?
■ Stay calm and try not to get angry or emotional. Stick to the facts and be reasonable with your complaints and requests.
■ If you don't get what you require, complain in writing to the head office. Address your letter to the chief executive—you can usually find the name and the address you need online.
■ Be civil, but demand a response within a fixed time—a week or two. Explain that you've already tried and failed to get satisfaction at a local level and give the names of the employees you have spoken to.

find your way with a Compass

To use a compass, stand in an open space and hold the compass level in your hand.

The colored end of the needle will always point north once it settles.

Align the dial with the needle, as shown, and you can read off any other direction you need.

■ Make sure that there are no large metal objects nearby that may interfere with the reading.
■ Once the needle has settled, turn the body of the compass until the colored end of the needle (usually red) lines up with north.
■ Once you know which way is north, you can read off any other direction from the dial.
■ Bear in mind that a compass gives magnetic north; true north, the axis of the earth's rotation, is slightly to the east of magnetic north. The degree of difference varies with time and place. For most country hikes it isn't significant enough to matter, but if you're setting a bearing for a long journey, such as an ocean crossing, you should be aware of it, and compensate accordingly.

C

clean your
Computer

Screens and keyboards become dusty and grimy with daily use. It's worth spending a few minutes cleaning them up from time to time.

■ First, turn off your machine and unplug it—you shouldn't clean your computer when it's on.

■ A flat-screen monitor or laptop display needs delicate treatment. Lightly dampen a soft, lint-free cloth (don't use paper towels), and wipe from side to side, never in a circle. Never clean your screen with products containing acetone, ethyl alcohol, toluene, ethyl acid, ammonia or methyl chloride.

■ Keyboards tend to fill up with dust, fluff, crumbs and other detritus that can damage the inner workings. Unplug it (if yours is freestanding), turn it upside down and shake, then vacuum it with the brush attachment. Cans of compressed air, available at camera stores, can be used to blow dust from between the keys. Don't use household cleaners or a wet cloth on a keyboard.

✳ golden rules

SUCCESS WITH COMPOST

■ **Keep your heap damp— a dry pile won't rot.**
■ **When cold, cover the heap with old carpet, blankets, plastic or bubble wrap.**
■ **Except for eggshells, never put in animal products. They will attract rats.**

make Compost to feed your garden

Compost can be made in a heap, piled on ground that has been well forked over, but a bin is more convenient and gives better results. It can be made of plastic or from slats of wood as a 3 ft (1 m) cube. It takes up to a year for garden waste to rot down to usable compost, so ideally you will need three bins: one filling, one rotting and one with well-rotted compost, ready for use (see below). Many plastic bins have a flap at the base for access to the ready-to-use compost, while you continue to add fresh waste at the top.

What can you compost? The best compost is made from quick-rotting green waste—vegetable peelings, grass cuttings and soft-stemmed annual weeds—plus an equal quantity of more fibrous material, such as trimmings of garden plants. If you can, add them in alternate layers, chopping or discarding any thick woody stems that will be slow to rot. Don't add a lot of grass cuttings all at once: Try layering them with shredded newspaper.

As it rots, turn the heap a few times, ideally into a second bin, or simply into a pile and then back into the original bin. If it's slimy or smelly, add some straw or newspaper. If it doesn't seem to be rotting, add more green matter, a compost accelerator or ammonia sulphate from the garden center.

Vary what you add to your heap: Don't make any one layer too thick.

Leave a full cube to rot for up to a year, turning every few months.

Use compost in the garden to improve soil texture and add nutrients.

1 Bin being filled   **2** Decomposition   **3** Compost being used

What not to compost Perennial weeds, such as dandelions and morning glory, will grow from the smallest pieces of root left in compost. Put them in a strong plastic bag with grass mowings or soft annual weeds, tie the bag and let sit for at least six months. They can then be added safely to your compost heap. Burn diseased plants or throw them away.

Leaf mold Decomposed leaves make an excellent soil improver, but they can take two years to rot in a compost heap. Try these methods instead.
■ Put leaves into heavy-duty plastic bags, punch holes in the sides, tie them and leave for a year. If necessary, allow another six months before using.
■ To speed rotting, spread leaves out on the lawn and mow them to chop them up before packing them into bags.

unfreeze a Windows Computer

▪ If just one program has locked up, go to **Windows Task Manager** and click on the **Applications** tab. You should see the status "Not Responding" against the frozen application: Click on **End Task** to quit.

▪ If no programs are responding and the cursor is frozen too, reboot your computer. Press the **CTRL**, **ALT** and **DEL** keys simultaneously, and shut down when prompted. If this doesn't work, press and hold the power switch for five seconds to turn it off. Wait a minute or two before restarting.

free up Computer disk space

To keep your computer working smoothly you need at least 700 megabytes (Mb) of available hard drive space. On Windows, you can check how much space you have left (usually on drive C) by clicking on the **Start** button then **Computer**. On a Mac, double-click the icon to open your hard drive (Macintosh HD) and note the available space quoted at the bottom of the window. If you need to make more space, try some of the following tips.

▪ Regularly go through old files and delete any that you don't need.

▪ Uninstall any software that you don't use. To do this on a PC, go to **Start**, then **Control Panel**, then **Uninstall a program**. Follow the instructions from there. On a Mac, go to the hard disk, then **Applications** and drag and drop unwanted programs into **Trash**. Empty the Trash when you have finished, otherwise you will have only moved the files to a different place.

▪ Move big files to an external hard drive. This is a good idea for movies, photos or music files that you want to keep but don't need to access all the time. Move or copy the files, delete the originals from your computer—and simply plug in the external drive when you need it.

guard against Computer viruses

Viruses can get onto your computer via email messages, downloads from the internet and from sharing portable storage devices, such as memory sticks.

Symptoms and cures If your computer has a virus it may run slowly or crash frequently; dialog boxes and other elements on screen may look different; you may hear the hard disk whirring when it should be inactive. Run your antivirus software immediately or seek help from a computer professional.

Beating off viruses Install antivirus software and keep it up to date. Be careful about what you allow onto your computer: Only download from reputable websites, and be wary of unsolicited or weird-looking emails, even if they appear to have come from a friend. Delete any that seem suspect without opening them (viruses are often hidden in an attachment).

deal with Concussion

If a blow to the head has rendered someone briefly unconscious, or if they are staggering or look dazed and confused, they may have a concussion.

Quick action

▪ If the person is unconscious, don't move them: Call 911. If the person is conscious, help them to sit up and place a cold pack of ice wrapped in a clean cloth on any injury to reduce swelling.

▪ Call 911 if the victim's condition deteriorates.

▪ Get the victim assessed by a doctor even if they were only unconscious for a few moments.

▪ Continue to monitor the victim's condition: They should rest under supervision for 24 hours. Call the doctor or 911 if they suffer nausea or vomiting, visual problems, breathing difficulties or disorientation.

C

deal with
Condensation

Condensation occurs when warm, moist air comes into contact with a cold surface, like an external wall or single pane of glass. It's most common in bathrooms and kitchens. To reduce condensation, you must tackle both the humid air and the cold surfaces.

- Open a window while you shower or immediately after.
- Cover saucepans with a lid when you cook.
- Install an extractor fan in your kitchen and bathroom and use them. Leave bathroom fans running for a while after you finish to clear the moisture.
- Keep your bathroom warm for the first hour or two of the day, when it's most in use.
- Use anticondensation paint (which contains a fungicide) on bathroom walls.
- Ensure adequate ventilation in rooms fitted with draftproof windows. Have trickle vents installed in the frames if necessary.

write a letter of Condolence

Getting started is often the hardest part of writing a letter of condolence, but it's best to be straightforward. Try a simple *I am writing to say how sorry I am to hear about David's death*. Explain what the deceased meant to you and why you loved or admired them *He was the center of any gathering*, *She taught me so much about ...* or just *He always had a friendly smile*. If you can, include a story about the deceased that the bereaved person might not know, a fond anecdote that sums up their personality. If that story happens to be funny, then so much the better: In times of grief, it's wonderful to be reminded that there were moments of joy and laughter.

treat Conjunctivitis (aka pinkeye)

Allergy, irritation or infection in the eye can cause a gritty sensation, itching, sharp pain or just a persistent feeling of "something in my eye." There may also be a discharge, causing blurred vision or causing eyelids to stick together when you wake up. Soothe the irritation as follows.

- Soak a clean washcloth or cotton ball in cool, boiled water and hold it to the eye to relieve itchiness and clean away any discharge. Wash the cloth after use and between eyes, and don't share washcloths or towels until the infection clears up: Conjunctivitis is very contagious.
- Consult a doctor, who may prescribe an oral medication, cream or eye drops. If you wear contact lenses, stop until you're better.

conquer at Conkers (aka Chestnuts)

This traditional English game was once popular in parts of the US and Canada, where it was also called "chestnuts." Looking for a little old-time fun? Arm yourself with a horse chestnut that's firm, of even shape and free of cracks. Drop it in a bowl of water: If it floats, find a better one. Drive a hole through your chestnut with a skewer or hand drill, and thread and knot a length of string.

- One opponent dangles their chestnut while the other takes a swing at it.
- If a player spins their opponent's chestnut full circle, they get an extra crack at it. The winner is the one whose chestnut is left on their string when the other has been smashed.

plant out flower Containers

Flowering plants in containers will thrive for longer than many border displays and need minimal maintenance. Plus, you can pack the plants in more tightly for a really striking splash of color.

First, choose a pot. Too small, and it will quickly become rootbound, too large and it will be prone to waterlogging. Plastic retains water better than terra-cotta, which must be treated to be frostproof. Next, choose your potting soil. A multipurpose mix is fine for short-term displays, but for permanent plantings, mix this with a good potting soil. Look for one with added feed and water-retaining compounds, which can reduce maintenance when you're away (see next page).

1 Fill the pot with drainage material to a tenth of its height. Use coarse gravel, bits of broken terra-cotta pot or Styrofoam plant trays. Add compost until the pot is about two-thirds full and push it down with your fingers. If using a large pot, water it now.

2 Position plants in their individual pots until you're happy with the display, then start planting, beginning with the largest. Set the plants in the container, planting them to the same depth as they were in their previous pots.

3 Fill in with soil as you go, leaving at least 1 in. (2.5 cm) between the finished surface and pot rim. Pack the soil around the roots.

4 Gently firm, water well and put the container in position, ideally on "feet" to keep drainage holes clear and help prevent waterlogging.

avoid and treat Constipation

A diet that provides insufficient fluid and fiber is a prime cause of this condition. It's normally easy to treat, but also to prevent.

■ The best way to avoid constipation is to drink six to eight glasses of fluid a day, preferably water, and eat plenty of fruit and vegetables, whole-wheat bread and brown rice. Get regular brisk exercise, too. This same advice can also help to treat the problem.

■ Your doctor may prescribe laxatives, but if you don't respond, you may require a suppository.

■ Some experts recommend taking a psyllium supplement with plenty of water in the early evening. Ask your doctor if this is appropriate for you.

■ Never ignore or rush the call of nature, and don't strain yourself.

golden rules

DAZZLING DISPLAYS IN CONTAINERS

■ **Don't over-compress the soil as you plant.**

■ **Reduce maintenance by adding water-retaining gel and slow-release fertilizer.**

■ **Use special ericaceous compost for acid-loving plants, such as camellias.**

■ **Prevent pots from blowing over by putting heavy stones in their bases.**

C

be confident holding a
Conversation

Maintaining a conversation is a skill, like driving a car, that anyone can master.

A conversation is more about engaged listening than talking. Often the hardest thing is getting started, but a reliable technique is to ask a few questions about the person in front of you.

- If you're a guest at a wedding, for example, inquire as to how they know the couple.
- In a social situation, paying a mild compliment is a good way to get a chat started. *I like that brooch, where did you get it?* or *Your children are behaving beautifully— how old are they?*
- If it's a professional situation, ask a question that might establish some common ground. *Are you in X's team?* or *Do you work on the Y account?*

Keep the conversation going
- If the conversation moves on to personal matters, listen, but resist the temptation to offer advice.
- When talk turns to big questions—religion or politics— state your view honestly, modestly and with good humor. An argument is the worst form of conversation.
- Never talk for more than a minute at a time without letting someone else have a say. A monologue isn't a conversation.

Time to move on It's perfectly polite to bring a conversation to a close when you need to. You should say something like: *I'm sorry, I really have to go now—but thank you so much. I really enjoyed talking with you.*

keep Containers blooming without you

If you don't have a neighbor to water your pots while you're away, cut off any surplus growth to reduce water loss, then try the following methods.

- Sink small pots into larger ones filled with wet sand or compost.
- Group them in a shady spot or bury them in a damp compost heap or empty flowerbed.
- Incorporate water-retaining gel into the soil when you plant.
- Sit pots in troughs covered with dampened capillary matting dipped into a bucket of water at one end.
- False-bottomed pots and troughs have a water reservoir in the base that will last longer than if you water from above.
- Cut off the base of a plastic bottle, remove the cap and stuff the neck with plenty of cotton wool. Push the bottle neck downward into the soil and tie it to a stake to keep it upright. Fill with water just before you leave and it will drain through slowly. Make one for each container.

- If you're away for long periods, install an automatic watering system that delivers a fine spray of water to each container. Some have a timer to control the watering.

bake Cookies for all occasions

Cookies can be made in endless variety. They can be cut into fancy shapes, iced or flavored with fruit, nuts, spices or chocolate. Whatever you choose, they should be crumbly and flavorful.

Oatmeal raisin cookies

MAKES ABOUT 30

½ cup butter, plus extra
   for greasing
½ cup sugar
1⅔ cups whole wheat self-
   rising flour

½ cup rolled oats
pinch of salt
⅓ cup raisins, packed
1½ tbsp corn syrup plus
   ½ tbsp molasses
1 medium egg, beaten

1 Preheat the oven to 350°F (180°C). Grease three baking sheets with a little of the butter and melt the remainder in a large pan over gentle heat. Take off the heat, add the remaining ingredients and stir until well mixed.

2 Use a teaspoon to form the mixture into small balls and place well apart on the baking sheets—they will spread. Bake for 12–15 minutes until golden and set. Leave to sit for 1–2 minutes, then transfer to a wire rack to cool completely.

Chocolate chip cookies

MAKES ABOUT 24

¾ cup soft margarine or softened
butter, plus extra for greasing
1 cup sugar
2 eggs
2¾ cups self-rising flour
1½ cups chocolate chips or roughly
chopped chocolate
½ tsp vanilla extract

1 Preheat the oven to 350°F (180°C).
Grease three large baking sheets with
a little butter.

2 Put all of the ingredients in a bowl
and mix to make a smooth dough. A
food processor will do this quickly.

**VARIATIONS Substitute half the
chocolate chips with chopped
toasted hazelnuts or pecans.
Use 1 tsp instant coffee powder
in place of the vanilla. Use brown
sugar for a deeper flavor.**

3 Place the dough on the trays in large
spoonfuls, pressing them down with
the back of the spoon dipped in flour.

4 Bake for 15–20 minutes until golden
brown and just firm to the touch.
Cool on a wire rack.

Cut-and-come-again cookies

MAKES ABOUT 50

1 cup softened butter
1 cup icing (confectioner's)
sugar, sifted
3 cups all-purpose flour
¼ cup dried apricots,
finely chopped

⅔ cup roasted hazelnuts, finely
chopped
**VARIATION Substitute other
fruit and nut combinations for
the apricots and hazelnuts. For
children, add a handful of small
candies to the dough mixture.**

1 Preheat the oven to
350°F (180°C). Line
two baking sheets with
parchment paper.

2 Put the butter and
icing (confectioner's)
sugar in a large bowl. Beat
until light and creamy,
scraping sides. Sift in the
flour and combine.

3 Add the fruit and nuts
to this basic dough and
mix together gently. Turn
the dough onto a lightly
floured surface and knead
until smooth. Divide in
two and roll each portion
into a log.

4 Wrap each log in plastic wrap and
refrigerate for an hour. The dough
will keep in the fridge for 7 to 10 days,
or freeze for three months.

5 Slice the logs into disks ½ in. (1 cm)
thick; place on sheets, 1 in. (2.5 cm)
apart. Bake for 10 minutes until just
firm. Cool on sheets, then a wire rack.

clean tarnished
Copper

Decorative copper items are usually
lacquered. Cookware is unlacquered.

For lacquered copper Wipe with a
damp cloth. Use warm soapy water
to remove grease and a medium
bristled brush to get into crevices.

For unlacquered copper Never use
a scouring pad and avoid bleach,
which causes discoloration. Instead,
sprinkle with salt and a little white
vinegar, or use the cut side of half a
lemon dipped in salt.

■ For ovenproof items, boil in a
large pan of water with ½ cup white
vinegar and 3 tbsp salt. Rinse well
and dry with a dish towel.
■ For grimy crevices, use an old soft
toothbrush and denatured alcohol.
■ Remove green corrosion by
soaking in washing soda.
■ Swab small items with ketchup,
using a makeup sponge. Rinse.

✳ golden rules
IRRESISTIBLE COOKIES

■ **Space cookies far enough
apart to allow them to spread.**
■ **Time cooking carefully;
cookies burn easily. When in
doubt, lower the temperature.**
■ **Cookies will crisp up as they
cool, so don't overcook.**
■ **Don't add too much egg or
other liquid—the mixture
should be stiff.**
■ **Most cookies will keep for a
week in an airtight container.
Finished cookies and uncooked
dough both freeze well.**

C

treat Corns on feet

A corn is an area of thick, dry skin that develops due to excessive pressure or friction.

- First identify and avoid the cause, such as shoes that rub or pinch.
- Use a pumice stone to rub down skin that's getting thick, but never cut away a corn yourself. That's a job for a doctor or podiatrist.
- If you talk to a doctor, podiatrist or pharmacist, ask about creams to rehydrate thick skin, and padding and insoles to ease or redistribute pressure on your foot.
- To prevent a recurrence, change socks or tights daily, choose comfortable footwear, thoroughly wash and dry your feet every night and apply foot-moisturizing cream.

---

tackle a Cough

A cough is the body's way of clearing mucus or irritants from the throat and lungs. It's usually caused by a respiratory tract infection resulting from a virus, such as a cold, flu or bronchitis.

- For a dry, throaty cough (one that produces no phlegm), make a warm drink of honey and lemon. The honey coats the throat, relieving the irritation that causes coughing.
- For a chesty cough that produces phlegm, ask your pharmacist to recommend an expectorant cough medicine. This helps to loosen up mucus, making it easier to cough up and out of your system.
- Avoid spreading germs; cough into your elbow. If you cough into your hands, wash them (*see* HANDS).
- If you have had a cough for more than two weeks, it's getting progressively worse or you cough blood, see your doctor.

produce a classic Coq au vin

SERVES 4

1 chicken (3-4 lb/1.5-2 kg)
2¼ cups red wine, ideally Burgundy
salt and freshly ground black pepper
1 tbsp olive oil
6 strips bacon, sliced
2 tbsp brandy
six pearl onions, peeled
1¼ cups mushrooms, sliced
2 cloves of garlic, minced

1¼ cups chicken stock
2 tbsp butter, softened
about 4 tbsp all-purpose flour

TO GARNISH

4 small white onions
2 tbsp unsalted butter
1 tsp sugar
4 button mushrooms
1 tbsp chopped parsley

1 Tenderize an older bird by marinating in the red wine for 24 hours, then clean, truss and season the bird (saving the wine for use during cooking). Heat the oil in an ovenproof casserole and fry the bacon until just cooked. Remove and set aside. Add the bird and brown. Pour off all but 3 tbsp fat.

2 Warm the brandy in a small pan, set it on fire and pour it over the bird. When the flames subside, pour in the wine and add the bacon, onions, mushrooms and garlic plus enough stock to come halfway up the bird.

3 Cover with a lid and cook on the top of the stove or in an oven preheated to 300°F (150°C) for 1½–2 hours, or until the thigh juices run clear when pierced with a skewer.

4 Meanwhile, mix the butter and flour with a fork. Set aside. Boil the white onions for 5 minutes, then toss them in butter in a frying pan for 3 minutes. Add the sugar and cook for 3–4 minutes until caramelized. Fry the mushrooms to be used for the garnish.

5 Remove the chicken, divide into pieces and place on a serving dish. Lift the mushrooms, onions and bacon from the casserole with a slotted spoon and arrange over the meat. Keep warm.

6 Place the casserole over high heat and boil hard to reduce by a third. Lower the heat and add the butter and flour mix bit by bit, stirring, until the sauce thickens. Check the seasoning and pour over the bird. Garnish with the onions, button mushrooms and parsley.

---

perform CPR

Cardiopulmonary resuscitation (CPR) is used to treat someone who has stopped breathing, but the method varies depending on the cause.

CPR always involves chest compressions, but in some cases mouth-to-mouth resuscitation via "rescue breaths" should also be given. Your first step must be to assess the victim's condition.

Assess the scene

- Tap or gently shake the victim. Shout *Can you hear me? Open your eyes. Squeeze my hand*. If there's no response, shout for help. Get someone to call 911. Make sure they tell the 911 operator that a cardiac arrest is suspected.
- Kneel by the victim and roll them onto their back, pulling from the hip. Tilt the head back, lifting the chin with your fingers to open the airway.

■ Put your ear close to their mouth and listen for breathing. If the victim is breathing normally, place them in the recovery position (*see* RECOVERY POSITION) and don't start CPR.

■ If the patient isn't breathing normally, or is coughing, breathless or motionless, apply CPR. If drowning or asphyxiation is suspected, alternate chest compressions with two rescue breaths. Otherwise, start by applying compressions only.

Chest compressions

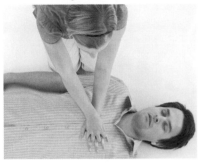

1 Kneeling over the victim, place the heel of your hand at the center of their chest. Cover that hand with the other and lace your fingers, keeping the fingers of the lower hand raised, away from the victim's ribcage.

2 Lean forward with your arms straight till your shoulders are over the chest, and press straight down 2 in. (5 cm). Keep your hands in place but ease the pressure to let the chest rise. Repeat 30 times at a rate of 100 per minute.

3 If the victim starts breathing normally again, place him or her in the recovery position. If the victim isn't responsive after six minutes of compressions, continue by alternating two rescue breaths (see below) with 30 compressions until help arrives. If you cannot or do not want to give rescue breaths, give chest compressions on their own. Carry on until help arrives or the victim regains consciousness or starts breathing again—or until you are too tired to continue.

Rescue breaths

1 Place a hand on the person's forehead and tilt the head back, supporting the chin with your fingers. Pinch their nose to close it, draw a normal breath, seal your lips around their mouth and blow until the chest rises.

2 Watch the chest fall—the complete cycle should take about one second —and repeat once more before resuming chest compressions. If you have enlisted a fellow first-aider, take turns; stop pumping the chest while your partner gives rescue breaths, and vice versa.

make a Corsage

A corsage is essentially three boutonnières tied with a bow, pinned to a dress or worn on the wrist. Be careful not to make it too heavy—you don't want it to sag.

YOU WILL NEED Three perfect rosebuds, pruning shears, corsage wire, wire cutters, floral tape, baby's breath as a filler flower, fronds of foliage, safety pin and ribbon

1 Dethorn and trim each rose stem to around 2 in. (5 cm) in length. Poke a wire about 4 in. (10 cm) long halfway through the fleshy base of each rose, bend downward in a U-shape and tape to the stem.

2 Add a spray of filler flower and a frond of foliage to each rose. Bind to the stem with floral tape.

3 Tape all three rose bundles together into a triangle and twist the wires together at the base. Wrap floral tape around the wires.

4 Wrap the safety pin in wire and tape. Secure the pin by twisting its wire to the back of the corsage just beneath the top rose. This ensures that, when pinned, the corsage remains upright.

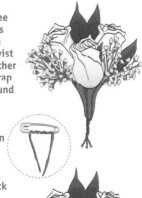

5 Finish with a ribbon tied in a bow around the stem tops.

C

go Crabbing

There are various ways to go about crabbing, some more high tech and equipment-heavy than others. If you're crabbing just for the fun of it, the easiest and simplest way to catch crabs is to attach some bait—rancid bacon works well—to a length of string or twine, and lower it into a rock pool or the water below a dock.

■ When you get a bite, gently lift the line and the crab will come with it, clinging onto the bait.
■ Keep your catch in a bucket of seawater, away from the sun. Don't put too many crabs in together; they will fight.

treat Cradle cap

In their first three months or so, babies may develop yellow, greasy, scaly patches on the scalp. The condition is harmless, rarely causes discomfort and usually lasts for no more than a few weeks or months.

■ Massage a little petroleum jelly, olive oil or baby oil into the scalp at night to soften the patches. Use a soft baby brush or a cloth in the morning to remove particles, then wash the hair and scalp with a gentle baby shampoo.
■ If the cradle cap doesn't clear up on its own, or becomes inflamed or infected, consult a doctor, who may prescribe medication.

prepare and dress a Crab

The meat of a crab is well guarded by its tough armored shell, but cooking, extracting and presenting it is a satisfying culinary challenge.

YOU WILL NEED **Large saucepan, claw cracker or small hammer, skewer or lobster pick, two bowls, teaspoon**

1 Cook a fresh crab in boiling water with 1 tbsp lemon juice, a bay leaf, some parsley stalks and a few black peppercorns. Allow 15–20 minutes for a 2–3 lb (1–1.5 kg) crab. Let it cool. Lay the crab on its back and twist off the legs and claws. Open the claws with the cracker or hammer, remove the meat using the skewer or lobster pick and put it in a bowl. Do the same with any other reasonably sized legs.

2 Twist off the tail flap and discard. Then push out the flesh of the central body chamber from the upper shell with your hands.

3 Remove and discard the gills from around the body. Pick up the back shell and remove and discard the stomach sac from just below the head.

4 Break the body into halves or quarters and pry out the white meat, discarding any small pieces of membrane that may remain.

5 Spoon the brown meat and any coral in the shell into a separate bowl.

6 Trim the washed empty shell, cutting around the edge to neaten. Season the meat and replace in the shell, white to the sides and brown down the middle. Serve with mayonnaise, lemon and brown bread, or with a salad.

create the perfect Crème brûlée

Crème brûlée perfection lies in the crispness of its sugar crust and the richness of its custard filling. Fruit such as raspberries, blueberries or nectarines can also be added below the custard mixture.

SERVES 4

2½ cups heavy cream
8 egg yolks
1 tbsp superfine sugar
½ tsp vanilla extract
about ¼ cup superfine sugar,
   to finish

1 Put the cream in an ovenproof bowl over a pan of simmering water. Beat the egg yolks with the superfine sugar and vanilla extract, then stir into the warm cream. Cook, stirring continuously, until the custard thickens enough to coat the back of a spoon.

2 Strain through a fine sieve into 4 ovenproof ramekins. Refrigerate for at least 4 hours, or overnight.

3 Cover each custard with a thick, even layer of sugar then use a cook's blowtorch or broiler to melt and caramelize the sugar. Let them chill for 2–3 hours before serving.

golden rules

CRÈME BRÛLÉE PERFECTION

■ When making the custard, don't let the water boil or the custard will overheat and the egg yolks will become curdled or scrambled.
■ Chill the custard thoroughly before the final broiling and again before serving.
■ Watch carefully during broiling—the caramel can burn quickly and easily.

make classic Crêpes suzette

Best finished on a tableside burner amid a flourish of flame, these sumptuous pancakes are a dinner party classic.

SERVES 4

8 pancakes made with sugar added
(see PANCAKES)
2 tbsp unsalted butter
¼ cup superfine sugar

juice of 2 large oranges, strained
juice of ½ lemon, strained
2–3 tbsp orange liqueur

1 Heat the oven to 250°F (120°C). Cook the pancakes and place between layers of waxed paper. Put on a large plate, cover with foil and keep warm in the oven.

2 Melt the butter in a large frying pan, stir in the sugar and cook until it becomes golden brown and caramelized. Add the orange and lemon juice and stir until the caramel has dissolved and the sauce is thick.

3 Put a pancake into the pan and fold it in half, then in half again. Push to the side of the pan, then add the next pancake and fold in the same way. Continue until all the pancakes are in the pan. If you have a table-side burner, switch the pan to it now and lower the lights for a touch more drama.

4 Add the liqueur, allow it to warm for a few seconds, then set it alight, shaking the pan so that the sauce becomes well mixed. Serve the pancakes with the still-burning sauce spooned over.

treat Cramps

Most cramps are brief episodes of intensely absorbing pain, when muscles go into involuntary spasm. You need to stretch the affected muscles to reverse the effect. Drink plenty of fluids if you're prone to cramps, as it can sometimes help.

Quick action

■ For a cramped foot, stand on it and lean forward to stretch the muscles on the sole. Rub firmly.
■ For cramps of the front of the thigh, lie down and bend the knee. Rub the front of the leg.
■ For cramps of the back of the thigh, straighten the leg and massage the back of it.
■ Relieve cramps in a calf by flexing the ankle, pointing the toes up.

play
Crazy eights

This card game is fast-moving and easy to master. Just remember that eights are always wild.

■ Deal seven cards to each player if two are playing; deal five cards each for three or four players. Place the remainder of the deck facedown on the table and turn the top card faceup beside it to start a discard pile.

■ Each player, in turn, discards a card that matches either the suit or the rank of the top card on the discard pile. For example, if the top card is the 7 of spades, you can discard any 7 or any spade on top of it. You can also discard any 8 and name the suit you want it to be. If you don't have a proper card to discard (you don't necessarily have to use an 8), you must draw from the stockpile until you come to a card you can play.

■ The first player to discard all of their cards gets points for all the cards remaining in the other players' hands. Each 8 counts for 50, each face card is a 10 and aces are 1 point each. Other cards score at face value. A game is 100 points.

make sense of Cricket

Cricket is one of the world's most popular games. It's played in many countries, as well as some communities in North America. Here's how to figure it out the next time you come across a match at the park.

Cricket is played between two teams of 11 players. Two batsmen take to the field at any one time. Each has a "wicket" to guard made up of three upright pieces of wood ("stumps") with two smaller pieces ("bails") laid across the top. The two wickets are positioned at either end of a thin rectangular pitch 22 yd (20.12 m) long, in the center of the playing field.

The bowler delivers the ball overarm from one wicket to the other. The batsman aims to hit it before or after it bounces, and then both batsmen run as many times as possible between the two sets of stumps before the ball can be returned to the wicket. Each must reach the safety of the opposite "crease" (a line drawn 4 ft/1.2 m forward of the stumps) for a run to be scored. After every six deliveries (an "over"), a new bowler takes aim from the other end.

Cricket fielding positions (right-handed batsman)

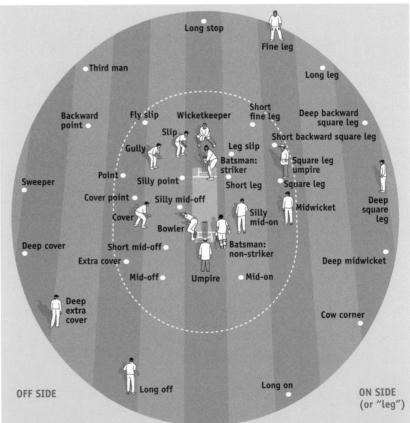

The captain and bowler "set a field," placing fielders where they are most likely to catch or inhibit the batsman. The figures above show a "defensive field," intended to limit the runs a batsman might score. An "attacking field" would include more "slips" close to the batsman, ready for a catch.

Understanding the ins and outs

The bowler's primary aim is to "bowl" the batsman out by hitting his wicket with the ball, but he may also try to trick the batsman into hitting the ball high so that he can be caught out by a fielder. The batsman must choose whether to try to score runs or just to guard his wicket until an easier ball comes along. If he manages to hit the ball to the boundary of the playing area (usually no less than 75½ yd/69 m from the wicket), he scores four runs, or six if the ball doesn't bounce before it clears the boundary.

An inning ends when ten batsmen are out. The opposing team then tries to beat the first team's score. Games consist of one innings each (a one-day game), or two innings (played over three-, four- or five-day games).

---

learn basic Crochet

Crochet is a way of making fabric by linking together loops of yarn or string. One loop is held in position by a hook (*crochet* in French) while another loop is fed through it. These instructions show how to make a foundation chain of loops, the base for all further stitches, and how to work a basic stitch into it. Reverse the hand positions if you are left-handed.

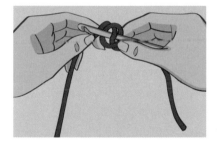

1 Make a slip knot about 6 in. (15 cm) from the yarn end and insert the hook through it from right to left.

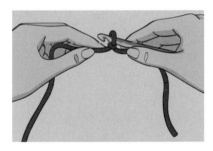

2 Pulling both yarn ends, draw in the loop until it's close but not tight to the hook.

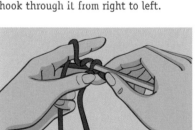

3 Holding the slip knot with your left thumb and middle finger, and pulling the yarn tight over your index finger, push the hook forward and twist it so that the yarn passes over the hook and is caught in its slot.

4 Draw the yarn through the loop, thereby forming a new loop (chain) on the hook. This should be loose enough for the next chain to be drawn through it in the same way. Repeat until you have the desired number of chains.

continued on the next page ➔

win at Croquet

Croquet looks like a genteel game, but its rules reward players who show no mercy.

Croquet is a game for two players, or two pairs of players. Each has two balls (black and blue, or red and yellow), which they must hit through six hoops twice in a set order and direction and, finally, against a central peg (as shown).

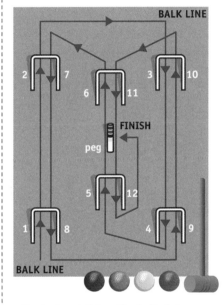

■ Begin by striking the balls into play from one of two "balk" (start) lines, diagonally opposite one another on the lawn.
■ In turn, players strike a ball to go through ("run") the next hoop or hit ("roquet") another ball.
■ For running a hoop, take an extra stroke. A roquet wins two; place your ball next to the roqueted ball and propel both at once.
■ If both balls are yours, direct them to your advantage. If one is your opponent's, despatch it to the most inconvenient spot you can find.
■ A turn ends when you have made all the strokes you are entitled to, or if you send a ball off the court.

master the
Cross-stitch

Cross-stitch is a form of counted thread embroidery, which, as the name suggests, involves counting fabric threads. It's usually stitched on Aida cloth or evenweave fabric that has easy-to-count threads. Often the stitcher follows a chart where the cross-stitches are displayed as clearly marked symbols.

Both the simplicity of the cross-stitch technique itself—each stitch is worked over the same number of threads to form a neat X shape—and the easy-to-follow charts mean you can stitch designs that are perfect in every detail, even if you're a beginner.

1 To start working from right to left, push the needle through a hole from the back of the fabric to the front. Insert it one hole up and to the left, and bring it out to the front again one hole down. Continue like this to form a row of diagonal stitches.

2 Now work from left to right to turn each diagonal stitch into a cross. Bring the needle out one hole below the top of the last stitch. Insert it one hole up and to the right. Bring it out one hole down. Continue to form a row of completed cross-stitches.

continued from page 91

 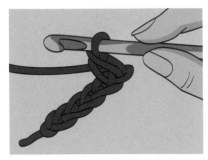

5 To begin a second row, keep the last chain on the hook and feed the hook through the second knot down on the chain. Then catch the yarn as before.

6 Pull the yarn through both loops on the hook to complete a turning stitch, then continue as before to add stitches to your new row.

7 When you're finished, trim the remaining yarn to 4 in. (10 cm), then pull through the loop. Work back along your final row, using the hook to pull the yarn through each stitch in turn, weaving it into the crochet. Partway along, make a knot. Trim the loose end and repeat with the tail left from the start of the crochet.

---

tackle a cryptic Crossword puzzle

Cryptic crosswords are an immensely satisfying form of mental exercise, a battle of wits between you and the puzzle designer.

The key to cryptic crosswords is that no element of a clue is superfluous. A crossword writer will call on a number of conventions when devising a clue. The ones listed here could account for perhaps half the answers.

Synonyms The answer is often a synonym for the first or last word or phrase in the clue. In "Roughly put down cheap wine (5)," the answer is a synonym for both parts of the clue: PLONK.

Anagrams Many clues are disguised anagrams, and these are often the easiest to spot. Look out for words that might point to an anagram, such as "confused," "about" or "mixed," then see if there are words in the clue that add up to the right number of letters. The solution to "Claimed USA plotted conflict (10)" is POSTULATED—an anagram of "USA plotted" signaled by the word "conflict" (and a synonym for "claimed").

Abbreviations Cryptic clues make great use of common abbreviations or colloquialisms. "Politician" can imply the letters MP, Dem or Rep; "fashionable" or "home" suggest IN; "about" implies CA or RE; C can be derived from "hundred" (Roman numeral) or "cold"; "father" can be PA; "mother," MA; "soldier," GI. If interpreted correctly, these letters, combined with other elements of the clue, will be featured in the solution.

Hidden words Sometimes the solution is actually spelled out in the clue, but split across one or more word breaks. The solution to "Find a seat in stalls of arena (4)," for example, is SOFA, its letters hidden in "stallS OF Arena."

get around on Crutches

Crutches are invaluable for staying mobile when you injure your leg, but using them takes some practice to perfect.

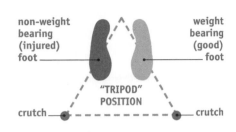

non-weight bearing (injured) foot

weight bearing (good) foot

"TRIPOD" POSITION

crutch   crutch

To get out of a chair, hold both crutches upright with the hand on your injured side and push against the chair with your free hand to stand on the uninjured leg. Move a crutch around to that side and get a comfortable grip. The crutches should be angled outward slightly, about 4–6 in. (10–15 cm) to the side, in front of your feet—the "tripod" position.

Share the load between crutches and injured leg.

Step forward with the sound leg.

To get moving, shift the crutches and injured leg forward together to share the load, then step forward with the sound leg. If you cannot put any weight on your injured leg, your arms and shoulders will have to work hard. Move both crutches forward, put your weight on them, swing your bad leg level then step forward with the other leg.

To go upstairs, if there's no handrail to hold, push down through your hands and mount the first step with your good leg. Stand firm on that leg, push down through your hands, bring your weight over the step, draw your bad leg up beside the good one, followed by the crutches—and so on. Coming down, crutches advance a step, followed by the bad leg. Balance your weight down through the crutches and lift yourself down with your good leg. Alternatively, you can negotiate stairs by sitting.

Step down by placing crutches first, then bad leg, then good.

Step up by moving good leg first, then bad, then crutches.

---

organize your Cupboards and closets

Use your cabinets only for everyday items. Don't pack them with things that can go into storage.

- Make the most of your kitchen corner storage unit by fitting carousel shelving to the doors to hold pots and pans. Nesting pots and pans together also saves space.
- To optimize cabinet space for storing canned food, dry goods and so on, install cheap, freestanding shelving or display steps.
- Where you have similar perishable items, put those with the longest shelf life at the back.
- When storing toxic cleaning products under the sink, secure the doors if you have young children.
- Take care of an overflowing closet. Remove all the clothes and divide into piles of "yes," "maybe" and "discard": the clothes that fit and are regularly worn, those you might wear occasionally and the has-beens for the thrift store or recycling bin. The exercise can reveal some forgotten garments, to be promoted from "maybe" to "yes."
- Keep linen closets tidy, with bed linens in sets or with sheets of similar size all together. Sort towels into colors and sizes and lay them with the folded side toward the front. Always rotate clean sheets and towels: Put the newly laundered ones on the bottom of the pile and take clean ones from the top.

C

write a winning
Curriculum vitae or résumé

Your CV, or résumé, needs to catch the eye of a prospective employer. Pay attention to presentation, choose a clear, easy-to-read font and keep it succinct. Always tailor your résumé to each individual application. Study the job ad to see what strengths are required and concentrate on displaying your relevant abilities.

■ Start by giving your personal details—name and contact information—and relating briefly and positively (not boastfully) what skills you possess that make you good for the job. Focus on your achievements. Bring your top selling points to the fore. And, throughout your résumé, recount your successes rather than belaboring the responsibilities.

■ Follow up with your training, education and employment history, starting with the most recent. Keep it relevant. Don't mention every night class or Boy Scout badge, but do include anything that might set you apart from other candidates— fluency in languages, IT skills…

✴ golden rules
IMPROVE YOUR CV/RESUME

■ **Run a spell and grammar check, then read and reread to iron out any errors.**
■ **Avoid jargon and clichés like "team player" and "think outside the box," in favor of clear, lucid language.**
■ **Don't start every sentence with "I," "me" or "my." That repetition gets old fast.**

bake delicious Cupcakes

Cupcakes have never been more popular. Ice them simply or dress them up with fancy piping or toppings for a special occasion.

MAKES 12
½ cup softened butter or soft margarine
½ cup superfine sugar
2 eggs
¾ cup self-rising flour
1 tsp baking powder
1 tbsp milk (optional)

FOR THE ICING
⅓ cup butter, softened
1¼ cup icing (confectioner's) sugar
1–2 tbsp milk
1 tsp vanilla extract

1 Preheat the oven to 350°F (180°C). Put 12 paper muffin cups into a muffin pan. Place all the ingredients in a food processor or mixing bowl and beat until smooth. If the mixture seems too thick, add the milk. Spoon into the paper cases, filling to about two-thirds. Bake for 15–20 minutes until risen, golden brown and springy to the touch. Cool on a wire rack before decorating.

2 Cream the butter and icing (confectioner's) sugar, adding enough milk to give a creamy texture, and the vanilla extract, plus any coloring or alternative flavoring you like. Smooth or pipe over the cakes. Or decorate in any other way (*see* CAKE).

Variations

■ Replace ¼ cup of flour with cocoa powder for chocolate cupcakes.
■ Add the grated zest of two lemons or a large orange for citrus flavors.
■ Fold in 1 tbsp instant coffee powder or strong espresso, and/or a handful of chopped nuts.

cook an authentic Indian Curry

The hallmark of Indian curry lies in its spices, which are mixed with a thickening agent, such as onions, yogurt, coconut milk, tomatoes or split peas. The heat will depend on the amount of chili or cayenne you use. An authentic recipe such as the one below takes some time and effort.

Lamb rogan josh

SERVES 4
4 tbsp plain yogurt
½–1 tsp cayenne
2 tsp ground coriander
1½ tsp ground cumin
2 large cloves of garlic, minced
2 tsp grated fresh ginger

1 tsp paprika
½ tsp ground turmeric
2 tbsp canola oil
1¼ lb (550 g) lamb, cubed
1¾ cup onions, finely chopped
1½ tbsp tomato paste
salt

2 tbsp unsalted butter
2 bay leaves, crumbled
2 green cardamom pods, split open
2 in. (5 cm) cinnamon stick, broken in half
4 whole cloves
½ tsp grated nutmeg

TO SERVE Rice and accompaniments such as papadums, nan bread, fruit chutney and a raita made with yogurt, cucumber and mint

1 Mix the yogurt, cayenne, coriander, cumin, garlic, ginger, paprika and turmeric. Heat the oil in a heavy-bottomed saucepan, add the lamb and onions and stir until lightly browned. Add the yogurt mixture and cook for a few minutes. Then lower the heat, cover and cook for 30 minutes or until the lamb has released its juices.

2 Remove the lid and cook on a high heat, stirring for about 5 minutes until the sauce has a paste-like consistency. Add the tomato paste, salt and half the butter, reduce the heat and simmer for 3–4 minutes. Pour in 1½ cups boiling water, cover and simmer for 15 minutes more.

3 Melt the remaining butter over a low heat, add the bay leaves, cardamom, cinnamon and cloves and sizzle for 40 seconds. Add the nutmeg, stir and then pour over the meat. Mix well, cover and cook for another 10–12 minutes.

---

measure and hang Curtains

Use these general guidelines to calculate length and width.

Length Measure from the bottom of the track to 1 in. (2.5 cm) above the floor (A), to 4 in. (10 cm) below a window sill (B) or 2 in. (5 cm) above a radiator (C). Add 6 in. (15 cm) for a hem and 3 in. (7.5 cm) for a top turning, plus enough fabric for a heading to conceal the track. If using a rod, alter the heading to conceal all or part of it, as preferred.

Width Multiply the width of the track or rod (D) by the factor required for your heading style:
■ 1.5–2 for gathers
■ 2.25–2.5 for pencil pleats
■ 2 for pinch pleats.
For made-to-measure curtains add 12 in. (30 cm) for side turnings and overlaps where curtains meet.

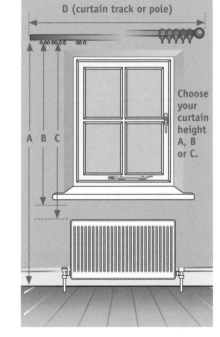

D (curtain track or pole)

Choose your curtain height A, B or C.

A B C

Curtain rod Any rod or track must be strong enough for your chosen fabric and be securely fastened to the wall or ceiling.
■ Most tracks are fixed with brackets spaced about 8 in. (20 cm) apart, but rods are held with one bracket at each end and, for heavy curtains, may need an extra central bracket.
■ Buy a rod or track that will extend at least 6 in. (15 cm) beyond the window at each end. In bay windows, fit rod to run beyond the bay and onto the wall at each side.

To keep heavy curtains hanging straight, sew small lead-free or covered lead weights to the hem on the wrong (reverse) side. Weighted beads threaded through the hems of sheer curtains will prevent them from billowing.

serve up a Thai
Curry

Thai curries are typified by their mixture of dried spices and fresh ingredients, spiked with the acidity of lime and the heat of chili.

Thai shrimp curry

SERVES 4

2 in. (5 cm) fresh ginger, peeled and chopped
2 stems lemongrass, bruised and chopped
3 cloves garlic, minced
1 tsp ground coriander
1 tsp ground cumin
2 kaffir lime leaves
3 tbsp canola oil
1 bunch scallions, chopped
3 large green chili peppers, seeded and shredded
⅔ cup coconut milk
juice of 2 limes
1 lb (500 g) cooked, shelled shrimp
2 tbsp chopped cilantro
freshly ground black pepper

TO SERVE **Plain boiled basmati rice**

1 Put the ginger, lemongrass, garlic, coriander, cilantro, cumin, lime leaves and half the oil into a food processor with 3 tbsp of cold water and blend to a paste.

2 Heat the remaining oil in a large pan. Add the scallions, chili peppers and spice paste and stir fry for 2–3 minutes until aromatic. Stir in the coconut milk and lime juice and simmer, stirring regularly, for 10–15 minutes, or until reduced and thickened. Add the shrimp and cook until just heated through. Adjust the seasoning and serve.

C

lengthen and shorten Curtains

YOU WILL NEED **Tape measure, scissors, tailor's chalk, pins, thread, needle, seam ripper, curtain and lining fabrics, iron. Optional: decorative tape**

■ Let down hems and clean curtains according to manufacturer's instructions, before making alterations.
■ Double check that both curtains are exactly the same length.

To shorten Measure the new length, adding 6 in. (15 cm) for the hem. Cut off unwanted fabric from the bottom. Fold up the seam allowances then tack (*see* TACK) and stitch the new hems into position.

To lengthen If there's enough fabric, make a smaller hem. If the previous hem mark is very obvious, disguise it with decorative tape. Replace or regather the heading tape.

■ Match new and old fabrics according to weight and laundering requirements.

■ Alternatively, insert extra contrasting fabric. Measure the new length, adding 1 in. (2.5 cm) for each additional seam, then unpick any lining. Cut a strip of the new fabric to the width of the curtain, allowing 1 in. (2.5 cm) allowances at each side. Mark cutting lines on the reverse of the curtains with chalk, then cut. Pin, tack and stitch in the new fabric bands, right sides together, then press the seams. Lengthen the linings by the same amount, working from the bottom. Turn up and stitch lining hems. Restitch the linings into place.

create a simple Cushion cover

This project shows you how to cover a square cushion. Making the cover slightly smaller than the cushion allows it to plump up when filled.

YOU WILL NEED **Cushion, fabric, tape measure, scissors, pins, thread, needle, sewing machine, iron**

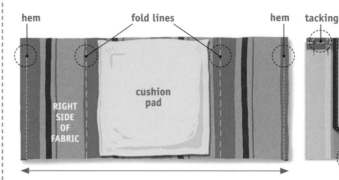

hem   fold lines   hem   tacking   Sew along raw edges top and bottom.

RIGHT SIDE OF FABRIC   cushion pad   REVERSE SIDE OF FABRIC

twice the length of cushion + 4 in. (10 cm)   doubled-over hems

1 Measure the cushion. Cut a piece of fabric the right height and twice the length, plus 4 in. (10 cm). Mark two fold lines the same distance in from the sides —10 in. (25 cm) for a 16 in. (40 cm) cushion, 11 in. (27.5 cm) for an 18 in. (45 cm) cushion or 14 in. (35 cm) for a 24 in. (60 cm) cushion. Turn under ¼ in. (5 mm), then ¼ in. (5 mm) again at each end to form hems. Pin, tack and sew. Remove tacking and press.

2 Fold fabric, right sides in, at fold lines. Allow 3 in. (8 cm) overlap at the join. Pin and tack the two raw edges then sew a ½ in. (1 cm) seam along each. Trim the hem diagonally at the corners to make them neater once the fabric is right side out. Remove tacking. Turn right side out and press. Insert the cushion in the slit at the back of the cover.

make real Custard

Custard can be served with any hot dessert or cold with fruit. It makes a delicious whipped cream replacement or pastry filling.

MAKES 2 CUPS

2 cups whole milk
1 vanilla pod, split
5 egg yolks
3 tbsp sugar

Bring the milk to a boil slowly in a heavy-bottomed saucepan. Add the vanilla pod, leave to infuse for 10 minutes then remove. Whisk egg yolks and sugar until thick, and stir in the hot milk. Pour the mixture into a bowl, then clean the pan. Strain the mixture back into it, then heat gently, stirring with a wooden spoon until it thickens.

■ Don't custard to boil, or it will curdle. If it starts to "turn," remove it from the heat at once and put it into a blender or processor. Or strain it into a bowl sitting in an outer bowl of ice cubes and beat vigorously.
■ If you don't have a heavy-bottomed saucepan, cook the custard over a pan of barely simmering water.

take plant Cuttings

Use cuttings to save money and propagate your garden favorites, selecting your method according to the type of plant.

YOU WILL NEED **Sharp knife, shears, plastic bags, rooting hormone, pots filled with a mixture of loam-based compost and sharp sand, trowel**

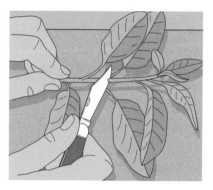

Softwood cuttings Before midsummer, cut off the soft, sappy tips of nonflowering shoots, with four or five pairs of leaves on each. Remove the lowest pair and the top pair just below the leaf joint. Pot and cover with a plastic bag. Keep warm until rooted. Use for plants such as geraniums and impatiens.

Basal cuttings In early spring, dig away soil from plant bases and cut off young growth. Pot as for softwood cuttings, making sure that cuttings don't touch in the pot when planted. Use this method for species such as lupins, chrysanthemums and delphiniums.

Semi-ripe cuttings Take cuttings in late summer from shoots that have begun to harden at the base. Prepare and root as for softwood cuttings, but dip into rooting hormone before planting. Use for shrubs. For clematis, trim between, not just below, leaf joints (below, left).

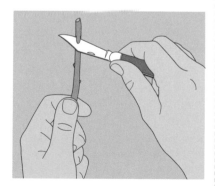

Hardwood cuttings Take cuttings in winter from the youngest shoots. Cut to about 10–12 in. (25–30 cm) and remove a thin sliver of wood from the base of each (above, right). Dip into rooting hormone and insert into a large pot or a shallow trench lined with coarse sand or grit. Ideal for roses.

deal with Cuts

A small surface cut or abrasion can be dealt with at home. Before you dress the wound, wash and dry your hands thoroughly (*see* HANDS).

Clean the wound under warm running water using a cotton swab, and pat dry with a fresh towel. If you need several swabs, discard each one after one use. Don't use antiseptic as this can damage the tissue and slow the healing process, but do apply a sterile bandage.

Change the bandage frequently and remove it at night if the wound is unlikely to rub on bedclothes. To keep the wound dry choose a waterproof bandage that can withstand light wetting such as a shower. When the wound is no longer moist and in need of protection, don't bandage it, but watch for signs of infection.

See a doctor if you notice any swelling, redness spreading around the wound, the formation of pus or an increase in pain, or if you feel unwell, develop a fever or have swollen glands.

If a cut is deep, though it may not appear large, there may be underlying damage to blood vessels, nerves, muscles, tendons and ligaments. Act quickly to stem the bleeding (*see* BLEEDING) and seek medical attention, because of the risk of complications, such as tetanus.

D

tackle Dandruff

Although harmless, dandruff can be itchy, and the appearance of white flakes of dead skin in hair and on clothing is unsightly and can be embarrassing. Dandruff's exact cause is unknown, but experts say it isn't linked to poor hygiene.

■ Treat with medicated shampoo or tea tree oil shampoo. Wash at least three times a week and rinse thoroughly.

■ Massage rather than scratch your scalp when using shampoo, to avoid causing unnecessary irritation.

■ Brush hair daily to help remove flakes of dead skin, but avoid scraping the scalp too roughly.

■ Change or stop using hair products, such as gels and sprays, and see if your dandruff improves.

■ See a doctor if the dandruff does not respond to home treatment, if your scalp is irritated or if it is infected by scratching.

■ Continue using medicated shampoo at least once a week after your dandruff clears up.

weave a pretty Daisy chain

Kids love to wear necklaces and garlands of daisy or dandelion chains, and will enjoy the process of making them.

■ Gather flowers with thick, strong, long stems.

1 Use a thumbnail to make a split in a stem just big enough to allow you to poke another stem through and continue until you have your chain.

2 Try to make each split the same distance from the flower head. The closer to the head, the more dense and colorful the chain.

3 To close the circle, poke the last stem through a small split in the top of the first flower and pull.

spot signs of Dampness

There are two main causes of dampness in the home: condensation inside the house, and a leak coming in from outside.

If you have crumbling plaster or peeling wallpaper in cold, dry weather, chances are that the moisture is caused by condensation (*see* CONDENSATION). If the dampness problem manifests itself in warm, rainy weather, then it's more likely that the moisture is coming in from outside, and is due to a structural problem in your home.

Damp patches at baseboard level, or a tidemark on wallpaper anywhere up to 3 ft (1 m) from the floor, may indicate that moisture is leaking in from outside through the base of the wall. Check to see if there's visible damage to the outside. Repairing this is a job for a professional.

Damp can also climb in if, say, a path or a flower bed is bridging (or overlapping) the base of the outside wall and letting rainwater in. In such instances, the flowerbed or path must be lowered, or a channel must be cut so that it doesn't touch the walls of the house.

Dampness higher up the walls can be caused by cracked or missing shingles on the roof, or by leaky or blocked eavestroughs. Get a professional to assess the cause, and have it repaired right away.

throw Darts well

double ring
triple ring
single score
outer bull (score=25)

5½ ft (1.7 m)

7¾ ft (2.37 m)

oche

inner bull (score=50)

out of play area

Players stand behind a line (the "oche") and take turns to throw three darts each.

There are many games that can be played on a standard dartboard. The most common is called 501.

■ Two players take turns ("legs") to throw three darts each. The score from each set of three darts is subtracted from 501, and the winner is the player who first reduces their tally to exactly zero.

■ Players must end on a "double," a dart landed in the double ring, for which the score is twice the number shown in that segment.

■ The triple ring scores three times the number shown. It follows that the highest, most valuable score that can be made with three darts is 180 (a triple 20 scored with each of your three throws).

■ If you score more points in a leg than you need, you "bust" and the total at the end of your previous leg is reinstated.

---

impress your Date

Dates, especially first dates, are fraught with potential disaster. Most pitfalls can be avoided if you're polite and honest about yourself.

■ If you're a man, does your date expect a little old-fashioned chivalry? If so, compliment your date's appearance and hold open doors.

■ Don't bail early if the date isn't going well or you don't have chemistry. It's rude, for one thing, but, more importantly, a bad start isn't always fatal.

■ Dress up a little. It's polite to make some effort, however casual the date.

■ Avoid any remark that sounds like a pick-up line. The only worthwhile pick-up line in all the world is *Tell me about yourself*, so be a good listener.

■ Don't brag. And don't tell self-aggrandizing fibs that you might have to retract later (i.e., *I'm in the special forces*).

■ Don't talk about exes, divorces or failed relationships. Be positive and happy. Cheerfulness is always more attractive than sadness.

■ Pay attention. Maintain eye contact, and don't look around to see who else might be available.

D

Darn a sock

The basic darning technique is essentially reweaving, and can be used on wool and woven fabrics of all kinds.

An old-fashioned "darning egg" or "mushroom" gives you a firm base for the job, but the smooth underside of a small jar is a good substitute. Don't stretch the fabric over the mushroom or jar, otherwise the darned section won't fit the hole.

YOU WILL NEED Darning needle, matching wool or thread, darning egg (or equivalent), scissors

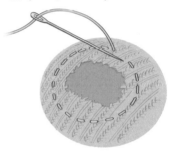

1 With the sock right side out, insert the darning egg or jar. Then thread the needle and run a neat frame of small stitches around the hole, working in a strong, undamaged area of the fabric.

2 Lay a warp of threads across the hole in one direction, leaving a small loop at the end of each row to allow for any shrinkage. Then weave a series of weft threads at right angles to the first set, doing a small anchoring stitch at each side. Fasten securely on the wrong side, out of sight.

DEADHEAD GARDEN PLANTS
- **Use sharp pruning shears for deadheading, working neatly, and clean them well afterward to remove any sap or disease-carrying organisms.**

clean a Decanter

Wash dust and grime from a decorative decanter from time to time and clean thoroughly inside after each use.

Outside Wash by hand in warm, soapy water using a sponge and a soft-bristled brush. If it is antique or made of crystal or cut glass, lay a folded dish towel in the bottom of the sink to protect against chipping.

Inside Half fill with warm, soapy water and shake gently with your hand over the top. If still stained, try swirling around a mixture of vinegar and coarse sea salt. Or buy special abrasive-coated cleaning balls to swirl around inside. For stubborn wine stains, use warm water mixed with coarse salt and baking soda. Alternatively, fill with water, add a denture-cleaning tablet and leave to soak overnight.

To dry Effective drying is essential to prevent fogging and contamination by microorganisms lingering in any water. Drain thoroughly, then insert a long-handled wooden spoon wrapped in paper towel. Leave overnight. Or dry with warm air from a blowdryer—but beware of overheating, which could crack the glass.

Deadhead your garden plants

Deadheading makes your garden look tidier and is the best way of lengthening the flowering season of many plants. Because plants put a lot of energy into seed formation, stopping this can strengthen the plants and encourage healthy foliage. Resist deadheading any plants whose seedheads make good winter shapes or food for birds if left uncut.

Bulbs and corms Cut flowers down to ground level as soon as they fade to divert resources into the underground storage organs. Keep well watered until the foliage dies down.

Perennials Remove dead flower spikes. In plants such as lupins and delphiniums, this will encourage the growth of flowering side shoots. Cut spring and early summer flowering perennials, such as hardy geraniums and poppies, down to ground level after flowering. Some will even flower a second time.

Annuals Because they will stop flowering once they have set seed, deadhead pansies, snapdragons and petunias to ensure continued blooms. Tidy up other annuals, such as carnations and marigolds, as flowers fade.

Roses Remove flowers down to the first pair of leaves.

prepare surfaces for Decorative paint

Whatever the surface, the time and effort you put into preparing for decoration make a world of difference to the finished look.

Painted wood should be stripped only if more coats would affect the functions—as with sash windows, for example. Wood doesn't need stripping if it's in good condition, but it should be cleaned with trisodium phosphate (TSP) and water. Glossy surfaces should be roughened with sandpaper so that the new paint adheres.

Exposed brick should be brushed to remove dust. Interior brick surfaces can be painted.

Old wallpaper should be removed before new paper is hung. Soften the paper with wallpaper removed or warm water containing dish soap, then scrape off with a scraper. Painted wallpaper may need to be scored with the corner of your scraper, especially if there are several layers. A steam stripper makes the whole job much easier, but take care not to oversteam, which can soften the plaster underneath. *See also* WALLPAPER.

Old, bare plaster might need some repair before it's primed then painted. Cracks and small holes left by picture hooks should be filled with spackle. Crumbly patches should be removed back to sound plaster and replastered with a repair plaster (*see* PLASTER).

Newly plastered ceilings can be prined and painted directly. *See also* CEILING.

build a simple Deck in your backyard

There's nothing like relaxing on the deck after a long day at work. After some initial setting out and leveling, it's quick and easy to construct a basic structure.

YOU WILL NEED **4 x 4 in. support posts, premixed concrete, landscape cloth to cover the area, 2 x 6 in. treated lumber for joists and perimeter frame, 2 x 4 in. treated lumber boards for cross-blocking, joist hangers, bolts, 3½ in. common nails, decking planks, deck screws, level, string line, hammer, screwdriver, saw**

Start by drawing a plan so that you can calculate how much lumber you need. Follow the minimum spacings between joists and support posts indicated on the plan below. Don't be tempted to stretch these distances to suit your final measurement; instead, put in additional supports. Lay down landscape fabric to cover the area that will be directly beneath the deck.

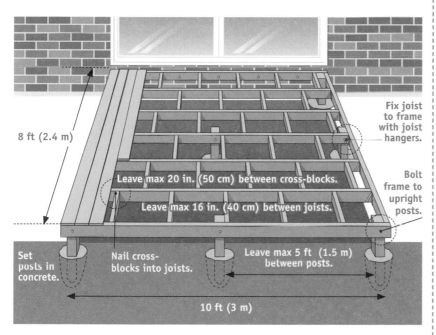

Fix joist to frame with joist hangers.

Bolt frame to upright posts.

8 ft (2.4 m)

Leave max 20 in. (50 cm) between cross-blocks.

Leave max 16 in. (40 cm) between joists.

Set posts in concrete.

Nail cross-blocks into joists.

Leave max 5 ft (1.5 m) between posts.

10 ft (3 m)

1 Set support posts in concrete, no more than 5 ft (1.5 m) apart in each direction. Use a spirit level to make sure they're perpendicular.

2 When the concrete sets, bolt the outer frame to the posts, checking carefully with the longest level you have. Saw off the support posts flush with the frame.

3 Use joist hangers to fix joists within the main frame, no more than 16 in. (40 cm) apart, and nails to fix cross-members, no more than 20 in. (50 cm) apart. Decking planks must be laid at right angles to joists.

4 Cut the decking and "dry lay" it in place to make sure that the joints between boards are staggered

continued on next page ➜

---

avoid Deep vein thrombosis
when flying

During air travel, prolonged immobility can cause blood to clot in a deep vein, usually in the leg or pelvis. Part of the clot may detach and travel to the lung, causing a life-threatening blockage.

■ Avoid alcohol and drink plenty of water to avoid dehydration.
■ To improve circulation, take short walks and perform the exercises below. Wear elastic compression socks or stockings.
■ Consult a member of the crew if you have any swelling in your limbs.

Exercise your legs for 3–4 minutes every hour. Lift your feet off the floor and flex them by pointing your toes up and down.

Raise each knee in turn, so that the back of your thigh is lifted off the seat.

With your knee raised, rotate your ankle by moving your outstretched toes in a circle. Switch legs and repeat.

Descale a kettle or showerhead

Special descaling solutions are available to buy, but white vinegar is ideal for attacking lime scale.

For a kettle, dilute white vinegar 50:50 with water. Fill the kettle and leave it overnight. Empty, rinse, refill with water, reboil and empty. It's now ready to use. No taste of vinegar will remain.

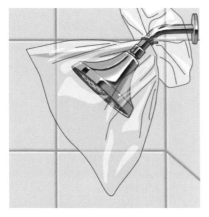

For a shower head unscrew the head and soak overnight in a bowl of white vinegar (if it has several parts, unscrew these if possible and soak them separately). Remove any remaining deposits with an old toothbrush. If the shower head can't be unscrewed, pour the vinegar into a plastic bag and pull it up around the head to immerse it. Secure firmly in place with twist ties or string and leave overnight before finishing off with the toothbrush.

continued from page 101

(optimally by 4 ft/1.2 m or more) to evenly distribute the load. If you will not be finishing the edges with an end-strip, leave a 1 in. (2.5 cm) overhang.

5 Use a power drill to screw two 2½ in. (6.5 cm) screws suitable for treated wood through the board and into the joist at each fixing point; a string line helps you keep the screws straight. With cardboard as spacers, leave a ⅛–¼ in. (3-7 mm) drainage gap between boards.

6 If not using an overhang, finish the deck edges with a cover strip of matching wood nailed in place. Check with your local authority to see the rules about railings.

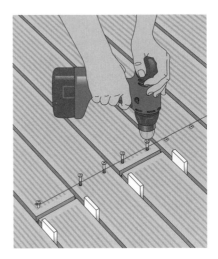

Defrost food safely

When food is defrosting, as soon as it rises above 39°F (4°C) any bacteria it contained before freezing begin to multiply. Poultry, especially large birds, must always be completely thawed before cooking to remove the risk of salmonella being activated during cooking.

Defrosting in the refrigerator is the safest method. If using the microwave, cook food immediately after defrosting because some parts may become warm and stimulate bacterial growth during the process.

Timing is crucial

■ For meat and poultry, allow 6 hours per pound (500 g) in the fridge, and half that time at room temperature.
■ For fish and shellfish, allow 4 hours per pound (500 g) in the fridge, or 2 hours per pound (500 g) at room temperature.

deal with Diarrhea

Although the symptoms of diarrhea can be extremely uncomfortable, the main danger of the condition is the dehydration it can cause.

■ Take small, frequent sips of water or diluted juice.
■ Talk to the pharmacist about rehydration preparations, such as Pedialyte or sports drinks, which have the right balance of water, salt and sugar.
■ Eat low-fiber food (bananas, cottage cheese and white bread, rice or potatoes) as soon as possible, adding in other foods when you're ready.
■ New research suggests that taking a probiotic will reduce the length of a bout of diarrhea and slash the risk of it lasting more than four days.
■ If symptoms persist for two weeks (five days in children, 48 hours in babies) or if you see blood or pus in your diarrhea, see a doctor.

eat a healthy, balanced Diet

Here is an easy way to visualize your daily plate, based on a well-balanced diet. The United States and Canada each have their own official food guides, which you can use to hone your food choices.

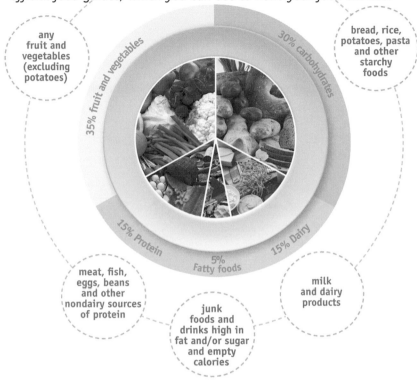

any fruit and vegetables (excluding potatoes)

35% fruit and vegetables

30% carbohydrates

bread, rice, potatoes, pasta and other starchy foods

15% Protein

5% Fatty foods

15% Dairy

meat, fish, eggs, beans and other nondairy sources of protein

junk foods and drinks high in fat and/or sugar and empty calories

milk and dairy products

A healthy meal should be based on starchy foods, such as whole-wheat bread, cereals, potatoes and pasta. They are the fuel on which our bodies run and are a prime source of nutrients and dietary fiber, which makes for good bowel and colon health and helps to control cholesterol. Try to choose whole-wheat or whole-grain varieties. They contain more fiber, vitamins and minerals than white varieties do.

Fruit and vegetables should make up more than a third of your diet. Fresh plants contain phytochemicals, powerful antidotes to the rogue oxygen molecules called free radicals that damage cells and cause disease. A little less meat and more veggies on your plate will make a real difference.

Cut right down on fatty, sugary snacks and soda—they are fattening sources of empty calories. Try dried fruit for a snack rather than a chocolate bar, and drink diluted fruit juice rather than soda.

Meat, fish, eggs and beans are good sources of protein, needed for the growth and repair of our bodies. Try to choose lean cuts of meat and skinless poultry to cut down on fat, and aim for at least two portions of fish a week.

Dairy products are also a good source of protein and contain the calcium we need to keep our bones healthy. Choose lower-fat options to avoid raising your blood-cholesterol levels and increasing your risk of heart disease.

throw a faultless Dinner party

There are two vital ground rules for a smooth-running dinner party: Plan ahead, and don't over-exert yourself.

■ Invite no more people than your table can accommodate. Six is a good number (including yourself) that facilitates around-the-table conversation. Eight is a sensible maximum number.

■ Ask in advance if your guests are vegetarian or have other special dietary requirements. (A polite guest will volunteer this information, rather than come and refuse your food.)

■ Plan your menu so it's full of contrasts: veggie starter, fish main; rich main, light dessert; no more than one spicy course, etc. Avoid repetition: Don't serve a creamy chicken casserole followed by a vanilla pudding, say, or a pot pie followed by apple pie.

■ Choose tried-and-true recipes that you know you can duplicate on the night. Don't treat your guests as guinea pigs for your culinary experimentation.

■ Serve one course that you can prepare entirely in advance—say, a chilled soup. You don't want to neglect your guests while you slave away at the stove. Avoid dishes, such as individual steaks, that require last-minute attention.

■ Make sure there are enough drinks—don't rely on guests to bring bottles. As a rule, keep white wine chilled, allow red wine to breathe and be sure to have soft drinks and water on hand.

■ Above all, be attentive to your guests. Making them feel at home and at ease is at least as important as the food you put on the table.

load a
Dishwasher

For maximum efficiency it pays to run a dishwasher fully and properly loaded. Make sure items won't prevent the spray arms moving freely or obstruct tubes, nozzles or the opening of the soap dispenser, and that breakables won't touch if they vibrate during the cycle. Check that all items are dishwasher safe.

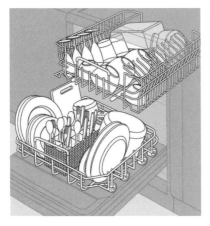

Plates Insert in slots in lower section, facing toward the center.

Cups, glasses and bowls Place in the top section. Stack bowls on an incline. Put glasses upside down between, not over, prongs.

Plastic items Place on top rack away from the heating element in the lower section that can cause melting.

Pots and pans Place upside down in the lower section.

Cutlery Place fork and spoon handles downward into utensil baskets, and knive handles upward. Mix them so that they don't "nest" into one another. Lay larger utensils horizontally across the top section.

Cutting boards and baking sheets Place on the outermost edges of the bottom section.

clear a blockage in your Dishwasher

Your dishwasher has filters where the water goes in and where it flows out. This is where blockages can occur.

The outlet filters, set inside each other like cups, are to be found at the bottom inside the dishwasher cabinet. They collect grease and food particles, so are prone to blockages.

Unclip the filters as advised in the manual, rinse them clean under warm running water, soak and wash in warm soapy water, using dish soap to disperse the grease. Return to their place.

To clear the inlet filter, turn off the water at the valve then disconnect the inlet hose. Remove any rubber seals and pull out the filter with long-nosed pliers. Clean it with a nail brush. Inlet filters rarely get blocked.

Dive into a swimming pool

A well-executed dive is by far the most graceful way to launch yourself into a pool and can generate momentum for your swimming stroke.

Hook your thumbs, and lay the fingers of the upper hand on top of the other hand.

Push your chin into your chest.

Bend slightly at the waist.

Fix your eyes on a point about 3 ft (1 m) into the pool; this is what you're aiming for.

Always check that the water is deep enough for diving. Never dive into water less than 5 ft (1.5 m) deep.

1 Stand with the toes of one leg (the one you kick off with) at the pool edge. Set your other foot slightly back from the edge.

2 Bend both knees slightly and allow yourself to tip forward.

3 As you strike the water, straighten your legs, keep your hands linked, your arms aloft, and your body in a straight line.

4 As your downward momentum slows, steer your body up toward the surface, kicking your legs for added speed.

take care of your Dog

Keeping your dog clean and well-groomed is one of the key things you can do to keep it happy and healthy. Regular grooming can become a special and affectionate ritual that strengthens your emotional bond, but it also allows you to spot new lumps or tumors, skin complaints and parasites, such as fleas or ticks, and tackle them before the problem becomes severe.

Grooming the coat

When grooming a long coat, hold the hair down at the roots so you don't tug the skin. Don't yank at knots; work patiently.
■ Use a flat, wide-tooth steel comb when the slicker brush fails.
■ A dematting comb, which has blades, can be used to cut through stubborn mat. Alternatively, cut with scissors and brush out.

Short coats are easier to groom than long ones, but can be prone to matting.
■ Use a slicker brush to remove tangles. Apply firm, long strokes down the body and tail.

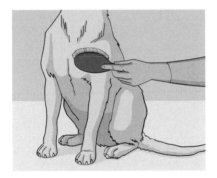

■ Next brush the entire coat, not forgetting tail and legs, with a bristle brush to remove dirt and dead hair.

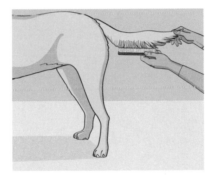

■ Run a fine comb through feathery hair on the legs and tail.

Bath time Always brush and comb your dog before you put them in the bath, and check the feet for grass seeds. Bathe them only when they are dirty or need a flea bath. Too much bathing can leave the skin dry and flaky. Use a gentle dog shampoo, or one designed for a specific problem, such as fleas or a skin condition.
■ Put a rubber mat in the tub so your dog doesn't slip. Use lukewarm water to wet them from neck to tail. Shampoo the hind legs, tail and rear end, then the body, chest and front legs.
■ Carefully wet the head, then shampoo, covering your dog's ears and eyes so that no lather gets in. Check ears for wax, which can indicate mites.
■ Rinse until the water runs clear: head, face and ears, then body, hind quarters and tail and, finally, the underside.
■ Wrap the dog in a towel to soak up excess, then dry from top to tail. Finish with a hairdryer on low, taking care not to hold it too close.

continued on next page →

seek out water with a Divining rod

To perform this esoteric art you'll need a Y-shaped stick (ideally willow), called a "water witch," or an L-shaped "dowsing rod" from a supplier (search online).

■ If using a stick, hold it pointed-end down, with your palms face up and thumbs pointing outward. Walk over the chosen area. If the stick is drawn convulsively down, it's telling you there's water beneath the surface.

■ If using rods, hold them loosely in each hand with the top wire pointing slightly down. If they swing apart or cross, start digging.

This ancient skill requires practice and sensitivity. Scientists dismiss it but Einstein believed it worked— although nobody knew how.

treat a Dog bite

All dog bites pose an infection risk, and the most savage may cause severe lacerations, tendon and nerve damage—even broken bones. Treat bleeding (*see* BLEEDING) and watch for shock (*see* SHOCK).

Quick action

For a small bite, thoroughly wash under warm, running water, gently squeeze to encourage bleeding, pat dry and cover with a sterile bandage. Unless you are certain that the victim is up-to-date on rabies and other shots, consult a doctor. If the bite is to the face, hands or feet, if a tooth has punctured deeply into the flesh or if any signs of infection develop, such as high temperature or chills, seek medical advice right away.

For a serious bite, wash as above and call 911 If a finger or other body part has been bitten off, wash it with tap water, and put it in a plastic bag or sealed container in a tub of iced water; a surgeon may be able to reattach it.

golden rules
DOG TRAINING
■ **Reward good behavior rather than punishing bad.**
■ **Be consistent. Apply the same rules at all times, using the same commands and the same rewards.**
■ **Short but regular training sessions are more effective than one long one.**

continued from page 105

Trimming claws A dog's nails are softer after a bath, so that is the time to trim them if necessary. Most dogs' nails wear down naturally.
■ Use canine nail clippers to cut the nails diagonally, taking off no more than an eighth of an inch or so (a few millimeters). Or ask your vet to show you how much to cut. Gently smooth the edges with a nail file or sandpaper.
■ Take great care not to cut the nails to the "quick," the pink area inside the nail; it's living tissue with blood supply and nerves.

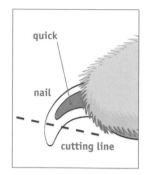

quick

nail

cutting line

House training Use reward, not punishment, to teach your puppy good toilet habits. Go for frequent walks—first thing in the morning, last thing at night, after meals, even every hour—to give them opportunities to learn where to go to the toilet. Watch for signs that they need to go out, such as fidgeting, sniffing, going around in circles or squatting. Once outside and in a suitable place, wait with and encourage the dog. When they have finished, collect the waste (if need be), praise them, then continue the walk for a while so they learn that walks don't end when they have been to the toilet. It's important to ignore mistakes; if you give a dog attention (even if it isn't "nice" attention) when they get it wrong, you'll only confuse them and the training will take longer.

---

train your Dog

A well-trained dog is a happy dog, so it's worth taking the time to build a confident relationship between you and your pet.

Sit, stay and come

The sit command is one of the easiest to teach a dog.
■ Face the dog with a treat in your hand and, as they trot toward you, hold it over their head. Keeping their eyes on the treat, the dog will back up and sit down. As they do so, say "Sit!" Reward them with the treat. Don't say "sit down," as this will confuse the dog when you try to teach them "down."
■ Don't push the dog's bottom down to make them sit, just keep repeating the command and give lots of praise.

Teaching to stay then come is trickier, since "stay" is an abstract concept for a dog, whereas sitting is a physical act.
■ Have a reward in each hand.
■ Tell the dog to sit and give them a treat.
■ Hold up your empty hand as if you were stopping traffic and back slowly away, issuing a firm, clear command of "Stay!"

Back slowly away, saying a firm, clear "Stay!"

Call out an enthusiastic "Come!"

When the dog comes, give them a reward.

■ Keep facing and looking at the dog. When you've put a small distance between you, call out an enthusiastic "Come!" When the dog comes to you, reward them with the other treat.

■ If they try to get up and approach you before you call, say a definite "No!", ask them to sit again, and start the exercise over.

Bring a dog to heel
In the excitement of a walk a dog may naturally tug. If your dog starts to pull the instant you clip the leash on, stand still and wait. Don't go anywhere until they have calmed down.

■ Choose which side you want your dog to walk on and stick to it. Hold the leash in the opposite hand and put a few treats in the other hand. Show the dog the treat to get their attention and walk forward. As the dog follows your hand, say "heel" and give a treat. Keep going, repeat "heel" and give another treat. Don't stop walking.

■ If the dog doesn't keep up with you or pulls in a different direction, suddenly change direction and encourage the dog to come with you.

■ Whenever your dog falls in step with you, praise them.

Start your training in your back yard, if you have one. Work up to going to the park at quiet times when there are few distractions. Get someone to drive you to the park, and walk home; your dog is less likely to pull on the way back. Gradually the dog will get the message.

If your dog has lots of energy, let them burn off a bit of it in the back yard before going for a walk.

If the dog pulls, change direction and say "Heel."

Stop jumping up
In natural exuberance, your dog may jump up to greet you or others. To discourage this undesirable behavior, you and all the family must take the same line. When the dog jumps up, don't make eye contact with them, don't touch them or talk to them. Instead, walk away or gently push them away. If a dog is ignored they will learn that this isn't the way to get attention, and that it's calm behavior that wins rewards.

play Dominoes

Twenty-eight solid domino pieces are "shuffled" face down on a table. Each domino's face is split into two halves, bearing a set of between zero and six dots (pips). Players draw a piece each and the one who scores closest to the highest pip count of 12 gets to start.

■ Each of the two, three or four players draws seven pieces. Any remaining pieces are left in "the boneyard."

■ The leader lays a piece—usually of the highest count.

■ The next player has to match one of the two pip counts on the piece by laying a domino bearing the same pip count end to end with it. Doubles are placed crosswise.

■ A player who cannot make a match draws a tile from the boneyard, and plays it if they can, until no tiles remain.

■ The first player to lay down all their pieces wins. If nobody can make a match, the winner is the one with the lowest pip count in their "hand."

Doubles are placed crossways.

Players lay pieces with the same pip count end to end.

paint a paneled
Door

Always open a door before you paint, and slide plenty of newspaper underneath to catch the drips.
■ Remove handles and other door hardware.

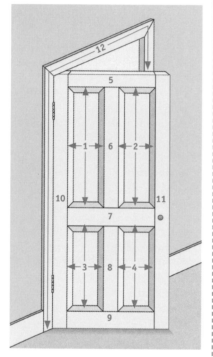

Solid doors Paint the panels first, in the order shown above. Use a thin brush for the moldings, one that's no wider than the moldings themselves. Don't overload the brush; this leads to drips and runs. Once you've done the panels, do the horizontal sections between them (eliminating any drips as you go), then the vertical sections and trim.

Glass doors If there are glass panels in the door, use masking tape or plastic to help keep paint off the glass. If any paint does dry on the glass, it should be carefully scraped off with a glass scraping tool or a razor blade.

change your Door locks

If, for security reasons, you want to change a cylinder lock (of which the night latch is the most common type) you need only replace the working parts. The same applies to mortise locks.

YOU WILL NEED Screwdrivers, locking pliers, pliers, new cylinder and keys (for a night latch), junior hacksaw (if necessary), hammer, new set of levers and keys (for a mortise)

Changing a cylinder lock Be aware that you cannot change the cylinder on a night latch with a locking interior handle; this method works only for the simple night latch design like the one illustrated below.

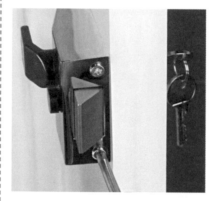

1 Unscrew the lock cover on the inside of the door so that you can get at the screws that hold the cylinder in place.

2 Unscrew the cylinder and pull it out. The connecting bar will come with it.

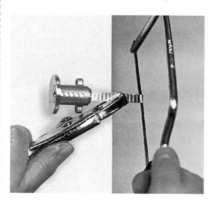

3 Take your new cylinder; this too has a bar attached. The bar is divided into segments along its length. Hold the new connecting bar tightly in locking pliers and use the junior hacksaw to cut it to the same length as the old one.

4 Make sure that the new connecting screws are the right length. If they aren't, you'll have to trim them with a junior hacksaw. Insert the new cylinder into the hole. Tighten the screws and then screw the cover back in place, making sure that the handle of the lock has slotted onto the bar.

Changing a mortise lock Mortise locks come in various shapes and sizes. Take the old one with you when you go to buy a new one to avoid having to chisel out a larger slot in the door.

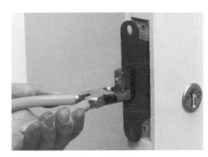

1 Unscrew the two screws that fix the cover plate and lock face to the edge of the door. Turn the key so that the bolt shoots out, then remove the key.

2 Use a pair of pliers to grip the projecting bolt and slide the lock out of the door.

3 Put the new lock back in the slot, making sure it is the right way around. Screw it and the cover plate in place, and make sure that the key turns smoothly.

fix a Door that squeaks or sticks

When a door squeaks, the problem is with the hinges. Squirt a tiny amount of aerosol lubricant onto the hinge pins then work the door back and forth a few times. With rising-butt hinges (*see* HINGE), lift the door off the hinge pins, lightly smear them with grease or petroleum jelly, then replace the door (this is a job much more easily done by two people).

A sticking door is usually caused by a buildup of paint on one edge. The problem usually arises in damp, wet weather, when the wood of an exterior door is liable to swell. Rubbing the edge of the door with a candle may cure slight sticking. Otherwise, wait for a dry spell, then strip the paint from the door edge and frame. Repaint only when the door is completely dry. If the door sticks on the bottom edge, which is often the case, the only solution is to take the door off (in a dry spell) and plane or file with a rasp to shave a whisker off the bottom.

Download music and videos online

If you have plenty of free disk space on your computer (*see* COMPUTER DISK SPACE) and a good internet connection (*see* BROADBAND SPEED), downloading music and video is a convenient, quick and simple process.

Open an account with a website that offers a download service, such as 7digital, Amazon or iTunes, the best-known music download site. Some sites ask you to pay a monthly subscription, in return for which you can download unlimited amounts of music; others ask you to pay individually for each track, album or movie that you buy.

Your payment details will be stored securely by the website so that no unauthorized transactions can take place. You'll be asked to provide security details, such as a password, before any transaction is completed. This also gives you an opportunity to check that you have selected the intended song or film before proceeding.

Before playing a purchased file, you may need to download a piece of software such as Microsoft Media Player—which is itself freely available from Microsoft's own site (*see* DOWNLOAD SOFTWARE). You may be provided with this software automatically when you open an account with a download site. If not, check the site for details of which software you require.

Files can be stored on your PC, iPod or MP3 player, or, depending on the download site you're using, can be transferred to disk (*see* CD).

Download software
from the internet

Many software manufacturers now sell their products in the form of internet downloads, rather than on disks retailed through stores.

■ Browse the manufacturer's website to locate the desired software. Look for and click on a button marked "download."

■ Enter your payment details (they will be stored securely on the site).

■ Confirm where on your computer you want to store the software and then click to begin downloading.

■ Click on the downloaded file to complete the installation process.

Look for free trials, at the end of which you can often pay to be given a code that you can enter to "unlock" the program permanently.

find free
Downloads

Many programs are available as "freeware." For example, you can freely download word-processing software that has almost as much functionality and flexibility as the commercially available packages that you must pay for. But most freeware is small programs such as games and antivirus scanners.

■ Free software can be browsed and downloaded through websites such as Tucows, Jumbo! and CNET.

■ Compare reviews on several sites before you download.

■ Make certain that the item you want is compatible with your computer's operating system.

Draw a face

Learn the basics of symmetry and proportion and you have the beginnings of a portrait that you can flesh out into a true likeness.

YOU WILL NEED Sketch pad, hard and soft pencils, ruler, eraser

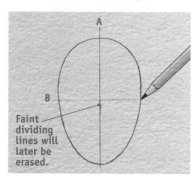

1 Draw an oval, tapered at the chin. Add faint lines to divide it in half vertically (A) and horizontally (B).

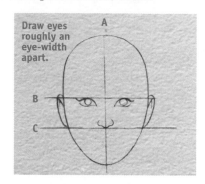

2 Bisect the bottom half with another line (C) and sketch the ears roughly between lines B and C. Add the eyes just under line B.

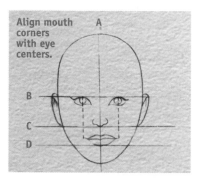

3 Add another line (D), halfway between C and the point of the chin. Sketch the nose and mouth—the nose so its tip rests on the intersection of A and C, and the mouth so the bottom lip sits on D.

5 Take a softer pencil and add shadow and detail, such as the irises and pupils of the eye, to bring your portrait to life. Imagine that the light is coming from top left, so add soft shadows on the right side of the nose and face, and under the mouth, chin, eyebrows and cheekbones.

4 Add eyebrows and hair. Erase your guide lines, taking care not to lose any of the facial detail you've drawn.

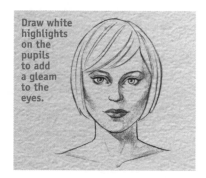

contruct basic Drawers

YOU WILL NEED **wood for drawer box and face, drawer slides, screws, clamps, framing square, glue, brads (thin nails)**

A box within a box, well-made drawers are a triumph of planning and layout. Build the cabinet first, then size the drawer to the case opening. For metal drawer slides, subtract 1 in. (2.5 cm) from the opening's width and about ¼ in. (6 mm) for height.

You can use rabbets and grooves throughout or use dadoes at the rear and dovetails or box joints at the front for extra strength. A false-front drawer makes it easier to fit the front for even visual gaps, or reveals.

1 Glue, assemble and square the drawer box. With clamps in place, nudge the box against a framing square and push a brad through the bottom near each corner. Let the glue dry before you mount the hardware.

2 Side-mounted slides separate for easy mounting. Screw the cabinet member inside the case, through the horizontal slots in the slide. Screw the drawer member to the drawer slide using the vertical slots. Adjust the drawer's tilt before adding more screws.

3 Use a spacer to position the drawer front evenly. Drive temporary screws through the existing hardware holes and into the drawer box. Then pull out the drawer and attach the front with permanent screws from the inside.

prevent Drafts

Draft-proofing doors and windows makes your home a more comfortable place to be —and cheaper to heat or cool.

Casement windows can be sealed using a foam strip or a self-adhesive rubber strip. Foam strips tend to wear out more quickly than rubber ones. Apply the adhesive strip to the window frame. For large or uneven gaps use silicone sealant, following the manufacturer's instructions on the tube.

Sash windows are notoriously drafty. Fit a foam strip along the top and bottom of the frame. Use a brush strip or a V-shaped plastic strip to create a seal along the moving parts of the window.

Front doors are a prime source of drafts in winter. A traditional sprung strip of copper tacked to the frame is the most durable choice. The metal strip is tacked along one side, then bent slightly outward so that it presses against the door's edge when it's shut and thus forms a seal. Rubber, foam or brush weatherstripping is more commonly available today.

■ Fix threshold draft weather-stripping at the bottom of your front door. This comes in two interlocking parts, one for the door and the other for the threshold, and it keeps out rain as well as wind.

■ A surprisingly strong current of cold air can come through the mail slot. A brush strip fitted on the inside will solve the problem.

■ For an effective additional barrier, you can also mount a thick curtain behind the door. Be sure to leave enough room on the rail or pole to allow the curtain to be drawn aside when opening the door.

D

Drive in bad weather

When hitting the road in adverse weather conditions, always put safety before punctuality. Better to arrive late, and in one piece, than take unnecessary risks.

Before you go ... Know your vehicle. Familiarize yourself with the position and operation of its controls. Plan your route to avoid back roads, and memorize it, so that you're not distracted by looking at directions or a map. Tune the radio to pick up travel bulletins.

WHATEVER THE WEATHER

The cardinal rules in any kind of bad weather are to limit your speed and keep your distance. In wet weather you need to allow more room, and when roads are frozen stopping distances can increase tenfold. Where visibility is reduced by mist, fog, driving rain or blizzards, hold well back from the vehicle ahead. Also, always use your headlights.

DRY   40 ft (12 m)   80 ft (24 m)

WET   40 ft (12 m)   160 ft (48 m)

Thinking distance

Braking distance

STOPPING DISTANCES AT 40 MPH On wet roads, the braking distance is least twice as long as in the dry. At 40 mph/65km/h (above), allow at least 200 ft. (60 m) total stopping distance in the wet (six car lengths more than in the dry); and as much as three times the braking distance.

IN HIGH WINDS

Buffeting winds can rock a car and make steering difficult, as well as blowing tree branches and other debris into your path. Keep your eyes peeled for hazards and grasp the wheel firmly with both hands, especially when overtaking another vehicle. Be particularly careful around campers and bikes, which may be blown off course.

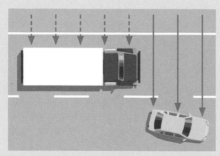

A high-sided vehicle may act as a windbreak while you're overtaking it. You should expect to encounter a sudden gust of wind as you complete the maneuver.

PREPARE YOUR VEHICLE FOR BAD WEATHER

Ask yourself if your journey is really necessary. Never drive in extreme weather if you don't have to. Prepare your vehicle by making the following checks.

Clean the windshield and mirrors, scrape ice off all windows.

In winter, top up antifreeze and windshield deicer.

Check the battery, since heaters, lights and wipers will drain it.

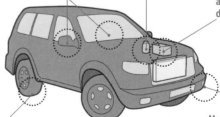

Check the pressure and tread of the tires, including the spare.

Make sure that all lights are working, including fog lights.

Ensure you have all you might need in an emergency: deicer, scraper, cell phone, flashlight, tow ropes, jumper cables, jack and spare wheel, shovel, warning triangles, sacking to lay under stuck wheels, extra clothing, blanket. In heavy snow, you might need snow chains.

IN SNOW AND ICE

Make patient preparations to ready yourself for your journey and drive cautiously to avoid having to deal with hazards such as skidding (*see* SKID).

Wear comfortable, dry shoes that won't slip on the pedals, and bring a pair of boots. Don't drive in heavy boots that might make you clumsy when using the pedals. Give a frosted windshield time to clear completely: Don't drive off peering through a small "porthole" (*see* WINDSHIELD). Brush snow off the roof so that it can't slide down the windshield.

Gentle maneuvers and a steady pace are the way forward. Move off in second gear to avoid wheelspin. If you drive an automatic, check that you know how to downshift into a lower gear, to reduce dependence on the brakes. If you have a "winter" gear mode, select it; it locks out first gear to reduce wheelspin.

Drive at low speed in as high a gear as possible and don't brake or accelerate sharply. Before braking, drop into low gear sooner than normal to slow the car then, if you don't have antilock braking, apply a gentle, pumping pressure.

If the steering feels light or the tires on the road surface are eerily silent, suspect black ice and shift to reduce speed. If the car skids when you brake, and you're driving a manual car, release the brake and press the clutch.

To climb a hill, drop a gear to build momentum on the approach, then take it at a steady pace. Coming down, use a low gear to avoid having to brake.

Brake well before a curve, where it's all too easy to lose control. Don't wrench the wheel; steer smoothly.

If the car gets bogged down in snow, straighten the steering, clear snow from under the wheels, use burlap or an old rug in front of the driving wheels to give them something to bite, and accelerate gently. Once you get going, try to continue until you find better road conditions.

In a blizzard, when the wipers can't work hard enough to clear the windshield, abandon your journey and seek shelter. A heavy snowfall can make roads impassable in minutes.

If you're trapped in your car, wrap up in rugs, coats, blankets—even newspaper. Use gas sparingly, running the engine and heater for 15 minutes each hour, with the window open a crack. Try to stay awake as you wait for help. If other drivers are also are trapped, "car share" to increase warmth, save gas and keep your spirits up.

Always clear your windshield and car roof as thoroughly as possible before you set off.

IN HEAVY RAIN

Don't underestimate the twin risks of poor visibility and slippery road surfaces. Allow twice the normal stopping distance and test your brakes. Lightly press the brake pedal from time to time, as the friction will help to keep them dry. Don't use the high beams, so as to decrease glare, and put your wipers on fast mode.

If the tires can't get a grip and you find yourself hydroplaning, don't brake but ease off the accelerator to slow down gradually. Grip the wheel and get ready; when the tires regain their hold it can cause the car to swerve and you should prepare to steer through it.

Never drive into standing water too deep for your car. Drive through shallow water at a steady crawl, keeping the revs high by using a low gear, then test your brakes as soon afterward as it's safe to do so. If you can't tell how deep the water is, don't drive in.

D

use a Drill properly

Always disconnect a drill from the power source when you're changing bits, or when you're leaving the drill unattended (this applies to all power tools).

- When working with a drill, grip it firmly with both hands; this is safer, and it will make your drill hole neater and more accurate.
- When drilling holes in walls or floors, check first for cables and pipes below the surface using a battery-operated detector.
- When using the hammer-drilling function, wear safety goggles to protect against the increased risk of flying debris, and ear protectors to shield you from the noise.
- When sanding with a drill, wear a dust mask.
- Always use the right kind of bit for the material that you're drilling, whether it is wood, masonry, concrete, metal or glass.

interpret your Dreams

Dreams are rich with metaphor and symbols. Two of the most common recurring themes are dreams of being naked or flying.

A dream that you are naked may express a fear of exposure, of being left defenseless—perhaps you dread disgrace or ridicule, or have been pretending to be something you're not.

If you dream you're flying and looking down, you may have gained a new perspective. If you can control your flight perhaps you enjoy an exalted sense of power—but falling could suggest insecurity, instability or loss of control.

Dream dictionaries can help you to understand common symbolism, but you're uniquely placed to interpret your own dreams, so try to hold onto them. On waking, lie still, gather in dream remnants and then jot them down at once. Within a few minutes they can have faded. Look out for puns and wordplay, rather like deciphering a cryptic crossword clue.

Keep a dream journal in which you write down not just what you dreamt, but the location, your emotional responses and physical sensations. You may find enlightening patterns or cycles that emerge.

save someone from Drowning

Don't try to leap into the water and rescue someone unless you're a trained lifesaver. You could easily become a casualty yourself.

Rescue from water

- Shout for help.
- Call 911 or, ideally, get someone else to do it so you keep your eyes on the victim.
- If there's a buoyancy aid—a life preserver belt or another object that floats, such as a ball—throw it. Look around for a life preserver ring on a rope, or tie a life jacket to a rope.
- If there's no lifesaving equipment nearby, throw something as a lifeline, such as a tow rope, or reach out with a pole, oar, fishing rod or tree branch.
- Don't go into the water unless you're trained in rescue. If you have to wade out, stay within your depth and ask someone onshore to hold a rope tied around your waist. Take a buoyancy aid for the person to hold onto.

Treat the victim

Pull the person to safety and out of the water. Remove any mud or weeds from the nose and throat and perform CPR if needed (*see* CPR).

If vomiting or regurgitation occurs after you begin CPR, roll the victim onto their side to clear their airway. Treat for hypothermia (*see* HYPOTHERMIA).

Keep trying to revive the victim until professional help arrives.

---

build a Drystone wall

A drystone wall is one constructed from stones without any mortar to bind them. If care is taken over the selection and positioning of each stone, a drystone wall can stand for hundreds of years.

YOU WILL NEED **Wooden A-frames shaped like the finished wall, string, stones sorted into piles of various sizes**

1 First dig out a trench 8 in. (20 cm) deep, corresponding to the dimensions of the wall you intend to build. Line the bottom of the trench with big, flat heavy stones.

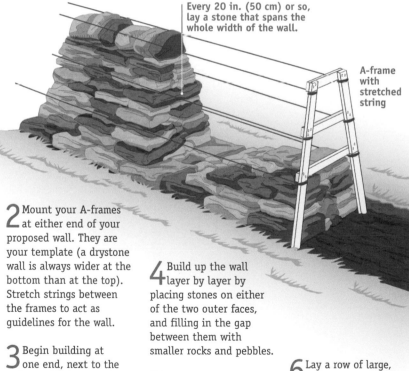

Every 20 in. (50 cm) or so, lay a stone that spans the whole width of the wall.

A-frame with stretched string

2 Mount your A-frames at either end of your proposed wall. They are your template (a drystone wall is always wider at the bottom than at the top). Stretch strings between the frames to act as guidelines for the wall.

3 Begin building at one end, next to the A-frame. The butt-end (known as the quoin) must be perfectly square and solid, so take extra care when choosing and laying your stones.

4 Build up the wall layer by layer by placing stones on either of the two outer faces, and filling in the gap between them with smaller rocks and pebbles.

5 When you position the next layer, be sure that each stone bridges the joint between the two beneath it, as in an ordinary brick wall.

6 Lay a row of large, heavy stones on top of the wall. Their weight serves to press together the stones beneath, making the whole structure more stable.

---

recognize and tackle a
Drug overdose

Any drug—legal, illegal, prescribed or bought over-the-counter—can cause adverse reactions, even at the recommended dose. Reactions are even more severe when the drug is taken in excess, in combination with other drugs or alcohol or by susceptible individuals.

Acute symptoms can range from drowsiness, shallow breathing, racing pulse, abdominal pain, vomiting, profuse sweating, dilated pupils, hallucinations, paranoia, irrational behavior, disorientation, tremors, tinnitus and seizures, to loss of consciousness and heart failure. Over hours or days acetaminophen poisoning can cause jaundice and liver damage.

If you suspect an overdose, make the victim comfortable, lying on their side to guard against choking on vomit, and ask what they have taken, when and how much. Ask others who may know, or look for bottles, packaging or other evidence. If you find a hypodermic needle don't touch it. Call 911, telling the operator all you can.

Note down changes in the victim while you wait, checking breathing, pulse and level of consciousness. If the patient falls unconscious, check their breathing and be ready to give CPR (*see* CPR). If they are breathing, place them in the recovery position (*see* RECOVERY POSITION). If they vomit, keep a sample for analysis, but don't try to make them sick.

Drive in bad weather
see pages 112-113

get rid of Dust

The aim of good dusting is to remove dust, not disperse it.

- Vacuum as many surfaces as possible before you dust.
- Use a just-damp microfiber cloth for most surfaces. For a highly polished surface, on which water may leave a permanent mark, use a dry cloth and furniture polish.
- Dust from the top of a room down so settling dust can be removed.
- A feather duster is good for blinds, but must be shaken outside frequently as you work. Or wipe slats with a cloth dampened with vinegar (which also disinfects).
- For tricky crevices, use a small, medium-bristled paintbrush.
- To remove stubborn dust from upholstery or clothing, wind masking or packing tape around your hand, sticky side out, then rub.

Dye clothes

Take care when dyeing. Wear rubber gloves and an apron, and cover work surfaces and floors with newspaper.

Hot water dyes Wash item and leave it damp. Submerge in dye mixture, bring slowly to a boil and simmer. Cool in the water. Rinse in warm water.

Cold water dyes Dissolve powder in hot water, add fixative and salt. Soak for an hour before rinsing. (For wool, substitute vinegar for salt and fixative.) *See also* TIE-DYE.

Machine dyes Ideal for bulky items. After dyeing, run through wash cycle with detergent at hottest temperature, then again with the machine empty to clear dye residue that could stain other washing.

avoid a fight with a Duvet cover

With the right technique, inserting a duvet into its cover is a simple process, involving a second or two of preparation, a straightforward flick of the wrists and a few moments more to complete the job.

1 Put the duvet flat on the bed. Turn the cover inside out then reach inside to grasp the two corners farthest from the opening.

2 With your hands inside the cover, take hold of the top corners of the duvet and lift both of them together.

3 Flick your wrists and shake the two corners you're holding so that the duvet cover unfurls over the duvet the right way out.

4 Hold the corners in the air; continue shaking. If you're not very tall, you may need to stand on the bed. Then smooth out the cover and close the end.

calculate the date of Easter

Easter, unlike Christmas, is a "moveable feast." It occurs on a different calendar date each year, determined by a complex compromise between astronomy and ecclesiastical necessity.

In its simplest terms, Easter falls on the first Sunday after the first full moon after March 21 (the vernal equinox). In practice, the calculation is not so straightforward, because the full moon appears at different times depending on where you are in the world. If the first full moon after March 21 were to appear late on Saturday in some places, and early on Sunday elsewhere, Easter would end up being celebrated a week apart in those locations.

To get around this problem, the Church publishes tables of "paschal full moons," in which the calendar is superimposed on a cycle of 19 years consisting of lunar months that are 29 or 30 days long. This scheme yields a rough model of the astronomical facts; the actual first full moon after the spring equinox is never more than a day or two removed from the notional paschal full moon.

Once you know the date of the paschal full moon, the rest is easy: The following Sunday is Easter Day.

buy and sell on eBay

eBay is the biggest and best-known internet auction house. It's easy to sell unwanted possessions and to bid for items that other people have put up for sale—all through your home computer.

To use eBay you must first register with the site. Go to the website and fill in the online registration form. If you're planning to sell, or if you're using an anonymous email address, you'll be asked to provide credit card details. This is purely for identification purposes.

Looking to buy
You're now ready to look for items; browse categories or use eBay's search function. If you find something, read the description carefully and verify that you're happy with the delivery arrangements and payment options.
■ You can email the seller to ask questions before you place a bid.
■ Check the seller's feedback from other transactions for clues to their reliability and service. As with a "brick-and-mortar" auction house, once you bid, you're obliged to buy if your bid wins.
■ Note when the auction is due to end. It's often worth waiting before bidding, so that you don't push the price up early. Online software (like Auction Sniper) can best the last price in the auction's final seconds.

Looking to sell
If you're planning to sell on eBay, click on **Sell** and follow the instructions for creating "listings." Take great care over the descriptions that you write and the starting price that you set. Also, check postage costs if you plan to send times to buyers by mail.

treat Earache

Pain in the ear is commonly caused by infection, or by a buildup of mucus after a cold. It will usually clear within two to three days, but there are steps you can take to help to alleviate the discomfort.

Quick action
■ Try holding a warmed, soft cloth over the ear, but avoid getting water in it.
■ Drink plenty of fluids and avoid cigarette smoke, which can irritate the membranes in the ear.
■ See a doctor if the pain is intense, if you have blood or fluid draining from the ear, if you are generally unwell, have a high temperature or if something lodged in your ear.
■ Never poke a cotton swab or anything else into your ear to attempt to clear a blockage; you could cause serious damage.

Doctors try not to use antibiotic ear drops, especially in young children, as they can lead to a buildup of drug-resistant bacteria and fungi. However, sometimes you or your child may be prescribed antibiotics, steroids or other drops to help to speed recovery.

golden rules
eBAY BUYING AND SELLING
■ **When selling, include good, clear photographs of your goods and write an honest, detailed description.**
■ **Don't get carried away. You can sometimes buy a brand new item from another online retailer or a store for only a little more, but with more consumer protection.**

organize an
Egg hunt

A treasure hunt with chocolate eggs for prizes is a fun Easter activity for young children.

■ Choose places around the house or garden to hide groups of tiny chocolate eggs, one for every child in each location. They might be behind a clock, in the fruit bowl, under a bush, in a tulip leaf ...
■ Make sure all hiding places are accessible to the smallest child.
■ Devise a series of clues to the hiding places, give each child something to put their treasure in, and send them on a bunny trail, with one clue leading to another.
■ Give them the runaround: back and forth, up and down. The first to come back to "base" with their full complement of eggs wins a prize.

Alternatively, forget about clues and just let children scour the place for as many eggs as they can find. Don't make the hiding places too obvious; kids are masterful hunters when on the trail of hidden treasures.

observe an Eclipse safely

The only time it's safe to train the naked eye on the sun is during the brief darkness of a total eclipse, when the moon completely covers the sun. To observe a partial eclipse you need a filter to prevent damage to your eyes. Some people use inexpensive shade 14 welding goggles (sunglasses aren't adequate), but the cheapest method is to use a pinhole projector.

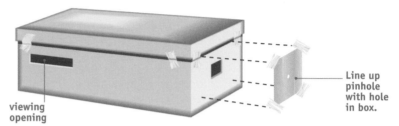

viewing opening

Line up pinhole with hole in box.

1 Cut a ⅓ in. (1 cm) square opening at the end of a cardboard box, such as a shoebox, and another, large enough to look through, in the side.

2 Tape down the lid of the box. Use a pin to make a hole in a piece of tin foil and tape it over the end opening.

image of the sun

3 Place the box on your shoulder and aim the pinhole at the sun, while peering through the side opening. You'll see the eclipse projected on the inside of the box. Never look through the pinhole directly at the sun.

get creative with Egg decorating

White-shelled eggs are best for decorating, as they show the color best. Place eggs in a single layer in a pan with dye and 2 tbsp vinegar for every quart (liter) of water.

Adding color Use spinach water for green, beet water for crimson, cranberry juice for pink, paprika for orange-red, turmeric for yellow, blueberries or red grape juice for lavender, strong coffee for brown, red wine for deep purple. Or add a few drops of food coloring. For a mottled brown effect, wrap onion skins tied with cotton thread around eggs. Simmer eggs for 15-20 minutes. For more intense color, let cool in the pan.

Adding a pattern before boiling For a marbled effect, add 1 tbsp olive oil to the dye water, draw on a pattern with a white wax crayon or wrap the egg in rubber bands before boiling. You can repeat the wax crayon method in several stages, dipping the eggs into dyes of increasing intensity for about 5 minutes each time. To wipe away any unwanted wax, put in a warm oven with the door open until the wax melts then dab off with a paper towel.

rubber band patterns

marbled effect with olive oil in water

wax crayon patterns

masking tape patterns

hand painted

metallic spray paint

Creating designs For geometric patterns, stick on masking tape before dyeing; when peeled off it will leave white areas. Use the same method for fancy shapes, such as leaves and flowers. Use crayons, pens, quick-drying acrylic paint or watercolors to create designs by hand, or spray with paint from a can.

---

treat Electric shock

If you find someone unconscious, look for clues as to what has happened, particularly any electrical equipment that could have given them a shock. Take care not to endanger yourself. Always make the situation safe first.

Quick action

■ If someone has been electrocuted in the home, don't touch them before you break the current. Unplug the appliance at the outlet or cut off the household current entirely at the breaker panel or fuse box. Don't touch the switch on the device itself: It may be faulty.

■ If this isn't possible, stand on some insulating material, such as a pile of newspapers or a rubber mat, and use something nonconductive, such as a wooden broom (never a damp mop), to separate the victim from the electrical source.

continued on next page →

---

test Eggs for freshness

A fresh egg feels heavy in the hand, but without another egg to compare, the easiest testing method is to put it in a bowl of cold water. A fresh egg will sink to the bottom and lie flat on its side. As it starts to lose its freshness, more air accumulates inside and the egg will stand upright with the broader end uppermost. If it floats to the surface it should be discarded.

As a double check, break an egg into a bowl or saucer before you use it. A stale egg has a flat (not firm and rounded) yolk and a runny white. If it's bad, it will smell.

---

separate Eggs

An egg separator (above) allows the white to drain through holes while retaining the yolk, but you don't need any special equipment to perform this simple task. Wash your eggs and hands before cooking to minimize any risk of infection.

■ Working over a bowl, crack the egg at its broadest point. Use your thumbs to pry the shell apart, letting the white fall into the bowl, but retaining the yolk. Tip the egg from shell to shell until only the yolk is left. Pinch off any threads of white with your fingertips.

E

Exfoliate your face

Sloughing off dead skin cells from the face boosts circulation and lends a radiance to the complexion. There's no need for salon visits or expensive products. Always cleanse your face first to avoid rubbing dirt into the skin.

- Make a paste of 2 tsp oatmeal, 1 tsp baking soda and water.
- Gently massage the paste into the skin with circular motions, avoiding the eye area. Rinse and pat dry.
- For a luxury treatment, use equal parts sugar and vegetable oil, scented with almond oil or vanilla extract. Step into the shower and apply when you're thoroughly wet; massage in and rinse off.
- Always moisturize after exfoliating and don't exfoliate the face more than once a week.

continued from page 119

- Assess the victim's condition. They may have suffered superficial or more serious burns (*see* BURNS), internal injuries, fractures from having been thrown, shock (*see* SHOCK), unconsciousness or cardiac arrest. Unless the electric shock was mild, call 911.
- Check their pulse and breathing and give CPR if needed (*see* CPR).

Shock from a power line Even domestic electricity can kill, but high-voltage electric shock, from power lines, for example, is usually fatal. Don't go within 60 ft (18 m) of someone who has been felled by such a shock and keep others away, too. The current can travel a considerable distance.
- Call 911 and the local electricity supply authority (you should find the number on a nearby cable support or pole).
- If the victim is conscious, give them verbal reassurance. Don't attempt first aid until the scene is declared safe.

create Embroidery stitches

Embroidery can be used to decorate everything from table linen to clothes and cushions. As you grow in confidence, you can embroider pictures or simple samplers to frame and display.

Materials Choose tightly woven plain fabrics, evenweaves such as linen, which have the same number of threads in both warp and weft, or regularly patterned fabrics, such as gingham.

Threads and needles Stranded cottons or silks, which can be separated to give a finer thread, are most versatile. Or choose 2-, 3- or 4-ply wool. For fine work use a sharp-pointed, medium length crewel needle. For heavier threads choose chenille needles. For thicker wool, select a tapestry needle.

Securing the thread To start a new thread, hold the end against the reverse side of the fabric and work 1.5 in. (4 cm) of stitches over it. To finish off at a thread end, slide it through about 1.5 in (4 cm) of stitches on the reverse.

Stitches

Chain stitch is a commonly used stitch for outlines, but also for filling.

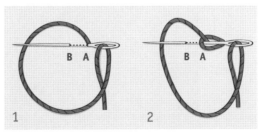
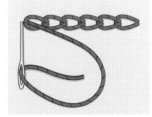

- Bring the needle out at A. Insert very close to the same hole and out at B, carrying the thread under the needle point. Pull the thread through to make the first chain link. Insert needle very close to B and repeat the stitch to sew a chain.

- Finish off by making a small stitch over the end of the last loop in the chain.

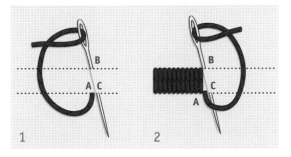

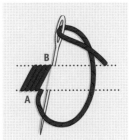

Satin stitch is a filling stitch. Working from left to right, bring the needle up at A and insert it directly above at B. Bring it up at C, just to the right of A and continue in a neat row.

You can also work on a slant, offsetting the position of A and B.

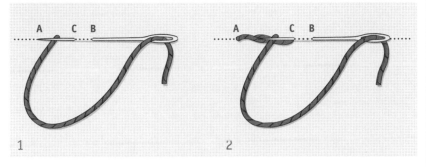

Stem stitch is an invaluable outline stitch for floral designs. Working left to right, bring the needle out at A, insert it at B and bring it out at C, half a stitch length back. Repeat, keeping thread below the needle and to the left.
■ Outlines sewn in stem stitch are often filled in with satin stitch, above. For a leaf, for example, fill in half at a time, each slanted a different way to emulate the pattern of veins in an actual leaf.

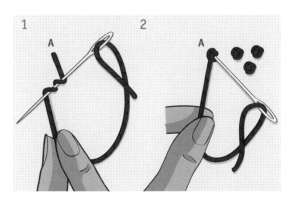

French knots create raised and textured effects. Bring the needle up at A. Holding the thread in one hand, wrap it around the needle twice, then tighten. Insert the needle near A, hold the thread taut and pull through to make a knot.

Other useful stitches Cross-stitch can be used for decorative borders and as a filling stitch (*see* CROSS-STITCH) and to sew entire patterns. Backstitch creates a neat line for outlining shapes, and herringbone stitch is used for decorative borders (*see* SEWING *for both*).

shape your
Eyebrows

A beautifully arched brow lightens and opens up your eyes, but work carefully. If you pluck too much you'll look permanently startled.

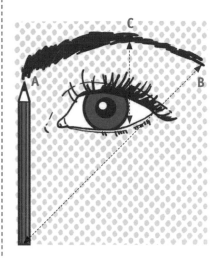

■ Hold a pencil straight up against one nostril. This will show you where your eyebrow should begin (A).
■ Hold it diagonally from the nostril so it crosses the outer corner of the eye; this is where it will end (B). Your aim is to achieve an arch directly above the outside of the iris when you are looking straight on (C). The brow should then taper.
■ Comb out your eyebrows and use an eyebrow pencil to draw the shape you want.
■ Tweeze unwanted eyebrow hairs one at a time, pulling in the direction of growth.
■ Soothe the area with toner when you've finished.

apply false
Eyelashes

YOU WILL NEED **Tweezers, eyelash strips and glue, small scissors, eyebrow pencil, mascara, eyeliner**

1 Use tweezers to hold the eyelash strip. Measure it against your own eye and trim the ends to fit. Draw a fine line with dark eyebrow pencil along your upper lid and smudge it a little.

2 Squeeze eyelash glue onto the back of your hand and draw the base of the strip through it. Using tweezers, apply the lashes as close to the natural eyelash line as you can.

3 Press from end to end and wait for the glue to dry.

4 Apply mascara to blend the false eyelashes with the natural ones and use eyeliner to fill any gap between the false and the natural lashes.

make Eyes up beautifully

You can enhance the natural beauty of your eyes with subtle highlighting and shadow, or create a more dramatic, smoky effect.

Sit in front of a magnifying mirror in good light and set out your palette: eyeliner, three complementary tones of shadow, highlighter, brushes and mascara. Be prepared to take your time and experiment to get the right look.

Eyeliner

1 Use your eyeliner of choice—pencil or brush—to frame your eyes. Start from the outside corners of the upper eyelids and work inward, as close as you can to the lashes.

2 Line under the eye, as close as possible to the lashes, starting only from the middle and working outward. Gently smudge this bottom line with a cotton swab so that it isn't too stark.

Eyeshadow

1 Apply a base color of shadow that almost matches your eyelids, sweeping it across the lid from the inside out and up to the brow bones.

2 Add a slightly darker shade to the lid only, not up to the brow bone. Finally, add the darkest shade in the crease at the top of your eyelid.

3 Blend the three shades into one another to create a subtle grading effect, using a cotton swab or blending sponge. Apply a dab of highlighter to your brow bone and blend from the mid brow outwards. Now try a professional tip from makeup artists: Brighten the eye by adding a dab of highlighter to the inner corner of each eye where upper and lower lids meet.

Mascara

1 First, remove excess mascara from the brush. With your chin pulled downward and your eyes looking up, brush the lower lashes of each eye with mascara.

2 Look down and stroke mascara onto the upper lashes, separating them as you work. Move the brush side to side at the roots, then outward so that the lashes fan out.

3 Mascara looks best when applied in thin layers. Let each layer dry before building on it. If the lashes clump, brush them out with a eyelash comb once they are dry.

keep your personal information safe on Facebook

The whole point of Facebook is to let people know that you're out there and tell them what you're doing. But you might not want to reveal everything to everybody.

Facebook is equipped with privacy settings that allow you to decide exactly who sees which parts of your "profile": the sum total of all that you write on the site, the pictures you post, and the information you give about your life.

■ At the top right of your home or profile page you'll find a tab that directs you to your privacy settings. Go through each element of your profile and choose how wide a circle of people can see it: just you, just your Facebook friends, your Facebook friends and all their Facebook friends, or anyone who happens upon your profile while browsing the internet. If you're concerned about your privacy, choose **Friends Only** as your default setting.
■ If, as most people do, you accepted some distant acquaintances as friends when you first joined Facebook, you might want to bar them from seeing personal details such as your home. You can do this through the "Customize" setting. No one will know that they have been excluded from your inner circle.

treat a child to Face-painting

Face-painting is always a hit with children. Use your imagination or follow one of our simple designs for a tiger or a butterfly.

YOU WILL NEED **Soft paintbrushes or makeup brushes, water, sponges, nontoxic face paints**

A tiger face

 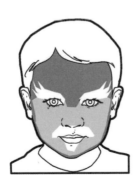 

1 Add yellow from the eyebrows down to the chin. Use a sponge to paint a white muzzle.

2 Use bright orange to frame the middle of the face. Then, from the brow line, paint in a pair of white eyebrows.

3 Add white stripes to the cheeks and paint in whiskers. Paint a black tip on the nose, a black mouth and stripes.

continued on next page

cleanse your Face

You should cleanse your face gently, no more than twice a day, to remove dirt, makeup and other debris without robbing the skin of its natural moisturizers.

■ Avoid normal hand soap, which contains detergents that dry out the skin.
■ Choose a cleanser formulated for your skin type. Moisten your face with lukewarm water, and apply cleanser with your fingertips, lightly massaging it in with tight circular motions. Thoroughly rinse off with lukewarm water (hot water is dehydrating), leaving no residue, and use a soft towel to pat—not rub—dry.
■ If you're using moisturizer, apply it while the skin is still slightly damp. *See also* EXFOLIATE SKIN.

☀ golden rules

FACE-PAINT TIPS
■ **Test the paint before use on anyone with an allergy.**
■ **Don't apply paint if the child has any cuts or sores or an infectious skin condition.**
■ **Use a sponge to shade in a large area and brushes for more detailed work.**
■ **Apply each color with a different brush or sponge, or wash brushes between uses.**

read Facial expressions

There are certain facial expressions that are the same in all cultures. Among them are happiness, sadness, surprise, fear and disgust. These universal expressions are easy to read, but people may also often say one thing while their face is sending a different message. When a person smiles at you, look at the eyes; unless you see crow's-feet wrinkles and movement in the muscle that surrounds the eye, the smile isn't genuine. You should also watch out for "micro-expressions," moments when a person's real feelings flit across their face. They are only fleetingly visible, but extremely revealing if you can spot them.

deal with Fainting

Someone is feeling sick and dizzy —they could be about to pass out.

Quick action

- Help them to lie on the floor, on their back. Kneel by them, lift their legs and rest them on one of your shoulders.
- If you cannot get the person to lie down, have them sit, head between their knees, and tell them to push their head up against your hand while you apply firm, gentle downward pressure. This encourages blood flow to the brain.
- If the person faints and doesn't come around in one to two minutes, put them in the recovery position (*see* RECOVERY POSITION) and call 911. The reason behind the fainting episode may need to –be investigated.

continued from page 123

4 Add an outline of black to define the whiskers and eyebrows. Finally, stipple the muzzle with dots.

Or paint on a butterfly face

Paint the outline of a butterfly wing on either side of the face. Fill in the wings, blending two pretty colors, then outline the wings in another color. Paint the butterfly's body on the nose, and add a round head and elegant feelers on the forehead. Finish by embellishing the wings.

draw up your Family tree

A family tree is an instantly readable representation of your personal heritage, linking you back to your ancestors.

Start by jotting down the names and dates of birth, marriage and death for all of the relatives you knkow about. Ask everyone in the family what they remember. Take a large sheet of paper and make a rough draft. To begin, you might find it helps to write the names on index cards, and move them around till you have everyone in place.

Making a simple tree In its most basic form, a family tree is called a "pedigree chart" or "birth brief," which begins with one individual (yourself), and goes backward, to include only direct ancestors—two parents, four grandparents, eight great-grandparents and so on, but no aunts, uncles, cousins or siblings. It might be arranged horizontally, from left to right (as below) or vertically, from top to bottom.

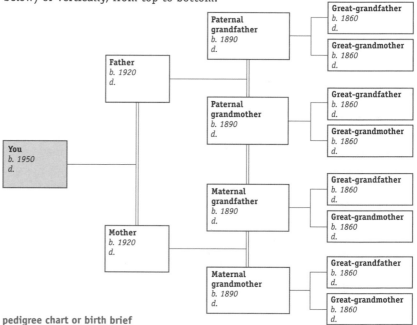

pedigree chart or birth brief

Embrace the wider family When you start to research your family history, you may want to move both forward and back in time, to include your own children and grandchildren and even aunts, uncles and cousins, back into the distant past. For this, you want the "drop-line" format (see below), in which the most distant relatives are listed at the top and the lines of descent drop down the chart from one generation to the next.

drop-line chart

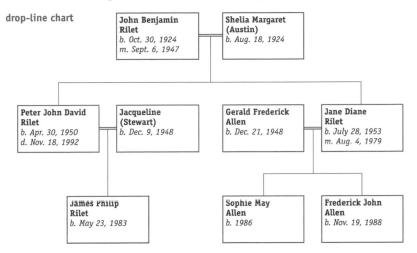

Family tree conventions

■ List women by their maiden names and use double lines to join spouses. List second spouses to the partner's other side, and number them 1 and 2.

■ Use a vertical line to link parents to children and a horizontal line to link siblings, listing them chronologically from left to right.

■ Save space by using the common abbreviations shown at right.

COMMON ABBREVIATIONS	
b.	born
bap.	baptized
m.	married
d.	died
bur.	buried
d.s.p.	died childless (*decessit sine prole*)
ob. inf.	died in infancy (*obiit*)
(c.)	approximately (*circa*)
?	uncertain or unknown
2	second marriage
═══	married
= = = =	unmarried

A drop-line chart can help you understand family relationships such as first and second cousins and first cousin once removed.

---

create a children's
Fancy dress-up box

Children love to get in costume and act out their fantasies. Delight them by filling a dress-up box or closet, and enjoy the characters they then create.

There's no need to splurge on store-bought costumes; it's more fun to mix and match. Start by bringing together old family hand-me-downs or thrift store finds, cleaned or laundered. Hats, a velvet muff, a silk kimono, a bridal veil, a poncho ... anything to fuel a child's imagination. Add accessories such as handbags, wigs, a parasol, sunglasses, a feather boa, baubles, bangles and beads.

Get the kids to help you to improvise more costumes for their burgeoning closet.

■ For a wicked witch, you might scare up a dark dress with a ragged net skirt underneath—and add a toy black cat for her "familiar."

■ For a swashbuckling pirate, bring together cut-off jeans, a striped top, a bandana and an eye patch.

■ For a fairy princess, adorn a pink leotard with silk or tissue-paper flowers, then add a net skirt, white tights and a tiara.

■ To make gossamer wings, use fine-gauge aluminium wire for the frame, and cover with the cut-off legs from a large pair of pantyhose. Tie with ribbons, so that the wings can be worn like a backpack.

■ A pointy hat for a wizard? Roll a newspaper into a cone, hold it together with tape and roll up the bottom edge until it's a snug fit for a small head.

■ A nightdress, a tiara and strings of fake pearls creates a princess.

respond to a Fever

A fever—when the sustained body temperature is above 100°F (38°C) or 99.5°F (37.5°C) in children under five—is an immune response to illness or infection and can usually be managed at home with pain relief and bed rest.

Quick action

■ Contact your doctor if a child with a fever is showing any additional symptoms of serious illness, such as severe pain, persistent and unusual crying, drowsiness, failure to drink, a non-blanching rash (*see* SPOTS AND RASHES), stiff neck or difficulty breathing.

■ For a baby under three months old, contact your doctor if their temperature is 100°F (38°C) or higher. Do the same for a baby from three to six months old with a temperature of 102°F (39°C) or up.

■ Don't overheat the person's room, and make sure fresh air circulates.

■ Cover the person with no more than a thin sheet, and keep nightclothes to a minimum.

■ If the fever is making the person uncomfortable, offer medication, such as acetaminophen or ibuprofen, to bring the temperature down. Make sure to check the label for the appropriate dose.

■ Provide plenty of cool, clear drinks to replace lost fluids.

■ Check the person's temperature (*see* TEMPERATURE) every few hours. Consult a doctor if it remains high or if other symptoms (see above) give cause for concern.

■ Be especially vigilant with young children. Fever in the under-fives can cause convulsions (*see* FITS).

replace an old Fence panel

Panel fences will rot if they haven't been properly treated, and they are subject to damage in storms and high winds. But it's not difficult to replace individual panels that are beyond repair.

1 Before you insert the new panel, paint it with a wood preservative, taking care to treat any joints or end grain that will be inaccessible once the panel is in place. You should apply preservative even if the panel has been pretreated by the manufacturer. Use an old paintbrush then throw it away.

2 It's simple to replace a fence panel that's supported by slotted concrete posts. The panels come in a standard length of 6 ft (1.8 m), so you need only buy a new one and slide it into the slots from above. For this you'll need a ladder and the help of another person.

3 If you're fitting a panel between wooden posts, the new section has to fit exactly in the gap. If it's too big, you may have to plane a small amount off the frame on both sides. If it's a little too small, then you'll have to fill the gap with a narrow strip of wood inserted between the post and the panel. Treat the strip with preservative. Drive in the new nails at a slight angle through frame, strip and post. This is easier if you drill pilot holes for the nails before you fit the panel. Three on each side should be sufficient.

change computer File formats

"File format" refers to the program in which any given document was created, and also the version of that program.

You'll sometimes need to change the file format of a document to make it readable on computers that with programs different—or older—than yours. Someone using Word 97, say, won't be able to open a document that you've created in Word 2010—unless you first change the file format.

To do this, go to **File** and select **Save As.** Click on the **Format** drop-down menu and select **Word 97-2003**. Check that the **Append File Extension** box is checked. Click **Save.** You'll now have created a copy of your Word 2010 document that's readable by the older Word 97 program. It will have the file extension ".doc." It's important to include the file extension, because sometimes another computer won't be able to recognize the file type unless the extension is present, and so won't be able to open it.

This example using Word is just one instance. Most programs have a **Save As** option that allows you to "save back" to older versions, or to change the file format in other ways.

shoot a Film worth watching

Technology has made it easy for anyone to try their hand at being a videographer or film director. But it's not so easy to make a movie that's really worth sharing with others.

Keep still The first and worst mistake that most people make is allowing the camera to shake and jiggle. It distracts viewers and affects the quality of the shot. Brace your camera in both hands and, if you can, lean on a fence or other immovable object. Alternatively, for fixed-position shots, use a tripod.

Take your time Don't pan quickly from side to side. This is known as "firehosing," and it makes your film impossible to watch. The same applies to zooming in and out; do it in a measured way and not too often. Let the camera roll: a three-second videobite of someone blowing out the candles on their cake isn't interesting. Capture the buildup, then the aftermath.

Get plenty of material Shoot lots of footage, then edit it on your computer. Invest in some good video-editing software and use it to rearrange your film into a narrative. Pick out only the very best bits, and ruthlessly discard everything else. When you edit, mix things up so as to vary the pace and the mood of your film. This is the time to add effects such as wipes (where one scene changes to another as if "wiped" from the screen) and fades (where the action dissolves gradually from the screen).

Be scared of the dark Camcorders work best in bright light. Films made in the evening or in the dim light of a party can easily end up looking like they were shot in a coal mine.

Change the angle
Don't shoot everything from shoulder height: this soon gets boring. Get up on a balcony from time to time or crouch down. If someone is talking to the camera, position yourself so that their head is not in the dead center of the frame.

Crouch down so that you film children at their level (not always with their faces turned upward to the camera). Or change the point of view even further by filming from a position below the children's eyeline.

transfer Files
to and from your PC

Sometimes you'll want to move documents and other files onto your PC, or from your PC to another storage device. The simplest way to copy files is to "drag and drop" them onto a different drive.

■ Plug a storage device—a memory stick or an external hard disk—into one of the USB ports on your computer. Click on the **Start** button, then on **Computer** from the Start menu. Your storage device will be displayed in the left pane, below Computer. Navigate on the "C:" drive to the files that you want to move. Highlight the folders or individual files, drag them over to the **Removable Disk (E:)** icon, and drop them. They will all be copied over.
■ If your aim is to free up space on your computer, you should now delete those same files from "Local Disk (C:)."

When you buy a new computer, you'll want to transfer all your files to the new machine. You can do this "manually," but it's easier and safer to use the Files and Settings Transfer Wizard, a built-in program designed specifically for this purpose. The Wizard works on older versions of Windows, so it is ideal if you're upgrading to a better, newer machine.

choose the right
Fire extinguisher

For small fires involving paper, wood or soft furnishings you can use water extinguishers, though they are unwieldy. Never use for cooking-oil or electrical fires.

For flammable liquids such as gasoline, and synthetic fibers in soft furnishings and carpets, use aqueous, film-forming foam extinguishers.

For kitchen fires involving burning oil or small, localized fires, use wet chemical extinguishers. They deliver a cooling layer of foam via a hose.

On burning liquids, and for fires involving computer and other electrical equipment, carbon dioxide extinguishers can be used without causing any damage. Don't use for cooking-oil fires; the jet of gas will blast the fat out of the frying pan.

Powder extinguishers are a powerful tool for all types of fires, but do not use them in confined spaces, where powder might be inhaled. They also cause a great mess and do damage.

The label on a fire extinguisher explains the type of fires on which it can be used and gives operating instructions. Commit this information to memory before you have reason to use the extinguisher.

tackle a Fire in the home

A house fire is potentially devastating. Take every precaution to avoid one, and be ready to act if the worst should happen.

No home is completely fireproof, but faulty wiring and appliances, overloaded outlets, inattention to the stove, negligent smoking and badly placed candles are all fire hazards that are easily avoided. A working smoke detector, a fire blanket and extinguisher (see left) can prove vital in saving your life and possessions. Learn how to use them by heart; you won't have time to learn in the event of a blaze. Plan escape routes and ensure they are kept clear.

Press the test button once a month to check that your smoke alarm is working.

When there's a fire in the home

If you smell smoke, or the smoke alarm sounds or you see flames, call everyone together and lead them out by the safest route without pausing to investigate. Close doors behind you to help to contain the fire. The instant you're clear of the building, call 911. Follow the simple rules below to stay safe while you're in the building.

■ In a choking cloud of smoke, stoop low where the air is clearer.
■ Don't waste time trying to salvage your possessions.

■ Check the top and handle of a door with the back of your hand. If it's warm, there's fire on the other side. If cool, stand behind it and open it a crack. If it opens toward you, brace your foot against it so that hot gases don't blow it wide.

■ If smoke and fire block your progress and there's no other way out, marshal everyone into a refuge room. Use bedding, rugs or rolled-up carpet to block the gap under the door to keep out smoke and fumes. If you can get to a phone, call 911. Open a window and shout for help. Wave a "flag" of some fabric to attract attention.

Kitchen fires

■ More than half of domestic fires arise from cooking accidents, and most commonly start as a cooking-oil fire. If a pan of oil catches fire on the stove, don't try to move it, but turn off the heat at the stove or at the main power source (the electrical box or the gas valve, for example) if you can't get at the stove knobs. Get out of the room and close the door. Evacuate the house and call 911.

■ Never use water on an oil fire as it can cause a fireball, while a fire extinguisher can spread the flames. Fire departments caution against the old technique of covering the pan with a damp dish towel and rolling it over the flames, away from you; it's simply too risky. Even the use of a fire blanket isn't advised. Call the professionals.

Electrical fires

■ Faulty wiring carries the risks of both shock (*see* ELECTRIC SHOCK) and fire. Maintain wiring and appliances to a high standard with regular checks, and watch for warning signs of faults, such as fuses that frequently blow, lights that flicker and scorch marks around outlets. The best advice for avoiding electrical fires is to unplug appliances whenever they are not in use.
■ In the case of an electrical fire, if you can get to the circuit breakers without endangering yourself, cut off the power. Don't touch or try to pull out a plug or remove an appliance until you've done this. A fire blanket, or a dry powder or carbon dioxide fire extinguisher (see left), can be used on a small, localized electrical fire. Otherwise, evacuate the house as quickly as possible and call 911.

lay and light a fire in your Fireplace

■ Make sure that the flue is open before you begin, otherwise you'll fill your house with smoke.
■ Place one or two fire starters or some twists of newspaper in the bottom of the grate.
■ On top, lay some twigs or thin scraps of wood in a crisscross pattern, so that plenty of air can circulate. The more of this kindling you have, the better.

■ Lean two smallish logs against each other in a tent-shaped arrangement on top of the kindling, disturbing it as little as possible.
■ Hardwoods such as oak and apple will burn hotter and longer than softwoods such as pine and cedar.
■ Light a match or long taper and hold it to your newspapers or fire starters. Once the fire is well established, add some bigger logs.

clean your Fireplace

If you have a working fireplace in your home, you should have your chimney professionally swept once a year—during the warmer months when it's not in use. This is also the time to do a thorough cleaning of the firebox (the area where you build the fire). Remove the firescreen and the grate, then sweep up all the ashes; it's a good idea to sprinkle damp tea leaves on first, to reduce dust. Clean any buildup of creosote with a wire brush. If that doesn't get the firebox clean enough, dissolve 3 tbsp of washing soda in 4 qt (4 L) of water, and apply with a sponge—then attack it with the wire brush, and rinse with clean water.

chop Firewood

Frozen logs are easiest to split—but warm an ax that has been left in the cold before use to prevent the blade from chipping.

■ Stand your log upright on a platform, such as a tree stump.

■ Set your feet so that you wield the ax with force and accuracy. Tee up to the log, then bring your ax over the shoulder of your dominant hand, swinging down hard. Your dominant hand should slide down the shaft of the ax as you swing. ■ If the log doesn't split at the first blow, repeat your swing. Try to strike in the same spot or in any crack that appears in the log.
■ Always wear safety shoes with steel toes when using an ax. They will not only protect your toes if you miss with the ax, but will also protect them from falling pieces of wood.

put together a
First-aid kit

Keep your first-aid kit in a cool, dry place, locked away from children, and replenished as necessary. Include a first-aid manual and useful information, such as family blood groups and contact details for your doctor or poison control center.

A household first-aid kit for routine emergencies should contain:

- Adhesive bandages and tape
- Sterile gauze dressings
- Sterile eye dressings
- Triangular, elasticated and crepe bandages; clips and safety pins
- Disposable sterile gloves
- Sharp scissors
- Tweezers
- Alcohol-free wipes to clean cuts and scrapes
- Digital thermometer
- Skin-rash cream
- Antiseptic cream and liquid
- Insect bite or sting relief
- Ibuprofen or acetaminophen
- Antihistamine tablets
- Calamine lotion for burns, rashes
- Distilled water
- Eyebath

For a first-aid kit in a car add an emergency thermal blanket, hand sanitizer gel, a disposable hot/cold pack and a clinical waste bag.

When traveling abroad, add laxatives; diarrhea medicine and rehydration salts; antacids; sunscreen and soothers; motion sickness pills and antihistamines. For certain destinations, health professionals recommend carrying a supply of sterile syringes and scalpels; water purification tablets and a single 500 mg antibiotic tablet, which must be obtained by prescription.

cook Fish

Always test that fish is properly cooked by prodding it gently with the tines of a fork. The flesh should be just opaque and flake easily. The exception is tuna, which can be served rare.

Method	Suitable for	Cooking tips	Timing
SAUTÉING AND PAN FRYING	Any firm fish	Use a hot oil and butter mixture. Put in pan skin side down. Can be dusted with seasoned flour then rolled into egg and bread crumbs.	2-3 minutes each side
DEEP FRYING	Any firm fish	Can be covered in batter or egg and bread crumbs. Use a frying basket and vegetable oil heated so that a bread cube browns in 1 minute.	6-7 minutes for a fillet
STEAMING	Any fish fillet, steak or small to medium whole fish	Use fish stock (*see* FISH STOCK) or a court bouillon (water with onions, herbs and seasoning added).	8-12 minutes for fillets or steaks
POACHING	Any fish or cut, including whole fish	Cook in a court bouillon on the stovetop or in the oven at 350°F (180°C). Use a fish poacher for large fish. Let cool in the poaching liquid.	10 minutes for fillets, 10 minutes per pound (500 g) for whole fish
BROILING AND BARBECUING	Whole oily fish; firm textured steaks or fillets	Brush with oil and add fresh herbs. Ensure broiler or barbecue is very hot.	4-5 minutes per side
BAKING	Any fish, whole or cut, especially delicate fish	Bake in a shallow buttered dish. Or wrap loosely in foil or parchment paper. Score (make deep cuts) whole fish.	15-20 minutes for fillets or medium whole fish

Batter for fried fish To make a basic batter, whisk together or mix in a food processor 1 cup all-purpose flour, a pinch of salt, 1 egg and ½ cup milk or beer. Let stand for 30 minutes before using.

create a classic Fish soup

Both white fish and shellfish make excellent soups. Choose from a hearty, rustic version or a creamy smooth, sophisticated bisque.

Fish soup Provençal

SERVES 4-6

3 tbsp olive oil
1 large onion, chopped
2 cloves garlic, minced
1 celery stick, chopped
1 small head fennel, chopped
14 oz (540 mL) can chopped
   tomatoes
2 tbsp tomato paste
juice of 1 orange
1 strip orange zest
2 cups fish stock (see fish stock)

6 oz (150 g) each pollock, hake
   and fillets of other white fish,
   skinned and trimmed, cut into
   2in. (5 cm) pieces
bouquet garni of 2 sprigs each
   parsley, thyme and rosemary and
   2 bay leaves, tied with string
salt and freshly ground pepper

TO GARNISH

1 bread baguette, sliced
   olive oil
4 tbsp heavy cream

1 Heat the oil in a heavy-bottomed pan and cook the onion until soft but not browned. Add the garlic and cook for another 1-2 minutes before adding the celery, fennel, tomatoes, tomato paste, orange juice and zest. Simmer for about 15 minutes, stirring occasionally.

2 Add the fish, stock and bouquet garni and bring to a boil. Cover and simmer for 20 minutes. Remove the bouquet garni and orange zest, let cool for a few minutes, then process until smooth. Return to the pan, bring back nearly to a boil and adjust the seasoning.

3 Brush slices of baguette with olive oil and grill until golden brown, turning once. Ladle soup into bowls. Swirl 1 tbsp cream into each bowl and top with the baguette slices.

Shrimp bisque

SERVES 4-6

1 tbsp butter
1 carrot, diced
1 small onion, diced
1 lb (500 g) uncooked shrimp
½ cup white wine
1½ tbsp brandy
4 cups fish or shellfish stock
   (*see* FISH STOCK)

bouquet garni (as above)
2 tbsp rice
salt and freshly ground pepper

TO SERVE

4 tbsp heavy cream
4 tsp sherry or Madeira
pinches of cayenne pepper
a few extra cooked shrimp, unpeeled
croutons

1 Melt the butter in a large saucepan. Add the vegetables and cook until soft. Add the shellfish and cook, stirring for 2-3 minutes. Pour in the wine and brandy and boil for 1-2 minutes to reduce. Add about ½ cup stock and simmer until the shrimp are tender. Remove and peel them, discarding any intestinal veins (*see* PRAWNS).

2 Return the shrimp to the pan with the remaining stock, rice, salt and pepper. Cover and simmer for 15-20 minutes. Discard the bouquet garni, purée the mixture then pass it through a sieve. Return to the pan, bring almost to a boil and check the seasoning. Pour into bowls, then stir in the cream and sherry or Madeira and a pinch of cayenne. Decorate with the additional shrimp and croutons.

make a versatile Fish stock

Bones and trimmings, such as heads and skin, are ideal for fish stock, but remove the gills from fish heads before using.

White fish are the best choice for making stock—darker ones can impart a bitter taste. For a shellfish stock, substitute shells of shrimp, crab, mussels or lobster. Fish stock freezes well but should be used within three months of being made.

MAKES ABOUT 1.5 QT/L

2 lb (1 kg) white fish scraps (can
   include inexpensive white fish
   such as pollack) or shells
1 onion, thinly sliced
4 sprigs parsley
2 bay leaves
2 carrots, chopped
2 sticks celery, chopped
4 black peppercorns
6 cups boiling water or 4 cups water
   and 2 cups dry white wine

1 Rinse the fish trimmings well and place in a large saucepan with the onion, parsley, bay leaves, carrots, celery and peppercorns. Pour in the boiling water and wine (if using). Return to a boil and simmer gently for about 30 minutes, skimming off any scum from the surface.

2 Remove from the heat, cool for 10 minutes, then strain through a fine sieve (plus cheesecloth if using shellfish, to catch any fine particles of grit). Use at once or chill.

master
Fish preparation
see pages 132-133

master Fish preparation

Good fishmongers will usually prepare fish, but it's useful to know how to do it yourself, particularly if you have the chance to buy it fresh from a market or harborside stall.

smells of the sea rather than "fishy"

tight scales

bright red gills

clear eyes

bright slippery skin

YOU WILL NEED Scissors, small sharp knife, plastic bag, chopping board, large cook's knife, teaspoon, filleting or medium-sized chef's knife, tweezers

A fresh fish has bright, slippery skin, tight scales and bright eyes and gills. It should feel firm to the touch and should smell of the sea rather than "fishy." Before cooking, fish may need to be trimmed and scaled, cleaned (gutted), boned and skinned. The methods used for most of these tasks differ depending on whether you're preparing round fish or flatfish.

Prepare a round fish

Before handling any fish, wash your hands thoroughly and improve your grip by dipping your fingers into salt. Wash your hands again when you're finished.

Trimming Use scissors or a small sharp knife to cut fins from both sides and along the back.

Scaling Put the fish into a plastic bag and onto a chopping board. Hold the tail in one hand and work the knife from tail to head, using the bag to catch the scales.

Skinning You need only skin fish if your recipe requires it. With a sharp knife, loosen the skin around the head then gently insert and draw the knife beneath the skin towards the tail. Repeat for the other side.

CLEANING A WHOLE ROUND FISH

1 Hold the fish on its side and slit it along the belly with a small sharp knife until you reach the head.
2 Pull the opening apart to widen it then scrape out the intestines with a knife or teaspoon.
3 Rinse the fish well under cold running water, running a teaspoon along the backbone to remove any blood clots.

BONING A WHOLE ROUND FISH
A filleting knife with a flexible blade makes this job easier. If you don't have one, use a medium-sized chef's knife. If you leave the head on it will help the fish to keep its shape during cooking.

1 Hold the fish with its cleaned cavity toward you. Slide the knife between the ribs and the flesh on both sides, freeing all the ribs down the backbone and taking care not to cut through to the skin.
2 Use scissors to cut through and release each end of the backbone. Then gently peel it away from the flesh, beginning at the head, using a small knife to ease it if necessary.
3 Check that no small bones remain, especially around the edges. Use tweezers to remove any left behind. Bones can be kept and used to make fish stock (*see* FISH STOCK).

CUTTING FISH STEAKS Use a large chef's knife to cut steaks ¾-1¼ in. (2-3 cm) thick, starting from the widest part of the body. Only remove the central bone after cooking.

F

FILLETING A WHOLE ROUND FISH

A round fish provides two fillets, one on each side of the backbone. Remove the head before you start, but leave the skin in place. The head can be used when making stock (*see* FISH STOCK).

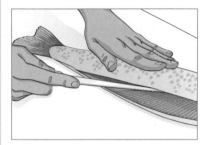

1 Put the fish on its side with the tail toward you. Working from head to tail, cut along the length of its back right through to the backbone with the knife, parallel to the work surface.

2 Starting at the head end, free the flesh from the rib bones on one side. Work the knife along the underside until the top fillet comes away.

3 Then, pulling on it gently, cut away the second lower fillet. Remove any bones with tweezers.

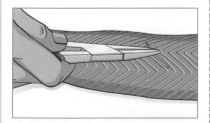

Prepare a flatfish

After being scaled, cleaned and trimmed, a flatfish can be cooked whole, with or without the head. Wash your hands before and after preparation.

Scaling Use the same method as for round fish.

Cleaning Make a semicircular slit just behind the head on the dark side to open up the body cavity. Scrape the entrails out with a small, sharp knife or a teaspoon. Wash well under cold running water. Cut off the fins with scissors, close to the body.

Skinning Put the fish on a board, dark side facing up. Make a slit across the skin just above the tail. Holding the tail tightly, pull the skin toward the head. Remove the white skin in the same way.

Boning Only large flatfish such as Dover sole, shown right, are suitable for boning. Smaller ones like plaice are too delicate. Once a fish has been boned, it can be stuffed.

FILLETING A FLATFISH A flatfish will make four fillets, two from each side. Keep the knife as close to the bones as possible and make bold strokes—tentative ones are more likely to damage delicate flesh. There will already be a small incision in the fish where the guts were removed at sea.

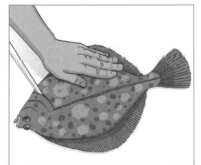

1 Put the fish dark side up on a board and cut off the fins. Working from head to tail, cut along the backbone. Make a semicircular cut just below the head, through half the thickness of the fish.

2 Slant the knife against the backbone and use short strokes to separate the left-hand fillet from the bone.

3 Make a thick cut just above the tail and remove the fillet. Repeat for the right-hand fillet and for the two fillets on the other side.

make Fish cakes

You can use white fish, salmon or smoked fish to make fish cakes.

SERVES 4

1 lb (400 g) potatoes, cooked and mashed with 2 tbsp butter
1 lb (375 g) white fish, poached in milk
3 scallions, finely chopped
3 tbsp chopped parsley
salt and freshly ground pepper
¼ cup all-purpose flour
1 large egg, beaten
¼ cup fine fresh whole wheat bread crumbs combined with 3 tbsp freshly grated Parmesan cheese

1 Heat the oven to 375°F (190°C).

2 Mix the potatoes with 2 tbsp poaching milk, fish, scallions and parsley to make a soft mixture. Season with salt and pepper.

3 Form into eight cakes. Dust cakes with the flour, dip into the beaten egg then into the bread crumb mixture.

4 Cook on a nonstick baking sheet for 20 minutes until golden. Alternatively, fry in canola oil.

cast a Fishing line

In freshwater fishing, the goal is to land your bait at a point in the water where you believe the fish are feeding. The technique used for casting your fishing line is the same whether you are using a weight or a float.

1 Hold the rod in front of you at an angle that's a little below the vertical, with a short play of line dangling from the end. Grip the rod near the reel seat using the hand you write with. Place the other hand at the butt of the rod.

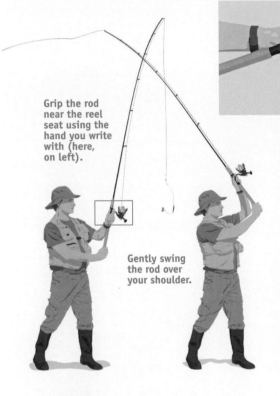

Grip the rod near the reel seat using the hand you write with (here, on left).

Gently swing the rod over your shoulder.

2 Using your index finger, hold the fishing line against the rim of the spool and flip over the bail so that the line can feed out freely once it has been cast.

3 If you're holding the line with your left hand, gently swing the rod over your left shoulder. If holding with your right hand, swing over your right shoulder. Allow the hanging line to swing away from your back.

The line should fly out over the water.

4 Now bring the rod forward in one smooth motion, simultaneously releasing the line from under your finger. The line should now be flying out over the water.

5 As the line reaches the point where you want to fish, tap the spool with your index finger to slow it down and drop it in the water without too big a splash. Close the bail arm.

deal with Fits & seizures

Witnessing a seizure is frightening, but they are not dificult to deal with. Stay calm and follow these tips to keep the patient safe from injury.

Quick action

Seizures may be recurrent, as in epilepsy (often triggered by flashing or flickering lights), or isolated. A sufferer may stagger, utter meaningless sounds or fall to the floor and convulse. Never restrain their movements or put anything in their mouth.

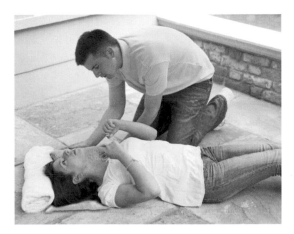

■ If the person suffering the fit is on the floor, provide padding with clothing, rugs and blankets to prevent injury, particularly to the head (left). If possible, move any nearby furniture.

■ When the jerking stops, roll the person onto their side and check that the airway is clear (see RECOVERY POSITION). Let them lie quietly to recover.
■ Call 911 if the fit is someone's first, lasts for more than five minutes or recurs. Call also if the person has been injured or is unconscious for ten minutes or more.

When a child has a febrile convulsion

Before the age of five a child may suffer convulsions caused by a fever (see FEVER). Though these are usually harmless and last no more than two minutes, you should take the following measures.

■ Call an ambulance if a child shows other symptoms of serious illness, such as a rash or stiff neck, if the fit lasts more than five minutes, or if they have not fully recovered within an hour. Seek medical advice if this is a first fit.
■ During the fit, to help prevent any injury lie the child on a soft surface if you can move them safely. If possible, lie them on their side to keep the airway open and avoid choking if they vomit.
■ As soon as you can, remove warm clothing or bedclothes and loosen tight clothing. Don't allow the child to get too cold and don't sponge the skin with cold water. Let them cool down naturally.
■ When the child is fully conscious, give acetaminophen or ibuprofen, if you wish, to help bring the temperature down.
■ Monitor the child's pulse, breathing and temperature every 10-15 minutes until the temperature starts to fall.

raise a Flag

The act of running a flag up a pole is a technical task, but there are also matters of etiquette.

Some poles feature snap hooks, which make the task pretty straightforward.

1 Attach the higher snap hook to the grommet (brass ring) at the flag's upper right.

2 Raise the flag a little, then attach the lower snap hook to the grommet at the bottom corner of the flag.

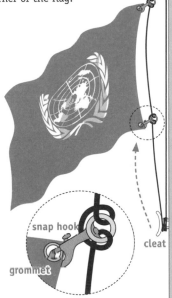

snap hook

cleat

grommet

3 Hoist the flag to the top of the pole, then secure the rope at the base using the cleat.

Etiquette

■ During raising or lowering, neither the American or Canadian flags should touch the ground.
■ The American flag may be flown with a state flag on the same halyard, so long as the state flag is below. Canada's national flag should never be flown with another flaq on the same mast.

deal with Fleas

If you have fleas in your home, start by treating your dog or cat to remove the initial cause.

■ Consult your vet for the safest and most suitable treatment. Never use a treatment intended for a dog on a cat or vice versa.

■ Wash your pet's bedding, then wash or thoroughly vacuum any furniture where your pet is allowed to sit. Remove the vacuum bag as soon as you've finished, seal in a plastic bag and throw away.

■ For serious flea infestations you may need to call in a professional pest-control company.

get a Flight upgrade

Free upgrades are rare, but to stand any chance of getting one you need to look the part.

■ If you're dressed scruffily, your chances of wangling your way into Business Class are slim.

■ An appearance that says SFU ("suitable for upgrade") is more likely to pay dividends if you check in late, once the cheap seats are full. But this is a risky strategy: You might just end up with the worst seat in Economy.

■ You're more likely to be upgraded if you're traveling alone.

■ The best tactic is to join an airline's loyalty program and try to use that carrier whenever you fly. Frequent flyers tend to go to the front of the upgrade line.

get ready for a Flood

When a flood threatens your home, there are measures you can take to minimize the risk of damage and keep you safe.

■ Have drinking water at hand. Fill jugs and saucepans from the kitchen tap before the flood hits; the water supply may become contaminated.

■ If water gets inside the house, turn off the electricity at the circuit breakers before you begin to clean up, and open windows if you smell gas.

■ Never leave your house during the flood, unless you feel your life is in danger there. Move upstairs and wait for help.

■ In high-risk flood areas, choose easy-to-clean ceramic tiles and loose rugs for flooring, rather than fitted carpets downstairs, which will need to be replaced after a flood.

■ If your house regularly floods, raise electrical outlets and switches to at least 5 ft (1.5 m) above the floor and run ground floor cabling through the ceiling void and down the wall to keep the wiring above water level.

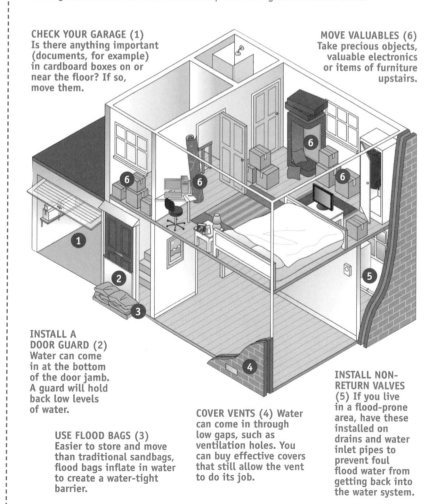

CHECK YOUR GARAGE (1) Is there anything important (documents, for example) in cardboard boxes on or near the floor? If so, move them.

MOVE VALUABLES (6) Take precious objects, valuable electronics or items of furniture upstairs.

INSTALL A DOOR GUARD (2) Water can come in at the bottom of the door jamb. A guard will hold back low levels of water.

USE FLOOD BAGS (3) Easier to store and move than traditional sandbags, flood bags inflate in water to create a water-tight barrier.

COVER VENTS (4) Water can come in through low gaps, such as ventilation holes. You can buy effective covers that still allow the vent to do its job.

INSTALL NON-RETURN VALVES (5) If you live in a flood-prone area, have these installed on drains and water inlet pipes to prevent foul flood water from getting back into the water system.

prepare and sand Floorboards

YOU WILL NEED **Dust mask and ear protectors, claw hammer, nail punch, floor sander, sanding belts (coarse, medium and fine), edging sander**

1 Sanding floors is a noisy business that creates lots of dust, so wear a dust mask and ear protectors. Before you begin, make sure that the room is entirely empty of furnishings, which includes taking down the curtains.

2 Carefully check over the floor, and use your claw hammer to remove any tacks that may remain from previous floor coverings. Look at all the floorboard nails; if any are protruding, firmly nail them down with the punch and hammer.

3 Now you can begin to sand. Fit a coarse-grade sanding belt first. Beginning at one edge of the room, work along the length of the boards. You'll feel the sander drag you forward; hold it slightly in check so that it moves at a controlled rate.

4 If any of your boards are curled (a common problem in old houses), then do your first pass diagonally (as left) to smooth the edges.

5 When you have finished one strip, move on to the adjacent section of floor. Take care to lift the belt from the floor as you turn the machine around, and never try to pull it backward. Once you have covered the whole floor, repeat the process with the medium belt, and then the fine-grade belt (don't sand diagonally with these finer belts).

6 The edges of the room have to be tackled separately with an edging sander. The corners must be done with a scraper, or with a handheld sander designed specifically for the task. When you have finished, vacuum the floor thoroughly, then wipe over with a clean, dry, lint-free cloth to remove the last of the dust. Finish with several coats of oil, varnish, stain or paint.

replace damaged Floorboards

YOU WILL NEED **Claw hammer, steel bolster, scrap wood strips, new floorboard, nails, stain or varnish**

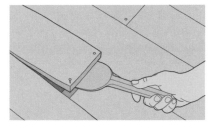

1 Lift the damaged board. Take a hammer and a steel bolster (a wide chisel). Tap the chisel into the gap at the end of the board and lever up the board a little, so that the nearest nails are partly pulled out. Then ease them out with the claw hammer.

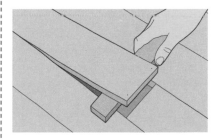

2 Lift the board again and slip strips of scrap wood under to hold it up while you free the subsequent sets of nails until the board itself comes free.

3 If the damage is superficial (a burn, say, or a bad dent) it may be enough just to turn the floorboard over and nail it back down. If your board needs replacing, take it to a lumberyard and get a new board made up to the same width and thickness—this varies greatly with the age and style of a house, so don't try to guess.

4 Put the new board in place and nail it down, using the old nails if they are good enough. Stain or varnish the new board so that it looks the same as the rest of the floor if you aren't going to carpet over it.

press Flowers

YOU WILL NEED **Blotting paper, tray, newspaper or paper towels, heavy books or heavy microwave-proof dish and microwave**

Pressing with books

■ Put three or four sheets of newspaper on a tray and cover with a sheet of blotting paper. Place the flowers on top, well spaced out.

■ Cover with another sheet of blotting paper and three or four sheets of newspaper. Place heavy books on top and leave for two weeks in a cool, dry place.

■ Remove blotting paper carefully to avoid damaging flowers. Leave for another week if not completely dry.

In the microwave

■ Prepare as above, but using paper towels rather than newspaper and a microwave-proof plate or the turntable rather than a tray. Place a heavy dish on top, then microwave on medium power in one-minute bursts, checking for dryness each time. Flowers should be stiff and the paper still slightly damp—it should take 3-4 minutes.

make cut Flowers
last longer

■ Pick flowers early in the morning or in the evening.

■ Remove all lower leaves that will be under water.

■ Cut off the bottom ½–1 in. (1.5–2.5 cm) of each stem at a sharp angle, then soak stems in lukewarm water for at least 2 hours (use cold for flowers from bulbs, such as tulips and lilies).

■ Make sure vases are scrupulously clean before use.

■ Change the water every two days.

create a beautiful
Flower arrangement

The key to making a flower arrangement is to think of it as a three-dimensional triangle built up in a series of layers. Using odd numbers of each stem helps to achieve this.

YOU WILL NEED **Flowers, vase, flower food, scissors, florists' tape. Optional: florist's foam, bucket, knife**

1 Fill the vase with water and add flower food. Arrange three long stems (usually foliage) to make the basic shape of your arrangement.

2 Add more foliage to fill out the shape. Some florists make a grid of clear tape over the neck of the vase to help to support the stems.

3 Start adding tapered flowers to enhance the arrangement's shape. Choose slender flowers, such as delphiniums, or unopened buds.

4 Fill in gaps with rounder flowers, which form the bulk of the arrangement and add volume and color.

5 Next, position one or three eye-catching focal flowers, such as large lilies or bright sunflowers.

6 Finish with fillers for additional texture or an airy contrast to bold flowers. Try baby's breath or even grasses.

Using florist's foam For shallow and flat arrangements a block of foam allows stems to be inserted at any angle. Soak the foam in cold water and submerge for about five minutes or until wet through. Use a sharp knife to cut to shape, 1 in. (2.5 cm) higher than the container, and remove a V from one corner for adding water. Secure with florist's tape.

dry Flowers

YOU WILL NEED Cut flowers, rubber bands, string and coat hangers, or silica gel crystals, shallow airtight glass or plastic container. Optional: microwave oven.

Air drying
- Strip off untidy lower leaves.
- Secure bunches of up to ten stems with a rubber band (the stems will shrink as they dry and fall out if tied with string), tie to hangers with string of different lengths and hang in a dark, warm, well-ventilated place for up to two weeks.

Using silica gel
- Line the base of an airtight container with 1 in. (2.5 cm) of silica gel then push in trimmed flower heads, face upwards and spaced well apart.
- Cover with another 1 in. (2.5 cm) layer of gel, seal and leave for three to five days. Alternatively, microwave on high for two minutes for delicate blooms and four minutes for fleshier ones.
- Cool for 20 minutes. Check that flowers are totally dry before removing.

---

be safe with Food storage

To store food safely you need to control the multiplication of bacteria, which contaminate food and produce harmful toxins. Similar toxins are also produced by the molds (fungi) that flourish on poorly stored food.

In the fridge
- Keep the temperature no higher than 40°F (5°C) to help keep bacteria and molds from spawning.
- Store dairy foods at the top of the fridge or in the door space.
- Cover cooked foods with plastic wrap or store in sealed containers at the top of the fridge.
- Cool cooked foods before storing.
- Store raw meats on the bottom shelf or in the meat drawer.
- Don't mix different meats in the same container, or meat with fish.
- Keep fruit, vegetables, dairy and any food that won't be cooked away from raw meat and fish.

- Keep fruit and vegetables in salad drawers.
- Put fresher items behind older ones to use them in order.

In a cupboard or pantry
- Keep dry ingredients in airtight containers to prevent deterioration and deter insects. Clothespins or chip clips are ideal for sealing opened packages.

Basic food hygiene
- Reheat cooked food thoroughly. Most bacteria are killed at 160°F (70°C), so heat until steaming hot and keep food at that temperature

continued on next page →

distinguish the Flu from a cold

You have a sore throat and a cough. Your head is pounding, you can't eat and you ache all over. Is it a cold or the flu? The two share many of the same symptoms, but are caused by different viruses—and influenza is far more serious.

- The flu comes on suddenly, with a high fever (see FEVER).
- There may be aching muscles, a dry cough and exhaustion.
- With a cold, you should start feeling better within a few days. Flu symptoms persist for up to a week and leave you still feeling tired.
- If you have the flu, you know it! With a cold it's still possible to move around and function; with the flu you won't want to get out of bed.

If you have the flu or a bad cold, always cough or sneeze into a tissue and wash your hands after. Avoid close contact with others, if possible. Seek medical advice for those over 65, under five, pregnant women and otherwise vulnerable people, such as those with asthma, heart or other chest complaints, diabetes or a weakened immune system.

---

golden rules
FRESH FOOD, SAFE FOOD
- The best-before dates on foods are just a guideline. Use your eyes and nose as well to tell whether food is safe.
- In hot weather, take a cooler to the supermarket to keep fresh food as chilled as possible on your way home.
- Clean the fridge once a week.

F

cut Food miles

The purpose of cutting your food miles is to reduce the fuel consumption involved in transporting food from its place of production to your plate. In doing this, you help to reduce the emission of the greenhouse gas, carbon dioxide, into the atmosphere. Food labels stating place and country of origin can reveal much about the eco-friendliness of your purchases.

Calculate food miles on the basis that, on average, transporting 2 lb (1 kg) of food 600 miles (1,000 km) by air generates 2½ lbs (1.1 kg) of carbon dioxide compared with 1 oz (23 g) if transported by boat, 10 oz (290 g) if carried by road and less than 1 oz (30 g) if moved by rail. As a rule, highly perishable foods such as strawberries and green beans are air freighted, while less perishable ones such as onions, potatoes and canned goods, are carried by boat, road or rail.

Cut food miles by buying local produce whenever possible and eating seasonally. Out-of-season foods are invariably transported long distances, grown in heated greenhouses or both. When you can, grow your own food and preserve any surplus for use throughout the year.

continued from page 139

for at least 2 minutes, even if you then let it cool again slightly before serving.

■ Once opened, transfer perishable foods, such as preserves, to the fridge. Always follow the storage instructions on a product's label.

■ Wash your hands thoroughly before and after handling food, even when shopping and unpacking your groceries (*see* HANDS).

■ To avoid contaminating food or spreading bacteria, never use the same knife for different kinds of food unless you wash it thoroughly in between. Keep a separate chopping board just for use with raw meat and poultry.

puree with a Food mill

A food mill—a metal bowl with a perforated bottom—not only purees food but, unlike a food processor, it strains out seeds, pulp and skins. A blade fitted closely to the bottom is turned by a crank to force food through the perforations. If the blade jams, you just reverse its direction and scrape away the residue with a spoon.

A food mill is ideal for jams, baby food, applesauce and riced potatoes. Just be aware that you should cut food into chunks and, except for soft foods, cook it.

These appliances are available in different sizes. Some include three different perforated disks for a fine, medium and coarse puree.

treat Food poisoning

The body can react violently to contaminated food, with diarrhea, vomiting, stomach cramps, abdominal and muscle pains, fever and chills. The symptoms, though unpleasant, can generally be soothed and usually abate within a week.

Seek medical help if symptoms persist or are extreme, if being unable to keep liquids down lasts for longer than a day, if the patient is very young or old, is pregnant or has other medical conditions that make them vulnerable, such as a weakened immune system.

■ Sip slowly at least 8 cups of water a day, plus 1 cup for every loose stool.
■ For elderly or vulnerable people, include rehydration salts, available from a pharmacist.

■ When appetite starts to return, introduce small portions of plain food, such as rice, bread or pasta in the first 24 hours.

know Football from "football"

There aren't may things as American as football, right? Well, it turns out that the word means many things to many people. The gridiron sport watched by millions of Americans every year is played by two teams of eleven players on a field that is 100 yards from end zone to end zone and grew out of the older "rugby football" game in the 19th century. Canadian football is a similar game with 12 players per team, 110 yards between end zones and three downs to the US game's four. The two games feature slightly different rules (Canadian football makes no allowance for fair catch, for instance), but are broadly similar.

In an increasingly international world, switching your TV to a sports channel may show you any one of several games called "football" across the world. For instance, Australian rules football bears scant resemblance to the North American game, beyond using an oval-shaped ball. Australian football is played on huge, oval fields by teams that field 18 players at a time and feature no padding. But in most countries, if you hear two people talking about football, they're referring to the game we call "soccer."

use correct Forms of address

Pete or *Mr. Brown*? Will you be court-martialled if you muddle your majors and generals? Even in these less formal times, it helps to know how to address people of certain ranks and professions. Here are some hints for modern manners.

Ms. or Miss? *Miss* is used mainly to address girls under 18. Use *Ms.* if you aren't certain of a woman's marital status. If a woman retains her maiden name after marriage, she usually uses the prefix *Ms.*, rather than *Miss* or *Mrs.*

First-name basis How do you feel when a stranger addresses you by your first name? Or when an email arrives with a strangely formal *Dear Mr. Smith?* Let common sense be your guide, reserving formality for more senior colleagues, people you don't know or people you know would appreciate the gesture.

Doctors, both medical and academic, are Doctor (*Dr.*, in writing).

A military officer is addressed by full rank in writing, with letters after their name to denote orders and decorations. In speech, address all Generals (generals, lieutenant generals and major generals) as *General* and likewise with other groups of ranks.

Mixing with Majesty Planning a trip across the pond? Even the Royal Family is moving with the times. While senior royals should still be addressed as *Your Majesty*, *Ma'am*, *Your Royal Highness* or something similar, many of the younger royals prefer a less stuffy approach.

apply
Foundation

As its name suggests, foundation provides the background to your makeup and shouldn't stand out. Aim for a subtle, dewy finish, not an unnatural glow.

- Choose the ideal shade by testing on your jawline; check it in daylight, not just artificial light.
- Apply a thin veil of moisturizer and wait for it to be absorbed.

- Use a brush or your middle finger to spread foundation. Work outward from the center of your face, covering a small area at a time.
- Blend into the hairline and jawline to avoid an obvious "seam" between foundation and your natural skin tone. Use a clean sponge instead of your fingers, if you prefer.
- If you have dry skin, "set" the foundation by blotting with a tissue. For medium or oily skin, use a light dusting of powder.

keep Foxes out of your garden

Foxes can be a nuisance in gardens by digging and soiling, and also keep you up at night with their barking and calling during the main breeding seasons.

- Think twice about paying a pest controller to remove or destroy the trespasser; a successor is likely to move in within weeks.
- A fox uses scent-marking to identify territory, so fool it by using an artificial scent-mark product, available from garden centers. Some people claim that collecting your own urine and distributing it around the perimeter of your property will deter a fox from crossing your territory.
- Close sheds to avoid providing shelter for the animal, and keep food waste inside garbage cans with secure lids to limit scavenging.
- Avoid fertilizers that contain fish bone or blood products. These can attract hungry foxes, who will dig up lawns and borders in search of the food they think is nearby.
- Use netting over fruit and vegetable crops, pick up windfalls and keep pet rabbits and chickens secure to deny foxes an easy meal (*see* CHICKENS).

dance a Fox trot like Fred Astaire

Put on some evocative swing music—"You Make Me Feel so Young," "Night and Day," "Cheek to Cheek." Ladies, place your right hand in his left, your left hand resting on his right arm. Gentlemen, place your right hand on her left shoulder blade.

- - - - ◄ slow step
━━━━ ◄ quick step

SMOOTH AND SOPHISTICATED
The slow fox trot is danced with grace and flair—think Fred Astaire and Ginger Rogers. It should flow, with a natural rise and fall created by the changing pace of the steps. Go low with the slow steps and rise up with the quicks. A "social fox trot" (right) is easier, with no rise and fall.

SLOW SLOW Start by taking two slow steps, forward for the gentleman (1) and (2), left then right.

QUICK QUICK Take one quick sidestep, gentleman to the left (3), and another to bring feet together (4).

SLOW SLOW The gentleman takes two slow steps backward, left then right (5) and (6). Ladies move forward, right then left.

QUICK QUICK Another quick sidestep—gentleman to the left (7) and (8), lady to the right. And a quick step to bring feet together before starting again. Repeat the sequence as you move around the floor.

Freeze food safely for storage

A well-stocked freezer can save you money and time but is wasteful if you aren't selective or don't use the food in time. Many premade dishes can be cooked from frozen, as can small pieces of raw fish; otherwise defrost food slowly and thoroughly first.

The more water a food contains, the less likely it is to freeze well. Many fruits and vegetables, including tomatoes, are better pureed or made into sauces, soups or cooked dishes. Vegetables need blanching in boiling water, then cooling quickly in cold water to inhibit the enzymes that detract from their color, flavor and nutritional value. Freeze food in watertight bags or rigid containers that will make the best use of your freezer space. Items can also be wrapped in foil or plastic.

Tips for a safe and efficient freezer

- A full freezer runs most efficiently.
- Freeze foods when they are as fresh as possible.
- Allow room for liquids to expand as they freeze.
- Never refreeze any food already defrosted.
- Label and date items you freeze.

Food and maximum keeping time		Comments
MEAT AND POULTRY		
Beef, lamb, poultry (uncooked)	12 months	Buy in bulk from a butcher, farmer or market.
Pork	9 months	Buy in bulk.
Ground meat (uncooked)	2 months	Shape into burgers before freezing.
Sausages, bacon, ham	3 months	Ideally, freeze uncooked.
Cooked meat	4 months	Same as for casseroles and other cooked meat dishes.
SOUPS AND STOCKS	3-6 months	Use shorter time for soups.
FISH AND SHELLFISH		
Fish (uncooked)	4 months	White fish can keep up to 6 months.
Shellfish (uncooked)	3 months	Bought, cooked or frozen shrimp share the same time frame.
VEGETABLES, FRUIT, HERBS		
Asparagus, peas, corn, and broad, french and runner beans	12 months	Blanch for 2-3 minutes before freezing.
Spinach	12 months	Blanch for 2 minutes then squeeze out excess water.
Herbs	12 months	Chop and freeze in ice cube trays, then bag for easy use.
Fruit	12 months	*See* FRUIT for best methods for freezing.
DAIRY AND EGGS		
Heavy cream, unsalted butter	8 months	Reduce by 2 months for salted butter.
Cheese	4 months	Best frozen grated; becomes more flaky after freezing.
Eggs	10 months	Must be out of their shells.
Ice cream	3 months	Same as for frozen yogurt.
BREAD, PASTA, PASTRY AND CAKES		
Bread	6 months	Freeze sliced and as bread crumbs for easy use.
Pizza	2 months	Freeze according to the topping ingredients.
Pasta, uncooked	4 months	Same timing for lasagne and similar cooked dishes.
Cakes	6 months	Freeze before frosting if possible.
Pastry, uncooked	3	Pre-roll for easy use.
Cooked pastry dishes		Freeze according to the filling ingredients.

F

defrost your Freezer

An iced-up freezer won't run efficiently, so it's worth defrosting regularly. Use up your frozen foods first, so you have less food to keep cold while you defrost.

1 Choose a cold day. Turn off and unplug the freezer. Remove ice trays, racks and containers. Pack food into garbage bags and put them outside. Or wrap in newspaper and blankets and leave in the coolest place indoors. Use coolers and ice packs for ice cream or soup, which melt quickly, and pack them tightly—this way, food should stay frozen for several hours.

2 Put old towels covered with newspaper on the floor and your largest roasting pan on the bottom shelf inside the freezer to catch excess moisture. Leave the door open. Mop up as the ice melts. Don't chip away ice with a knife—use a plastic scraper.

3 To remove lingering smells, clean the freezer with 2 tsp baking soda in 4 cups of warm water, then dry thoroughly. Wash racks and drawers in warm, soapy water and dry. Rub the inside with glycerine before you put them back—ice will come away much more easily next time you defrost.

4 Inspect the food before you replace it and discard anything that's out of date or has deteriorated. Repack with the oldest food most readily accessible.

To speed defrosting
- Put saucepans of hot water inside the freezer and refill as necessary.
- Spray the inside with a store-bought defroster.
- Use a steam cleaner sold as safe for the purpose—never use a hair dryer, which could electrocute you if it gets wet.

throw a Frisbee

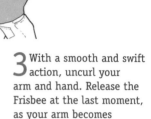

1 First you need to get the grip right. Your thumb rests on top of the Frisbee, your index finger lies along the curved rim, and the other three fingers support the disk underneath.

2 With this grip, curl your arm in toward your body, holding the Frisbee level with the ground. Point your shoulder toward your target.

3 With a smooth and swift action, uncurl your arm and hand. Release the Frisbee at the last moment, as your arm becomes completely straight.

4 The Frisbee should fly true and level to the catcher, who should pluck it out of the air by grabbing the rim.

preserve Fruit

Fruit seasons are short, but harvests plentiful, so try preserving your crops for use when the fresh fruit has passed its best.

Make jams or chutneys (*see* JAM *and* CHUTNEY) or use one of these methods. Wash and dry fruit first.

Freezing is the easiest method. Although it may sacrifice some of the fruits' texture, frozen fruit retains all the flavor of fresh.

Dry freezing Use this method for berries. Spread on trays lined with wax paper, freeze for 1 hour then pack into boxes and return to the freezer.

In sugar Pack fruit between layers of sugar. Allow about ¾ cup sugar per pound (500 g) of fruit.

In syrup Put fruits, mixed in with the syrup, into rigid containers before freezing. Make a simple syrup using 1 cup sugar to every cup of water.

Poached or pureed This method is ideal for less-than-perfect specimens. Poach fruit for a few minutes in a sugar syrup then cool before freezing. Or puree in a blender and freeze in batches.

Bottling Most fruits can be bottled, either in a sugar syrup or in alcohol, but only use unblemished fruits. Use ovenproof bottles with an airtight seal—those with a rubber ring and metal spring clip are best. Peel, core and slice apples and pears; skin, halve and pit apricots and peaches; and bottle plums and berries whole. Pack them in sterilized bottles and top up with boiling syrup (left). Put lids on loosely and sterilize the bottles again in the oven. Stand them on cardboard in the center of the oven at 300°F (150°C) for 40-60 minutes, then seal. To bottle in alcohol, layer fruit with sugar then top up with any spirit more than 40 percent proof, shaking every few days for a month to dissolve the sugar.

make a traditional Fruitcake

Covered with marzipan and iced, this is a perfect special-occasion cake for Christmas or a celebration. Or eat it plain for afternoon tea.

If you don't plan to ice the cake, press some almonds or candied cherries (or both) into the top before baking. This cake is best left to mature for six weeks after cooking, tightly wrapped in a double layer of waxed paper, then in foil. You can add more brandy over this period if you wish.

MAKES AN 8 IN. (20 cm) ROUND CAKE

½ **cup candied cherries, washed and dried**
½ **cup mixed peel, finely chopped**
1 **cup currants**
1 **cup large raisins**
1 **cup sultanas**
¾ **cup ground almonds**
2 **tbsp whole almonds, roughly chopped**
1 **cup all-purpose flour**

½ **tsp salt**
1 **tsp pumpkin pie spice**
1 **cup salted butter**
1 **cup soft brown sugar**
4 **eggs, lightly beaten**
1 **tbsp molasses**
½ **tsp vanilla extract**
finely grated zest of 1 orange or lemon
2 **tbsp milk**
2 **tbsp brandy**

1 Heat the oven to 300°F (150°C). Grease an 8 in. (20 cm) round cake pan and line it with a double layer of parchment paper. Tie a double layer of brown paper around the outside of the pan. Mix the cherries with the peel, dried fruits and almonds. Sift the flour, salt and pumpkin pie spice into a bowl, add 4 tbsp of the fruit mixture and toss together.

2 Cream the butter and sugar together until the mixture is light and fluffy. Add the eggs a little at a time, plus a spoonful of the flour mixture at each addition to stop the batter from curdling. Once all the egg has been incorporated, fold in the remaining flour. Then add the rest of the fruit mixture, the molasses, vanilla, zest and milk and mix well.

3 Carefully spoon the batter into the prepared pan and smooth it level. Arrange some almonds or cherries in the top if you wish (see above). Bake for 2 hours then lower the temperature to 285°F (140°C) and cook for another 1½-2 hours, or until a skewer pushed into the center of the cake comes out clean. If the top of the cake is browning too quickly, cover it loosely with foil.

4 Cool in the pan for 1 hour, then turn out the cake and continue cooling on a wire rack. When completely cool, pierce the top several times with a skewer and spoon over the brandy, allowing it to soak in.

thaw Frozen pipes

Find the pipe that's blocked with ice, which will naturally be in a cold part of the house. Be prepared to turn off the water supply in case the thawing process reveals a burst joint or a pipe has split in the freeze.

If no taps are working, the problem is with the cold-supply pipe. If a single tap runs dry, then the blockage is in the pipe leading to that faucet.

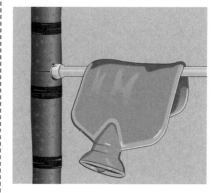

Remove any insulation from the affected pipe and open the tap, so that you will know when the water is flowing again. If the pipe is copper, use a hair dryer to heat it until the water starts to flow, or hang a partly filled hot water bottle on it. If the pipe is plastic, wrap it in towels soaked in hot water.

golden rule
STOP FRUIT FROM SINKING
■ **Always wash and dry the candied cherries thoroughly before adding them to the cake mixture. This will prevent them from sinking to the bottom of the cake.**

F

make Fudge

MAKES 64 SQUARES

1 lb (500 g) light brown sugar
1 cup milk
½ cup unsalted butter, plus extra for greasing pan
1 tsp vanilla extract
½ cup chopped nuts (optional)

1 Line a 8 x 8 x 2 in. (20 x 20 x 5 cm) square pan with foil and brush with melted butter. Put the sugar, milk and butter in a large saucepan and stir over low heat until the sugar dissolves.

2 Bring to a boil and boil for about 20 minutes, stirring constantly, until the mixture reaches 235°F (114°C) on a candy thermometer or when a teaspoon of mixture dropped into cold water forms a soft ball. Remove from the heat and stir in the vanilla and nuts (if using).

3 Leave until lukewarm, beat until creamy, then pour into the pan. When nearly set, mark squares with a knife. Break into squares when set.

protect Fruit trees and bushes from hungry birds

Birds have voracious appetites for soft fruit of all kinds, which makes protecting crops essential. Protection is easiest for bush fruit, such as raspberries and black currants, and for low-growing strawberries.

Trees such as cherries and plums are hard to protect, but you can throw netting over a small tree for short periods. Or hang old CDs, strands of cassette tape or pieces of scrunched-up foil secured with string onto the branches. These may work for awhile but birds quickly become immune to them.

For individual bushes set three or four poles around each bush, top with glass jars and drape netting over the top. Pull it taut, then secure at the base with pegs.

For strawberries make a cane framework for netting around the whole bed or push sturdy hoops into the ground and stretch netting over.

For a large area construct a fruit cage high enough to walk inside. Buy a kit with metal uprights or make a frame using 2 x 3 in. pressure-treated wood for the corner posts and 2 x 2 in. wood for intermediate posts placed 6½ ft. (2 m) apart. Link all posts with heavy-duty wire stretched taut and allow for a door of some kind, which can be well-overlapped pieces of netting or a wooden construction. Attach the netting with staples and secure at ground level with pegs, bricks or stones.

prune and train Fruit trees and bushes for a good crop

Well-pruned fruit bushes will stay healthy and produce maximum yields. Training fruit trees against walls and fences saves space and is ideal for warmth-loving varieties, such as peaches and apricots.

Soft fruit bushes

Prune soft fruits according to their time of harvest and the type of wood on which the fruits grow.

Raspberries For summer harvest types, remove dead canes after fruiting. For autumn harvest varieties, cut back to ground level in autumn or early spring.

Currants Black currants fruit on new wood, so prune the bushes as you harvest, leaving eight to ten branches less than three years old to grow and fruit next year. Red and white currants fruit on old wood. Prune them in winter, shortening tall new growth by half. Cut side branches (laterals) back to one bud.

Fruit trees

Winter pruning Prune to create a strong framework. Remove crossing branches, those blocking light or air, and any dead wood. To promote new growth, prune back main growing shoots (leaders) to just above a healthy growth bud, slanting the cut upwards. Prune back side shoots (laterals) to form a fruiting spur or let them grow into new branches. Growth buds are easily distinguished from fruit ones because they lie flat to the stem; fruit buds are plumper and stand prouder by comparison.

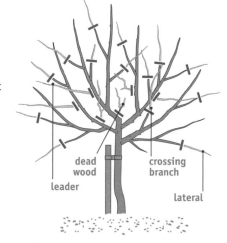

dead wood

leader

crossing branch

lateral

 fruit bud

 growth bud

 pruning cuts just above a bud

fruiting spur

Summer pruning Apple trees can be pruned to promote fruiting. Prune new side shoots to about six or seven buds, cutting just above a plump fruit bud.

Training Blackberries, loganberries and other bushes that grow untidily are best trained onto wires spaced 8 in. (20 cm) apart, cutting out dead wood each autumn after fruiting. For other fruit use one of the following methods.

Espaliers Plant 8 in. (20 cm) from a wall or fence. In early summer, select three shoots, one at the top (to be trained vertically) and one on either side of the main stem, 12 in. (30 cm) above ground level. Remove all other shoots and buds. As side shoots grow, attach them to wires on the wall. In early spring select more side shoots for training and remove unwanted growth. Allow shoots to grow every 4-6 in. (10-15 cm) on the side shoots, removing the rest. On new growth, cut back shoots with flower buds at their base to one or two leaves.

Cordons This method is ideal for apples and pears that bear fruit on short side shoots (spurs). Cordons are best established with trees planted 2-3 ft. (60-90 cm) apart at a 45-degree angle against a fence or wall onto which you've secured horizontal wires 2 ft (60 cm) apart. After planting, leave the leader and any short laterals intact. Cut back all laterals longer than 4 in. (10 cm) to three buds. Between July and September cut back all laterals to one good leaf from the base and sub-laterals to one or two buds.

cut down your Fuel consumption

There are lots of small things you can do to make your car more fuel-efficient, but the most significant is to drive smoothly. Going fast then braking hard wastes gas.

Check your tire pressure at least once a month. Tires only have to be a little underinflated for gas consumption to rise noticeably.

Don't use your trunk as a closet Take out the toys, the toolbox and anything else that doesn't have to be there. Extra weight sucks gas.

Keep short trips to a mimimum Cars use more gas when they are running cold, so if you're taking the car out, run as many errands as possible with each trip.

Plan your route There's no more pointless waste of gas than driving around looking for your destination because you didn't look up the route before you set out.

Use the gears to slow down gradually, and the brakes only to bring your car to a stop. Try to change gear up at 2,000-2,500 revs to make the best use of your fuel.

Negotiate traffic-slowing obstacles at a constant speed rather than braking suddenly and then accelerating.

Use air-conditioning sparingly, as it burns a lot of gas. At low speeds an open window is better. Don't open windows at high speeds, though, as this increases drag on the car and, therefore, increases fuel consumption.

illuminate
Garden features

With the right type of lighting, features such as ornaments and statues, as well as individual plants, can become the stars of your nighttime garden.

The simplest option is to use lighting that doesn't need cables, such as garden candles or solar-powered lamps.

Wired lighting should be installed by a professional. To protect cables from damage, they should be buried under walls, lawns and paths, which is easiest when creating a new garden.

Low-voltage lights are easier to install, as the wires don't need to be buried. DIY kits are available with a transformer that just plugs into an existing electrical outlet in the house or garage.

Uplighting works particularly well for picking out individual garden features. Simply place a light right at the base of the item.

Spike-mounted lights are good for illuminating pathways or providing light for a garden bench.

Water features give the garden an enchanting new appeal when lit at night. Submersible lights are especially effective.

✦ golden rule

GARDEN LIGHTING SAFETY
■ **Have the wiring checked by a professional every few years.**
■ **Know where the wires run so you can avoid accidentally damaging them when digging in the garden.**

create Garnishes

A well-chosen garnish will contrast with a dish in color and texture. It should enhance both the dish's look and its taste.

Savory garnishes These can be as simple as slices of lemon cut into butterfly shapes, parsley sprigs or a sprinkling of fried breadcrumbs. Alternatively, use croutons or fried sage leaves.

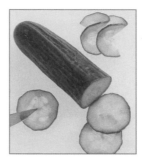  

Cucumber twists Use a small, sharp knife to cut the cucumber into thin slices. Make a single radial cut from the edge to the center of each slice, then twist either side of the cut in opposite directions.

Fluted mushrooms Score each cap from the center to the edge with a small, sharp knife, tracing a curved shape and removing a narrow strip of flesh each time. Remove the stem.

Radish roses Remove most of the stalk and slice across the top so that the radish stands upright. Make partial scalloped incisions in the radish. Place in iced water for an hour. Dry before use.

Sweet garnishes **Frosted fruit** Brush fruit such as grapes, cherries (with stalks), sprigs of red currants or mint leaves with lightly beaten egg white, dredge with superfine sugar then dry on wire racks. **Citrus strips** Remove the rind from lemons or oranges without pith and cut into thin strips. Boil in a sugar syrup, drain and dry. **Dipped fruit** Half-dip fruit such as strawberries into melted chocolate and place on baking parchment to dry. **Chocolate curls** *see* CAKE.

deal with a Gas leak

If you smell gas indoors it's time for fast action
■ **Don't turn on a light** or use any electrical switch.
■ **Don't strike a match** or use any naked flame.
■ **Open doors** and windows right away.
■ **Turn off any gas appliance** that has been left on—a stove burner, say.
■ **Shut off the gas supply** at the meter or main valve if the source of the gas is not immediately apparent, but don't try this if the meter is located in the basement, where levels of gas may be higher.
■ **Call your gas provider** or 911.

cut a pane of Glass

YOU WILL NEED Pane of glass, newspaper, grease pencil, glasscutter's wheel, mineral spirits, straightedge

1 Lay your pane of glass on an open newspaper. Using the rules and lines of print on the page, align your glass. With a grease pencil, mark the line along which you plan to cut.

2 Lubricate a glasscutter's wheel with mineral spirits. Position a straightedge on the cutting line. Hold the cutter so that your index finger applies pressure to the wheel. Starting at the furthest point from you, run the cutter the full length of the glass without stopping.

3 Lift the glass and tap lightly underneath with the ball-end of the cutter. Then place the glass so that the scored line is immediately above the edge of the straightedge. Press firmly on both sides, and the glass will snap cleanly along the scored line.

clean Glass ornaments

Glass can be hard to wash because it's so easily broken. Caution and patience are the key to cleaning ornaments with the minimum of risk.

Always wash fine glassware by hand, and with the utmost care. Remove any jewelry that may scratch the glass—diamonds are particularly dangerous. Wash your ornaments in soapy water, having first placed a rubber mat in the bottom of the sink (remember to swing the tap head out of the way, too). Always wash one item at a time. Rinse items in a bowl of clean water. Don't attempt to wipe glass objets d'art, particularly if they have delicate parts. Allow them to dry naturally in the air.

Dealing with really delicate glass Some ornaments may be too precious or fragile to wash as above, but they can still be cleaned. Put on rubber or disposable latex gloves. Make up a solution consisting of equal parts denatured alcohol and water, then add a few drops of ammonia. Apply the solution with cotton balls. Don't use this technique on glass that has decorative gilt, as it may make the gold come off.

bake Gingerbread men

Children love helping to make these traditional treats, which taste just as good whatever size and shape of cutter you use.

MAKES ABOUT 16
¾ cup plus 2 tbsp brown sugar
4 tbsp molasses
1½ tsp ground ginger
½ tsp cinnamon
1½ tbsp water
8 tbsp butter, diced
½ tsp baking soda
3 cups all-purpose flour
currants, to decorate

1 Put the sugar, molasses, spices and water into a large saucepan and bring to a boil, stirring constantly. Remove from the heat and add the butter and baking soda. Stir in the flour (add some extra if necessary) to make a smooth dough. Cover and refrigerate for 20 minutes.

2 Heat the oven to 350°F (180°C). Roll out the dough on a floured surface to ¼ in. (5 mm) thick, then cut into shapes using a gingerbread man cookie cutter. Place on greased baking sheets and add currants for eyes and buttons. Bake for 12-15 minutes until the edges are brown. Cool slightly before transferring to a wire rack.

G

take care of
Goldfish

These colorful creatures can be rewarding pets, especially for children, and are relatively easy to keep. Look after a goldfish and it could live for 20 years or more.

Provide enough space You should allow 5 gal (20 L) of water for each goldfish you keep, so use a tank rather than a traditional bowl.

Keep the water clean Goldfish swim in their own waste, and polluted water will make them sick. Even traces of the ammonia in their urine can be deadly to them.
■ Use a small net to skim off any fish waste or leftover food flakes.
■ Every two weeks, replace a third of the water with treated water (*see* AQUARIUM), at the same temperature as that in the tank.
■ Buy a siphon to vacuum dirt from the gravel. Make sure any equipment that you use with the fish is kept clean.
■ Add plants to the tank. Living plants oxygenate the water, while plastic ones attract algae, an additional feeding source for the fish. They also make for a more interesting environment.

Feed them well Buy food specifically prepared for goldfish from a pet shop or supermarket.
■ Don't overfeed; leftover food will go bad in the water.
■ If you have to go away for more than a couple of days, ask someone to feed your fish.

get your Gold to gleam

Gold needs regular cleaning to keep it shiny. Avoid immersing delicate gold jewelry in chlorinated water (swimming pools, for instance), which can make it deteriorate. For a really professional cleaning, take gold to a jeweler or invest in an ultrasonic cleaning machine. Or try these two methods, which will have your gold looking great.

Mild method Make a bowl of suds with warm water and a little dish soap. Soak the gold item briefly then scrub gently with a soft toothbrush or eyebrow brush. Rinse in a wire strainer under warm running water. Dry with a soft, clean cloth or chamois.

Stronger method Mix equal parts of cold water and ammonia and soak the gold piece for 30 minutes. Then scrub, rinse and dry as above.

choose the right Glue for the job

To bind two materials together effectively you must first select the right adhesive for the task, a choice that depends on the materials you want to bind. You must then follow the manufacturer's instructions for preparing the surfaces and applying the adhesive correctly.

Type	Uses
RUBBER CEMENT	Good for flexible materials such as card, leather and fabric-backed plastic.
CONTACT GLUE	Use with nonporous sheet materials—for example, laminate trims for kitchen worktops.
EPOXY RESIN	Use for metal, china or glass. Good for mixed materials—for example, a glass pendant in a metal setting.
WHITE (CARPENTER'S) GLUE	Suitable for paper and wood, also for fixing ceramic to other materials, such as felt.
PVC ADHESIVE	Use to glue plastic to plastic. Good for repairing plastic raincoats, inflatable toys and so on.
FABRIC GLUE	Best used for fabrics and leather—for example, fashion embellishments or carpet edges.
SUPERGLUE	Good for small objects, such as china ornaments and rigid plastic toys, and for binding metal parts to other materials.

make an authentic Goulash

SERVES 4

2 tbsp olive oil
2 lb (1 kg) boneless veal or braising
   steak, cubed
1½ tbsp butter
2 large onions, thinly sliced
2 cloves garlic, minced
2 large red peppers, in chunks
2 tbsp paprika (plain or smoked)
1 tbsp caraway seeds
1 tbsp all-purpose flour
2 cups tomato sauce
1 cup beef stock—for best results,
   use homemade (*see* BEEF STOCK)
1 tsp dried marjoram or oregano,
   plus a few fresh leaves

1 Heat the oil in a large frying pan over medium heat, brown the meat in batches and set aside. Melt the butter over medium-low heat in a large, deep saucepan. Add the onions, garlic and peppers and cook for 2 minutes, or until the onion is soft, stirring occasionally. Add the paprika and caraway seeds. Stir for 30 seconds, then add the flour and stir constantly for 1 minute.

2 Stir in the tomato sauce, stock and dried marjoram or oregano. Bring to a boil, then reduce the heat to low. Add the meat and simmer, uncovered, for 1½ hours, or until the meat is tender. Stir occasionally and add a little more stock or water, if needed, to keep the meat covered. Garnish with fresh oregano or marjoram and serve with mashed potatoes or noodles. A dollop of sour cream adds a little richness.

treat an attack of Gout

Gout is a form of arthritis caused by a build up of uric acid in the blood. Too much uric acid, a waste product usually excreted by the kidneys, can cause crystals to form in the joints, which then become inflamed and painful.

When pain strikes
- Rest, with the affected limb elevated.
- Keep the joint cool. Don't cover it. Remove clothing from around it and apply ice packs wrapped in a dish towel for 20 minutes at a time.
- Drink plenty of water and a couple of glasses of black cherry juice a day.

Managing your gout
- Maintain your ideal weight (*see* BODY MASS INDEX) and avoid alcohol.
- Eat plenty of fresh fruit and vegetables.
- Be very sparing with: meat (especially liver, kidneys, veal and turkey); seafood (especially anchovies, herrings, mackerel, sardines, mussels, scallops and roe); asparagus; kidney beans; lentils; spinach; and yeast extract.

speak the language of Golf scores

Golf, like cricket, is a game of eccentric charm, with jargon to match. This is especially true when it comes to describing the score.

Par The number of shots you're expected to take to complete an individual hole or an entire round.

Birdie One shot fewer than the par amount ("under par") for a hole.

Eagle Two shots under par for a hole.

Albatross Three shots under par.

Bogey One shot over par.

Double bogey Two shots over par.

say Grace

When offering this prayer of thanks before a meal, make an effort to be gracious. Thank the Almighty for the food on the table, the company of family and friends, and perhaps for one other thing specifically related to the occasion, such as the presence of a much-missed relative or the safe conclusion of another year. Those at the table should listen in silence—so don't tempt them by making jokes. Everyone should have their hands folded in front of them. As with any other kind of speech, keep it pithy and brief; dinner is getting cold, after all.

come to grips with
Golf
see pages 152-153

G

come to grips with Golf

The game of golf involves hitting a tiny ball into a tiny hole hundreds of yards away while playing as few shots as possible. Power, precision—and stoicism—are key.

Swing is king The best golfers are simply the ones who hit the ball the right distance in the right direction more often than most. A good set of clubs helps but, whether you need to hit the ball 22 yards (20 m) or 220 yards (200 m), it's consistency of grip and swing that really matters. Master those basics and you'll get better with every round you play.

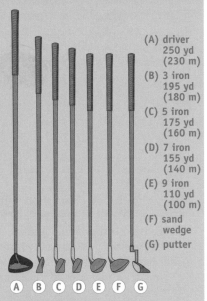

(A) driver
250 yd
(230 m)

(B) 3 iron
195 yd
(180 m)

(C) 5 iron
175 yd
(160 m)

(D) 7 iron
155 yd
(140 m)

(E) 9 iron
110 yd
(100 m)

(F) sand wedge

(G) putter

Ⓐ Ⓑ Ⓒ Ⓓ Ⓔ Ⓕ Ⓖ

BEGINNER'S SET OF CLUBS showing men's average distance achieved.

CLUBS FOR THE OCCASION
To play golf you will need a set of clubs. Seven is enough for most beginners: a putter, a driver, a sand wedge and four irons—numbers 3, 5, 7 and 9—are a good initial selection. It makes sense to buy secondhand if you're an absolute beginner, but be sure that your clubs are all of the same type or make, so that they all "feel" the same when you play: Don't just buy a ragbag set of oddments. Take advice on equipment from a more experienced player, or from the golf pro at your golf club.

HOW TO GRIP
You should also get some initial advice on your grip. It's impossible to play accurate shots if your grip is bad—so invest in a few lessons at the start of your golfing life. This will pay dividends later on, when you begin to improve through regular practice sessions. By far the most popular method of holding a club is the "Vardon grip" (see below), and like every aspect of the game it takes time to perfect. The grip locks the two hands together on the shaft of the club so that they act as a single dynamic unit when you swing.

THE VARDON GRIP These instructions are for a right-handed golfer but can be reversed for a left-hander.

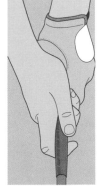

BACK VIEW Put the little finger of your right hand between the middle and index fingers of the left.

FRONT VIEW Use your right hand to grip both the club shaft and the thumb of your left hand.

DRIVING: POWER AND ACCURACY
Your aim when you drive a golf ball off the tee is to strike that ball with maximum force and send it in a precise direction.

It's important to stay relaxed. Don't allow tension to build up in your hands and forearms. This is why some professionals waggle the club before they drive to loosen up. To achieve power, you have to twist your body

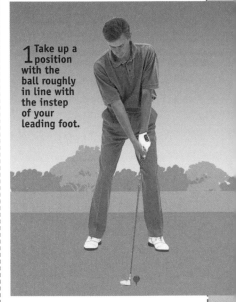

1 Take up a position with the ball roughly in line with the instep of your leading foot.

and lift your club so that, when you unwind, all the energy in your body and in the moving head of the club is delivered sweetly to the ball at the moment of impact. In order to have accuracy at the same time, your club must make the same smooth arc through the air on the way down as it did when you (slowly) lifted it up and back. All parts of your body, as well as the club (which should be seen as a kind of extension of your body), must be aligned in the instant when you make contact. The ball should be slightly forward of your center, level with your left instep (if you're right-handed), so that it's hoisted into the air by the strike.

PUTTING: THE GAME WITHIN A GAME

A round of golf is won or lost on the green. That's to say, missed putts are what make the difference in a competitive situation—so it makes sense to concentrate a good deal of your practice time on putting. But there are other things you can do to improve your putting game. One is to make a habit of "walking the green," as it's called. When you have a putt to make, pace out the distance between the ball and the hole, so that you get a feel for how far the ball needs to go, and weight your shot accordingly. It also helps to visualize a point beyond the hole as your target. Aim for an imaginary flag half a yard (0.5 m) beyond a line connecting your ball and the hole: This will help you keep the ball on track when you putt.

2 Keep your head still and slowly twist your body to swing the club back.

3 Unwind your body to swing the club toward the ball at speed.

4 Keep your head still until the point of contact and then allow it to follow the movement of your body.

THE SECOND SHOT: THINKING STRATEGICALLY

Don't just slam the ball down the middle of the fairway. Consider what you're going to do next. Think about how you're going to approach the hole. Sometimes you have to tack, or zigzag, towards it. Consider hazards such as water and bunkers, and whether you dare risk placing your ball close to them. This is a question of measuring your own confidence and ability, as well as gauging the lie of the course.

TO COMPLETE THIS PAR 5 HOLE, you're expected to make three approach shots and two putts.

GETTING OUT OF A BUNKER: DAMAGE LIMITATION

If it all goes wrong, and you find yourself in a sand trap, take a moment to assess the situation. Your main objective is to get out of the bunker so you can continue toward the hole. If you're in a fairway bunker, you may have to escape by lofting the ball high over the lip of the bunker. You'll need the correct club to clear the lip, but this means you might not be able to get enough distance to reach the green. The same is true if the ball is lying deep in the sand: To get it out at all, you'll have to sacrifice distance.

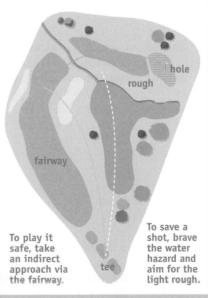

To play it safe, take an indirect approach via the fairway.

To save a shot, brave the water hazard and aim for the light rough.

protect
Greenhouse
plants from scorching

Although greenhouses are designed to provide a higher temperature for raising delicate plants and seedlings, at the height of summer they can reach oven temperatures that will bake the plants inside. Keep a watch on heat levels with a maximum/minimum thermometer.

Provide shade In midsummer heat, greenhouse plants need protection from the sun, and even on a bright spring day seedlings may benefit from some shade. The cheapest solution is to brush greenhouse shade paint onto the outside of the glass. Choose one of the new paints that turns opaque in bright sunlight but becomes more transparent on dull days and is impervious to rain.

Allow air to circulate On warm days open greenhouse vents and doors, then shut them before the evening temperature drops. Automatic vent openers are inexpensive and easy to fit and will open and close the windows according to the temperature inside the greenhouse.

Water regularly Watering is essential for plants to survive hot weather inside a greenhouse. Water at the beginning or end of the day, when the temperatures are at their lowest, to minimize the amount of water lost through evaporation before it can get to the plant. Use a plant mister to spray water on leaves as well as watering at the roots, and water the greenhouse floor, too, if it's stone—this water will evaporate in the sun and help to raise the humidity inside.

make perfect Gravy

Using a good stock makes all the difference when making gravy, and won't mask the true flavors of your roast meat (*see* BEEF STOCK *or* VEGETABLE STOCK). No stock available? Save the water in which vegetables have been cooked, or use a can of beef or poultry consommé.

1 Pour excess fat from the roasting pan, leaving the drippings and enough fat for a thin layer on top. Gradually stir in 2 cups hot stock or vegetable water, and blend thoroughly over medium heat, scraping up all the sediment.

2 Pour the mixture into a saucepan. Blend some flour or cornstarch with a little water to make into a smooth paste and add to the pan juices. Cook, stirring over medium heat, until the gravy has reduced and thickened.

For extra flavor add red or white wine or sherry to match the meat you're serving. For lamb or game, stir in a few spoonfuls of red currant jelly. Mustard and spices, such as nutmeg, can also be used. If you add herbs such as rosemary or thyme the gravy will need straining.

clean a Greenhouse

A thorough annual cleaning will help to keep your greenhouse free of pests and diseases and allow maximum light penetration. Early autumn, once crops such as tomatoes have finished, is the best time to do this.

1 Before you begin, remove all plants, except those growing in fixed borders, and take out all pots, boxes and trays, and any shelves that can be dismantled. Turn off the electricity and protect any outlets with masking tape.

2 Using a brush and a hose, or buckets of water, clean the outside of the glass, then the inside. Use the edge of a plant marker or an old knife to pry dirt from between overlapping panes and wash away with a jet of water.

3 Disinfect all the interior surfaces. You can use a strong chemical cleaner, but even better are biodegradable products that combine cleaning with disinfecting and attack algae, mosses and fungi as well as bacteria and viruses. Follow the manufacturer's instructions to the letter.

4 Wash and scrub all pots, trays and shelves, and disinfect in a similar way. Replace all these, plus the plants, and close all the vents.

create Greeting cards

Save interesting images of all kinds, pressed flowers and even pieces of fabric to stick on cards, either alone or as collages. Or be more ambitious with these effective but easy ideas.

YOU WILL NEED Card, cutting board, scissors or metal ruler and craft knife, leaves or petals, low-tack adhesive spray, white glue, spray paint, thick colored paper, pencil, eraser. Optional: crayons, pens or paints.

Stenciled card As well as leaves or petals you can use any cut-out shapes as stencils in this method.

1 Place the base card on a cutting board and cut it to size using scissors or a metal ruler and knife. Then fix one or more leaves or petals to it with low-tack spray adhesive.

2 Spray paint over the plant material, following the manufacturer's instructions, and let dry. Peel off the leaves or petals and carefully rub off any traces of glue. Finish by folding the card ready for use.

Pop-Up Valentine card

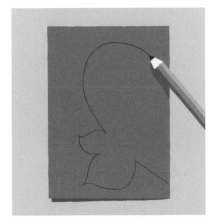

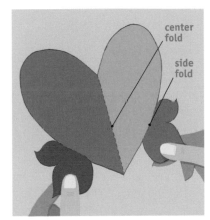

center fold

side fold

1 Choose a piece of thick colored paper to contrast with your base card (see over) and fold it in half, pressing it down flat. Draw one half of the "winged heart" design with the center of the design against the fold. Cut it out, just inside your drawing line to make a symmetrical piece that will be used to create the pop-up element of your card.

2 Fold and unfold along the center fold line several times to make it flexible. Fold in the "wings" at the sides of the heart to crease them, then open them out to the sides. Hold with the main center fold pointing forward as shown. Add any further decorations to the heart using crayons, pens or paints and allow them to dry thoroughly.

continued on next page →

---

tune a Guitar

It doesn't matter how good a guitar player you are; if the strings on your guitar are out of tune, it will sound awful. The action of playing a guitar can easily cause the strings to lose the correct tension, so every time you pick your instrument up, you should spend a couple of minutes tuning it up. The best way to tune your guitar to itself is to use the 4th/5th fret method, where you use the note at the 5th fret (or 4th fret on the G string) of a given string to tune the next open string.

Start by tuning the bottom E string as precisely as you can, using a piano or an E tuning fork.

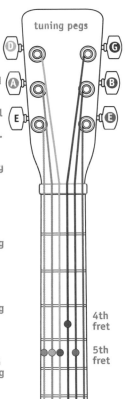

tuning pegs

● **A STRING** Fret bottom E at 5. Play the open A string. If it sounds lower or higher than the fretted E string, gently adjust the A tuning peg until the two strings sound the same.

● **D STRING** Fret the A string at 5. Tune the open D string until you have the same note.

● **G STRING** Fret the D string at 5. Tune the open G string to it.

● **B STRING** Fret the G string at 4 and tune the open B string to it.

● **TOP E STRING** Fret the B string at 5 and tune the open top E string.

4th fret

5th fret

E A D G B E

clear Gutters

Clearing gutters is a maintenance job best done late in autumn, after all the leaves (the most likely cause of a blockage) have fallen. But your gutters can suddenly start overflowing at any time of year.

Place the ladder at the downpipe, climb up and stuff a piece of rag into the top to prevent debris from plugging up the pipe.

Check the contents of your gutter Scoop out any silt, leaves, moss, old tennis balls or other debris—and put it in a bucket. Don't allow any of the debris to go down the wall of your house, where it will make an unsightly stain.

Once you have removed all the debris, remove the rag plugging the downpipe. Reposition your ladder at the far end, away from the downpipe, and pour three or four buckets of water into the gutter to sluice it through. You might find it easier to use a hose for this part of the job.

continued from page 155

3 Measure the rectangular base card to at least 2 in. (5 cm) larger all around than the pop-up shape and cut it out. Using a ruler and pencil for accuracy, fold it exactly in half width-wise. Rub off any pencil marks. Place the pop-up piece inside of the card, standing proud as it will be in the finished item, and use a pencil to mark where the "wings" will be stuck to the card (right). The pop-up piece needs to fold neatly into the finished card, or can protrude a little if desired. Apply glue to these areas, then immediately fix the pop-up design in place.

4 Allow to dry, then carefully rub off any excess adhesive with your fingertips and erase any pencil marks. Carefully close the card, folding the pop-up along its center line. The outside of the base card can be decorated further if you wish.

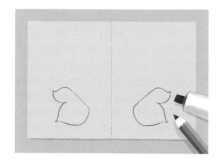

replace a Guitar string

If you're changing a string on a steel-string acoustic, turn the appropriate capstan to loosen the old string so that it isn't under tension, and have a cloth ready to clean the guitar beneath where the string usually sits.

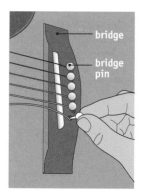

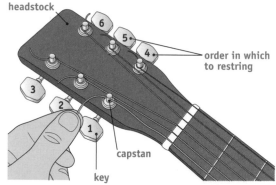

headstock

order in which to restring

capstan

key

1 First pull up the little peg (bridge pin) that holds the string in place. You may need a pair of pliers or wirecutters to do this. Insert the ball-end of the new string into the hole, and replace the pin.

2 Thread the other end of the string tip into the capstan on the headstock, and pull through so that there's about 2 in. (5 cm) of slack. Bend the string to one side, then tighten by winding the key attached to the capstan. Trim the excess with wirecutters, or wind it into a neat loop. If you're changing all the strings at once, begin with the one nearest the neck on the near side and follow the order shown above.

write a Haiku

A haiku is a minimal Japanese verse form consisting of three lines and 17 syllables. Beyond that, everything is entirely up to you.

In Japan, strict rules govern the elements of the haiku. It has to consist of three unrhyming lines of five, seven and five syllables, respectively. There should be "cutting"—a division of the poem into two ideas that contrast and illuminate each other. The haiku should allusively describe a concrete scene or image or event, and it should contain a word, called a *kigo*, that hints at the season in which it's set (the "green" that suggests spring in the example below). Metaphors and personal emotions aren't allowed, though the odd one may creep in. Here's a translation of a classical haiku about a frog:

> *At the ancient pond*
> *A sudden flash of green legs;*
> *The ghost of a splash.*

Some will say you must stick to the classical form, or it's not a haiku. But in poetry you're at liberty to meddle with the form if you feel that the result will be a better poem. So, if you wish, you can give your haiku a title, make it rhyme, use imagery ... Above all, you should feel free to express any feelings or make any point that inspires you.

remove unwanted Hair

If you don't want an expensive salon habit, there are a number of ways to remove unwanted facial and body hair in the privacy of your own home.

Shaving is quick and inexpensive, but it's a temporary solution as it cuts the hair off only at the surface of the skin. When the hair grows back it can be more noticeable, because it has blunt tips rather than a natural taper. Always moisturize first to minimize snagging and razor burn.

Epilators are electrical devices that roll over the skin plucking out hairs, so results are longer lasting than with a razor. They are only moderately expensive, quick and effective. Most are for use on clean, dry skin. Before you start, stroke the hairs against the direction of growth so they stand on end.

Waxing kits for use at home also work by pulling out hairs at the root. Practice on your legs before you try this on more sensitive areas, where waxing may irritate the skin.

Sugaring works on a similar principle to waxing, but is a less messy and more natural method, first used in ancient Egypt. Products are available over the counter. Like waxing, sugaring can irritate the skin.

Depilatory creams dissolve hairs at the skin's surface. They contain harsh chemicals, so always test a new product on a small patch before wider use.

Tweezers are ideal for plucking out stubborn facial hairs and tidying

understand British Hallmarks

Wondering what those marks are on grandma's prized silver from the old country? Here are the basics.

SPONSOR'S MARK (A) There will always be a sponsor's mark, identifying the craftsman who made the object.

STANDARD MARK (B) A standard mark (below) indicates the purity of the metal and the background shape identifies the metal. A lion (on pendant, right) indicates sterling silver, 92.5 percent.

925 Sterling silver   **750** Gold 18 carat   **900** Platinum 90 percent

ASSAY OFFICE MARK (C) This records where the silver was assayed, or checked.

Birmingham   London

Edinburgh   Sheffield

DATE MARK (D) A letter of the alphabet indicates the year of manufacture. The same letters recur every 25 years (J isn't used), but often in minutely altered styles that take years of experience to decipher. Date marks are no longer compulsory.

 2000
 1900
 1800

Together with a reference guide for each Assay Office (or an online search), these marks give you some of the history of any piece of silver, gold, platinum or palladium.

wash your Hands

Thorough washing is vital to prevent the spread of infection. Use liquid soap, not a shared bar, and a clean towel.

■ Wet hands and apply soap. Rub hands together for 15-30 seconds under warm running water, paying attention to fingertips, nails, thumbs and right up to the wrist.
■ Work the hands together, palm to palm, palm to back and fingers interlacing, for as long as it takes to sing "Happy Birthday" twice.
■ Dry thoroughly; moist hands spread germs. Choose clean paper towels over a hand dryer—it may recycle dirty air and take a long time to dry hands thoroughly, encouraging you to walk away without completing the job.

choose and use a Hammer correctly

Make sure you have the right hammer for the job.

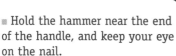

CLUB HAMMER
Good for light demolition work.

CROSS-PEEN HAMMER For nailing in tacks and pins.

CLAW HAMMER For driving nails into wood and removing old nails.

■ Hold the hammer near the end of the handle, and keep your eye on the nail.
■ Tap gently at first to fix the nail in position. For the heavier blows, pivot your arm from the elbow, so that the handle is at right angles to the nail at the moment of impact.

make a great Hamburger

The secret of a good hamburger is to use best-quality lean beef and grind it yourself, in a grinder using a coarse blade or in a food processor. Alternatively, chop it by hand with a large knife, occasionally turning and lifting the meat until it resembles ground beef. Always cook store-bought ground beef until no pink remains.

SERVES 4
1⅔ lbs (750 g) lean ground beef
salt and freshly ground
     black pepper
1 small onion, grated (optional)
½ tbsp oil (optional)
1 tsp mixed herbs
1 tbsp Worcestershire sauce

1 Season the beef. Sweat the onion lightly in heated oil (if using) and add with the herbs and Worcestershire sauce. Mix very well.
2 Using wet hands, form into even-sized patties 1 in. (2.5 cm) thick. Cook under a preheated grill for 4-6 minutes per side or to taste.

plant a Hanging basket

Choose drought-tolerant plants for a hanging basket and add water-retaining gel and slow-release plant food granules to the potting mix to reduce watering. This will let you enjoy months of color with minimal maintenance.

YOU WILL NEED **Hanging basket, bucket, liner, utility knife, trailing plants and some bushy varieties for the top, newspaper, soilless potting mix, filled watering can. Optional: hairpins, moss**

1 Remove the detachable hanging chains, if possible, and stand the basket on top of the bucket. Line the basket with moss, if you have it, then insert the liner: rigid cardboard or flexible cellulose made of felt, jute or other fibers.

2 Starting from the bottom, use the knife to make holes in the lining. If plants are delicate, wrap them in newspaper to protect the stems. Push the plants in roots-first from the outside, filling in with potting mix as you go. Space plants evenly, staggering them in rows.

3 Put the tallest plants in the center at the top, making a depression in the soil around them to help retain moisture. Plant more trailing plants around the rim, using hairpins if necessary, to attach stems to the frame, encouraging them to hang down.

4 Drench the basket with water and allow excess water to drain through. Attach the chains, then hang the basket, taking care not to squash any stems with the chains.

play Hangman

This simple word game is ideal for two to four players and easy for children to learn. You can play it anywhere with only a pencil and paper. Players take turns to be the hangman, who must have a word in mind. Their opponents, condemned to hang, hope to earn a reprieve by guessing the word.

■ The hangman marks out the appropriate number of dashes—for instance, _ _ _ _ _ _ _ _ .

■ The condemned players guess, one at a time, letters that might be in the word. Say the word is GERANIUM and the first suggested letter a vowel, A. The hangman enters it thus: _ _ _ A _ _ _ _ .

■ Say the next suggested letter is a C. With this first wrong guess the hanging begins. The gallows are drawn in bit by bit: base, upright, crossbar, diagonal bar, noose. Then, with each subsequent wrong guess, the hangman adds head, body, one arm, one leg, a second arm —and with the second leg the execution is complete.

■ To help younger players, keep track of wrong guesses and maybe decide on a theme for the game, or a minimum or maximum number of letters.

Winning tip Obscure words and little-used letters can be winners for either hangman or guesser (XEROX would be make or break), but a three-letter word with two letters contained in lots of other words can be a real killer.

cure a Hangover

Nausea, a pounding head, dry mouth, light sensitivity, shame, self-reproach ... It's the morning after the night before!

Rehydrate Alcohol is a diuretic, promoting the production of urine, so drink lots of water to get rid of that furry tongue and headache. Avoid caffeinated drinks, which are also diuretic.

Honey on toast The concentrated sugar in honey converts toxins left in the body from alcohol to acetic acid, which is burned as part of the normal metabolic cycle. Toast adds potassium and sodium, which also help the body to cope.

Eggs for breakfast You might crave a big fried breakfast, but it's the eggs you really need. They contain cysteine, an amino acid that can help to mop up the toxins.

Never again! Of course, the best "cure" is prevention. Try alternating alcoholic drinks with soft drinks or water, and avoid red wine, brandy or whiskey in excess—these contain chemicals known as "congeners" that contribute to the agony the next morning. After drinking, rehydrate with two glasses of water before going to bed.

dazzle with
Hair up-dos
see pages 160-161

dazzle with Hair up-dos

"Up-do" hairstyles have a timeless appeal. Think of Audrey Hepburn's chignon in Breakfast at Tiffany's, *as desirable today as it was in 1961. Not that you need to be up for an Oscar to create a film-star look. If you can manage a ponytail, you can create any of the styles here.*

YOU WILL NEED Natural bristle brush, hairspray, hair elastic, hairpins and possibly a straightening iron. Optional: hair gel or wax, flowers, hair jewels or ornamental combs for embellishment

GET TO KNOW YOUR HAIR

It's easiest to put your hair up the day after it has been washed. Silky, newly shampooed hair can be difficult to work with. If you have just washed your hair, apply gel when it's still damp, blow dry and then mist it with hairspray, in sections, to make it more malleable.

Plan the look Dragging your hair into a tight top-knot can create too severe an effect, so start by experimenting with what best suits you. Study yourself in the mirror as you sweep your hair backward, upward, and downward; choose a flattering line. How will you frame your face? With bangs, half-bangs or none? Stray tendrils, curls or ringlets? Will you go for a side or center part, or sweep your hair straight back? How much height do you want?

Dressy or messy? Practice makes perfect—but imperfections can be part of the charm. Artful dishevelment (below), an off-center "do" and stray ends can lend a more modern look to a traditional style. You can also embellish your hair with flowers, jeweled pins, ornamental combs, or skewer with lacquered chopsticks.

CLASSIC BUN

The style favored by ballet dancers, a formal bun (below left) should be centered on the back of the head, lying flat to it and firmly secured. Trace the line of your cheekbones; the bun will sit on the point where these lines meet.

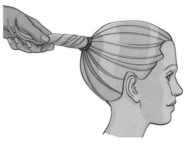

1 Dampen, then smooth the hair and form a ponytail, secured with a hair elastic. Give a couple of twists to the top of the ponytail to form a short section of "rope."

2 Working in the same direction as your twist, start to coil the "rope" around the base of the ponytail. Twist and wrap, twist and wrap, until the hair is all neatly coiled.

3 Tuck the ends under and secure the bun with hairpins close to the scalp.

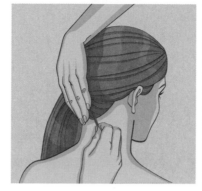

SOPHISTICATED FRENCH TWIST

For a formal occasion, a French twist can be dressed with flowers or jewels along the line of pins. If you prefer, curl the ends of the ponytail and leave them loose, or pin them in loose curls or loops around the crown of the head.

1 Brush the hair completely smooth across to one side at the back, applying a veil of hairspray in the direction that you brush. Use hair pins to grip the hair at the nape of the neck to keep it in place. The twist will come back across these pins.

ELEGANT CHIGNON

The word "chignon" derives from *chignon du cou*, meaning nape of the neck. This soft style is worn low, showing off the neck and shoulders and accentuating cheekbones.

Don't brush the hair too smooth or pull it too tight—a chignon looks best when it's a little loose.

1 Brush your hair and apply a mist of hairspray. Brush it back into a ponytail and secure it with an elastic towards the nape of the neck.

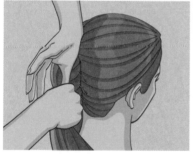

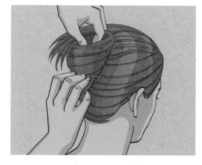

2 Grasp the hair gently, then lay your left thumb against the head and pull the hair over and around it to create a twist. For a twist that lies the other way, use your right thumb.

3 As you twist, use the fingers of the left hand to coil the hair upward. Fix with pins, picking up a little of the twisted hair and pushing pins into the hair under the twist.

2 Divide the ponytail into two and push the hair in each section back up towards the head, as if gently backcombing it to add volume. Twist the two sections around each other in a two-strand "plait."

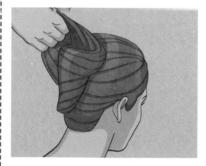

4 Coil the ends of the hair and tuck into the twist then pin to close the loose top of the coil.

5 Lightly brush the surface to smooth any loose hairs. Add more pins to secure and a final fix of spray.

3 Coil the twisted hair around the base of the ponytail in a loose bun at the nape of the neck.

4 Secure the hair with pins as you coil it, then tuck the end back into and under the chignon and pin it all in place.

treat and avoid
Hay fever

This common allergic disorder can be a minor irritation or more severe. Pollen stimulates the production of histamines—one of the body's defenses against infection—leading to streaming noses and puffy eyes.

As hay fever season nears, start taking a daily spoonful of raw (unpasteurized) locally-made honey. Traces of pollen in it can help to desensitize the body.

Reduce exposure to pollen. Keep away from grassy areas and stay indoors with windows closed when the pollen count is high. Damp-dust and vacuum regularly. When you go out, wear sunglasses and keep car windows closed. If you suffer badly, consider fitting a pollen filter to the car's ventilation system. Change clothes and take a shower as soon as you arrive back home.

Spread petroleum jelly inside your nostrils to intercept the pollen.

Eat onions They are rich in quercetin, which is said to help to ward off hay fever.

Try butterbur, a traditional herbal remedy that has been used for centuries and has shown promise in a Swiss clinical trial.

Talk to your doctor about which prescription and over-the-counter treatments might help you. Make sure you tell them about any natural remedies you already take.

If you find no relief, ask your doctor about allergy shots, a highly specialized procedure in which minute amounts of allergens are introduced to accustom the body to them and lessen the allergic reaction they normally trigger.

make a paper Hat

YOU WILL NEED **Double page of a broadsheet newspaper, tape**

1 Fold the newspaper pages back on themselves to form a double layer. Fold in half, top to bottom.

2 Fold the corners in to the middle to form a pointed top and a triangular body for the hat.

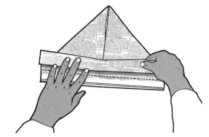

3 Now for the brim. Fold one side of the bottom of the paper up to meet the bottom of the triangle. Fold again so that it overlaps. Turn it over and do the same with the other side. Secure with tape, then pull the bottom of the brim apart. Wear side to side, front to back, or at a rakish angle.

relieve a painful Headache

In a common tension headache, pressure is felt on both sides of the head, sometimes with sensitivity to light and noise. Here's what to do to bring relief, without necessarily having to take a pill.

■ Drink water. A lot of headaches are caused by dehydration.
■ Take a hot shower, letting the water play on your neck and lower back to help to relax tense muscles that may be causing the headache. If this isn't possible, apply a warm washcloth to the forehead or neck.
■ Put a few drops of lavender oil on a handkerchief and sniff it to relax you, or try rubbing peppermint oil onto your neck—it will energize you and help to relieve any congestion that may be causing a sinus headache.
■ Try a drink of coffee, tea or cola. Caffeine will constrict your blood vessels and can relieve an aching head as well as providing a helpful pick-me-up.
■ As a last resort take a painkiller, such as acetaminophen or ibuprofen, but beware overuse of medications and always stick to the stated dose.

recognize and deal with a Heart attack

With a heart attack every second counts, so learn to spot the signs and act at once. A victim is three times more likely to survive if medical help is given within the hour.

Should you call an ambulance? If someone appears unwell and exhibits any of the following symptoms, dial 911 immediately, saying clearly that you suspect a heart attack, or enlist someone else to do so while you stay with the victim. Comfort the victim and monitor their condition while you wait for the emergency services.

Symptoms
■ Vice-like chest pains that may spread to the jaw and down one or both arms, although not all heart attacks are accompanied by chest pain.
■ The patient feels dizzy and faint, and is stricken with panic or a sense of impending doom.
■ Their skin is ashen and clammy, their lips are turning blue and they are gasping for air.
■ Their pulse is weak, racing or erratic.
■ They experience discomfort high in the abdomen or suffer nausea, vomiting or loss of consciousness.

If the victim remains conscious

Help them into a half-seated position with head and shoulders supported, legs raised and knees bent to ease strain on the heart. If possible, support the knees on pillows, cushions or rolled-up coats for comfort.

Loosen clothing at the collar, chest and waist.

Offer reassurance that help will soon arrive. If you're in a public place, call out to see whether there's a doctor nearby who could help, but try to keep intrusive bystanders away from the patient.

Give medication if the victim suffers from angina and has their medication on them. They may need you to help to find their meds and administer them.

Continuously monitor the victim, checking their breathing, pulse and state of consciousness. Don't leave them alone.

continued on next page ➜

deal with
Head injuries

Severe head injuries or a patient who has been knocked unconscious need immediate medical attention. A minor bump, though it may cause mild swelling, bruising, nausea, headache and dizziness, is unlikely to do long-term damage.

Quick action
■ Sit the victim down and give reassurance.
■ If there's swelling at the site, apply an ice pack (*see* CONCUSSION).
■ Bleeding from a scalp wound can be heavy. Place a sterile pad over it and apply gentle pressure for a couple of minutes to staunch the flow. Secure with a bandage wrapped around the head.
■ Avoid excitement and offer acetaminophen as a painkiller (not aspirin or ibuprofen, which can increase the risk of bleeding within the skull). Keep meals light.

Delayed symptoms
■ Keep an eye on the patient for 48 hours for signs of more serious injury: slurred speech, drowsiness, difficulty in writing or understanding, loss of consciousness, seizure, double vision, unequal pupils, loss of balance, weakness, clear or bloody fluid leaking from nose or ear, severe headache or stiff neck, or unusual behaviour.

Be safe, rather than sorry
■ If you're in any doubt following a head injury, seek medical advice.
■ If a child vomits or seems drowsy after a bang on the head, take them to hospital to be checked.
■ Stay off work and rest until you have completely recovered. Don't drive or operate machinery.

relieve the pain of
Heartburn

This common condition occurs when stomach acids pass upward into the esophagus. Try these natural remedies to douse the burning pain.
■ Sip soda water, lemonade or a little baking soda dissolved in water.
■ Try ginger or camomile tea.
■ Suck a peppermint.
■ Chew a small handful of almonds—unsalted, of course.

Over-the-counter antacids will usually relieve a bout of heartburn quickly, but overuse of them has been linked to increased risk of infection, nutritional deficiencies and the very symptoms they are designed to assuage.

To minimize the risk of heartburn avoid eating too much fatty food or chocolate and drinking excessive amounts of alcohol or coffee. Smoking can also be a trigger. Raise the head of your bed, and try to avoid large meals, being overweight, tight waistbands and bending over or lying down after a meal.

See also INDIGESTION.

continued from page 163

If the victim is unconscious
Open their airway, check for breathing and prepare to begin CPR (*see* CPR).

Call for a defibrillator Public buildings may be equipped with an automated external defibrillator (AED), which comes with clear instructions and can deliver a shock to correct an abnormal heart rhythm (ventricular fibrillation or cardiac arrest). Don't be tentative, but trust this smart machine: It will deliver a shock only if necessary. Leave the pads in place until the ambulance arrives, even if the victim seems to be recovering. If an AED is provided there should also be trained staff available.

treat Heat stroke

Heat stroke and its precursor, heat exhaustion, can be fatal. Act immediately to lower body temperature and stop the overheating.

Heat exhaustion occurs when the body's core temperature rises above 98.6°F (37°C). Water and salt levels in the body drop, causing nausea, heavy sweating and faintness. There may also be fatigue, confusion, vomiting and a racing heartbeat. Ultimately, it can lead to organ failure from heat stroke.

■ Get the sufferer to rest in a cool place and give fluids—water or rehydrating sports drinks, but never coffee or alcohol.
■ Loosen their clothing and make sure they have air.
■ Cool them with cold water—a shower or bath, or wet washcloths applied to the skin.
■ Call an ambulance if the person is no better within half an hour. Heat exhaustion can lead to heat stroke.

Heat stroke occurs when the body temperature exceeds 104°F (40°C). Symptoms include rapid heartbeat and breathing, cramps, mental confusion, loss of coordination, anxiety, hallucinations, seizures and unconsciousness. Untreated, it can cause brain damage, organ failure and death.

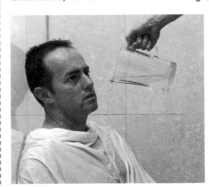

■ Call an ambulance.
■ Move the patient to a cool place. Fan them and give fluids, as above.
■ Shower or immerse the patient in cool (not cold) water, or cover the skin with cool, damp towels.
■ Massage gently to encourage circulation.
■ Be prepared for their condition to deteriorate. *See also* CPR *and* RECOVERY POSITION.

plant a Hedge for privacy and shelter

A hedge, if chosen well, will be an attractive boundary all year round. Always avoid Leyland cypress, which is too vigorous in any domestic setting.

1 Prepare the soil in late summer. Dig deeply and thoroughly, then allow the soil a few weeks to settle. In autumn, buy plants. Water container-grown plants well and soak bare-rooted plants for two hours. Tease out the roots and trim any that are damaged or overlong.

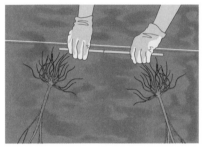

2 Mark the line of the hedge with string. Lay out the plants, spacing them an even distance apart. Use a length of stake to ensure that the spacings are even.

3 Make planting holes and position plants at the same depth as they were growing previously. Firm the soil around each plant and water them. Add a layer of mulch if you wish, to lock in the moisture.

perform the Heimlich maneuver

Otherwise known as an abdominal thrust, the Heimlich maneuver can be a lifesaver for a choking patient if applied correctly.

Use this procedure to expel a blockage in a person's airway that cannot be shifted by pressure applied to the back (*see* CHOKING). If not carried out properly it can cause injury, so this should be seen only as a last resort and should not be used on babies under one year old or pregnant women.

- Stand behind the victim, wrap your arms around them.
- Place a clenched fist just above the navel. Grasp the fist with your other hand and pull sharply upwards and inwards. Don't squeeze the ribs; let your hands do the work. Repeat as necessary.
- If you yourself are choking, lean over a table or chair back and press your abdomen against it to create the thrust.

trim a Hedge

Trimming a hedge in mid to late summer allows new growth to harden off before winter sets in.

- Quick-growing conifers need trimming at about eight-week intervals through the growing season.
- When possible, trim small conifer hedges with shears to avoid cutting across leaf sprays.

Preparation Tie strong string along the hedge on one side to mark the desired height, making sure it's taut and horizontal. Fix the string to long bamboo canes, if you have some tall enough, or to strong stems within the hedge.

Trimming Cut the sides of the hedge with shears or a hedge trimmer using an upward motion. Taper the hedge slightly toward the top. Cut the top to the string level.

golden rules

TIPS FOR A TIDY HEDGE

- Sharpen shears before you begin.
- Trim a wide hedge in two stages, working to the centre from each side.
- Wear safety goggles and gloves when using an electric hedge trimmer and make long, sweeping strokes.

turn up a skirt Hem

Take down and iron flat an existing hem then mark the new length with pins and turn the skirt inside out.

YOU WILL NEED Skirt, tape measure, pins, needle, tacking thread, chalk, scissors, sewing thread

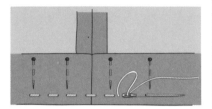

1 Lay the skirt flat, fold up and pin hem at right angles to the edge. Check skirt for length then tack close to the fold (*see* TACK). Remove pins and press.

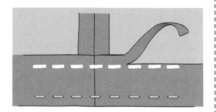

2 Measure and mark with chalk the hem allowance (how deep the hem is): 2¾ in. (7 cm) for a straight skirt, less for a flared one. Trim excess fabric.

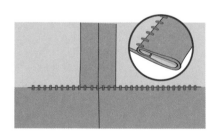

3 Turn the hem edge under ¼ in. (5 mm), iron flat, then hemstitch in place (*see* SEWING). Remove the tacking.

plan and plant a Herbaceous border

Carefully planned and planted, a herbaceous border will give color from spring right through to fall. And if you choose the right plants for your conditions, a border will last for many years.

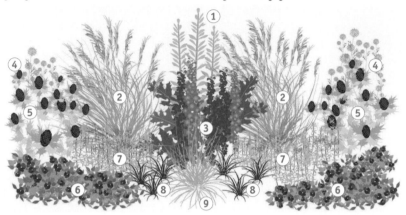

Plan first, plant later To make an impact, a border should be at least 5 ft (1.5 m) deep. Draw a plan before you buy any plants.

■ Even if you want a mixed color scheme, choose a dominant shade or two: pastel lilacs and pinks (good in light shade); hot reds and golds; cool blues and whites; or purples, limes and oranges. Work out how these will link with the seasons and your garden conditions.

■ Start with plants that work well together, using them in groups of odd numbers and repeat patterns along the border.

■ Spring and autumn bulbs set between perennials will add extra color.

1 Bear's breeches
  Acanthus mollis
2 *Miscanthus sinensis* 'Morning Light'
3 *Delphinium* 'Magic Fountains Dark Blue'
4 Globe thistle *Echinops ritro*
5 *Eryngium giganteum*
6 Horned violet *Viola cornuta*
7 *Thymus vulgaris* 'Silver Posie'
8 Lily turf *Ophiopogon planiscapus* 'Nigrescens'
9 *Festuca glauca* 'Elijah Blue'

Don't forget foliage Choose a variety of foliage types, colors and textures from deep to pale green—including variegated leaves—and from smooth and shiny to almost furry. Make use of grasses with textural foliage and consider including a few edible plants, such as cut-and-come-again lettuces or strawberries, plus chives, fennel and other herbs.

Height and impact Put the tallest plants at the back of the border and lower, ground-covering ones toward the front. For an island bed, position the tallest plants in the center. To lead your eye along a long border, use architectural plants and splashes of bright color at intervals.

Planting Enrich the soil with a balanced fertilizer, such as bonemeal, before planting and dig in some well-rotted manure. Insert plants to the same depth as they were growing when they were purchased.

choose Herbs to match food

The distinctive tastes of herbs work well with many foods. Choose the right ones and they will boost flavor, livening up relatively bland ingredients such as pasta, fish and chicken.

Herb	Goes best with	Tips
BASIL	Tomatoes, peppers, eggplant, cheese dishes, pasta, poultry, eggs	Tear immediately before using. Blend with oil, garlic, pine nuts and parmesan for a pesto sauce.
BAY LEAVES	Fish, red meat, game, goose, pâtés, beans, lentils	A pronounced flavor, especially when dried. Best used sparingly.
CHIVES	Leafy salads, potatoes, mayonnaise	Mild onion flavor. Also available in a garlic version.
DILL	Fish, seafood, lamb, cucumber	Mild anise flavor. Best used fresh. Use seeds for a stronger flavor and in breads.
CILANTRO	Curries and all other spiced dishes, salsas	Use stalks as well as leaves for extra flavor. Cook minimally.
MARJORAM	Tomatoes, lamb, pork, poultry, beans and legumes, pasta	Very useful dried. Similar in flavor to oregano.
MINT	Lamb, peas, carrots, potatoes, cucumber	Best fresh. Pour boiling water on fresh leaves for mint tea.
PARSLEY	Fish, poultry, stuffings, vegetables of all kinds, béchamel sauce	Flat-leaved parsley has more flavor. Perfect as a garnish for almost every dish.
ROSEMARY	Fish, lamb, pork, poultry, game, potatoes and other root vegetables	Coarse leaves may need to be finely chopped.
SAGE	Oily fish, pork, duck, cheese, pasta	Dries well, intense flavor. Leaves are delicious fried.
TARRAGON	Fish, seafood, poultry, eggs, mushrooms, mayonnaise	Choose the French variety for best flavor. Buy freeze-dried.
THYME	All meats and fish, tomatoes	Dries well, very versatile.

maintain a
Herbaceous border

Keep a herbaceous border neat with regular deadheading (*see* DEADHEAD). In addition, cut back to their bases the stalks of plants that bloom before midsummer to stimulate a second flush of flowers. Later-flowering plants can be neatened after flowering or left to provide winter interest (where snow doesn't bury the garden) then cut down in spring. Weed regularly. Mulching in spring will suppress weed growth.

Moving plants Autumn and early spring, when plants are dormant, are the best times for moving them, and for lifting and dividing those that have become too large. After being dug up, smaller plants can be pulled apart with your hands. Trim off any damaged or rotten roots and replant. For large, matted perennials, use two forks back to back to separate them once they have been dug up. Cut away any woody shoots and dead roots before replanting.

golden rules

COOKING WITH HERBS
- Add delicately flavored fresh herbs such as basil and tarragon at the end of cooking.
- Use strongly flavored herbs such as sage to cut through the oiliness of foods like pork.
- Use finely chopped stalks of fresh tender-stemmed herbs for an even better flavor.
- Buy herbs in small quantities and use quickly to prevent them from going stale.

stop Hiccups

A sliver of unpeeled lemon dredged with Worcestershire sauce and sugar, chewed and swallowed, is strangely effective. Alternatively, stir a teaspoon of sugar or honey in warm water, hold the mixture on the back of the tongue and then swallow it. If you have no such ingredients, take a deep breath and hold it for as long as you can. Take quick sips of cold water, or try bending over, head down, and drinking from the "wrong" side of a glass. Breathe in and out of a paper (never plastic) bag. See your doctor if hiccups persist for more than 48 hours.

---

walk in
High heels

High heels aren't worn for comfort or practicality, they are designed to make an impression. Learning how to walk in them with style is essential if you want to be noticed for the right reasons.

■ Buy shoes that are a perfect fit—ideally ones that can be firmly strapped to your feet.
■ Begin with lower heels with a thicker base and work up. Keep torturous high heels for "best." If you're going out, wear flat shoes there and back and change when you arrive.
■ Avoid tights or pantyhose that cause your feet to slip in the shoes.
■ Practise at home before braving the outside world. Stand tall; the heels will stop you from falling backward.
■ Keep your legs close together. Take short steps, coming down with a heel-toe motion and placing most of the weight on the ball of the foot. Swing your hips to help you move.

dry Herbs

YOU WILL NEED String, **wire rack, paper towels, airtight storage jars, labels. Optional: microwave**

Air drying Tie in bunches and hang upside down in a dark, dry airy place until leaves snap easily. Or spread sprigs on a wire rack and put in a warm dry place, turning several times for the first two days. Remove leaves by rubbing stems between your hands over paper towels. Store herbs immediately in jars and keep in the dark to prevent flavors

deteriorating. Add a label to each jar identifying the herb for future use.

Microwave drying Place herbs on paper towels and heat gently for about 3 minutes, watching all the time, as some herbs can catch fire. Check dryness after the first minute and then every 30 seconds. Cool before removing leaves.

Strip ripe seeds from herbs such as fennel and dill and air dry on trays following the same method for storing as used after air drying.

---

install a simple Hinge on a door

Mounting hinges is the trickiest part of hanging a replacement door. It requires accurate measuring, and some basic carpentry skills.

YOU WILL NEED Hinges, utility knife, marking gauge, chisel, screws, **screwdriver, shims**

1 If your door is new, you must first cut recesses in which the hinges will sit, matching them with the hinge positions on the door frame. Hold the door against the frame, supporting it on shims, and mark the positions of the hinges. Then hold the hinges in place, and mark around the flap of each with a knife.

2 Set the marking gauge to the thickness of the hinge flap, and use it to mark the depth of the recess required on the edge of the door.

3 Cut around the perimeter of your recess with a sharp chisel, then make a series of cuts about ⅕ in.(5 mm) apart across the grain of the wood. Carefully pare away the waste with the chisel, bevel side downward. Try to leave as level a surface as possible on which to mount the hinge, but take care not to make so many adjustments that the recess becomes too deep.

4 Screw the hinge flaps into the door recesses with just one or two screws.

5 Put the door up to the frame, using shims to support it, open. Screw the free hinge flaps to the recesses in the frame with two screws. Check that the door swings freely. If it does, insert the remaining hinge screws. If it doesn't open or close properly, the hinge positions may have to be adjusted.

make and rescue Hollandaise sauce

A double boiler is ideal for making this variation on mayonnaise, served hot with fish, eggs or vegetables such as asparagus. Béarnaise sauce is similar but flavored with tarragon and served cold with grilled meat or fish.

MAKES 1¼ CUPS

3 tbsp lemon juice or
   white wine vinegar
1 tbsp water
6 black peppercorns

1 bay leaf
3 egg yolks
¾ cup butter, softened
salt and freshly ground
   black pepper

1 Before you start, partly fill a large basin with cold water (see "Rescue the sauce" below).

2 Boil the lemon juice or white wine vinegar, water, peppercorns and bay leaf together until the liquid is reduced to about 1 tbsp. Cool.

3 Cream the egg yolks with 1 tbsp butter and a pinch of salt in an ovenproof bowl. Strain in the lemon juice, set over a pan of barely simmering water and turn off the heat. Whisk in the remaining butter about 1 tsp at a time until the sauce is glossy and has the consistency of thick cream. Season.

Make in a food processor Lightly blend the egg yolks and lemon or vinegar reduction, then pour in melted butter in a thin stream, keeping the motor of the processor running.

Rescue the sauce If the sauce becomes granular or starts to curdle, immediately put the bowl into the basin of cold water and stir vigorously to cool. Or remove from the heat and beat in 1 tbsp of cold water.

Béarnaise Reduce 2 tbsp white wine vinegar and 2 tbsp tarragon vinegar with half a small onion, finely chopped. Cool, then follow step 3 above.

play Hopscotch

This simple playground game can be played by two to four people and requires only some hard ground, a piece of chalk and some stones.

Start by chalking out ten numbered squares in seven rows, alternately made up of a single and then two squares.

As you get better, you can vary the layout of the grid as you like.

Begin to play

■ Give each player a stone to mark their progress.

■ Throw your stone into square 1 and hop over it into square 2. Then proceed to 10 and back, hopping in rows with only one square, putting two feet down in rows with two.

■ Once back at square 2, balance on one foot and retrieve your stone. Then, hop back into square 1.

■ Turn and throw your stone into square 2, then hop directly from 1 to 3, and proceed as before. Next time throw the stone into square 3, then 4 and so on, always hopping over the square with the stone in it.

■ Continue until you put a foot wrong, or your stone misses a square. Then place it on that square and stand down while the next player has a turn.

■ The game gets progressively more challenging, as no player may enter any square with a stone on it. First to claim square 10 is the winner.

repair a garden
Hose

You can temporarily repair a pinhole leak in a rubber hose by jamming a wooden toothpick into the hole, breaking it off flush, and taping over with insulating tape. For a long-term repair, the only effective way is to use a hose repair connector.

■ Disconnect your hose from the tap, and cut through it on either side of the damage with a sharp knife, so that you leave a clean edge on both parts.
■ Fit the connector according to the manufacturer's instructions. Since your connector is going to be permanent, screw the sections together as tightly as possible.

✦ golden rules

HORSE-GROOMING ROUTINE
■ **Always give a quick groom before riding. Dried mud caught beneath a saddle can give your horse sores.**
■ **Have all your grooming tools to hand before you start, but not so close that they could be kicked by the horse.**
■ **Make sure that your horse is securely tethered before you begin your grooming routine.**
■ **Think about safety at all times when handling and grooming the horse.**

groom a Horse

Grooming is not just for show. It ensures a horse's well-being and allows you to check it over for minor injuries. Follow these techniques for horses that live outside or horses that are not clipped.

YOU WILL NEED **Rubber curry comb or grooming mitt, dandy brush, body brush, face brush, clean sponges or soft cloth, plastic mane comb, hoof pick, hoof oil**

1 Start on one side, working down from the neck, using the rubber curry comb (above) or grooming mitt in circular sweeps to loosen dirt, following the direction of the hair. Go gently over bony parts and sensitive spots, such as the belly and between the hind legs. Do the same on the other side. Then use a dandy brush to sweep out the loosened dirt, and a body brush to remove any residues and to smooth the coat.

2 Gently whisk the broader parts of the face, ears and throat clean with the face brush and use it to remove any remaining dust that you missed with the body brush. Clean carefully around the eyes, ears and muzzle with a damp sponge or soft cloth (above).

3 Hold the tail out and up then clean the dock with a damp sponge. Then gently comb out the mane and the tail. If necessary, use the body brush (above) to remove loosened dirt from the mane or tail.

4 Use the hoof pick to scrape out mud and stones, which can cause lameness. Work from heel to toe, as you're less likely to dig into the horny pad in the sole—the "frog." If your farrier recommends it, oil the hooves to prevent cracking.

get started with riding a Horse

Before you get on a horse, you should get into the right clothes; a riding safety helmet that conforms to current safety standards is essential, and it's advisable to wear strong boots and a body protector.

Mounting a horse

As with all riding skills, mounting is best learned at a riding school. If available, a mounting block makes it easier to get on, especially for children and beginners, and puts less strain on the horse. The guidelines below apply whether or not you use a block.

1 Mount from the left. Ensure the girth is tight enough to stop the saddle slipping then take the reins in your left hand just behind the mane. Turn the stirrup (so that it isn't twisted once you're seated) and put the toes of your left foot in.

2 Grasp the pommel at the front of the saddle with your right hand. You'll now be facing the horse's flank, with your left foot up.

3 Spring up off the right foot and swing your right leg over the horse's back (taking care not to kick it by mistake). Land as gently as you can on the saddle and take up the reins.

Sitting on a horse

■ Double-check the stirrup length. Take your feet out and let them hang straight; the bottom of the stirrup iron should be level with your ankles.

■ Once checked, place your feet securely in the stirrups.

■ Make sure you're seated in the deepest part of the saddle.

■ Keep your upper body straight, but not stiff.

■ Hold reins in both hands above the withers, thumbs on top facing forwards.

■ Keep a firm, not tight, pressure.

Walking and halting a horse

TO WALK, squeeze gently with your lower legs. Relax once the horse responds. Be flexible from the elbows, so your arms and hands move back and forth with the nod of the horse's head.

TO HALT, sit up tall, squeeze with your legs, brace the hands and clench your fingers on the reins as if squeezing water out of a sponge. Relax your legs and reins once you've stopped.

---

deal with
Hot flashes

Hot flashes and night sweats are an uncomfortable, at times embarrassing, symptom of menopause. But you can develop practical coping strategies to get you through.

■ Wear lightweight fabrics made from cotton or linen. Avoid silk, synthetics and high-necked tops. Dress in layers so you can shed clothing if necessary.
■ In the morning, try a tepid bath for 20 minutes. Throughout the day, turn the central heating down, carry a small battery-operated fan and have iced water to hand to sip if you feel a flash coming on.
■ Every day, do at least 20 minutes of aerobic exercise (*see* AEROBIC EXERCISE). Its impact on hot flashes is just one of the many benefits. A low-fat diet, over time, and loss of excess weight can also help, but losing too much weight makes symptoms worse.
■ Keep a record of the things that trigger your hot flashes and avoid them, where possible. For instance, caffeine, alcohol and spicy foods are all prime suspects.
■ Stress is another major factor. Anxiety can increase the frequency and severity of hot flashes, so try to relax. Yoga (*see* YOGA), meditation (*see* MEDITATE) and breathing exercises can help to put you back in control.
■ Try drinking soothing sage tea. Many women report that it helps, particularly with night sweats.
■ Before bed take a cool shower, then sleep on cotton sheets in cotton nightwear.

make a
Hot toddy

A roaring fire and a hot drink are just the thing on a bitter winter's night. Pour 1½ fl. oz of whiskey, rum or brandy into a glass or pottery mug. Add a teaspoon of dark-brown sugar, a teaspoon of runny honey, a cinnamon stick, the juice of half an orange or lemon and a strip of pared rind. A toddy may not be a cure for a cold or flu, but it can certainly make you feel better. Sip slowly and let the vapors do their stuff.

treat
Hypothermia

When core temperature drops below 95°F (35°C), the body diverts blood supply from the surface of the skin to the vital organs, leading to hypothermia. In severe cases, a victim may seem confused, lethargic and disorientated, drawing slow and shallow breaths. Their skin will look and feel cold.

Quick action
■ Call 911 and, while you wait, try to warm the person gradually, but don't apply heat directly.
■ Move them quickly to the warmest place available.
■ Remove any wet clothing, dry them and swaddle them in layers of blankets, in particular wrapping head and torso. Hug the person gently to share your own warmth.
■ Provide warm (not hot) drinks and a high-energy food, such as a chocolate bar.

keep Houseplants alive

Houseplants need careful attention, but if you look after them they will reward your investment with years of attractive, healthy growth.

Water Don't overwater (the commonest cause of houseplant death). It kills the roots, making plants collapse. Always let the surface of the soil dry out before watering and allow excess to drain away. Or water from below by standing plants in a bowl of water. Reduce watering to a minimum during winter. Mist regularly in dry conditions, such as in centrally heated rooms.

Temperature Provide stable conditions away from drafts. If necessary, move plants away from open fires or from cold windows at night.

Light and air Bright filtered light, not scorching direct sunlight, is ideal. Foliage plants are best suited to low light levels.

Food Use a store-bought liquid fertilizer from spring through to autumn, while plants are growing actively.

impress with a Hula hoop

Hula-hooping is fun and challenging. It's also a great form of exercise, providing a low-intensity workout, increasing strength and flexibility.

Choose a size and weight of hoop that feels comfortable. It should be between stomach and chest height when you stand it on the floor in front of you. A child's hoop from a toy store is no good for an adult. A large hoop is great for a beginner, as it will spin more slowly, giving you more time to get the feel of the technique.

Getting the hoop habit The aim is to use the momentum of your body to keep the hoop revolving around it. For a great toning exercise, as you become proficient, periodically alternate the direction of spin.

Raise your forearms.

Thrust your hips forward (don't circle them).

Slightly bend and straighten the forward leg to shift your weight.

Keep one foot forward.

■ Stand with one foot a little forward and, with both hands, hold the hoop horizontally against the small of your back.
■ Give it a whirl in your preferred direction to set it in motion and raise your forearms. As the hoop crosses your belly, thrust your hips forward (don't circle them). Round and round goes the hoop as you thrust your hips and belly forward then pull back, slightly bending and straightening the forward leg to shift your weight.

make delicious Ice cream

Homemade ice cream, using the best-quality ingredients, has top-notch taste, is of the highest purity and quality and is easily made by hand—you don't need a special machine.

The classic base for most ice cream is a simple custard (below), with fruit or other flavors added according to taste or what you have on hand. But you can also make quick and easy frozen desserts based on just cream or yogurt (bottom). Try traditional favorite flavors or invent your own combinations.

Vanilla ice cream

SERVES 4-6

2 cups heavy cream
1 vanilla pod, split
½ cup sugar
⅔ cup water
4 egg yolks

Variations Instead of the vanilla pod use 1½ tsp vanilla extract, adding it directly to the cream. Before freezing, add nuts, coffee essence, chocolate buttons or chopped chocolate.

1 Bring the cream almost to the boiling point, remove from the heat and drop in the vanilla pod. Let cool. Scrape the seeds from the pod and leave them in the mixture, discarding the pod itself.

2 Dissolve the sugar in the water and boil until syrupy (it should form threads between finger and thumb when cooled). Whisk the egg yolks in a large bowl, gradually pouring in the syrup, followed by the cream. Pour into a plastic container and freeze for 1-2 hours or until the edges are frozen.

3 Tip the mixture into a bowl and whisk well; this breaks down any ice crystals in the mix. Return to the container and freeze again. Repeat the freezing and whisking twice more until the ice cream is smooth and completely frozen.

Summer fruit ice cream

SERVES 4

1 lb (500 g) mixed berries
   (e.g. blackberries, raspberries)
1 tbsp lemon juice
1½ cups icing (confectioner's) sugar
1¼ cups heavy cream

Variation Substitute full-fat yogurt for half the cream.

1 Blend the fruit, lemon juice and icing (confectioner's) sugar in a food processor until smooth. Press through a nylon strainer into a large bowl. Discard the seeds. Whip the cream to form soft peaks. Fold gently into fruit mixture.

2 Pour into a container and freeze as for vanilla ice cream (above), freezing and whisking in turn.

deal with Ice on paths

In winter, icy paths and driveways can become potentially dangerous skating rinks. You can prevent the ice forming in the first place or take simple measures to clear it.

Start early As soon as snow has settled, or first thing in the morning after an overnight fall, clear your paths. Snow is easier to move when fresh rather than compacted. If the sun comes out it will help to melt any uncovered ice.

Clear the ice
■ If you use water to melt ice, remember it could refreeze and turn into black ice, which is even more hazardous.
■ Chip away at the ice with a shovel and spread salt on any area you have cleared. Ordinary table or dishwasher salt will do, but take care not to spread any on grass or plants or they will be damaged. If you don't have enough salt, you can use sand or ash, though they aren't as effective.
■ Cover cleared paths with more salt, sand or ash before nightfall to give a grip in case of overnight freezing temperatures.

✴ golden rules

ICE CREAM TIPS
■ **Chill all equipment and ingredients before you start.**
■ **If your freezer has a fast freeze setting, use it.**
■ **Measure accurately—too little sugar or cream will make the mixture granular.**

I

protect your Identity

Identity theft is increasingly common. But you can make it harder for the criminals.

■ The misuse of credit card details is one of the most common forms of identity theft, so check credit card statements as soon as you receive them. If there are any unauthorized or inexplicable purchases, inform the card provider immediately and check any other cardit card, bank and online accounts you have.

■ Be suspicious if you're refused a loan despite a good credit history, or if important letters from your bank fail to arrive.

■ Tell the police if you lose any documents that contain your name, address and date of birth—such as your driver's licence or passport.

■ Shred anything containing personal information: official letters, credit card receipts, bank statements and even junk mail.

■ Never give personal information to cold callers, and never, ever give out your PIN over the phone: No one should be asking for it.

■ If you move house, redirect your mail for at least six months and promptly inform your bank and any other financial organizations you deal with, so that all letters go to the right address.

stand and move on Ice skates

When you first put on skates it feels impossible to stand, let alone move. But the knack for it comes quickly, with just a little practice.

How to stay upright Spend a minute or two getting used to your skates before you venture out onto the rink. Stand in them, and walk around in them (if you have covers for the blades). Find your balance. When you're ready, remove the covers and go out onto the ice. Keep a hold of the boards and pull yourself away from the entrance, sliding on your skates as you go. Don't attempt to take normal steps, and don't worry that your grip on the boards is the only thing keeping you upright at this point.

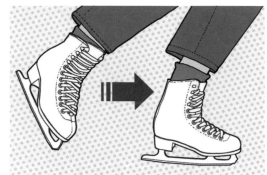

How to make your first move Hold your head up and your body straight, but bend your knees slightly. Position your feet so that they form an inverted T, with your left heel touching your right instep. Shift your weight slightly to the left foot, while digging into the ice with the inside of your right skate. Push off by straightening your right leg—and you'll sail off, slowly and, with luck, gracefully across the ice.

treat painful Indigestion

You could take an antacid, but there are also some simple, natural remedies that can swiftly ease your discomfort.

Drink a cup of herbal tea The warmth itself will be soothing, but the herbs you choose will also have an effect. Try ginger, which has long been used to relieve the bloating and flatulence that can make indigestion so uncomfortable. Peppermint and camomile teas are also good choices.

A tablespoon of apple-cider vinegar in a glass of water, sipped slowly, can also bring relief—especially when taken with a meal.

For better digestion, naturally, take a regular probiotic supplement of beneficial bacteria, including *lactobacillus* and *Bifidobacterium* to inhibit the growth of harmful bacteria in the gut. Avoid big, rich, spicy meals, don't bolt your food and try to avoid eating too late at night. If you smoke, quit, and keep your alcohol consumption at a moderate level (*see* ALCOHOL).

put Insomnia to bed

Sleeping pills may knock you out, but they provide poor-quality sleep, may stay in your system in the daytime, encourage dependency and don't get to the root cause of your wakefulness. Try these drug-free solutions instead.

Stress and worry can come between you and your sleep, so address these first, with simple relaxation techniques or a course of cognitive behavioral therapy (*see* STRESS *and* RELAXATION).

Get daily exercise—but not within four hours of bedtime. This helps to combat stress and encourages restful sleep.

Adopt a bedtime routine and don't take daytime naps. A warm bath and a milky drink or camomile tea before going to bed can help to make you drowsy.

Avoid watching the clock and fretting as the minutes—and hours—tick by. If it takes you more than 30 minutes to drift off, get up and go to another room. Read or watch television for a while. Write down your worries and possible resolutions then put them from your mind until morning.

Address the fundamentals: peace, quiet and comfort. Choose a mattress and pillows that allow you the best sleeping posture (*see* MATTRESS *and* PILLOWS), have freshly laundered bedding, put up heavy curtains to exclude the light and use earplugs if noise is a problem. *See also* SLEEP.

Insulate water pipes

There are two types of protection—tubing and wrap—that provide good insulation for pipes. Never leave a joint or corner exposed; these are the points most likely to freeze—and burst—in a cold snap.

Snap-on foam tubing is the quickest and simplest choice for lagging straight runs of pipe. The insulation is made to fit standard diameters of pipe and is slit along its length so that you just need to cut it to length and snap it onto the pipes. Make neat, notched joints with a knife at corners and T-junctions (right), and wrap the joints in insulation tape to keep them closed.

Self-adhesive foam wrap is good for pipes that have lots of bends or are otherwise difficult to clad in tubing. Wrap the foam round the pipe like a bandage with a generous overlap of about a third of the width of the wrap. Be sure to wrap valves as you go, leaving only the handle or turn screw exposed so that it can still be operated.

protect against Infections

Frequent hand-washing is the single most important factor in combating the spread of infectious diseases (*see* HANDS). Throughout the day, as you open a door, exchange money, pet a dog, handle raw food, flush the toilet, tap the keyboard and answer the phone, you pick up and spread germs, which can infect you if you then touch your eyes, nose or mouth. Much of this is unavoidable, but good hygiene can help to protect you from infection.

Try not to sneeze into your hands and, if you do so, wash them immediately. Be cautious about shaking hands with someone who obviously has a cold; be sure not to touch your face until you have washed.

At home, respect the rules of basic food hygiene (*see* FOOD), and avoid restaurants that you suspect of poor hygiene practices.

Hospitals are breeding grounds for viruses and bacteria. Always use the alcohol-based hand sanitizers provided on arrival and leaving. Don't visit a patient if you have sickness or diarrhea; unwell people are particularly vulnerable to infection.

Your immune system is your first line of defense against disease, so give it the best fighting chance by adopting a good diet (*see* DIET) and getting regular exercise (*see* AEROBIC EXERCISE).

protect children on the
Internet

Take these simple steps to make the web a safe place for your children to explore.

■ Have your computer somewhere in the house where you can keep an eye on it, and on anyone using it. There's no substitute for in-person parental supervision.

■ Monitor your children's internet use by checking the "History" function in your web browser. This is a complete list of all the sites that have been accessed recently. Bear in mind that a reasonably adept user (that is, any teenager) will know how to disable or edit the History list.

■ Make use of the "Content Advisor" that comes with Windows. From the **Start** menu, open the **Control Panel**. Select **Network and Internet** then **Internet Options**. In the Internet Properties dialogue box click on the **Content** tab, then the **Enable** button under Content Advisor. Click the **Ratings** tab and use the slider to set a level of access that excludes categories such as nudity, depiction of weapon use and so forth. You'll be asked to create a supervisor password so that only you can amend the settings.

■ Many internet browsers have a built-in content filter, but you can also buy software such as Net Nanny and Cyber Patrol that filters inappropriate content, blocks access to chat rooms, and creates an activity log that only the approved supervisor can access. Some such programs can be installed on internet-enabled mobile phones.

Insulate your attic

Good attic insulation is essential to keeping valuable heat inside your house in winter—and keeping it out at the height of summer, too. Your insulation should be at least 8½ in. (about 220 mm) thick.

Choosing insulation The quickest and easiest type of attic insulation to use is blanket roll. Sold in widths that match the standard gaps between joists, the insulation is rolled out in the attic and cut to length; it can also be laid at right angles to the joists. It comes in different thicknesses.

■ Of utmost importance is an insulation's R-value. The higher the R-value, the warmer the home. An R-28 will usually be 8½ in. (220 mm) thick, while at the upper end, R-49 is about 16 in. (280 mm) thick.

■ Blown-in insulation is another good solution. This style of insulation comes in large plastic bags, and must be put into a special blowing machine before being installed via a forced-air hose.

YOU WILL NEED **Scissors or utility knife, face mask, protective gloves, rolls of insulating blanket**

The fibers in plain insulation can irritate the skin, so wear a mask and tuck your sleeves into gloves, and trousers into socks. Only open the packaging in the attic, and do all the cutting there, to minimize the spread of fibers.

1 Start at one end of the attic, leaving a gap of about 2 in. (5 cm) in the eaves for ventilation. Unroll the blanket between two joists, pressing lightly so that it lies flat. Don't squash it down, as this will reduce the insulation's heat-isolating effect.

2 Cut the roll as necessary, butting the ends up tight against each other when making a join.

3 Keep cables above the insulation so that they don't overheat, but water pipes below it, to keep them warm. Never insulate under the cold-water tank, or it will be more likely to freeze in winter, but do stick a square of insulation on the attic hatch.

pay safely on the Internet

Buying products over the internet can be quick, easy, convenient and perfectly safe, so long as you follow a few golden rules.

Check out the website that you're planning to buy from. Look for a link entitled "Contact us" or something similar, and make a note of the physical address or phone number. Call the number and see if anyone answers. If the page only gives an email address, send a short message; if it's a genuine and reputable site, someone should respond to your query promptly.

The payment process should take place on a secure webpage. Look at the address; it should begin with the letters https rather than just http. In Windows 7 you should also be able to see a padlock symbol at the top of the page; double-click on it to see the site's security certificate. Avoid any sites without a certificate or where the certificate has expired.

Check the delivery times and costs before you commit. The postage and handling costs might negate any saving you're hoping to make by buying on the internet, or you may have a long wait for delivery.

Pay for big items by credit card for the consumer protection that your card issuer provides. For small transactions, use "electronic cash" with an e-cash account. PayPal is the best known and most universally accepted.

---

make a success of Internet dating

The internet is a marvellous way to meet people when you're looking for love or simply companionship. Be sure that you make the most of its potential and avoid the possible pitfalls.

Post a photo Most people will be keenly interested in what you look like and you'll have a much better response rate if you make a picture available. Choose one in which you look your best, and make it a recent and honest headshot (not a snap of you sitting in your friend's Ferrari ten years ago).

Craft a good statement All sites allow you to write something about yourself. Be reasonably open and frank, and make it meaningful. *I love cooking for my friends—especially Thai food* ... tells others about your interests and the kind of person you are. Avoid clichés like *I enjoy candlelit dinners or I'm a glass-half-full person*, as they are unlikely to set you apart from others. Similarly, steer clear of bald statements, like *My friends say I have a good sense of humor.* It's much more telling if you prove your humor through the information you give and the way you give it.

Stay close to home There's no point in striking up an online friendship with someone who lives at the other end of the country; remember, the aim is to find someone you can have a real relationship with.

Get together If the signs look good, meet up for a drink (rather than a meal—save that for the second date). Even if romance doesn't spark, you might end up enlarging your circle of friends, which itself increases the odds that you'll meet someone you want to be with.

Be careful Meet your new date in a public place, and don't accept an offer of a lift, especially to or from your home. Always tell a family member or friend where you're going to be and what time you expect to be home, and make sure your cell phone is fully charged so that you can make contact if you need to. Avoid the temptation to drink too much—you need to like the person sober. If you're at all uncomfortable, make your excuses and leave.

carry out an effective Internet search

When looking for information on the internet, your aim should be to define your search as narrowly as possible to generate the best and most appropriate results.

Use four or five key words If you're looking to find a store in your area that sells Fender guitars, for instance, it's not enough to type the words "guitar" and "store," as you'll get suggestions of shops all over the world. Try something that better defines your wishes, such as: "Fender guitar retailer Boston."

Use quotes If you put double quotes around a phrase, the search engine will prioritize hits where those words occur together. This is useful if you want something with a specific name—a 1973 Fender Jazz Bass, for example. Put exactly that in double quotes: "1973 Fender Jazz Bass". Quote marks are helpful if your search naturally takes the form of a phrase—a line of a poem you want to identify or the title of an out-of-print book you want to find.

Exclude words Sometimes a search can be overwhelmed by sites that contain the right word in the wrong context. If you're searching for a guitar shop in Boston, you'll get lots of hits, for both Boston, Massachusetts, and Boston, Lincolnshire. You can hone your search by adding words you don't want and putting a minus sign in front of them, for example, "-Lincolnshire,"or "-Massachussetts," and any other variations, such as "-Mass" and "-MA".

I

Introduce people to each other

Provide names to both of the people being introduced, and explain who they are—just enough information to kick off a conversation. Your primary aim is to put people at ease, but there are some etiquette conventions to follow.

■ Always introduce a man to a woman: *Jane Brown, I would like to introduce Jack Black.*
■ The older or more senior person should "receive" the younger. *Dad, this is my former French teacher, John Stewart; John, this is my father, Harry Smith.*

----

send and reply to Invitations

■ Make sure that any invitation, however informal, contains all the vital information: the name of the host; the nature of the occasion; the time, date and venue (including directions or a full address and postal or ZIP code); a time that the event finishes; an address, phone number or email for RSVPs; and any special information, such as a dress code or request to bring something.
■ Include the names of all invitees, and make it clear whether children are invited too. If you're inviting friends by email or through Facebook, take extra care not to invite the wrong people by mistake.
■ For big events, send invitations 10-12 weeks in advance. Include an RSVP date to give you time to invite more people if some decline.
■ If you're replying to an RSVP be prompt, especially if the occasion is something formal, like a wedding, that requires a lot of planning.

conduct a job Interview

Your job as an interviewer is to allow interviewees to make a case for themselves and get them to reveal something of their personality.

Set the tone and take control Explain the purpose of the interview and give an indication of how long it will last. Introduce yourself and anyone else who is taking part by name. But don't speak for too long at the start; get the interviewee involved as soon as possible.

Ask open-ended questions A good question is *What would you say has been your finest achievement?* This allows candidates to showcase their strong points, while their manner when answering will give you a good idea of what they are like, what qualities they value and how articulate they are.

Keep your responses neutral Encourage the candidate with occasional nods of the head. Be interested and try not to look surprised by any of the interviewee's responses.

Record the interview It's hard to take notes and stay engaged with the interviewee. If a sound recording isn't possible or appropriate, have someone on hand to take detailed notes for you.

Make notes afterwards As soon as the interviewee leaves, jot down a few thoughts while the impression of that person is still fresh in your mind.

----

perform well in a job Interview

Preparation is the secret of making a good impression at an interview. Be sure of your facts and confident in your abilities.

Prepare yourself Think about why you're qualified for the job, and write down your strong points. Identify triumphs and successes from previous jobs, and be ready to talk about them succinctly and convincingly.

Practise your interview technique If possible, get a friend to conduct a trial interview with you and give you honest feedback.

Know the firm Read up on the company that you're applying to work with and, if possible, talk to people who already work there. Then you can tailor your responses to the way the company works and ask relevant questions.

Sell yourself on the day Smile, maintain eye contact and a relaxed pose, be courteous and speak clearly. Remember the interviewer's name and use it.

Remember some critical "Don'ts" These all-too-common pitfalls could cost you the job, but are easy to avoid.

■ Don't be late. No excuse is good enough to counteract the bad impression this makes.
■ Don't dress casually. If anything, dress more smartly and formally than you would in a normal work situation.
■ Don't be overly familiar. You won't get the job by trying to make friends.

save battery life on your iPhone

Your iPhone may be carrying out lots of little tasks that you don't require. Turn off these functions, and your battery will last longer between charges.

■ Disable "push notifications" on applications. These alert you to things going on within your applications ("apps") that might be of interest to you. If you turn them off you'll still get the information when you open the app.
■ Check for mail less frequently. Set the default to check hourly.
■ Lock your phone. Put your iPhone to sleep whenever it's not in use, and set the Auto-Lock function to the shortest possible time.
■ Turn down the brightness. Keep the screen as dim as you can manage.

remove scratches from your iPod

The iPod is a desirable object that gets a battering with day-to-day use. There are steps you can take to restore some of its original gloss.

■ Always use a soft, dry, lint-free cloth to avoid making more scratches as you clean. Polish regularly to remove the lightest scratches.
■ Some people recommend banana or toothpaste to remove scratches, but you'll get the best results with store-bought cleaning products.
■ Scratch removers work by rubbing down the surrounding area to the depth of the scratch, so deep scratches can only be removed with very abrasive products that could damage the rest of the device.

Protect your Touch The iPod Touch relies on the sensitivity of its screen, so fit an adhesive screen protector as soon as you take it out of the box. They are sold in packs of 12, so that you can replace them as they get scratched.

Earlier iPods, with the clickwheel interface, are fast becoming design classics—and so are worth looking after. Buff the back gently with Brasso but use a store-bought cleaning fluid for the front.

unfreeze an iPod

If your iPod Touch freezes or crashes, the problem is likely to be with an application rather than the iPod itself. For a classic iPod, try turning it off and on again to reboot the software.

■ Try to force-quit the current application by pressing and holding the sleep/wake button for a few seconds, then pressing and holding the home button when the red slider appears.
■ If that doesn't work, the time-honoured method of turning the device off and on again should do the trick. If not, you can "reset" an iPod Touch (and an iPad, too) by holding down both the sleep/wake and the home button for at least 10 seconds, until the Apple logo appears.

compile an iTunes playlist

In iTunes, it's easy to make manual playlists for different moods and occasions by selecting albums or individual songs and dragging them into folders. But you can also use iTunes to generate other kinds of playlists for you.

Smart Playlist In iTunes, go to **File** then select **New Smart Playlist**. Here you can set search parameters, such as artist, year or genre, and iTunes will compile the songs in your library that fit the bill.
  Smart Playlist can be set to exclude all sound files that aren't actually music (such as podcasts or audio books). You can set the "Last Played" option to exclude any songs that you've listened to in the last week or month, or tag songs according to categories of your own (party favorites, music for jogging) so that you always get the right sounds for the occasion.

Genius The iTunes "Genius" function automatically generates playlists from the songs in your library. Choose one track and Genius finds other similar songs, and also makes recommendations of songs that you might like to purchase.

remove lids from Jars

If a jar lid seems to have been welded on, wear rubber gloves or try placing a rubber band around the lid rim to give yourself a better grip.

Still no luck? Run hot (not boiling) water over the lid for 20 seconds, directing the stream onto the center rather than the rim so that it expands a lot more than the glass. Dry it off and try again.

- Three good whacks to the base of the jar with the heel of the hand can break the vacuum seal.
- Alternatively, try inverting the jar and banging it (not too hard) on the countertop, or tapping around the side of the lid with the handle of a knife to loosen the seal.

golden rules

MAKE GREAT JAM
- Avoid using moldy or over-ripe fruit.
- Warm the sugar before use to speed dissolving.
- Wash and sterilize jars and lids before using them (*see* STERILIZE).
- Fill jars as full as possible and put on lids when jam is still hot to reduce the risk of condensation, which encourages mold.
- Label and date jars before storing in a cool, dark place.

make great Jam

Jam is often made using equal weights of fruit and sugar, but the secret of a good set is pectin, a natural fruit sugar.

Fruit such as apples, red currants and plums are pectin-rich and can be added in small quantities to low-pectin fruits such as strawberries and raspberries. Alternatively, you can add lemon juice or jam sugar (it has pectin added), or use ready-made pectin powder or liquid, following the instructions on the label. A preserving pan, sugar thermometer and a wide-necked funnel for filling jars are good investments if you make jam regularly.

YOU WILL NEED **Jam ingredients, preserving pan or large heavy-bottomed saucepan, sugar thermometer, saucer, skimming spoon, ladle, sterilized jars, canning lids or waxed disks, labels. Optional: wide-necked funnel**

Raspberry jam

MAKES 4 X 1-PINT (500 ML) JARS

2 lbs (1 kg) raspberries
2 lbs (1 kg) granulated or gelling sugar, warmed in a low oven
¼ cup lemon juice (if not using gelling sugar)

1 Put the fruit into a preserving pan. Add the lemon juice (if using) and heat gently until the juices run. Simmer until the liquid is reduced by about a third. Add the sugar and boil rapidly for about 20 minutes until the setting point is reached (220°F/104°C on a sugar thermometer—see right).

2 To test for set, put a teaspoon of jam onto a cooled saucer. If the skin crinkles when pushed with a finger, it's ready.

3 Quickly skim off any scum with a skimming tool or spoon then ladle into warm, sterilized jars. The jam can be covered with waxed disks (wax side down) if you wish.

make Jelly

Jelly is both a preserve and a dish made with gelatin or agar. Preserves are an excellent way of using summer and fall soft fruits, including blackberries and apples, and are well worth the effort of straining the juice. As a dish, dessert jelly is a traditional and easy-to-make favorite.

Preserve jellies Jelly is best made in small quantities, no more than can be accommodated in one jelly bag. A purpose-made bag (right) is ideal for straining, but you can make one yourself from a piece of cheesecloth.

Red currant jelly

MAKES 4 X 1-CUP JARS

2 lbs (1 kg) currants, including stalks, rinsed
1 cup water
granulated sugar (see recipe for amount required)

YOU WILL NEED **Jelly ingredients, preserving pan or large heavy-bottomed saucepan, bowl, jelly bag and stand (or equivalent), measuring jug, saucer, skimming spoon, ladle, sterilized jars and lids, labels. Optional: wide-necked funnel, sugar thermometer, waxed disks, cellophane covers, rubber bands**

1 Put the fruit into a preserving pan with the water. Simmer for about 30 minutes. Strain into a bowl overnight through a jelly bag suspended on a purpose-made stand or an improvised alternative such as an upended stool. Measure the juice into a jug and allow 1 cup sugar for every cup.

2 Reheat the juice until nearly boiling, stir in the sugar and boil rapidly until setting point is reached (*see* JAM). Pour into jars, label and store.

Dessert jellies Strained fruit juices make an ideal base for jelly. They can be used alone, with wine or spirits added, or with cream to give a slightly denser texture. Dessert jellies are made with the animal extract gelatin or with agar, a vegetarian alternative derived from seaweed.

Gelatin comes as powder or sheets. If using powder, allow 1 tbsp per 2½ cups of liquid for a firm set. Sprinkle into a little cold water in a heatproof bowl and leave, without stirring, until spongy. Set over simmering water and stir until dissolved. Add to warm liquid. If using sheets, remember that six sheets equal 1 tbsp of powder. Soak in cold water for 15-20 minutes until soft. Squeeze lightly to extract surplus water, and add to the amount of liquid recommended by the recipe you're using. Let stand in a bowl over hot water and heat, without boiling, until the gelatin has dissolved.

Agar tends to set more firmly and at a higher temperature than gelatin. Always check the package for advice on quantities and method.

beat Jet lag

■ Don't drink alcohol on the flight and avoid caffeine too. But drink lots of water while you're airborne.
■ If you're flying while it's nighttime at your destination, do all you can to sleep. Use an eyeshade and earplugs, and turn the cold air to high; a cooler temperature tells your body it's night.
■ When it's daylight where you're going, try to stay awake—in sunlight if you can.
■ Switch to local time as soon as you can if you're staying more than a day or two. Stay up until local bedtime, and don't take an afternoon nap.
■ Eat carbohydrates before bed when you arrive. Food such as pasta helps you to sleep.
■ Eat eggs for breakfast. The protein will help you through that first day in a new time zone.
■ Get some exercise; a swim, or jog in the hotel gym, will encourage natural sleep.

clean Jewelry

For diamonds and hard stones such as rubies and emeralds, if settings are secure, use dish soap and soak for ten minutes in hot, sudsy water in a small bowl. Use an old toothbrush to remove ingrained dirt around settings. Rinse, then dry with a soft cloth.

For soft stones such as opals and coral, wipe with a silk cloth but never wash.

For pearls and strung beads, wipe after each wearing with a barely damp, really soft cloth. Very occasionally, wash quickly in mild soap suds in lukewarm water. Rinse, then dry with a soft cloth.

J

tell a funny Joke

Telling a joke is like singing a song: it requires rhythm and a confident delivery—and you have to know the whole thing from start to finish.

Don't spoil the joke before you start If you've just said *You know that joke where it turns out he's the old lady's butler?* then don't bother telling it. And don't begin by saying *I know this really hilarious joke*—a phrase guaranteed to make everyone's heart sink.

Have your joke down pat If you find yourself saying things like *Oh, I should've said earlier that the second man had an ostrich on a leash ...* then your joke is already dead and buried.

Don't laugh at the joke yourself— at least until you've got the punchline out. Laughing at all is poor form, but giggling just as you get to the best bit wrecks the timing, and may mean that nobody hears the payoff line.

Don't recycle half-remembered incidents from *The Simpsons*, *Seinfeld* or any other TV show. They are not jokes and, however funny they were to watch, it will be torture to listen to your retelling.

Know your audience A joke that was hilarious in the bar with your friends may clang like a cracked bell at lunch with the in-laws.

If all else fails, and all your jokes seem old and tired, make that the point of your joke. *A wrestler, a bald priest and a piece of string walk into a bar. The bartender takes one look and says, "Sorry, but is this some sort of joke?"*

do the Jive

This dance developed from the jitterbug and boogie woogie. It should be performed with great verve, with legs pumping, the music loud and the dance sassy.

The basic count of six beats begins with a "rock step" (beats 1 and 2), followed by two triple steps that are counted 3-a-4, 5-a-6. Put on a CD of jive music (such as Elvis Presley's "Hound Dog" or Dion's "Runaround Sue") and feel the beat. Study the steps described below and count them in time to the music. When you have them fixed in your mind, start the music again, get up and rock around the clock till it's broad daylight.

Starting position Stand facing each other. The man takes his partner's right hand loosely in his left, holds it aloft, and leads her through the steps shown below. As she follows, her every step mirrors his; if the man steps back with his left foot, the woman also steps back, but with her right, and so on.

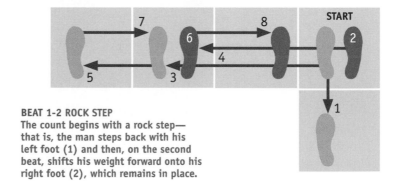

BEAT 1-2 ROCK STEP
The count begins with a rock step— that is, the man steps back with his left foot (1) and then, on the second beat, shifts his weight forward onto his right foot (2), which remains in place.

BEAT 3-a-4, 5-a-6 THREE SIDE CHASSÉS
There's now a gliding three-step sequence. The man chassés to the left—that is, sidesteps with his left foot (3). He then brings his right foot across next to his left (4).
He takes another sidestep to the left with his left foot (5). Then he shifts his weight back onto his right foot (6).
Finally he sidesteps to the right with his left foot (7) and then sidesteps to the right with his right foot (8).

Advanced When you have perfected these steps, try adding the spins so characteristic of this dance. Start with one or both partners performing a spin instead of a second chassé. If only one partner spins, the other should complete the second chassé as usual but keep their sideways movement to a minimum.

master some essential Judo moves

Judo is a combat sport, a form of wrestling derived from the Japanese martial art of jujitsu. Your aim is to win by throwing or immobilizing your opponent, while defending yourself from attack.

Safe landings Before you learn to win at judo, you should learn how to lose at judo—that is, you need to know how to fall when you're thrown. This is the first thing that you'll be taught if you join a judo class. The essence of the "breakfall," as it's known, is to roll rather than hit the mat flat.

Keep your chin tucked in, so that you don't strike the back of your head against the floor.

Use your arms to strike the mat before you hit the ground, and so absorb some of the impact.

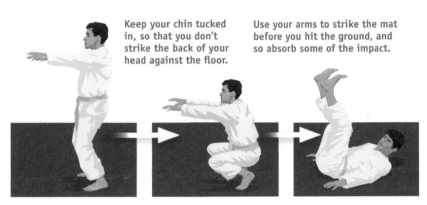

Learning to throw There are many effective ways of throwing an opponent. But in competitive judo you're aiming not merely to land your opponent on the mat, but to do so with good technique, since this is what wins points. *Osoto-gari* is one of the basic judo throws.

1 Pull downward on your opponent's right sleeve with your left hand, while using your right hand to push on their left shoulder.

2 Swing your right leg behind your opponent's. Use your forward motion to push with your arms and unbalance your opponent.

3 As your opponent's left leg lifts, rotate your body so that your opponent falls swiftly and unstoppably on their back.

Winning the bout A controlled throw that lifts an opponent off their feet and onto their back scores an *ippon*—a full point—and the match is won. There are other ways of scoring an *ippon*: knocking your opponent on their back, pinning them for 25 seconds, or applying an armlock or a stranglehold. **Armlocks and strangleholds can be dangerous;** they should only be performed by experienced *judoka* (judo fighters).

---

learn to Juggle

Stand with your back against a wall to discourage a tendency to move forward. The pattern should be an arc, not a circle, with balls crossing paths in the air.

1 Hold your hands at waist level, and start by tossing a single ball from one hand to the other, cresting at eye level, and allowing it to plop down into your palm. As you toss it back and forth the ball should always describe the same arc.

2 When this exercise is second nature, bring another ball into play. Toss the first ball from one hand and, as it loops at the top of its arc, toss the other one from the other hand. Pause. Do the same thing in reverse. Practice to make perfect.

3 Add a third ball. Hold balls 1 and 3 in the hand you favor (usually the right) and ball 2 in the other (left). Launch ball 1, cross it with ball 2 and catch ball 1. As ball 2 reaches its high point, launch ball 3. As ball 3 reaches its high point, send ball 1 left to right Catch 3 in your left hand, and so on.

prepare Kabobs

Any meat, fish or vegetables suitable for broiling will make good kabobs, which can also be barbecued. Or try fruit brushed with melted butter and sprinkled with sugar for an unusual dessert. Marinating ingredients before cooking adds greatly to their flavor and tenderness.

Choose ingredients that will complement each other in terms of their taste (sweet pepper with salty pork) and texture (crunchy onion with succulent beef). Three or four ingredients is usually plenty.

Prepare a marinade based on an acidic ingredient, such as tomato, vinegar or lemon juice, which helps to tenderize the meat or fish. Add other ingredients for their flavor, such as garlic, fresh ginger, olive oil, sherry, brown sugar or soy sauce. Place cubes of meat or fish in the marinade, cover and leave to stand in a refrigerator for at least 30 minutes—or even overnight.

Before cooking remove the meat or fish from the marinade and thread onto skewers, interspersing the fruit or vegetable ingredients as you do so. While cooking, brush the remaining marinade on the kabobs to keep them moist. Make sure the meat is cooked through and then serve immediately.

golden rules

PREPARE KABOBS
- **Soak wooden skewers for 20-30 minutes before using so that they don't burn.**
- **Cut ingredients into chunky equal-sized pieces to ensure even cooking.**

understand the principles of Karate

Students of karate learn to channel their own or an opponent's energy to maximum effect—in order to deliver a powerful blow or unbalance that opponent.

Karate is a form of self-defense that has an almost balletic grace. If you take up karate, you'll spend a great deal of time performing *katas*, set sequences of fight moves that, to an outside observer, look like a rather warlike dance routine. The purpose of the *katas* is to teach you to concentrate all the energy you can muster into fight-winning blows. The idea at the core of karate is that a strong strike, delivered with precision to the weakest points on an opponent's body, can make a decisive difference. By applying this approach, a smaller, physically less powerful protagonist can overcome a much larger, stronger enemy. However, in modern karate the focus is more on discipline, self-control, fitness and confidence than in actual self-defense.

Making an impact One way to make a strike as strong as it can be is to reduce the area of impact, so that the force of the blow is concentrated in a small spot. To this end, karate practitioners (*karatekas*) recognize certain "points of contact," which are the weapons in the practitioner's armory; the knifehand, often termed the "karate chop," is perhaps the best known. *Karatekas* also stress the importance of following through the blow beyond the moment of contact, and they practice resisting the temptation to pull punches (hence the spectacular feats of smashing tiles or planks with the hand or forehead).

Positive energy When you practice karate, you should think about your opponent's power as well as your own. You must learn to block intelligently and effectively, so as to deflect blows aimed at you. You can also use an opponent's energetic movement against them, to tip their balance and topple them over. When karate is practiced as a sport (as it usually is) all these skills are honed through *kumite*, or freestyle sparring, in which two *karatekas* fight—but deliberately avoid making contact with their blows.

retrieve a broken Key

This method can be used for the locks found on car doors and for the cylinder locks on front doors.

- Spray the lock with aerosol lubricant (not generally recommended for cylinder locks—but this is an emergency).
- Insert a thin piece of fretsaw blade into the keyhole. Position the blade so that its serrated teeth are pointing back toward you.
- Maneuver the blade so that its teeth catch on the notches in the key, then gently pull back to draw the key out slightly.
- As soon as a small part of the shaft is protruding, use needlenose pliers to get hold of it and extract it from the lock.

make a simple paper Kite

This simple paper kite costs next to nothing and is quick to make. You could have liftoff within 15-20 minutes.

YOU WILL NEED **Sheet of letter paper, tape, wooden skewer (about 10 in./ 25 cm long), ribbon, hole punch, ball of fine string**

1 Lay the sheet of paper on a work surface in front of you with the long sides at the top and bottom, fold it in half from right to left, and make a firm crease down the middle.

2 Rotate the paper so that the folded edge is facing you. Make a diagonal fold so that two triangles of paper protrude from beneath the folded section, one about four times larger than the other. Make a firm crease.

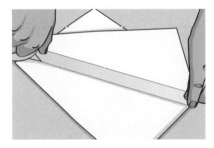

3 Turn the paper over and unfurl one leaf of the uppermost folded section. Apply tape along the join revealed to create the spine of your kite.

4 To hold the wings in place on either side of the spine, tape the wooden skewer across the widest section of the paper at right angles to the spine.

5 Tape the ribbon to the bottom of the spine, then turn the kite over. The fold of paper beneath the wings is the kite's keel. Fold it back and forth so that it stands at right angles to the wings.

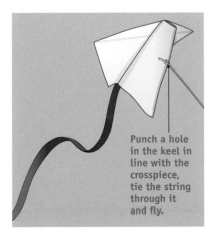

Punch a hole in the keel in line with the crosspiece, tie the string through it and fly.

fly a Kite

Find a wide open space, a safe distance from roads or power lines and well away from hills, trees and buildings, which cause turbulence.

How much wind a kite needs depends on its design. Heavy kites require more wind to get off the ground. Some are made especially to fly in light wind, but most are designed for average wind speeds. If you can feel wind in your face, or see fluttering leaves, there should be enough puff to launch your kite.

■ Stand with your back to the wind and hold your kite as high as you can, its nose pointing straight up
■ Gently give it over to the wind. If the breeze is strong enough, it will start to ascend. Pay out a little line and the kite will drop. Before it lands, tighten your grip and it will rise again. Repeat this until it's high enough to find steady winds.
■ If the line slackens, bring it in a little. If the kite tugs hard, pay more line out. Don't feed your kite too much line; about 100-200 ft (30-60 m) is enough.
■ Watch the kite like a hawk to avert a crash. A dive-bombing kite can cause injury.

choose the right
Knife

Using the correct knife for the job will make food preparation easier. A basic set of kitchen knives will meet most of your needs.

■ Hold a knife before you buy, to check its comfort and balance.

■ Choose knives with handles riveted to the blade or made all in one piece.

■ A few good knives are better than many of poor quality. High-carbon stainless steel is easy to sharpen and stays sharp longest (see opposite).

LARGE CHEF'S KNIFE (A) An especially versatile knife used for chopping, slicing and paring.

SMALL VEGETABLE KNIFE (B) A knife for more intricate jobs such as boning meat or fish or making garnishes—as well as for preparing vegetables.

SMALL FRUIT KNIFE (C) For cutting through skins without tearing delicate flesh.

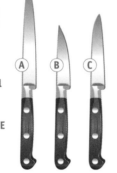

PALETTE KNIFE (D) For smoothing and lifting. It's particularly useful when applying icing, and for lifting cookies from baking sheets.

BREAD KNIFE (E) The best bread knives come with deep serrations and a long, straight 12 in. (30 cm) blade.

CARVING KNIFE (F) Best with a broad, tapering blade of at least 8 in. (20 cm).

learn the basics of Knitting

Knitting is creative, absorbing—and easy to master. And it enables you to make things that are totally individual in color and style.

The basic process of knitting starts with "casting on" a first row of stitches (see steps below) using your chosen yarn and a pair of needles. You then build up the work, row by row, using a combination of stitches: knit (plain) and purl (hence the phrase "knit one, purl one"). When you have reached the desired length, you "cast off" the finished rows to prevent your knitting unraveling.

The basic tools Knitting can be done with almost any yarn, including wool, wool mixtures, cotton, linen and silk—or you can mix them as you wish. You can choose needles in metal, plastic and also in bamboo and wood, which are the most expensive but the easiest to use. For best results you need to match yarn and needles. As a rule the thicker the yarn, the larger the needles should be. You'll need to practice to achieve the correct tension—the number of stitches and rows to a given measurement—stated in the knitting pattern.

Knowing the stitches
Knit and purl stitches are used in combination to create three basic styles of knitted work.

Garter stitch Knit stitches on every row—creates horizontal ridges.
Stocking stitch Alternate rows of knit and purl—resulting in a basic smooth knitting stitch.
Ribbing Alternate knits and purls with the pattern reversed on alternate rows—producing firm but stretchy ridges useful for edges, such as cuffs.

Casting on

1 Tie a slipknot around a needle and hold that needle in your right hand. Wrap the yarn from the ball end around your left thumb, then grasp the yarn firmly between the palm of your hand and the tips of your fingers.

2 Turn your hand so that the back of your thumb is facing you, forming a loose loop. Insert the needle from front to back through the loop.

3 Slip your thumb out of the loop and, at the same time, pull the yarn downward to close the loop around the needle. Repeat to make first row.

Stitches

Knit (plain) stitch

1 Insert the right needle into the first cast-on stitch and behind the left needle. Loop the ball-end yarn counterclockwise around the right needle.

2 Use the right needle to draw the loop forward through the stitch. At the same time, push the stitch on the left needle up toward the tip.

3 As you pull the loop away with the right needle, allow the stitch on the left needle to slip off. Pull it tight to the right needle to make the stitch.

Purl stitch

1 Insert the right needle in front of the left needle (not behind) and behind the ball-end yarn rather than in front.

2 Wrap the yarn around the right needle as before, pull it through and push the stitch on the left needle toward the tip.

3 Allow the stitch to slip off the left needle and tighten it against the loop on the right needle to complete a purl stitch.

Casting off

1 Knit the first two stitches in the row. Insert the tip of the left needle into the front of the first stitch knitted.

2 Lift the first stitch over the second, allowing it to slip off the right needle, and withdraw the left needle. Knit the next stitch and repeat the process. Continue to the end, then cut off the yarn and draw the cut end through the last stitch.

sharpen
Knives

The extra chromium in a stainless steel knife keeps it sharp for longer than ordinary steel, but all knives become blunt with use and should be sharpened regularly.

Purpose-made wheel sharpener
Simply draw the blade through the V formed by the two sets of hardened blades.

On a sharpending steel Hold the steel at a slight angle, point down. Place the widest part of the knife blade at the top of the steel, at an angle of about 20 degrees.

■ Draw the knife down the steel, keeping it at the same angle but gradually pulling the blade toward you so that, when you complete the stroke, only the tip of the knife is touching the end of the steel.

■ To sharpen the other side of the knife blade, place it at the same angle against the underside of the steel and then draw it down in the same way. Alternate these diagonal strokes until both sides of the knife blade are sharp.

Knot garden

The fragrant knot garden, a favorite in Elizabethan times, will work well in both large and smaller spaces. Within its low hedges—trained to mimic the shapes of Celtic knots—you can grow aromatic herbs such as thyme, sage, rosemary and camomile.

Design Draw a design, to scale, on squared paper, marking key measurements and plant choices. The garden should be at least 6 ft (2 m) square, or 9 ft (3 m) in diameter for a circular plan.

Plants Select boxes of different varieties, including variegated types, and hardy English lavenders. Other good choices are germander, rosemary, hyssop and the gray-leaved cotton lavender. You can also add purple sage or a purple-leaved berberis.

Preparation and planting Dig over the area, adding plenty of compost. Mark out your design using stakes and string. Set plants in place, allowing growing room, with "crossing" plants placed appropriately within each line. Box plants need to be 12-14 in. (30-35 cm) apart, lavenders and rosemary 12-18 in. (30-45 cm) apart. Keep well watered. Fill in open areas with gravel.

Training and care Cut back "underneath" plants at crossing points and allow the "over" ones to grow continuously. Enhance the knot effect by allowing the plants in the upper lines to grow taller than those below.

tie Knots

There are scores of different knots, but five basic types will cover most of your needs. Practice tying them with pieces of string and try to remember the tasks for which each type of knot is suitable.

Uses for knots

Reef, or square, knot This simple knot lies flat when finished, so is useful for tying bandages. It's also used for joining two ropes of equal thickness, but works well only with natural rope, not rope made out of synthetic fibers.

Sheet bend An essential knot for securely joining ropes. If they are of different thicknesses, the thinner rope should be the active partner in tying the knot.

Bowline If you need to make a loop that won't slip at the end of a length of rope—for instance, as a rescue knot when throwing a line to someone in trouble in the water—this one is quick to tie.

Round turn, two half hitches A knot that's useful for tethering a horse or mooring a boat to a post or ring.

Constrictor This is used to tie a rope around a fixed object such as a post, rail or jetty post.

How to tie knots

Reef knot Wind the "working" rope end (A) in your right hand over and then under the "standing" rope end (B) in your left. Swap hands, so that the working rope is in your left hand, then loop it back over and under the end of the standing rope and pull tight.

Bow line Form a small loop (A) near the rope end. Pass the end (B) through the loop, hook it around the standing rope and then back through the loop. Pull the standing rope and rope end to tighten the knot and form a fixed loop.

Sheet bend Make a loop in the thicker rope (A). Feed the end of the thinner rope (B) through the loop; wrap it round the two lengths of thicker rope and under its own standing part. Pull the lengths of thicker rope to tighten.

Round turn Loop the rope twice around the post or ring, with the second loop overlapping the first. Make a half hitch by taking the end around the main rope and passing it through between the post and the rope. Repeat, then slide the two half hitches up and pull tight.

Constrictor knot Wind the rope around the post or rail in a figure of eight. Feed the end of the rope under the second loop, then over and under the first loop and pull to tighten.

choose cuts of Lamb

Lamb is a tender meat that is extra sweet when it's from the youngest animals, with a pale pink flesh and creamy white fat. Meat from older animals is darker in color.

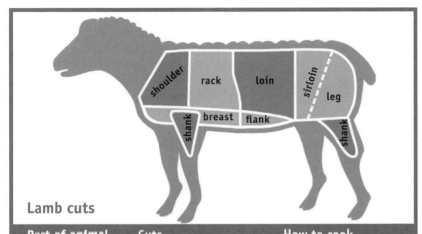

Lamb cuts

Part of animal	Cuts	How to cook
SHOULDER	Whole Shoulder blade chops Shoulder arm chops	Shoulder: roast. Shoulder chops: braise, broil or grill.
SHANKS	Shank	Braise or cook in liquid.
RACK	Rib roast Rib chops Rib crown roast	Roast: as the name implies, roast. Chops: broil, grill, pan fry, roast or bake. Crown roast: roast.
BREAST	Whole Breast riblets	Breast: braise or roast. Riblets: braise or cook in liquid.
LOIN	Whole Chops or Double chops	Broil, grill, pan broil or pan fry.
FLANK	Flank steak	Grill.
SIRLOIN	Whole Sirloin with leg Sirloin steak	Sirloin/with leg: roast. Sirloin steak: grill or broil.
LEG	Leg shank (half) Leg, bone in/boneless Leg steaks	Leg steaks: broil or grill. All other cuts: roast.

use a Ladder safely

- Set straight ladders at a 75-degree angle—for example, if you're putting a ladder 13 ft (4 m) up a wall, stand it about 3 ft (1 m) out from the wall.
- For time-consuming jobs, tie the ladder to sturdy pegs driven into the ground on either side.
- On hard surfaces, get someone to stand on the bottom rung to prevent slippage.
- Use cordless tools—cables are a hazard when working on a ladder.
- Hold the rungs when climbing up or down the ladder.
- Don't climb a ladder with your hands full. Raise and lower items in a bucket on a rope, and hang the bucket on an S-hook.
- The top four rungs are for holding only—don't stand on them.
- Don't set up a ladder in front of an unlocked door.
- Never leave a raised ladder unattended, even for a moment.

---

treat Laryngitis

An inflamed larynx, or voice box, is usually caused by a virus, and will often get better with simple home treatments. Persistent cases may be due to bacteria and will require antibiotics.

- Drink plenty of fluids, especially water, and try not to swallow or cough excessively.
- If you are hoarse, rest your vocal cords. Don't shout, talk, sing or whisper for long periods.
- Gargling with mouthwash or salt-water can help to ease a sore throat (*see* SORE THROAT). A menthol inhaler and air humidifier can help to clear your airways.
- If you smoke, it's time to stop.

fix a central heating
Leaking pipe

If your home is heated using hot-water-based central heating, fix any leaky pipes right away—not just to prevent water damage, but because leaks let in air, which can cause the components to rust.

It's most likely that the leak is in a compression fitting. This consists of a nut attached to a fitting that has a screw thread around its outside. A small ring of soft metal, called a ferrule, forms a seal between these two parts. To stop a leak, it may be enough just to tighten the nut a quarter of a turn (no more than that, or you'll damage the ferrule).

Still leaking? Fit a new ferrule, or try wrapping the old one with PTFE pipe joint tape.
■ Drain the system, or isolate the leak by closing valves on either side.
■ Undo the leaky joint and drain any residual water into a bucket.
■ Pull the pipe slightly away from the nut. Wrap two or three turns of pipe joint tape around the ferrule.
■ Reinsert the pipe, tighten up the nut and refill the system.

⚡ golden rules
LAYING A LAWN
■ **Choose a seed treated with a bird repellent.**
■ **Check sod samples for firmness, color and absence of weeds.**
■ **Keep a new lawn well watered in dry spells.**
■ **Don't mow until the grass is 2 in. (5 cm) high.**

install a Lawn

Spring and autumn are the best times to get started on your lawn. You'll need to prepare the ground at least a month in advance, and decide whether to grow a lawn from seed or lay sod.

Prepare the ground
■ A firm, level surface is essential. Trample the earth and break up dirt clods with a rake, removing weeds and large rocks.
■ Compact the soil to make it firm by taking small overlapping steps with your weight on your heels.
■ Rake over the ground several times in different directions to create a crumbly, even surface.
■ Select seed or sod to meet your requirements—lawns that will get repeated use by a family need hard-wearing grass mixtures. Fine grasses will be less resilient.

Laying sod Putting down sod has the advantage of giving you an immediate, more predictable result and can be done in the summer if necessary, but it is much more expensive than sowing seed.

1 Buy sod and set in a shaded area. If you can't lay it within 24 hours of purchase, water it lightly.

2 Set a plank on your prepared area and lay the first sod against the straight edge. Lay alternate courses of sod in staggered rows, working from the plank.

3 Bang the surface with the back of a rake to pack it in. Brush fine topsoil into the cracks. Water thoroughly. Repeat if any cracks open up later.

4 At this stage, don't worry about shaping sod to fit your lawn area. Wait until it settles in, then trim any excess with a knife or lawn edger.

Sowing This method is quick and inexpensive, and there is a wider range of grass types to choose from, but this type of lawn can take six months to mature and is susceptible to bird and cat damage. The kind you choose will depend on your region's climate. Any seeds should have a germination rate of at least 75 percent—that's how many are expected to sprout.

Peg out strings 3 ft (1 m) apart, then place bamboo canes across them to form a square. Sprinkle the seed evenly across the square. Repeat for the remaining area, repositioning the bamboo canes as you go. Rake in seed lightly and evenly. Deter birds with scarecrows, or crisscross black cotton thread 2–3 in. (5–8 cm) above the surface, between pegs.

patch a Lawn

A lawn can be repaired with seed or sod, ideally in spring or autumn. If a replacement patch is needed, try to use the same grass type.

Broken edges Make three neat cuts in the sod around the broken edge. Lift the cut section and turn it around so that the ragged edge is on the inside.

Seeding bare patches
■ Use a half moon edging tool to cut out the damaged area in a neat square or rectangle. Lightly fork over the soil and add some replacement topsoil or compost. Scatter grass seed, using about 1–2 oz per 3¼ sq ft (30–60 g/m²). Sprinkle lightly with topsoil and protect from birds as for a new lawn (see above). Water if necessary.
■ Alternatively, pre-germinate the seed: Mix with moist compost in a bucket, cover with plastic wrap and put in a warm place for three days or until you see roots beginning to develop. Then sow as above.

Sodding bare patches
■ Cut away the damaged area and prepare the patch as above. Cut a piece of sod to size, place in position and brush in some topsoil. Press it in neatly with the back of a rake. Water well. Alternatively, use an identically sized piece of sod from a less conspicuous area of your lawn.

make Lemonade

Nothing is more refreshing on a sweltering summer afternoon than a glass of homemade lemonade—so much better than the artificial stuff. This syrup will keep in the fridge for up to a week.

1 cup superfine sugar (or to taste)
3 cups boiling water
juice of 8 large lemons
2 tbsp finely grated lemon zest

TO SERVE
ice cubes
sprigs of lemon balm, lemon verbena or mint

Put the sugar in a saucepan with the water and stir until the sugar has dissolved. Leave to cool. Stir in the lemon juice and zest until well blended. Strain if desired. Chill before serving, dilute with water to taste, pour over ice cubes and top with herbs.

clean Leather

Leather comes either untreated or dyed and coated with polyurethane, as in shoes, leather garments and upholstery. The two need different treatment—as does suede, a leather with a fuzzy finish usually used for shoes (*see* SHOES) and handbags.

Untreated leather Dust frequently with a soft cloth. Try removing any dirt or marks with an eraser, but be aware that it may still leave a smudge.

Coated leather Dust regularly with a cloth, and occasionally with one dampened with cold water. Wash every six months or so with saddle soap. First, remove any loose dirt with a stiff brush or damp cloth. Then rub a damp cloth on saddle soap and work up a lather on the leather, rubbing with a circular motion. Allow to air dry, then buff with a clean, soft cloth. Finish with a protective leather cream, or waterproof with mink oil.

Suede Brush regularly with a suede brush or a clean, dry kitchen sponge to restore the nap. Use a slow, circular brushing motion.

Lift items safely

Before lifting anything heavy, assess it carefully. Note anything that might snag, scratch or slip through your fingers. Try to never strain yourself too much and, if possible, use mechanical help, such as a dolly.

■ If you're worried that the load might be too heavy and you have no mechanical help, don't take a chance—recruit a helper.
■ If you have a helper, take control. Issue clear, concise instructions for lifting, moving and setting down, such as *up*, *left*, *right*, *down*.
■ Stand close to the load, with feet apart and one slightly in front of the other, for stability.

Bend at the knees, not the waist, and tuck your chin in. Keep your back as vertical as possible and get a firm hold on the object.

Don't lift with straight legs and a bent back—you risk hurting your back and abdomen.

Make your legs do the work: Begin to straighten them as you slowly lift, taking care not to twist your torso.

Once you're standing, hold the object close to your body to minimize stress to your lower back.

find the perfect Level

Establishing a correct horizontal line is vital for putting up shelving as well as building decks and fences. A good level will help you keep things straight, both horizontally and vertically.

A level is the essential tool for any job requiring a horizontal line. You will need a full-size one, at least 2 ft (60 cm) long, for large projects, such as building a fence and laying concrete. A shorter torpedo level will help you mount shelving. A line level, one that hooks onto a taut string, is useful for bricklaying. Most levels have clear vials filled with liquid. When the level is horizontal or vertical, a bubble in the liquid floats between two lines marked on the vial. (Laser levels project a line of light instead.)

A water level, or transparent hose, can be used across long distances—say, between two walls of a room. Fill the hose with water. Tip a little out so there's a small amount of air in the hose. Hold your thumb over one end of the hose and ask a helper to do the same at the other end, then each takes up position at the points between which you want to fix a level. Hold each end upward and remove your thumbs from the hose. Ask your helper to align the water level inside the hose with the first reference point. The surface of the water at your end will always be at the same height as your helper's, allowing you to determine a straight line.

compose a witty Limerick

A limerick is a funny five-line poem. It has a characteristic galloping rhythm. The fourth and fifth lines are short, and rhyme with each other; the three longer lines also share a rhyme. Here's an early classic of the genre, by 19th-century English poet Edward Lear:

> There was an Old Man of Calcutta,
> Who perpetually ate bread and butter,
> Till a great bit of muffin,
> On which he was stuffing,
> Choked that horrid Old Man of Calcutta.

To modern tastes this is not hilarious, and the repeat of the rhyme-word Calcutta is a little disappointing. When you attempt to write your own limerick, make sure that the first line ends in a word that has plenty of rhyming possibilities. Try to retain the central character introduced in the first line: *There once was a ... person of some kind, from somewhere.* Then just use the five lines to tell a miniature short story.

Modern limericks tend to be a little bawdy. They don't have to be ribald at all, but they should be entertaining:

> There was a young man from Argyll,
> Who sharpened his teeth with a file.
> It meant he could eat
> The most leathery meat,
> But it made for an unnerving smile.

cook, prepare and eat Lobster

YOU WILL NEED Plastic bag, large pan, salt, chopping board, chef's knife, large napkin, finger bowl of warm water and lemon slices, fork, small hammer or lobster (or nut) crackers, lobster fork or skewer

Cooking The most humane way to treat a live lobster is to rinse it, put it in a plastic bag and freeze it for 2 hours before plunging it into boiling water to which you've added ¼ cup salt salt per qt/L. Cook for 12 minutes for the first pound (500 g) weight, 10 minutes for the next pound and 5 minutes for each additional pound. Drain off water and let cool.

Preparation

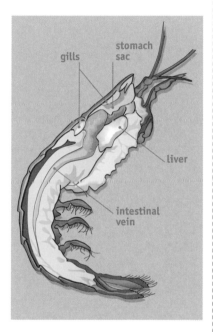

gills
stomach sac
liver
intestinal vein

■ Lie the lobster on its back on a chopping board and slice in half from head to tail.
■ Spread out the two halves and remove the gills, stomach sac (in the head) and the dark intestinal veins running down the tail.
■ Remove the liver (also in the head) and, from female lobsters, the coral-red roe in the tail. Set aside for garnish.

Eating Protect your shirt with in a large napkin and prepare a finger bowl. Serve with mayonnaise, melted garlic butter, lemon wedges or with a hollandaise sauce (*see* HOLLANDAISE SAUCE).

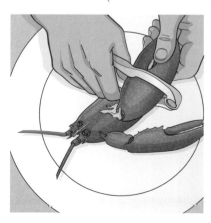

■ Use a fork to remove as much meat as possible from the tail. Then crack the claws in several places using a small hammer or lobster cracker, and use the lobster fork or skewer to extract as much meat as possible from either side of the thin membrane running down the center of each claw.
■ Break off the smaller side feelers. Crack open and suck out the meat.

apply
Lipstick

YOU WILL NEED Lip liner pencil in a nude or neutral shade, lip brushes, lipstick, clear lip gloss

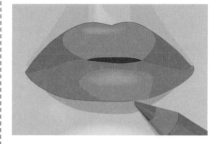

1 Carefully outline the shape of your mouth with the lip liner, using gentle strokes.

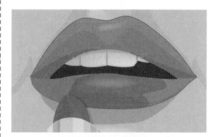

2 Next, fill in with your lipstick. You can apply it directly from the tube, but a lip brush gives you more control. Start from the middle of your bottom lip and work out, applying an even layer. Then do the same with your top lip. Use the brush to blend lipstick and lip liner.

3 Blot with a tissue and apply a second light coating of lipstick. Press your lips together to ensure even coverage.

4 Finish by adding a layer of clear lip gloss, starting at the center of the lips and moving outward.

create a company
Logo

A well-designed logo should help you to stand out from the crowd and tell your customers what kind of business you run. It's worth hiring a professional graphic designer to create your logo.

Find a designer Ask around or look online for designers who do work for businesses. Contact three and arrange some initial meetings.

Create a brief Think about what the designer needs to know.
■ What's your business, and what are its values? Are you modern and innovative? Caring and customer-focused? Reassuringly traditional? This will affect the images and typography that the designer uses.
■ Where will your logo appear—on your letterhead, business cards, websites, billboards, packaging or even on a van?
■ What's your budget? Have a figure in mind, then agree on a price before the designer starts work.

Protect your logo All logos are protected under copyright law. For better protection, register your logo as a trademark with the United States Trademark Office or Canadian Intellectual Property Office.

The FedEx logo is modern, efficient and clever (spot the hidden arrow)—qualities the company would like customers to associate with its courier service.

free up a stiff door Lock

Various things can make a lock mechanism stiffen up, but most problems are easily fixed. If your problem is with a latch that won't close properly, it could be that the door has sagged slightly, so the bolt is out of alignment with the slot in the strike plate. A small misalignment can be fixed by filing down the bottom edge of the slot with a metal file. If the misalignment is larger, you'll have to remove the strike plate from the door frame and reposition it.

Mortise locks on exterior doors may dry out or corrode if the wind and rain get at the mechanism. In the first instance, spray a lubricant into the keyhole and operate the lock a few times to allow the grease to disperse. If that doesn't work, you'll have to take out the lock mechanism.
■ Remove the door handles and the two screws holding the lock in the doorframe, then pry the mechanism out (*see* DOOR LOCKS). Carefully open the casing by removing the screws.
■ Apply grease or petroleum jelly to all working parts, and put them back in the order that you took them out. Close the casing and reattach the lock.

Cylinder locks Don't use aerosol lubricant on a Yale cylinder lock. They should be treated with a dry lubricant, such as graphite or PTFE powder, available from hardware stores.

make emergency repairs to Luggage

A suitcase can get battered during baggage handling or succumb to long-term wear and tear. But you can make running repairs.

A breaking handle can be temporarily fixed by binding it with self-adhesive fabric tape or filament (strapping) tape. If a handle breaks completely and is attached by D rings, pry them open with pliers, remove the handle and replace it with an old tie or other makeshift solution. Keep the handle. You can later take it to a leather store and buy a similar one. If the handle is retractable and screwed in on the inside, you'll need to open up the case to locate and remove the fixings, which may mean detaching the lining.

If the case itself tears, undo any lining around the tear, and patch it with leather or fabric. For a vinyl case, you can buy vinyl cement and patches. Apply the appropriate adhesive to the case interior and patch. Wait until it's dry to the touch, then position the patch and press on the surface. Hammer lightly at the edges to affix it. Use fabric glue to reattach the lining.

A broken zipper can be a nightmare, but a removable luggage strap bound around your case gives you security—and makes it easier to spot your bag on a baggage carousel.

A dent in a metal suitcase can be knocked out by gentle tapping on the inside with a piece of wood.

dance the Macarena

The Spanish song "Macarena," by Los del Rio, became an instant hit when it came out in 1995, inspiring a craze for this exuberant dance.

Don't worry if you have two left feet or no willing dance partner. This dance requires only that you move your hands, arms and body—with a Latin swing and sway. Every movement is sensuous. Put on "Macarena" and feel the beat. *Oh, when I dance, they call me Macarena / And the boys, they say that I am buena ...*

BEAT 1 Stretch your right arm out in front of you at shoulder height, palm down.
BEAT 2 Follow with your left arm.

BEAT 3 Turn up your right palm.
BEAT 4 Turn up your left palm.

BEAT 5 Put your right hand on your left shoulder.
BEAT 6 Put your left hand on your right shoulder.

BEAT 7 Clasp your right hand to the back of your head.
BEAT 8 Clasp your left hand to the back of your head.

BEAT 9 Right hand to front of left hip.
BEAT 10 Left hand to right front hip.

BEAT 11 Right hand to right buttock.
BEAT 12 Left hand to left buttock.

BEATS 13, 14, 15 Swing your hips to the right, left, then right again.

BEAT 16 Clap hands and jump-turn 90 degrees to the right—then start again.

remove Makeup

Remove makeup as carefully as you apply it. Use cotton pads and separate products specially formulated for eyes and face, or try using milk, plain yogurt or olive oil for removing eye makeup.

■ Start with your eyes, working gently around each one. Close your eyes and work from eyelash root to tip to remove mascara. Then use a cleanser (not soap) or milk to remove foundation, powder, lipstick and blusher. Rinse with warm (not hot) water and pat dry with a soft towel. Finish with toner.

peel and cut a Mango

A mango is easiest to prepare when it's fully ripe. The skin should yield slightly when pressed gently, and it should smell sweet and fruity.

1 Hold the mango horizontally and cut into two lengthwise, on one side of the stone. Repeat on the other side, leaving a thin layer near the stone.

2 Slash the flesh in a lattice pattern, cutting down to, but not through, the peel. Holding the flesh upward, push the center of the peel with your thumb, turning it inside out and opening up the cubes of flesh so they can be easily cut off.

3 Cut remaining pulp from the outer two edges of the seed, pare away the skin and cut the mango into chunks.

Alternatively, remove the peel with a potato peeler or sharp knife and cut off the flesh in slices until you reach the stone. Cut away any remaining flesh in chunks.

conjure up
Magic tricks
see pages 198–199

read topographic
Maps

A short walk isn't necessarily an easy stroll if it's all uphill. Learn how to interpret topographic maps so you can figure out the gradient before you set off.

Topographic maps show variations in the height of the ground with brown contour lines, which group places of the same height above sea level.

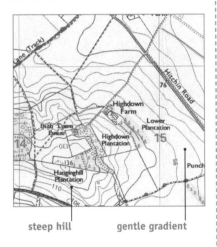

steep hill   gentle gradient

■ Each line indicates a rise or fall of a set height, which depends on the map's scale.
■ Numbered lines indicate the actual height of the ground. Use these to figure out whether the ground is rising or falling with the direction of your route.
■ Tightly packed contour lines indicate a steep hill. If the contour lines are widely spaced, then the slope is less steep.
■ The highest number is always at the top of the hill, but the bottom of the hill is rarely at sea level. To calculate how high you'll climb, subtract the starting height from the height at the top.

treat yourself to a French Manicure

A French manicure achieves a refined, natural look using pearly tinted polish and white-painted tips on carefully tended nails.

YOU WILL NEED **Warm water, towel, cotton balls, nail-polish remover, emery boards, cuticle conditioner, rubber-tipped cuticle stick, nail buffer, hand cream, pink or peachy nail polish, white polish, clear top coat. Optional: self-adhesive tip guides**

1 If your nails are already polished, remove all polish, paying particular attention to cuticles. Wash and dry your hands.

2 Shape nails with the emery board, using the fine side at a 45-degree angle, working from the outer corners to the center. Aim for smooth, rounded tips or a slightly square finish, if you prefer. Smooth rough edges with light downward strokes starting from the top of each nail and upward strokes from the bottom.

3 Gently work cuticle cream into the base of each nail. Using the rubber-tipped stick, loosen the skin around each nail bed, then immerse hands in warm water for a few minutes before drying them. Use your stick to ease the cuticles back, working from the center out.

4 Use a buffer to buff your nails, working in one direction only.

5 Apply a light hand cream that will soak in quickly to smooth hands.

6 Apply a base coat of the colored polish to each nail, let it dry and apply a top coat. *See also* NAILS.

7 Use tip guides or work freehand to apply white polish. The length of the tips will depend on the length of your nails, but keep them uniform.

8 Once the tips are dry, finish off with a top coat of hard-wearing, clear polish to protect the tips from chipping.

get started on Marathon training

To run a marathon, you must first be able to tackle a half-marathon. The key to success is to run regularly. Training with friends or a running club can make it more enjoyable and help you stay committed. Build your stamina with one long run a week, with shorter or less strenuous sessions in between, plus some gym-based strength and conditioning sessions and one full rest day. *See also* AEROBIC EXERCISE *and* RUNNING ROUTINE.

Training program for beginners The program below will take you from a standing start to your first half-marathon in 21 weeks.

Week	TUESDAY	THURSDAY	FRIDAY	SUNDAY
1	5 mile walk		20 min jog	5 mile walk
2	10 min jog		20 min jog	10 min jog
3	20 min jog		20 min jog	20 min jog
4	10 min jog		25 min jog	30 min jog
5	25 min jog		25 min jog	30 min jog
6	30 min jog		30 min jog	40 min jog
7	35 min jog		35 min jog	45 min jog
8	50 min jog		50 min jog	60 min jog
9	50 min jog		50 min jog	60 min jog
10	60 min jog		60 min jog	70 min jog
11	60 min jog	5 mile jog	70 min jog	70 min jog
12	60 min jog	5 mile jog	70 min jog	70 min jog
13	5 mile run	6 mile jog	70 min jog	60 min run on grass
14	5 mile run	6 mile jog	70 min jog	60 min run on grass
15	60 min run	6 mile run	5 mile run	60 min run
16	60 min run	6 mile run	5 mile run	70 min run
17	60 min run	7 mile run	60 min run	85 min run
18	60 min run	7 mile run	60 min run	85 min run
19	60 min run, 10 min hard	60 min run, 10 min hard	6 mile easy	95 min run
20	60 min run, 10 min hard	60 min run, 10 min hard	6 mile easy	6 miles with friends
21	6 mile jog	3 mile jog	3 mile jog	HALF-MARATHON DAY

What next? Allow a few weeks to recover, but don't stop running or you'll lose your hard-won fitness. Go out three or four times a week and run for at least an hour, increasing your distance week by week. Do cross-training or go swimming once a week to minimize wear on your joints. It's important to build in *fartlek* ("speed play" in Swedish) sessions, where you run hard for short bursts as part of a longer run. Joining a local running club could also help you work toward running a full marathon.

clean Marble

Because marble is porous, it needs care and gentle treatment. Always wipe away any spills immediately, then rinse and dry thoroughly. Never apply abrasive cleaners, ammonia or any acid, such as vinegar. It also marks easily, so seal the surface annually with stone sealer, available online.

General cleaning Mix about 2 tbsp of mild liquid soap in 2 qt/L of water and apply with a soft sponge or sponge mop. Rinse, then dry with a soft cloth.

Surface stains Use a marble-polishing powder such as tin oxide, available from hardware stores. If the item isn't valuable, try a thick paste of baking soda and water. Leave for ten to 15 minutes, then rinse off with warm water and dry.

play Marbles

This old-school marbles game is known as "ringer."

- First, draw a ring on the ground, about 10 ft (3 m) across. Arrange 13 equally sized marbles in a cross at the center of the ring, leaving about 4 in. (10 cm) between each marble.
- Two to six players, positioned at the edge of the ring, take turns trying to knock marbles out of the circle using a "shooter" marble. A point is awarded for each knocked out of the ring, and players can keep point-scoring marbles. A player's turn ends when they fail to knock a marble out of the ring or if their own shooter is knocked out of the ring.
- The player with the highest score when the last marble is knocked out wins.

conjure up Magic tricks

It's amazing how impressive a simple magic trick can be. With a little knowledge and a few hours of practice, you can astonish and impress your family and friends.

Tricks of the trade **You must rehearse until your routine is smooth and fault-free. And you need to develop a good patter: Many tricks depend on distracting the audience—so you have to be able to talk and joke as you perform. Here are some magic tricks that are easy to learn and require no specialized props.**

PICK A CARD
Here's a classic find-the-card trick. You'll need a rubber band.

1 Shuffle a deck of cards and ask a volunteer to take one and show it to the audience. Turn your back to assure them you can't see it.

2 While your back is to the audience, turn the pack of cards faceup, and turn the top card over and place it facedown on the pack.

3 Turn back to the audience, and showily wrap the rubber band round the pack. With the pack in your left hand, ask the volunteer to push their card facedown into the pack.

4 Now, pass the pack from your left hand to your right, left palm down. Pass it back to your left hand. Ask the volunteer to twang the rubber band to "release the magic."

5 Remove the band and fan the cards out (but don't let the audience look too closely). The volunteer's card will be faceup in the middle of the pack —allowing you to name it with a triumphant flourish.

MIND READING
Ask a volunteer to do the following calculation in their head, so you can zero in on their brainwaves.

Say, "Pick a number between one and ten...multiply it by nine...if it's a two-digit number, add them together... subtract five."

Now say, "Pick the letter of the alphabet that corresponds to that letter, whatever it may be: A for 1, B for 2, and so on.

"Now think of a country that begins with that letter. Think of an animal that begins with the second letter of that country. Think of the color of that animal."

Now say, "That's odd: I'm getting a vision of a gray elephant in Denmark!" Nine times out of ten you'll be right, because the answer to the calculation is always four, Denmark is the obvious country beginning with D and an elephant is the obvious animal that starts with E—but they don't know that.

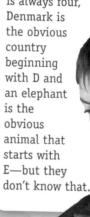

THE OBEDIENT WAND

A great trick to do early in your set—it will establish your magician's credentials.

The audience sees that your wand wondrously sticks to the palm of your hand though you aren't holding onto it. They don't see that the wand is held in place by a pencil you're holding in your other hand. You could try tucking the pencil into the band of your wristwatch, but you'll have to practice hiding it at the end of the trick.

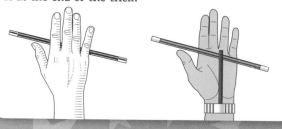

THE MYSTIC BANANA

Pulling off this trick is simply a matter of planning ahead.

Take a banana and insert a needle through the skin near the top. Twist the needle from side to side, keeping it level, so as to neatly slice the banana. Repeat down the length of the banana. The pinholes will be barely visible. During your performance take a knife, and mime chopping the banana—without the knife ever touching the fruit. Now unpeel the banana. The pieces of fruit will fall out, as if chopped by magic inside the skin.

THE DISAPPEARING COIN

The ability to palm a coin is crucial to the magician's art, and all it takes is lots of practice.

1 Hold a small coin between the thumb, index and middle fingers of your right hand.

2 Pretend to take it into your left hand, but instead push it into the palm of your right hand, wedging it into the folds of skin, and slightly cupping your palm if necessary (it's hard to make this look natural; use a mirror to see how it looks from the audience's point of view).

3 Keep it there until you're ready to make it "reappear" in an unexpected place—behind someone's ear, for example. Look surprised when you find it there.

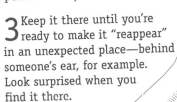

THE INDESTRUCTIBLE SHOELACE

In this trick you clearly cut a shoelace in half, but somehow it remains in one piece.

1 You need one whole shoelace, and a 2 in. (5 cm) length of an identical shoelace.

2 Make a loop in the short piece, and conceal it behind the fingers of your left hand. Pick up the long lace in such a way that the two ends dangle down. The loop of the long lace should remain concealed behind your fingers, but unnoticed. Move the short loop into view, so it appears to be part of the long lace.

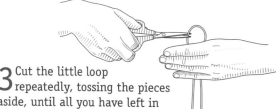

3 Cut the little loop repeatedly, tossing the pieces aside, until all you have left in your hand is the long lace. Take one end and triumphantly pull it through your fingers to show that it's whole.

create a flavor-packed
Marinade

The aim of marinating is to tenderize and add flavor to meat and fish. It's particularly useful for some of the otherwise tough, cheaper cuts of meat.

Marinades must include acid ingredients (wine, lemon juice or vinegar), herbs or spices and oil, plus vegetables, such as onions. Yogurt or heavy cream can also be used, particularly in Indian tikka dishes (*see* CURRY). A marinade will help to keep chunks of kebab meat tender (*see* KEBABS).

When marinating red meat, use red wine and red wine vinegar with a bouquet garni of parsley, rosemary, thyme and a bay leaf. Leave in the fridge for up to three days, turning from time to time.

Drain and pat the food dry before cooking or it won't brown. Save the marinade, though, for basting or cooking up in a sauce.

White wine marinade for chicken or fish

MAKES ABOUT 2¼ CUPS

1 small onion, sliced
1 small carrot, diced
½ stalk celery, sliced
1 clove of garlic, minced (optional)
¼ cup olive oil
¼ cup dry white wine
½ cup white wine vinegar
juice of 2 lemons or 4 limes
bouquet garni of parsley, rosemary and thyme
6 whole peppercorns

Mix all the ingredients well and pour over the chicken or fish. Cover and leave in the fridge for at least 30 minutes before cooking, but no longer than 24 hours.

serve up classic breakfast Marmalade

Marmalade can be made from most citrus fruits, alone or mixed, but bitter Seville oranges give the best flavor to this classic orange preserve. They have only a short season; look for them in late winter.

YOU WILL NEED Oranges (or other citrus fruit), stiff brush for scrubbing fruit, dish towel, small sharp knife, citrus squeezer, bowl, cheesecloth, string, preserving pan or large saucepan, sieve, skimming spoon, sterilized jars and lids, labels. Optional: potato peeler, sugar thermometer

Chunky Seville orange marmalade

MAKES ABOUT TEN 1 LB (500 g) JARS
3⅓ lb (1.5 kg) bitter oranges
juice of 2 lemons
3⅔ qt (3.5 L) water
6⅔ lb (3 kg) preserving sugar

1 Remove any stalks from the oranges, scrub and dry with the dish towel. Peel off the rind using a sharp knife or potato peeler, avoiding the pith. Cut into strips, as chunky as you like in your marmalade, and set aside. Halve and squeeze the oranges, saving the membranes and seeds (removing the pith) and bundling them together in a square of cheesecloth tied with string.

2 Put the cheesecloth bag of pits and membranes into the preserving pan with the peel. Strain the orange juice into the pan and add the strained lemon juice and water. Bring to a boil and simmer, uncovered, for about 2 hours or until the peel is soft and the pan contents reduced by about half. Remove the cheesecloth bag and let it cool a little while you add the sugar, stirring constantly over low heat until it has dissolved.

3 Squeeze the jelly-like juices from the cheesecloth bag into the pan— these are high in pectin and will help the marmalade to set. Turn up the heat and boil hard until the mixture reaches setting point and wrinkles when tested on a cool saucer (*see* JAM) or registers 217°F (103°C) on the thermometer. Skim, let stand for 30 minutes then pot in prepared jars (*see* JAM). The rind will float if you pot it too hot. When cool, seal the lids, label the jars and store them in a cool, dry place.

surefire lump-free Mashed potatoes

For smooth and fluffy mash, select either Russets or Yukon Gold potatoes. Boil in lightly salted water for 15-20 minutes until just tender and drain. Then:

By hand Add a little milk (warm is best, but cold will do) and a pat of butter. Mash thoroughly until all lumps have gone, moving the mixture from the sides to the center of the pan as you work.

Potato ricer or food mill Press the cooked potatoes through the sieve or mill and return to the pan with a little milk and a pat of butter.

After mashing, adjust seasoning, and warm through just long enough to remove any excess moisture, if necessary. Add seasonings or other ingredients to taste, such as mustard, grated cheese, roasted garlic, fresh parsley or pesto.

give a neck and shoulder Massage

You don't need special training or equipment to give someone this wonderfully relaxing treatment in your own home. Choose a warm, quiet room with soft lighting, and even add some soothing music.

1 Ask the person you want to massage to lie facedown on a firm, comfortable surface with a pillow under their chest. Pour a little massage oil such as sweet almond (check for nut allergies first) into your palm and rub your hands together to warm it. Spread the oil smoothly and evenly over the shoulders and neck.

 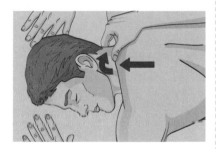

2 Squeeze and knead the shoulders, moving from the outside toward the neck. Do this for five to ten minutes, working harder as you feel the muscles relax. Ask how it feels to see how much pressure the person wants.

3 Move to the base of the neck, making small circular motions with your right thumb on the left side, for a few minutes, gradually increasing the pressure. Repeat with the left thumb on the right side of the neck.

4 With your hands on the shoulders, use both thumbs and the same small circular motions across the base of the neck. Work your thumbs up the sides of the neck. Perform this sequence a few times, easing up on the pressure toward the end.

make and use Marzipan

Marzipan, usually covered with icing, is a traditional topping to a rich fruitcake such as a Christmas or wedding cake. It can also be molded into shapes of all kinds, which can be tinted with food coloring, dipped in chocolate or both. *See also* CAKE.

FOR 7 IN. (18 CM) CAKE

¾ cup icing (confectioner's) sugar, sifted, plus extra for rolling
½ cup superfine sugar
8 oz (225 g) ground almonds
1 tsp lemon juice
few drops almond extract
1 egg, beaten

1 Put the sugars and ground almonds into a bowl and mix. Add lemon juice and almond extract and gradually stir in the beaten egg until the mixture is firm but manageable. Knead gently. Store for up to one week in an airtight container.

2 To make the marzipan stick to the cake, it's best to apply it over an apricot glaze.

FOR THE GLAZE

¾ cup apricot jam
½ tbsp lemon juice
2 tbsp water

1 Bring all the ingredients to a boil, stirring. Rub through a strainer, return to the pan and boil for 2 minutes. Cool. Place your cake on a rack and brush glaze over the top and sides of the cake.

2 Dust the work surface with icing sugar and roll out the marzipan until large enough to cover the top and sides of the cake. Wrap around the rolling pin and unroll it over the cake. Press gently all over, and trim off any excess. If not being covered with icing, the marzipan can be grilled to brown it, although take care as it scorches easily

give a face Massage

This is a great way to relieve stress, improve facial tone and bring a radiant glow to the complexion. Spend no more than 20 minutes overall and cleanse the face first. Ask the person to lie on their back and stand behind them as you work.

1 Apply a massage oil formulated for the face with a gliding movement and a deft, light touch. Stroke the face with your fingertips, upward and outward toward the temples.

2 Massage along the jaw line with your fingertips.

3 Work on the nose, mouth, forehead and around the eyes. Use a circular motion to massage the temples.

4 Use thumbs and forefingers to give little pinches along the eyebrows. Finish by massaging the neck muscles with firm upward strokes.

get bed bugs out of a Mattress

If you wake with an itchy rash or find bloodstains or dark spots of insect fecal waste on the sheet, it could be that a bug has moved into your mattress. A smell of almonds or overripe raspberries is another clue.

■ Once the bugs are in, they mean to stay. There are a number of old wives' remedies and modern gadgets, such as UV hand wands, that claim to move them, but the best way to do it yourself is to steam-clean the bed and the surrounding room, including baseboards, where the bugs hide in the day.
■ If steam-cleaning fails, call a professional pest controller.

choose the best Mattress for you

Sit on the edge of your mattress. If it sags, it's time for a new one. No more waking up feeling ragged and racked with aches and pains.

You get what you pay for Even a good mattress needs replacing after seven to ten years. Cheap ones may be good for just a couple of years.

If you have back trouble, you may be tempted by an "orthopedic" mattress, but this simply means a firm one and you need both support and comfort. A mattress that's too hard will not be comfortable and a too-soft mattress will not offer enough support. The right mattress will conform to the shape of your body, allowing for the curves of your hips, spine and shoulders.

Little and large Body weight is a major factor in getting the right firmness. If you're a 120-pound woman married to a bodybuilder, choose a combination mattress with a softer side for you and firmer side for him. Zip-together single mattresses are another option. Always go together to choose.

If your bedmate is a fidgeter, avoid "continuous coil" mattresses, in which a single looped wire moves as one, with a trampoline effect. Choose an open-coil mattress, made from single springs wired together, or, better yet, a pocket-sprung mattress, which has individual springs, each supporting a small part of the sleeper.

If you have painful joints, a memory foam mattress may help. The foam is affected by room temperature, body heat and pressure, so the mattress can feel cold and hard when you first get into bed. As it warms, it softens and molds to your body shape, which feels cozy but may inhibit movement.

If you suffer from allergies, a hypoallergenic pure foam or latex mattress is a wise choice.

Try before you buy Take off your coat and shoes and lie down in your normal sleeping position for at least ten minutes. On your back, you should be able to slide your hand under the small of your back. If there's a large gap, the mattress is too hard. If there's no gap, it's too soft. When trying a memory foam mattress, lie still for a few minutes then see if you can move freely.

See also SLEEP.

convert Measurements

Thanks to the calculator on your smart phone, you don't have to be a latter-day Einstein to convert metric and imperial or US measurements—you just need to employ these basic formulas. Enter the original value and multiply by the appropriate conversion factor.

LENGTH AND AREA		
FROM	TO	MULTIPLY
inches	mm	25.4
mm	inches	0.0394
inches	cm	2.54
cm	inches	0.3937
feet	meters	0.3048
meters	feet	3.2808
yards	meters	0.9144
meters	yards	1.0936
miles	km	1.6093
km	miles	0.6214
sq inches	cm²	6.4516
cm²	sq inches	0.155
sq feet	m²	0.0929
m²	sq feet	10.7639
sq yards	m²	0.8361
m²	sq yards	1.196
sq miles	km²	2.5899
km²	sq miles	0.3861
acres	hectares	0.4047
hectares	acres	2.471

VOLUMES		
FROM	TO	MULTIPLY
imp. pints	liters	0.5682
US pints	liters	0.4731
liters	imp. pints	1.7598
liters	US pints	2.114
imp. gallons	liters	4.546
US gallons	liters	3.785
liters	imp. gallons	0.22
liters	US gallons	0.2642
fl oz	liters	0.0284
liters	fl oz	35.195

WEIGHTS		
FROM	TO	MULTIPLY
ounces	grams	28.3495
grams	ounces	0.0352
pounds	grams	453.6
grams	pounds	0.0022
pounds	kg	0.4536
kg	pounds	2.2046

Temperature conversion
  Fahrenheit to Celsius: subtract 32, then divide by 1.8.
  Celsius to Fahrenheit: multiply by 1.8, then add 32.

In the kitchen Most recipes use round measurements—rendering 1 oz as 25 g, for example—rather than the exact mathematical conversion. This is close enough for recipes to work, but always use either the metric or imperial quantities, and not a mix in any one dish.

■ In this age of easy shipping be aware of transatlantic differences if your cookbook came from across the pond; "pint-sized" might mean an imperial pint (20 oz, a little more than half a liter) in Canada or the UK, or a US pint (16 oz, a little less than half a liter) in the US. A European cookbook will often measure ingredients by weight (specifically, grams or kilos) rather than by volume (cups). One cup of flour is 150 g; white sugar is 225 g and brown sugar 175 g; one cup of uncooked rice weighs 200 g; and butter, 225 g.

mix your own
Mayonnaise

Homemade mayonnaise is far nicer than anything out of a jar. It's easy to make and you can add your own flavors. A light olive oil is the best base, or you can use a mixture of vegetable oils. Extra virgin oil gives a really strong flavor.

MAKES 1¼ CUPS
2 egg yolks or 1 whole egg
½ tsp Dijon mustard
½ tsp salt
1¼ cups olive oil
1-2 tbsp white wine vinegar
   or lemon juice

By hand Beat egg yolks (or whole egg), mustard and salt in a bowl using a whisk or electric beater. Add half the oil, drop by drop, beating continuously until the mixture begins to thicken. Add the vinegar or lemon juice, then drizzle in the remaining oil, still beating all the time.

In a blender Blend yolks or whole egg with mustard, salt and vinegar or lemon juice for a few seconds. With the motor running, add the oil, first drop by drop then in a steady light stream.

Rescuing curdled mayonnaise
If the mixture begins to separate, add a tablespoon of warm water. Or beat one additional egg yolk and gradually add the curdled mixture.

Adding flavors Spice up a basic mayonnaise by adding finely chopped garlic or herbs—basil, chives, dill, parsley, tarragon and thyme are all good on their own or as a mixture. Try using a tablespoon of Dijon mustard and the same of honey, or make a paste of sun-dried tomatoes and garlic in a blender and stir into the finished mayonnaise.

learn to Meditate

Regular meditation is deeply relaxing and restorative, with a multitude of health benefits for both body and mind.

Don't try to meditate too soon after eating or drinking. Set aside a quiet space for your meditation practice.

1 Sit comfortably, upright on a supportive chair, and rest your hands, palms down, on your lap. Some people choose to lie down with their eyes closed, but this can induce sleep.

2 Clear your mind of "chatter." To do so you might fix on one calmly pleasing thought, or repeat to yourself over and over, in your head, some meaningless syllable (what some call a mantra). Alternatively, focus on your breathing; count the breaths in and out, taking as long to exhale as to inhale, expelling all the air.

3 Thoughts and worries will steal in. Acknowledge that they have come and just bat them away like balloons.

4 Try imagining that you're in a place of great beauty and peace. Hear the splashing of a stream and the breeze rustling the trees, smell the roses—transport yourself mentally away from your actual domestic surroundings.

5 After about 20 minutes, come back into yourself. Shuffle in your chair. Flex your muscles. Get up slowly. Don't spring to your feet. Meditation can lower blood pressure, so you may feel dizzy if you stand too quickly.

chair a Meeting effectively

Keep it small Invite only people who are directly involved with the subject to be discussed.

Circulate an agenda beforehand Summarize at the beginning of the meeting what is to be discussed and what you aim to achieve. Then work through the agenda point by point.

Stay on track Your task as chair is to channel the flow of ideas. Don't allow the discussion to deviate. If there are six points on the agenda, and you have scheduled an hour, insist that the discussion moves on to a new point every ten minutes.

Take minutes Appoint someone else to take notes—you cannot both chair and take minutes effectively.

Make sure all action points are written down, and assign someone to take on each task.

Make it brief The longer the meeting, the less productive it becomes. Don't aim to tackle too much at once. Better to have a follow-up meeting at a later date.

Timing is everything Try to avoid organizing meetings for first thing in the morning, when people are most busy, or late afternoon, when energy levels have flagged.

Outlaw monologues No one person should be allowed to dominate proceedings—especially not you. Make sure everyone has their say.

See also MINUTES.

improve your Memory

There are tricks—known as mnemonics—that use verse, phrases and acronyms to assist mental recall. These are useful props, but there are much simpler things you can do to boost the power of your memory.

Stretch your brain Tackle a new skill. Take a course in a subject about which you know little but that fascinates you. Perhaps learn a new language.

Stretch your legs Research among older adults has shown that walking six to nine miles (10-15 km) a week reduces the risk of memory loss.

Practise neurobics New routines activate new brain circuitry. If you're right-handed, try doing things with your left. Eat with your eyes closed. Take a new route to work. Go to new stores.

Cut down or cut out alcohol The old saying "I drink to forget" is all too true.

Feed the gray matter A diet rich in nutrients will boost brain function. Eat plenty of fresh fruit, vegetables and whole grains. Increase your intake of omega-3 fatty acids, found in oily fish, such as herring and mackerel, and walnut and flax oils.

Sleep on it Many studies have shown that taking a daytime nap after studying speeds up long-term memory consolidation. In one experiment, two groups of participants were asked to learn a task. One group then stayed awake, while the other took a 90-minute nap. The group that was allowed to sleep showed a significant improvement in their task performance by the evening.

make wafer-thin Melba toast

This makes a sophisticated accompaniment to pâtés of all kinds, or soup. It's also a good way of using thick or medium slices of stale white bread that you might otherwise throw away.

Toast slices lightly in a toaster or under the broiler, cut off the crusts and use a sharp thin knife to cut each in half horizontally into two very thin slices. Broil uncooked sides until crisp and curly. Alternatively, cut crusts from wafer-thin slices of bread and bake in the oven at 350°F (180°C) until evenly brown. Once cool, store the slices in an airtight container.

whip up the perfect Meringue

Absolute cleanliness of equipment and scrupulous care when you separate your eggs are the keys to making perfect meringues.

MAKES 20 MERINGUE SHELLS

3 egg whites
⅔ cup superfine sugar, plus extra for sprinkling

1 Heat the oven to 230°F (110°C). Whip the egg whites until stiff in a large, grease-free copper, stainless steel, glass or china bowl. You can do this with a hand whisk, but it will be quicker with an electric beater. Gradually blend in half the sugar, whipping well after each addition, then fold in the remaining sugar using a large, clean metal spoon.

2 Spoon or pipe the glossy mixture onto a baking sheet lined with parchment paper, sprinkle lightly with sugar and bake for 2½–3 hours or until crisp. When cooled, store the shells in an airtight container, ideally at room temperature. For serving, they can be sandwiched together with whipped cream flavored with vanilla and sugar, if you wish, or topped with fresh fruit.

Bake immediately after mixing or meringues may "weep" a watery syrup. Don't be tempted to raise the oven temperature to speed up baking—this is another common cause of "weeping." To make more room for filling, press the base of each shell lightly with your finger halfway through cooking.

spot the signs of Meningitis

The onset of meningitis is usually sudden. If you suspect meningitis or if any of the symptoms below are accompanied by a fever, call 911.

Symptoms

Meningitis is most common in children, but can strike an any age. Early symptoms can be similar to those for flu. They include:

- cold hands and feet
- limb pains or neck stiffness
- pallor
- blotchy skin
- vomiting

More alarming symptoms may follow, such as:

- severe headache
- stomach cramps
- a blank stare and delirium
- sensitivity to light

The glass test The most serious form of meningitis may be accompanied by a telltale rash of red or brown pinpricks on the limbs, which may develop into red or purple blotches or blood blisters.

If you press the side of a glass to the rash and it doesn't fade, call 911. If someone is feeling seriously unwell, don't wait to see whether a rash develops before calling 911.

find treasure with a
Metal detector

Be legal Make sure you know the law regarding metal-detecting wherever you happen to be. Different laws in different jurisdictions mean that you cannot necessarily keep what you find, and in some places you need a permit even to search. Be careful, too, not to trespass on private property. Check with local authorities before you start.

Develop a technique Long, slow sweeps close to the ground yield the best results. Practice covering the ground methodically.

Pick your spot Focus on areas where there's known to have been human activity in the past. A beach or the site of a forgotten village is more likely to yield treasure—or at least something of interest—than a barren mountaintop.

Stay safe If you discover anything that looks like live ammunition or an unexploded bomb, stop digging or searching, mark the site carefully, and inform the police.

get rid of Mice

Mice breed rapidly. If you see any sign of infestation—such as rod-shaped droppings about ¼ in. (5 mm) long—you must act as soon as possible.

■ Clean your kitchen thoroughly. Leave no food out, and seal garbage pails.
■ Seal cracks or holes in walls and baseboards with steel wool, which mice cannot chew through.
■ Set traps around the perimeter of the room, baited side facing the wall. For bait, use small pieces of bacon or a little peanut butter.

treat and prevent a Migraine

All migraine sufferers have their own particular symptoms and tried-and-tested relief remedies, often retreating to a quiet, darkened room with an icepack as a first resort. These tips, though, may also help.

■ At the first signs of an aura (flashing lights or zigzags), take a spoonful of apple cider vinegar or honey.
■ Eat regular, light meals to keep blood sugar levels constant. Keep a food diary to identify potential triggers in your diet.
■ Stay active. Although strenuous exercise can bring on migraines, moderate aerobic exercise promotes general well-being and can reduce the frequency and severity of attacks.
■ Painkillers can help to nip an attack in the bud, but avoid those containing codeine, which can cause rebound headaches. Painkillers containing caffeine, or even just a cup of strong coffee, may help some sufferers.
■ The herb feverfew—available as a supplement from pharmacies—is a much-used headache remedy and some people find that it can help to prevent migraines, though medical studies are inconclusive.
■ If you're taking the contraceptive pill, consider trying another brand, as hormone cycles can be linked to migraine. If you experience migraines with an aura, avoid the pill altogether, as this can increase the risk of stroke.

See also HEADACHE.

take the Minutes of a meeting

■ Talk to the person chairing the meeting (*see* MEETING) beforehand. Find out the purpose of the meeting, and get a copy of the agenda and a list of invitees.
■ During the meeting, don't try to record every remark. Concentrate on actions to be taken (noting who they are assigned to), and write down any decisions that are made. These two categories—actions and decisions—should form the bulk of your minutes.
■ Show a draft of your finished document to the chair of the meeting before circulating it to the invitees and any other relevant recipients.

clean a Mirror for a clear view

Don't just treat your mirror like a pane of glass. A store-bought glass cleaner, sprayed liberally onto the mirror, can seep around the edges and affect the backing, oxidizing the silver and making it black, brittle and flaky. It can also damage the frame. Spray cleaning fluids onto a lint-free cloth and use this to clean and polish the surface, or try these household tips.

■ Use a leather chamois, dipped in a solution of 1 tbsp white vinegar in 2⅔ qt (2.5 L) of warm water and squeezed out.
■ If hairspray has become caked on the mirror, wipe it off with a little rubbing alcohol on a soft cloth.
■ Avoid abrasive cleaners and acidic ones too, as they can damage the reflective backing.

hang a Mirror

Large framed mirrors are heavy and should be hung on wood supports. Make an interlocking support from a length of wood approximately 2 x 1 in. (5 x 2 cm) and slightly shorter than the width of the mirror. Cut along its length at an angle, as shown (right). Attach one part to the wall studs and the other to the back of the mirror so that they slot together when the mirror is hung.

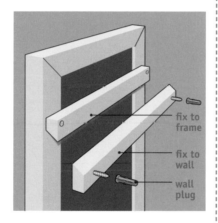

fix to frame
fix to wall
wall plug

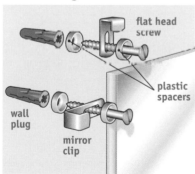

flat head screw
plastic spacers
wall plug
mirror clip

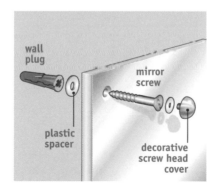

wall plug
mirror screw
plastic spacer
decorative screw head cover

Sliding mirror clips are used for frameless mirrors. Use fixed clips at the bottom and two sliding clips at the top. For large mirrors, put two clips on each side. Position clips so the screws are hidden and they can slide in and out for fitting or removing the mirror.

Use mirror screws to hang a mirror with screw holes. Use plastic spacers between the back of the mirror and the wall to allow air to circulate and avoid cracking the mirror as you tighten the screws. Don't attempt to drill holes in a mirror yourself: This is a job for a specialist.

make a Mobile

A mobile is a delicately balanced assemblage of lightweight objects suspended by strings. The slightest movement of the air will set a mobile in motion.
■ To make a simple mobile, tie or glue various shapes (circles, squares, animal forms) to a central string. Cut the shapes from construction paper or medium-weight cardboard.
■ To add texture and interest, incorporate balsa wood, colored glass, or natural objects like shells and nuts.
■ More complex and interesting mobiles can be created by incorporating one or move horizontal arms into the structure. The arms should be rigid, but lightweight. Slender wooden dowels or 14- to 20-gauge steel wire make good arms.
■ Use string or nylon fishing line to hang an object or shape from each end of an arm. Hold the arm between your thumb and forefinger to determine the balance point, knot a string there, and lift the mobile by the string to make sure it hangs level.
■ Create other arms by the same method and add them to the structure. Work from the bottom up, checking the balance whenever a new arm is added. For visual interest, vary the size of the shapes and the lengths of the threads.
■ Display the finished mobile in an open area where it can move freely.

keep Money safe when you travel

Don't keep all your money, cards and ID in one place.

Do take out only as much cash as you need for the day, and spread it around your person: in a money belt, a neck pouch inside your clothes, or hard-to-access pockets.

Don't flash your wallet around, especially in busy places.

Do carry your wallet or purse in the front pocket of your pants: It's almost impossible for a pickpocket to steal it from there.

Do leave the rest of your cash at your hotel in a safe. If there's no safe, lock your cash in a suitcase.

---

win at Monopoly

It's partly a game of chance. But there are winning strategies.

■ Buy as much property as you can early on. You're then in a strong position to trade to complete a set of three properties.

■ Aim to get the orange properties; they're cheap to build on (just $100 per house), and so provide a high return. Moreover, their position on the board, on the run after "Jail," means that they have a high probability of being visited. The red properties are also good, but avoid green, yellow or blue: The odds are against your getting rich with them.

■ When you build, stop at four houses; converting to hotels doesn't bring that much additional revenue. More importantly, it's a good tactic to create a housing shortage so that your opponents cannot build on their own properties easily. If you're pulling in the rent while preventing your opponents from doing the same, then sooner or later you'll win.

read and send Morse code

Morse code is a method of transmitting messages using sound or a flashing light. It's a useful way of communicating over long distances, or when face-to-face communication is impossible.

Letters of the alphabet

Morse code provides a means of representing each letter of the alphabet using combinations of dots (short bursts of light or sound) or dashes (longer bursts, equivalent to three dots). The sender spells out the message letter by letter, leaving an interval the length of one dash between letters, two dashes between words. To write or read Morse code fluently takes time and practice, and there's no shortcut to mastering it. In the days when Morse code was widely used in wireless telegraphy and by ships at sea, there were many skilled operators. Knowledge of Morse code is now rare—but it's still worth everyone's while to know the Morse distress signal, which is the three letters SOS (Save Our Souls)—or dot-dot-dot, dash-dash-dash, dot-dot-dot.

A	● ▬	M	▬ ▬	Y	▬ ● ▬ ▬	3	● ● ● ▬ ▬
B	▬ ● ● ●	N	▬ ●	Z	▬ ▬ ● ●	4	● ● ● ● ▬
C	▬ ● ▬ ●	O	▬ ▬ ▬	.	● ▬ ● ▬ ● ▬	5	● ● ● ● ●
D	▬ ● ●	P	● ▬ ▬ ●	,	▬ ▬ ● ● ▬ ▬	6	▬ ● ● ● ●
E	●	Q	▬ ▬ ● ▬	?	● ● ▬ ▬ ● ●	7	▬ ▬ ● ● ●
F	● ● ▬ ●	R	● ▬ ●	/	▬ ● ● ▬ ●	8	▬ ▬ ▬ ● ●
G	▬ ▬ ●	S	● ● ●	@	● ▬ ▬ ● ▬ ●	9	▬ ▬ ▬ ▬ ●
H	● ● ● ●	T	▬	1	● ▬ ▬ ▬ ▬	0	▬ ▬ ▬ ▬ ▬
I	● ●	U	● ● ▬	2	● ● ▬ ▬ ▬		
J	● ▬ ▬ ▬	V	● ● ● ▬				
K	▬ ● ▬	W	● ▬ ▬				
L	● ▬ ● ●	X	▬ ● ● ▬				

● ● ●	▬ ▬ ▬	● ● ●
S	O	S

---

make a beautiful Mosaic

Craft shops or internet sites sell all the basic materials needed for making mosaics, but you can also use your own collections of stones, shells or even pieces of broken pottery.

YOU WILL NEED Pencil, paper, safety glasses, tiles (or other material such as broken-up plates), tile cutter, wood glue or tile adhesive, tweezers, plywood backing cut to size, cement-based grout, rubber scraper or palette knife, strips of wood, masking tape, brown craft paper, water-soluble glue or wallpaper paste, brush, heavy books, stiff-bristled brush

Direct method—for simple geometric designs

Draw your design on paper. Put on safety glasses and cut tiles to shape and size, coat with adhesive and use tweezers to place pieces in position on the plywood. Let dry. Apply grout with the scraper or palette knife. Allow to dry overnight. Scrape off any excess. Trim backing.

Indirect method—for building a picture

1 Draw your design, then tape wood strips around the edge. Arrange unglued pieces in place, cutting them as you go, beginning with the shape outline. Apply glue to the craft paper and lay it over the mosaic, taking care not to move the pieces. Let dry, loosen the tape, then turn the mosaic over.

Stick craft paper over finished design.

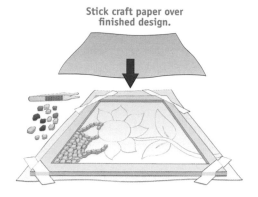

Apply plywood to back of mosaic.

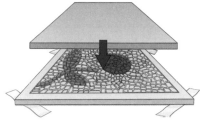

2 Apply wood glue to the plywood backing and place over back of mosaic. Weight with books and let dry.

Peel back paper to reveal design.

3 Moisten the craft paper and peel off. Grout as for direct method and grout a second time, if necessary.

keep Mosquitoes at bay

■ Mosquitoes are attracted by the carbon dioxide in human breath, but also by floral fragrances in perfumes and toiletry products. Avoid fragrant lotions to reduce your chance of being bitten.

■ If mosquitoes trouble you around your home, eliminate all pools of stagnant or dirty water. Be sure to change the water in fountains and birdbaths. Empty buckets, plant pots and wheelbarrows of accumulated rainwater. Drain any puddles that form on patios or lawns. Remember that even a pet's drinking bowl can become a breeding ground for mosquitoes.

■ Citronella oil, the active ingredient in most "natural" mosquito repellents, can work for a hour or two when applied to the skin. However, citronella candles, often used outdoors in the evening, are no more effective against mosquitoes than ordinary candles: It seems the flame—a source of warmth and light—acts as a decoy.

■ By far the most effective "topical" repellents are those containing the chemical DEET. A repellent with a DEET concentration of 35 percent is adequate for most situations, but travelers in countries where malaria is endemic should use a more concentrated formula.

deal with Mosquito bites

In parts of Africa, Asia and South America, a "bite" from one of these parasitic bloodsuckers can cause malaria. In temperate regions, itchy lumps, and possibly blisters and inflammation, are usually as bad as it gets.

■ Don't scratch! It can make the bite more itchy and swollen and cause a secondary infection.
■ Wash the area with soap and water.
■ Apply a cold compress, such as a bag of ice or frozen peas wrapped in a cloth, to reduce swelling. Don't apply ice directly to the skin.
■ Soothe the itch. Calamine lotion, ibuprofen gel or antihistamine cream can bring relief and reduce the likelihood of infection and swelling—but don't use them on broken skin. Alternatively a paste of baking soda and witch hazel is a trusted natural remedy.
■ Watch for an allergic reaction (*see* ALLERGY EMERGENCY).
■ Mosquitoes are at their busiest from two hours before dusk and again at dawn—so go indoors before the sun goes down and don't venture out too early without protection.

avoid Moths

Regular cleaning of clothes is the best way of avoiding moths, but it's far from foolproof. Sweat, hair oil and food attract moths and make attack more likely. Wool and cashmere are most vulnerable, but moth larvae will munch on cotton and even heavily stained synthetics.

Clothes
- Never put clothes away dirty.
- Store valuable items, such as cashmere sweaters, in plastic storage bags all year. Do the same for clothes you're storing for a season.
- Store-bought moth-killer strips work better as a deterrent than mothballs and are odor-free. Cedar balls can work well, too. Sprays are also available for treating the inside of closets and drawers.

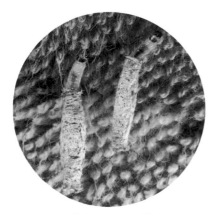

moth larvae, magnified

Carpets and furniture
- Shampoo or clean items regularly.
- Purpose-made chemical sprays are available but must be applied following the manufacturer's specific instructions.
- Carpet areas that get the least traffic need most attention.
- If buying secondhand carpets, look for the telltale white threads left by moth larvae.

ride a Motorcycle safely

While riding
- If your helmet has no face shield, wear goggles while riding.
- Protect your body from abrasion in the case of a spill by wearing a leather jacket and pants, or the newer lightweight protective wear sold by many companies.
- Drive defensively; a motorist often won't even see a motorcyclist until it's too late. Look far ahead, use your mirrors and be prepared to stop or swerve even when you have the right of way.
- If you're at a stop and see a car coming up quickly in your mirror, tap the brakes repeatedly to blink your brake light in case the driver doesn't see you.

Preventative maintenance
- Keep an eye on your tires' tread and make sure that they are always properly inflated.
- Check the oil and brake fluid regularly.

make an authentic Moussaka

Beef can be used in place of lamb in this recipe, to cut down on salt and fat. Modern eggplant varieties aren't as bitter as they once were, so it isn't necessary to salt them before cooking. If you have time, cook and refrigerate the meat in advance, then skim any fat from the surface. Serve with a salad.

SERVES 4-6

3-4 tbsp olive oil
1 large onion, finely chopped
1 lb (500 g) lean ground lamb
2 tsp tomato paste
2/3 cup vegetable stock

salt and freshly ground black pepper
4 medium eggplants, thinly sliced
2 tbsp butter
3 tbsp all-purpose flour
1 cup plus 2 tbsp milk
1 egg

1 Heat 1 tbsp oil in a heavy-bottomed pan and gently cook the onion for about 5 minutes. Gradually add the lamb and cook, stirring, until thoroughly sealed. Stir in the tomato paste and stock, season then bring to a boil and simmer for 30 minutes, or until the meat is tender and the liquid almost absorbed. Cool and remove any fat.

2 Lightly brush the eggplant with the remaining oil and broil on both sides until soft and golden brown. Beginning and ending with eggplant, layer them with the meat in a large, lightly greased ovenproof dish.

3 Heat the oven to 350°F (180°C). Melt the butter over low heat and stir in the flour. Cook for 1 minute then mix in the milk. Season then simmer for 1-2 minutes. Take the pan off the heat and beat in the egg. Spoon over the moussaka and bake in the oven for 35-40 minutes, until brown and bubbling.

minimize the stress of Moving

Moving from one house or apartment to another is notoriously stressful. To minimize the worry, you should plan well in advance.

Three weeks, or more, before you move
- If you're moving yourself, get boxes and begin packing non-essentials such as books, pictures and ornaments.
- Get at least three quotes for a truck rental.
- If you're using movers (a far less stressful option), ask some companies to give a quote for the job. Be sure to discuss matters such as parking problems and items that will need special handling, such as a piano or aquarium.
- Arrange to have your mail redirected to your new address.

A week before you move
- Whether you're using a moving company or not, pack your precious, fragile items—jewelry, heirlooms, ornaments—ready to take them with you in your car, so that they're not sitting at the bottom of a stack of boxes.
- If you're moving yourself, consider taking out moving insurance.

On the day
- Get an early start; it takes longer than you think.
- Make sure all boxes are labeled.
- Speak to the mover in charge when he arrives and give instructions only to him. Keep the workers supplied with snacks.
- Pack a small box of essentials, such as a coffeemaker or kettle, cups, coffee or teabags, toilet paper and a utility knife, which you can access immediately once you've moved.
- Phone through all utility meter readings to the relevant companies.

Before you go
- Lock all doors and windows before you hand over the keys.
- Check you have done everything you agreed upon with the new owners.
- Leave your new address, so that they can forward stray mail.

mix up your own Muesli

You can vary muesli ingredients to suit your taste, but a generous base of cereal is always required.

MAKES 8-10 BREAKFAST PORTIONS

1 cup wheat bran
½ cup sunflower seeds
1 cup nuts (Brazils, hazelnuts, almonds), chopped
1 cup mixed dried fruit (raisins, apricots, figs), chopped
½ cup dried banana chips
2½ cups rolled oats
½ cup barley flakes
2 tsp ground cinnamon (optional)

Dry fry the bran and sunflower seeds in a large nonstick frying pan for 3-4 minutes until golden and aromatic. Cool, then mix with the remaining ingredients. Store in an airtight container. Serve with milk or yogurt and, if you wish, fresh fruit such as grated apple, raspberries or banana. Also, you can vary the ingredient amounts to taste.

choose and use a Mulch

Mulches are soil coverings that come in two types—biodegradable and non-biodegradable. All help to retain moisture, suppress weeds, protect plant roots from extreme heat and cold, and encourage earthworms and other beneficial soil organisms.

Biodegradable mulches, such as leaf mold, mushroom compost or wood chippings, also release additional nutrients into the soil as they rot.

Non-biodegradable options include gravel or pebbles, and plastic or fabric sheets. The latter are good at suppressing weeds and retaining moisture but can be unattractive and, unless you choose a permeable fabric, cut slits or leave gaps, won't let water penetrate.

- Apply mulch from late spring to autumn when the soil is moist and warm. Lay it over an entire bed or border, or around individual plants.
- Lay biodegradable mulches to a thickness of at least 2 in. (5 cm).
- Weed thoroughly before mulching.
- Don't smother small plants.
- Don't pile mulch up the stems of shrubs and other woody plants.

golden rules

- **Never cook a wild mushroom unless you're totally sure you have identified it correctly.**
- **Remember that mushrooms can produce large amounts of liquid, especially when cooked slowly.**

warm up with
Mulled wine

Sweet and spicy mulled wine is wonderfully reviving on a cold winter's night. The Germans call it Glühwein—glow wine—a name that couldn't be more apt.

SERVES 12

4 bottles fruity, dry red wine
⅔ cup sugar
thinly pared rind of 2 lemons and 2 oranges
juice of 2 oranges
12 cloves
generous grating of nutmeg
2 cinnamon sticks
½ cup brandy
thinly sliced lemon

1 Pour the wine into a large pan and add the sugar, citrus peel and juices, and spices. Set over low heat and stir occasionally until the sugar is dissolved.

2 Remove the pan from the heat and let stand for half an hour to allow the flavors to mingle.

3 Return the pan to low heat, warm until the liquid is just beginning to steam, then add the brandy.

4 Strain into a punch bowl, garnish with the slices of lemon and ladle into heatproof glasses.

prepare and cook Mushrooms

Mushrooms are versatile ingredients that can be cooked and served on their own or added to everything from soups to casseroles. As well as cultivated mushrooms, wild varieties such as shiitake and chanterelles are widely available, especially in autumn. Their delicate flavor makes them ideal for serving on toast or as accompaniments to chicken and fish. Dried porcini mushrooms, with their robust flavor, are excellent for risottos (*see* RISOTTO) and meat dishes, and make a useful pantry ingredient.

Wipe with a damp cloth to clean If covered with excessive dirt, plunge into cold water then shake. Morels and other mushrooms with deep indentations should be left in water for 5 minutes before cleaning. But don't let other kinds of mushroom soak or they will absorb too much liquid.

Trim the stalks Peel the skins from large field mushrooms. Then quarter, slice or dice as required. Pour boiling water over dried mushrooms, soak for 20 minutes, then strain and dry on paper towels. (The flavor-rich soaking liquid can be restrained through cheesecloth and used in stock or soup.)

Fry in a mixture of oil and butter Add mushrooms to a hot pan and cook over medium heat. As juices appear, turn the heat to high to boil them off quickly. Season well with salt and freshly ground black pepper. Tarragon is also an excellent flavoring, or add lemon juice or a dash of chili. Or brush with butter and grill for 6-8 minutes, turning once. Stuff large flat mushrooms with a breadcrumb-based stuffing or a cheese mixture and broil or bake.

compose a perfect Music compilation

Creating a music mix is fun and absorbing. It allows you to include only your favorite tracks and makes a very personal gift.

Use online music stores such as iTunes for digital singles. The choice is almost limitless.

Make a playlist Search for songs by name or title, listen to them and drag those you want into your playlist. This will be a rough draft. Edit it as you go; add to it, drop things, change the playing order.

Start with a couple of stunners to draw the listener in.

Vary the pace Follow a soft and dreamy track with something loud and electrifying.

Make it meaningful Choose songs that evoke memories of the day you met, a romantic holiday, that first date—or that show how you feel.

Don't get carried away Anything more than 16-20 tracks, however good the music, is too long.

Make the final track count Choose something that stays in the mind. Let it impart something significant to the listener.

When you're thrilled with your mix, burn a disk (*see* CD).

Add finishing touches Create artwork for your CD and give it a title. You can print off artwork from iTunes. Go to the **Advanced** menu and choose **Get Album Artwork**.

master the basics of Music notation

When reading or playing music from the page, there are two things you need to know about every note: what the pitch is (how high or low it is), and how long you should play the note for. Musical notation conveys this information, and much more, using a highly readable and economical system. The short example below is taken from the horn part of J.S. Bach's Mass in B Minor.

The length of a note is signified by the precise shape of the tadpole-like symbols on the page. A black note with a stick-like tail is played for one beat.

A note with a curly hook on its tail (or, when they occur in pairs, with a thick horizontal lid) is played for half a beat.

A note with a doubled tail or lid is played for a quarter of a beat.

The five lines of the stave, and the four gaps between them, represent the notes of the scale. The higher up the stave the note is placed, the higher the note to be played.

Each space or line on the stave is one note up the scale from the one below.

Other symbols represent rests: an instruction to the player to be silent for a set duration such as one beat (a vertical squiggle, right) or half a beat (above, shaped like a curly "7").

The symbols for standard notes and rests are shown in the table opposite. There are many other symbols signifying, for example, how to play rather than what to play—quietly, crisply, running the notes together.

NUMBER OF BEATS	STANDARD NOTATION	REST	NAME
4	𝅝		semibreve
3	𝅗𝅥.		dotted minim
2	𝅗𝅥		minim
1	♩	𝄽	crotchet
½	♪ 𝅘𝅥𝅮		quaver
¼	𝅘𝅥𝅯		semiquaver

grow Mustard and watercress

These little plants are so easy to grow. They are great fun for children—and a tasty addition to a salad.

YOU WILL NEED **Plastic tray without drainage holes, paper towels, seeds, scissors**

■ Line the tray with paper towels and dampen.
■ Sprinkle in the mustard seeds and leave in a light place for three or four days, keeping the paper moist but not sodden. Then add the watercress seeds (which germinate faster).
■ Leave until well grown, moistening as necessary. Harvest with scissors.

tackle and cook Mussels

Hidden within the hinged darkness of a mussel's shell lies a succulent morsel of orange flesh.

To store As soon as you get them home, put mussels into the fridge or a large bucket of cold, salted water.

To prepare Scrub with a stiff brush to remove grit, and scrape off any barnacles with a sharp knife. Rinse well. Finally, scrape away the strands of the "beard" emerging from the shell (pictured).

To cook Put in a large pan with about ½ in. (1 cm) water or white wine, plus some chopped parsley and chopped shallots or onions. Cover; cook on high heat, shaking occasionally, for about 5 minutes or until the mussels open. Remove mussels with a slotted spoon. Strain the cooking liquid through a cheesecloth-lined strainer to remove grit, then serve.

golden rules

SPOTTING BAD MUSSELS
■ **Discard any mussels with broken shells, or that float when soaked in water.**
■ **Before cooking, discard any mussel that doesn't close after being pried open a little, or that opens easily.**
■ **Never eat a mussel that doesn't open once cooked.**

polish your Nails

YOU WILL NEED Nail polish remover, cotton balls, cotton swabs, protective base polish, colored polish

■ Remove any remnants of old polish from the nails with a cotton ball. Dip a cotton swab into the polish remover and work around the cuticles.

■ Rest one hand at a time on a firm surface. Work from the little finger in. Apply the base coat in three strokes—center, right, left—right to the edges. Wait for it to dry.

■ Roll the polish bottle between your palms to mix. Paint on a thin layer in three strokes. Be sure the first coat is dry. Apply a second, covering any gaps in the first.

Start your first stroke at the point shown.

Brush back toward the cuticle.

Then brush forward to your nail tip.

Make a parallel stroke to one side, brushing from cuticle to tip.

Apply a third stroke on the other side, again from cuticle to tip.

Once the whole nail is covered, dry, then repeat to apply a second coat.

use the right Nails

You should select the correct nails for the job at hand—and then take care hammering them in.

Use	Nail type
ROUGH CARPENTRY 	**Common nails** are best for fixing large pieces of wood together in situations where appearance isn't key. They come in various sizes. Always nail the thinner piece of wood to the thicker one.
FINE CARPENTRY 	Use **finishing nails** where you want the nail to be invisible. Sink the head with a nail punch and fill the hole. These are good for wood that you might want to paint, such as a piece of furniture.
PLYWOOD OR MDF	Use **paneling nails** for fixing sheet materials to wood framing. Paneling nails, being small and unobtrusive, are also good for installing wooden moldings. You can sink the head with a nail punch and fill the hole.
ROOFING FELT/ WIRE FENCING 	**Roofing nails** have large heads that hold pliable materials firmly in place. Use galvanized ones for outdoor jobs.
DRYWALL 	There are special **drywall nails** that have jagged shanks and large heads to increase their holding power. Use the ringed (annular) type for plasterboarding ceilings.
BRICKWORK	**Masonry nails** are specially hardened so that they can penetrate brick. Drive them into the body of the brick, not into the mortar courses between them. The nails may shatter if not struck straight, so wear safety glasses when using them.

stop Nail-biting

Nibbling your nails is a largely unconscious act. Keep a record of when you do it. This will increase your awareness and interrupt the process. If you find, for instance, that you bite your nails when you're alone, reading, wear gloves before you pick up a book.

Give yourself a weekly manicure Pride in your hands can discourage biting (*see left and* MANICURE).

Keep your fingers busy with fidget toys, sewing, doodling or worry beads —any handicraft or activity that provides an alternative.

Try a bitter-tasting anti-biting solution This can be painted onto nails and is available from pharmacies.

---

change your Name

There are many reasons to want to change your name. And in some countries, it's a very simple deal. However, where you live dictates just how easy—or hard—changing your name will be.

In Common Law jurisdictions, like the US and most of Canada, an official name change follows the basic guidelines below; for specifics, call your local government. An unofficial name change is easy: just call yourself whatever you like!

In the US, name changes are handled at the state level. Not all states have the same requirements, but generally you should start by registering an official name change with your state social security office and department of motor vehicles. It is important to find out, at the time of registering your new name, which agencies you will have to notify.

In most of Canada, a woman can choose to take her husband's name using her marriage certificate as proof. Other name changes in most provinces and territories must be submitted to the appropriate government ministry, the court or some other approved agency.

Quebec operates on Civil Law rather than Common Law. As such, a married woman may not take her husband's name. Any other name-change requests must have a valid reason and be approved by the director of civil status.

---

remember Names

If you say you have a head like a sieve when it comes to names, consider this: It might be more like a brick wall. Demolish those mental barriers.

Take an interest When you're introduced to someone, study them and want to know more about them.

If you don't quite catch a name, ask to hear it again. If necessary you should ask for the spelling.

Repetition, repetition Say their name back to them, repeat it mentally to yourself and drop it subtly into the conversation.

If you've forgotten a name, apologize and ask to be reminded.

Make associations Think of someone else with the same name. Picture that person. If someone is called Basil, Rose or Ruby, visualize those things.

On leaving, say goodbye to your new friend by name. Write their name down afterward.

---

fold a
Napkin

A crisp linen napkin, sharply folded, adds an elegant finishing touch to a dinner table setting.

Pyramid napkin

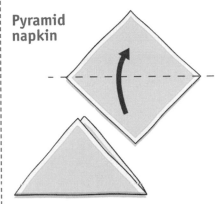

1 Use a spotless starched napkin that will take a shape and stand, not flop. Lay it out in front of you on the diagonal and fold the bottom corner to the top to form a triangle. Smooth the crease.

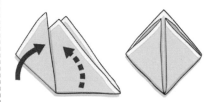

2 Bring the bottom corners up to meet at the top point.

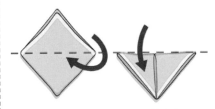

3 Turn the napkin over and fold it in half by bringing the top point of the diamond toward you.

4 Turn the napkin over again, fold along the center line and stand it on the base of the triangle with the crease facing the diner.

repair a Necklace

It's best to have valuable jewelry professionally repaired, but there are some problems you can solve yourself. A broken necklace is best totally restrung (*see* BEAD NECKLACE). Replacement clasps can be obtained from jewelers, bead stores or specialty suppliers.

Untangling Sprinkle a knot with talcum powder, cornstarch or vegetable oil to lubricate the links. Then place on a firm surface and use the points of two pins to pry knots apart. Wash in a mild detergent, rinse and dry with a soft cloth.

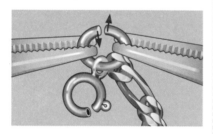

Repairing or replacing a clasp or loop Use a single pair of pliers to close up a gap in a clasp or loop. To replace a clasp, use two pairs of small pliers to twist open the loop attached to the clasp. Remove the old clasp and replace with a new one, then use the pliers to close the loop.

Tightening a V-spring Insert a knife blade between the two parts of the V-spring and turn it a little to push the leaves apart. Test to make sure it fits the clasp sheath and repeat as necessary.

thread a Needle easily

- Choose a needle with an eye of appropriate size for the thickness of thread you're planning to use.
- Hold the thread against a background with a contrasting color.
- Lick or dampen the end of the thread, or apply some hairspray.
- For thick thread such as wool, tie on a length of thin cotton thread and stick that through the needle first, pulling the wool through behind it.
- Use an old-fashioned wire needle-threader. Pass the thin loop of wire through the needle, feed the thread through the loop and pull back through.
- Use an automatic threader (available online).

---

start basic Needlepoint

Needlepoint, or tapestry, is stitching done on canvas. It's versatile and easy to master, and can be done almost anywhere.

The mesh of the canvas provides a grid onto which you can stitch differently colored threads to create a pattern or picture. You begin with simple stitches, then add more as you progress. The completed canvas can be incorporated into a cushion or chair cover, or framed as a wall hanging or picture.

YOU WILL NEED **Canvas, yarns, round-ended tapestry needle**

Patterns, yarns and stitches Canvases with preprinted patterns on them can be found at craft stores or online, or you can work from printed charts. Tapestry wool, viscose, cotton and silk are all suitable yarns for needlepoint, and should match the size of the canvas holes (its "gauge"). Yarn should be thick enough to cover the canvas when stitches are formed, but slip easily through the holes without distorting the canvas or scuffing the yarn. Cross-stitch (*see* CROSS-STITCH) and tent stitch are the most common needlepoint stitches.

Continental tent stitch

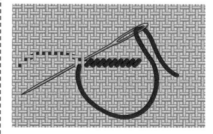

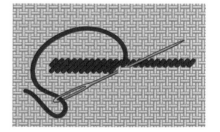

1 Pull the needle through the canvas to the right side, leaving about 2 in. (5 cm) of yarn at the back. Stitch the first row from right to left as shown, catching in the tail of yarn with the first few stitches.

2 Add the next row of stitches below the first one, working from left to right as shown. Continue working alternately from right to left and then from left to right.

Basketweave tent stitch

 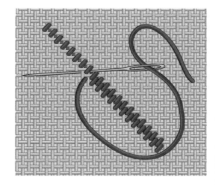

1 Beginning at the upper left of the area to be worked, bring the needle out to the front and insert it one square up to the right. Bring it back out again two squares down, then repeat until you've made the required number of stitches diagonally down the mesh.

2 To begin the "up" row, complete your last down stitch by bringing the needle out two squares down, but one to the left. Put the needle in one square up to the right, then out again two to the left. Repeat until you have the required number of diagonal rows up and down.

Finishing Bring needle and yarn to the back of the canvas. Weave yarn through the underside of the last few stitches you did. Cut off excess.

---

use Newsgroups to keep in touch

Newsgroups work like online bulletin boards, allowing you to have discussions with like-minded people all over the world.

The term "newsgroups" is a little misleading, because they don't have to be about the news. A newsgroup is a forum dedicated to talking about a particular subject—it could be anything from movies to human rights, crafts, bicycles, computer programming or parenting. You post a message that all subscribers to that group can see and reply to. It's a great way to find answers to problems and make online friends.

To find a newsgroup, search online for a key word describing your interest and a newsgroup comes up in the search results. Alternatively, browse the list of categories online on **Google Groups** (groups.google.com).

To use a newsgroup, you must register with a valid email address, which will be kept private. You then set up a username and password. Some forums require payment, but most are free to use. You'll then be ready to read all the discussions that have taken place, receive new posts as they're written and make contributions of your own. Take care to follow the golden rule of newsgroups: Only post the kind of messages that you'd like to see posted by others. Posts are monitored by moderators, who will remove unsuitable content, but always remember that these are open forums—be cautious about the information you share and the advice you follow.

Negotiate
a better price

It's amazing how many stores will offer you a discount if you ask for it. You just have to know the right things to say.

Most stores will negotiate on large items such as fridges and TVs. When it comes to secondhand items, such as cars and antiques, the seller usually expects to haggle, and will have set the price accordingly.

Build rapport with the seller. Be warm, but don't make friends. Conversely, don't try to bully the retailer into selling (*I'm not paying that price!*); you're trying to reach an agreement, not win an argument.

Make it clear you're not wasting their time, and imply that the price is just a small obstacle standing in the way of a sale. Say something like *I'm really interested, but I'd need you to give me a deal on that.*

Don't accept the first offer. In fact, don't say anything about it at all. Just look doubtful or wince, and wait to see what the seller says next. They may name a lower price.

Look for ways to add value that don't affect the price; ask for free delivery if you're buying appliances or a better stereo if it's a car.

detect and deal with
Nits (aka lice)

There's no disgrace in having head lice. They are spread by head-to-head contact and can live in both clean and unwashed hair—so it's not about hygiene.

If your child can't stop scratching his or her scalp, it could be a sign of a head lice infestation—and it may have been present for weeks, even months. These parasites are most common among kids under 11, especially girls. Lice eggs, or nits, stick to the hair close to the scalp until they hatch. Your child may get a rash on the back of his or her beck as an allergic reaction to lice feces.

Search and destroy
If your child displays symptoms, inspect their scalp minutely. Live lice are the only sure sign of a current infestation, and they are hard to see. Look for the tear-shaped eggs or shells, which can be mistaken for dandruff. Inspect collars and pillows for black specks of droppings.

Coming the hair while it's wet with a fine-toothed lice comb is an effective and nontoxic (if time-consuming) way to eradicate lice. Apply plenty of conditioner, then comb thoroughly.

- Comb through first with an ordinary comb.
- Divide the hair into sections and work through each in turn with the lice comb.
- Start each stroke as close to the scalp as possible and wipe the comb with a tissue after each stroke. If you find lice on the tissue, repeat every three to four days for the next two weeks to eliminate any new lice hatchlings.

create a Newsletter on your computer

A family newsletter is a great way to stay in touch with distant family friends, and it's easy to produce.

First, gather together your material. You'll need articles or snippets of news about your life—written by you or family members—and a selection of eye-catching photographs. Decide how long your newsletter will be. Four pages is probably enough.

Edit your text carefully and thoughtfully. When you mention triumphs and successes, try not to sound smug (*Alice was chosen to dance the lead in her ballet show—again!!!*). Modesty, ideally laced with some humor, is the best policy. And concentrate on events of common interest: A detailed chronology of your vacation, however thrilling it was at the time, is unlikely to make interesting reading for others. Save paper and postage by emailing your newsletter whenever possible instead of using snail mail.

1 Microsoft Word has a selection of newsletter templates you can use. They come with spaces for the words and pictures, and with decorative details such as borders and panels. Access all the templates by opening the Project Gallery, then selecting **Newsletters** from the dialogue box.

2 In your template, replace the default text with your own by clicking in the text box and typing. You can resize the box by clicking on it and dragging the corners and small points on its borders.

3 To add your own pictures, click in a picture box and use the dialogue box to locate your digital image. You can resize the picture boxes in the same way you did the text boxes.

cure Noisy pipes

There's no need to put up with bumps, bangs and hisses from your household plumbing. Most noises can be diagnosed and cured.

Creaking and clicking This kind of noise is caused by the pipes rubbing against wood, or against each other, as they expand and contract. One likely source of the noise is the point where the pipes come up through the floorboards. If you can raise the floorboards, use a file to enlarge the hole slightly, and cover the pipes with felt. If the noise is coming from under the floor, lift the board above it. It may be that the pipes are running through a notch that's too tight. Use a tenon saw to make the notch wider, and pack the space with lagging.

Rushing water There's air in the system. Turn the heating off and vent the radiators (*see* RADIATOR). With a rag ready to catch drips, use a radiator key to loosen the vent. The air will hiss as it emerges. As soon as the hissing stops and water comes out, tighten the vent. Check for leaks, then vent the next radiator.

Banging If you hear loud banging noises from your plumbing system, the most likely cause is "water hammer"—a shock wave caused by water being shut off too quickly. It can usually be cured by replacing worn tap washers, closing the cold-water stop valve or replacing a piston-type ball valve on the cold water cistern with an equilibrium-type ball valve.

remember Numbers

We live in a world of numbers, and it's practically impossible to remember them all. There are some simple tricks, though, to keep a random series of numbers—such as your credit card number—in your head.

- Break them down. Just as phone numbers would be harder to recall if they didn't divide into area codes and sets of numbers, any long numbers can be divided into manageable chunks. Instead of trying to memorize a 16-digit bank card number, memorize four 4-digit numbers.
- Use rhythm and repetition. Reciting numbers in threes is effective because it resembles normal speech patterns. If the long number doesn't divide into threes, add "and" or "and a"—for example, "146 289 722 and a 9."
- Use rhyme. Substitute bun (one), shoe (two), tree (three), paw (four), hive (five), bricks (six), heaven (seven), gate (eight), line (nine), hen (ten) —pictures you can visualize—for the digits.

stop a Nosebleed

Unless they are frequent and persistent, or caused by a serious blow to the face, nosebleeds are more of an inconvenience than a medical emergency. They can usually be halted in a matter of minutes.

Do lean forward—ideally over a basin—so the blood can drain down and out of your nose.
Don't tilt your head back—it will cause the blood to drain down the back of your throat. If any blood does reach your throat, spit it out, don't swallow it.
Do breathe through your mouth and pinch the soft part of the nose to stem the flow.
Don't sniff, swallow or cough while clots are forming.
Do continue to pinch for ten minutes, then release and see if bleeding has stopped. If not, pinch again. A covered ice pack held against your cheek can also help reduce bleeding.
Don't blow your nose after the bleeding has stopped. Use a damp cloth to clean around the nose.
Don't put a coin in your mouth, tie string around your little finger or use any other crazy folk remedies. They don't work!

follow the Offside rule in soccer

The offside rule isn't as complex as people think. But in some cases, its enforcement relies on the judgment of the referee.

An offside player is one who is nearer to the opponents' goal line than both the ball and the two last opponents. One defending player will usually, but not necessarily, be the goalkeeper. The ball must be played forward to the offside player for the foul to be called.

An attacking player (A) isn't offside if there's an opposition player (B), other than the goalkeeper, in line with or in front of them at the moment the passing player (C) kicks the ball.

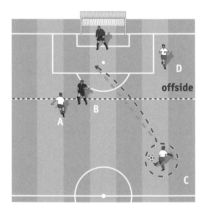
offside

There is some gray area, however. A player in an offside position (D) isn't deemed to be offside if not interfering with play. If they were far from the action of an attack that resulted in a goal (above), that goal would most likely stand.

The problem is, even if a player is utterly uninvolved in an attack, their mere presence might be enough to attract the attention of a defender, who then plays differently. It's for the referee to judge if an attacker's position or actions amount to "interfering with play." This is the source of much of the confusion around this rule.

get started with Oil painting

The rich pigments of oil paints make them a joy to work with. Learn the basics and you'll soon be producing your own masterpieces.

YOU WILL NEED **Bristle brushes and soft brush (see below), canvas, easel, charcoal, palette, student-grade oil paints, turpentine**

Select your brushes The strong, springy bristles of hog-bristle brushes are ideal for the heavy texture of oil paint. Bristle brushes come in different shapes, such as flat, round and bright, and in numbered sizes; the largest is 12 and 00 is smallest. For a beginner, the three shown below will cover most tasks. One soft synthetic brush is also useful for small-scale or detailed work.

NO. 5 FLAT Ideal for applying broad, rectangular strokes and areas of thick, bold color as well as short dabs of color. Use the side of the brush for thin lines and sharp details.

NO. 8 ROUND Suitable for early composition, making long, bold marks and laying in large areas of color.

NO. 2 BRIGHT Good for detailed work thanks to its shorter, stiffer bristles. A round-ended No. 4 synthetic brush is also useful for fine detail or for laying in an area of thin color.

Set the scene Decide on your subject—for instance, a landscape. Place the canvas level and perpendicular. When painting outdoors, position the canvas so that the sun doesn't shine on it.

Do the groundwork Use charcoal or thinned paint to sketch the composition. Include one dominant element, such as a barn, and some subordinate items, such as trees or livestock. Give the dominant element due prominence in size or position. The horizon should be one-third or two-thirds up the canvas. Keep it low if you want to paint tall trees or close-up buildings.

Prepare your palette The colors you plan to use should go to the sides. Mix them in the middle to make an infinity of new shades.

Start painting If you have a dark sky, keep the landscape light, or vice versa. Paint the foreground in detail; keep the background vague—as the eye sees it. Make most use of contrast in the foreground. Oil paints can be applied as is, straight from the tube, but are easier to use when mixed ("thinned") with turpentine. Simply stir in turpentine until you have the desired consistency.

Wet-on-wet painting requires a single layer of paint, and is usually executed in one sitting ("direct"). Think of the fluid energy of Impressionist painters such as Monet and Cézanne. Blending wet colors can produce subtle changes.

Fat over lean is slower and more controlled ("indirect") painting, often starting with a tonal under-painting in grey or brown. Think of such Old Masters as Rembrandt. "Fat" describes the buttery paint straight from the tube. Start with thin paint then gradually build in thickness, waiting for each layer to dry. So which are you—a Monet or a Rembrandt?

---

appreciate Opera

Opera is all about intense emotion—that of the composer, the characters and the spectator, who is swept away on a flood of music and spectacle. Best of all, there's no need rent a tux.

An opera is a drama in music, with dance, lavish costumes and sets. Like any stage play, it has multiple acts and scene changes. Unlike a musical, most operas have no spoken lines and are entirely composed of song, with musical overture and interludes.

Understanding the language of opera
The written lyric is called the *libretto*, delivered as melodic solo arias, duets and dialogue between the various players. The greatest operas combine several memorable arias, a tragic tale and intriguing characters. A female star of great rank or pretension is called a diva—a goddess. "Tenor" describes the highest natural male voice; "basso profundo," the lowest. "Soprano" is the highest female voice, followed by "mezzo soprano" and "contralto." The varied singing styles and techniques give opera its rich texture and complexity.

What's it all about? Driven humanity, passion and towering emotion.

But isn't it elitist? No matter what income bracket you're in, you'll find yourself singing along to the Toreador Song from Georges Bizet's *Carmen* (1875), or "La donna è mobile" from Giuseppe Verdi's *Rigoletto* (1851). Opera may even have persuaded you to buy sneakers, aftershave, cereal or soda. Advertisers use it because it evokes an emotional response.

But it's in a foreign language! There are English operas, too, but the language of opera is the universal language of the heart.

Where do I start? The most accessible operas are from the Romantic period in the second half of the 19th century, usually sung in Italian. Try anything by Giacomo Puccini (*Tosca, La Bohème, Madama Butterfly*), or Verdi's *Aida, Rigoletto, La Traviata* or *Falstaff*. For an English-language opera, try *Peter Grimes* by Benjamin Britten. Before seeing your chosen opera live, get to know it on DVD first. This will increase your appreciation of the show and add to your sense of anticipation, which is a powerful part of the experience.

make a perfect
Omelet

You can add herbs to this omelet mixture if you wish and, before folding, toss in ingredients such as grated cheese, sliced cooked mushrooms or diced ham, to taste. Cook in a small frying pan or a special omelet pan.

SERVES 1

2 eggs
1 tbsp milk or water
¼ tsp salt
freshly ground black pepper
1 tbsp butter

Beat the first four ingredients together with a fork. Melt the butter until hot, but not brown. Pour in the mixture, lifting it up around the edges and pulling the cooked parts to the middle with a spatula, letting any uncooked mixture run into the gap created, tipping the pan as necessary.

When the entire mixture is almost set, and the underside is golden, fold in half or into thirds with the spatula. Remove from the pan and serve immediately.

grow and care for
Orchids

The exoticism and beauty of orchids can make them expensive to buy, but with the right care they can flower again and again. They can be grown as houseplants or in a greenhouse with equal success.

Orchids are extremely difficult to grow from seed so it's best to buy them pre-grown. For the best repeat flowering, choose the white-flowered moth orchid, or *phalaenopsis*.

■ Position orchids in good light but not full sun, in a humid environment, ideally provided by standing pots in trays filled with moist gravel.

■ Mist them regularly with rainwater. Keep plants moist between spring and autumn by plunging pots into a bucket of rainwater once a week, but water only sparingly (about once every 14 days) in the winter months.

■ Orchid's above-ground roots are good indicators of health. If yellow or brown at their ends, the plants need attention. Try repotting them in specially formulated mix from a garden store. But because orchid needs vary widely from species to species, feed only according to the guidelines provided by the grower.

fold an Origami frog

In origami, a wide variety of finished pieces are based on set initial folds. There is, for example, a bird base and frog base. Here we use the frog base to make ... a frog.

Make the preliminary fold

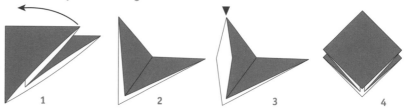

Fold a square piece of paper in half diagonally to make a triangle, then fold that in half again to make two smaller triangles (1). Lie the paper on a flat surface and lift the top triangle so it stands perpendicular to the bottom one (2). Press the upper point of this triangle directly down (3) until it meets the fold line dividing the two triangles. Flatten the paper out to either side to make a diamond shape. Turn the model over, lift the other triangle and repeat to complete the preliminary fold (4).

Turn preliminary fold into a frog

1 Raise one flap so it's perpendicular, and squash it flat as shown to make an inverted kite shape.

2 Fold in the left and right points of the kite so they make two small flaps that meet at the center line.

3 Fold the whole base in half and unfold again. Open up the flaps you just made, and take hold of the horizontal edge beneath. Lift this edge, making the two flaps "yawn." Continue lifting the edge until the two flaps meet at the center again to make another, smaller kite shape. Repeat steps 1–3 on back and both sides.

4 You'll now have a neat diamond shape. Turn the left flap of your diamond as if you were turning a page, to reveal a flat surface. Turn the diamond over and repeat on the back. You'll now have a flat surface front and back and four flaps on each side.

5 Fold in the right and left tips of the top layer to meet in the middle. Repeat on the back and sides.

6 Turn the top right flap to the left, again like a page. Turn the model over and repeat on the back. The four long thin flaps at the bottom of the model will be the frog's limbs.

  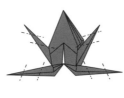

7 Fold and unfold the front limbs to make a crease in both. Open slightly and push out the inner fold line to switch the direction of the fold (a "reverse fold") so that the two limbs point up diagonally. Crease the back limbs along the different lines indicated above, and make a reverse fold in each to bring them up into a horizontal line.

8 Make further creases in each of the four limbs as shown. Then make two more reverse folds in each limb along those lines. You'll now have four fully jointed limbs.

9 To complete the frog, blow into the opening at the base of the model to inflate its head and torso, then draw on a froggy face if you wish.

---

prepare and eat Oysters

Oysters are a delicacy usually eaten live. If eaten uncooked, they must be opened just before serving and always on the day they are bought.

YOU WILL NEED **Stiff brush, thick dish towel, strong short-bladed or specially made oyster knife, bowl, plates, crushed ice, serving accompaniments and cooking ingredients, small fork, finger bowl with lemon**

Preparation

1 Scrub and scrape shells to remove any sand and dirt. Wrap your hand in the dish towel then grip the oyster in the protected hand, rounded side down. Insert the tip of the knife into the hinge and twist it to pry the shell apart.

2 Run the knife between the shells to cut through the muscles holding them together. Lift off the top shell, then cut out the oyster with the knife. If you're going to serve it raw, carefully retain all the juices. If not, drain into the bowl.

Serving and eating Present on a plate, on a bed of crushed ice, with lemon wedges, salt and pepper, Tabasco, finely chopped shallots and brown bread and butter. Supply a small fork and finger bowl for each diner.

Cooking Trickle over a little melted butter and broil for 3–4 minutes, or until just opaque. Serve right away, or cool and add to a seafood salad. Good toppings to add before broiling include breadcrumbs, herbs (dill, chervil or fennel), or grated parmesan or pecorino cheese.

---

banish grease from your Oven

Regular, thorough cleaning improves an oven's efficiency, extends its life and prevents a smoke-filled kitchen or even the risk of fire.

Prevention To avoid grease buildup:

■ Wipe spills with a moist sponge immediately, while the surface of the oven is still warm.
■ Regularly wipe the inside of the oven with a vinegar-soaked cloth.
■ When possible, cover food with a lid or foil while it cooks.
■ Don't overfill dishes—put any that may spill onto baking sheets.

Cleaning routine

1 Remove oven racks and broiler pan. Wash with cleaning liquid, using a nonabrasive scrubber. Or you can leave your racks to soak inside a specially designed cleaning bag filled with oven-cleaning solution.

2 Fill a glass bowl with about ½ cup of full-strength ammonia. Put into a cold oven, close the door and leave overnight. Remove the bowl, then clean off the loosened deposits with a cloth or sponge.

3 Pry off stubborn grease with a silicone spatula and/or scour with a nonabrasive scrubber dipped in kitchen surface cleaner.

Caustic commercial cleaners Use only as a last-ditch solution and always in a cold oven. Wear long sleeves and rubber gloves, keep the kitchen well-ventilated and follow the instructions.

make Paella

Traditionally, this Spanish rice dish is cooked and served in a two-handled iron pan. A big skillet or wok will also work well.

SERVES 6

about 1 qt (1 L) chicken stock
¾ lb (350 g) mussels
3–4 tbsp olive oil
1½ lb (750 g) boneless chicken
¼ lb (100 g) chorizo, cut into chunks
1 large onion, chopped
2 cloves garlic, minced
1¾ cups paella or risotto rice
1¼ cups (225 g) tomatoes, skinned and chopped
1 red pepper, seeded and chopped
⅓ lb (175 g) large peeled cooked shrimp
1⅔ cups frozen peas, defrosted
pinch of saffron strands
salt and freshly ground black pepper

TO GARNISH

6 large unshelled cooked shrimp
6 lemon wedges

1 Heat 1¼ cups stock in a large pan. Add the mussels, cover and simmer for 5–7 minutes until opened. Strain the stock through a cheesecloth-lined sieve and set it aside. Remove the mussels' top shells, discarding any that didn't open.

2 Heat the oil in the pan over moderate heat and cook the chicken until golden. Remove and cut into smaller chunks. Cook the chorizo and remove when browned. Cook the onion and garlic, add the rice and stir until pale brown.

3 Return chicken and chorizo to the pan with tomatoes and pepper. Add mussel stock plus chicken stock to cover. Bring to a boil, reduce heat, cover and simmer for 30–40 minutes, or until rice is tender and stock absorbed (add more if necessary). Five minutes before serving, add seafood, peas and saffron. Garnish with the shrimp and lemon.

match Paint to surfaces

It's important to use the correct paint for the job, both for aesthetic and practical reasons. Most paints now come in versions that are low in VOCs (volatile organic compounds), which are less polluting than traditional paints. You can also buy quick-drying, water-based undercoat and topcoat paints.

Surface	Application and paint type
BARE WOOD/METAL	The surface should be clean and dry, then painted with **primer**.
BARE DRYWALL	Newly drywalled interior walls can be painted with **latex interior** paint so long as the surface is primed. If the surface is old or slightly damaged, repair with drywall compound before painting.
BATHROOM AND KITCHEN WALLS	Use **mildew-resistant** paint in bathrooms and steamy kitchens. It won't stop condensation, but it will inhibit the buildup of water droplets on the painted surface, and it won't peel away when exposed to moisture.
PRIMED WOOD/METAL	One or two additional coats of **primer** should be applied first when painting primed wood or metal.
BRICKS/ STUCCO	Specially formulated **masonry** paint should be used on the outsides of houses. Two main kinds are available: oil- and water-based. Masonry primers are generally oil-based.
FLOORS	Ordinary paint isn't hard-wearing enough for wooden floorboards. Use a dedicated **floor paint** or **varnish** and thin down the first coat.
WINDOWS/DOORS	Interior wooden surfaces, including window frames, doors, doorjambs, baseboards and banisters, should be finished with a **topcoat** in the desired color. **Gloss** is shiny, while **semigloss** (also known as **satin**, **silk** or **eggshell**) is slightly more understated. The same topcoat can be used on primed metal.
CHILDREN'S TOYS AND FURNITURE	Use nontoxic **enamel** paint on metallic or wooden toys or furniture. No primer or undercoat required.

strip away old Paint

Most paint-stripping jobs require the old paint to be softened up by applying heat or chemicals. Then it's all about laborious scraping.

■ You'll need a variety of scrapers if you're removing paint from moldings on, say, a window frame: flat-blade scrapers, large and small; extra narrow scrapers, for small spaces; a long-handled scraper with a replaceable blade.
■ A hot-air gun works well on wooden doors—apply heat until the paint begins to bubble. Wear gloves while scraping and make sure the hot paint doesn't fall on you as you work. Protect the floors with dropcloths.
■ If you're using a chemical stripper, apply, then begin scraping when the paint becomes wrinkled and broken. Start too soon, and the paint won't come off; leave it too long, and the paint will dry out and get hard again.
■ Chemical strippers are best for objects with awkward nooks and crannies —old cast-iron fireplaces, for example. But you should also consider having these objects professionally sandblasted. It may be worth the expense, because it will save you many tedious hours of work.
■ When scraping wood, work along the grain as much as possible. If you're going to repaint, you don't need to get off every scrap of the old paint.

choose Paintbrushes and rollers

Buy the best brushes you can afford. Cheaper ones give worse coverage, and the bristles tend to fall out and stick to the surface you're painting. You're likely to need a number of brushes in varying widths—you should have a set of four at least. Synthetic bristles are generally a better choice for painting surfaces such as walls and fences, especially when using latex paint.

4 in. for large expanses of wall or fencing

2 in. for smaller areas such as door panels, as well as some corners and edges

1 in. and ½ in. for windows and other tricky areas

Angled brush with slanted tip for painting windows without getting paint on the glass

Paint rollers take much of the effort out of painting walls. The synthetic pile type is good for most jobs. Invest in an extension pole to paint ceilings or the high parts of walls, and a little roller for painting behind radiators without removing them. You can also rent "power rollers" that use a pump to feed paint to the head, so you don't have to stop to reload.

calculate how much Paint you need

Most paint cans indicate the area that the contents can be expected to cover. Bear in mind that you'll have to double the amount for a second coat, and bare plaster soaks up paint like a sponge, so the first coat on a fresh wall will require more paint than the tin suggests.

1 Calculate wall area (sq. ft/m²) = height x width (in ft/m)

2 Add ceiling area (sq. ft/m²) = length x width (in ft/m)

3 Subtract area of doors (sq. ft/m²)

4 Subtract area of windows (sq. ft/m²) = total area to paint

Always add a little to the total figure—better to have paint left over than to run out before you're done.

clean your Paintbrushes

Remove as much excess paint as possible before cleaning. Lay the brush on newspaper, and use an old knife to scrape along the bristles from the base to the tip. Wash out latex paint under running water. Rub a little cleaning liquid into the bristles as you work the brush with your fingers.

Oil-based paints should be cleaned off with paintbrush cleaner. Half-fill a jar with the cleaner and soak small brushes for a few minutes, then wash the brushes in running water and cleaning liquid, and rinse. Shake off water outdoors, allow the brushes to air-dry and put away.

cook the thinnest
Pancakes

Thin pancakes, also called crepes, are delicious with a variety of toppings or rolled around fillings like fruit or cheese.

MAKES 8–10 PANCAKES

1 cup all-purpose flour
pinch of salt
2 eggs, lightly beaten
1¼ cups 1% milk
oil or melted butter for frying

1 Sift flour and salt into a large bowl, make a well in the center and add the lightly beaten eggs. Slowly work in half the milk, then beat with a whisk until smooth. Then add the rest of the milk, beating until bubbly. (Or put all the ingredients into a blender and mix for 1–2 minutes until smooth, scraping down any mixture from the sides with a spatula.) Rest the batter for 30–60 minutes, then stir well and add a little more milk if the mixture is too thick.

2 Brush enough oil or butter on a frying pan to coat lightly. Heat until hot, then ladle in just enough batter to form a thin layer. Cook for about 1 minute or until the underside is golden, then turn over and cook the other side. Stack, separated with wax paper, and serve warm.

build a Paper plane that flies

Paper planes have become ever more sophisticated. The fascination may begin in childhood, but grown men compete to set new records. All you need is a crisp sheet of paper. Success depends on making precise, sharp creases to ensure the integrity of the structure.

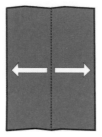 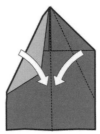 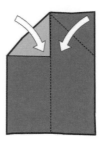 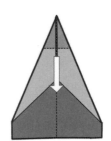

1 Lay the paper on the table lengthwise, and make a fold in it along the middle, matching corner to corner and smoothing the crease. Open it out and lay it so the creased edge forms a valley.

2 Fold the top corners in so they meet at the center line and form two triangles and a point. Smooth down the creases.

3 Fold in again from the outer point of each triangle, so the two points meet on the center line to make a more streamlined shape.

4 The next step is unexpected if you were picturing a dart. Fold the point of the plane down to meet the points on the center line.

5 Fold the whole paper back on itself along the center line so all the folded parts are on the outside. Fold down a wing on either side of the plane.

When you fly your plane, angle the wings slightly upward before you launch it. If the plane climbs, stalls and plummets to earth, angle the wings downward a little. If the plane then nosedives, angle the wing tips up slightly.

mold a Papier-mâché piggy bank

YOU WILL NEED Old newspapers, cold water, white glue, plastic bowl, balloon, scissors, egg box, tape, paints, brushes

Preparation Protect your work area. Lay down an old tablecloth, some newspaper or other covering—you will make a mess.
■ Tear the newpaper into short, uneven strips.
■ Pour 1 cup of cold water and 1 tbsp of glue into your plastic bowl, and mix to make a weak, gluey solution.
■ To make your papier-mâché mix, immerse a handful of paper strips in the glue. Be ready to add more strips to the mix as you go along.

Make your piggy bank

1 Blow up your balloon to the size of piggy bank you want. Then spread the gluey strips of paper one at a time over the balloon.

2 Apply five or six layers of papier-mâché, leaving the knot to stick out at one end. Leave overnight to dry the paper out completely.

3 Pop the balloon and remove it through the hole. Cut out feet, snout and ears from an egg carton and stick them to the pig's body with tape.

4 Cover ears, feet and snout with more papier-mâché and let dry. Paint the pig, let dry again and cut a slot in the top big enough to put coins in. Getting money out might be a little trickier...

Park a car in a tight space

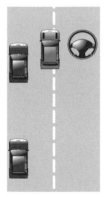 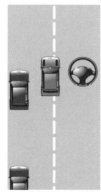 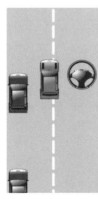 

1 Position yourself parallel to the curb and slightly in front of the car that's in front of the space you want to occupy—you're going to back in. Check that it's safe to begin the maneuver.

2 Reverse slowly, and when the rear of your car is level with the rear of the other car, turn your steering wheel one full turn toward the curb, until the front of your car is pointing to about 2 o'clock.

3 Straighten the steering wheel and reverse until the front corner of your car passes the back of the car in front. Turn the wheel two full turns in the other direction and continue reversing.

4 Reverse slowly into the space, being sure not to clip the car in front. Straighten the wheel as your front end nears the curb. Make adjustments so the car is parallel and fairly close (1 ft/ 30 cm) to the curb.

---

wrap a Parcel efficiently

When you want to send a package in the mail, your two aims should be to protect its contents and keep the weight to an absolute minimum.

■ Use a padded envelope for any items that are irregularly shaped or have hard edges.

■ Unbreakable, rectangular items are best wrapped in brown paper, which is very light, keeping the cost of postage down. Seal folds with clear packing tape—ordinary tape may not be strong enough.

■ The binding and corners of books can easily get crushed or otherwise damaged in the mail. Don't wrap books in brown paper—instead, use a corrugated cardboard book package. Small books can be sent in padded envelopes.

■ Perishable items must be clearly marked as such.

■ Prominently label any breakable items with a "FRAGILE" sticker.

■ Always write a return address on the back of a parcel or important package in case it can't be delivered for some reason.

■ The safest way to send maps, posters and plans is in a rigid cardboard tube.

■ Liquids and creams should be wrapped in plastic and sealed with tape, then sent in a leakproof container. (Both USPS and Canada Post include instructions for mailing liquids on their websites.) Powders and grains, including items such as loose-leaf tea, should be sealed in a strong plastic bag and shipped in a rigid, corrugated cardboard box.

calculate quantities
for Parties

Every party planner wants to make just the right amount of food, without a lot of leftovers and wasted food and expense. Work out your quantities by person and timing.

Canapés Allow four pieces per person to accompany drinks before dinner, 12–15 per head for a two-hour cocktail party (*see* CANAPÉS).

Food Allow just under 1½ lb (700 g) of food per person for a three-course meal. Serve a main course consisting of around ½ lb (200 g) of protein such as meat or fish, 1 cup of carbohydrates such as potatoes, rice or pasta, and ¾ cup of vegetables.

Drinks A standard bottle of wine will yield four to six glasses. Calculate on the basis of three to four glasses per person for a two-hour cocktail party, evening meal or celebration lunch. A 25 fl. oz (750 mL) bottle of liquor will make about 25 shots. Allow four shots per person for a cocktail party, plus 4 fl. oz (100 mL) of mixer for each shot. For drinks such as orange juice, allow about 1½ cups per person.

golden rules
PARTIES ON A BUDGET

■ **To save money, serve a sit-down meal—quantities are easier to calculate than they are for a buffet.**
■ **Buy wine in bulk, and opt for a large case (or keg) of beer—it'll come out cheaper than buying many small cases.**

choose a secure Password

You need to think of a password that you can easily remember, but nobody else can guess. That means you should avoid your mother's maiden name and the names of your children or pets. The worst password in the world is PASSWORD. To be effective, passwords should be at least six characters long and include a combination of letters, numbers and punctuation. If you choose your favorite city, for example, add the year you first went there, and replace one of the letters with a punctuation mark: NEWY*RK98. If you must use the name of a loved one, add the year of their birth in some unguessable way, such as mid-word: M!CH11AEL.

produce your own Pasta

Pasta is hugely versatile and simple to make at home. It can be frozen after making, or dried completely and kept in an airtight jar. It's even quicker and easier to make if you invest in a pasta machine.

SERVES 4

2 cups all-purpose flour, plus extra for working and rolling
3 medium eggs, lightly beaten
pinch of salt
1 tsp olive oil

1 Mound the flour on a clean work surface and make a well in the center. Add the eggs, salt and oil, then use a fork to draw in flour from the rim. Use your fingers to form a moist but not sticky dough.

2 Lightly flour your work surface, then knead the dough for about 10 minutes, alternately folding it using your fingers and pressing it with the heel of your hand. Form into a ball, wrap in plastic wrap and let rest in a cool place for 20 minutes.

3 Divide dough into four portions (roll each separately). Flour both your work surface and rolling pin. Pat the dough down, then roll, lifting and turning the dough occasionally to form a neat oblong or square. Let dry for about 10 minutes. For flat pasta such as lasagne, use a large knife to cut it as required. Let dry for at least 15 minutes before cooking.

4 For ribbon noodles, flour the dough and fold it several times to make a loose roll. Cut into strips about ¼ in. (5 mm) thick before unraveling them and leaving them to dry on a clean, floured dish towel for at least 15 minutes before using.

Using a pasta machine
Make the dough using durum wheat (Italian "00") flour if possible. Divide into batches and pass through the machine's rollers six to eight times, starting with the thickest setting, then adjusting the machine with each rolling until you have the required thinness. Dry for 10 minutes then, if you wish, attach a cutting head to make noodles. Dry as described above.

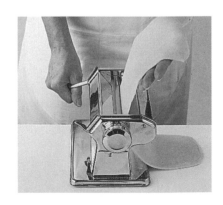

match Pasta with the right sauce

Choose sauce for pasta according to the texture, shape and size of the pasta and the thickness or chunkiness of the sauce. As a rule, the thinner the pasta, the lighter the sauce. Never drown the pasta in sauce—stir in enough to give the pasta a light coating.

Pasta	Sauce
THIN PASTAS spaghetti, linguine, vermicelli and fine bucatini 	Thinner sauces or those containing oil, cream, cheese or tomatoes. Examples include carbonara (eggs, garlic, pancetta and cheese), puttanesca (tomatoes, olives, capers and garlic), bolognese and pesto (*see* BOLOGNESE SAUCE *and* PESTO).
RIBBON PASTAS tagliatelle, linguine, fettucine and other ribbon pastas	The most versatile. Match with meat, seafood or vegetable sauces, as long as they aren't too thick.
TUBULAR SHAPES penne, rigatoni, macaroni and shells 	Chunky meat and vegetable sauces that fit into the crevices of the pasta, including sauces with small meatballs. Also good with thick cheese sauce or eggplant and tomato, for baking in the oven.
SHAPED PASTAS farfalle (bow ties), fusilli (spirals) and radiatore (ruffled) 	Versatile, but best with thicker sauces such as mushroom, sausage and tomato or meat ragout.
LASAGNE 	Thick sauces such as bolognese, or sauces made with heavier meats. Usually baked in the oven.

make piecrusts and Pastry

Homemade pastry has a better taste and texture than the store-bought kind—it's worth the extra effort. It also freezes well.

This all-purpose pie dough is best made with equal parts butter and lard, but can be made just with butter or block margarine if you want. For a rich, sweet pastry, add 2 tbsp superfine sugar to the mixture after rubbing in, and one egg yolk in place of 1 tbsp of water. It's usually cooked at 350°F (180°C).

MAKES ENOUGH TO FILL 9 X 9 IN. (22 X 22 CM) TART PAN

1½ cups all-purpose flour
1 tsp salt
6 tbsp unsalted butter, chilled, cubed
6 tbsp vegetable shortening, cubed
about 4 tbsp cold water

1 Sift flour and salt into a bowl. Add the butter and fat and rub in with your fingertips until the mixture resembles fine breadcrumbs. Make a well in the center and pour in the water.

2 Use a round-bladed knife to mix, adding another 1–2 tbsp water if too dry. Press with your fingers to make a ball of soft, not sticky, dough. Cover with plastic wrap and refrigerate for 15–20 minutes before rolling out.

make a simple Pâté

A pâté is usually made from liver, but you can also use mushrooms or other vegetables, or smoked fish such as salmon or mackerel, as the main ingredient. Pâté might not sound too appetizing if you're not used to eating liver, but don't worry—it's delicious. It should have a smooth texture.

Chicken liver pâté

SERVES 6

1 lb (500 g) chicken livers
4 tbsp butter
1 small onion, finely chopped
2 bay leaves
2 tsp chopped thyme
salt and freshly ground black pepper
2 tbsp brandy or balsamic vinegar

1 Trim the chicken livers, cutting away any green or gristly bits. Divide into small pieces and set aside. Melt the butter and cook the onion, bay leaves and thyme for 2–3 minutes. Add the chicken pieces and cook gently for 5 minutes or until they are just cooked through. Remove and discard the bay leaves.

2 Transfer the mixture to a food processor and process until smooth. Season to taste and stir in the brandy or balsamic vinegar. Transfer to a dish, cover and refrigerate for several hours, preferably overnight.

Alternatives Cook 1 lb (500 g) mushrooms with seasonings such as mace and paprika, then drain off any liquid and process with 1 cup cream cheese. Or blend 5 oz (150 g) smoked salmon or mackerel with 3 tbsp low-fat crème fraîche or sour cream, 1 tbsp lemon juice and 1 tsp horseradish.

play Patience (aka Solitaire)

This take on the well-known solo card game may have French origins—Napoleon played it while he was in exile.

The aim is to build up four full suits of cards, from ace up to king.

To start, deal out a pack of cards to form a tableau (see below). There should be seven columns of cards, with one card in the far left column and one more in each subsequent column so that there are seven in the far right one.

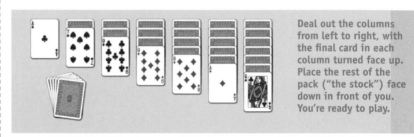

Deal out the columns from left to right, with the final card in each column turned face up. Place the rest of the pack ("the stock") face down in front of you. You're ready to play.

■ Study the tableau. If there's an ace showing, put it aside as a "foundation card" and turn the card immediately underneath it face up.
■ Move exposed cards onto other columns if you can—red on black, black on red, in descending rank or value. Turn up any face down card you uncover at the foot of a column. Sequences of cards in the tableau can be moved from column to column according to the same rules.
■ If you empty a column you can start a new one by moving a king, or a sequence beginning with a king, into the space.
■ Whenever possible, move cards onto the foundations sequentially within suits, ace to king.
■ If you can't move any of the exposed cards, take three cards from the stock and fan them face up on the table. If the top card—and subsequently those under it—can be added to the tableau or foundation piles, do so. Then turn another three cards face up on top of these and continue that way.
■ When you've worked through the stock, turn the pack over and go through as before. You win if you liberate four full suits of cards. Whether you succeed depends on key cards becoming exposed during the course of play.

Here, the ace of clubs and ace of diamonds have been moved from the tableau to start foundations. Sequences have been built on the columns using turned-up or stock cards. The three available stock cards can all be played—red three on the black four, red jack on black queen and red queen on black king.

lay Paving slabs

No matter which materials you're using, the most important parts of paving are a firm foundation and a level surface. Plan the layout before you start, to avoid awkward cuts or poor alignment with features such as a door or path. Allow for a ½ in. (1 cm) joint between slabs. If you're laying irregularly sized slabs, draw a plan before you begin.

Prepare the foundation

1 Mark out the area to be paved with pegs and string. Drive pegs into the ground to the depth that you need to dig out (depending on the kind of surface you're laying). Mark pegs with the proposed depth of subgrade improvement layer (crushed concrete/gravel laid over the soil), concrete subbase and paving slabs or bricks.

2 All paving materials need a solid subgrade improvement layer, about 4 in. (10 cm) deep. Spread it in the excavated area, and tamp it down using a plate compactor.

3 Spread a ½ in. (1 cm) layer of ballast or sand to fill the gaps, and tamp down. Use a string line to ensure that the surface is smooth and flat, with a slight slope away from any building for drainage.

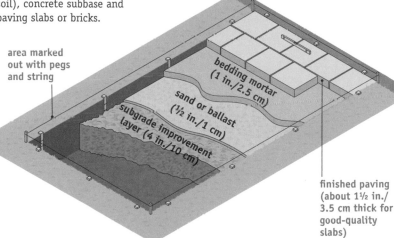

area marked out with pegs and string

bedding mortar (1 in./2.5 cm)

sand or ballast (½ in./1 cm)

subgrade improvement layer (4 in./10 cm)

finished paving (about 1½ in./ 3.5 cm thick for good-quality slabs)

Lay the slabs

1 To create mortar, buy a premixed package or combine six parts sand to one part cement and add water (with just a little dish soap) a little at a time until the mortar is like a stiff cake mix. Spread a 1½ in. (3.5 cm) layer over the sand.

2 Position the slabs one small area at a time, then tamp down with a piece of wood and a mallet until the mortar bed is just 1 in. (2.5 cm) deep, and the slabs are level and firm. Make any cuts using an angle grinder with a masonry cutting blade. (Wear gloves and goggles while you do this.)

3 Wait two days before filling the gaps between slabs with a dry mortar mix of one part cement to two parts building sand, using a trowel to get a neat finish.

whip up a Pavlova

A pavlova makes a perfect dinner party or celebration dessert. The vinegar and cornstarch added to the meringue help to make it crisp on the outside and soft and sticky in the center.

Summer berry pavlova

SERVES 6-8

3 egg whites
¾ cup superfine sugar
a few drops vanilla extract
½ tsp white wine vinegar
1 tsp cornstarch
1¼ cups heavy cream
¼ cup icing (confectioner's) sugar, sifted
2 cups fresh berries, such as raspberries, strawberries, blueberries or blackberries

1 Heat the oven to 300°F (150°C). Draw a 7 in. (18 cm) circle on a piece of parchment paper and place this, marked side down, on a baking sheet. In a large bowl, whisk the egg whites until stiff. Gradually add half the sugar, whisking well. Fold in the remaining sugar with the vanilla extract, vinegar and cornstarch.

2 Spread or pipe the meringue over the circle, piling it up at the edges to form a rim. Bake for about 1 hour, or until crisp on the outside. Transfer to a rack to dry. Alternatively, for an extra-crunchy exterior, turn off the oven and leave the meringue to dry for several hours or overnight. Remove the paper and place the meringue on a serving plate.

3 Whip the cream until stiff and add the icing (confectioner's) sugar. Pile or pipe it onto the pavlova, then put the fruit on top and serve immediately.

whip up a Pesto

This Italian pasta sauce, originally from Genoa, is also good mixed into salad dressing or added to mashed potato.

MAKES ABOUT 2 CUPS

1 bunch basil, roughly chopped
6 cloves garlic, minced
3–4 tbsp pine nuts
½ cup parmesan, grated
¾ cup extra-virgin olive oil,
   plus extra for sealing
salt and freshly ground black pepper

Puree the basil, garlic, nuts and cheese in a food processor with 2–3 tbsp oil. Then, on low speed, add the remaining oil in a steady stream. Season to taste. Alternatively, pound the basil, garlic, nuts and cheese with a pestle and mortar, gradually add the oil, and season. Store in an airtight jar with a little oil poured on top to seal. Pesto also freezes well.

indulge yourself with a Pedicure

Looking after your feet is an essential and often neglected part of any beauty routine, especially in warmer weather when you're planning to wear sandals or peep-toe shoes.

YOU WILL NEED **Nail polish remover, exfoliating cream, bath oil, pumice, toenail clippers, emery board, cuticle remover, cotton swabs, body moisturizer, cotton wool, nail polish**

■ Remove any trace of nail polish to make a smooth, clean surface.
■ Use exfoliating cream to rub away dead skin.
■ Let your feet soak in a bowl of warm water laced with bath oil for a relaxing five minutes to soften skin and nails.
■ Use pumice to rub away hard skin from the heels and balls of your feet.
■ Dry your feet completely and trim your toenails. Smooth them with the coarse side of the emery board. The nails should be even and square-ish.
■ Apply cuticle remover to the cuticles and use a cotton swab to ease them back gently. Wash off any excess and dry thoroughly once more.
■ Massage moisturizer into your feet.

■ Use cotton balls or a store-bought toe separator to hold your toes apart and—working from left to right if you're right-handed, vice versa if you're left-handed—apply a base coat of polish in three strokes: one down the center and one to each side. Allow to dry and apply another coat or two.
■ Put your best foot forward.

choose a Pet for kids

Pets give children a valuable sense of responsibility and are an outlet for affection. They need looking after, though, and you need to choose one that suits your child—and you.

■ Talk it over. Find out what your child wants from a pet. Stress that animals aren't toys.
■ Wait a few months to see if the desire was more than just a whim.
■ Set a budget. Decide what expenses you can meet.
■ Consider your home. A small apartment with no access to the outside is an unhappy environment for dogs and cats who, in turn, can become messy and destructive.
■ Consider safety. Cats can scratch. Dogs can bite. Young children may accidentally hurt small animals.
■ Do your homework. Study different animals' needs.

■ Start small. Cats and dogs can demand time and money (*see* CATS *and* DOGS). Lower-maintenance animals, such as the ones below, can provide a good introduction to caring for a furry friend.

Mice, hamsters and gerbils look sweet and need only small cages, but they require gentle handling and are generally more active at night.

Guinea pigs need shelter, hiding places and an exercise area safe from predators. They are loveable and responsive; the more they are handled (gently), the tamer they become. They are extremely active, will get bored if cooped up and crave the company of other guinea pigs.

Domestic rats have a bad rep, but they do become attached to their owners, and love to snuggle in a pocket or up a sleeve. They're intelligent and crave handling. They rarely bite. They should be kept in same-sex pairs—ideally, siblings. Don't let them run all over the house, though.

Rabbits are endearing, cuddly and sociable. They need space and companionship—both human and bunny. They may be kept outdoors with a hutch and an exercise run, but can also live indoors and be house-trained.

Prepare for bereavement. Rabbits can live five to ten years, guinea pigs five to seven years; mice, rats, hamsters and gerbils only live two to three. For real longevity, choose a tortoise—they can live up to 100 years!

See also AQUARIUM *and* GOLDFISH.

- -

take more professional Photos

Photography is an art, so there are no hard-and-fast rules. But keeping certain principles in mind will help you get the best possible shot out of any situation.

Be camera-ready Carry your camera with you at all times—there's nothing more frustrating than seeing something that would make a great picture, but not being able to capture it.

Be aware of the light If the light is behind your subjects, they will be underexposed or silhouetted; if the light is in front of your subjects, they may come out overexposed or washed out (and sunlight tends to make people squint). It's best to have your light source coming in from the side.

Keep it off-center Good composition makes the difference between a dull photograph and a memorable one. The most basic principle is: Don't put the subject in the dead center of the frame. The girl on the beach, the Eiffel Tower, the jumping basketball player—they will all look more interesting in the left- or right-hand third of the frame.

Look past the subject The background is always important. Avoid a cluttered backdrop. Make sure no construction pylons are sprouting from your subject's head. Make use of attractive or dramatic cloud formations.

master the
Photographic portrait

Portraits are one of the hardest photographic genres, because the act of taking a picture affects the way that the sitter behaves, making the photo much less natural.

Put the sitter at ease Talk to them as you set up and shoot. Tell them how well they're doing. Flatter them shamelessly.

Don't say, "Say cheese!" A natural expression is generally better than a pose. Get your sitter to tell a joke or talk about something that interests them. Take lots of shots, so that you catch the moment when emotion shows on their face.

Vary the angle Don't always shoot straight on at eye level. Shoot upward from chest height or climb a ladder to catch the sitter from above.

Get in close Sometimes the face is everything. Experiment with close-ups—the results can be stunning.

Frame the subject Think of ways to draw attention to the subject's face. Have them look through a window or peep from behind a tree. Think of what suits the sitter's personality and the feeling you want to convey.

store Photos safely

Photographic prints are fragile and need to be handled and stored with care. Digital images are easier to look after.

If you have a lot of digital images, it's worth investing in an external hard drive on which to keep them. Having your photographs on a drive of their own has several advantages: They won't take up large amounts of space on your computer's internal hard drive, aren't in danger of being lost or damaged if your computer breaks down, and you'll never have to transfer all your pictures if you change or upgrade your computer.

Printed or film photos

You should store these in a bone-dry part of your house where the temperature doesn't fluctuate—such as a closet, rather than a basement or attic. Your best shots should be mounted in an album, using plastic or paper photo corners, and shouldn't be viewed in strong sunlight. Other photographs can be stored in plastic sleeves or paper envelopes, but the plastic should be non-PVC and the paper should be acid-free. You can buy plastic boxes that are specially designed for containing envelopes of photographs. Ask at your local photo store.

share Photos over the internet

The simplest way to share individual digital photographs with loved ones is to send them directly as email attachments. But there are more sophisticated and public ways to share large numbers of photographs. Websites such as Flickr (flickr.com) and Picasa (picasa.google.com) invite you to edit and manipulate your photos, which you can then post as albums on the internet. Here anyone—or anyone you want—can see your pictures and even comment on them. These sites operate much like social networking sites such as Facebook, but with photography as the main focus of activity. Flickr is also a great resource for other people's photos—try using its search function.

transfer Photos to your computer

If you take pictures on a digital camera, it's easy to transfer them to your computer. This might involve connecting your camera to a USB port, or removing the camera's memory card and inserting it into your computer. Some computers have a slot designed for the SD memory cards found in many cameras; if your computer doesn't, you might need a USB adapter to connect your memory card to your computer. Photos taken on cell phones can be transferred using Bluetooth (*see* BLUETOOTH). Generally, your computer will automatically launch a picture transfer program when it detects the camera or memory card. This program will also ask if you want to delete the transferred pictures from the camera's memory, to make room for new shots.

Turning paper photos digital

To transfer the printed pictures in your photo album onto your computer, you will need a scanner, a machine that turns physical pictures into digital computer files. Scanners are relatively inexpensive, and many modern printers include a scanning function. You can scan only one photograph at a time on a home scanner, so it's a time-consuming process. But it's worthwhile: Snapshots taken 30 or even 80 years ago tend to fade away, but by scanning the pictures, you're ensuring that you have the image forever. And antique photographs, once scanned, can be digitally restored using programs such as Adobe Photoshop. You can edit out creases or tears, and, if you want, even make prints that look like new.

play a tune on the Piano

Learning the basics of piano is a little like learning to type on a computer keyboard. Once you have the position of the keys at your fingertips, it's as easy as A, B, C, D, E, F, G.

One of the advantages of learning to play the piano is that, unlike wind and reed instruments, it's easy to produce a pleasing note right from the start—just press a key! It takes a little longer to learn the principles of scales, chords and tunes but, as with all instruments, practice makes perfect.

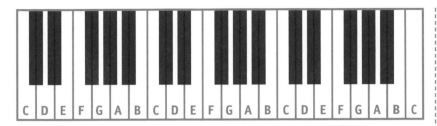

C D E F G A B C D E F G A B C D E F G A B C

Get to know the keyboard A full keyboard consists of 88 black and white keys that form a repeating pattern. The black keys—the sharps and flats, or half notes—are grouped in twos and threes. The white notes are named alphabetically: A, B, C, D, E, F, G. At the center is middle C, so the preceding keys are A and B, the following are D, E, F, G—then you start over at A again.

Play the scales The underpinning of popular and classical music, the scales are a series of eight ascending or descending notes, always ending on the starting note—otherwise known as "tonic." Play the C major scale: do, re, mi, fa, so, la, ti, do—C, D, E, F, G, A, B, C. Play it up, play it down. Keep your mind focused on the notes as you strike them. This is just an introduction. There are 12 major scales to learn, but you're getting a feel for your piano.

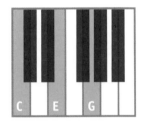

C MAJOR SCALE Use thumb, middle finger and little finger to play the scale.

Now for chords Of course, making music on the piano requires more than pressing random keys. Look at the C-major scale (see above). Play C, E and G together. Hear how much more depth it has. That's your C-major chord. Playing the first, third and fifth notes from any major scale gives you a major chord with the same name as the scale you're using. Practice the major chords at the same time as you practise scales.

Play your first tune All right, it's only "Chopsticks," not beautiful music, but it helps to get you used to the keys.

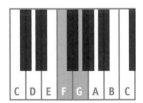

C D E F G A B C

1 Index fingers on F and G —play it six times.

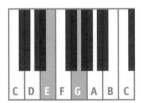

C D E F G A B C

2 Left finger on E, right on G—play six times.

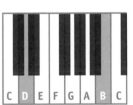

C D E F G A B C

3 Left on D, right moves up to B—play six times.

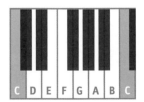

C D E F G A B C

4 Move each finger out one note to the next C— play four times.

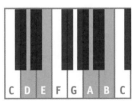

C D E F G A B C

5 Moving your fingers back towards each other, play D–B and E–A once each.

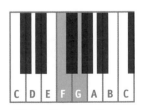

C D E F G A B C

6 Index fingers on F and G—play six times and you're off again.

make Pickled onions

Pickled onions should be left to mature for six months before eating. They go best with cheese, bread and cold meats, such as ham.

MAKES 2 X 1 PINT (500 mL) JARS

4 lb (2 kg) small white pickling onions or shallots
1 cup salt
10 black peppercorns
4 bay leaves
2 qt/L cider or white wine vinegar

1 Put the onions or shallots in a bowl, cover with boiling water and leave for 5 minutes. Remove the outer skins and trim neatly. Cover with cold water, add the salt, mix well and leave for 12 hours or overnight. Drain.

2 Pack with the peppercorns and bay leaves into sterilized jars (*see* STERILIZE). Cover with the vinegar, seal and keep in a cool dark place.

pack Picnic food

Carefully packed, picnic food will arrive at its destination fresh, wholesome and intact. If you picnic often, invest in good-quality containers. And don't forget to include napkins, utensils and condiments, too.

Choose plastic containers with sealable lids. Each can contain a personal "mini meal" such as a salad. Or cover food well with foil or plastic wrap to keep it fresh and bug-proof.

Pack food in coolers or bags If you're taking both hot and cold food, have one box or bag for each. Keep food extra cool with freezer packs. If you don't have a cooler, line a picnic bag or basket with a large sheet of bubble wrap, plus cold soda cans or bags of ice cubes—they will keep food cool for an hour or so.

Thermoses are ideal for hot or cold drinks. Choose wide-necked thermoses for soup.

On a hot day, prefreeze sandwiches and yogurt and put directly into the cooler. They will defrost as you travel. Avoid foods such as egg salad, potato salad, fish, pasta and rice dishes, which are most prone to food-poisoning bacteria.

hang a Picture

Pictures add life to a room. Plan their positioning carefully so they have room to breathe and sufficient light to be enjoyed.

Use mounts that are strong enough to support your picture, and check that the wall is solid. Picture hooks, driven in by a hammer, usually suffice. Or drill into the wall and insert a screw into a wall plug.

A heavy or wide picture should hang on two hooks positioned near each end instead of one central hook. The hooks must be at the same level—use a level to mark a true horizontal line on the wall and put the hooks along it.

To hang a picture on a single hook, get someone to hold it up against the wall, and lightly mark the wall with a pencil where the top of the frame is, at the central point. Lay the picture facedown, mark the top middle and use your picture hook to pull the wire tight toward the mark. Measure the distance between the top of the frame and the top of the hook. Measure this same distance down from the mark you made on the wall and make a new mark. Hammer in the hook so that its top is level with this new mark.

Heavy pictures and large framed mirrors should be hung on a narrow strip of wood rather than hooks (*see* MIRROR).

choose the right kind of Picture frame

A picture frame should play a full supporting role—not just structurally, but visually. It can give a more finished look to a painting and define the boundaries of an artwork.

Stealing beauty A frame that draws attention to itself will distance the viewer from a painting, rendering it a mere object. An eye-catching frame can work with a strong painting, but remember: It should complete, not compete.

A large frame for a small picture is possible, provided the picture has sufficient impact not to be overwhelmed. Indeed, where a small painting might be lost on a wall, a wide frame can give it presence.

Choose a frame color to complement the hues of the painting or picture, not to blend with the room. Paintings with predominantly warm pigments such as reds can sit happily in a gilt frame. For studies in black and white, go for black or silver. Complement pale hues with a light wood frame. Cool colors such as blues, lilacs and whites are beautifully set off by silver.

Gilding and moldings send a message. Save them for grand, formal, rich oil paintings, not delicate watercolors.

For perspective pictures, choose an inward-sloping border that seems to retreat towards the horizon, drawing your eye in.

For contemporary paintings, generally choose simple, flat frames that project the work out toward the viewer.

make a Pie crust

YOU WILL NEED **Pie bird/vent, dish, pastry brush, pastry or pie dough, flour, rolling pin, knife, fork. Optional: beaten egg, milk**

Before you begin To prevent the top crust from becoming soggy, put a pie bird or vent through it—this will allow steam to escape. For a pie without a pastry lining, brush the rim of the dish with a little cold water. For a pie with a lining, brush the edge of the pastry where it meets the rim.

Rolling out If your pie doesn't have a pastry lining, roll out and cut a strip of pastry. Place the pastry strip all around the rim and brush with water. Then roll out the pastry for the top of the pie on a floured surface, and use the rolling pin to transfer it into position. Press the edges together to seal.

Finishing
■ Make edges by holding a knife horizontally and tapping it against the outside rim of the pastry while pressing the top on the inside of the rim with the back of your index finger. Repeat all around the rim. Then use the tines of a flour-covered fork to make a pattern all around.

Alternatively, pinch the edges of the pastry between thumb and finger for a crimped edge, or use a knife to make a scalloped edge. Use any leftover pastry to cut diamonds or other shapes for decoration. Brush with water, then place in a pattern on the crust. Finally, brush with beaten egg or milk for a glazed effect if desired.

learn simple Pilates exercises

This subtle but powerful exercise method builds core strength and improves posture, giving you a long, lean and more toned figure. It's suitable for all ages, and enhances agility, mobility and stamina.

These elementary exercises will give you a feel for Pilates. Wear clothing that allows freedom of movement. You will also need an exercise mat. Before starting any exercise, relax your body and focus on the muscles you'll be using.

Belly button-to-spine breathing technique
This is fundamental to creating stability and allowing centered movement. Practice it: Breathe in and, as you exhale, draw your abdominal muscles up and in; visualize your belly button being drawn to your spine. Notice how the technique is incorporated into the following exercises.

continued on next page ➜

choose Pillows

A good pillow provides both comfort and support. A squishy one that lets your head flop, or one so hard it gives you a crick, can result in neck pain.

The volume of filling in a pillow will determine its level of softness; tightly packed filling makes for a firmer pillow. If you sleep on your back, try using a flatter pillow than you would if you slept on your side or stomach.

Down and feather pillows can be molded to a shape that fits you. They feel luxurious but aren't good for allergy sufferers unless the pillow is hypoallergenic. Choose a closely woven covering so the sharp feather ends won't poke through.

Latex foam pillows hold their shape and give good support— helpful if you have neck or back pain. They are also resistant to dust mites—good news if you have a dust allergy.

Polyester filling in a variety of thicknesses is recommended if you're asthmatic or allergic.

Memory foam pillows are designed to mold to the contours of the head and neck, giving strong support and relief to neck and shoulder muscles.

golden rules
PILLOW WISDOM
■ **Plump your pillow every day.**
■ **Protect with a good-quality pillowcase, and wash often.**
■ **Replace pillows as they become stained, shrunken or misshapen—it's worth it.**

choose a memorable
PIN number

Since they all consist of four digits, there are only 10,000 possible PIN numbers. To make yours as secure as possible, avoid obvious combinations, such as the day and month of your own birth. It's much better to think of a memorable four-word phrase in which each word contains the same number of letters as the digits in your PIN. So if your PIN is 1455, a good phrase might be: *I LOVE FRIED BREAD*. Choose something unforgettable.
Or select a simple letter and trace its shape on the keypad—for example, "C" could be 3179.

prepare and cut a
Pineapple

For rings Slice off the leafy top and stem end. Using a sharp knife, cut off the skin and woody "eyes" from the flesh. Cut into slices ½ in. (1 cm) thick. Then use a small, apple corer to remove the center of each ring, or cut out using a knife.

For chunks Leave the top and stem in place and cut the pineapple in half lengthwise. Use a small sharp knife to remove the core and a serrated fruit knife to cut out the flesh. Cut into chunks. If desired, serve in the pineapple shell.

continued from page 237

Roll down—roll up

1 Sit tall on the mat with your knees up, feet flat on the floor in front of you and arms outstretched.

2 Breathe out as you begin to roll down, curling your lower back in a C shape and drawing your navel to your spine. Keep your feet firmly planted as you roll slowly all the way down. Rest your arms by your sides.

3 Take a deep breath, filling your lungs and expanding your back. Exhale as you peel yourself off the floor, rolling up as you rolled down, arms outstretched by your sides. Keep your chin tucked in and lift your head first, drawing navel to spine.

4 Reach your arms forward to rest on your feet and use those hollowed abdominals to hold you in a C curve. Then inhale and lift up from the base of your spine to take up your original position. Do this three times.

Pelvic curl

1 Lie on your back with your knees bent, feet flat on the floor and arms resting by your sides.

2 Exhale and draw your navel to your spine, moving your tailbone upward. Continue to lift your spine from the floor—not straight, but one vertebra at a time. Keep your feet firmly planted on the ground.

3 When you have raised yourself onto your shoulders, with your body forming a straight line from knees to shoulders, hold the position, inhaling. Relax your neck, shoulders and rib cage while bracing hips, thighs and ankles.

4 Exhale, drawing your navel to your spine, and uncoil slowly back down to your starting position, vertebra by vertebra, working from the top of your spine.

bend a copper Pipe

To bend a copper pipe, you'll need bending springs (available from a hardware store) of the right diameter. If the pipe is longer than the spring, you'll also need a length of string. Tie it to the end of the spring.

■ Grease the spring well and push it into the pipe, making sure it reaches the point where you'll make the bend. Pull the spring through with string if the pipe is long. The pipe can then be easily bent across your knee.
■ It's best to bend it slightly further than the required angle, then ease it back. This makes it easier to withdraw the spring: Insert a screwdriver through the spring loop or the end of the string, and pull.

make a great Pizza

Homemade pizza is not only tastier than frozen, but is lower in fat and salt. It's worth making large batches of dough, dividing them up and keeping them in the freezer. Pizza toppings, usually set onto a tomato base, can easily be varied according to individual tastes. Variations on this recipe could include finely sliced mushrooms, capers, peppers, anchovies or artichoke hearts.

MAKES 1 LARGE OR 2 SMALL PIZZAS, TO SERVE 2–4

BASE
2¼ cups all-purpose flour
½ tsp salt
½ tsp fast-rising yeast
⅔ cup warm water
1 tbsp olive oil

TOPPING
14 oz (540 mL) can chopped tomatoes
2 garlic cloves, crushed
2 tbsp chopped fresh basil and/or oregano
pinch of sugar
3 tbsp olive oil
salt and freshly ground black pepper
¼ lb (150 g) mozzarella cheese, sliced thin
⅛ lb (75 g) chorizo, sliced thin
16 black olives

1 Sift the flour and salt into a large bowl. Add the yeast. Make a well in the center and gradually work in the water and oil to form a soft dough. Knead lightly on a floured surface. Place in an oiled bowl, cover with plastic wrap and leave to rise for about 1 hour, or until doubled in size.

2 Meanwhile, put the tomatoes, oil, garlic, herbs and sugar in a pan and simmer for 20 minutes, or until thickened. Season to taste, then cool.

3 Heat the oven to 450°F (230°C). Punch down the dough (*see* BREAD) and roll out into one thin 12–14 in. (30–35 cm) or two 6–8 in. (15–20 cm) rounds on a floured surface. Place on floured baking sheets. Top with the tomato sauce, mozzarella, chorizo and olives. Bake for 8-10 minutes, or until the dough is crisp and golden and the cheese is melted.
For extra crispness Preheat extra baking sheets in the oven and put the pizzas (on their trays) on top of these. The additional heat will cook the bases quickly and evenly.

make Place mats
from fabric

■ Place mats provide a special finishing touch for a well-laid table; they have the power to make the table look great, even if you're using your regular flatware. It's easy to make your own to match the rest of your decor.
■ Place mats must be sturdy enough to form a stable base for dishes and utensils. Reversible quilted material is especially suitable, but you could also use two layers of firmly woven fabric back to back. Avoid slippery or very thin fabrics.
■ Each mat should measure at least 10 x 15 in. (25 cm x 40 cm) to provide sufficient space for a place setting. Choose an oval shape if your table is round, and a rectangle if it's rectangular or square. Add ⅝ in. (1.5 cm) all around for seam allowances.

1 Stitch two fabric layers, right sides together, leaving a 4 in. (10 cm) opening along one edge.

2 Trim the seam allowances to half; trim the corners diagonally or clip Vs along the curves.

3 Press the seam allowances flat, then press them open. Turn the place mat right-side out, pushing out corners and bringing the seams out to the edges.

4 Slip stitch the opening closed. Press mat flat.

Plane wood

Your jack plane will have a lateral adjustment lever behind the blade; use it to make sure that the blade is square to the plane body. You can set how far the blade projects —and therefore the thickness of each cut—using the adjuster.

■ Mark a cutting line on both sides of the piece of wood you want to plane. Clamp it firmly in a vice.
■ Position your plane so it's ready to run the full length of your piece of wood. Your stronger hand should be on the handle at the back of the plane, while your other hand guides the front.

■ Plane from one end to the other, always working with the grain, in long, smooth strokes. Regularly check how close you are to your marked cutting lines.

tackle common Plant diseases

Diseases can make plants look unsightly or even kill them, marring the beauty of your flower garden and reducing the yield of crops. As well as the diseases included here, both roses (*see* ROSES) and seedlings (*see* SEEDS AND SEEDLINGS) are particularly prone to attack.

Disease	Signs and treatment
BLIGHT *summer, especially when wet*	Leaves turn brown and rot. Tubers and fruit also rot. Affects potatoes and tomatoes. **Treatment** Spray with a copper-based fungicide or mancozeb every seven to 10 days.
CANKER *anytime*	Brown, cracked and sunken patches on bark. Oozing slime from affected areas, which die. Affects many trees and shrubs, including apple, oak and poplar. **Treatment** Spray with copper-based fungicide. Destroy a badly infected tree.
CHLOROSIS *growing season*	Foliage turns yellow all over, on margins or veins or in lines or rings. Affects a large range of plants. **Treatment** Dig in peat and/or a lime-free fertilizer. Add a chelated iron compound (iron formulated for easy absorption). Control aphids, which spread viral disease (*see* APHIDS).
CLUB ROOT *growing season*	Roots become swollen and distorted. Leaves of cabbages turn red, purple or yellow. Affects cabbages, wallflowers, turnips, radishes. **Treatment** Lime soil in winter to keep it neutral or slightly alkaline. Raise plants in sterilized compost. Don't regrow on affected soil.
CORAL SPOT *anytime when plants under stress*	Rashes of pink or coral-red spots on dead twigs. Plants vulnerable when over-dry, waterlogged or recently transplanted. Affects many trees and shrubs, including maples, beeches and magnolias. **Treatment** Prune to 6 in. (15 cm) below affected area. Avoid injuries to bark, through which infection can enter.

Disease	Signs and treatment
ARMILLARIA ROOT ROT *autumn* 	Mushrooms at base of trunk. Black bootlace threads on diseased roots. Plants die. Affects most trees and shrubs and some herbaceous perennials and bulbs. **Treatment** No chemical control.
LEAF CURL *before bud burst*	Leaves develop big red blisters, turn white, then brown and fall prematurely. Affects flowering cherries and other ornamental *Prunus* species, as well as apricots and peaches. **Treatment** Treat with mancozeb or a copper-based fungicide in late winter.
LEAF SPOT *late spring onwards*	Leaves and stems develop round or oval brown spots that may have a black pinpoint. Leaves fall prematurely. Affects chestnut trees, celery, spinach, black currants and gooseberries. **Treatment** Treat with mancozeb or a copper-based fungicide.
POWDERY MILDEW *growing season*	White powdery patches spreading on leaves, flowers and fruit. Affects many ornamental plants, fruits and vegetables. **Treatment** Treat with fungicides such as difenoconazole or myclobutanil.
ROOT ROT *warm, wet periods*	Foliage dies back and plants may die. Roots may look black and mushy. Affects trees and shrubs, including rhododendrons and azaleas. **Treatment** No cure for some pathogens, but try applying an anti-pythium fungicide.
RUSTS *spring and summer*	Shoots covered with orange fungal spores; may become malformed. Affects leeks, mint, apples and decorative plants such as fuschias. **Treatment** Spray with mancozeb or myclobutanil at first signs of attack.
SCAB *growing season*	Ragged-edged scabs on tubers or roots. Affects potatoes, beets, radishes, rutabagas and turnips. **Treatment** Compost well before planting; avoid adding lime.

apply a coat of
Plaster

For any large plastering job, you need a hawk (a large flat tray with a handle on the bottom) and a steel plastering trowel. You carry the plaster to the wall on the hawk, and apply it with the trowel. Plastering takes skill and practice to get a smooth finish.

■ Mix the plaster in a clean bucket to a consistency between oatmeal and whipped cream. If the plaster is too wet or thick, it won't adhere to the wall. Alternatively, use a premixed plaster.

■ Load a manageable amount of plaster onto your hawk. With the hawk close to the wall, scoop a little at a time onto your trowel and, holding the trowel at roughly 45 degrees, sweep upward to push the plaster onto the wall, flattening it slightly at the end of the stroke.
■ Apply a finishing coat about two hours after the undercoat. Mix it to the consistency of melting ice cream, and spread with the same kind of motion as before. About 20 minutes after application, spray with a spray bottle and use the trowel to smooth to a perfect finish.

Pluck poultry

Game birds, such as grouse and wild turkeys, may still be sold with their feathers at some traditional butchers. If you live in the country, you may get them fresh from the field, either from a breeder or after a day of hunting. Either way, you'll need to pluck them. Ideally, they should be hung in a cool, dark place for seven to ten days before they are plucked, to allow the muscle to slacken and flavor to develop.

■ The method for plucking poultry is the same, no matter what bird you have.
■ Sit with the bird on your lap. Starting with the legs and wings, pull out two or three feathers at a time using sharp, backward tugs against the direction of growth. Be careful not to tear the skin.
■ Leave the breast feathers until last. Start at the top and pull toward the head.
■ Using a cooking or propane blowtorch, quickly singe off any remaining down or hairs.
■ Wipe the bird with a damp cloth and use tweezers to pull out any remaining long hairs or feather ends.

repair damaged Plaster

Repairing small areas of damaged plaster is relatively easy, and a good way to learn the craft.

YOU WILL NEED **Brick set chisel, hammer, paintbrush, premixed patching plaster, spray bottle, finishing trowel, thin strip of wood wider than the area to be patched, fine sandpaper**

1 Use the chisel and hammer to chip away loose or crumbling plaster until you have an area that's firm all around the edges. Brush the entire area with an old paintbrush to remove any remaining dust and spray lightly with water.

2 Apply the patching plaster using a trowel (above). Build up the damaged surface in thin layers, waiting for each layer to stiffen (but not dry out) before applying the next.

3 If the wall will be papered, level with the strip of wood. Work fast, keeping both ends in contact with the solid wall, as you move it from side to side and up across the repaired area. Sand smooth when dry.

4 If the wall is to be painted, fill to a ¼ in. (5 mm) below surface, then apply a layer of finishing plaster. Use a large brush and upward strokes, then spread and smooth. Sand when dry.

Poach fish

Poaching is especially good for white fish, which can dry out when broiled, or for whole salmon or trout. Use a large saucepan, or cover a shallow dish with foil and poach in the oven.

Preparation A court bouillon—a flavored poaching liquid that's discarded after use—will give poached fish the best possible taste.

MAKES ABOUT 1½ QT/L

2 carrots, finely chopped
1 large onion, finely chopped
2 ribs celery, finely chopped
1 bay leaf
3 parsley stems, chopped
2 sprigs thyme
1 bay leaf

2 tbsp lemon juice
long strip of lemon rind
1 cup dry white wine, dry cider
    or water
1¼ qt/L water
6 black peppercorns
1½ tsp salt

Put all the ingredients in a large saucepan, bring to a boil, skim off any scum and simmer on low heat for 15 minutes. Let cool slightly, then strain. Pour it over the fish to be poached. Tie a whole fish in cheesecloth before poaching, securing it at each end with string. (Leave long ends on the string to help you lift out the bundle when the fish is cooked.)

Complete poaching If a whole fish is to be cooked and served cold, poaching is the perfect method. Simmer the fish slowly in the court bouillon, either on the stove or in an oven set to 350°F (180°C), allowing 8–10 minutes per pound (500 g). Allow the fish to cool in the liquid, then lift out with broad spatulas and drain on paper towels to prevent it from leaking liquid onto the serving plate. To serve, carefully scrape off skin with a sharp knife, stopping at the gills so the head remains intact, and just before the tail. (Or remove the head and tail, if you prefer.) Thinly sliced cucumber is a traditional garnish—you can either cover the entire fish with cucumber, or just serve it, sliced, on the side. Watercress and lemon are other good choices for accompaniments.

create your own Podcast

A podcast is a little bit like a homemade radio show, distributed on the internet rather than broadcast over the airwaves. You can listen to it on your computer or download it onto your MP3 player. A good podcast requires both a creative idea (something to say) and some technical expertise—you have to know how to record, edit and publish your work.

Your subject The content is up to you. It might be a dramatic monologue, a spoken-voice tour of your town or nearest museum, or an oral-history project for which you interview local people, war veterans or family members.

Equipment A microphone is vital, preferably a USB microphone that plugs directly into your computer and records a digital file. Use an omnidirectional microphone if you plan to feature more than one voice at a time, or a unidirectional one if your podcast consists of just one person talking. You might also need a USB mixer, so that you can modify the sound as you record, and a pop filter to soften "P" sounds.

Software Editing software allows you to make the elements of your podcast into a professional-sounding finished product. This is where you add background music, cut and edit interviews, add your commentary and clean up background noise. If you have a Mac, all this can be done with the Garage Band application. Other available programs include Adobe Soundbooth and Audacity (which is free to download).

Publishing To distribute your podcast, you must upload it to a web server or blog. You must also create a web feed, or RSS, which allows people to subscribe to your podcasts and alerts them whenever you post a new installment. Many servers or blogs automatically generate the web feed for you. Finally, advertise your podcast by posting a link on your own website, on a social networking site, or by mailing the link to your friends and family.

cook the perfect
Poached egg

The perfect poached egg, with a just-firm white and a runny yolk, is as delicious eaten on toast as it is on your eggs Benedict. Add vinegar to the poaching water to help eggs keep their shape.

1 Fill a large, deep frying pan or large saucepan with about 3 in. (7.5 cm) of water. Bring water to a boil and add 2 tsp white vinegar.

2 Break an egg into a cup. Make a small whirlpool in the water with a spoon, and gently slip the egg into the middle of the spiral.

3 Reduce the heat and simmer for 4 minutes, or until the white is set and the yolk is soft. To test, lift out the egg on a slotted spoon and press it gently with your fingertip—the yolk should give a little.

4 Lift out the cooked egg, then trim any ragged edges with a knife or scissors before serving.

golden rule
PERFECT EGG POACHING
- **Never add salt to the poaching water, or the egg whites will break down.**

learn a Poem

Memorizing and reciting poetry by heart is a rewarding challenge and a great exercise for your brain.

To begin, browse an anthology and choose a poem that appeals to you, or that contains a line you like. Pick a piece that has a memorable rhyme scheme and is manageably short—say, two or three stanzas.

Write it out by hand. Keep the paper with you and look at it whenever you have a spare moment.

Learn the first two lines, testing yourself throughout the day so that you have them word-perfect by evening. The next day, learn two lines more. That way, you can master a sonnet in a week.

Recite the whole poem out loud to yourself and doodle it during your idle moments in newspaper margins or on scraps of paper until it's firmly rooted in your mind.

deal with Poisoning

Cases of poisoning are rarely fatal. But most homes do contain an array of toxic substances, so it's important to be familiar with the symptoms and know what action to take. Most poisoning involves small children, but ingesting tainted food or accidentally taking the wrong dose of medicine can happen to anyone.

Quick action If you think someone has swallowed a poisonous substance, call an ambulance right away.

- If the victim is unconscious, don't put your finger into their mouth to make them vomit. Try to wake them up, then encourage them to vomit what they swallowed.
- If the person vomits, keep a sample for examination.
- Put the victim in the recovery position (*see* RECOVERY POSITION).
- Look for clues as to what might be the cause, such as open bottles of household chemicals, nearby plants or vials of medication. Take them with you to the hospital.

At the hospital Be prepared to give medical staff as much information as you can to help them to treat the victim appropriately. Be ready with the following information—write it down while you wait for the ambulance. If you're stressed, it will help to calm you down as well as assist the doctors.

- The substance that you think may have been swallowed (or inhaled, or splashed on the skin).
- Precisely when it was taken.
- How much of it was ingested.
- The symptoms you've noticed.
- The age of the patient and any known medical conditions.

Carbon monoxide poisoning Tasteless, colorless, odorless and poisonous, carbon monoxide (CO) is a major cause of brain damage and death due to poisoning. As well as vehicle exhaust, common sources in the home include faulty furnaces, gas appliances and fires, and blocked chimneys.

The symptoms of mild CO poisoning are similar to those of flu or food poisoning: headache, nausea, abdominal pain and dizziness, shortness of breath and a cough (but with no fever). More severe poisoning induces a racing and irregular heartbeat, hyperventilation (fast breathing), confusion, drowsiness, respiratory problems, seizures, chest pain, clumsiness and unconsciousness.

If you, your colleagues, family or pets experience any of these, get everyone into the fresh air and call 911. Ask them to check the premises for possible sources of a leak. Anyone who has displayed any of the symptoms listed above should see a doctor right away. And of course, all homes should have CO detectors.

understand the basics of Poker

No card game has a greater aura of glamour, mystique and James-Bond cool than poker.

Players bet on having the highest-scoring hand, but only they know what cards they hold. With nerve, a cool exterior and good judgment, the player with the lowest hand might tough it out and win. It's all about reading your opponents' body language while keeping your own "poker face" inscrutable.

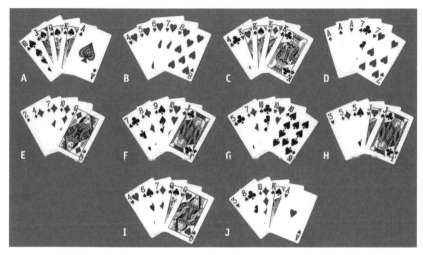

ASSESSING YOUR HAND The highest-scoring hand in poker is a "royal flush" (A): 10, jack, queen, king and ace, all of the same suit. Next comes a "straight flush" (B), a single-suit run of any other consecutive cards. "Four of a kind" (C) is next, with the highest-value card set winning in a tie, followed by a "full house" (D): three of a kind, plus a pair. Any five cards of a suit is a "flush" (E), just beating a "straight" (F)—any five consecutive cards, whatever the suit. Next come "three of a kind" (G), "two pairs" (H) and a "pair" (I). If you have no scoring groups of cards (J), your hand is valued by its highest card—here, the ace.

For straight poker, you need six to eight players (ideally) and one 52-card deck. A jack may be added as a wild card, or the dealer may designate any card as wild ("dealer's choice"). Aces are high except in a straight or straight flush (5-4-3-2-A).

To start Players buy into the game with a stake in the pot (the "ante"). One player takes the deck and starts to deal cards face up. The first to receive a jack is dealer. Any player may shuffle the pack but the dealer takes last shuffle. The turn to deal passes one to the left with every game. Cards are dealt clockwise. Each new deal is a separate game so you're betting on your current hand.

The play Each player receives five cards. The player to the left of the dealer stakes money on his hand or discards it ("folds"). The next player must match the bet ("call"), make a higher one ("raise" it, in a show of confidence or bravado) or fold.

The showdown Every player has a chance to bid—the "betting interval." Since a player may not raise their own bet, an interval ends when the betting has returned to the player who made the last raise. Players left in the game then show their hands, and the winner takes all the stake money in the pot. In the event of a tie the pot is split. A fresh game begins with a new deal.

grow lettuce in
Polytunnels
(aka hoophouses)

Polytunnels, or hoophouses, are plastic substitutes for a small greenhouse or row of cloches. They offer warmth and light and extend the growing season of many crops, providing homegrown lettuce through the winter and the earliest crops of summer fruits.

What to sow Oriental greens such as mizuna (Japanese mustard greens), as well as arugula, radicchio and endive, are ideal choices. Scallions and cold-hardy lettuces such as romaine will also do well. Seeds can be bought in packaged mixtures or as packages of a single variety.

Prepare the growing area Choose a double-skinned model for the best insulation, and ensure that it has a free flow of air within. For extra insulation, line the inside of the tunnel with bubble wrap, held in place with duct or strong masking tape. Make sure the tunnel is firmly secured to the ground.

Sow the seeds Make shallow drills ¼ in. (5 mm) deep and sow directly into the ground from autumn onward, allowing 8–12 in. (20–30 cm) between rows. Water as necessary, and apply liquid compost or manure every two weeks. If the weather is warm enough, sow again in early winter and spring. If the weather is very cold, protect plants with fleece.

Harvest the crop Loose-leaved greens can be cut with scissors. Larger ones such as lettuce and radicchio can be pulled out. If plants are closely packed, thin them out, eating the thinnings.

play Pool

There are many forms of pool, but eightball is one of the most popular.

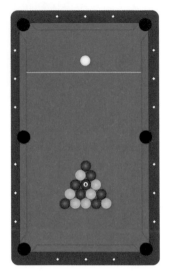

There are two sets of seven "object" balls, either striped and solid (as is now most common), or the traditional yellow and red (as seen on early televised pool tournaments).

The object balls are arranged in a triangle, so the base is parallel with the end of the table. The eight ball must be in the middle of the third row, and positioned over the spot on the table. The other balls are arranged as shown here.

The game One player breaks, striking the cue ball from a point behind the "balkline" on the table. If one or more balls are pocketed off the break, the player must nominate which color they want to play. The first legal shot after this determines which color they are for the rest of the frame. If they pocket nothing, the other player takes a shot. The first player to pocket all seven of their balls, then the eight ball, wins. A player who pockets the eight ball before the other balls loses.

create a simple garden Pond

Water adds an extra dimension to any backyard, and a pond is easy to install using a premade flexible liner. If you're not used to digging, work in short spurts so you don't injure your back.

YOU WILL NEED **Hose, sand, shovel, plank, level, landscape fabric, flexible pond liner, large scissors, paving or edging stones**

1 Lay out the shape with the hose, then trickle sand around the edge and remove the hose. Dig out, sloping the sides at a 20-degree angle. Remove turf around it to make room for an edge.

2 Make a 10 in.- (25 cm) wide ledge for marginal plants, the same length from the top. Use a level on a plank to check that sides are level all around, building them back up as necessary.

3 Line the hole with damp sand, then fabric. This will protect the liner from sharp rocks and root growth. Put the lining in place, hold down edges with rocks or bricks and fill with water, easing the liner into the corners of the ledge.

4 Trim the liner to within 4 in. (10 cm) of the water's edge. Cover with soil and lay paving stones or other decorative stones around the perimeter.

How much lining? Measure the width, length and depth of the pond. Then double the depth, and add it to the length and width measurements. So a pool that's 6½ ft. (2 m) wide, 13 ft. (4 m) long and 1½ ft. (0.5 m) deep needs a lining sheet that's about 10 ft. x 16 ft. (3 m x 5 m). Then add an extra 1–1½ ft. (30–50 cm) all around for overlap.

Planting Adding plants to the pond in containers prevents muddying the water and allows you to move them around until you're happy. Line and cover the tops of pots with stones or heavy pebbles.
- **Underwater plants** Choose American pondweed, which is excellent at aerating the water and keeping down algae.
- **Marginal plants** Colorful choices include marsh marigolds, irises and water mint. Set them on the ledge at the rim of the pond. Rushes are also suitable.
- **Surface plants** Water lilies are ideal and come in a wide variety of colors and shapes. If a water lily is too short to reach the water surface, cut off the leaves before immersing it.

choose and cook cuts of Pork

Almost every bit of the pig, from snout to tail, can be eaten, although the least tender cuts require long, slow cooking. Here's how to cook some of the most common pork cuts for the best results.

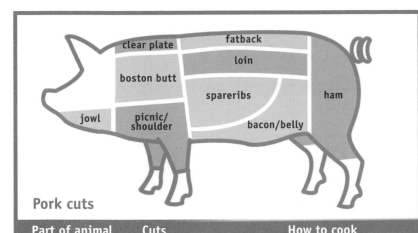

Pork cuts

Part of animal	Cuts	How to cook
JOWL	Jowl	Use in sausages or as bacon.
BOSTON BUTT	Blade steak Roast	Roast, braise or stew. Make pulled pork.
CLEAR PLATE/ FATBACK	Fatback Streak o' lean Rinds/cracklings	Use to make lard, salt pork, sausages or bacon. Fry or stew.
PICNIC/SHOULDER	Picnic roast Arm steak Hock	Roast: roast. Arm steak: braise. Hock: braise.
LOIN	Rib/sirloin/loin chops Top loin roast Tenderloin Center loin Sirloin cutlet	Chops: grill, broil, panfry or braise. Loin cuts: Grill, roast or broil (don't overcook).
SPARERIBS	Spareribs	Grill or braise—long, slow cooking.
BACON/BELLY	Bacon Belly	Bacon: fry. Belly: roast or braise.
HAM	Ham, bone-in or boneless	Roast, panfry, grill or simmer in liquid.

make crisp and crunchy
Pork cracklings

Perfect cracklings, made from pork rinds, are definitely delicious. Many cooks have their own secret techniques for making them, but one important rule is that the skin needs to be completely dry and scored with deep parallel cuts before cooking. Some cooks rub olive oil and sea salt liberally into the skin before putting the meat in the oven; others recommend raising the temperature for the last 20 minutes of the roasting time to 425°F (220°C).

If your crackling fails, you can rescue it by carefully cutting the skin away from the cooked meat with a sharp knife and crisping it under a hot broiler or in the microwave for a couple of minutes.

----

golden rules
GET THE BEST FROM PORK

■ **Tangy accompaniments, such as applesauce or sage and onion stuffing, counter the fattiness of the pork and make the meat more digestible.**
■ **Good-quality pork is pale pink with a fine grain. The fat should be white with a milky tinge and pink skin.**

improve your
Posture

Standing tall boosts well-being and self-confidence and staves off aches and pains. Try these exercises in front of a long mirror.

FEET Stand with your feet apart and firmly planted. Rock back and forth and side to side to get centered and put weight on the balls of your feet, not the heels.

KNEES Stand with knees relaxed, not locked, and your body weight "dropping" through your feet.

PELVIS Circle your pelvis one way then the other to release tension in your lower back.

SHOULDERS Bring your shoulders up to your ears, hold—1, 2, 3—and let them drop. Repeat. Pull shoulders down from the ears and relax them. As your hands hang by your sides see if your shoulders are level. If not, there's work to do.

NECK Loll your head gently to one side, to the front and then to the other side. Do it twice. Extend your neck so your head sits easily balanced and freely on the top of your spine, with your chin neither thrust forward nor tucked in.

STAND TALL Imagine there's an invisible cord linking the top of your head to the ceiling. Picture how it draws you up so you stand tall but still relaxed, not ramrod straight. Enjoy the feeling. Practice daily.

grow Potatoes

When it comes to flavor there's no contest between homegrown and store-bought potatoes. They are one of the easiest vegetables to cultivate, come in dozens of varieties and have the added advantage of helping to clear the ground of weeds.

Potatoes are bred to mature at different times of the year and to resist diseases such as scab and blight, as well as pests. Select for disease-resistance first and then choose early varieties, which will be ready in early and midsummer, as well as varieties that are harvested in late summer or early autumn for winter storage. That way it's easy to enjoy homegrown potatoes nearly all year round.

Chitting or sprouting In late winter, set seed potatoes nose end up in cardboard boxes or slatted trays. Leave in a cool, light place for about six weeks until strong, short shoots develop.

Planting Dig trenches about 4 in. (10 cm) deep and 18-24 in. (45-60 cm) apart, using well dug and composted soil. Rub off all but the strongest two or three shoots and plant, shoots uppermost, along the trenches 10-12 in. (25-30 cm) apart.

Earthing up Use a rake to draw the soil up over the row into a ridge. Continue to earth up when leaves appear and as foliage grows. Cover any potatoes near the surface or they will turn green and be inedible.

Harvesting Harvest after flowers appear. Use a fork and work from the edge of the row to avoid piercing. Before lifting the crop, test one or two potatoes by rubbing the skin with your thumb. If it doesn't rub off, the crop is ready.

In a barrel Grow potatoes in a barrel with holes in the base for drainage. Put in a 6 in. (15 cm) layer of soil, then add the potatoes and cover with 3 in. (7.5 cm) of soil. Once the stems have grown so that they protrude about 6 in. (15 cm) above the surface, add another layer of soil. Keep well watered and continue adding soil layers until the barrel is almost full, then harvest.

freshen your home with Potpourri

Fill bowls with potpourri to scent your rooms. Or use it to fill pillows or sachets to put into closets and drawers.

YOU WILL NEED **Fragrant flowers and herbs, newspaper, scissors, orange or lemon peel, cardboard box with a lid, whole crushed spices such as cloves, cinnamon and coriander, orris root fixative. Optional: essential oils**

1 Dry flowers and herbs by hanging them in a warm dark place (*see* HERBS *and* FLOWERS) or spread on newspaper, removing petals from large flowers and cutting up large leaves.

3 Put the dried material into the box and add 2 tsp orris root fixative and 4 tbsp of crushed spices for every 4 oz (100 g) of dried material. Cover and leave for four weeks, shaking occasionally.

2 Leave the flowers or herbs for three or four weeks, turning every day to ensure even drying. Cut the citrus peel into slivers and dry separately over the same period.

In place of spices, you can use a few drops of an essential oil such as lavender or lemon verbena. But avoid using this potpourri for pillows or sachets as the oil will leak out.

---

prepare and cook Prawns & shrimp

Whereas it seems like "shrimp" and "prawn" are transatlantic names for the same creature, the fact is that the two are different, though similar animals. But preparation depends more on size than species: Small shrimp are shelled after cooking, but shells of large shrimp and prawns are best removed before.

Small shrimp If not bought precooked, plunge into boiling water for 5 minutes and cool in their liquid. Drain. Hold the tail tightly and pull it off. Twist off the head then peel off the body shell. Remove the intestinal vein, if necessary.

Large prawns Before cooking, remove the head and shell but leave the end of the tail in place (see below). Make a shallow cut along the back with a small, sharp knife and pry out the intestinal vein. To cook, brush with oil and broil, barbecue or fry, or add to curries or other dishes.

Power-walk
for fitness

Power-walking is faster than a stroll, slower than a run, and an all-round good way to get some fitness-building exercise.

■ Wear good running shoes, not walking shoes. Also wear synthetic sports socks that are designed to prevent blisters.

■ Start slowly, so as to warm up your muscles. A sudden start to any aerobic exercise puts you at risk of pulled muscles or other injuries.

■ Don't carry weights, and certainly don't place weights on your ankles; it will hamper your natural gait and place undue stress on your ligaments, tendons and joints.

■ Breathe normally. If you get out of breath, slow down or rest. You should be able to maintain a conversation as you power-walk.

■ Fix your gaze on a point about 25 ft (8 m) ahead of you. Don't stare at your feet.

■ When you power-walk, think about standing tall with your head high—as though suspended from a string.

■ Don't lean forward or hunch your shoulders.

■ Swing your arms in a relaxed and natural way, keeping your elbows bent at a right angle and your hands loosely curled.

■ Don't elongate your stride to increase your speed. Instead, move your legs faster. Keep your steps small and even.

treat Prickly heat

This intensely irritating skin rash is thought to be caused by excessive sweat leaking from glands into surrounding tissue. The medical term *miliaria rubra*, or "red millet," describes the appearance. In some cases salt crystals form in sweat gland ducts, causing blisters.

■ To reduce sweating, avoid excessive heat and humidity. If you have to go out in really hot weather, wear loose clothing made of natural fibers. Taking a cool bath or shower will provide some relief.
■ Antihistamine pills or creams can help to reduce itching. Or try applying hydrocortisone cream (not to the face) or calamine lotion. Aloe vera gel is pleasantly soothing. Plain yogurt spread on the rash is messy but often effective.

Publicize an event

Once you've settled on the who, what, when, where and why of your event, it's time to spread the word.

Create a "hub" Put all the details of the event on a website (*see* WEBSITE) or a Facebook page. Mention this hub in every other form of publicity you use.

Use your contacts Email or "tweet" details of the event to everyone you know, and ask them to pass the news on (*see* TWITTER).

Use traditional media Contact local papers and broadcasters, sending a press release or a letter to the editor. Say you're available for an interview. Notify the "what's on" columns.

Be seen Print posters and ask local store owners to display them. Print a flyer to be delivered door to door.

prepare an effective Presentation

Whether you use PowerPoint, an overhead projector or a flip chart, presentations are all about employing the material effectively, and with a touch of visual flair.

■ Before you begin to make slides or other visual material, work out your presentation on paper. How long will you be talking? How many slides or pictures will your presentation need to contain? What photographs, graphs or other artwork do you intend to use? Make rough sketches of your ideas.
■ Only put the headline information on your slides. If you have three points, just give the headings, then expand on them in your talk. The slide is there primarily to remind your audience of the structure of what you're saying. Don't simply stand there and read out what's on the slides.
■ Use alliteration and acronyms to bind your points together. A slide that says "Strategy, Security, Sanity" is punchier than one that says: "Have a plan, try to make sure it won't go wrong, and use your head when you implement it."
■ Turn any statistics into a chart or diagram, with minimal labeling, and then explain what it means as part of your speech. Make the visual as large as you can: a graphic can never be too big.
■ If you're working in PowerPoint, use the "theme" facility to give a unified visual look to design elements, such as colors and fonts. Use the software to add video and audio—but do so sparingly. Keep clips brief, and use them to illustrate your point rather than as a substitute for speaking yourself.
■ Know what you're going to say. Write out your entire script if that helps, and rehearse it so that you know exactly how long your presentation lasts.
■ Above all, speak clearly. Don't ramble on, and never mumble.

repair a bicycle Puncture

1 Remove the wheel by unscrewing the nuts or opening the quick-release lever, working a rear wheel free from any gear cogs as you go. Let the air out of the tire.

2 Insert a tire lever between the wheel rim and the tire, taking care not to catch the inner tube. Pry the bead of the tire away from the rim, and hook the lever on a spoke. Insert a second lever about 6 in. (15 cm) further on to release the next section of the tire. Repeat until you can pull out the inner tube.

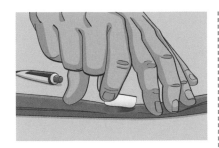

3 Pump up the inner tube and listen for hissing air to locate the puncture, or immerse the tube in a bowl of water and look for bubbles. Mark the hole with chalk or crayon, deflate the tire, and roughen the area around the puncture with sandpaper. Apply rubber solution, wait until touch-dry, then stick on a patch.

4 Inflate the tube slightly, insert the valve into its hole, and slide the tube little by little under the wheel rim. Push the bead over the rim with your thumbs, working your way around until it's in place. Refit the wheel on the bike, then pump up the tire.

carve a Pumpkin for Halloween

YOU WILL NEED **Big round pumpkin, sharp serrated knife, serving spoon, marker pen, tea light**

1 Set the pumpkin stalk side up and scalp it. Use a careful, deliberate sawing motion. Set the top aside.

2 Scoop out the seeds and fibers, holding the bowl of the spoon for leverage.

3 Draw triangular eyes, nose and a grinning, toothy mouth. Cut around the features and press them out with your thumb from the inside.

4 Put a tea light into the base of the pumpkin, light with a fireplace match or lighter and pop the top back on. Dim the lights. Spooky!

take a Pulse

Your pulse is your heart rate and is measured in beats per minute. It's lower when you're at rest and raised by exertion. To take it, you need a watch or clock with a second hand, or a minute timer.

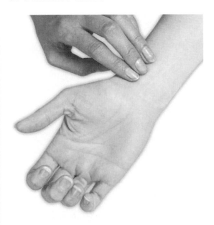

■ Lay your index, second and third fingers lightly on the inside of the wrist, close to the base of the thumb. Alternatively, place the tips of the index and second finger on the neck to the side of the windpipe. Move them around until you feel the insistent rhythm of coursing blood.

■ Count the beats for a full minute, or for 15 seconds multiplied by four. The normal adult pulse rate at rest is 60-80 beats for men, 65-85 for women. It's considerably faster in children.

escape from
Quicksand

This viscous, waterlogged sand is rarely deep, so you're unlikely to drown. But you'll need to find a way to get out—quick.

Quicksand is loose wet sand that yields easily to pressure. You sink into it slowly, especially if you're standing up.

■ If you step onto quicksand and your feet start to sink, sit down or fall backward so that your upper body is on dry land.
■ Pull out your feet one at a time—sacrificing your shoes if need be.

■ If you sink in to your midriff, don't panic and don't thrash about. Lean back and paddle very slowly with your legs to inch yourself toward firmer ground. Then turn over and crawl on your elbows and stomach until you're clear.

dance the Quickstep

The quickstep evolved in the 1920s from the foxtrot and Charleston, and contains elements of both. It's fun and lively, to be danced with gusto.

Put on some catchy quickstep music: "It Don't Mean a Thing," "Too Hot to Hold," "Let's Face the Music and Dance." Get to know the rhythm: slow, quick, quick, slow ... slow, quick, quick, slow ...

Posture and movement Because of the speed of this dance, you'll be mostly up on your toes for the quick steps and should move like a cat on hot bricks. Longer, slow steps are taken on the heel. The upper body should remain smooth and unaffected, as the feet work quickly underneath.

Get started Engage your partner in a classic ballroom hold (the lady slightly offset to the man's right). The man leads, the lady follows. The example below shows the basic man's steps, without any turns around the floor—the woman's steps are the mirror image of these.

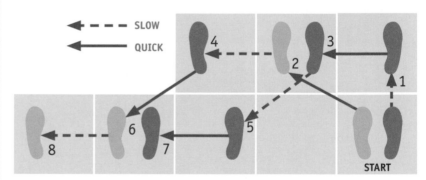

SLOW Take a good step forward with your right foot (1).

QUICK QUICK SLOW Now for a chassé (sidestep-slide-sidestep). Step forward and to the left with your left foot (2) and close your right foot to meet your left (3), then step left again with your left foot (4).

SLOW Take a long step back and to the left with your right foot (5).

QUICK QUICK SLOW Step back and to the left with your left foot (6) and close your right to meet your left (7), then take another step to the left with your left foot (8).

Change the angle As you take any of the slow steps, try rotating your foot so that it lands at an angle to where it was originally pointing. You can then use this foot as a pivot to execute a simple turn. As you grow in confidence, you can also add "lock steps" by crossing one foot behind or in front of the other, and "variations" by throwing in some fast little hopping movements. Have fun!

Quilt a simple cover

Warm quilted covers can easily be created using plain or patterned fabrics or sheets of patchwork.

YOU WILL NEED **Smooth light- or medium-weight fabric, tape measure, scissors, polyester fiber batting, dressmaker's pencil, ruler, masking tape, pins, ordinary sharp and quilting needles, quilting thread**

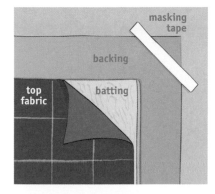

1 Cut out fabric for the quilt top and backing, adding at least 4 in. (10 cm) to the desired width and depth to allow for the "shrinkage" the quilting will cause. Make the backing 2 in. (5 cm) larger all round than the front. Cut the batting to the same size as the quilt top. Use a dressmaker's pencil and a ruler to mark a geometric pattern on the top fabric. Lay the backing fabric, wrong side up, on a hard, flat surface. Pull it taut and attach with masking tape. Spread the batting on top. Put on the top fabric, right side up.

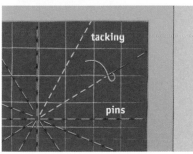

2 Pin through all three layers, starting at the center of the quilt and working outward to make a sunburst effect. Once all the pins are in place, remove the masking tape from the backing fabric. Then apply tacking stitches along the pin lines to hold the layers together more firmly. Remove the pins as you go.

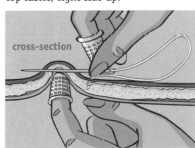

3 Thread the needle and make a small knot at the thread end. Starting at the center, insert the needle through the top layer only, bring it back up on a quilting line and pull to lodge the knot in the batting. Sew through all three layers along your pencil lines, using running stitch (*see* SEWING). Secure the thread end with a few backstitches on the underside. Remove tacking as you go.

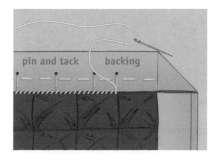

4 Fold the excess backing over the top layer, turning the raw edge under by ⅓ in. (10 mm), then pin and tack into place through all three layers. With the sharp needle, use a slipstitch (*see* SEWING) to attach the backing to the front of the finished quilt. Turn corners in on the diagonal before folding in backing edges to finish with neat mitered corners.

host a Quiz night

To host a good quiz night you need to do more than shout out a few questions.

■ Get your questions from an impeccable source. Check all facts if you're writing them yourself, and make sure that there's only one correct answer. So if the question is *In what year was "Hound Dog" released?*—specify whether you mean the Willie Mae "Big Mamma" Thornton version or Elvis Presley's.

■ Don't make the quiz too long. Try eight sets of ten questions—plus perhaps a picture round or two that teams can work on at their tables.

■ Get the technical side set up well in advance. Designate a technically savvy helper to test and operate the sound system, the overhead projector, the electronic scoresheet.

■ Have at least two other helpers on hand—to do the marking and collate the scores.

■ Practice reading the questions so that you're aware of awkward turns of phrase. Check the pronunciation of any obscure words or names.

■ On the night, read each question twice, with a gap of, say, 30 seconds. Don't rush; discussing possible answers is the bit participants love.

■ Speak with authority, and don't be put off by hecklers or know-it-alls. Your decision is final. At the same time, don't terrorize the participants; you are a quizmaster, not a taskmaster, and everyone is there to have fun.

■ If the answer to a question appears to be wrong, declare that question void so that no points are scored. Explain that this is the fairest way to proceed, and apologize graciously.

■ Make a bit of a show of announcing the winners and presenting the prize.

■ Take rabbits to the vet for regular health checks.
■ Rabbits are happiest as a compatible pair. Keep a neutered male with a neutered female.
■ Provide an exercise run, where rabbits have enough room to run around.

---

bleed a Radiator

You should bleed a radiator if it remains cold at the top when the heat is turned on and the rest of the radiator is hot. This means there's air trapped inside that has to be released. You'll need a radiator key and a rag.

■ Turn off the heat.
■ Fit the key over the air vent that's situated on one end of the radiator, at the top.
■ Turn it slightly counterclockwise. Air should start to hiss out. Stop turning as soon as you hear the hissing—if you turn the key too much the vent will screw right out.
■ Hold the rag underneath to catch any drops of water that escape as the last of the air is released. As soon as water starts to appear, turn the key back to close the vent.
■ Turn the heat on again.

look after pet Rabbits

Happy bunnies have a roomy purpose-made hutch with a wire-mesh door in a sheltered spot, with access to a secure pen for exercise.

Food
■ Feed rabbits two meals a day, at regular times, in a heavy earthenware dish that won't move as they eat. Use a second dish for fresh water.
■ Hay and grass should make up most of your rabbits' diet, or a good food from a pet-supply store. Feed them at least their own body weight every day. The only treat you should give is a root vegetable or fruit, in small amounts.
■ Don't give rabbits rhubarb, potato shoots, mown grass, buttercups, daisies or any weeds or wildflowers sprayed with pesticide.

Housing
■ Line the hutch floor with newspaper or clean wood shavings, with soft hay or straw on top. Clean the hutch every day by removing any wet and dirty shavings or bedding, remove any uneaten fresh food and clean the food and water containers before refilling them.
■ A hutch must have separate areas for eating, sleeping and toilet, and be large enough for a rabbit to stand on its hind legs without the ears touching the top. Ensure a hutch has safe places where rabbits can hide when afraid.

Handling
■ Lift a rabbit with one hand under its abdomen then support it under the rump with the other hand. Hold it to your chest, supporting the head and ears. Keep movements slow and gentle; don't startle your pet. Never lift a rabbit by its ears as this causes unnecessary suffering. With correct and frequent handling from a young age you can build a relationship of affection and trust.

---

stop wild Rabbits feasting in your garden

Rabbits can eat through an entire crop in one night or destroy your prize flowers just for a snack. Your first line of defense is a chicken-wire fence, which must enclose the entire garden or vegetable patch.

■ Hammer meter- or yard-long stakes into the ground about 5 ft (1.5 m) apart. Unroll a meter- or yard-wide roll of chicken wire and make a bend about 8 in. (20 cm) deep along its length. Stand the wire against the stakes so that the bent portion faces outwards to stop the rabbits from digging underneath. Another tactic is to bury the bottom 8 in. (20 cm) of the wire fence in the ground. Attach the wire to the stakes.
■ In addition, use commercial repellents—which should be applied in the evenings (when rabbits come out to feed) and after rain. Serious rabbit infestations may need to be dealt with by professional pest controllers.

construct a Raised bed

Raised beds are ideal for growing vegetables and fruit such as strawberries. Once built, they don't need to be tilled, help to combat perennial weeds and can be tended without walking on the soil.

YOU WILL NEED **Tape measure, stakes, string, shovel, saw, eight 50 x 6 in. lengths of treated wood, four 30-in. long 4 x 4 in. posts, 16 x 3 in galvanized nails, hammer, soil, rake. Optional: bark mulch, landscape fabric**

1 Mark out an area 4 ft (1.2 m) square. Measure diagonally from corner to corner—if the bed is square the diagonals will be equal. Clear all weeds and dig to a depth of 8-12 in. (20-30 cm), piling the soil in the center.

2 Nail corner posts flush with the tops and edges of two pieces of board, then fix a second, lower board to each. Position the edging boards on opposite sides of the bed, 4 ft (1.2 m) apart, and tap down until the lower edge of the lower board is flush with the surface level.

3 Nail the side boards into place. Mix compost into the dug soil and rake level. Surround the bed with bark mulch if you wish. Water well, if necessary, and add plants.

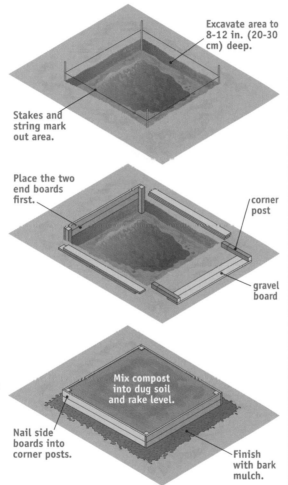

Excavate area to 8-12 in. (20-30 cm) deep.

Stakes and string mark out area.

Place the two end boards first.

corner post

gravel board

Mix compost into dug soil and rake level.

Nail side boards into corner posts.

Finish with bark mulch.

Tips and alternatives

■ Railroad ties make excellent raised beds and don't need nailing to corner posts. But make sure you buy new ties; reclaimed railroad stock will be steeped in toxic oil that's harmful to plants and people.

■ If your ground is weed prone, remove all the soil as you dig and line the bed with landscape fabric. Fill the bed with fresh topsoil and compost.

■ Make sure beds are small enough for you to reach across without walking or kneeling on the soil. For a higher bed (and less bending) use longer corner posts and more boards.

■ Make paths between beds wide enough to push a wheelbarrow through.

learn to Rap

Freestyle rap involves improvised rhythmic speaking to a beat. You need the ability to think on your feet and impeccable timing.

Learn the language Rap rejoices in the use of street slang and is woven through with terms such as *cupcakin* (acting lovey-dovey), *burbalatin* (happening), *livin large* (doing big *thangs*), *off the hook* (crazy and wild), *scallywag* (uncool) and *parlayin* (relaxing with friends). Remember that *-ing* is always said as *-in*, or you'll ruin the effect of what you say.

■ Build a stock of rhyming words, and words with similar sounds or endings. Search for "rap dictionary" online to find a wide selection of rap, or hip hop, slang.

■ Work out a narrative. Your rap should tell a story or state a case, expressing your opinion. Decide what you want to say.

■ To begin with, forget about rhyme. Practice flowing until you get the hang of improvising, or "freestyling" to a rhythm.

■ Now start to introduce rhyme. Don't worry if you make mistakes or talk yourself into dead ends; this is how to learn. Accomplished rappers are able to acknowledge a slip and build it into the rap. Let your mind run ahead a little; as you finish line one you should have line two in your head.

■ A neat rappers' trick is to have a store of all-purpose fill-in rhyming couplets that you can throw into the mix to buy yourself some time to think of the next few lines.

R

make Ratatouille

Slow simmering is the key to a good ratatouille. The dish is best in late summer, when all the main ingredients are in season.

SERVES 6-8

**3 small egplants, cut into
 ¼ in. (5 mm) slices
5 tbsp olive oil
1 large onion, chopped
2 cloves of garlic, minced
2 large zucchini, cut into
 ¼ in. (5 mm) slices
5 large tomatoes, skinned,
 seeded and chopped
1 green pepper, seeded
 and cut up
1 red pepper, seeded and cut up
salt and freshly ground black pepper**

1 Brush the eggplant slices with oil and broil on high until lightly browned on each side but not softened.

2 Heat the remaining oil in a large lidded frying pan or shallow casserole dish that's suitable for use on the stovetop. Cook the onions and garlic until the onion is softened.

3 Add the zucchini, tomatoes and peppers, season and simmer for about 35 minutes, stirring occasionally, until vegetables are just soft, but not pulpy. Stir in the grilled eggplant and heat thoroughly before serving.

get rid of Rats

Rats inside the home are a serious health risk, since they spread diseases such as salmonella, *E. coli* and leptospirosis (Weil's disease), which is potentially fatal. You can help to discourage rats by never leaving pet bowls or garbage bags outside and not putting meat on your compost heap.

Act fast if you detect signs of rats in the garden, under the deck (a favorite nesting spot) or in a garage. You may see rod-shaped droppings ⅓-½ in. (8-12 mm) long or holes gnawed in baseboards and packaging, or notice a distinctive musky smell.

Set a large number of traps with poisoned bait, such as sausage or bacon. Bait the traps unset for a week before activating them, since rats tend to avoid anything new. If the infestation doesn't clear up quickly, call in a pest-control specialist before the rats multiply.

use the Recovery position

Someone is unconscious but breathing. Once you have dealt with any potentially life-threatening issues, and while you wait for the ambulance, you must make them safe, to prevent choking (*see* CHOKING). If the victim is left lying on their back, there's a danger that vomit, saliva, blood or their own tongue could block the windpipe. Don't roll the person if there's any possibility of a spinal injury, and keep the airway open by lifting the jaw carefully and tilting the head back without moving the neck.

1 Keep the person's airway open (see above). Straighten their legs. Kneel at their side, at chest level, and place the arm nearest to you at right angles to the body.

2 Take the other arm across the chest and support the head, resting the cheek on the back of the victim's hand. Bend the farther knee upward and pull it to roll the person toward you.

3 Take great care to protect the head while rolling the person over. Ensure that the one knee remains bent to prevent them from rolling too far.

4 If you have rolled the victim onto their left side, the bent right knee and right arm will provide support—and vice versa.

5 Continue to support the head and tilt the chin up and head back to keep the airway open and to allow fluids to drain without risk of choking.

6 Monitor the pulse (*see* PULSE) and breathing until help arrives. If help is delayed, switch the person to the other side every 30 minutes.

---

write an effective Reference letter

When you write a reference for someone, whether they are applying for a job, a university or any position of responsibility, your must be fair and truthful. Never say anything libelous. If you have doubts about the person or their suitability, it's better to decline to write them a reference altogether.

■ Your reference letter should begin by stating your connection to the applicant, and should say something positive early on. *I was Georgina's line manager at the Acme Corporation for four years, and in that time I found her to be thoroughly trustworthy/hard-working/efficient/...* Make sure you mention how long you have known the candidate.

■ You should say something specific about why you feel that this person is right for the role in question—so make sure you know what the job or position is. Ask the applicant or the person who has approached you for more information if necessary.

■ End on a high note: *I recommend Georgina wholeheartedly, and know she is a fine candidate for the post.*

---

keep your Refrigerator clean and cool

Regular cleaning is essential to prevent the buildup of potentially dangerous bacteria and fungi and to eliminate unwanted odors. You should also keep the temperature low enough to prevent the growth of harmful bacteria.

Cleaning

■ A quick wipe once a week will keep your fridge clean, but every six months do a thorough cleaning of all the shelves, drawers and storage areas.

■ Remove food from shelves and keep in a cool place. On a really hot day, put perishable items into a cooler or work one shelf at a time, so that most of the food can stay in the fridge.

continued on next page →

banish Red-eye from photos

The curse of red-eye is easy to avoid and, nowadays, not difficult to put right.

Red-eye in photographs occurs when you use a flash, so take your pictures in natural light if possible.

■ A camera with internal flash is more likely to lead to red-eye, because the source of the light is close to the lens—which is where the subject tends to be looking. Have your subjects look away from the camera if that suits your shot; if you need them to be looking directly at the camera, use an external flash.

■ Some cameras have a red-eye reduction setting, which produces a small blink of light before the main flash. This causes the subjects' pupils to contract, and so restricts the amount of light reflecting off the retina (which is the cause of red-eye).

Easy computer fix Red-eye removal pens can touch up the telltale red stare on photo prints, but with digital photographs it's an easy thing to put right using your computer. Import your pictures onto your computer (or scan the prints if your camera isn't digital).

■ Open the images in the image-editing software that came with your camera or your computer. Many have a built-in red-eye function; it's simply a matter of highlighting the eyes in your image, and clicking on the button.

Repoint
damaged brickwork

Repointing is a straightforward job so long as the affected area is small.

The trickiest part of repointing is making mortar that matches the surrounding joints. The only way to do this is to experiment by making up small batches using varying amounts of sand and lime with the cement. Repoint a small area with each different batch, having first taken note of the quantities. Wait for the mortar to dry—for a week at least—before settling on the mix that's the best match. You may have to scrape out your unsuccessful experiments.

1 The first task is to remove cracked or crumbling mortar from between the bricks. This can be done with a chisel that has a tapered edge specially designed for this task—use it with a club hammer. If you own an angle grinder, a special diamond cutting wheel does the trick. Whichever method you use, you should cleanly remove the old mortar to a depth of ½ in. (15 mm).

2 Brush the bricks to remove dust and debris, then wet them. Copy the shape of the mortar in the surrounding joints, using a pointing trowel or a special pointing tool (see above)—or you can improvise with a wooden stick or even a length of hose.

continued from page 257
■ Remove shelves and disinfect to reduce the risk of salmonella and *E. coli* infection. Rinse shelves and dry with a clean dish towel or paper towel.
■ Clean the interior surfaces, including the door storage areas, with the same cleaner. A little white vinegar will quickly cut through any grease.
■ Remove drawers, squirt in some dish soap and soak in the sink in hot water for ten minutes. Use a brush to remove any stubborn or trapped pieces of dirt. Rinse and dry.

Maintenance
■ Check the temperature regularly. For safety it should always be between 35°F and 40°F (2°C and 4°C). If your fridge doesn't have a built-in thermometer, buy a fridge thermometer and store it inside.
■ If the door doesn't close properly, your fridge won't operate efficiently and may not be cool enough. Try shutting a piece of paper in the door—the seal around it should be strong enough to make it difficult to pull the paper out. If the seal doesn't seem good enough, use a mild detergent solution to clean the rubber sealing strip, making sure to clean in all the grooves.
■ Dust and dirt on the condenser coils will also reduce the efficiency. Every six months, pull out the fridge and gently vacuum the back.

practice deep Relaxation

The pace of modern life can lead to stress and exhaustion, but just minutes of the right kind of relaxation can be enough to calm the mind and refresh the body.

Find a quiet space, take off your shoes, loosen your clothing and try the following techniques.

Take a deep breath Breathing exercises promote calm and clarity of mind, and ease tension. Lie on your back on the floor with your head cushioned and with something to rest the backs of your knees on.

From the diaphragm Rest your hands on your abdomen and use your diaphragm to draw air into and then completely out of your lungs; your hands will move up and down with the rhythm. Deep abdominal breathing can be done in any comfortable position, sitting or lying down.

Sink into the floor Lie on your back with your spine aligned from neck to tailbone, toes pointed up and arms a little way from your body.
■ Start to isolate, tense and relax different muscles from top to toe, concentrating in turn on each part of your body.
■ Crease your forehead for a count of five and relax. Do it again. Squeeze your eyes tight shut. Then move down your body.
■ When you have worked your way down to your ankles—one arm, one leg at a time—lie still, release all tension and imagine yourself floating.

organize a Reunion

An exchange of holiday cards is all very well, but bringing together a group of old classmates or colleagues is better—if you get it right. Here are some tips for a successful gathering.

Who will be there? Make your list then start to spread the word. Even if you have lost touch with a friend, chances are that someone else is still in contact. Try asking whoever organized the last reunion for their list.
■ Approach an alumni representative at your old school, college or university.
■ Don't overlook the phone book. Your friend may have moved on, but their parents might still live at the old address.
■ Use the internet and reach out across the world. Try social networking sites such as Facebook or Twitter. Try dedicated reunion websites such as Friends Reunited, and people searches such as yaba.com.

When? If years have slipped by, what's another six months? Give everyone plenty of notice of your intention and gauge enthusiasm. Suggest a couple of possible dates and ask for feedback before settling on a final day.

Where? Is it to be at a restaurant, bar, your own home? You might decide to meet up informally in a bar, then move on for a meal nearby. Consider the type of venue; you're going to want to talk above all, catch up, show photographs and bring news, so avoid anywhere too busy or loud. Wherever you decide to meet, make it somewhere central and accessible to all.

Set a budget Remember some partygoers will have to bear the cost of travel and possibly overnight accommodation, so be practical about your plans.
■ For a large gathering, allow for food, drink, venue rental and music.
■ Don't hand over your own credit card without firm promises from attendees. Explain that acceptance is a commitment—or consider selling tickets.

When everything is booked send around a confirmation. State the time, date, venue and who else so far has signed up for the do.

- -

write a Resignation letter

If you are resigning from a company where you've held a position of authority or where you've worked for a long time, it is appropriate to write a letter of resignation. Set it up like any other business letter, and send a copy to the president (of a small corporation) or the HR director (for a large company), and CC your immediate supervisor.

Be clear Your letter should state your intent to resign and the date your resignation will be effective. Give the reason for your leaving, and express appreciation for the experience you've gained while working there. You may want to modestly mention some of your accomplishments, in case you plan to ask for a reference letter at some point in the future.

Be careful Your letter will become part of your permanent work record, and may arise again at any point in the future, so be careful if you are leaving under less than ideal circumstances. Be polite, be clear and don't be negative.

cook perfect white Rice

Perfect rice is light and fluffy, not soggy and gluey. It's easy when you know how.

Rice can be cooked in a large pan of boiling, salted water for 10-15 minutes and then drained, but this 2:1 absorption method gives even better results.

SERVES 4

1 Put 1 cup long-grain white rice in a heavy-bottomed saucepan with 2 cups of cold water and a pinch of salt.

2 Bring to a boil, stir once, cover, then simmer on very low heat for 10 minutes.

3 Remove from the heat and let sit, with the lid on, for another 10 minutes. Fork through to separate the grains and serve immediately.

golden rules
RICE TRICKS AND TIPS
■ **Make sure the pan lid fits tightly.**
■ **If the rice sticks, transfer it to a sieve, rinse thoroughly with boiling water, shake off any excess liquid, return to the pan, cover and leave undisturbed for 5 minutes.**

remove a stuck Ring

When a ring is so tight you can't get it off, the worst thing you can do is to wrench at it in panic. Stay calm.

Run it under cold water, raise your hand above your head to decrease blood flow, use a lubricant—olive oil, dish soap, hair conditioner—then twist the ring back and forth to ease it off.

Try dental floss

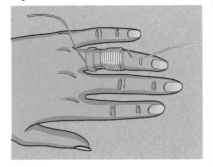

Poke the end of a length of dental floss under the ring, then wind the floss from the dispenser firmly around and up the finger from the ring towards and over the knuckle.

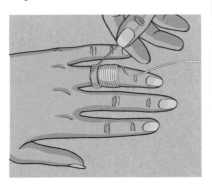

Then start to unwind the string by pulling on the loose end beneath the ring to edge it up your finger and over the knuckle.

Take care Don't tie a knot in the floss or leave it on for more than five minutes. Remove the floss at once if your fingertip turns blue.

make a simple Risotto

The round grains of risotto rice are essential for absorbing the stock in a risotto. You can add vegetables, chicken or seafood to this basic recipe, but if you are using seafood, omit the parmesan.

SERVES 4-6

4 tbsp butter
1 tbsp olive oil
1 small onion, finely chopped
1 small clove of garlic, minced
1 cup risotto rice
½ cup dry white wine
about 5 cups hot chicken or vegetable stock
¾ cup parmesan cheese, freshly grated
salt and freshly ground black pepper

1 Melt half the butter with the oil in a large, shallow pan. Add the onion and garlic and cook over moderate heat until the onion is transparent. Add the rice and cook, stirring, until the grains begin to change color. Pour in the wine and a quarter of the stock and bring to a boil.

2 Put the remaining stock into a separate pan and keep at the simmering point. As stock is absorbed into the risotto add more, a ladleful at a time, stirring constantly for about 20 minutes. The risotto is done when the rice is just tender, the liquid absorbed and the mixture creamy. Stir in the remaining butter and the cheese, check the seasoning and serve at once.

■ Use good—preferably homemade—stock (*see* CHICKEN SOUP *and* VEGETABLE STOCK).
■ Make sure the risotto doesn't dry out.

---

avoid a Road rage incident

If another driver becomes angry with you as a result of an accident or a near miss, your main goal should be to keep yourself safe. If in doubt, stay in your car.

■ Try to defuse the situation. Hold up your hands as a conciliatory gesture, though avoid saying sorry as this could be seen as admitting liability.
■ Don't make the situation worse by arguing.
■ If you've stopped and got out of your car, get back in and lock the doors at any point that you feel threatened.
■ Don't hesitate to drive away if you feel that the driver is becoming violent.
■ If the driver follows you, don't head home. Instead, drive straight to the nearest police station or a public place such as a gas station or drive-through restaurant, sticking to busy, well-lit roads. If the situation remains dangerous, stop and use your cell phone to call the police from your car.

Roast meat **without worry**

Before cooking but after they have been prepared and had any stuffing added, all cuts or birds need to be weighed. Season the meat, brush with a little oil if it's very lean, then put it on a rack to allow fat to drip and air to circulate freely. The meat can be loosely wrapped in foil to stop it from drying out, but always remove foil for the last 30 minutes of cooking to allow the surface of the meat to brown.

A meat thermometer is a handy tester. Insert it into the thickest part of the meat, making sure it doesn't touch either bone or the roasting pan.

Meat	Cooking times	Meat temperature

Cooking times below are from when the oven is preheated.

BEEF AND LAMB	350°F (180°C)	
■ Rare	15 mins/lb (35 mins/kg) + 15 min	140°F (60°C)
■ Medium	20 mins/lb (45 mins/kg) + 20 min	160°F (71°C)
■ Well done	24 mins/lb (55 mins/kg) + 25 min	175°F (80°C)

Cook at 425°F (220°C) for the first 20 minutes to brown. The rarer the meat the more it will give when pressed (*see* STEAK).

PORK	400°F (200°C)	165°F (75°C)
	25 mins/lb (55 mins/kg)	

Must be well cooked all through. For good crackling, score the skin with deep parallel cuts. Cook for last 15-20 minutes at 425°F (220°C) (*see* PORK CRACKLING).

CHICKEN	400°F (200°C)	160°F (71°C)
	15-20 mins/lb (35-45 mins/kg)	
	+ 15-20 mins	

Baste often. When the thickest part is pricked, the juices should run clear.

TURKEY	350°F (180°C)	160°F (71°C)
	25 mins/lb (45 mins/kg)	
	+ 20 mins	

Baste often. When the thickest part is pricked, the juices should run clear.

■ For meat on the bone add 5 minutes per pound (500 g), plus 5 minutes overall.
■ Bring meat to room temperature before roasting.
■ Ensure that the surface of the meat is completely dry.
■ When the cooking time is up, rest the roast on a warm serving platter in a warm place for at least 15 minutes before carving. This allows the fibers of the meat to firm up, making it easier to carve.

cook the perfect
Roast potatoes

For roast potatoes that are crisp on the outside and fluffy within, use floury potatoes such as Yukon Gold or Russet, and cook them in some sort of fat (traditionally lard or goose fat). For a healthier or vegetarian version, use canola oil. Shaking them well roughens the surface and helps to make them extra crunchy.

SERVES 6

**3½ lb (1.5 kg) potatoes, peeled
    and cut into pieces
salt
½ cup lard or canola oil**

Heat the oven to 425°F (220°C). Boil the potatoes in salted water for 5 minutes then drain. With the lid on the pan, shake them well. Heat the fat in a roasting pan until very hot, add the potatoes and baste well. Cook for 40-50 minutes until crisp and golden brown, turning once.

golden rules
BEST ROAST POTATOES
■ **Keep potato pieces an even size.**
■ **Make sure each piece is completely covered with fat when you baste.**

build and plant a
Rock garden

A rock garden adds a bit of rugged drama to sunny, open sites and is a good way to plant on an awkward slope.

For best results, the soil shouldn't be too rich and you should avoid overhanging trees, which will drop leaves on your display.

YOU WILL NEED Shovel, crushed stone, sharp sand, assortment of large and small rocks and stones, trowel, plants, bulbs. Optional: pea gravel

Start with the stones Get your stones from a garden center or quarry; they will deliver if you're buying a large enough quantity. Limestone resists frosts and weathers attractively but isn't good for acid-loving plants, such as summer-flowering heathers. Sandstone is lighter and cheaper but less frost resistant, and tufa is excellent but expensive.

1 Dig the topsoil to 12 in. (30 cm), creating a slope downward from a plateau. Add 6 in. (15 cm) of crushed stone to help drainage. Cover this with 2 in. (5 cm) of sharp sand, then 4 in. (10 cm) of topsoil. Place rocks and stones in tiers, embedding two-thirds of each below the surface and placing all grooves and fissures running in the same direction. Butt some up closely and leave planting spaces between others.

2 Allow soil to settle for three to four weeks, then plant with alpines, such as alyssums, sedums and saxifrages. Mulch with small stones or pea gravel. Plant bulbs such as miniature daffodils, alliums and tulips in early autumn, followed by heathers, dwarf shrubs and conifers in late autumn.

launch your own Rocket

This simple rocket won't go into Earth orbit, but it flies using exactly the same ballistic principles as the Apollo spaceship.

YOU WILL NEED Sheet of 8½ x 11 in. paper, pencil, scissors, plastic canister with a lid that fits inside the tube (an old-fashioned 35 mm film canister is ideal), tape, water, measuring cup or spoons, antacid tablet (such as Alka Seltzer) or effervescent salts (Epsom salts)

1 Mark up the paper as shown, and cut out the shapes. Use a lid or saucer to draw a circle for the nose cone (experiment to find the right size for your canister) and keep all the fins the same size. Decorate the paper components if you want them to look even more like a rocket.

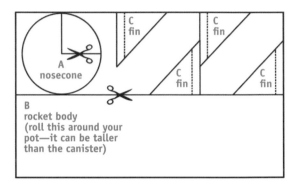

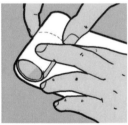

2 Take the long oblong of paper and wrap it around the canister, securing it in place with tape. The canister should be positioned at the bottom of the paper cylinder you have made, with its open end pointing upward.

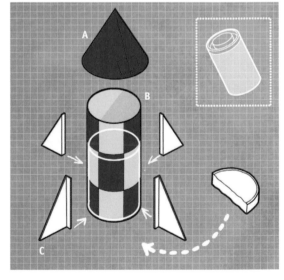

3 Cut a quarter out of the circular piece of paper, and discard. Use tape to stick the two straight edges together—this is your nosecone (A). Tape the nose cone to the top of the body (B) of the rocket (the opposite end to the canister).

4 Make a fold in the long edge of each of the rocket's fins (C) and secure them to the base of the rocket with tape, spacing them evenly.

5 Turn your rocket over, and carefully fill the canister one-third full with water. Then put in half an antacid tablet or ½ tsp effervescent salts for each 2 tsp (10 ml) of water and very quickly snap on the lid. Place your rocket on a hard, level surface and stand well back. In a few seconds, it will launch itself into the air.

climb a Rope ladder

Climbing a rope ladder with wooden rungs isn't the same as climbing a "stiff" ladder (*see* LADDER). If the ladder is hanging free—that is, not resting against a tree or a wall—then you should tackle the ascent from the side, not the front: left arm and leg to one face of the ladder, right arm and leg to the other. That way, the ladder does not swing away from your body as you climb. If the ladder rests against a vertical surface, you can only climb up the front. Move your left arm and right leg together, and vice versa, to keep more or less equal pressure on both ropes as you move and minimize the sway.

handle Ropes properly on a boat

Coil a rope All sailors need to know how to coil a rope for safe, tangle-free stowage. This method offers a secure way of stowing ropes that won't be hung up. Coil clockwise, beginning from the fixed end and working your way to the free end. Make each loop the same size—about the length of your outstretched arm—and twist the rope as you go if you need to work out any kinks. When you have 5 ft (1.5 m) left, make three or four turns around the bundle, then push a loop of the free end through the coil (1) and pull it back over the top (2). Pull the free end to tighten (3) then tuck it through the coil to finish off (4).

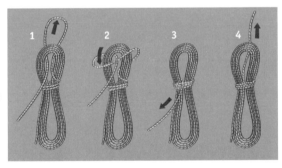

Throw a rope First uncoil and recoil the rope. Making sure that the line is attached to the boat (see left), split the coil into two with slack between. Hold the fixed end of the rope in your left hand (if you're right-handed) and throw the first half and then release the second immediately after. This will reach the greatest distance and make the rope easier to catch. Don't aim straight at the receiver, but just to one side.

Tying up To tie the free end of the line when mooring, for instance, use a round turn and two half hitches to make fast to a bollard or a mooring ring, or a bowline for dropping a loop over a post (*see* KNOTS). These are the two most essential knots for part-time sailors. To make fast to a cleat, take the rope around the cleat, add one or two more figure-eights and make another round turn to secure.

read Roman numerals

The Romans had a numerical system based on seven letters, representing seven numbers.

These letters are:

I (one)
V (five)
X (ten)
L (fifty)
C (one hundred)
D (five hundred)
M (one thousand)

Other numbers can be generated by adding these together, with the largest figure coming first:

MCCLVI stands for **1,256**.

M (1,000) + **CC** (200) + **L** (50) + **VI** (6) = **1,256**

If a smaller number comes before a larger one, then the lesser figure is subtracted from the higher one:

XC means 90 (100 – 10)
IV means 4 (5 – 1)

This was a cumbersome and inefficient way of counting, but Roman numerals continued to be used long after Roman times to express dates on civic monuments, such as buildings and statues.

grow perfect
Roses
see pages 264-265

R

grow perfect Roses

A rose is not simply a rose. The plant comes in an extraordinary range of colors and forms, often combined with a heady scent, and will climb up walls and over trellises, as well as thrive in borders alongside other shrubs and herbaceous perennials, or in pots.

Choosing and siting roses **All roses need sunshine for at least part of the day and do best in well-manured, slightly acid, water-retentive soil. Choose the right type of rose for your needs from the categories listed below, considering color and scent as well as growing habit.**

Rosa 'Excelsa' (climber)

BUYING GUIDE Roses can be bought container-grown or bare-rooted, and should do well as long as you follow these guidelines:
- Buy from a reputable grower and ask for disease-resistant varieties.
- Check plant details carefully if buying by mail order or online, to ensure it's what you want.
- Always unwrap mail-order plants promptly when they are delivered, check their condition and plant them as soon as possible.
- When choosing a variety, check that it's repeat flowering (blooms more than once each season) if you want a long-lasting display.
- Choose plants with at least three or four strong shoots and plenty of roots. Avoid old, pot-bound ones.
- Never buy roses showing signs of pests or disease.

A ROSE FOR EVERY PLACE

Rosa 'Ballerina' (shrub)

Shrub roses This group includes many well-known types, such as China, damask and Old English roses, which mostly flower only once a year. They are good in mixed borders and can be trained up posts. Also in this group are rugosa roses, which are good for hedges and have large attractive hips, and ground cover roses, many of which are repeat flowering.

Hybrid teas These are smaller than shrub roses, with large, usually scented double blooms. Hybrid teas are easy to grow, come in many colors, and flower in two main flushes in early and late summer, and even through to the first frosts. They are the ideal roses for a dedicated rose bed but can also be mixed with other plants.

Climbers You usually get fewer but larger blooms with climbers, borne on young wood made in the same year. They make a framework of long, strong shoots, which look excellent growing through a tree or on pergolas and trellises.

Patio and miniature roses These roses are bred for small spaces and containers. They bear pretty, small blooms but tend to be prone to blackspot and mildew.

Ramblers Vigorous growers with large trusses of small flowers borne once each season on flexible wood made in the previous year. Easily trained, but best around pillars and over arches.

Floribundas Usually unscented, but flower in profusion over a long period. They are easy to grow in a dedicated bed or in a mixed border in the same way as hybrid teas.

Rosa 'Iceberg' (floribunda)

PLANTING Plant bare-rooted roses in mid to late autumn (see TREE), and container-grown ones at any time, as for other shrubs (see SHRUB).

■ Soak roots of bare-rooted plants overnight in a bucket of water before planting, or water container-grown plants thoroughly.

■ Trim back all stems to about 6 in. (15 cm) above outward-facing buds and remove any thick, coarse roots. Try not to damage thin, fibrous roots.

■ Most roses are grafted and the "union" between the rootstock and the grafted stems must be below ground, but not planted too deeply. Lay a stick across the hole to help you to gauge the depth.

PRUNING The methods for pruning roses vary according to their type, but it's an essential routine to encourage strong growth and abundant flowers.

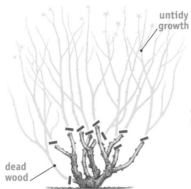

untidy growth

dead wood

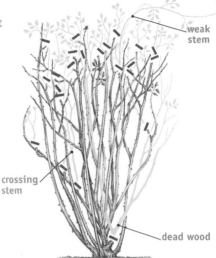

weak stem

crossing stem

dead wood

Shrub roses Prune every two years. Thin out and trim back untidy growth in early winter or spring to leave strong new shoots. Remove all dead wood and old weak stems. You can use sharp shears for this.

Hybrid tea, floribunda and patio roses Cut out dead wood and weak or crossing stems; prune to healthy buds in late winter. Prune hybrid teas and miniatures to 4 in. (10 cm), floribundas to about 12 in. (30 cm).

Climbers Immediately after blooming, trim back shoots that have flowered to new buds—don't wait until energy-sapping hips form. Then in early winter cut spindly, dead and diseased wood back to strong new shoots. Prune back old shoots that haven't produced any new growth by about half.

Ramblers In early autumn, cut some of the old flowered shoots ("canes") down to ground level, leaving new growth springing from the base. If there aren't enough new shoots to maintain the shape of the plant, leave more old stems in place, but cut back to a strong shoot (right) higher up.

PESTS AND DISEASES Good health is the best prevention, but roses are still vulnerable to attack. Aphids (*see* APHIDS) are a problem, as are rusts and powdery mildew (*see* PLANT DISEASES). The following are also major problems for roses.

black spot

Black spot A common fungal disease causing unsightly dark spots on leaves. Spray every two weeks from late winter onward with rose fungicide, according to the manufacturer's instructions. Burn fallen leaves and all prunings to stop the fungus from spreading.

Rose sickness Sometimes roses suddenly die back for no apparent reason, possibly as a result of fungal buildup in the soil. Remove a dead rose with its root ball and burn it, then dig out all the surrounding soil to a depth and diameter of 20 in. (50 cm). Replace with fresh compost, then wait three years before planting another rose in the same spot.

Row a boat

The aim is to combine a series of movements into a cyclical action in which the blades of the oars move in a smooth oval.

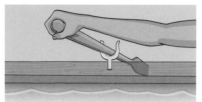

1 Grip the oars with your arms held straight out in front of you, parallel to the water. The blades should be vertical, and just out of the water. Your wrists should be straight.

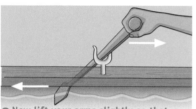

2 Now lift your arms slightly so that the blades dip into the water and, once buried, lean back with your body, keeping your arms parallel. This will get you moving. Finally, bend your arms to complete the stroke.

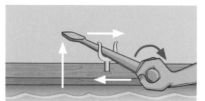

3 At the end of this first stroke, push down on the oars to raise the blades out of the water; bend your wrists, as if revving a motorbike, so the blades are horizontal, and simultaneously push your arms forward to make ready for the next stroke.

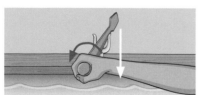

4 As your arms straighten, turn your wrists back so that the blades are vertical once more. Lift your arms slightly to drop the blades into the water, and pull again.

place bets in Roulette

You bet against the "House" in this casino game, predicting which of 38 slots on a wheel (37 on European wheels) a ball will land in when the croupier spins it.

To bet, place chips on a table layout of red and black boxes representing each number on the wheel, and outer boxes representing various combinations of numbers.

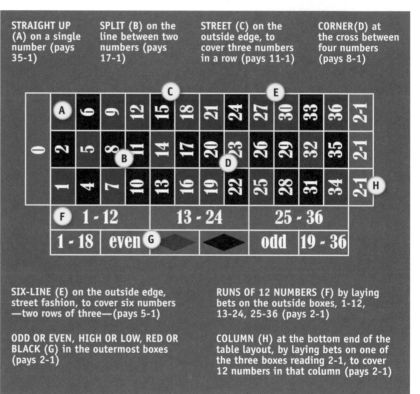

STRAIGHT UP (A) on a single number (pays 35-1)

SPLIT (B) on the line between two numbers (pays 17-1)

STREET (C) on the outside edge, to cover three numbers in a row (pays 11-1)

CORNER(D) at the cross between four numbers (pays 8-1)

SIX-LINE (E) on the outside edge, street fashion, to cover six numbers —two rows of three—(pays 5-1)

ODD OR EVEN, HIGH OR LOW, RED OR BLACK (G) in the outermost boxes (pays 2-1)

RUNS OF 12 NUMBERS (F) by laying bets on the outside boxes, 1-12, 13-24, 25-36 (pays 2-1)

COLUMN (H) at the bottom end of the table layout, by laying bets on one of the three boxes reading 2-1, to cover 12 numbers in that column (pays 2-1)

use a Router

A router consists of a motor mounted vertically on a horizontal base plate. As you slide the base over wood, a rotating bit carves out a path. The many bits available allow you to make decorative edges and fluting, to cut designs and lettering, to trim veneer and plastic laminate, and to make interlocking joints. A router can make mortices for hinges and locks, or cut dado, rabbet and tongue-and-groove joints for furniture. A router rated under

½ horsepower is fine for many jobs.

- For a deep cut, you simply make a series of shallow cuts. But cuts that must be made in one pass, like a dovetail, for instance, must be made with a higher-power model.
- To keep a cut straight, many bits have a tip, or pilot, that rolls along the edge.
- For cuts parallel to the edge, you can attach an edge-guide accessory to the router base. Otherwise, clamp a straight board to your work as a guide: Measure from the router base's center to its edge, then align the board the same distance from the cut's center.
- For a cut wider than the bit, which requires side-by-side passes, mark the cut's edges with lines. Place the edge of the bit along one line. Then mark the router's edge and draw a line parallel to the cut. Align the board along it, then clamp another board the same distance away on the other side of the cut.
- Always cut from left to right to keep the bit from bucking. Hold the router firmly, and move it fast enough that the bit doesn't ripple the side of the cut, but slow enough that the motor doesn't strain.

---

understand the basics of Rugby

The game of rugby has two distinct versions—Union and League. The skills are similar, but there are some key differences.

In both forms of rugby football (to give it its full title), the aim of the game is to score points by taking the ball over the goal line, which stretches over the entire width of the field, or to kick it between the uprights and over the cross-bar of the tall H-shaped posts. The ovoid ball may be kicked, but it's mostly carried and passed between players by throwing (see right).

The Union game A Rugby Union team consists of 15 players. A game begins when one side kicks the ball deep into the opposing half. The team in that half collects the ball and works it forward by running with the ball while passing it sideways or backward. It's against the rules to pass the ball forward with the hands, though it can be kicked toward the goal line. The defending team attempts to regain possession of the ball either by intercepting the ball or by bodily tackling the player holding the ball —who's obliged to release it after falling to the ground. A scrum—called for technical infringements—is one of the distinctive features of the game. Eight players from each side lock together in a kind of tense huddle then the ball is thrown into the gap between the two front rows. The "hooker" drags it back with their foot so as to win possession of the ball. A try—five points—

continued on next page →

make a
Rugby pass

1 Hold the ball firmly with the thumbs and fingers of each hand positioned on the seams. The fingers should be splayed, and your palms shouldn't touch the ball. Aim to pass at chest height, so that the receiver doesn't have to take their eye off their run, and so that you're passing over the head of any opponent tackling you at waist height.

2 Draw your arms and the ball to one side of your body, then swing them across and release the ball directly at the target. The ball must not travel forward to the receiving player. The referee will penalize a "forward pass" by awarding a scrum (see left) to the opposition.

work out a
Running routine

Running is a straightforward way to get fitter. Just pull on your shoes, and you're ready to go.

The only special equipment you need if you want to run is a good pair of running shoes. Go to a dedicated running shop, where the experts will watch your running technique and advise you on what pair to buy.

The health benefits of running will come to you if you do it regularly and build up slowly. Three ten-minute runs over the course of the week will do you more good than one half-hour run—and are far less likely to cause injury. Rest for a day between every run (so the maximum is three or four runs in a week). Don't increase the time or distance that you run by more than ten percent from one week to the next. If you get breathless when you run, stop and walk for 30 seconds or so.

Make a regular time to run Early mornings can be an exhilarating time to be out—but beware; your muscles may be stiff, so do some dynamic warm-up exercises before you start (*see* AEROBIC EXERCISE). Never run on a full stomach. Motivation is important, so find yourself a "running buddy," and choose a pleasant route for your run: along the ocean or boardwalk, through the park, down a path.

See also MARATHON.

continued from page 267
is scored if a team places the ball on the ground beyond the opposing goal line. Three points are scored for a "drop goal" or "penalty goal" (kicking a ball over the crossbar and between the goalposts). After each try, two additional points can be scored for a "conversion," which is a kick taken in the same way as a penalty goal.

The League game Rugby League differs from Rugby Union in several significant ways. In the League game, teams consist of 13 players, and there's a rule that the team in possession must concede the ball if tackled six times in succession. The scoring system differs too: four points for a try, two for a kicked goal.

---

stop Rugs from slipping

A rug on a polished surface is prone to slip, which can be dangerous. The best way to prevent this from happening is to put a rubber mat or rubberized backing underneath. The backing should be cut to a size that's a little shorter and narrower than the rug itself. Another way of achieving the same result is to apply spray-on rug adhesive to the back of a rug or mat. The rug will stick to the floor without harming the surface, but can still easily be lifted and repositioned. Don't use carpet adhesive on valuable or antique rugs.

---

prevent and remove Rust

This flaky corrosive coating damages tools and machinery, and is an unsightly blemish on metalwork—but you can prevent it.

Rust occurs when water and air chemically react with iron or steel. The best way to prevent rust is to stop the water and air coming into contact with the metal in the first place. Painting metal fixtures, such as railings and window frames, is the obvious way to keep the corrosive elements at bay, but the paint must be kept in good condition. Even small scratches in paint will allow rust patches to form. If this happens, you need to repair and repaint promptly.
- Scrape away the damaged paint, making sure that all the rust is exposed.
- Remove surface rust with emery paper, cleaning back to bare, bright metal. Use an old paintbrush to remove all dust.
- Repaint with a zinc-rich metal primer, followed by undercoat and topcoat.

Large areas of rust on outdoor items, such as wheelbarrows or barbecues, can be treated in the same way.
- Wearing safety glasses, gloves and mask, remove the rust scales using a power drill with wire-brush attachment.
- Rub down the surface with emery paper. Dust clean, then fill the pitted area with two-part epoxy adhesive before repainting as above.
- Alternatively, use a rust-inhibiting paint (such as Rust-Oleum) directly on the rusted metal. No primer or undercoat is needed; paint can be brushed on or sprayed from an aerosol.

take a first step in Salsa

Salsa is fun, sexy and great exercise. It's easy to pick up, with a simple eight-beat rhythm. Here's a basic step for you to practice.

Holding your partner If you're leading, face your partner (the follower) and place your right hand on the small of their back. Lift your left arm to chest height, bend the elbow at a right angle and raise your palm. Take your partner's right hand in a loose grip and place their left hand on your right shoulder. This is known as the "closed" position. Alternatively, you can simply hold your partner's hands, with one raised to shoulder height—the "open" position.

Basic forward and back These are the steps for the leader. Start with your feet together and your weight on your right foot. The follower starts with feet together and their weight on the left foot, using the backward step as in beat 5.

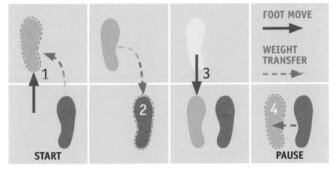

BEAT 1 Step forward with your left foot, shifting your weight onto that foot (1).

BEAT 2 Rock your weight back from your left foot to your right (2).

BEAT 3 Step back with your left foot, keeping your weight on your right (3).

BEAT 4 Pause for the fourth beat, but transfer your weight onto your left foot (4).

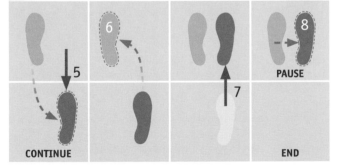

BEAT 5 Step back with your right foot and shift your weight onto it (5).

BEAT 6 Transfer weight from your right foot to your left (6).

BEAT 7 Step forward with your right foot (7).

BEAT 8 Shift your weight to your right foot (8), then begin again.

mix a classic
Salad dressing

MAKES ¾ CUP

9 tbsp extra virgin olive oil
3 tbsp white (or red) wine vinegar
2 tsp Dijon mustard
½ tsp salt
½ tsp black pepper
½ tsp sugar (optional)

Whisk or shake all the ingredients together. You can add a twist with any of the following ingredients: one or two crushed garlic cloves, 2 tbsp chopped tarragon or chives, 1 tbsp puréed tomatoes and a pinch of paprika, 1 tbsp honey.

---

spice up a party with
Salsa dip

SERVES 12

4 large tomatoes, diced
½ large onion, finely chopped
3 cloves garlic, minced
handful chopped cilantro
2 tbsp fresh lime juice
1 jalapeño pepper, seeded and minced
salt to taste

Mix the tomatoes, onion, garlic, cilantro and juice. Add the jalapeño half a teaspoon at a time, tasting after each addition to see how hot the salsa is. Add salt to your taste.

Sand by hand

It may take longer, but sometimes sanding is a job best done with your own hands. Different tasks require different techniques—and the right choice of sanding material.

■ Sandpaper or glasspaper are the cheapest options for hand sanding. Aluminum oxide paper is more expensive, but works better and lasts longer. Silicon-carbide paper—sometimes called wet-and-dry—is primarily used for smoothing metal surfaces and keying painted wood before decoration. Garnet paper is for the fine finishing of furniture that's to be varnished or polished.
■ If you're sanding a flat surface by hand, wrap the paper around a sanding block made of cork or wood (a scrap piece will do for many purposes). Always work along the grain of the wood. Scratches across the grain are hard to remove, and will show up if the wood is later varnished.
■ It's best to hand-sand furniture; it takes longer but gives a better finish. When you're sanding curved areas, shape the paper with your palm rather than using a block.
■ Use the right grade of paper. A coarse grade is adequate for rubbing down paintwork before painting, but use only fine grades for finishing planed lumber.
■ Don't use sandpaper to remove paint; the friction will quickly melt the paint and clog up the abrasive surface, making it useless.

launch into
Sailing
see pages 272-273

be the king of the Sand castle

Sandcastle building keeps the kids amused for hours and you can be the envy of all on the beach. Choose a site below the tide line but away from the incoming tide.

YOU WILL NEED **Good-quality shovel (preferably with a metal blade), two buckets (one full of sea water, to keep sand damp), small funnel, old plastic or wooden spatula, or picnic knife**

1 Scoop up plenty of wet sand to form a circular flat-topped base for the castle. Build in layers, packing each one down and pouring on water to keep moist.

2 Dig down into the center of the mound and clear the sand to reveal a circular courtyard and inner castle walls. Use a spatula to finish the inner and outer walls of the castle off to a smooth face.

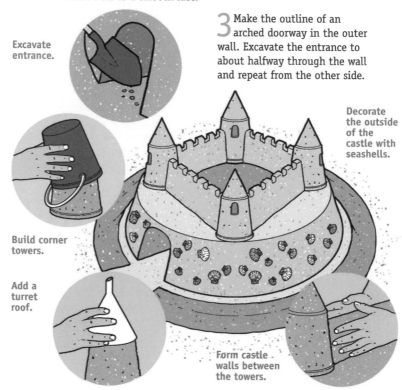

3 Make the outline of an arched doorway in the outer wall. Excavate the entrance to about halfway through the wall and repeat from the other side.

Excavate entrance.

Decorate the outside of the castle with seashells.

Build corner towers.

Add a turret roof.

Form castle walls between the towers.

4 Use your bucket to make the first tower near the edge of the mound. Repeat to make more towers.

5 To make roofs for your towers, fill a funnel with moist sand, pack it down, and place on top of each tower. Use a picnic knife to carve details such as stairs and slits for windows.

6 Build up castle walls between the towers with your hands. With a knife carve crenellations along the top.

7 Dig a moat around the outer wall and fill with water.

play the game of Sardines

Sardines is similar to the old favorite hide-and-seek, but with a twist—it starts with only one person hiding, while everyone else seeks.

The game is great fun to play indoors or outdoors. As few as three people can take part, but the more who join in the better.

Begin by deciding who's going to hide. Then, the seekers close their eyes and count to a predetermined number—say, 20 or 50—while the hider hides. When the time is up, the seekers spread out and the hunt begins. As each seeker finds the hiding place, they join the hider, cramming together like, well, sardines in a can. The last person to discover the hider is the loser and becomes the hider in the next game. Play sardines indoors, using closets, under the stairs and even under beds, and the game really lives up to its tightly packed name.

---

rescue Sauces

Even the best cooks can have problems with sauces, so it pays to know what to do when trouble arises.

Lumpy sauce or gravy Off the heat, whisk hard in the pan with a balloon whisk or smoothing whisk. If this doesn't work, process in a blender or rub through a strainer, then reheat.

Too thin In a bowl, use a fork to mix 2 tbsp of all-purpose flour into 1 tbsp of butter. Add to the sauce a little at a time, stirring, until it thickens.

Too salty Add 1-2 tsp sugar or a little milk or yogurt.

Too sweet Add a little lemon juice.

Curdled custard Blend or process, or strain into a cold dish sitting in a bowl of ice cubes and beat vigorously.

Separated mayonnaise Add 1 tbsp of warm water. Or start again with one egg yolk and gradually add the curdled mixture.

Curdled hollandaise Remove from the heat, then beat in 1 tbsp of cold water a little at a time until the sauce becomes smooth. Or, off the heat, stir an ice cube into the warm sauce. Or beat in an additional egg yolk in a clean pan until thick, then, over low heat, gradually beat in the curdled sauce until smooth.

Grainy or "seized" chocolate sauce Try adding warm water, a little at a time, while stirring vigorously.

cook perfect Sauté potatoes

The best sauté potatoes are crisp on the outside and soft within. Really hot fat is critical.

SERVES 2-4

1 lb (500 g) potatoes, peeled
2¼ tsp butter
3-4 tbsp canola or olive oil
sea salt

1 Boil potatoes in salted water for about 10 minutes until barely tender. Cut into small, even chunks.

2 Heat the butter and oil in a large frying pan, add the potatoes and fry quickly, shaking the pan and turning them two or three times until well browned all over.

3 Lift out with a broad spatula and drain on paper towels. Sprinkle with sea salt and serve immediately.

☆ golden rules

SAUTÉ SECRETS
- Make sure the fat is really hot before adding the potatoes.
- Don't lower the cooking temperature or the potatoes will "stew" and become soggy.
- For larger quantities, cook in two or more batches.

S

launch into Sailing

Sailing of any kind demands a certain amount of seamanship; you need to be able to read the moods of the sea or lake, and you need to learn how to catch the wind in the sails so as to propel the boat.

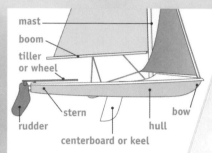

PARTS OF A BOAT Sailboats come in all shapes and sizes but most share a core set of common parts.

Labels: mast, boom, tiller or wheel, stern, rudder, centerboard or keel, hull, bow

Know the ropes You should start on a small boat. Most have two sails—the mainsail and the jib—or try a dinghy, which has a mainsail alone. The best way to learn to sail is to spend time on the water with an experienced and responsible sailor, perhaps as part of a training course.

THE WIND The wind is your boat's engine. The skill of sailing lies in harnessing the wind to take you in your chosen direction. Sailing in the same direction as the wind ("running") is a simple matter; the wind naturally pushes you along, and you go where it leads you. Sailing "upwind" is much trickier. You have to work hard to manipulate the sails, so as to catch the wind and drive the boat against its natural inclination.

SHEETS AND SAILS When sailing you need to constantly adjust or "trim" the sails. You have to do this when the boat changes direction, when the wind itself changes direction, or when you want to slow down or speed up. The sails are controlled by ropes known (confusingly for nonsailors) as sheets. When you complete a tacking maneuver (see opposite), the jib must be moved across to the other side of the boat by slackening one of the sheets that control it and tightening the other. This must be done swiftly, and at the right moment; judging and executing this correctly is one of the key skills of sailing.

Diagram labels: wind direction, into wind (in irons), close hauled, close hauled, close reach, close reach, no go zone, beam reach, beam reach, broad reach, broad reach, dead run

HOW TO SAIL By angling the mainsail and jib, you can run with the wind or "reach" across it. The only direction you can't travel in directly is the 45-degree "no go zone" to either side of the headwind. Instead you must use a zigzag approach called "tacking" (see opposite).

Labels: mainsail, wind direction, jib sail, jib sheet, main sheet

TACKING

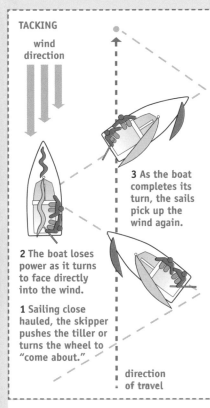

wind direction

3 As the boat completes its turn, the sails pick up the wind again.

2 The boat loses power as it turns to face directly into the wind.

1 Sailing close hauled, the skipper pushes the tiller or turns the wheel to "come about."

direction of travel

TACKING You can't sail a boat directly into the wind; you have to zigzag to and fro, like a slalom skier. This means sailing close hauled on, say, a starboard tack (with the wind hitting the right-hand side of the boat first) then turning the boat through the wind to sail on a port tack. As you pass through the wind, there will be a moment when there's no force in the sails. For this reason you should build up speed before you make your move, so that the momentum will carry you through from one side of the tack to the other.

JIBING Jibing (or gybing) means taking the stern of the boat across the wind. This is trickier than tacking because it causes the boom—the heavy horizontal pole to which the mainsail is attached—to swing forcefully right across the boat. Timing is everything when you jibe—not just to make sure that the boat keeps moving, but also to make sure that you don't get hit by the boom when it swings. You have to be ready to duck out of the way.

JIBING

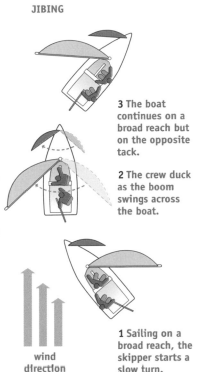

3 The boat continues on a broad reach but on the opposite tack.

2 The crew duck as the boom swings across the boat.

1 Sailing on a broad reach, the skipper starts a slow turn.

wind direction

DOCKING You should come into a dock or mooring with the wind as nearly ahead of you as possible. Come to a stop by slackening the main sheet, so that the sail flaps. If you must dock with the wind behind you, lower the sail when you're 50-65 ft (15-20 m) away, so that the boat loses momentum and coasts in, guided by the tiller. *See also* ROPES.

THE TILLER Some boats have steering wheels, as on a car. Others have a tiller, a long pole attached directly to the rudder. With a tiller (but not with a wheel), you steer to the right by pushing to the left, and vice versa. Do this very gently and smoothly, especially when changing tack, or you run the risk of capsizing.

SAFETY Always wear a buoyancy aid when sailing, and always hold on with one hand when moving around a boat.

■ If your boat capsizes and is lying on its side, free the sheets then climb onto the centerboard. With your feet close to the hull, take hold of the gunwale (the rim of the boat) and lean back—your weight should pull the boat upright. Move around to the stern, keeping hold of the boat, and climb back in.

RULES OF THE ROAD Where differently powered boats of differing sizes use the same body of water, it's important that everybody knows who has right of way. There are certain rules that all boat users must observe.

■ You must give way to boats that can't change course without the risk of running aground.
■ Powerboats give way to boats under sail.
■ A sailboat with the wind on its port side (the left of the boat if you're facing the bow) gives way to a sailboat with the wind on its starboard (right-hand) side.
■ A boat that's overtaking gives way to the boat being overtaken.
■ If in doubt, take a positive course of action, make it obvious to the other vessel and perform it in plenty of time.

choose the right
Saw for the job

hacksaw

CUTTING METAL Replaceable hacksaw blades have extra-hard teeth, designed to cut through metal. Hacksaws are ideal for cutting pipes.

tenon saw

WOOD JOINTS A tenon saw has a small blade with a solid metal strip along the top. It's designed for making woodworking joints. It can be used for any small wood-cutting task.

crosscut saw

CUTTING WOOD A crosscut saw is the one to choose for most DIY jobs. Its long, flexible blade, usually around 20 in. (50 cm) in length, is ideal for cutting up panels of wood or boards.

coping saw

CUTTING SHAPES The blade on a coping saw can be rotated to any angle, so as to cut shapes and slots in wood, plastic and fiberglass.

ROUGH-CUT LOGS A bow saw is designed for rough-cutting logs and greenwood branches. Two-handed saws can be used to cut through large logs.

bow saw

use a hand Saw correctly

Safety and accuracy should be your watchwords when sawing. Always use a workbench or sawhorses to support the wood as you cut.

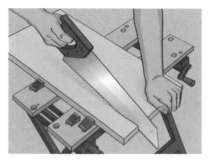

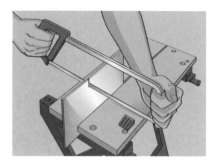

Crosscut saw Begin with a few short backstrokes to create a nick. Guide the blade with the thumb knuckle of your free hand. Once the cut is started, move your free hand, hold the saw at 45 degrees to the wood and saw in even strokes. Use the full length of the blade and keep your arm relaxed. Move the wood forward as you cut.

Coping saw Be sure that the work is gripped firmly in a vice. Use short strokes, adjusting the angle of the blade as necessary as you go.

Hacksaw Use your free hand to hold the front of the D-frame and steady your stroke. Friction might make the blade hot as you work; allow it to cool from time to time.

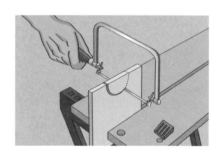

sharpen a blunt pair of Scissors

YOU WILL NEED **Fine file, whetstone, light machine oil**

1 Open the scissors and hold them firmly. Use the file to remove any nicks in the blades of the scissors until you have two straight edges.

2 Put a few drops of oil on the whetstone. Hold the scissors firmly, and brace the back of the blade against a solid surface, such as a tabletop.

3 Run the whetstone along the cutting edge of the blade, keeping the stone at the same angle as the edge of the blade. Work in smooth strokes. Then run the stone flat along the inner face of the blade to remove any raised "burr" that may have formed.

4 Sharpen the other blade then tighten the securing screw if necessary.

win at Scrabble

It may not be the player who knows all the long words who wins this highly competitive game, but the crafty technician with an arsenal of short ones and a mastery of letter combinations.

In this crossword game, two to four players hold a running stock of seven lettered tiles of different values, and use them to build word on word. Premium squares, such as "double word score" and "triple letter score," yield extra points. There is a bonus of 50 for laying down all seven tiles in one go. Here are some of the secrets of the champions.

- Learn two-letter words (*al, ai, em, en, ax, ex ...*) and you'll rarely be stuck for something to put down.
- Learn where "Q" can be used without a "U"—*the Faqir chews qat while typing on his qwerty keyboard.*
- Try to use "S" to make a plural at the same time as a new word and score two words for the price of one.
- Focus on the board, not on your rack. Where you put a word and the options it opens up is at least as important as what you put down.
- Keep abreast of which tiles have been used—or used up.
- Aim to use a premium square with every move.
- Don't hoard high-score tiles. As play progresses it gets ever harder

to lay them down, and any you're left with count against you.
- When laying down the high-scorers you'll want to place them where others can't make use of them—but then nor can you. Consider your tactics and whether to take a chance on a second crack which risks your opponent laying down a feeble spoiler.
- Get the best score you can with every turn. Holding back because you have nearly got a seven-letter word, or because you might be able to get that triple-word bonus, is a loser's game. While you're holding out in the hope of something, others can be notching up consistently good scores.

make perfect Scrambled eggs

Gentle cooking and meticulous timing are the keys to the best scrambled eggs. Use a heavy-bottomed pan—a nonstick one is ideal. The freshest eggs are best cooked with a little milk.

SERVES 1-2

2-3 eggs
1 tbsp milk (optional)
salt and freshly ground black pepper
2 tbsp butter plus (optional) extra to finish
1 tbsp cream (optional)

- Whisk the eggs lightly. Melt the butter over medium heat, add the eggs, lower the heat and

cook, stirring constantly with a wooden spoon. As the eggs begin to solidify, scrape them away from the base and sides of the pan.
- When they are creamy and a little runny, remove from the heat. Serve at once. They will finish cooking in their own heat.
- For extra richness, add a little more butter and the cream at the end of cooking if you wish.

remove Scratches
from furniture

There are various ways to remove or disguise scratches, depending on the damage and the surface.

Waxed wood You can remove a light scratch in waxed wood with a retouch crayon or pen, or by sanding with fine sandpaper or garnet paper (available from craft shops) dipped in linseed oil. Repolish the area, taking care to blend the newly waxed area with its surroundings.
- A deep scratch can be filled with a wax filler stick, available in various wood colors. Apply by hand, following the instructions, and remove excess with a cloth, making sure that it fills the scratch. Once it has set, polish with wax polish.

Varnished wood Dilute matching varnish with mineral spirits and apply with a soft brush (above).
- Work along the length of scratch, brushing in the direction of the grain. Let the varnish dry, then re-apply until surface is slightly raised.
- Level off with fine sandpaper, dust and apply more varnish to blend with the surface.

Dents in solid wood You can restore a dent in solid wood (not veneer) using a household iron over a damp cloth. The wood will swell, then dry, then you can sand and repolish.

choose the right
Screws

It's important to select the right type and size of screw for the job.

Wood screw For fixing to wood. Use countersinking screws (right) when joining wood to wood, roundhead screws (left) for other fittings.

Coach screw A large screw for fastening bulky pieces of wood together. Has a head like a bolt, so that it can be tightly fixed.

Masonry screw Has a wide thread that can be driven straight into concrete or brick. Some masonry screws have hexagonal washer heads.

Self-tapping screw Cuts its own thread as it's screwed in. Good for fixing to sheet metal and plastic.

raise
Seeds and seedlings
see pages 282-283

Seal gaps around the home

Gaps around door and window frames, holes where pipes go through walls and warped or poorly fitted baseboards let heat escape and moisture creep in. Seal them with these simple techniques.

Choose the right sealant for the job. For gaps between different materials (brick and wood, for example), you need a flexible acrylic or silicone-based sealant that will allow for any slight movement in future. Flexible sealants come in cylindrical cartridges that fit into a trigger-operated cartridge gun for use. For larger gaps, use expanding foam filler or decorating filler, built up in stages.

Before you start, make sure that the area you're going to work on is clean and solid, otherwise the sealant won't stick.
- Clean off dirt and dust with a cloth and check that any paintwork is in good condition. Rub it down and repaint it, if necessary, before tackling the sealing.
- Scrape out any old sealant with a putty knife, screwdriver or a razor blade, taking care to remove it all.

Applying sealant Snip off the end of the nozzle at a 45-degree angle so that the hole at the tip is about half as wide as the crack you have to fill. Don't make it too wide.
- Squeeze the trigger of the cartridge gun to start the flow of sealant.
- Start at one end of the gap and, with a steady hand, move slowly and evenly along the gap. You'll need to release and squeeze the trigger again from time to time.
- Use your thumb to release the locking bar on the piston to stop the sealant flowing when you have finished or need to stop.
- Use a wet finger or a special sealant-shaping tool to make sure that the sealant has a neat finish and is well embedded into the crack.

Expanding foam filler For deep, wide or awkward-shaped gaps, expanding foam is the easiest solution for a neat finish.
- Always wear the gloves supplied, as the filler is very sticky when wet.
- Practice with the can before you start the job. The foam comes out surprisingly fast and expands to up to 60 times its original volume.
- Spray the gap with a little water to dampen it before filling.
- Squirt a bead of foam into the gap and allow it to expand.
- Let it dry for up to two hours, then cut away the excess with a hacksaw or sharp knife. Wear a face mask to protect you from the dust.
- Sand the surface smooth if you want to paint over the repair.

make a Seam to join fabric

Seams are used to sew pieces of fabric together. The width of the seam, or seam allowance, is usually about ½ in. (1.5 cm). After stitching, the raw edges need to be finished in some way. Stitch seams by machine, backstitch or, on very fine fabric, the smallest possible running stitch (*see* SEWING).

Basic plain seam Place fabric pieces right sides together and secure with pins at right angles to the seam. Tack, then remove the pins and stitch by machine or by hand close to the tacking stitches, following the line exactly (*see* TACK).

WRONG SIDE   BACK

Pressing and finishing Remove tacking. If a seam is curved—at the top of a sleeve, for example—use small, sharp scissors to make small cuts in the seam allowance to help it to lie flat. Keep well clear of the stitching. Press seam open.

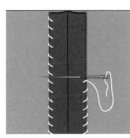

■ For non-fraying fabrics, use pinking shears to cut along the edges of the seam allowance.

■ For fabrics that will fray, use machine overlocking, or sew a zigzag stitch close to the raw edge. Cut off any excess fabric close to the stitching.

■ To finish by hand, if you prefer, or if machine stitching is impractical, use overcasting. Make ⅛ in. (3 mm) even stitches ¼ in. (6 mm) apart over the raw edges.

ward off Seasickness

If you don't have an over-the-counter remedy at hand, try these strategies to quell your nausea.
■ Get up on deck, preferably at the middle of the vessel, and breathe fresh air. Face toward the direction of travel and focus on something other than the pitching ship—the nearest land or the horizon.
■ Keep busy and occupy your mind, but avoid close work such as reading.

■ If it's warm and sunny lie in a deck chair and close your eyes.
■ Ginger is a trusted herbal remedy for nausea. Crystallized ginger is fine, but some ginger ales don't contain the real thing.
■ Drink plenty of water.
■ Console yourself with the fact that your brain will eventually adjust and you'll find your sea legs—if you don't reach dry land again first.

understand Semaphore

As long as two people can see one another, they can use flags and arm movements to send short, simple messages over long distances.

There are eight arm positions: straight up and down; horizontal, diagonally up and diagonally down (left and right).

Each letter of the alphabet is a combination of two arm positions —imagine hands pointing to an eight-hour clock face. Once you have learned the semaphore alphabet, you simply spell out your message, one letter at a time.

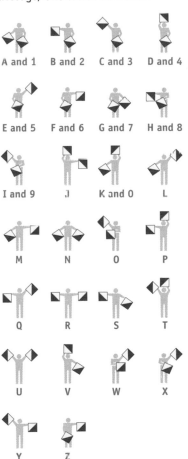

A and 1   B and 2   C and 3   D and 4

E and 5   F and 6   G and 7   H and 8

I and 9   J   K and 0   L

M   N   O   P

Q   R   S   T

U   V   W   X

Y   Z

S

put on a Shadow puppet show

Shadow puppets are silhouettes of animals made by forming a shape with the hands. To make shadow puppets you need only a reading lamp and an expanse of white or light-colored wall. When you put on your show, position yourself and the light source so that the shadows—not your hands—are the center of attention. Put on some music to add atmosphere. Withdraw your hands from the light as you form the puppets, so that each one enters the limelight with a flourish.

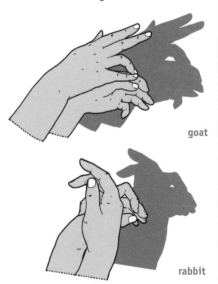

goat

rabbit

grasp the basics of Sewing by hand

Sewing is the means of joining and decorating pieces of fabric by drawing a threaded needle in and out of the fabric in a variety of ways. By practicing and perfecting a few essential stitches it's possible to create clothes and furnishings and make repairs and alterations. Even if you use a sewing machine, hand stitching is essential to many sewing tasks.

Needle types Needles are sized in numbers 1-28 (the higher the number, the thinner the needle), and described according to their type of point. For most jobs "sharps" in sizes 7 and 8 are the best choice but have small eyes. "Crewel" needles in these sizes have larger eyes and are easier to thread. Larger crewels have blunter points and are used for jobs such as wool work and needlepoint. Tapestry needles have blunt ends. "Betweens" are good for fine fabric.

Starting and finishing For hand stitching and quilting, the thread needs to be secured on the wrong (reverse) side of the fabric with a small knot at the thread end, or with a few stitches worked over each other. Except for herringbone, always work from right to left. Finish off with a few stitches worked over each other, then cut the thread close to the fabric.

Running stitch Used for tacking, quilting and making gathers. Weave the point of the needle in and out of the fabric several times, then pull the whole needle through. Weave the needle so that both the stitches and the spaces between them are small and even for quilting and gathering, longer for tacking.

Backstitch Used for seams and embroidery. Pull the thread through from the wrong to the right side. Insert the needle ⅛ in. or less (1.5-3 mm) behind the point where the thread emerges. Bring it out again at the same distance in front of that point and repeat.

Herringbone Firm and flat for hems. Working left to right, insert the needle diagonally across and above the hem edge and bring it through just to the left of that point. Take the needle back diagonally over the hem edge and insert it, bringing it up just to the left of that point. Repeat as necessary.

Hemstitch (vertical)

Used for a near-invisible finish on hems. Start by bringing the needle through the hem edge. Directly opposite this point,

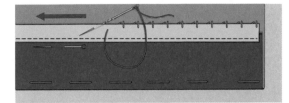

catch a single thread of the fabric. Then direct the needle diagonally to go through the hem edge ¼-½ in. (6-10 mm) to the left. Continue along the hem in this way for succeeding stitches.

Blind hemstitch

For an invisible finish, fold back the hem edge and secure the thread inside it. Take very small stitches ¼ in. (6 mm) apart, catching a single thread of first the

garment fabric, then the hem fabric. Continue to alternate stitches in this way. Be careful not to pull the stitches too tightly as you go or the material will become gathered.

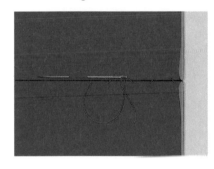

Slipstitch For joining two folded edges (left) or a folded edge to a flat surface. Fasten thread and bring the needle through the folded edge. Make a very small stitch into the flat surface, then take the needle back through the folded edge, bringing it out about ¼ in. (6 mm) away. Continue in this way so that most of the thread is hidden.

See also APPLIQUÉ, CROSS-STITCH, CUSHION COVER, EMBROIDERY, HEM, NEEDLEPOINT, QUILT, SEAM, TACK, ZIPPER.

---

put up adjustable Shelving

Upright-and-bracket adjustable shelving is economical, versatile, strong and durable—a good option for most domestic purposes.

YOU WILL NEED **Tape measure, uprights and brackets, pencil, spirit level or plumb bob, drill, wall plugs, screws, screwdriver, bradawl**

1 Measure the wall for the uprights. You'll need two uprights for shelves up to 35 in. (90 cm) long, three (or more) for longer shelves. Hold the first upright to the wall, and mark the position of the top screw with a pencil. Using a spirit level or plumb line, draw a vertical line.

continued on next page ➔

S

build a survival
Shelter

If you're stranded outdoors for the night, you must find a way to keep warm and dry.

Don't wait until it's getting dark. Find a safe place in daylight, while there's a chance to check for hazards such as rockfalls or a hornets' nest. If you have a tarpaulin or a groundsheet and a length of rope, then you have the makings of a basic shelter.
■ Tie your line between two trees, and lay the tarp over it.
■ Peg the lower edges to the ground to make a tent; most tarps have eyelets for this purpose.

If you have no tarp, build an A-frame.

1 Find a dry spot, a branch 6-10 ft (2-3 m) long and two shorter ones of 5 ft (1.5 m) or so. Use the two shorter branches to make an A by pushing both branches into the ground and tying their tops together. Then push one end of your longer "ridgepole" into the ground, and tie the other end to the apex of your A. Make sure it's aligned so that the lower end faces the prevailing wind.

2 Attach more branches to the ridgepole, and weave twigs between them. Fill the gaps with evergreen branches or bracken, and cover the ground inside with ferns or conifer branches to provide additional insulation

S

soothe Shingles

After a chickenpox infection, the virus can lie dormant and cause shingles later. It's known as *herpes zoster*, from the Greek "to creep" and "girdle," because it manifests as a blistering rash that spreads around one side of the body, most often on the trunk. A doctor will prescribe medication, but you can help yourself. If shingles appear on the face, though, consult a doctor at once as the eyes may be affected.

■ Wear loose clothing that doesn't catch or rub.
■ Take two or three cool baths a day (don't apply talcum powder).
■ Apply calamine lotion.
■ Try adding three drops each of geranium, sage and thyme oil to 4 tsp of vegetable oil and dab it on.

clean and revive a
Shirt collar

The collars of shirts are prone to attracting stains from hair gel, makeup and the like. Try treating them with these methods.

■ Use a clean nailbrush to apply a little shampoo (greasy-hair formula) or some liquid detergent. Leave for 15 minutes then machine wash at the hottest setting. For a quick treatment, wash the collar only by hand, rinse well, rub as dry as possible in a thick towel then iron completely dry.
■ Spray with a stain remover, leave for ten minutes, or as directed, then machine wash, again at the hottest safe setting.
■ For lipstick, rub in some white toothpaste as a prewash treatment or use a stain remover as above.

continued from page 279

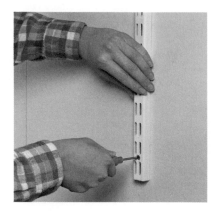

2 Draw a parallel vertical line for the second upright. Use a spirit level to pinpoint the exact point at which the top screwhole for the second upright should be drilled. It's crucial that the two top screwholes are made at precisely the same height, otherwise the shelves won't be level.

3 Drill and plug the top two screwholes. Screw the uprights temporarily in position. Use a bradawl to mark the positions of the other screwholes, then swing the uprights aside to drill and plug each one. Then screw the uprights permanently in position.

4 Fit the brackets at the required height, and place the shelves on top, making sure they are all in line. Use the bradawl to mark screwholes in the underside of the shelves, then take them off and make pilot holes. Put them back on the brackets and screw them firmly in place.

fold a Shirt

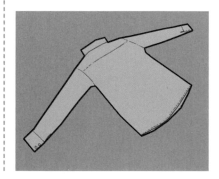

Properly folded shirts and blouses will stay wrinkle-free. They are also easier to store neatly on shelves and in drawers. Always start with a well-ironed shirt or blouse (see opposite).

1 If the shirt has buttons, fasten them and smooth out any wrinkles. Then place the shirt face down on a flat surface with the arms extended.

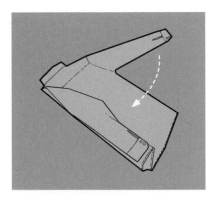

2 Fold in the left shirt side to the center line of the shirt back, then fold back the sleeve so that its upper edge meets the shirt side seam. Repeat for the other side.

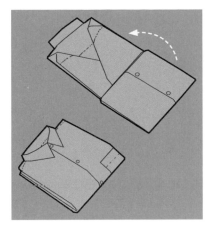

3 Fold up the bottom third of the fabric, then fold over again. Turn the shirt over.

recognize and deal with Shock

This clinical term doesn't describe emotional trauma, but a dangerous physical response to illness or injury, a complication that itself needs urgent intervention.

Shock occurs most usually as the result of a drop in circulation, often due to blood loss, depriving the vital organs of oxygen. Severe burns, vomiting, a heart attack, bacterial infection or allergy, near-drowning, extreme pain and blood poisoning are among other possible causes.

Suspect shock if the patient is:
- pale, cold and clammy—or sweating profusely
- breathing rapidly, yawning or sighing
- weak and dizzy
- feeling sick or vomiting
- complaining of thirst

Quick action
- Call an ambulance.
- Be prepared to administer cardio-pulmonary resuscitation (*see* CPR).
- Treat any injuries appropriately (*see* BLEEDING, BURNS AND SCALDS, DROWNING *and* HEART ATTACK).

If the casualty is conscious and their injuries allow it:
- Lie them down with their head lower than their heart to increase blood flow to the brain.
- Unless it interferes with breathing, raise and support their legs.
- Keep them warm—cover with a coat or blanket but don't swaddle them tightly.
- Offer comfort and reassurance.

If the patient is unconscious:
- Place them in the recovery position (*see* RECOVERY POSITION).
- Keep them warm (as above).

In all cases, don't give anything to eat or drink.

See also ALLERGIC EMERGENCY, INFECTIONS.

iron a Shirt

Ironing each part of the shirt in the correct order is the key to success: first collar, then cuffs, yoke, sleeves, back and front.

1 Using a preheated iron, iron the outside then the inside (the side visible when worn) of the collar (1). Next, iron the inside then the outside of both cuffs (2).

2 Slide the shirt over the pointed end of the ironing board and iron one shoulder of the yoke (3) and then the other.

3 Iron the sleeves (4) on each side, followed by the back (5), again with the fabric spread over the end of the ironing board. Turn the shirt over and iron the front (6), the right side followed by the left side. Button up and then hang or fold the shirt neatly (see opposite).

S

raise Seeds and seedlings

Growing plants from seed is rewarding and economical, but all seeds and seedlings need careful treatment if young plants are to grow and thrive. Perennials take a long time to establish from seed, but vegetables and annual and biennial flowers offer a better chance of success.

Sowing seed Seeds can be sown in pots or trays, or directly into the ground in the warmer months. Sow in spring or summer for a summer or autumn harvest, and autumn for crops that will mature the following year.

START IN POTS OR TRAYS

1 Mix one part sand or vermiculite with every two parts of soilless potting mix to help drainage. Fill seed trays or small pots, level and tamp down.

2 Moisten mix, then sow seeds, either individually by hand or by tapping them out of your palm or a folded piece of card using your finger. If seeds are very small, mix them with sand or coffee grounds before planting to make it easier to spread them evenly.

3 Except for very fine seeds, cover with a fine layer of sifted potting mix. Mist with water. Finish, if you wish, with a layer of finely ground vermiculite to help to keep the temperature even. Label the pots.

4 Cover each tray with a lid or a sheet of glass or fabric. Place plastic bags over individual pots and secure with elastic bands.

5 Once growth appears, remove the lid or coverings.

SOW DIRECTLY INTO THE GROUND

Seeds of annuals such as cornflowers, clarkias and California poppies that don't transplant well are best scattered directly into garden beds and raked in lightly. Use sand to mark out areas for each plant, flowing and overlapping for a natural look, and sow in drifts across each section, not in regimented rows.

For vegetables use this method:

1 Rake well-prepared ground and use garden line to mark out rows for your crop, spaced according to the seed package instructions.

2 Use a hoe to scrape out seed drills to the recommended depth. Plant the seeds as for sowing in trays (left). Cover with soil, firm in with your fingers, water lightly and label. Add an additional covering of fabric or cloches if you wish. If using cloches, water regularly.

HELP THE GERMINATION PROCESS Use these tips to help seeds to germinate better and produce stronger, healthier plants.

- Soak hard-skinned seeds like lupins, beans and peas in warm water for 24 hours before planting to soften them.
- Rub sweet pea seeds with sandpaper or make a nick in each one with a clean sharp knife before planting.
- Plant flat seeds of melons, cucumbers and their relatives on their sides.
- Plant seeds that develop deep roots, such as runner beans, in root trainers—individual, reusable cells that can be folded open to remove seedlings without damage to roots or stems.

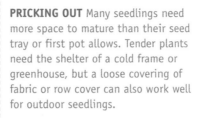

PRICKING OUT Many seedlings need more space to mature than their seed tray or first pot allows. Tender plants need the shelter of a cold frame or greenhouse, but a loose covering of fabric or row cover can also work well for outdoor seedlings.

1 Fill the bottom half of a tray or pots with a 2:1 mixture of moist multipurpose potting soil and sand or vermiculite. Top up with compost and firm down. Make planting holes at least 1-1½ in. (2.5-3.5 cm) apart using a dibble or pencil.

2 Lever up a clump of seedlings with the dibble or an old kitchen fork. Tease out seedlings individually, holding them by their seed leaves—the first to appear, which usually look different from the true leaves.

3 Plant in the holes and firm in with your fingers. Water lightly.

BUYING AND SAVING SEEDS
Seeds are usually sold loose in packets, but some vegetables are now also supplied on tapes that you bury in the ground, with no thinning or transplanting.

■ To save seed from garden plants, allow seed heads to ripen for as long as possible. Collect directly from the plants or cut off seed heads, dry them in a warm place then shake or pick off the seeds.

HARDENING OFF Frost-tender plants need hardening off before they are planted out. If they are being grown indoors, put them out during the day and bring them in again at night. If they are in a cold frame or greenhouse, open the ventilation for a few hours each day, and close it up at night. Gradually increase the ventilation until protection is no longer required. Watch out for late frosts.

THINNING AND TRANSPLANTING
Without thinning out and transplanting, young plants will grow weakly. These jobs are best done when the soil is damp (water it if necessary) but remember that seedlings of root vegetables such as carrots and beets won't transplant satisfactorily.

■ Use one hand to pull out an unwanted seedling while pressing the other down on the soil.
■ Firm in all remaining plants and water well.
■ Select the best seedlings with good, healthy leaves and strong roots for transplanting. Discard any weak or damaged plants.
■ Use a small dibble or trowel to make holes for new plants and insert them.
■ Firm in with your fingers and water well.

cure squeaky Shoes

Eliminating unwanted friction between parts of a shoe is the way to cure squeaks. Spraying the squeaky area with WD-40 or dusting it with talcum powder are two good cure-alls. If the squeak seems to be coming from the inside of the shoe, partially lift the inner sole and dust inside with powder. If the tongue is rubbing against the laces, apply saddle soap or a similar leather conditioner to the tongue and reapply as necessary. If a heel is loose, take it to be repaired professionally or try to secure it with bonding glue.

stretch tight Shoes

Nearly all shoes stretch in time, and if a little too tight it's worth wearing them around the house for a while to break them in. If this doesn't work, try one of these remedies before resorting to professional treatment.

- Stuff shoes as tightly as possible with crumpled, wet newspaper or peeled potatoes. Let dry slowly, then wear shoes for a few hours—they should have more "give."
- For leather shoes, put on thick socks and squeeze your feet in. Heat the troublesome area for 20 to 30 seconds with a hair dryer while bending and unbending your toes.
- Swab the insides of leather shoes with rubbing alcohol, concentrating on the tightest areas. Put the shoes on and walk around for a few minutes. Or soak an old pair of socks with alcohol, put them on and wear the shoes.

work out Shoe sizes around the world

ADULT'S		Sizes will vary, so use these two charts as a guide		
USA/CANADA Women	Men	UK/AUSTRALIA NEW ZEALAND	EUROPE	JAPAN
4½	-	2	34	21.5
5	-	2½	35	22
5½	-	3	35.5	22.5
6	-	3½	36	23
6½	-	4	37	23
7	-	4½	37.5	23.5
7½	5½	5	38	24
8	6	5½	38.5	24
8½	6½	6	39	24.5
9	7	6½	39.5	25
9½	7½	7	40	25.5
10	8	7½	41	26
10½	8½	8	42	26.5
-	9	8½	42.5	27
-	9½	9	43	27.5
-	10	9½	44	28
-	10½	10	44.5	28.5
-	11	10½	45	29
-	11½	11	46	29.5
-	12	11½	46.5	30
-	12½	12	47	30.5

CHILDREN'S			
USA/CANADA	UK/AUSTRALIA NEW ZEALAND	EUROPE	JAPAN
6½	5½	23	-
7	6	23.5	14
7½	6½	24	-
8	7	24.5	15
8½	7½	25	-
9	8	25.5	16
9½	8½	26	-
10	9	26.5	16.5
10½	9½	27	-
11	10	27.5	17.5
11½	10½	28	-
12	11	28.5	18.5
12½	11½	29	-
13	12	30	19
1	13	31	20
1½	13	31.5	20.5
2	1	32.5	21
2½	1½	33	21.5
3	2	33.5	22

lace and tie Shoes

Most of us learn to tie our shoes as children with a rudimentary bow —and spend the rest of our lives stooping to retie them. But it's never too late to learn better ways to lace and tie your shoes.

Ace lace This lacing method gives you a neat ladderlike finish on top of the shoe with tight and secure crisscrossing underneath.

1 Thread the lace ends down through the eyelets at the toe end.

2 Bring the orange end as shown up through the next but one eyelet on the opposite side; take it across, then down through the eyelet directly across.

3 Take the red end as shown diagonally over the other and bring it up through the next empty eyelet opposite, then draw it straight across and thread it down through the opposite eyelet.

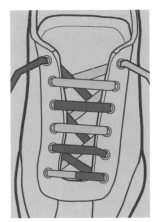

4 Repeat the actions of step 2 with each end in turn. You'll find that the orange lace will skip an eyelet one more time, while the red lace will perform the action twice.

5 Keep running lace ends in this way diagonally on the underside and straight across on the top until they reach the final eyelets at the top.

Tie the knot An easy variation of the basic knot, this is known as a "bunny ears" knot because you create two loops at once rather than work with a loop and a single strand.

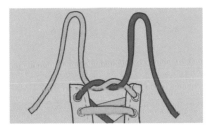

1 Start as normal, right over left and under; pull tight.

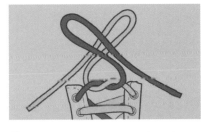

2 Make a loop in both strands and cross them over.

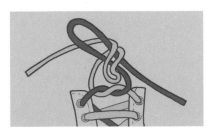

3 Wrap the lower loop around the upper and feed the end of it through the gap between the upper loop and the starter knot.

4 Take hold of both loops and draw tight. It will stay tied all day.

look after and clean Shoes

Shoes will keep their shape and last longer if well cared for and cleaned regularly. Take them to be repaired before heels wear right down into the body of the shoe and before soles become thin and uncomfortable.

Shoe care

- If possible, switch to a different pair of shoes every couple of days.
- Insert shoe trees into good leather shoes to keep their shape.
- Dry wet shoes away from direct heat. Stuff them with newspaper or rolled-up magazines to keep their shape and absorb moisture.
- Remove salt stains by rubbing with equal parts of water and vinegar applied with a cotton ball.
- Protect new shoes with a waterproof stain-repellent spray and repeat applications regularly before going out in bad weather.

Shoe cleaning

Leather Remove laces before cleaning. Brush off loose dirt with a stiff brush. Apply polish with a clean cotton cloth or soft brush. Let dry for ten minutes, then buff with a clean cloth or brush. If dirty, clean with saddle soap using given directions.

Patent leather Shine with purpose-made cream, baby oil or petroleum jelly using a clean cloth. Remove scuffs with a clean pencil eraser.

Suede Use a plastic or fine metal brush to clean and brush the nap. Dust oily stains with baby powder and brush off.

Canvas Spray with stain remover then scrub by hand with detergent. Or machine wash, adding towels to stop them from bouncing around.

S

bake the best
Shortbread

Butter is an essential ingredient of shortbread, a Scottish specialty. Add rice flour or semolina for a fine-grained but deliciously crunchy texture.

MAKES 8 WEDGES

2 cups all-purpose flour
⅓ cup rice flour or semolina
¼ cup icing (confectioner's) sugar,
**   plus extra for dusting**
7 tbsp salted butter, chilled

1 Sift the flours into a bowl, add the sugar and grate in the butter using a coarse grater. Rub in the butter until the dough resembles breadcrumbs. Press into an 7 in. (18 cm) straight-sided cake pan and level the top. Prick all over with a fork.

2 Chill in the fridge for 1 hour. Heat the oven to 300°F (150°C) and bake for about 1 hour or until straw-colored. Cool in the pan for 10 minutes then cool further on a wire rack. While it's still warm, mark into eight wedges. Sprinkle with icing (confectioner's) sugar and separate into wedges before serving.

✳ golden rules
PLANTING SHRUBS
- **Always choose shrubs to match your garden conditions. Check your soil type** (see SOIL) **and read labels carefully.**
- **Don't skimp on hole size.**
- **Water frequently and generously until established.**
- **Put in supports before, not after, planting.**

Shop responsibly

With a bit of thought you can use your buying choices to benefit causes that matter to you, such as the environment, local businesses, ethical trading, international development or animal welfare.

For the environment
- Buy less. If you're constantly throwing food away, edit your shopping list.
- Shop close to home. By using independent neighborhood stores and services, you can save on car use—and support your local community.
- Choose locally sourced goods. In general these will have required less transportation, and therefore had less impact on the environment.
- Opt for organic—but be discriminating. Organic food crops, free from chemical fertilizers and pesticides, confer benefits to the workforce, the consumer and the environment where they are grown. However, organic fare flown in from overseas may have a greater overall impact on the environment than non-organic foods grown locally.
- Think before you eat. There are plenty more fish in the sea, for example, than the most endangered species. Be adventurous, try new species, look for the "approved" certification. Buy "dolphin-friendly" tuna.
- Choose goods that are packaged in an efficient and easy-to-recycle way.
- Take your own shopping bags with you rather than accumulating a mountain of unwanted plastic bags back at home.

For ethical trading
- Favor Fair Trade. The label guarantees a better deal for developing world producers, while a portion of sales is invested in development projects.
- Favor manufacturers with a good company profile (read their mission statements) over makers of shoddy, cut-rate throwaway goods.
- Use charity shops. Pass unwanted clothing and goods on to a charity and buy from there yourself (you may be amazed at what you find).
- Shop at cooperative-style stores, where a greater percentage of the profits will go to the store workers.

For animal welfare
- Choose free-range meat, poultry and eggs rather than cheaper but intensively farmed alternatives.
- Avoid cosmetics or household goods that have been tested on animals. Look for the internationally recognized Leaping Bunny logo, a guarantee that no such testing has taken place during the product's development.

plant a Shrub

Shrubs are the backbone of the garden. They are best planted in autumn, while dormant, or in early spring before they sprout with growth. Except for acid lovers, such as azaleas and rhododendrons, all shrubs, including roses, will benefit from the addition of granules containing mycorrhizal fungi, which encourage root growth. Follow the manufacturer's instructions, making sure that roots and granules are in contact.

Before planting Prepare a planting mixture of 2⅔ qt (2.5 L) each of well-rotted manure and garden compost plus 4 oz (100 g) of sterilized bone meal. Dig over the planting area to one spade's depth, removing all perennial weeds. Have some mulch ready to cover the soil around the new shrub (*see* MULCH).

Planting Most shrubs are bought in containers, but can also be obtained bare-rooted (*see* TREE). Before buying container-grown shrubs, remove them from the pot and check that there are several white roots around the rootball.

1 Dig a hole as deep as, and slightly wider than, the plant's rootball. When you place the plant in the hole, the base of its stem should be at the same level as the surrounding soil.

2 Water the plant and remove its container, if applicable. If the roots are wound around the outside of the rootball, tease out some of the outer roots so that they will establish more quickly in the surrounding soil.

3 Holding the plant by its stem, and supporting the rootball, place it in the hole. Fill the hole to the top with the planting mixture and tamp down firmly. Top up and tamp down again, then water thoroughly.

master Shrub pruning

Regular light pruning is the best way to keep shrubs in good health and to ensure that they produce flowers each year. Rather than pruning them precisely, shrubs with many thin stems such as *Spiraea* and *Potentilla* are best cut back and shaped with shears.

Before pruning a shrub to shape, cut out all dead and diseased wood. (This can be done at any time of year.)

Shrubs that flower after midsummer Late bloomers such as *Lavatera* (mallow) and buddleia (right) should be pruned in early spring, before new growth starts. Cut back last year's flowering stems and any weak shoots. The harder you prune the more new growth—on which flowers will develop—will be produced.

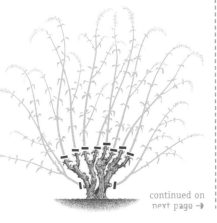

continued on next page →

overcome Shyness

Don't be a shrinking violet. Work on your confidence and blossom at work and play.

■ Understand your shyness, notice where and when it strikes and ask yourself what it is that you fear. Note down the negative messages that you send yourself then list the assumptions on which they are based. Remind yourself that they are assumptions, not facts.

■ Feel the fear and do it anyway. Strike up a conversation, go for that interview, make that phone call, go to that party. If you duck out of challenging situations you only reinforce your problem.

■ Set a target. Don't go to a party expecting to talk to every single guest. Challenge yourself to talk to, say, three people you don't know.

■ Break social encounters down into smaller, simpler steps. Start with everything but conversation: stand tall, look around you, make eye contact, smile. A friendly approach is usually welcome and reciprocated.

■ Keep conversation simple (see CONVERSATION). Say hello, introduce yourself, find out the other person's name, make a comment, ask a question. Above all, take an interest in what the other person has to say; don't worry what they think about you.

■ Remember that you have something in common with the other person; you are both in the same place at the same time. Think about why: Do you have a shared acquaintance, interest or job? Use this to fuel your conversation.

■ Be polite. Thank people warmly for any service they perform. Be appreciative. Make them feel good. It will help you to feel the same way.

S

PRUNE SHRUBS

■ Use sharp shears and make cuts as clean as possible.

■ Cut back to an outward-facing pair of buds if you can.

■ Remove all green shoots from variegated shrubs as soon as they appear. This prevents them from taking over the whole plant.

Shrubs that flower before midsummer Early bloomers such as forsythia, philadelphus and weigela (right) produce flowers on wood grown by the shrub the previous season. They should be pruned as soon as flowers fade, cutting back only to the highest new shoot or bud. This gives the shrub time to grow mature wood ready to flower again next season.

Shrubs grown for colored stems Prune in early spring, cutting back all the previous year's growth to near ground level or to an established framework of branches.

Evergreen shrubs Prune to keep them in shape, to shorten overlong shoots and to thin out congested plants in late spring and summer.

keep Silver clean

As well as pastes and liquid, you can buy polishing gloves and cloths to buff up silver regularly. For valuable items try a jeweler's rouge cloth (available online). Always wash silver by hand in warm water with mild dish soap and dry at once to avoid leaving marks.

Cutlery Clean with paste or polish applied and buffed off with a soft cloth. Solid silver—but never silver plate—can be immersed in a silver dip according to the instructions. The dip will strip off plating, especially if it's damaged.

Ornate pieces Sprinkle on some baking soda and rub off with a soft cloth. Use a soft brush to get into any crevices.

Jewelry Clean as for silver-plated cutlery. Dip an old toothbrush in baking soda for cleaning crevices. Wash in warm water and dry well.

empty a fish tank using a Siphon

Transferring liquid from one receptacle to another can be laborious and messy, especially when a container is really heavy and difficult to move—like an aquarium. The easy way is to siphon it out. All you need are flexible tubing, a bucket and a helping hand from gravity and atmospheric pressure.

1 Place your bucket on the ground, close to the tank. The bottom of the tank must be higher than the bucket—the greater the vertical distance, the quicker the liquid will flow. If there are any fish in the tank, transfer them to a safe place.

2 Find a length of flexible plastic tubing long enough to reach easily from the bottom of the tank to the bottom of the bucket. If possible, use transparent tubing so that you can monitor the flow of liquid. Holding the tubing in an even U shape, carefully fill it from a tap until the water reaches nearly to the top of each end. Cover each end with a thumb. This will be easier if you have someone to help.

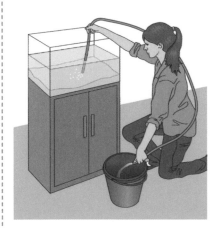

3 Move to the tank and, keeping your thumbs in place, insert one end of the tube into the bottom of the tank and the other into the bucket. Remove your thumb from the end in the tank and then do the same with the end in the bucket. The water will now flow out from the tank. The tube will also suck away mess at the bottom of the tank.

4 To stop the flow, if, for example, the bucket is full, lift the tube out of the tank water—the water left in the tube will empty out. To start again, refill the tube as in step 2. If the tank is large, you'll need several buckets.

unblock a Sink

If water isn't draining away from your sink, then there's a blockage somewhere below the drain.

First, try using a plunger If that works you won't have to dismantle any of the pipework. Place a sink plunger squarely over the drain, and hold a damp cloth tightly against the overflow. Pump the plunger sharply up and down.

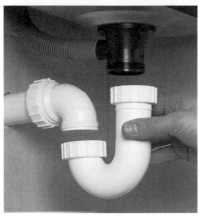

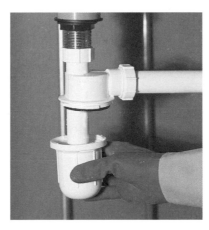

If plunging fails, look at the pipework underneath the sink or basin. Directly beneath the drain there will be a plastic "bottle trap" (above, right) or a P shaped sink trap (above, left). Put the plug in the drain of the sink, and place a bucket underneath the trap to catch any dirty water that may be blocked up in there. Unscrew the trap carefully (there's one central screw on a bottle trap, one on each end of a P trap). Wash it thoroughly if it's blocked with hair, grease or food debris, then screw it back into place.

If the sink or basin still won't drain, the blockage is farther down the pipe. You'll need a plumber's snake, a spiral device that can be bought or rented. Disconnect the trap once more, and feed the wire into the pipe. Turn the handle to rotate the spiral, which should break up any blockage it encounters. Reassemble the trap, remove the plug from the drain and run the tap to test.

alleviate Sinusitis

When infection causes the linings of the sinuses (small cavities behind the cheekbones and forehead, opening into the nose cavity) to become inflamed, it can cause fever, pain, tenderness and a blocked or runny nose. Sinusitis usually clears up on its own, but if symptoms persist you should see your doctor. In the meantime, there are a number of ways to ease the problem.

Try a steam inhalation of a decongestant. You can buy a ready-made mixture from a pharmacy or make one yourself at home.

■ Put two drops of tea tree, pine or eucalyptus essential oil in a bowl and pour in four cups of hot water.

■ Lean over the bowl with a towel draped over your head and breathe in the soothing vapors for ten minutes, inhaling as deeply as possible through the nose.

■ If you're having trouble breathing, rub a couple of drops of tea tree oil between your palms and inhale from your cupped hands.

Eat horseradish For a strong decongestant blast try chewing and swallowing ½ tsp of freshly grated horseradish root. To avoid stomach irritation, use this remedy only after a snack or meal.

Add pepper to a meal One of the quickest ways to loosen up blocked sinuses is to sprinkle cayenne pepper on your food.

embrace life after
Sixty

Once upon a time, 60 was "old." Advances in medicine, healthier lifestyles and a revolution in attitudes to age have changed all that, but there are still key actions you can take to give you the best chance of staying well after 60.

Worry less about losing weight
If you do drop weight after 60, you could be losing muscle and even bone density, making you weaker, with less balance and flexibility, and so more likely to have a fall. An obese person, though, should still be looking to lose some weight.

Eat more food but fewer calories
Concentrate on eating for good nutrition and disease prevention. Pile your plate high with fruit and vegetables, add beans and whole grains, and cut down on high-calorie culprits like burgers and cream sauces. *See also* DIET.

Keep excercising Even routine chores such as mowing the lawn or raking leaves a few times a week will keep you mobile and active for longer, and even stave off heart disease and diabetes. *See also* AEROBIC EXERCISE.

Do something interesting Join a choir, do charity work, take up painting and you'll have less stress, better moods and even lower blood pressure. Indulge in puzzles and other brain stretchers and you could even lower your risk of Alzheimer's and other forms of dementia.

Have a laugh Share plenty of time with friends, watch funny films, look on the bright side, and the endorphins released will make you more relaxed, less stressed and likely to fight off infections.

Sit properly

The teacher who told you to "sit up straight" had a point. Good sitting posture is important to your health—but holding yourself rigid can be as bad as slouching.

Change your sitting posture regularly to alter the forces on your joints and muscles. If you're reading a document or are on the phone, move in your chair, perhaps sit back and relax a little, or stand up to take a call.

Working at a computer Pay attention to the height of your chair in relation to your desk, your monitor and your own height.

Your head should be freely poised, shoulders relaxed, and your knees slightly apart.

Choose an ergonomic chair with lower-back support for good posture.

Avoid slouching, crossing your legs or twisting your body. To lean forward, keep your bottom on the chair and bend from the hip joint.

Aim to sit with your feet flat and your thighs parallel to the floor. Adjust your chair height with these factors in mind.

The top of the screen should be slightly below your eye level. If it's too low use a stand for it. The screen should be positioned so it doesn't reflect glare and cause avoidable eye strain.

Hold your forearms level or tilt them up slightly.

The work surface should be at about elbow level and afford clearance below for your knees.

Check and correct your posture periodically, and take regular breaks to stand up and walk around.

At the wheel Sitting incorrectly when you drive can not only cause back strain but affect the quality of your driving and place you in danger in an emergency. When you get into your vehicle make sure the seat is optimally positioned for you. Don't sit so far back that you can barely grasp the bottom of the wheel—or so far forward that you're hanging on to it.
■ Your legs should be comfortable when you press a pedal to the floor.
■ Hold the upper part of the steering wheel with your free hand and adjust the seat back so that you are as close to vertical as is comfortable, and your arms are slightly bent at the elbow when holding the wheel.

steer out of a Skid

You've lost control of your car; keep a grip on your nerves. A panic reaction will make the situation more dangerous.

Front-wheel skid You're approaching a bend in the road and turn the wheel but your car continues to travel straight.

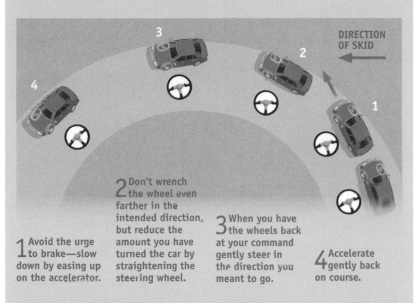

DIRECTION OF SKID

1 Avoid the urge to brake—slow down by easing up on the accelerator.

2 Don't wrench the wheel even farther in the intended direction, but reduce the amount you have turned the car by straightening the steering wheel.

3 When you have the wheels back at your command gently steer in the direction you meant to go.

4 Accelerate gently back on course.

Rear-wheel skid As you round a bend, the back of the car begins to skid as if it might break away or spin you around.

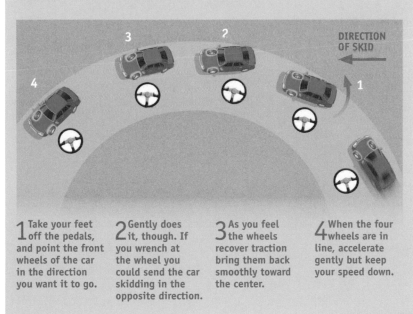

DIRECTION OF SKID

1 Take your feet off the pedals, and point the front wheels of the car in the direction you want it to go.

2 Gently does it, though. If you wrench at the wheel you could send the car skidding in the opposite direction.

3 As you feel the wheels recover traction bring them back smoothly toward the center.

4 When the four wheels are in line, accelerate gently but keep your speed down.

---

get on board with
Skateboarding

As with skating and bicycling, everything in skateboarding is easier once you're balanced.

■ All beginners fall off their skateboards, so invest in knee and elbow pads and a helmet. Specialized skateboarding shoes, designed to grip the board, might make the early stages easier for you.

■ First, get balanced. Stand, feet apart, on the flat section of the board. Your dominant foot should be at the front, or "nose," of the skateboard (this end is usually curved up slightly higher than the tail end). Place your feet at right angles to the length of the board, and turn body and head toward the front.

■ To "roll," or move forward, angle your front foot toward the nose and use your back foot to push, as with a child's scooter. When you pick up speed, put both feet on the board and adopt the balancing position.

■ To steer, move your center of gravity to one side of the board or the other. Shift your weight to the right, and you'll go into a wide, right-hand turn. To slow down, lean toward the back of the board.

Skip stones
across the water

Choose your stone carefully. Look for an oval that fits easily in your palm. It should be flat, thin and as light as possible. Bear in mind that you'll get more bounces if the surface of the water is calm.

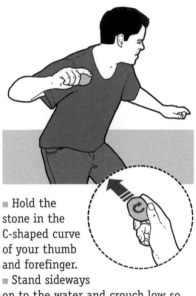

■ Hold the stone in the C-shaped curve of your thumb and forefinger.
■ Stand sideways on to the water and crouch low so that the stone, when you throw it, strikes the water's surface at an angle of no more than 20 degrees.
■ Whip your arm forward as fast and as strongly as you can, spinning the stone clockwise as you release it. Then watch it bounce, bounce, bounce toward the horizon …

master the basics of Skiing

The key to skiing well is good balance. Concentrate on that and everything else will follow.

In skiing, your gear makes a difference. Stood on end, your skis should come up to around eye level; long skis are harder to control. Buy the best boots that you can afford; good boots make skiing easier. Your poles, like your skis, should be the right length. Turn them upside down and grasp them below the basket (the hoop near the tip). With the poles resting on the ground, your elbow should be bent at a right angle.

In a starting position, ready to push off, your ankles, knees and hips should be slightly bent, and your weight should be in the center of your feet. But your body should be upright, and you shouldn't be leaning steeply forward from the waist.

To begin skiing down a gentle slope, push off with your poles, then hold them so that they are pointing backward, clear of the ground. Once you're gliding downhill, you shouldn't need to use the poles to propel you. Bend your ankles, knees and hips enough to feel the pressure on the tongues of your boots. Look ahead—not at your feet—and let your body take care of your balance.

To slow down, angle your legs so the tips of your skis are pointing at each other—a position known as the wedge or snowplow. Keep your knees apart and your weight forward and equal on both feet, and don't allow your ski tips to cross. The wider your wedge (the farther apart the back of the skis) the slower you'll go. Keep making it wider and, if you're on easy terrain, you'll come to a stop.

install Skype and make free calls

Skype is a computer program that lets you make free phone calls from one computer to another over the internet. You'll need to connect a microphone and speakers if they aren't built into your computer.

First go to www.skype.com and follow the instructions that you find there to download the software. Once the software has downloaded, run the installation "Wizard." You'll have to assign yourself a Skype name—your actual name is fine. This will be the equivalent of your Skype phone number.

When you launch for the first time, go to the **Contacts** menu and click on **Search for People on Skype**. Type in the name of a friend you know is on Skype already. Make sure you choose the right person from the list of people with that name (either by asking their username in advance, or by checking the name against that user's given location). Click **Add contact**, then click **OK**. That person will be added to your address book once they respond, and you'll be able to see when they are logged on to Skype.

To make a call, click on a name in your contacts list that's highlighted with a green tick. Then click on the phone icon if you want to speak to that person without a visual link—or on the camera icon if you'd like to see each other (both computers need webcams for this to work—*see* WEBCAM).

---

get a good night's Sleep

A good bed and bedding—and a clean, tidy, well-aired and fresh-smelling bedroom—are key to unbroken, restorative sleep.

Love your bedroom You spend about a third of your life there. Dedicate it to sleep. Banish the computer and television to other rooms. Eliminate dust and mess. Hang up clothes, return books to their shelves.

Launder the sheets often They should smell fresh. Also, lightly spray with lavender water—the perfume is said to aid sleep and relaxation.

Set a routine Keep regular hours and start to wind down as you look forward to going to bed. Create a ritual to prepare for bed. Read, write down your thoughts, watch some TV (but not thrillers or horror)—whatever relaxes you.

Not too hot, not too cold Set a comfortable temperature for your bedroom.

Sleep in complete darkness—and seek sunlight in the morning. As bedtime approaches start to dim your lights; don't sit in a glare.

Try to soundproof your bedroom Exposure to noise at night can suppress the immune system—even if it doesn't wake you.

Use an old-fashioned alarm clock Even a dimly luminous digital clock can be enough to disturb sleep, while the sheer visibility of digits as the hours tick away adds stress to a night of tossing and turning. Electrical alarms and other devices may also transmit electrical fields or faint sounds to disturb sleep and penetrate consciousness. *See also* INSOMNIA, MATTRESS, PILLOWS.

Skip
for health or for fun

Group skipping with a long rope is a popular playground game, but skipping isn't just child's play. Solo skipping is an exhilarating way to keep fit.

Solo skipping
- Use the right length of rope; if you stand on the middle you should be able to bring the ends of the rope up to your armpits.
- Start with the rope hanging to the floor behind your heels, arms angled out from the hips.
- Twirl the rope forward using small, circular wrist movements.
- Keep your feet together and bend your knees slightly as you jump.
- For a basic workout, skip for 30 seconds, rest for 30 seconds. Repeat ten times. Gradually progress to 60-second intervals over 20 minutes.

Playground games
Skippers do stints as "enders," to turn the rope for their playmates.

"I like …" First skipper ducks under the turning rope and starts to skip before calling in a friend (let's say Sam), by chanting *I like coffee, I like tea, I like Sam in with me*. Sam joins in and both jump rope. Then it's *I don't like coffee, I don't like tea, I don't like Sam in with me!* Sam has to exit and another friend is called. The aim is to keep going for as long as possible without a fault.

"Teddy bear …" Four players skip in time to a chant: *Teddy bear, teddy bear, turn around. Teddy bear, teddy bear, touch the ground. Teddy bear, teddy bear, go upstairs. Teddy bear, teddy bear, say your prayers.* The skippers have to both jump the rope and mime these actions.

S

win the battle against
Slugs and snails

These slimy little creatures destroy plants virtually overnight. Their particular penchant is for the soft foliage of salad vegetables and herbaceous perennials, such as hostas, and for strawberries. Although plants at soil level are most vulnerable, slugs and snails will also climb up and eat young clematis.

- Try to avoid having dark havens in the garden, such as behind pieces of wood or loose bricks.
- Sprinkle slug pellets sparingly. There are now organic versions available in most garden centers.
- Handpick and destroy slugs and snails, particularly when they emerge after rain and at dusk.
- Sink glass jars filled 50:50 with beer and water into the ground. The creatures will be lured into them and then drown.
- Surround plants with glass or gravel chippings, or with used coffee grounds.

- Wrap copper bands around pots (above). Slugs and snails can't tolerate the metal.
- Scoop out grapefruit halves and place them upside down beside vulnerable plants. Slugs and snails will accumulate overnight and can be removed and destroyed.

make a Sling for an injured person

If your first-aid kit doesn't have a sling, you can support an injured arm with a triangular bandage (*see* BANDAGE). Treat any wound before applying a sling.

1 Place the arm across the body with the hand slightly above the elbow and thumb uppermost. Handle with great care if you suspect a break. Slide a triangular bandage between the arm and chest so that the corner opposite the longest edge of the bandage is behind the elbow of the injured arm. Take the top corner around the back of the neck to the front of the shoulder on the injured side.

2 Carefully support the site of the injury with soft padding, such as a towel. Then bring the bottom corner of the bandage up and over the injured arm. Tie it to the top corner using a reef knot (*see* KNOTS) just over the hollow in front of the shoulder.

3 Twist the excess fabric at the elbow so that the sling fits snugly around the joint, then tuck the twisted end into the fabric. The weight of the arm in the sling will then hold the twisted end in place. Monitor the fingers to check that they aren't turning pale or blue. Check the pulse and ask the victim about any tingling—if there are signs of loss of circulation, loosen the sling.

Improvised jacket sling If the casualty is wearing a jacket, this will serve very well as a support for the injured arm.

For an injury to the forearm, hand or wrist
- Undo the jacket's fastenings.
- Ask the victim to support the injured arm as you bring the hem up and over, ensuring that the elbow is supported (see left).
- Fasten the hem to the jacket with safety pins.

For an upper-arm injury
- Gently unzip or unbutton the jacket a little way down from the top.
- Slide the victim's hand into the jacket opening and, if you're unsure of the solidity of the zipper or buttons, fasten beneath it with safety pins.

build your own fish Smoker

Hot-smoking is a great way to cook fish such as mackerel and salmon. A smoker is easy to make from everyday household equipment.

YOU WILL NEED **Roasting pan, bricks, sawdust, grill rack, cooking oil, fish, brine (water saturated with salt), baking sheet, alcohol burners**

1 Take an ordinary roasting pan and place it on four bricks, outdoors. Sprinkle in 2 tbsp of sawdust—hickory, oak or maple. (This "smoke dust" can be bought from fishing-tackle or barbecue stores.) Place a grill rack inside the roasting pan, so that it sits above the sawdust.

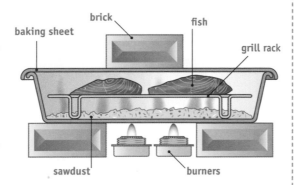

2 Wipe some oil on the rack to keep your food from sticking. Put the fish on the rack having first soaked it in brine for 30 minutes and patted it dry. If the fish is filleted, place it skin side down. Use a baking sheet to cover the roasting pan and weigh it down with another brick.

3 Half-fill two burners (available from camping shops) with alcohol. Position them underneath your homemade smoker, between the supporting bricks, and carefully light them with a match.

4 Don't worry if smoke seeps out of the burner; it's supposed to. Refill the burners if they run out of fuel—but be careful, as they will be hot. Cook the fish for 20 minutes or so, remove it from the smoker, and let it cool before serving.

---

prepare, cook and eat Snails

Although garden snails are edible, they need careful preparation to remove harmful toxins. It's best to buy *escargots* in cans. They are traditionally cooked with garlic butter in *escargotières*—earthenware dishes with indents to hold each snail individually. They are best eaten with the help of small, sharp forks.

SERVES 4

1 cup butter, softened
2 tbsp brandy or white wine
4 tbsp chopped parsley
2 large garlic cloves, minced
4 tbsp breadcrumbs
salt and freshly ground black
    pepper, to taste
24 canned snails, drained
    and rinsed, plus shells

Heat the oven to 400°F (200°C). Mix the butter, brandy, parsley, garlic and breadcrumbs well. With a teaspoon, put a little of the mixture into each indent of the *escargotières*, add a snail, then fill to the rim with more mixture. Bake for about 10 minutes, until the butter is bubbling.

quit Smoking

The addiction to tobacco is powerful—but so is the human will. Make up your mind to quit and you'll do so.

Set a date for quitting Tell everyone of your intention.

Write down the reasons why you want to quit They will be compelling.

Prepare for withdrawal symptoms For a while you may feel bad-tempered, confused, anxious or restless. You may have a headache or insomnia, but these don't last forever. Symptoms tend to peak in two to three days, reducing over two to four weeks. Nicotine patches or nicotine chewing gum can help. You may also, perversely, have a cough. All this just signals that your body is ridding itself of toxins.

Get some exercise It will reduce the symptoms, enhance your mood and improve your chances of success.

Try acupuncture It has a good track record for treating addictions and symptoms of withdrawal.

Get rid of ashtrays and lighters You have no more use for smokers' paraphernalia.

Avoid places and situations you associate with smoking And, whenever possible, avoid associating with continuing smokers.

Have your teeth cleaned by the dentist Enjoy the novelty of a fresh mouth.

Bank the money you would have spent on cigarettes If you have a 20-a-day habit, think what a vacation you can have after a year as a nonsmoker. Just don't celebrate with a cigarette!

use a Snorkel

Safe snorkeling means having the right equipment. The mask should fit snugly; the snorkel should be a J-shaped breathing tube with a mouthpiece that sits comfortably between your teeth. Only snorkel if you can swim well, and never snorkel alone.
■ Put on the mask and snorkel and check that they fit well.
■ With your head still above water, take a few practice breaths in and out of your snorkel. Get used to breathing only through your mouth rather than your nose.
■ Start swimming and duck your face just below the surface of the water. Continue breathing steadily through the mouthpiece and watch in wonder as a new world opens up to you beneath the waves.

It's possible to dive underwater with a snorkel, but you'll need to clear the tube of water afterward. Tilt your head well back as you rise to the surface. Exhale as you break the surface and keep on breathing out as you tilt your head forward.

If your mask fills with water, look up, press the top of the mask, and breathe out through your nose until the mask is clear.

learn the basics of Snooker

Snooker is a pool-like game in which you use a cue and a white cue ball to steer balls around a table. Points are scored by knocking ("potting") the balls into six pockets on the table edge.

■ There are 15 red balls, each worth one point, and six colored balls: yellow (two points), green (three), brown (four), blue (five), pink (six) and black (seven). The game begins with the balls arranged as shown.
■ A player must first pot a red, then a color, then another red, and so on.
■ If a color is potted after a red, it's placed back on its starting spot.
■ If a player fails to make a pot, the other player takes over and begins by attempting to pot any available red.
■ Once the reds are gone, the colors are potted in value order. The player with the most points by the time the black is potted wins the "frame."

Game within a game

Snooker is more than marksmanship, though. A good snooker player—like a chess player—must think ahead and map out all the many possibilities on the table. That way each shot can be played to set up the next one. And where there isn't a clear scoring opportunity, a good player will position the cue ball so that their opponent doesn't have a direct shot and has to use the angles of the table to hit a red or the next colored ball. This situation is called a "snooker" and, if not successfully escaped from, incurs a penalty of at least four points.

yellow
2 points

brown
4 points

green
3 points

blue
5 points

pink 6 points
reds 1 point

black 7 points

stop Snoring

See a doctor if snoring is extreme, and especially if breathing stops for a period and then restarts noisily. Otherwise, try the following to ease snoring.
■ Slightly raise the head of the bed on blocks.
■ Use only enough pillows to keep your neck straight (and airway open).
■ Sleep on your side with a pillow behind you as a wedge. If you still tend to roll onto your back, sew a small ball or marble to the back of your nightwear.
■ Avoid alcohol or sleeping pills that may further relax the muscles. And stop smoking (*see* SMOKING). Try nasal strips and other anti-snoring devices.
■ Excercise regularly, which may strengthen your head and neck, and help you to lose weight—the main contributing factor to snoring.

get started at Snowboarding

A snowboard looks like a short, fat ski, but snowboard technique is very different from skiing. It's an odd feeling to have your feet strapped to a board. Start by spending some time adjusting the bindings on your board, so that you feel comfortable and your body can move freely.

■ Skating is the snowboarder's means of moving around on flat terrain. Keep your front foot strapped into the binding, and use your back foot to push yourself along with short kicks, as if on a scooter. As you gain momentum, you can place your pushing foot on the board, in front of the back binding—a move known as gliding.

■ Zigzag down slopes, across the steepest part of the hillside (called the fall line). You control the direction of your board and its speed by pressing on the left foot to go left and right foot to go right. This is also a good way of getting down a slope that's too steep to turn on.

■ Turning involves changing the balance of the body from one edge of the board to the other, from the toes to the heels, to create a curving line down the slope like a series of linked S shapes.

■ As you move down a slope, keep your arms just slightly away from your sides so you can move them to aid balance.

---

build a Snowman

A snowman is a satisfying seasonal sculpture. Grab the chance to make one when you can.

1 Begin by making a large snowball in your hands. Place it on the ground and roll it so that it gathers more snow. Change the orientation of the ball frequently so that the ball remains spherical rather than barrel-shaped. Make three balls, of decreasing sizes, in this way.

2 Flatten the top of your largest ball to form a stable base. Place the second ball on top, taking care that it doesn't crumble. The head, being smaller, is easier to place.

3 Decorate the snowman. Be creative; the main thing is to ensure that your snowman (or snow-woman) has charm and character.

A hat and scarf always look good, and so does an old-fashioned pipe.

A carrot nose and coal eyes are traditional.

Equip him with some kind of a smile, using small stones.

twigs for arms

pebbles for buttons

flat top on which to place middle ball

A CLASSIC SNOWMAN consists primarily of three balls of snow sitting on top of each other. You can make a shorter, more rotund snowman out of two balls.

make Soda bread

This quick, simple bread made without yeast has a nutty taste thanks to the inclusion of whole wheat flour. If you don't have buttermilk, use 1% milk and add a tablespoon of lemon juice.

MAKES 1 LARGE LOAF TO SERVE 6-8

1¾ cups all-purpose flour
1¾ cups whole wheat flour, plus a little extra to sprinkle
1 tsp baking soda
½ tsp salt
1¼ cups buttermilk

1 Heat the oven to 400°F (200°C). Sift the flours, baking soda and salt into a bowl, tipping in any bran left in the sifter. Make a well in the center, pour in the buttermilk and use a wooden spoon to mix. Bring together with your hands into a soft dough.

2 On a floured surface, knead lightly and briefly. Place on a greased baking sheet and flatten into a domed loaf shape. Use a sharp knife to cut a deep cross in the top, cutting about halfway down into the dough. Sprinkle with a little whole wheat flour.

3 Bake for about 30 minutes or until well browned and the bread sounds hollow when tapped on the base. Leave to cool completely on a wire rack then serve at once.

learn soft
Soldering

If you want to join together two pieces of metal, such as wires or plumbing pipes, soft soldering is a useful skill to have. Solder is a soft alloy, usually supplied in wire form, with a melting point lower than the metal it's joining. The solder is applied to the join, melted using a hand tool called a soldering iron, and then resets to create the join. Soldering irons should only be used in a well-ventilated space. Keep the iron in its stand, away from the edge of your workbench. Wear safety goggles.

YOU WILL NEED Soldering iron, damp sponge, solder, safety goggles

1 Turn on your soldering iron. When it reaches operating temperature, wipe the tip with the damp sponge to clean off any debris. Now touch a piece of solder to the tip, so that it melts and coats the tip completely. This is called "tinning," and it helps the heat to flow to the joint.

2 Hold the iron as if it were a pen. Touch it to the joint to be made, making sure that both items to be joined are in contact with each other. Feed a little solder onto the joint—not the iron. If you're soldering twisted wires together, the solder should flow freely into the twist.

3 Withdraw the solder, then the iron, and keep the join still until it cools.

prepare and dig Soil

Digging in late autumn or early spring is the best way of preparing most soils. For large areas you can use a rototiller, as long as there aren't a lot of perennial weeds (*see* WEEDS) whose roots will be chopped up and spread around.

Single digging

1 Dig the first trench to one spade's depth. Put the soil in a wheelbarrow and take it to the far end of the plot. Spread the remaining area with well-rotted manure or compost.

2 Dig the next trench alongside the first, throwing soil into the first one. Continue over the whole plot. Fill the final trench with the reserved soil, mixed with some manure or compost.

Double digging

1 Use for a newly cultivated patch or to improve clay and other firm soils. For the first trench, dig to two spade depths, and remove soil as for single digging. Fork over the base of each trench.

2 Add plenty of compost or well-rotted manure before starting the next trench. Finish by filling in with your reserved soil.

No-dig gardening On light soils such as chalk and sand, and in raised beds, avoid digging. Cover in autumn with a thick layer of well-rotted compost, which worms will draw into the soil over the winter.

test and know your Soil

All soil is made up of sand, silt, clay and organic matter. Once you know what kind of soil you have, and its acidity level, you can work to improve it and will be able to choose the most appropriate plants.

Use a testing kit to measure the acidity of the soil on the pH scale. Follow the instructions and take samples of soil from different parts of the garden. A pH reading of 7 is neutral, lower than 6 very acid, above 8 very alkaline.

1	2	3	4	5	6	7	8	9	10	11	12	13	14

ACIDIC   NEUTRAL   ALKALINE

THE pH SCALE is usually shown as a strip of 14 colors. Test results may consist of the color or number, or both.

Acid soils are good for heathers, azaleas, rhododendrons and blueberries, which won't tolerate alkaline conditions. Most vegetables and fruit prefer slightly acid soils. Neutralize acid soils by adding lime as instructed on the package.

Alkaline soils are good for delphiniums, pinks, mulleins, sage, lilacs and privet. Organic matter will help to neutralize and acidify alkaline soils.

Soil type Test your soil at different locations in your garden by scooping up a handful and trying to make it into a ball with your hands.

Soil type	Properties and treatment
SANDY—won't form a ball, very loose and gritty.	Free draining, lacks fertility, needs generous composting.
SILT OR LOAM—holds some shape, smooth but slightly gritty in texture.	Fertile, holds water well but also free draining. Compost annually.
CHALKY—will hold some shape, pale in color often with white limestone visible.	Fertile but quick draining, alkaline. Compost well and never add lime.
CLAY—easily forms a firm ball, soapy in texture.	Tends to waterlog, bakes hard in hot weather and can be very fertile, usually acid. Add sand to help to break it up and compost generously.
PEATY OR ORGANIC—crumbly and fibrous, dark in color.	Very fertile, retains water well. Can be acid or alkaline.

make a refreshing Sorbet

All kinds of fruit and fruit juices can be used for good sorbets. These easy-to-make frozen desserts are a refreshingly healthy alternative to ice cream.

Strawberry sorbet

SERVES 4

- 1 cup sugar
- 1 cup water
- 1 lb (500 g) strawberries, hulled, plus extra to decorate
- 2 tsp lemon juice
- 1 egg white, lightly whipped

1 Put the sugar and water into a pan over low heat and stir until the sugar dissolves. Bring to a boil and simmer for 2 minutes. Leave to cool.

2 Purée the strawberries in a food processor, then press through a strainer. Stir in the sugar syrup and lemon juice. Pour into a freezable container and freeze until half-set. Break up the mixture with a fork, then whizz in the processor or beat until smooth. Fold in the egg white then refreeze until completely frozen. Serve garnished with slices of strawberry.

S

relieve a
Sore throat

Gargle with honey Soothing honey coats the throat and is mildly antibacterial. Stir a couple of teaspoons into a mug of warm water and gargle two to three times a day.

Try salt water To help cleanse your throat of phlegm, dissolve ½ tsp of sea salt in a mug of warm water, and gargle two to three times a day.

Drink plenty of fluids This helps to keep the mucous membrane moist and relieve a scratchy sore throat.

Take a mild painkiller You can help to dull the pain with a painkiller made for use during colds and flu.

Avoid cigarettes Now is a good time to stop smoking (*see* SMOKING).

See a doctor If your sore throat is accompanied by a fever, severe pain or difficulty in breathing or swallowing, see a doctor.

---

banish Spam emails

Spam is one of the irritations of the internet age. It's hard to avoid completely, but there are ways to stop it from clogging up your inbox.

■ Activate your email program's spam or junk filter.
■ Don't hit the "unsubscribe" button on spam emails. This only confirms that your email address is active.
■ Use a separate, free email address, such as Gmail, when buying online or subscribing to newsletters. Keep another email address for friends and colleagues.
■ Don't publish your email address on the web—a "spambot" might find it and start to bombard you.

make individual cheese Soufflé pots

A soufflé is impressive and not as difficult as you might think. You can make this in one large dish if you wish (with a capacity of about 1½ qt/L), but increase the cooking time to 40–45 minutes.

SERVES 4

2 tbsp salted butter, plus extra for greasing
¼ cup all-purpose flour
just under 1 cup milk
½ tsp Dijon mustard
4 eggs, separated, plus 2 egg whites
1 cup cheddar cheese, grated,
  plus extra for sprinkling
salt and freshly ground black pepper

1 Heat the oven to 350°F (180°C), grease four individual soufflé dishes and put a baking sheet in the oven. Melt the remaining butter in a saucepan. Stir in the flour and cook gently for 1–2 minutes, stirring continuously. Remove from the heat and stir in the milk until completely smooth. Return to the heat, bring slowly to a boil and simmer mixture for 10 minutes. Remove from the heat and beat in the mustard, egg yolks, cheese and seasonings.

2 In a large bowl, beat the egg whites until they form stiff peaks. Fold 2 tbsp into the soufflé base followed by the remainder, using a chopping and folding action until just combined.

3 Pour into the prepared dishes, sprinkle with the extra cheese, then put the dishes onto the hot baking sheet. Bake for 15–20 minutes, or until the soufflés are well-risen and golden brown. Serve immediately.

---

replace Spark plugs in a car

A spark plug is the device in your car's internal combustion engine that lights the fuel using an electric spark. Replace spark plugs according to the manufacturer's instructions. How often you need to replace them depends on what kind of car you drive—it could be anywhere from 10,000–30,000 miles (16,000–48,000 km).

■ If there is at least 2 in. (5 cm) of clearance above your spark plugs, you can do the job yourself. Make sure the engine is cool and the ignition is off before starting.
■ Tape identifying labels to the spark-plug cables before pulling them off, then grasp each at the nipple end, twist to break any heat seal and pull up. Never pull on the wire itself.
■ To remove the plugs, you need a ratchet wrench and either a ¹³⁄₁₆ or ⅝ in. spark-plug socket, depending on your car's plug size. A universal-joint drive-handle attachment and extension attachments can help you reach awkwardly placed plugs.
■ After cleaning around the spark plug with a soft brush, fit the socket firmly over the hex section of the plug and, with the ratchet set to unlock,

apply pressure counterclockwise. Hit the handle with the heel of your hand to unseat a stubborn plug. If it continues to stick, use penetrating oil.
■ Replace plugs with the brand and model number recommended by the manufacturer, or with a manufacturer's equivalent. If your engine has an aluminium head, apply a film of anti-seize compound to each new spark plug's threads.
■ Use a spark-plug gauge to adjust the gap between electrodes of each new plug. (Refer to your manual or gap specification on the decal under your car's hood.) The gauge wire should fit snugly. To adjust the gap, use the gauge's bracket to bend the L-shaped side electrode. Recheck with the wire.

arrange stereo Speakers

Speakers are what will ultimately determine the sound quality of your stereo—the best system in the world can't compensate for terrible speakers.

For the best performance, place two speakers roughly 8 ft (2.5 m) apart, facing the center of the room. In a rectangular room, locate the speakers along one of the shorter walls. Whatever the room's shape, however, the speakers should not face each other—that position doesn't make the most of their sound quality.
■ If, at certain frequencies (bass or treble), the surface under a speaker vibrates, check that all speaker connections are tight. You can also try placing a sound-dampening pad under the speaker.
■ If the speaker is too close to a record turntable or radio, you might find that it makes a loud howling noise. Try moving them further apart.
■ If your stereo system sounds muted, check each speaker; make sure all the wires at the back are firmly plugged in.

be successful at Speed dating

In speed dating, first impressions really count—even more than they would normally.

■ You have just 3 or 4 minutes to make your mark, so don't fill that time with a monologue or string of lame jokes. Make sure you allow your date to speak as much as you do, and be sure to listen and respond.
■ Approach each person with a smile and warm greeting, and try to project confidence, even if you're a bit nervous. Create the impression that, for the short duration of your date, he or she is the only other person in the room.
■ Think of some questions that will give you insight into your speed-date's personality: *What do you do on weekends? What's your favourite film/song/food?* Recent vacations and future plans are a rich and revealing topic.
■ Don't be afraid to talk about dating—that's what you are both there for, after all. *What are you looking for in a partner?* is a fair thing to ask, but don't get too personal—and don't bring up past relationships!
■ Find a way to compliment your date and make him or her feel good. *Wow, you went to Siberia? You must be adventurous.*

give a good Speech

Public speaking doesn't have to be scary, as long as you're well prepared and stay positive.

Practice beforehand A speech is a visual performance as well as a talk, so it pays to know how you appear to your audience. Rehearse your speech in front of a mirror, then run it past a harsh but trusted critic—someone who will tell you when you're getting boring.

Learn it by heart It's boring to watch someone reading pages of notes out loud, because then they can't make eye contact or engage emotionally with the audience. So learn your lines as if you were an actor. Your notes, if you need them, should be on unobtrusive index cards and used as prompts, at most.

Get off to a flying start Don't begin with thank-yous or a lengthy preamble. Make your first words a remark or story that will grab the attention of your audience. A well-received anecdote will put everyone at ease, including you.

Use your body Your facial expression and gestures can add warmth and meaning to what you're saying, so don't be too static. On the other hand, wild hand movements will be distracting to everyone. Strike a balance.

Keep it brief Short speeches are nearly always preferable to long ones, no matter how fascinating the subject matter.

remove Splinters

Use tweezers and pull out the way the splinter went in. If this fails, sterilize a needle and work along the line of the splinter to tease it out. Wash well. Apply antiseptic.

Use adhesive if you can't get the splinter out. Soak the area in warm water, dry and dab on a spot of white glue. Peel off the glue when dry, and the splinter should lift out.

Try a poultice to draw out a stubborn splinter. Make a paste with baking soda and a little water, and secure to the area overnight with a bandage—it will make the skin swell and push out the offending splinter.

See your doctor if you cannot remove it, if it was dirty or an animal spine, or if the surrounding area becomes infected.

---

soothe itchy Spots and rashes

Resist the urge to scratch an itchy rash. Instead, try these remedies.

Over-the-counter lotions such as calamine may help. Antihistamine pills could also help, but they can make you drowsy. Ask your pharmacist for advice.

Aloe vera gel smoothed on the skin has a cooling effect.

A cup of oatmeal sprinkled in a warm bath calms down angry spots and rashes—and it's good for the rest of your skin, too.

identify Spots and rashes

Your child came home with an angry red rash. Don't be alarmed, but do read these symptoms and take appropriate action.

What to do?

Before you do anything else, test for meningitis (*see* MENINGITIS).

Eliminate obvious triggers Rashes can be caused by irritants such as poison ivy, medication or polluted pool water. Also try to identify anything eaten that could have caused an acute anaphylactic reaction (*see also* ALLERGY EMERGENCY).

Check his or her temperature A child with an infectious disease may well have a fever. Keep your child at home, and wash their and your hands frequently to avoid the spread of infection (*see* HANDS).

Consult your pediatrician If a rash doesn't fade overnight, see a doctor.

Call an ambulance if your child has difficulty breathing or swallowing or is abnormally drowsy.

Cause	What to look for and do
MEASLES 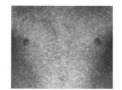 Acute, highly communicable viral disease	**Incubation period** About 10 days. **Look for** grayish-white "Koplik's spots" on a red background inside the cheeks and on the throat. Two to four days after initial symptoms, there will be a brown, spotted rash, usually starting behind the ears and around the hairline, spreading around the head and neck, then to the legs and over the body. The spots are initially small but quickly increase in size and may join together to form angry blotches. The measles rash isn't intensely itchy. **Spread by** contact with fluids from the respiratory tract, such as coughs and sneezes. **Stay at home** for four days after the first measles rash appears.
RUBELLA 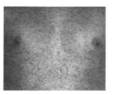 Also called German measles, often experienced as a milder illness than measles	**Incubation period** 14–21 days. **Look for** pink, flat rash made of very small spots, similar to a measles rash but less extensive. It starts at the hairline, face and neck, before spreading to the body, arms and legs. **Spread by** contact with fluids in the respiratory tract, such as coughs and sneezes. **Stay at home** for seven days after onset. **Pregnant women:** If you're expecting, you must not be exposed to rubella—it can seriously damage a developing fetus, especially in the early weeks.

Cause	What to look for and do
CHICKEN POX 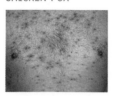 Highly communicable varicella zoster virus is most infectious from a day or two before rash appears *See also* SHINGLES.	**Incubation period** 14–16 days. **Look for** small, flat red spots, which become raised, forming fluid-filled round blisters ("vesicles") against a red background. In the third stage, the vesicles crust over. The rash is intensely itchy. It starts on the trunk before spreading to the face, arms and legs. Spots may also be found on the eyelids, and on the inside of the mouth and vagina. **Spread by** contact with fluids in the respiratory tract, or by contact with fluid from an infected person's blisters. **Stay at home** from when spots first appear until all sores are crusted over (about five days after the onset of blisters).
FIFTH DISEASE 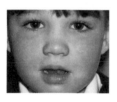 Viral illness also known as "slapped cheek syndrome"	**Incubation period** 13–18 days. **Look for** bright red and slightly raised rash on the cheeks, developing a lacy appearance that lends a blotchy look, and spreading to the body, arms and legs. Other symptoms—temperature, sore throat and headache—appear up to a week before the rash. **Spread by** contact with fluid in the respiratory tract. **Lasts for** around five days, but the rash may return for a few weeks. Once the rash appears, the disease is no longer infectious. **Pregnant women:** Exposure can damage the fetus.
ECZEMA 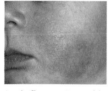 An inflammatory skin condition, also called atopic dermatitis	**Look for** itchy, dry and hot, or broken, raw and bleeding skin, most commonly on the face and neck, the inside of the elbows, and the knees and ankles. In infants, more typically found on the forehead, cheeks, scalp, neck, forearms and legs. Severity can vary. **Isn't contagious**—no need for your child to stay home from school.
RINGWORM 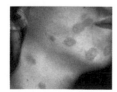 Caused by a fungus not a worm	**Look for** a burning ring that expands outwards. **Spreads by** skin contact with an infected person, shared towels, bedding and washcloths. Also passed on through pets. **No need to stay home** so long as your child sticks to their treatment—usually an anitfungal cream — and takes care with their hygiene.

treat Sprains and strains

A sprain is a stretched, twisted or torn ligament (or more than one). It can be even more painful and slower to heal than a break.

A strain occurs when a muscle is stretched beyond its limit or forced to contract too abruptly.

Apply PRICE therapy in both cases to speed recovery:

PROTECT the injured area. For an ankle injury, wear shoes that enclose and support the foot.

REST. Avoid activity in the first 48–72 hours. For a leg injury, your doctor may offer crutches.

ICE. For the first two to three days, apply an ice pack wrapped in a towel for 15–20 minutes every 2–3 hours during the daytime.

COMPRESS. Bandage the injury to reduce swelling and give support (*see* BANDAGE).

ELEVATE. Keep the injury raised and supported (below) on a pillow or chair to help to reduce swelling. This is especially important if your leg is injured: Don't spend long periods without it raised.

use a paint
Spray gun
correctly

Spray guns are a type of airbrush that are useful for painting large areas, rough surfaces and things that are awkward to paint with a brush. Older models used compressed air, forcing paint through the nozzle of the "gun." More compact, electrically operated airless versions are now also available.

■ Whichever gun you have, always prepare the equipment carefully. The gun should be scrupulously clean, and the paint should be thinned in accordance with the manufacturer's instructions.

■ If you have a spray gun that uses compressed air, adjust the airflow and compressor pressure, following the manufacturer's recommendations.

■ Adjust the fan pattern, then perform a test spray on a sheet of cardboard, away from whatever you want to paint.

■ When you're ready to start the job, spray in a wide, continuous sweeping motion that begins 6 in. (15 cm) or so to one side of the object, and ends the same distance on the other side. This ensures that the edges are properly painted.

■ The gun should be 6–8 in. (15–20 cm) away from the object you're painting, and you should move no faster than if you were painting with an ordinary paintbrush.

■ Each stroke with the spray gun should overlap about half the area covered by the preceding one.

■ Always wear safety goggles and a face mask.

■ Clean spray guns immediately after use, before the paint dries.

create a basic Spreadsheet

Computer spreadsheets are a great way to keep track of budgets and accounts because they make your data easy to read and compare. A spreadsheet is a grid of cells into which you put information in the form of words or numbers. Microsoft Excel is the best-known spreadsheet program.

Imagine the grid as a set of columns in an old-fashioned ledger.

■ To make a home budget, add a column for each month. In the example here (right), type the months of the year in row 3, beginning at column C.

■ Next, type the heading "Income" in column A, then add categories from all your various incomes into column B. Now type the heading "Expenses" and add your main categories of expenditure: mortgage, utilities, food and so on. It's easy to add categories as you go, such as vacation or birthday presents. Try to be specific and avoid a huge "miscellaneous" figure.

■ Now type in all the figures from your bank statements, pay stubs and receipts from the appropriate month.

Now you can get the program to do the math and analyze your finances. You can find out quickly if your spending exceeds your income and get an instant number for all food costs throughout a year, for example, or for all your expenditures in any given month. To calculate your monthly balance, in cell C4 in the example above, type the calculation "(C10–C19)" into the bar on top and press enter.

do some Spring cleaning

Spring cleaning is aptly named, because it's best to do it when bright light highlights dust and dirt that has accumulated over the winter. As you're cleaning, plan to de-clutter as much as possible.

De-cluttering and tidying Tackle clutter room by room, including drawers and cupboards, and assess and deal with things in the following way.

■ **Discard** Look for anything that can be thrown away, recycled, donated to a thrift store or sold online or at a garage sale. Don't forget the pantry, fridge and freezer (*see also* CUPBOARDS *and* FREEZER).

■ **Keep** Hold onto papers to be filed and anything that needs to be put away. Replace all items in their correct place. Use storage boxes.

■ **Take action** Identify anything that needs cleaning, repairing or replacing, paperwork that needs action or photos to put in albums, and so on.

Assemble your cleaning tools Before you start work, think about what you'll need to clean everything in the room you're tackling. Don't forget the windows, heavy-duty cleaners for any stains, something to reach cobwebs (such as a broom with its head wrapped in a clean, soft cloth), plenty of cloths and dusters, and stepladders for high places.

Your cleaning strategy Start at the top of the house and work down. Work through each room in the following pattern, always finishing a room before starting the next.
- Take down curtains and launder them, or take to the dry cleaner.
- Remove blinds and all pictures and other decorations from the walls.
- Think dry then wet—start with the dusting, sweeping and vacuuming, then move on to wet cleaning, such as that for windows and floors.
- Move all furniture to clean underneath it and blitz any neglected corners.
- Use the gentlest cleaning methods first, before moving onto something more aggressive for stubborn marks and stains.

---

understand the basics of Squash

Squash is a racket game played in an enclosed court. It's fast and furious—great for getting your heart pumping.

Two players hit a small rubber ball against the front, back and side walls of the court, aiming to hit the front wall without bouncing. Either player can score points, and the first to 11 wins the game. Matches are usually the best of five games. When you return the ball, it must hit the front wall between the "tin" at the bottom and the out line at the top. If it touches the line, it's out. A rally happens when both players correctly return the ball to each other, and you win a point if your opponent doesn't serve or return correctly.

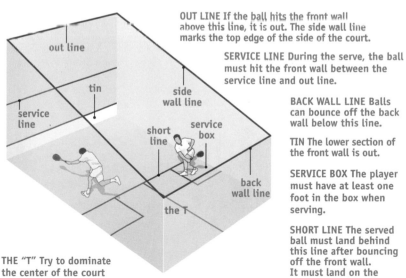

out line

OUT LINE If the ball hits the front wall above this line, it is out. The side wall line marks the top edge of the side of the court.

tin

SERVICE LINE During the serve, the ball must hit the front wall between the service line and out line.

service line

side wall line

BACK WALL LINE Balls can bounce off the back wall below this line.

TIN The lower section of the front wall is out.

short line

service box

SERVICE BOX The player must have at least one foot in the box when serving.

back wall line

the T

SHORT LINE The served ball must land behind this line after bouncing off the front wall. It must land on the opponent's side of the court.

THE "T" Try to dominate the center of the court so that your opponent has to do the running.

make a
Spun-sugar basket

Desserts served in spun-sugar baskets make an impressive display. They soften in a couple of hours, so don't make them too far ahead and only fill them just before serving.

YOU WILL NEED Sugar, water, pastry brush, vegetable oil, ladle, baking sheet, tablespoon. Optional: candy thermometer

1 Put ½ cup sugar and ⅔ cup water in a pan. Heat gently to dissolve, then boil rapidly until light brown in color and when a little syrup dropped into cold water immediately becomes hard and brittle; this is when the syrup reaches 300°F (150°C) (*see* SUGAR THERMOMETER). Plunge base of pan into cold water for a few seconds to stop the caramel from cooking. Leave for 1–2 minutes.

2 Use a pastry brush to grease the outside of the ladle and a baking sheet. With a tablespoon, trail thin threads of caramel over the ladle in a crisscross pattern. Finish by trailing a ring of caramel around the edge to make a rim. Leave to cool until crisp, then very gently ease off the rim with the point of a sharp knife. Lift off with the other hand and carefully transfer to the baking sheet to cool completely.

conquer
Stage fright

Actors aren't the only people who get stage fright. Anyone can get nervous when making a presentation or delivering a speech. A certain amount of nervousness is good, because it creates an adrenaline rush that makes you step up your game. But if you're crippled by stage fright, there are some things you can do that will help you to combat the fear.

■ Before you have to present a speech, find a quiet space and concentrate on breathing normally.
■ Mentally go over the first five minutes of your performance, whatever it may be. That is the crucial time, because your fear will evaporate once you get going.
■ Practice, practice and practice some more. Practice in front of friends and family to familiarize yourself with an audience, and practice in front of a mirror to build confidence and see how people will see you when you're on stage.
■ Sing or speak out loud before your performance to warm up your voice, and hum softly to keep it warm while you're waiting to speak.

apply **Stain** to wood

Staining is best done on light, undistinguished woods such as birch and new pine. Other, more distinctive woods—oak, beech, cherry, maple and mahogany—look best when left in their natural colors.

■ Before you stain bare wood, be sure that the finish is as smooth as it can be. Sand the surface with a fine sandpaper (*see* SAND), and use a soft brush to remove every speck of dust.
■ Test the wood stain on a scrap of the wood, or on a part of the object that will not usually be seen (the underside of a table, for example).

YOU WILL NEED **Wood stain, paintbrush, sponge or cloth, fine sandpaper**

■ Apply stain with a brush, new dish sponge or lint-free cloth. Work quickly in the direction of the grain, spreading liberally over the whole surface. Use a clean, lint-free cloth to wipe off the excess.

■ When dry, you may find that the liquid stain has raised the grain of the wood. Sand smooth with fine sandpaper. Reapply a very light coat of stain to any exposed grain, and wipe with a cloth, as before.

clean **Stainless steel**

Unless deeply scratched to expose its untreated center, stainless steel won't rust. But it does need a gentle touch to remove grease marks.

Pots and cutlery Use hot water and dish soap, removing stubborn food with a sponge or nylon-bristled brush. Polish with a clean, dry cloth. Remove any stubborn grease spots with a cloth soaked in white vinegar or use a store-bought stainless steel cleaner, following the instructions.

Sinks and appliances Use warm water and a squirt of dish soap on a sponge or soft cloth, working in the direction of the grain. Rinse with clear water and dry with paper towels or a soft cloth. If more cleaning is needed, scrub with a paste of baking soda and hot water, or with a solution of one part white vinegar in three parts of water. Baby oil or WD-40 wiped over the surface will also remove fingerprints and other marks.

remove Stains without leaving a trace

Quick, smart action is key to dealing with most stains. Always start with the gentlest cleaning tactics first and test any cleaning solution on an inconspicuous area before treating the stain. Remember that heat will almost always set a stain, so get something really clean before you tumble-dry or iron it. For nonwashable items, remove as much of the stain as possible, then get it dry cleaned. For stains on carpets, *see* CARPET.

Stain	Action	Tips and hints
FOOD (milk, cream and cheese-based foods; also feces and urine)	**Fresh stains on washable fabrics** Soak in cold water for 30 minutes. Put the stained area under cold running water and rub fabric gently against itself. Machine wash in warm water. **Dried-on stains on washable fabrics** Soak for 30 minutes in a solution of 1 tsp liquid detergent in 2 qt/L of cold water. Then machine wash in warm water. **Dried-on stains on upholstery** Lightly apply a solution of ½ tsp mild dish soap in 1 qt/L cold water onto a clean cloth. Blot the stain with the cloth, blot again with a paper towel, then rinse with a spray of cold water. Put a pad of paper towels over the area, weigh it down and allow to dry.	■ If stain persists after washing, don't dry. Soak for a further 30 minutes. ■ For persistent stains, try using oxygen bleach in the next wash cycle.
GREASE (including hand lotion, salad dressing and sunscreen)	**Washable fabrics** Pretreat with liquid laundry detergent or a prewash stain-removing spray applied directly onto the stain. Machine wash immediately in hot water. **Satin** Dust with flour, leave for an hour, then brush with a soft-bristled brush. Silk satin can be handwashed in ice-cold water with mild soap.	■ Blot up as much as possible with paper towels before treating. ■ Try ironing a fresh stain over blotting paper.
BLOOD	**Washable clothing** Blot with a clean rag wetted with cold water. Or mix a few drops of dish soap with cold water in a bowl and dab onto the stain. Leave for 30 minutes. Or try an oxygen-based cleaner, and wash as usual. **Washable upholstery** Spray with cold water and blot with a clean towel. Repeat until clean. **Bedding** Rub in shampoo until fully absorbed. Lather with a stiff brush, then rinse with cold water. Let air dry.	■ Always use cold water to prevent blood stains from setting. ■ Be gentle. Work from the outside in to avoid spreading the stain. ■ Take non-washable items to be dry cleaned.
WINE (red and white)	**Washable fabrics** Soak for half an hour in a solution of 1 tsp detergent in 2 qt/L warm water. Machine wash in the hottest possible water.	■ For stubborn stains, try an oxygen-based cleaner.
GRASS (also "dyes" such as beet, mustard and ink)	**Washable fabrics** Pretreat with pre-wash stain remover, or apply liquid laundry detergent and rinse well. Soak in oxygen bleach solution, following the package instructions, then launder as appropriate for the fabric. Hairspray is a great tool for removing ink stains; simply spray the stained area, making sure the spray penetrates the fabric, and let it sit for a few minutes. Then wash in the machine right away.	■ If stain persists, try soaking in chlorine bleach and water, but remember that this may cause irreparable damage to the fabric.

Stake plants

Without stakes, plants will sag and be more prone to damage from wind and weather. Once beaten down by the rain, they might never recover.

Slender stems
Push in a stake near the plant. Use string to gather the stems together near the crown and tie to the stake.

Tall perennials
Buy or make a cylinder of chicken wire tied to a couple of stakes, and place it over flopping plants.

Short and medium perennials
As plants begin to grow, ring them with bamboo canes or branches. Tie rings of green string at 6 in. (15 cm) intervals to support the growing stems. You can buy plastic-coated metal kits that link together in a similar way.

Protect your eyes Be careful not to put your eye out when bending over in the garden! Cover the stakes with plastic bottles or table tennis balls.

fix creaky Stairs

It's much easier to deal with a creak if you can access the stairs from underneath. To work from above, you'll need to lift the carpet (make sure you'll be able to put it back afterward).

From under the staircase, ask someone to walk up and down the stairs, so you can pinpoint the creaking step or steps.

■ Cut small blocks (right) from wood scraps—two for each squeaky step. Drill four holes in each block, with one pair at a right angle.
■ Use carpenter's glue to hold the blocks in the angle between the tread (the step) and riser (the upright part), then screw into place.
■ Take care that your screws are the right length so they don't poke through the step.

From above, use a chisel to pry away the tread from the top of the riser slightly, and insert some glue.
■ Drill clearance holes every 10 in. (25 cm) along the tread edge and pilot holes into the top of the riser. Countersink the holes, and screw down the tread.
■ Fill the holes with wood filler and smooth with sandpaper.

start a Stamp collection

Stamps are tiny works of art, expressions of nationhood and markers of history. They are often worth far more than their face value.

Tell everyone about your new hobby, and ask them to save any foreign or commemorative stamps. Stamps are fragile and need to be handled with care, so ask friends and family to send you stamps still attached to the corners of their envelopes and to not try to remove them for you.

For serious collecting, you will need an album, corner mounts, stamp tongs, scissors, a magnifying glass, reference books on correct care and preservation, and a recognized catalog of current stamp values.

To remove a stamp for collection, cut the stamp corner from the envelope (not too close) and float it in tepid water, or lay the stamp face up on damp blotting paper or newspaper until it peels off. Dry it face down on blotting paper, and flatten it between the pages of a book before you mount it.

Decide how you want to organize your stamps—for example, by region or theme. There's a peculiar excitement in coming by stamps from countries that no longer exist—from Abyssinia to Zanzibar via Bechuanaland, Ceylon, Prussia, Rhodesia and many more. They all tell a tale.

Start to buy Dealers and stores sell packages of used stamps. In the early stages of your collection, go for packs containing a wide range to lay down the basics of your album. Sell any stamps that don't interest you.

Use the internet—with care Websites make it easy to research and buy stamps to add to your collection. The most reputable will show clear photographs, but it's not always possible to discern quality and condition.

Join a collecting club Enthusiasts love to share their knowledge and experience. You can learn from them and take the opportunity to buy and sell or swap duplicates from your own and their collections.

cook a perfect Steak

What constitutes the perfect steak is really a matter of taste. For one person, it might require a quick flash in the pan; for another, only meat that is almost burnt will do.

Cooking Fry steak in a very hot, lightly oiled skillet. Lower the heat to medium after the first 3 minutes. For grilling, heat the grill to hot, brush the meat with oil or marinade, and cook for 1 minute on each side, about 3 in. (7.5 cm) from the flame. Then turn down the grill to medium and use the timings given below. Turn halfway through cooking.

Testing The cooking times given here are per side for round, filet mignon or sirloin steaks about 1 in. (2.5 cm) thick. The best way to test is by pressing the steak gently with your finger. Match the feel of the fleshy part at the base of your thumb (below). Touch your thumb to the tip of your first, middle, ring or little finger to emulate the feel of a rare to well-done steak.

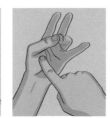

Rare
- Fry: 2 minutes.
- Grill: 2½ minutes.
- Finger test: offers little resistance when pressed.

Medium rare
- Fry: 3 minutes.
- Grill: 3½ minutes.
- Finger test: feels slightly firmer when pressed.

Medium
- Fry: 4½ minutes.
- Grill: 5½ minutes.
- Finger test: feels firm when pressed.

Well done
- Fry: 5–7 minutes.
- Grill: 6–8 minutes.
- Finger test: feels quite firm when pressed.

use a Staple gun

Staple guns are often quicker and neater than a hammer and nails when you need to attach something thin to a solid base. For example, they are good for repairing upholstery or picture frames, attaching chicken wire to posts, securing carpet underlay or insulation and sticking papers to a bulletin board.

Staple guns can be manual or electric, but all kinds fire the staple into the materials to be joined together, so they should always be used with care. Different grades and sizes of staple and stapler can be used, depending how heavy-duty the job is.

- Hold the gun firmly and make sure it's in the right position before you fire the staple.
- Take great care to observe safety procedures: Keep your fingers out of the way and never fire the gun toward anyone.

golden rules

STEAK SECRETS
- Allow meat to come to room temperature before cooking.
- Time cooking accurately.
- Add salt after cooking, but pepper before cooking.
- Plan your cooking times so everyone's steaks are ready at the same time.

get to know
Star constellations
see pages 310–311

S
get to know Star constellations

Humans have been finding patterns and meanings in the stars for millennia, and we scour the night skies with the same fascination today. Here's a selection of heavenly wonders for stargazing beginners.

Looking up For city dwellers used to skies awash with light pollution, a star-spangled, midnight-blue sky is a revelation. At first it looks like a blizzard of lights, but filter out the fainter stars and you'll start to see the constellations. There are 88 of these patterns of celestial bodies. They aren't scientifically significant, but the images appeal to the human imagination.

THE SKY IS EVER CHANGING You'll see different constellations at different times of year and hours of the night, depending on your latitude and the way the planet is facing. The moon, planets and most constellations, including those of the zodiac, are visible all over the world, but constellations close to the poles stay above the horizon all night and are only visible from one hemisphere. In the southern hemisphere you'll never see the Big Dipper, while people in the north have never experienced the glory of the Southern Cross and the jewel-box cluster within it. The southern hemisphere has 11 such constellations, the northern only five. Star charts can be a bit baffling at first, but once you pick out the more familiar and distinctive constellations, everything begins to fall into place and you can start to spot some of the big names up there in lights.

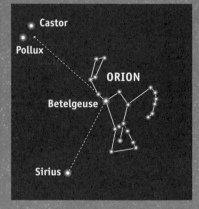

SCORPIUS The zodiacal constellation Scorpius rises in the sky as Orion sets—a nightly reminder that in Greek mythology, the hunter Orion was killed by the sting of a scorpion. At the heart of the constellation lies Antares, the thirteenth-brightest star in the night sky, with the body and tail of the scorpion arching below and the claws fanning out above. Every couple of years the planet Mars appears to travel closely past Antares, and their similarity in colour and brightness makes them easy to confuse. This is how Antares came by its name, which translates as "rival to Mars."

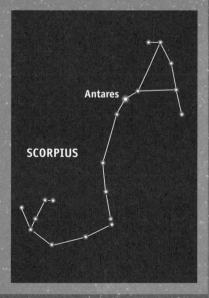

A HUNTER, THE TWINS AND A BIG DOG Orion, the celestial hunter, can be located in the winter months by the three bright stars that form his belt, from which hangs a sword. His left shoulder is represented by the bright star Betelgeuse. Move your eyes up and left from the belt to locate it, then onward to find Castor and Pollux, a constellation dominated by two bright stars visualised as the heads of the Gemini twins. Trace the slanting line of Orion's belt left and down to locate Sirius, the brightest star in the whole sky. It's also known as "the Dog Star" because it forms part of the constellation Canis Major ("the Big Dog"), Orion's faithful hound.

THE SEA SERPENT AND THE LITTLE DOG Another weird creature best seen from the southern hemisphere (although she rears her ugly heads in the north from January to May) is the Hydra, a giant mythological beast with the body of a dog and 100 snake-like heads. This is the longest constellation in the sky and covers the largest area. It's so long that it takes more than six hours to rise completely. It resembles a snake twisting its way toward Canis Minor ("Little Dog"), which is visible in the northern hemisphere from December until April, and in the southern from November to April. It represents the smaller of Orion's two hunting dogs. Within Canis Minor, Procyon is the eighth-brightest star in the night sky. The name means "before the dog," which it's called because it rises before Sirius.

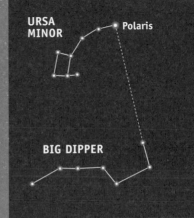

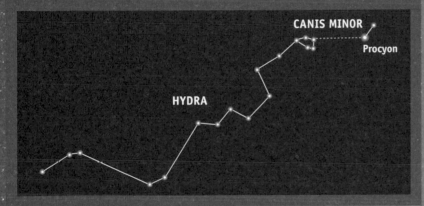

THE BIG DIPPER, GREAT BEAR AND LITTLE BEAR For star-spotters in the north, the Big Dipper, part of the constellation Ursa Major ("the Great Bear"), is a constant presence, one of the most easily recognizable star groups in the sky. It has the shape of a ladle: three stars for the handle, four for the bowl. The two stars farthest from the handle are known as "pointer stars." Follow their line and they draw your eye to Polaris, the North Star in the constellation Ursa Minor ("Little Bear") and the tip of the bear's implausibly long tail. Ursa Minor consists of seven main stars and is also known as the Little Dipper, also for its resemblance to a ladle. Wherever you are in the northern hemisphere, if you're facing Polaris, you're facing north.

A CROSS, A CENTAUR AND A WOLF Also known as "Crux," the Southern Cross is one of the best-known groups of stars, thanks to its appearance on the flags of Australia and New Zealand. Despite its nation-defining status, the constellation is quite small and

hard to spot. But once you learn to recognize it, you can use the Southern Cross as a point of reference for sky-watching. It's a compact formation of four bright stars (another less bright star, Epsilon, is included on the Australian flag). Helpfully, two "pointer stars," Beta Centauri and Alpha Centauri, are always nearby to show the viewer where to look. These are part of the constellation Centaurus ("the Centaur"). The mythical beast, half-man, half-horse, bears a lance, which he uses to kill Lupus, the wolf in front of him (visible from February to October). The dazzling Alpha Centauri is the third-brightest star in the southern sky and the closest to the Sun. Alpha Centauri actually comprises a double star and a nearby red dwarf called Proxima Centauri.

Steam food
for maximum goodness

Steaming is an excellent way of preserving the flavor, vitamins and color of vegetables, and can be used for delicate items, such as fish. The technique also works well for sweet and savory puddings or custards, cooked in a little liquid in a covered pan.

Equipment Specially made stacking steamer pans can be used on the stove, or you can buy standalone electric steamers. Alternatively, you can use a perforated basket with short legs, placed over a little water in a pot with a tightly fitting lid.

Steaming vegetables
Typical steaming times are:
5–10 minutes spinach, cabbage, zucchini.
10–15 minutes broccoli, green beans, cauliflower.
15–20 minutes: brussels sprouts, new potatoes.
40–45 minutes parsnips, beets, artichokes.

Fish and shellfish Wrap in parchment paper or foil before steaming, or place on a sheet of parchment paper in the steamer to make it easy to lift out without breaking.
5–10 minutes thin fillets, scallops, shrimp, mussels.
10–15 minutes thick fillets.
20–25 minutes whole trout or sea bass (longer for bigger fish).

Steamed puddings or custards
Use an ovenproof bowl covered with a double layer of parchment paper, then a layer of foil, all tied on tightly to prevent water from seeping in. Sit in a pan in a little water, topping up as necessary as it cooks. A sponge pudding will take 1½–2 hours to cook, depending on the recipe.

add a flourish with Stencils

Stenciled motifs lend a real touch of personality to your home. They can give new life to old furniture or transform a plain wall.

Before you start, practice on a piece of paper to perfect your technique. Working from the edges in helps to prevent paint from running under the stencil and losing definition.

■ When you remove the stencil, wipe off any excess paint. Make sure the stencil is clean and dry before reusing it.

YOU WILL NEED Stencil, masking tape, paint, stenciling brushes (with tightly packed, stiff bristles), synthetic sponge for a smooth finish or natural sponge for a more textured look

The brush method This technique is also known as "stippling," because of the jabbing movement you make with the brush.
■ Wipe clean and prepare the surface to be stenciled. Sand it lightly, if necessary, to remove loose old paint or smooth out surface imperfections.

■ Position the stencil and secure it with masking tape.
■ Dip the brush into the paint and tap off any excess on a sheet of scrap paper. If you overload it you risk drips, spoiling the effect.
■ Hold the brush at a right angle to the surface and start to stipple— that is, apply color with repeated light dabs of the bristle ends.
■ Aim to build color gradually, blending shades rather than changing abruptly. Use a different brush for each shade.

The sponge method This gives you good control over the paint texture.
■ Fold or cut the sponge to make a small pad, dip it in the paint and dab it on an old rag or paper towel to remove any excess.
■ Apply with light dabs or gentle swirls.

Sterilize jars and baby bottles

Whether you're making strawberry jam or preparing a baby bottle, wash containers thoroughly in soapy water before you sterilize them. You must also ensure that your hands and working area are clean (*see* HANDS).

Jam jars can be sterilized in the oven. Arrange the clean jars on a baking sheet, open end up, and make sure that they aren't touching. Put into a cold oven. Heat the oven to 225°F (110°C). Leave it on for 45 minutes, then turn off. Remove the jars when they're cool enough to handle, and place them upside down on a clean cloth till needed.

Baby equipment can be sterilized by boiling them in a pot—but check first that the bottles and nipples can handle it. It's best to keep a pot specially for this purpose. Fill the pot with water and submerge all the feeding equipment. Check that there are no air pockets inside the bottles. Bring the pot to a boil at 212°F (100°C) and keep it at that temperature for ten minutes, with the lid on.

A specialized steam sterilizer is the quickest and easiest way to sterilize baby bottles and feeding paraphernalia. The equipment will remain sterile inside the steamer for six hours, or until it's opened. You can also buy a microwave sterilizer. *See also* BABY.

make the most of Stick-on vinyl

A staple of many craft and organizational projects, stick-on or self-adhesive vinyl gives an easy but durable finish. It's usually sold as a roll, can be translucent or opaque and comes in a variety of colors. Cut the length you need and peel away the backing little by little, smoothing the plastic over the surface to prevent bubbles. Smooth out any bubbles with the edge of a ruler.

Covering books Self-adhesive vinyl makes a hard-wearing protective cover for books. (You have to commit to it, though—it isn't removable.)

Adding decoration You don't need to cover an entire object. Sheets can be cut into self-adhesive shapes to dress up shelves, storage boxes and more.

Window frosting Patterned clear or frosted vinyl can be used to cover windows for decoration or privacy, or to make a large plate-glass window more visible to any birds or humans who might run into it.

relieve a Stiff neck

Your neck has to carry the weight of your head all day long, and poor posture or a sagging mattress can lead to strain. See your doctor if the pain is sudden and severe or accompanied by other symptoms, such as high temperature, pins and needles, or numbness in your arms or hands. Otherwise, follow this simple advice to speed your recovery.

Keep moving Try to move as normally, but gently, as possible. Taking mild painkillers will help to make this more comfortable. Concentrate on not slumping or slouching, to avoid further strain.

Warm it A gentle massage in a hot shower will help (*see* MASSAGE). Or try wrapping a hot-water bottle and holding it to the source of pain. A compress made by soaking a small towel in hot water can also provide relief.

Sleep on it A special neck pillow can make a real difference if you have chronic pain, or it may just be time to replace your regular pillows.

Stir-fry
a quick, delicious meal

The key to a good stir-fry is fast cooking, allowing vegetables to keep their crunch and flavor.

Choosing a wok A rounded base is best for even cooking. For everyday use, stainless steel or nonstick woks are most practical—choose something that will be able to handle high temperatures.

Cooking tips There will be no time for chopping while you cook, so cut all ingredients into small, even-sized pieces before you start.
- Heat 2–3 tbsp of vegetable oil until very hot, swirling it to coat the whole surface of the wok.
- Begin with the meat and set aside when almost cooked. (You'll add it back in near the end of cooking.)
- Add vegetables in batches, according to cooking time. Start with dense vegetables, like broccoli and carrots, and add leafy ones last.
- Scoop, push and flip the pieces continuously, moving each piece of food over the entire surface of the wok. It should take no more than 5–10 minutes to cook a stir-fry.
- Add the reserved meat and any sauce. Heat thoroughly and serve.

grow juicy
Strawberries

Fresh strawberries are hard to beat. They're easy to grow, as long as the soil is well drained and the site is sunny. They also do well in pots and hanging baskets.

Choosing varieties Single-crop strawberries produce one flush of fruit in summer. Perpetual varieties grow from early summer to autumn.

Planting For an early summer crop, plant in early autumn and protect plants with cloches over winter. Spring plantings will produce fruit in late summer. Position plants 1½ ft (45 cm) apart.

Routine care Look out for slugs and snails that can devour your crop; put straw or a strawberry mat under each plant to keep the berries off the ground. Water plants regularly.

Propagating new plants In late summer, strawberries put out shoots, or runners, with new plants growing on them. Choose up to four of the strongest from each plant and use bent wire to peg them into the soil or pots of compost sunk into the bed. When the new plants are firmly rooted, cut them away from the parent plant to use next year.

take stock of your food Storage

You should always have the ingredients you need to make an impromptu meal—just make sure everything's stored properly.

Keep an eye on expiry dates and always put newly bought food at the back of the pantry. Airtight tins and jars with well-fitting lids are invaluable for storing dry goods once their packages have been opened, but write down the date and recommended storage time before you throw the packaging away. Clips and twist ties are useful for keeping bags tightly sealed.

How long to keep it	Typical food (unopened)
Less than 1 month	Cakes and other sweet baked goods
1 month	Coffee beans, cookies
2–3 months	Self-raising and whole-wheat flour, ground coffee, breakfast cereal, cooking oil, stock cubes, mayonnaise, potato chips
6 months	All-purpose flour, oats, icing (confectioner's) sugar, jam, honey, nuts (whole and ground), dried yeast, dried herbs, baking powder, dried mushrooms, peanut butter, olive/vegetable oil
1 year	Cocoa, instant coffee, chocolate, tea, dried fruit, brown sugar, spices, ketchup, mustard, dried beans and peas, lentils
2 years	Pasta, pickles, sauces, tomato paste, canned vegetables with low acidity (corn, for example), rice, gravy mix, sauces, vinegar
5 years	Canned fish in oil, canned vegetables with high acidity (tomatoes, for example)
Indefinitely	White sugar

Food dating Apart from some canned goods, foods are labeled in the following ways to give guidelines for safe storage.

Use by The last date recommended by the manufacturer for using the product. This is particularly important for yeast and baby food.

Best before The date after which food becomes stale, even if it's still edible. Applies to food such as cereal, jam, sauces and dried fruit.

Sell by The date before which a product should be sold to allow for some time before actual consumption—usually reserved for fresh foods.

practice basic Stretching exercises

Stretching can make you feel relaxed and help keep you limber, as well as preventing painful, tight muscles after exercise.

Stretch slowly, feeling your muscles tense but stopping before it's painful. Never bounce to extend a stretch, but maintain the pressure even as you gradually reach a little farther. Alternate sides, repeating five times on each.

For your chest and shoulders, stand at a right angle to a wall. Reach across to press against the wall. Make sure you're close enough to do this without leaning in. Keep your hips facing forward and twist your torso toward the wall to feel a stretch in the back of your shoulder. Hold for 15 seconds, then swap sides.

For your calves, stand arm's length from a wall and brace yourself with your palms flat against it. Step back with your left leg and lean in gently, bending the right leg at the knee, while keeping both heels firmly on the floor and your back and left leg straight. Press against the wall until you feel a stretch in your calf, and hold for 15 seconds. Push yourself upright and repeat with the other leg.

For a side stretch, stand with feet shoulder-width apart and raise your right arm. Relax your left arm in front of you. Gently lean to the left, curving your right arm over your head, palm down. Stop when you feel a pull from hip to shoulder. Hold for 15 seconds then straighten. Repeat on the other side.

combat Stress

A little stress can energize you for a while, but living with too much stress is exhausting and bad for your health. Deep relaxation, yoga or meditation (*see* MEDITATE, RELAXATION *and* YOGA) can help to relieve the symptoms, but to really conquer the problem, you have to take a practical approach to stress in everyday life.

Exercise releases tension, burns off adrenaline and other stress hormones that the body generates, and releases mood-enhancing endorphins.

A long walk in the country can really clear your head and put things in perspective.

A heart-to-heart with a friend will often bring solace. Don't bottle up your anxieties: Talk them through with friends and family, or ask your doctor about counseling.

Try aromatherapy using calming essential oils such as cardamom, camomile, lavender, rose, vetiver and ylang-ylang. Use them as perfume, bath oils or in an aromatherapy diffuser.

Alcohol, tobacco and drugs aren't the answer—no matter how badly you might want that kind of escape. All cause problems without solving any, and could give you serious health problems.

Review your values. Is it time to get out of the rat race and cool down your ambition? Should you move to a more modest home if you're having trouble keeping up with payments? Identify the main cause of your stress and think about what you can do to eradicate it.

S

treat a Sty

A sty is an inflamed red lump on the eyelid, caused by a clogged eyelash follicle. It may cause the eye to water, and can take several days before it ruptures and heals.

- Apply a compress such as a clean, soft facecloth soaked in warm water and wrung out.
- Or put 2 tsp of dried pot marigold flowers in a bowl, add 2 cups of boiling water and leave for 20 minutes. Strain the infusion and use it to soak the compress.

---

solve a Sudoku

The unalterable law of sudoku is that each number from 1 to 9 can appear only once in any row, column or box of nine squares. This means that the puzzle can be solved purely through logic and deduction.

Look at the puzzle below. In the box of nine squares in the top left-hand corner, the number 2 can only go in the third row, because there's already a 2 in the top two rows of the grid. This kind of thinking, applied repeatedly to different parts of the puzzle, should help you solve most sudokus.

1				(2)	8	3		
	8		1		4			(2)
7	2	6		8				
					7		5	
2	7		5				1	9
	3		9	4				6
		8		9		7		5
3			8		6		9	
	4	2	7					3

recognize the symptoms of a Stroke

A person has a stroke when a blood clot blocks the flow of blood to the brain, or a blood vessel in the brain bursts. The onset of symptoms is sudden and sometimes dramatic. Learn what to look for so you can take action right away.

Take FAST action A stroke causes numbness, weakness or paralysis on one side of the body. Speech may be slurred, and there may be blurred vision or loss of sight, unsteadiness and confusion or complete unconsciousness. If you suspect someone's having a stroke, use the FAST test.

FACE. Look at the face. Do you notice any weakness? Ask the casualty to smile. A one-sided smile, while the other side of the face droops, suggests stroke.

ARMS. Ask the casualty to lift each arm in turn. If they can't lift one of them, this is further evidence of stroke.

SPEAK. Ask the casualty to speak. If they have just had a stroke, they may not understand you or be able to respond at all.

TIME. Act quickly. If the casualty fails any of these tests, call 911. Offer reassurance. Check and make note of levels of consciousness. Prepare to give CPR (*see* CPR).

Risk factors for strokes include smoking, high blood pressure, heart disease, being overweight, high cholesterol, diabetes and excessive alcohol and caffeine consumption. It's not something that just happens to the elderly—even children can have strokes. A stroke is certainly alarming, but if you recognize the warning signs and act quickly to get fast medical help, the stroke victim can still have a solid recovery.

pack a Suitcase

Be a smart traveler and pack only what you'll need for your trip. The secret is to plan ahead, rather than packing half your wardrobe at the last minute. Bon voyage!

■ Make a list of everything you might want—then edit it.

■ Lay the items you want to take on your bed. Edit again.

■ Organize your items into four groups: smaller items, such as underwear and swimwear; pants that may crease; casual items, such as jeans and T-shirts; other items that may crease, such as dresses, blouses and skirts. Follow the guide below to pack each group layer by layer.

■ If you're taking casual jeans and T-shirts, the best way to save space is to roll them up tight before packing.

TOP LAYER
Clothes that will crease should be carefully folded and laid on top.

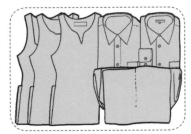

If items, such as jackets or dresses, can be laid flat rather than being folded, do so.

MIDDLE LAYER
Place a layer of jeans and T-shirts tightly rolled into cylinders. Pack any towels the same way.

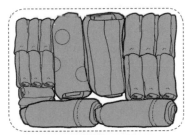

BOTTOM LAYER
Add toiletry bag, swimwear, underwear, socks and tights.

AT THE SPINE
Put shoes and belts at the spine. Tuck rolled socks inside shoes to save space.

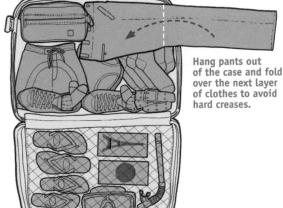

Hang pants out of the case and fold over the next layer of clothes to avoid hard creases.

IN LID
Place flat items in the flaps of the lid.

use a Sugar thermometer

(candy thermometer)

A sugar, or candy, thermometer helps to take the guesswork out of making jam, caramel and sweets of all kinds.

Before use, put the thermometer in a bowl of hot water to make it react faster. Quickly wash and dry the thermometer and submerge its bulb in the pot, tilting the pot's contents if necessary. After use, put it back in the hot water immediately to prevent sugar from drying on it. *See also* JAM *and* MARMALADE.

These are the temperatures and descriptions of hot sugar commonly referred to in recipes.

230°F (110°C)	Thread stage	Thin syrup, jam, marmalade
235°F (112°C)	Soft-ball stage	Fondants, fudge
245°F (118°C)	Firm-ball stage	Caramels
250°C (121°C)	Hard-ball stage	Nougat, marshmallows
270°F (132°C)	Soft-crack stage	Saltwater taffy, butterscotch
300°F (149°C)	Hard-crack stage	Toffee, nut brittle
338°F (170°C)	Caramel stage	Caramel coatings, praline

✧ golden rules

SUGAR THERMOMETER

■ **Always make sure the bulb is completely covered when testing temperatures.**

■ **Don't let the thermometer touch the base or sides of the pan.**

avoid and soothe
Sunburn

Sunburn is caused by overexposure to the ultraviolet rays in sunlight. It increases the risk of skin cancer and can age your skin.

Stay protected
- Children and fair-skinned people in particular should keep covered up in bright sun, wear a wide-brimmed hat and stay in the shade.
- Infants should be kept out of the sun entirely. Invest in covers for strollers and car windows, and consider buying a UV-protected tent for them to play in outside.
- Use a sunscreen with an SPF of at least 30, even if you never burn. Apply a generous amount before you go out in the sun. Reapply regularly —at least every 2–3 hours—and after getting wet.

If you do get burned...
- Cool the burn by sponging it with lukewarm water, or take a tepid shower.
- Stay hydrated. Drink plenty of fluids and avoid alcohol.
- Apply soothing lotion to moisturize the skin and prevent it from feeling tight. Calamine lotion relieves the irritation.
- More serious sunburns require aid. Seek medical attention.
- Always consult a doctor if a baby or small child has been sunburned.

Be aware that sunburn can occur even on overcast days, especially at high altitudes.

get on board with Surfing

You don't have to be a dedicated soul surfer to experience the thrill of catching a wave.

If you're a beginner, you should use a wide stable board, no less that 8¼ ft (2.5 m) long. This kind of board is easier to balance on than the shorter variety used by many experienced surfers. At first, you should surf only in "white water"—the part of the wave that has crested and broken, where it's a little easier.

Before you can surf, you have to paddle out to the waves. To paddle, arch your back, keep your head up, and propel yourself with long, alternate strokes of your arms, as if doing the crawl.

To catch a wave, turn your board toward the shore. As you feel a wave coming up behind you, paddle fast with your head low. If you pick up enough speed, the wave will carry you forward.

To stand up, place your hands on the outer edges of the board. When you feel the wave lifting the board behind you, bring your knees up to your chest.

Get up on your feet, letting go of the board as you do. Your feet should be shoulder-width apart, and at a right angle to the direction you're moving in.

roll your own Sushi

Sushi is made with special Japanese rice that's sticky when cooked, and can include vegetables, raw or cooked fish, or cooked shellfish.

YOU WILL NEED **Sushi ingredients, large plate, rolling mat, sharp knife**

MAKES ABOUT 20 ROLLS
⅔ **cup sushi rice, rinsed and cooked**
1½ **tbsp mirin (rice wine)**
1 **tbsp sugar**
3–4 **sheets of nori (dried seaweed)**
1½ **tsp wasabi paste, plus extra to serve**
1 **avocado, thinly sliced**

4 oz (100 g) **fresh raw fish such as tuna or salmon, thinly sliced**
½ **cucumber, seeded and cut into matchsticks**

TO SERVE
light soy sauce and pickled ginger

1 Spread the rice on a large plate to cool. Mix the mirin and sugar, and heat gently until the sugar dissolves. Spread a sheet of nori onto the sushi mat shiny side up, and add the rice in a thin layer, leaving a 1 in. (2.5 cm) gap at one end. Dab on a little wasabi paste. Add fish and vegetables in a single layer in the center.

2 With the help of the mat, and working away from you, roll up tightly, then squeeze firmly. Unwrap and cut into 1 in. (2.5 cm) rolls. Repeat with the remaining ingredients. Serve with the soy sauce, ginger and additional wasabi paste.

describe your Symptoms to a doctor

Visible symptoms such as a lump, rash, bruise or swelling speak for themselves. Underlying discomfort is harder to describe. Before you visit your doctor, prepare to answer these questions to help with the diagnosis.

- What exactly are you experiencing?
- When did you first notice something wrong?
- Are symptoms constant? If not, when do they occur?
- Does anything make symptoms better or worse?
- How do they affect your work and home life?
- Has anyone else in your household had the same symptoms?

Use plain language—say dull ache, stabbing pain, nausea, weakness— and use a scale of 1–10 if it helps. Be ready with information about any medication, supplements or herbal remedies you take. Your doctor might ask about habits and major life events that may have affected your health.

Swim the crawl

The crawl is the most useful swimming stroke—it's fast and efficient.

1 Extend your left arm forward. Pull your right arm along your body, crooking your elbow so that your hand passes beneath your body. Keep your hand flat and your fingers together. Your right arm should exit the water by your thigh with elbow high and wrist low.

2 Roll to your left with your face in the water. Arc your right arm forward so the upper arm passes close to your ear. Anchor your left hand in the water and pull down and back beneath your body, as in step 1.

3 As your left hand reaches your thigh, turn it so the little finger leads. Lift your left elbow so it leaves the water first. Spear your right arm into the water, fingers pointed.

4 As your left arm comes forward and your right goes back, roll to the right. Repeat steps 1–4 giving six strong scissor kicks during every cycle.

Breathing Your mouth clears the surface just before your hand exits on the same side. Take the chance to inhale deeply.

fix a wobbly leg
on a Table

Evening up the legs on a wobbly table isn't hard—but if the item is antique or valuable, you might want to call in a professional.

First, check the floor The problem may not be with the table, but an uneven floor. Place the table on a flat, level sheet of particleboard or plywood and check to see whether it still wobbles. Use a tape measure to see if all the legs are the same length.

If the table still wobbles, place thin squares of wood under the legs until the table is stable.

If just one leg is short, cut a piece of wood that fits the gap, and attach it to the base of the leg with glue and a countersunk screw. Use a chisel to shape the wood to match the leg and smooth the edges with sandpaper, then stain or paint to match the leg. If the table has decorative feet, detach the shortest leg, if possible, and position your piece of wood at the top.

If more than one leg is short, trim all legs to match the shortest one.

■ Identify the longest leg.
■ Set a pair of geometry compasses so that the point is touching the particleboard or plywood sheet, and the pencil is touching the bottom of the leg.
■ Mark the other three legs with the compass set at this distance. The compass point should always be in touch with the particleboard or plywood, while the pencil marks the leg at the point where it needs to be trimmed.
■ Saw or chisel the excess from each leg, and smooth with sandpaper. The table should now be level.

set a Table for dinner

A table set for a celebratory meal not only looks great, but serves a practical purpose by giving diners everything they need.

Flatware (knives, forks and spoons) Always arrange from the outside in, working in the order that implements will be used.
■ Knives and spoons go on the right of the setting; forks on the left. Forks should be placed with tines upward, knives with blades facing in.
■ Lay a dessert spoon and fork horizontally above the setting, spoon above fork, with the spoon pointing left and the fork pointing right.
■ Lay a butter knife on the side plate.

Plates and bowls
■ A side plate for bread should be laid to the left of the setting. The plate can sit right next to the dinner fork if there's space, or above and to the left.
■ Other plates will usually be brought with the food, but a base plate is often put in the middle of the setting. The folded napkin (see NAPKIN) should be placed on top of this—unless the first course has already been served, in which case place the napkin next to the fork.

Glassware Put a water glass above the knives. To its right, put a wine glass or even multiple glasses, if different kinds of beverages will be served.

have impeccable Table manners

Good table manners are mostly a matter of simple courtesy. Don't do anything to offend your hosts or the people you're dining with.

■ Never start to eat until everyone at the table has been served.
■ Talking is as important as eating, so never take a mouthful larger than you can swallow quickly. You need to be able to reply if someone asks you a question. Never speak with your mouth full.
■ Talk to the diners on either side of you, giving them equal attention. Don't shout across the table or dominate the conversation—listen attentively, ask

relevant questions and steer clear of controversial topics that could cause an argument (*see* CONVERSATION).

- Be alert to the needs of the people you're eating with and offer to pass sauces, condiments or other dishes without being asked.
- Praise the host's cooking in a meaningful way. *This is great* isn't very specific. Something like *What incredible fish—do I taste fennel?* will make your host happy, and could start an interesting conversation.
- If you feel out of place at a formal dinner, follow the host's lead. And, for goodness sake, don't drink more to compensate for your awkwardness—that definitely will not end well!

---

play Table tennis (aka Ping-Pong)

As in other racket sports, the aim of table tennis (or Ping-Pong) is to prevent your opponent from returning the ball. It's fast, furious and lots of fun.

Hold your bat however it feels most comfortable: the shakehands grip or penhold (right).

At the start of a game, the serving player tosses the ball up and hits it so it bounces once on their own side and onto the other side of the net. The opponent attempts to return the ball to bounce in the server's court.

shakehands grip front

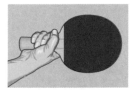
shakehands grip back

penhold grip front

penhold grip back

5 ft (1.52 m)
9 ft (2.74 m)
30 in. (76 cm)

A point is scored when a player fails to get the ball in the opponent's court (that is, fails to hit the ball or hits a shot that misses the opposing half of the table). A player wins when they reach 11 points—they must be two points higher than their opponent. A match usually consists of the best of five or seven sets. Service alternates every two points unless the score reaches 10-10, where it alternates every point until one player wins.

In doubles, the ball must be served diagonally, so that it bounces first in the right-hand half of the server's court, then in the right-hand half of the receiver's. After that, the four players must hit the ball in rotation.

learn shortcuts for times Tables

It can take hours of math classes to memorize the times tables, but there are some quick tricks that will speed up those on-the-spot calculations.

One or nothing Any number multiplied by 1 equals itself. Multiply anything by 0 and it will make zero.

Multiples of 2 Anything multiplied by 2 will be that number added to itself, so 2 x 8 will equal the same as 8 + 8: 16.

The law of 5 A number multiplied by 5 will always end in 5 or 0. If you multiply an even number by 5, the answer will be half that number, with 0 after it: 6 x 5 = 30 (half of 6 is 3; add a zero and you get 30). When multiplying an odd number by 5, take one away from that number, halve it and add a 5: to figure out 7 x 5, subtract one from 7 to get 6, halve 6 to get 3, then put a 5 after the 3 to reach 35.

To the power of 10 To multiply any number by 10, simply add a zero: 10 x 4 = 40.

Eleventh heaven Single-digit numbers multiplied by 11 are simply that number repeated: 4 x 11 = 44. For double-digit numbers, separate the two digits, add them together and put the result in the middle: 11 x 26, for example, is 2_6; fill in the middle digit by adding 2 and 6 (2 + 6 = 8). 11 x 26 = 286.

Tack fabric

Tacking, or basting, stitches are used to hold pieces of fabric in place before they're permanently sewn together, usually after pinning. Whatever you're sewing, accurate tacking is key to a good end result.

Starting off Thread a needle with thread that's a different color than your fabric. Cotton basting or tacking thread is cheaper than sewing thread because it's weaker, but you can use any kind of thread. Knot one end and insert the needle.

Even tacking/basting From right to left, make stitches about ¼ in. (5 mm) long and the same distance apart. Use even tacking/basting for smooth fabrics, on curved seams and all areas that need careful fitting.

Uneven tacking/basting Sew long stitches about 1 in. (2.5 cm) long with about ¼ in. (5 mm) between them. Use for straight seams and for holding pieces in place while quilting (*see* QUILT).

Finishing End each piece of tacking or basting stitch with two or three stitches worked over each other. The stitches needs to hold firm but must still be easy to remove once the fabric is stitched.

master some Tai chi moves

This gentle form of exercise is often described as "meditation in motion." It builds strength and agility and is suitable for all ages.

In tai chi, you perform a sequence of movements, called a "form," based on the defensive and attacking actions of martial arts. Tai chi is, in effect, a stylized fight sequence, performed as gracefully as a slow-motion ballet. The moves look easy but take many years to perfect; they require mental focus, physical strength, balance, good posture and controlled breathing.

Perfecting a sequence Tai chi moves evolve from one set posture, such as "bird's beak" (1) to another, such as "strumming the lute" (7), below. A full routine of the 100 or so movements of other styles of tai chi would take up to 40 minutes or so, but start by mastering a simple sequence.

■ Wear loose clothing that doesn't restrict your movements. Keep your feet bare, or wear thin-soled soft shoes.
■ Learn a basic tai chi form. There are a certain number of moves in the basic form, and you need to memorize these the same way you would a choreographed dance. This stage is best done in a tai chi class.
■ Be aware of your posture. Stand tall, then breathe out, relaxing any tension in your body before you start. Keep your knees slightly bent and imagine your weight dropping downward, through your legs into the floor.
■ Involve your whole body as you move. You never simply lift an arm in tai chi; the action unfolds from the abdominal region, and is coordinated with a turn of the waist. Each movement should flow seamlessly into the next.
■ Keep your breathing slow and rhythmic, exhaling and inhaling through the nostrils. Allow your abdomen to rise and fall with each breath.
■ Practice your tai chi every day—preferably first thing in the morning and again in the evening.

dance the Tango

It takes two to tango. To really master this sensuous and dramatic dance, both of you need to keep a straight face.

The music Tango was born in the working-class suburbs of Buenos Aires around the 1870s, and was banned in public places for being too voluptuous and improper. Start by thinking yourself into character. Dancer Isadora Duncan described the tango as "soft as a caress, toxic as love under the midday sun, cruel and dangerous as a tropical forest."

The hold The man rests his right hand between the woman's shoulder blades and holds her right hand to the side. Her left hand tucks behind his right arm at the armpit. Torsos are angled slightly away from one another, with the woman to the man's right. Both dancers hold their upper bodies straight and move using their hips.

The movement is decisive, staccato (step and stop) and "flat," with no obvious rise and fall. Although the dance is sexy, it isn't romantic—it has no graceful arcs or smooth rhythms.

■ The tempo is about 120 beats a minute and the count is slow, slow, quick, quick, slow. That's eight counts of music: two for each slow step and one for each quick. The slow steps have a stalking feeling; this dance is a game of cat and mouse, with the man pursuing the woman.
■ Feet are planted and don't swivel. The heel should hit the floor first.
■ The man faces away from the dance floor, and the dancers move counterclockwise around the room. Steps should curve slightly to the left and can be tailored to the music, with a run of slow or quick steps that break the basic rhythm, or by adding back-and-forth steps when turning.

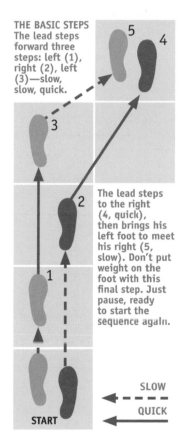

THE BASIC STEPS
The lead steps forward three steps: left (1), right (2), left (3)—slow, slow, quick.

The lead steps to the right (4, quick), then brings his left foot to meet his right (5, slow). Don't put weight on the foot with this final step. Just pause, ready to start the sequence again.

SLOW
QUICK
START

deal with Tantrums

Tantrums are to be expected if you have a toddler. They are just one way children learn to deal with their emotions.

■ Stay calm. Don't pick up on the anger and reflect it back.
■ Don't scold or try to reason with your child. When he or she is in the throes of a tantrum, a child is beyond reasoning.
■ Don't bribe your child or threaten him or her with punishment. Send the unspoken message that tantrums are pointless.
■ Don't give in to demands, or you'll teach your child that tantrums are a good way to get results.
■ It's embarrassing when your child throws a tantrum in public, but the same rules apply. If you pacify your child with a treat to keep them quiet, they will learn that this is a good way to get something nice. Instead, move to another place if your child is disturbing others, and let the tantrum run its course. Remember, most other parents have been in the same situation.
■ As the screams subside into sobs, offer hugs, warmth and praise for the child calming down.
■ Remember, this is just a phase —one that isn't fun for you or your child.

make the perfect cup of Tea

High-quality tea and a simple routine are essential to making the ideal relaxing treat.

■ Use fresh, cold water from the tap, not water in the kettle that has been previously boiled—the minerals will be more concentrated, and this can adversely affect the tea's flavor.

■ Boil the water and swirl a little of it in the pot to warm it.

■ Use one bag or one teaspoon of loose tea for each cup you're brewing, and a bit extra for the pot.

■ Give tea time to brew. Start at about two minutes and increase gradually to reach the strength you want. (See chart below for more specific brewing times.) After pouring, top it up with more boiling water.

■ It's up to you whether or not you add milk. Some people swear by pouring in milk before the tea.

■ Only buy tea in bulk if you can keep it in an airtight container in a cool location. If you do that, it should be good for up to two years.

TYPE OF TEA	BREWING TIME
English breakfast	3-4 minutes
Orange pekoe	2-3 minutes
Earl Grey	3 minutes
Darjeeling	2-3 minutes
Genmaicha	3-4 minutes
Gunpowder	3-4 minutes
Jasmine	2-3 minutes
Rooibos	5-7 minutes
Lapsang souchong	4-5 minutes
Oolong	5-7 minutes
Sencha (green)	2-2½ minutes

choose the right kind of Tape

Painter's tape, electrical tape, masking tape—with the right adhesive tape you can simplify your home repair task and get better results.

While tape doesn't usually have the holding power or permanence of glue or other adhesive, it does many jobs that a liquid can't—and it's important to use the right kind. Check the list below to find the right one for your purposes.

Anti-slip or anti-skid Heavy weatherproof plastic with rough-textured surface and strong adhesive. Typically used to add traction in tubs and showers, and on stairs and ladders.

Duct Strong, plastic-coated cloth with moderately strong adhesive. Resistant to moisture, heat and cold, and very versatile—often used for temporary repairs. Despite its name, should not be used on heat ducts.

Electrical Flame-retardant, stretchy vinyl with moderately strong adhesive. Helps insulate electrical connections, switches and outlets against shorts and shocks.

Masking Paper tape with minimal adhesive. Versatile—can be used to mark paint lines or hold glued parts of an object together till glue is dry.

Metal foil Heavyweight aluminum foil with strong adhesive. Used for sealing duct seams and joints, or temporarily repairing aluminum siding and gutters.

Weather-sealing Heavyweight weatherproof tape with strong, permanent adhesive. Can seal gaps around protruding pipes, cables and windows.

bake a Tart shell

A tart is a sweetened pastry shell filled with fresh or cooked fruit, usually a pastry cream or custard, and often a glaze. The pastry is not as flaky as pie crust. Here's a recipe for the basic shell, without filling.

⅓ cup butter
2 tbsp sugar
2 egg yolks
1¼ cups all-pupose flour, plus extra for rolling the dough
Pinch of salt

1 Work together butter, sugar and egg yolks. Gradually work in 1¼ cups flour and a pinch of salt. Knead for about 1 minute, then wrap in plastic and refrigerate for 1–2 hours.

2 Roll out the dough on a floured cloth or board. Fit it into a 9 in. (22 cm) tart pan, or cut and fit into six 4 in. (10 cm) tartlet pans. Alternatively, with the dough at room temperature, and press it evenly into the pan with your fingertips.

3 Prick the crust with a fork. Weight with pie weights (available at kitchen stores, or use dried beans) and bake at 350°F (180°C), or until golden. Let cool.

■ Fill the tart an only hour or two before serving, or the shell will get soggy.

manage a Team

■ **Be approachable.** Your subordinates should see you as an essential member of the group, not as a general commanding the troops from afar.
■ **Acknowledge hard work,** and give praise where it's due: Nothing demoralizes a team more quickly than feeling undervalued.
■ **Never reprimand** a member of your team publicly.
■ **Learn the strengths** of the individuals in your team, assign tasks accordingly and allow people to finish tasks their own way—don't just issue orders and insist on a particular way of working.
■ **When building a team**, resist the temptation to only pick people who are professional clones of yourself or share your values: The strength of any team lies in the diversity of its skills and ideas.

clean your Teeth

Flossing

■ Once a day, take a length of floss about 18 in. (45 cm) long and wind the ends around your middle fingers. Pinch between thumbs and pointer fingers to isolate around 1 in. (2.5 cm) of it, draw taut and slide it up and down in the gaps between your teeth (don't "saw" with it and risk cutting your gums —use a circular movement).
■ As you move on to the next pair of teeth, wind the floss along a little to expose a fresh piece.
■ Don't worry if your gums bleed a little at first. This should stop as your dental hygiene improves.

Brushing

■ Brush morning and night for at least two minutes, getting into all the nooks and crannies. Be thorough—it's worth your time.
■ Use a pea-sized blob of toothpaste.
■ Use small, circular movements rather than a scrubbing motion and make sure you work on all surfaces—don't neglect the insides.
■ Brush along your gum line and your tongue as well as your teeth.

ease the pain of Teething

When babies start teething, at about six months, it can make them tearful and grumpy. There are ways you can make it easier for them.

■ Use a water-filled teething ring. Chill it in the fridge (not the freezer) and offer it to your baby to chew on—it'll soothe painful gums. A clean, cold wet washcloth can also help.
■ Offer a piece of chilled raw fruit or vegetable, such as an apple slice or carrot stick, to gnaw on. You can also give your baby sugar-free teething biscuits. Always supervise your child closely to avoid choking.
■ If your baby has a temperature, you could use a liquid painkiller meant for infants. Follow the instructions on the package. Don't give them aspirin— babies are too young for that kind of medication.
■ Don't forget that a good, old-fashioned cuddle can relax both of you.

understand a Teenager

Teenagers are baffling—even to themselves. Keep the lines of communication open and before you know it, your teenager will be a young adult.

Remember your own teenage years. It will help you to deal with your teen's behavior if you think about when you were a less-than-charming presence in your own parents' home. Your teens might be interested to hear you talk about your own adolescent experiences, in a way that makes it clear that you know what they're going through.

Keep abreast of your adolescent's school and social life. Be a good listener, but don't pry. Know who their friends are, and encourage your teen to invite them over. When friends visit, quickly say hello, then leave them alone. But you should still set boundaries about unacceptable behavior.

Make time for your teens and allow them into your world; involve them in your adult conversations and activities. Spend time with them, doing something you can share and enjoy, such as shopping or going out for pizza.

Don't mock them or their views. You may not like your teenager's taste in music, clothes or posters, but keep your opinions to yourself. Saying that the music was better in your day, or anything along those lines, is a good way to alienate a teenager fast.

Above all, treat teens like adults, not unruly children—after all, they really will be grown up before long!

take someone's body
Temperature

A normal temperature under the tongue is around 98.6°F (37°C); under the arm it's about 1°F (0.5°C) lower. You should be able to buy a digital thermometer from any drugstore or large supermarket.

■ Before you start, thoroughly wash your hands (*see* HANDS) and clean the thermometer tip with a soft, damp cloth using soap and water.

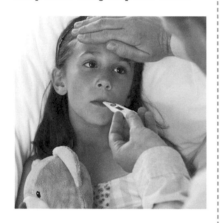

■ For kids under five, put the thermometer in either armpit and hold the arm against the body. This prevents a child from biting down on the thermometer. Otherwise, place it gently under the tongue (above). Follow the instructions on the package for guidance about the length of time you have to hold the thermometer in place.
■ Don't take a temperature reading for at least 20 minutes after drinking, eating or taking a bath.
■ A high temperature is anything above 100.4°F (38°C), or 99.5°F (37.5°C) in a child under five (*see* FEVER).

build a simple Telescope

It might not help you really see the stars, but this fun science project will entertain budding pirates and astronomers alike.

This telescope uses two lenses, meaning the image you see through it will be upside down—but kids will relish this crazy view of the world.

YOU WILL NEED **Two sheets of stiff paper flexible enough to roll into a tube (or use cardboard), scissors, two magnifying glasses (preferably the same size), clear tape**

1 Roll one sheet of stiff paper into a tube the same diameter as your first magnifying glass and use tape to hold it. The longer the tube, the more you'll be able to change the focus—but don't make it longer than you or a kid can manage to hold.

2 Hold the magnifying glass tight to one end of the tube. Then tape the paper around the frame of the magnifying glass to hold it firmly in place. (A second pair of hands would come in handy here.)

3 Make another tube with the other sheet of paper. This tube must be slightly narrower than the first, so it can slide inside it. Attach the second magnifying glass to one end of the narrower tube, then slide the narrower tube inside the other one.

4 If you want, decorate the tubes with markers, paint or stickers. Your telescope is now ready to use. Move the lenses apart or closer together to focus the image by sliding the tubes in and out.

get into the swing of Tennis

Tennis can be played indoors or out—on clay, grass or a synthetic surface— there may be courts at your local park.

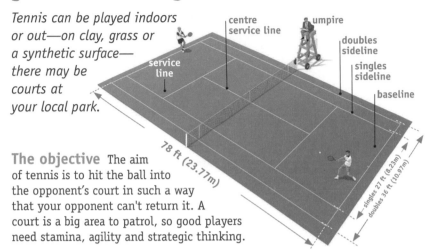

centre service line
umpire
doubles sideline
singles sideline
baseline
service line
78 ft (23.77m)
singles 27 ft (8.23m)
doubles 36 ft (10.97m)

The objective The aim of tennis is to hit the ball into the opponent's court in such a way that your opponent can't return it. A court is a big area to patrol, so good players need stamina, agility and strategic thinking.

Scoring A match is scored as a series of duels. Players have to win four points (counted as 15, 30, 40 and "game") to win. A 40:40 tie is called "deuce;" a player must then win two consecutive points ("advantage" and "game"). Service alternates with each game. The first to win six games or more, with a two-game advantage, wins the "set." Pro matches are played to the best of three or five sets. If, in any set other than the decider, the score reaches six games each, a "tie break" is played—the player who scores seven or more points, with a two-point advantage, wins.

Playing tennis shots In a long rally, you'll use forehand and backhand, lob high balls over your opponent's head and fire back quick volleys. Practice the basic shots on the next page, then work on your serve. A good serve should put your opponent on the defensive.

1 2 3 4 5 6

How to serve Stand at the baseline with your body sideways, and transfer some of your weight to your back foot (1). With a straight arm, toss the ball up and slightly forward (2), and bring your racket arm back into a "throwing" position (3). As the ball reaches its highest point, bring your racket arm forward overhead (4). Aim to strike the ball at as high a point as possible (5), as this maximizes power and the angle of the bounce, making the serve (6) harder for your opponent to reach and return.

continued on next page →

relieve the pain of
Tennis elbow

This is an occupational as well as a recreational problem. Factory workers, carpenters, tennis players and golfers—even politicians at the end of a long campaign of hand-shaking—can suffer as a result of repetitive, strenuous arm movement while gripping with one hand. The tendon that anchors the muscles to the bottom of the upper arm bone becomes inflamed, causing an acute pain at the elbow and a dull ache down the forearm.

Self-help remedies
■ Rest the arm and avoid the activity that caused the problem, if you can. Speak to your employer if work is the cause.
■ Apply ice packs (*see* SPRAINS AND STRAINS) and take NSAIDs (non-steroidal anti-inflammatory drugs), such as ibuprofen in cream or gel form, to ease the inflammation.
■ Try using natural cayenne ointment, applied four times a day.
■ If the pain persists, it's time to consult your doctor, who may prescribe stronger anti-inflammatory drugs, give you a shot of hydrocortisone in the affected tendon or suggest physical therapy (physiotherapy).

score a strike in
Tenpin bowling

To get strikes consistently, you need to rotate the ball. A rotated ball curves as it rolls down the lane and strikes the pins at an angle, greatly increasing the chances that they will bang into each other.

To roll a hook (as this technique is called), approach the moment of release with your fingers beneath the ball, then turn your hand into a "handshake" position as you release it. With practice, you'll be able to rotate the ball so it loops almost into the gutter, then curls in sharply as it approaches the pins. Make sure you try to hit the headpin every time.

continued from page 327

Forehand As the ball approaches you on your racket side (your right, if you're right-handed), bring the racket head back in a loop, so it reaches head height. Turn your body sideways, so you put all the muscle power of your legs and torso into the shot. Bring the racket around, aiming to make contact in front of your body as the ball bounces up to waist height. Follow through, so your racket arm comes across your body, finishing high.

Backhand If the ball is coming toward your non-racket side (your left, if you're right-handed) draw the racket across your body, so it lies horizontally across your midriff. Step up to meet the ball in front of the body, and strike it (double-handed style, above) as your weight comes onto your front foot, so your forward momentum adds power to your shot. Push with your legs as well as your arm at the moment of impact, finishing high.

understand a Tenpin bowling scorecard

There's more to bowling scores than just adding up the pins you knock down. On a scorecard, each big box corresponds to a "frame"—every time a player takes a turn, with two throws—and gives a running total. The number of pins knocked over with each throw is recorded in the two smaller boxes.

FRAME 1 The player knocked down 5 pins with the first, 3 with the second, making 8.

If a player knocks over all the pins with two throws (called a "spare"), it's depicted in the second small box as a diagonal slash.

When a spare is scored, the number of pins knocked over with the first ball of the following frame is added to a player's running total for the previous frame, then counted again in that next frame.

PLAYER NAME	1	2	3	4	5	6	7	8	9	10	TOTAL
	5 3	6 /	4 2	7 1	X	7 /	X	X	7 0	6 1	
Bella	8	22	28	36	56	76	103	120	127	134	134
	6 2	7 0	6 2	7 /	3 0	X	1 6	4 /	6 1	3 / 5	
Tilly	8	15	23	36	39	56	63	79	86	101	101

FRAME 2 The total of 22 equals 8 (frame 1) plus 10 (frame 2) plus 4 (first ball, frame 3).

If a player knocks over all ten pins with the first attempt (a "strike"), that's indicated by an X in the first small box. All the points made with the next two throws are added to the total.

FRAME 5 The total of 56 equals 36 (frame 4), plus 10 (the strike in frame 5), plus 10 (spare in frame 6).

If you score a strike with your first ball in frame 10, you get two more balls to complete your score. Throw a spare, and you get one more ball. The highest possible score is 300.

put up a dome Tent

Who wants to begin their vacation by struggling to erect the tent? Follow these basic rules—and do a test run in your backyard before you leave—and your camping trip will start smoothly.

1 Spread out an extra groundsheet if you have one, to prevent rocks from damaging your sewn-in groundsheet. Unfold and lay the tent on top.

2 Assemble the poles. Thread poles through loops or clips on top of the tent and through the central loop at the top. For some tents you pitch the flysheet, or outside, first—they may have long pockets that you can thread the poles through.

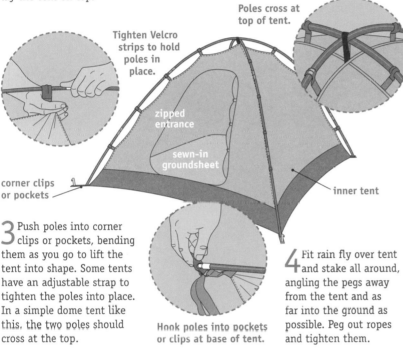

Poles cross at top of tent.

Tighten Velcro strips to hold poles in place.

zipped entrance

sewn-in groundsheet

corner clips or pockets

inner tent

3 Push poles into corner clips or pockets, bending them as you go to lift the tent into shape. Some tents have an adjustable strap to tighten the poles into place. In a simple dome tent like this, the two poles should cross at the top.

Hook poles into pockets or clips at base of tent.

4 Fit rain fly over tent and stake all around, angling the pegs away from the tent and as far into the ground as possible. Peg out ropes and tighten them.

examine your Testicles

Testicular cancer is almost always curable if detected early. Once a month, do this simple self-check-up after a warm bath or shower.

▪ Use all your fingers and thumbs to feel around one testicle at a time. After a few times of doing it, you'll know what feels normal for you.
▪ It's normal for one testicle to be a little larger and lower than the other.
▪ The soft lump at the top towards the back of each is the sperm-carrying tube.

▪ The testicles should be smooth and not swollen, with no unusual lumps or soreness.
▪ They should be no harder or softer than usual and should not have changed size or weight since the last time you checked.
▪ If you notice any changes, talk to a doctor. It may be nothing serious.

remove a Tick

Take precautions against being bitten by a tick in the first place. When out in the woods during the summer months, wear a long-sleeved shirt and long trousers, and tuck your trousers into your socks. Use DEET repellents, and check your skin carefully after a walk.

If you do get bitten, remove the tick as soon as you can. Wearing gloves, or covering the tick with a tissue to avoid contact with your fingers, grasp it with thin-ended tweezers as close to your skin as possible. Pull straight upward and don't squeeze the tick too hard, or you may force the contents of its stomach into the site of the bite. Pull gently, and it should come free. Make sure that its head and mouth parts haven't become detached.

After removing the tick, wash your hands and the bite with soap and water, and apply an antiseptic to the bite area. In rare cases, a tick bite can result in serious infection; if a rash appears around the bitten area, or you develop a fever, seek medical attention immediately. In areas where lyme disease is prevalent, it's best to put the tick in a jar and bring it with you to a medical center immediately.

deal with a Tire blowout

If a front tire bursts don't brake, since this will pull your car heavily to the side. Let the car slow naturally, if possible. Steer to counter the drag of the burst tire, and pull over if it's safe to do so. Try to stop on firm ground where you can change the tire.

If a back tire bursts, brake very gently if you must—but not too hard, or you risk losing control of the car. Be prepared for the back of the car to slide. Keep a firm grip on the wheel to maintain a straight course. Change down a gear to slow the car, and pull over.

---

check the condition of your Tires

Inspect your tires regularly and thoroughly. Make sure the hand brake is firmly on before you begin.
■ Look for cuts, bulges and embedded objects such as nails or glass shards.
■ Check the tread depth. It must be more than ²⁄₃₂" (1.6 mm) in many states and Canada. Any less and the tire must be replaced. Manufacturers often mold "tread bars" at ²⁄₃₂" (1.6 mm). If the tread has worn as far as the bars, replace the tire. If there are no bars, buy and use a tread depth gauge. In areas where winter brings snow, replace your tires earlier.

write a sincere Thank-you letter

Anyone who has made a gift or a gesture, offered hospitality or performed some kindness deserves a properly penned—yes, handwritten—note of gratitude.

Put pen to paper Take the trouble to show that a kindness has real meaning to you. In these days of texts and emails, it can be a lovely surprise to receive a letter or, perhaps even better, an attractively illustrated card. If you write a letter, make sure you use a good-quality paper and matching envelope—a piece of photocopy paper won't impress. And choose a pen that works—not one that's about to run out of ink or makes smudges. Don't wait too long to respond to a gift, treat or kindness. Send a letter or card within a few days. If you really don't have the time to send something in writing, an email is better than nothing, but should be sent as soon as possible.

Choose the right words The most important thing is to keep it personal. If you received 50 wedding gifts, that means 50 individual letters. Don't just change the name and address at the top; take time to craft each one. Do a few each day so you don't become jaded. Use the following basic framework.

1 Remember that it's a letter, not an email. Begin *Dear ... name.*

2 Say at once what it is that you're thankful for and why it's special. *The vase looks lovely filled with roses. I couldn't put the book down. How clever of you to pick just the right color! What a treat to get up into the hills again!*

3 Close with the hope that you'll see one another or be in touch soon. If you already have a date written down in your calendar, say how much you're looking forward to it.

4 Sign off on a warm note—*With love, With best wishes, Thanks again,* as appropriate. Avoid abbreviations—*LOL* or *xxxxxxx* will shriek of insincerity.

---

play Tiddlywinks

There's more to this traditional favorite than just popping counters into a cup. It's a game of strategy with complex rules. Have fun at home with this simplified version.

YOU WILL NEED **Six "winks" (that is, four small and two large counters) of each color (red, yellow, blue, green), felt mat measuring 6¼ x 3 ft (1.8 x 0.9 m), pot, four "squidgers" (small circular disks)**

To start Lay the mat on a hard surface, such as a table or wooden floor. Four players form two pairs. Blue partners red; green partners yellow. The pot is placed at the center of the mat, and colors occupy corners of the mat, in the order red, yellow, blue, green. Each player uses a squidger to press down on the edge of a wink and ping it towards the center. The wink nearest to the pot gets to start. All winks are returned to the corners; play proceeds clockwise.

To play The basic aim is to flip all one's winks into the pot ("pot out"). Players have one shot per turn; aiming toward the center, play their winks in any order. If a player pots a wink they get another turn, meaning that it's feasible to pot all six in one go. If a wink lands off the mat it's returned to the edge and the player's turn ends.

A wink is "squopped" if it's overlapped even slightly by another wink; it cannot be played. If a player's last wink is squopped they are stymied until the covering wink is flipped away by the player to whom it belongs.

If nobody pots out within 25 minutes, the score of "tiddlies" is counted thus:
3 for every potted wink
1 for each uncovered wink
0 for squopped and unplayed winks.

tie a Tie

There are many ways to tie a tie. The Windsor knot is particularly stylish, and the four-in-hand is easy to do.

Four-in-hand

1 Cross the tie on your shirtfront such that the wide end is about 12 in. (30 cm) longer than the narrow end. Wrap the wide end around the back of the narrow end.

2 Bring the wide end back across the front of the narrow end, so that the front of the tie is facing outward.

3 Take the wide end up through the gap between the tie and your collar button.

4 Pull the wide end down through the knot, and finish by sliding the knot up to your neck. The narrow end should come out fractionally shorter than the wide end.

continued on next page➔

Tie-dye successfully

It's easy to create colorful patterns on fabric, or on clothes, such as T-shirts and skirts, by folding, crumpling or tying the fabric before dyeing it. The way you prepare the material will determine the finished result.

Marbled effect Crumple the fabric into a ball, then tie it in a criss-cross pattern with string.

Irregular stripes Fold the fabric like an accordion and tie it at intervals with thread.

Irregular spots Scrunch up small areas of fabric and tie them around with thread to enclose them.

Patterns Try sewing or folding objects such as buttons, small pebbles and dried beans into folds of the fabric.

Dyeing Use commercial hot and cold water dyes (*see* DYE) according to the manufacturer's instructions. Immerse the fabric in the dye as recommended, rinse, unfold and dry the fabric a little. Then iron it while it's still damp. For a second color, allow the fabric to dry completely then repeat the process with a different dye.

golden rules

TIE-DYE TIPS
- **Start with easy-to-dye fabric such as soft cotton.**
- **Dampen the fabric a little before you fold it.**
- **For deep color areas mix dye and push it into creases and folds with a paintbrush or from a squeeze bottle.**

deal with Tinnitus

Many of us will at some time in our life experience mild tinnitus, a perception of buzzing or ringing in the ears when there's no external sound. If no underlying cause is found and treated, you can learn ways of coping with it.

- Don't worry. Anxiety is a major exacerbating factor (*see* RELAXATION *and* STRESS).
- Keep occupied. It really helps if you can take your mind off it.
- Use masking sound. In a quiet room, the brain will listen to random activity in the auditory pathway. Place a ticking clock in the room, or play some soft music, and the brain will filter out the unwanted buzzing or ringing.
- At bedtime try a "sound therapy system." This plays digital recordings of such soothing natural sounds as ocean waves and gentle rain as you drift off to sleep.
- Herbal remedies ginkgo biloba or lesser periwinkle may help in some cases.
- Try a cup of fenugreek-seed tea morning, noon and night.
- Avoid exposure to loud noises and the buildup of ear wax.
- Try reflexology, acupuncture, acupressure or meditation (*see* MEDITATE). All have been known to help in some cases.
- Join a support group. It helps to share your experience and to know you're not alone.

continued from page 331

Windsor knot

1 Cross the tie on your shirtfront such that the wide end is about 12 in. (30 cm) longer than the narrow end.

2 Bring the wide end up behind the narrow end, then pull it down toward the front to make a loose twist at the neck.

3 Bring the wide end behind the narrow end to point out to the left, then take it through the loop from front to back.

4 Bring the wide end across the front of the narrow end from right to left, then take it behind and through the loop.

5 Now tuck the wide end through the inverted triangular knot that has formed at the top.

6 Pull down on the wide end to tighten the knot, and on the narrow end to slide the knot up to your collar.

Tile a floor

Ceramic tiles can be laid directly onto a concrete floor. Wood floors must be overlaid with ¼-in. exterior plywood, firmly screwed down.

1 Place a tile at the exact center of the room. Dry lay single rows of tiles from this point to the walls to check that there will be no narrow slivers of tile at the edges. If there are, shift the rows so that you'll have half a tile or more at all edges.

Find the center of the room by marking diagonal lines from corner to corner and seeing where they cross. In an irregular-shaped room, center tiles on the largest area or align with a prominent feature.

2 Fix wood strips to the floor at one corner, where the outermost whole tile will go. Now dry-lay a square of nine tiles against the wood to check that they line up perfectly—if they don't, adjust the wood strips.

3 Spread enough adhesive on the floor for these tiles, lay them, with spacers between, and use a spirit level to check that they are level, measuring across each row and diagonally. Then lay the next set of nine.

4 Once the adhesive has set, remove the wood. Measure and cut the edge tiles (few rooms are exactly square), applying adhesive to the back of the tiles. Leave for 24 hours, then apply a waterproof, stain-resistant grout.

Tile a wall

Take time to plan the positioning of tiles before you begin and you will achieve a far more professional result, with fewer awkward cuts.

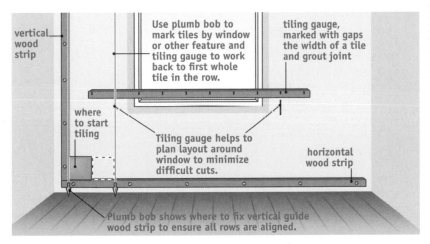

vertical wood strip

Use plumb bob to mark tiles by window or other feature and tiling gauge to work back to first whole tile in the row.

tiling gauge, marked with gaps the width of a tile and grout joint

where to start tiling

Tiling gauge helps to plan layout around window to minimize difficult cuts.

horizontal wood strip

Plumb bob shows where to fix vertical guide wood strip to ensure all rows are aligned.

Plan the layout Lay a row of tiles on the floor along the wall to be tiled, leaving gaps for spacers. Adjust the row so that the gap is even at either end. If there's a window, it may look better to center tiles around it and live with unequal cuts at the wall edges. Use a plumb bob to mark a vertical line at the point where the last whole tile goes, and nail a guide wood strip to the wall. Work out the vertical spacing in the same way and use a spirit level to mark a horizontal line under the lowest whole tile, and fix another wood strip. This creates a square corner that is the point from which you'll begin tiling.

continued on next page →

make
Toffee apples

If you buy apples from a store, you'll need to remove the preservative wax that covers them first, or else the toffee won't stick. If you use homegrown apples you can avoid this boiling water treatment (see step 1 below). A sugar thermometer makes it simple to judge the temperature.

MAKES 6

6 crisp eating apples
1½ cup sugar
½ cup water
2½ tbsp butter
2 tbsp molasses, maple syrup or corn syrup

1 Put the apples into a large bowl, cover with boiling water then remove and dry thoroughly. Spear each with a wooden skewer or craft stick and place on parchment paper.

2 Dissolve the sugar in the water over medium heat, add the butter and syrup and cook until the mixture reaches 300°F (150°C)—the hard crack stage (*see* SUGAR THERMOMETER). Remove from the heat and dip each apple in turn, twisting it to get an even coating of toffee. Place upside down on the parchment paper to cool. If the toffee starts to harden before all the apples are dipped, reheat it gently.

unblock a Toilet

■ If the blockage isn't caused by something out of the ordinary, there's a quick and clean way to clear it. Partly fill a bucket with water—not so much that it would fill the toilet bowl. With one swift movement, pour the water all at once into the center of the toilet bowl, where the pipework curves out of sight. The weight and the force of the water will probably be enough to shift the blockage.

■ If that doesn't work, use a special toilet plunger that's large enough to cover the entire toilet outlet.

■ For a really stubborn blockage, try a plumber's snake (above). Insert the cable end of the tool into the U-bend and turn the crank handle. This winds the cable through the toilet's trap and into the soil pipe. Its hooked spring tip allows you to grab the blockage and carefully pull it back out through the trap or to push and break up the clog.

■ If none of this works, get the help of a plumber.

continued from page 333

Fixing the tiles to the wall

1 Apply adhesive to the wall in a band a little more than one tile wide. Place a tile, then another, moving horizontally along the row, and fitting spacers between each tile. Push firmly and evenly into place, making sure tiles are well bedded into the adhesive and level with the adjacent tiles. Use waterproof adhesive (and grout) around sinks, baths, showers and other wet areas.

2 Continue up the wall with all the whole tiles. Wait 24 hours, then remove the wood and fill in the edges with cut tiles. It's easier to apply adhesive to the back of cut tiles than to the wall. Wait another 24 hours before removing the spacers and applying grout. Use a sponge or grouting tool to push grout between tiles and smooth it. Wipe tiles clean before the grout sets hard.

Toilet train a child

It can take a while to teach an infant to use the toilet. Be patient and relaxed about it. They all get there in the end.

Buy a large, comfortable potty ahead of time and put it in the bathroom. When the day comes to use it, the potty will be a familiar sight.

Choose your moment When your child can understand basic commands and exercise some bladder control by staying dry for a few hours—usually at about two years old—you can make a start. Don't expect nighttime dryness until much later. Avoid starting at times of stress, like when moving house.

Get them used to the potty After they eat or drink, put your child on the potty. If nothing happens, don't worry, but praise them if something does.

Phase out diapers As potty time becomes part of the routine, let your child go without a diaper. Choose a time when you can be at home or in the yard. Use potty training pants instead of diapers and put your child on the potty every hour. Always praise success; don't scold a child for failure.

Mark triumphs Make a chart and stick on gold stars when the potty is used.

Use picture books A fun story with lots of pictures helps toddlers to understand what's involved. Or there are free child-friendly images online.

Take a step up When your child can manage it, introduce a toddler step and trainer seat for the toilet. Teach correct wiping (with girls, particularly, teach to wipe from front to back) and thorough hand-washing (*see* HANDS).

grow a great Tomato

You don't need a greenhouse to grow flavor-packed tomatoes. The key is to choose a variety well suited to your space and situation.

There's a huge range of sizes and colors available, from big red beefsteak tomatoes to yellow cherry ones designed to tumble out of hanging baskets.

YOU WILL NEED Seeds or plants, compost, seed trays, pots, bamboo canes, soft string, watering can, tomato food

Start growing with seeds (*see* SEEDS AND SEEDLINGS) in trays or small pots; kept on a sunny windowsill if you don't have a greenhouse. Sow seed in mid-spring for outdoor varieties and late winter for indoor ones. They will need a temperature of 65°F (18°C) to germinate.

Transplant seedlings to 3 in. (7.5 cm) pots as soon as two true leaves have formed, then into permanent positions in the garden or into deep 3½-4¾ in. (9-12 cm) pots once the first flowers begin to form.

Support growing plants with a bamboo cane pushed in alongside each plant. Tie the stem to the cane with soft string in several places.

Pinching out is essential for vine tomatoes, but not for bush varieties. Remove sideshoots regularly to leave about seven good fruit trusses on indoor plants and four on outdoor ones. Remove the top of the main stem to stop any more growth and concentrate development into the fruits. Water regularly to keep soil moist. Once fruit on the second truss begins to form, feed every 7-14 days with a store-bought tomato fertilizer. Keep pinching out shoots that grow from the joint between the stem and other shoots.

make a fresh Tomato sauce

Tomato sauce is the base of many dishes, and the star of the show in a simple bowl of pasta. You can use fresh tomatoes when they are in season and full of flavor, or canned ones all year round. The sauce freezes well and can be supplemented with olives, tuna, chili flakes or any other ingredient you like.

MAKES ENOUGH FOR 4 SERVINGS OF PASTA

4 tbsp olive oil
1 medium onion, finely chopped
2 cloves garlic, minced
1 lb (500 g) fresh tomatoes, skinned, seeded and chopped (see right), with juice, or

15 oz (540 mL) can Italian chopped plum tomatoes, with juice
salt and freshly ground black pepper
2 tsp dried marjoram
handful of fresh basil, chopped

1 Heat the oil in a heavy-based saucepan and cook the onion until soft. Add the garlic, tomatoes, seasonings and marjoram. Cover and simmer for 20-30 minutes.

2 Just before the end of cooking, check the seasonings and add the basil. The sauce can be used as it is or processed for a totally smooth version.

skin and seed a Tomato

Skin tomatoes to prevent pieces of skin coming off during cooking and spoiling your sauce or casserole. As well as tomatoes, peaches and apricots can be skinned using this method.

1 With a small, sharp knife, lightly cut an "X" in the base of each tomato. Remove any stalks.

2 Fill a large bowl with boiling water then immerse each tomato for 30-60 seconds, or until the cut skin begins to curl up. Don't submerge the tomatoes for too long or they will get soggy.

3 Remove with a slotted spoon, drain and allow to cool a little, then peel away the skin with the knife.

To seed, quarter the tomatoes and remove the cores and seeds with a knife or a teaspoon.

golden rule
TOMATO SAUCE TIP
■ **If the sauce isn't thick enough, cook it uncovered on a high heat, stirring, until you have the right consistency.**

sharpen Tools

A blunt tool is less effective than a sharp one, but also more dangerous. It's likely to slip during use and cause injury or damage. Keeping chisels and plane blades sharp is simple, but worthwhile.

YOU WILL NEED Whetstone, honing guide, light machine oil

1 Prepare the stone by smearing a teaspoon of oil over it. Let it soak in, and then repeat the process.

2 Clamp the blade in the honing guide so that it projects the correct distance. Pour a little more oil on the stone to coat the surface.

3 Now move the guide up and down the whetstone, pressing down so that the tip of the blade to be sharpened is flat against the stone.

4 Take the blade out and rub its flat edge against the stone to remove the "burr"—the little curl of metal that will have formed on the cutting edge.

create simple Topiary shapes

Plants such as boxwood and bay are ideal subjects for making topiary shapes such as pyramids, globes and "lollipops." It's easiest to start with large potted plants before tackling hedge topiary.

YOU WILL NEED Potted plant, pruning shears, canes, wire rings, scissors

Pyramid or globe box Use scissors to trim the plant to roughly the desired shape. Leave it to grow for a year. Then use canes and wire to construct a cutting guide to place over the plant. Trim once or twice a year with shears, following the lines of the guide. To look effective, these shapes must be neat and geometrically accurate.

Lollipop bay tree When the young tree is a little taller than needed, use pruning shears to prune off the growing tip and cut off the side shoots from the lower trunk. When they are about 6 in. (15 cm) long, pinch or cut out the tips of side shoots in the "head" to encourage them to bush out. Continue to trim in this way as the tree grows.

relieve a Toothache

It's time to see a dentist, but you can manage the pain while you wait for an appointment.

At the first slight discomfort drink hot liquids. For a continuous ache, hold a cold pack to your jaw and take some painkillers.

Wash your mouth every hour with warm salt water. Hold the strong brine in your mouth and swish it around your teeth before spitting out. Unrefined gray sea salt, which is rich in minerals, is the most effective.

Clove oil is a natural dental painkiller. Dab a little on a cotton swab and hold it to the affected tooth (avoid touching it to your tongue, if possible).

Tea tree oil has natural antibacterial and pain-relieving properties; apply in the same way as clove oil.

avoid the rot of Tooth decay

To keep teeth in top condition, you must banish the bacteria that feed on food particles left on the teeth and produce corrosive acid.

- Keep teeth clean (*see* TEETH). Brush at least twice a day with a toothpaste that contains fluoride, and floss regularly between teeth.
- Ban sugary and starchy snacks, and soft drinks laced with sugar. Combine sugary foods with a meal, as this can limit the damage.
- Chewing gum that contains the sweetener xylitol may retard the growth of bacteria.
- See your dentist every six months to catch problems early on.
- Consider sealants, which apply a protective coating to the biting surfaces of the back teeth.

leave Travel sickness at home

Travel sickness pills are effective at quelling nausea, but can cause drowsiness. Try these simple strategies to minimize the problem instead.

- Try closing your eyes or looking into the distance at something in a fixed position or at the horizon.
- Try deep breathing.
- Play music and sing along.
- Ensure adequate ventilation.
- Take a flask of ginger tea; ginger is a tried-and-tested nausea relief.
- Schedule regular stops—at least once an hour.
- On arrival, lie down, close your eyes and keep your head still until the feeling of movement passes. *See also* SEASICKNESS.

drive safely with a Trailer

Driving with a trailer can be hazardous. So make sure you follow certain rules—before you set off and while you're driving.

Load up correctly There should more weight ahead of the trailer's axel than behind it. Check the tire pressures before every journey.

Go slowly and legally Laws vary by state, province or territory. In some places the speed limit for trailers is lower than the posted limit, and you must stay in the right lane. Elsewhere, maybe not. Either way, drive carefully and don't brake sharply on curves, or the trailer may jackknife.

Take special care when reversing This is best done with the help of a second person who can see what is behind you (*see* CAMPER).

Know how to stop snaking A trailer can weave from side to side if poorly loaded, you're going too fast or you get buffeted by side winds. Don't try to accelerate or steer out of trouble. Keep straight, change down a gear, take your foot off the accelerator and the clutch and let the car slow down gradually. Don't brake unless you're going downhill, and then only gently.

organize a Treasure hunt

Treasure hunts are terrific fun, but they require thoughtful advance planning. Ambiguous clues mean dead ends and lost treasure hunters.

The idea of a treasure hunt is to make a trail of clues that leads from one location to the next, and finally to a finish line. There need not be any "treasure" along the way, but there should be a prize for the person or team that completes the hunt and reaches the finish first.

- If you're doing a treasure hunt for children, keep the clues simple, make the hunt brief, and be sure that the area in which the hunt is to take place is safe and enclosed.
- If you're doing a hunt for adults, make use of the location—be it a country house, a historic town center or main street, or your own home—with cryptic clues, historical hints, puns and local knowledge to make clues harder.
- First work out the route of your hunt, then write clues to fit. Remember, each clue must refer to the next place the hunters must go, not where they are now.
- On private property, you can attach or even conceal the clues around the place. For a hunt in a public place, issue a complete list of all clues to the teams—each one in a sealed envelope, perhaps.
- Make your clues witty, baffling, intriguing—rhyming, if you like. A good clue is unfathomable on its own, but reasonably easy for a hunter who is in the right spot. If you need inspiration, search online for "treasure hunt clues" to find a selection of riddles and cryptic clues.

stake a young Tree

Until their roots are firmly anchored, which can take three years or more, young trees need to be staked. This prevents their roots from rocking around, which impairs their growth. Choose cushioned ties to protect the trunk, or add it yourself with a wad of sacking.

Sturdy and short-stemmed bare-rooted trees Use a short vertical stake that comes a third of the way up the trunk. Attach with a tie.

Container-grown trees Drive in a short stake angled so as to miss the rootball. Attach it about 18 in. (45 cm) above ground level.

For any tree Drive in two short upright stakes 2 ft (60 cm) apart on either side of the trunk and join them with a horizontal piece of wood. Attach the tree to the wood.

plant a Tree

Fall is the best season for planting deciduous trees, but frost-vulnerable container-grown evergreens are best planted in spring.

Before planting, make up a planting mixture as for shrubs and soak bare rooted trees in a bucket of water for several hours. If they are container-grown, water them well.

1 Work out the size of hole, allowing several extra inches in width and depth. Dig the hole and add the planting mixture (*see* SHRUB).

2 Put in the tree to check for correct depth—use a length of wood put across the hole and mark the trunk at the right position. Sprinkle in some granules of mycorrhizal root-stimulating compound following the manufacturer's instructions.

3 Add a stake (see left) then put in the tree and spread the roots out as much as possible. Backfill with soil, pressing it in well as you go. Firm in the tree with your foot. Water well, firm in again and add a layer of mulch.

cut off a Tree branch

Trees seldom benefit from pruning, because the wounds are vulnerable to infection. But sometimes it's necessary to remove lower branches to raise the crown, or take out boughs to thin the crown to allow more light through.

■ Don't prune when a tree is producing or dropping its leaves.
■ Always leave large, high or difficult-to-reach branches to a professional. Don't try to remove any branch you cannot reach from the ground.
■ Use a pruning saw and wear sturdy gloves and eye protection. Don't use a chainsaw for this job unless you have been trained to do so.
■ Remove branches where they meet the trunk or shorten them to a lateral stem (one branching off) that is at least one-third of the diameter of the branch you're removing.

1 Make sure the area into which the branch will fall is clear. Begin by cutting a third of the way through the branch from below, 1¼-2 in. (3-5 cm) from the trunk, using a pruning saw. Then repeat from above, 1¼-2 in. (3-5 cm) farther away from the trunk. This helps to prevent the branch from tearing from the tree.

2 Cut through the branch with an angled cut that is flush with the trunk at the top and slopes away slightly. If sap "bleeds" from the cut, don't dress or bandage it, or you may inhibit the natural healing processes.

shorten Trouser legs

Pants bought off the rack are often too long, but shortening them is easy with a little care. This method also works for unlined sleeves.

YOU WILL NEED Tape measure, pins, stitch ripper, iron, full-length mirror, needle and thread, scissors

1 Measure the depth of the existing hems. Try on the pants or jeans, turn up and mark the new length with pins on each leg (you may need to recruit a helper for this). Take them off, turn them inside out, undo the existing hems and press. Turn up to your pin marks, using the tape measure to make sure that both hems are equal. Try them on, checking in the mirror that legs match exactly for length. Adjust as necessary.

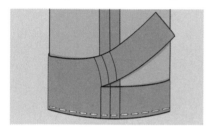 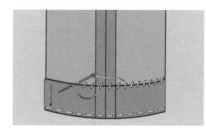

2 Tack new hems close to the turned-up edge, then cut off any excess fabric. If legs are tapered, open the side seams to make the fabric lie flat.

3 To neaten raw edges, make a small turning or finish as for seams (*see* SEAM). Pin, then hem using a hemming or blind hemming stitch (*see* SEWING).

get tweeting on Twitter

Anyone can say ("tweet") anything they like, and if it's interesting enough and anyone is reading ("following"), it may spark a conversation.

■ Once you have signed up at the Twitter website, identify some people to "follow"—each tweet they post will then appear on your "Home" page. Most people start by following friends and family or colleagues. Click on **Who To Follow**, type in people's names to find their accounts, then click **Follow**.
■ You also need followers of your own; otherwise your tweets will only be read if someone happens across them via the site's search engine. At first, you can start by hoping that the people you are following will reciprocate.
■ To tweet, click in the "What's happening?" text box, type your message and click **Tweet**, but remember you only have 140 characters; every letter, comma and space counts. A space-saving Twitter and text language is evolving, with shortcuts such as TY for "thank you" and IRL ("in real life").
■ Make your tweets as interesting as possible and one of your followers might "retweet" (RT) one of your messages—that is, forward it to their own followers, some of whom might then choose to follow you.
■ The hash tag (#readersdigest) before a name in your tweet will help users to search for more information about something you mention.
■ If you mention another twitter user, type "@" before their name and they will be more likely to see your tweet, as it will appear in a different place.

do a Tumble turn
in the pool

A tumble turn, or flip, is an underwater somersault and twist. The aim is to change direction quickly at the end of a lap.

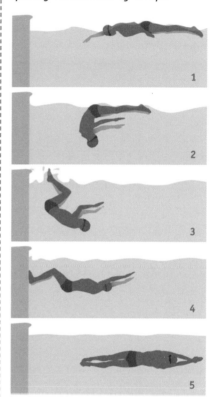

1 Make ready to turn when you see the "T" on the bottom of the pool.

2 Turn your palms to face the pool floor. Push your hands down, tuck your chin to your chest, and give a dolphin kick.

3 Perform a front somersault, tucking chin and chest close to your knees, with your feet just above the surface. As you rotate into the faceup position, start pulling your hands toward your head.

4 Plant feet against the wall, under the water, and push off. Stretch out your arms and press them against your ears.

5 Turn on to your front. Glide with the momentum of your push-off, then kick your legs and aim for the surface.

understand
Typefaces

Anyone who's ever launched a word-processing program to type a letter, only to end up scrolling through the font list looking for the perfect typeface, will appreciate that not all letterforms are created equal. Typefaces are divided into different categories, each of which is best for a particular use. The two largest categories are "serif" and "sans serif."

Serif These letters have small details at the ends of their main strokes, which are widely believed to improve legibility in body text on the printed page, as they help to guide the eye along from one letter to the next. Good examples of familiar serif typefaces are Times, Bodoni and Garamond.

Sans serif The sans serif category is best represented by its most famous member—Helvetica. Helvetica can be seen almost everywhere, from the names of Nasa's space shuttles or the US TV-rating icons, to the logos of Canada's federal departments. Sans serif fonts are generally best for applications where clarity and impact are important: titles, headlines and street signs, to name a few. Sans serif type is also best for computer operating systems and internet content, because it comes across clearer in smaller sizes and on screens.

Times (serif)

Helvetica (sans serif)

learn to Type

A QWERTY keyboard is ingeniously designed to facilitate touch typing. You'll soon have the skill at your fingertips.

This primer covers lower-case letters only. From here you can go on to learn numerals, unlock the mystery of the shift key and master punctuation marks and symbols.

LEARN THE HOME KEYS
■ Rest the fingers of the left hand on A S D F.
■ Rest the fingers of the right hand on J K L and semicolon.
■ These are your "home keys"—that is, the default position for your fingers.
■ Each of your fingers is responsible for its home key and one or two keys above and below it (see below); the space bar is controlled by either thumb.

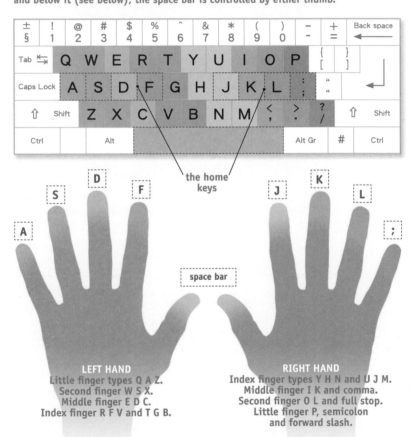

the home keys

LEFT HAND
Little finger types Q A Z.
Second finger W S X.
Middle finger E D C.
Index finger R F V and T G B.

RIGHT HAND
Index finger types Y H N and U J M.
Middle finger I K and comma.
Second finger O L and full stop.
Little finger P, semicolon and forward slash.

Look at the screen Use your fingers to press the keys for which they are responsible, working down in lines. Feel for the keys, don't look at them.

Pangrams make perfect Practice these phrases, which use every letter: *the quick brown fox jumps over a lazy dog; heavy boxes perform quick waltzes and jigs; the five boxing wizards jump quickly.*

Copy some written text Cover your hands with a scarf so you can't cheat.

relieve the pain of mouth Ulcers

Most people experience a painful sore, or ulcer, in their mouth at some time. It can be caused by damage to the mouth, such as an accidental bite to the cheek, sharp teeth and food, or stress. If you have recurrent mouth ulcers or cankers, seek advice from your doctor; you may have an underlying condition, such as a vitamin deficiency, or you may need to avoid certain foods or medications. Most mouth ulcers will clear up without treatment, but there are actions you can take to help yourself.

For pain relief
- Put a dab of peppermint oil on the affected area, but don't overdo it or you could cause further irritation.
- Use a mouthwash of cooled chamomile tea.
- Chew some fresh basil leaves.

To speed the healing process
- Avoid foods such as chips or toast, which may aggravate the ulcer.
- Use a soft toothbrush.
- Try relaxing activites such as yoga or meditation (*see* MEDITATE *and* YOGA) to reduce stress levels.

deal with Unconsciousness

A blow to the head, poisoning and shock are among the many reasons why someone might pass out (*see also* FAINTING). The cause may need medical attention, but first priority is to avert the risk that the person's tongue will fall back and block their windpipe, or that they will choke on saliva or vomit.

- Lie the person on their back and kneel by their shoulder. Place one hand on the forehead and tilt their head back so the mouth falls slightly open.
- Still holding the forehead, use two fingers of the other hand to lift the point of the chin, which moves the tongue away from the back of the mouth. Put your ear to their mouth and nose and listen for breathing. Look to see if their chest is moving.

If no regular breaths
- Call 911 or send someone to do so.
- Begin cardiopulmonary resuscitation (*see* CPR).

If the person is breathing
Treat any conditions that affect blood circulation (*see* BLEEDING *and* BURNS AND SCALDS). Place the person in the recovery position (*see* RECOVERY POSITION) and call for emergency help. Monitor their breathing and circulation closely.

repair an Umbrella

Not only is it raining, but a gust of wind catches your umbrella and tears the fabric from a spoke. Don't throw it away—take it home and make this simple repair instead.

YOU WILL NEED Strong, thick thread; needle

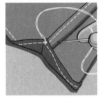

1 Check the corner seam of the umbrella where it's supposed to meet the spoke. If it's undone, repair with a few stitches.

2 Fold the seam corner about ¼ in. (6 mm) in toward the center, and add a few stitches to hold it in place.

3 Insert your needle into the edge seam just to one side of the folded corner.

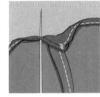

4 Pass the needle through the hole in the loose spoke of your umbrella.

5 Add a stitch in the seam on the opposite side of the folded corner. Then go back through the spoke hole again and repeat steps 4 and 5 once more.

6 Knot the end of your thread. Working close to the fabric, wrap the thread around the needle twice, then pull the needle through. Repeat for strength.

mark and record
Valuables

Take precautions to ensure that you can identify your property if it's stolen and found, or so that you can claim on contents insurance if you're the victim of theft.

■ Seek professional valuations of jewelry, antiques and rare objects, and keep a record. Have them revalued every few years, as valuations can quickly become out of date.
■ Certain objects can be indelibly marked with house number and postal or ZIP code using invisible fluorescent ink pens. Or you can simply etch your code and civic number on an object, such as a bicycle.
■ Make an inventory of all possessions of value, noting serial numbers, brand names and other identifying information.
■ Photograph important items against a plain background and next to a ruler to show scale. Note any distinguishing marks such as crests, initials, signatures, or chips or scratches.

---

golden rules
VEGETABLE GARDENING
■ **For variety, grow small amounts of many different vegetables.**
■ **Plan planting to have crops all year round.**
■ **Grow larger quantities of vegetables that will keep well over the winter, either fresh or frozen.**

make Vegetable stock

A well-flavored vegetable stock makes the world of difference to soups, braised dishes, casseroles and sauces. You can use almost any vegetables—and it's a great way of using up odds and ends from the bottom of the fridge.

TO MAKE 2.5 QT/L OF STOCK

3 tbsp olive oil	small bunch parsley
1½ lbs (750 g) onions, chopped	sprig of thyme
1 leek, chopped	a few sage leaves
1 clove garlic, chopped	salt and freshly ground
5–6 carrots, chopped	black pepper
2 sticks celery, chopped	2⅔ qt (2.5 L) water
8 mushrooms, quartered	

Heat the oil in a large saucepan and soften the onions, leek and garlic until the onions are golden. Add the remaining ingredients, bring to a boil and skim off any scum. Simmer, covered, for 2 hours before straining the stock through a fine sieve.

---

get started with a Vegetable garden

Freshly picked home-grown vegetables are full of flavor, nutritious and immensely satisfying to cultivate. You can grow them almost anywhere in the garden, in borders or in containers, but a traditional plot, if you have enough space, will give better results and be easier to maintain. Raised beds (*see* RAISED BED), which reduce the need for digging, are excellent for growing vegetables.

Site A sunny place is vital, ideally sheltered from the wind, which can impede plant growth. Vegetables prefer well-drained soil, so you'll need to add generous amounts of organic matter if it's heavy clay or very light sand or chalk (*see* SOIL). Easy access to water is also essential.

Permanent features You'll need one or two compost bins (*see* COMPOST), a space to stack manure or other bulky materials like leaf mold, paths for easy access and gardening tools. In a small garden, go for tall compost bins that take up less ground space.

What to plant Begin with the vegetables you most like to eat, and match them to your space. Quick-growing salads, spinach and snow peas are good to start with. On a small plot, choose vegetables that can be grown close together such as lettuces, beans, garlic and onions. Plant in blocks or rows.

How to plant Divide the plot roughly into quarters and plan to rotate crops to avoid buildup of pests and diseases. Each year, alternate positions of the four main types of crops: legumes (peas and beans), brassicas (such as broccoli and cabbage), potatoes, tomatoes and onions.

cook Vegetables perfectly

The art of cooking vegetables is to retain the maximum amount of nutrients and produce a pleasing taste and texture. Before cooking, vegetables need to be prepared by washing, peeling, slicing or podding to clean them and remove tough or inedible parts. Inedible bits can be kept for composting or adding to a wormery (*see* COMPOST *and* WORM COMPOST), and many are suitable for making stocks and soups.

Cut vegetables into even-sized pieces before cooking. Many vegetables are best cooked al dente; the exceptions are potatoes and root vegetables like parsnips, which should be tender but firm. Test that vegetables are cooked through by pricking them with the point of a sharp knife or skewer. Never overcook green vegetables—not only do they go mushy, but brassicas such as cabbage and Brussels sprouts take on an unpleasant, sulfurous taste.

Method	Cooking instructions and tips
BOILING	**Leafy vegetables, beans and peas** Use a minimal amount of water with ½ tsp salt added per 1¼ cups so that vegetables partly steam. Plunge into boiling water, cover and simmer for about 5 minutes. Drain well. **Root vegetables** Add just enough cold salted water to cover, bring to a boil then simmer for 10-20 minutes.
STEAMING	**Good for most vegetables** Put into a steamer with a tightly fitting lid over a little rapidly boiling water. Allow 3-5 minutes longer cooking time than for boiling. Add salt before or after cooking, as desired.
SHALLOW FRYING	**Good for soft-fleshed vegetables** such as mushrooms, eggplant and tomatoes, and for zucchini, peppers and celery. Use olive or canola oil, with a little butter added if desired, heated in a wide heavy-bottomed pan. Root vegetables, whole French beans and thick-stemmed vegetables such as broccoli are best parboiled (partly cooked by boiling) before being shallow fried.
DEEP FRYING	**Best for potatoes, onions, zucchini, peppers and eggplant** Vegetables, which may be coated in batter or egg and breadcrumbs, are immersed in hot vegetable oil and fried quickly. Fat should be at 375°F (190°C), or so hot that a cube of day-old bread browns in 1 minute.
BROILING	**Best for eggplant, zucchini, mushrooms, asparagus and tomatoes** Brush with a little oil and cook under theb broiler, turning once if necessary.
BRAISING	**Best for celery, leeks, lettuce, onions, carrots and celeriac** Blanch vegetables for 2-3 minutes in boiling water, drain and cover with stock. Cover with a tightly fitting lid and cook in the oven at 350°F (180°C) or on the stove top.
BAKING	**Best for potatoes, whole squash or pumpkins, peppers or tomatoes** Prick potatoes before baking to prevent them from exploding. Vegetables, which can be brushed with a little oil, are oven-cooked uncovered. Individual vegetables may be foil-wrapped and/or stuffed.
ROASTING	**Good for a wide range of vegetables, including root vegetables, onions, garlic, peppers, squash and zucchini** Vegetables are cooked in the oven in hot fat, either alone or around roast meat. Potatoes are best parboiled before roasting.

clean
Venetian blinds

They always look modern and stylish, but venetian blinds attract dust like a magnet and offer a real cleaning challenge. The trick is to maintain them regularly—it will avoid a much more difficult job later on.

Save yourself work by vacuuming venetian blinds regularly, ideally with the help of a purpose-made cleaning attachment, or use an old paintbrush to clean the slats.

Or put on an old pair of soft, absorbent gloves and run your hands along both sides of each slat. If you don't have an appropriate pair of gloves, use a couple of anti-static dusters. When the blind is pulled up, wipe the cords with a clean, dampened duster.

If washable blinds are really dirty, take them down and wash them in the bathtub with warm soapy water, using a small brush to work between the slats. Put a towel in the bottom of the bathtub to prevent damaging its surface. Rinse the blinds well and dry them with the help of a clean dish towel before re-hanging.

make the most of Velcro

Velcro, which comes in sew-on and adhesive-backed versions, is a handy substitute for zippers or buttons on garments—especially useful for quick-change stage costumes—and for cushion closures. But it can be used in many other situations, too. Each piece consists of a rough "hook" tape that joins tight to a softer "loop" tape.

On fabric pin and tack (*see* TACK) the hook part of the tape into position, making it the underneath part of the closure. Sew into place using backstitch (*see* SEWING), or by machine. Position the loop part of the tape then sew into place. Machine stitch or work backstitch by hand from the right side of the fabric to ensure a neat finish.
- Close Velcro fastenings before washing and ironing garments.

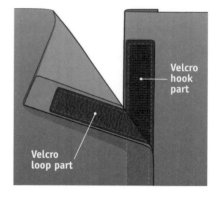

Velcro hook part

Velcro loop part

Hard surfaces Combine sew-on and stick-on types of Velcro for attaching fabric to hard surfaces, as when joining a curtain pelmet to a wooden support. Use adhesive-backed Velcro as a temporary closure for a door with a broken latch.

Other uses Use a hook strip of Velcro to remove fuzzy buildup on sweaters. Cut Velcro strips to create firm ties for securing plants to supports, or for holding electrical cables in neat bundles.

clean and restore Velvet

Velvet can be made from a variety of yarns, usually cotton or synthetics, but high quality velvet is made of silk. Dry cleaning, following the instructions given below, is always the safest cleaning method, and a must for crushed velvet, the surface of which will be ruined by water. Be sure to test an inconspicuous area of the fabric first. Specific stains should be removed with a dry-cleaning solvent, following the manufacturer's instructions.

- Brush the velvet gently against the nap to raise the pile or, for upholstery, use a vacuum cleaner.
- Mix half a teaspoon of dish soap with warm water to make a foam and use a sponge to apply the foam only. Be sure not to get the fabric wet or the backing may shrink.
- Leave for 24 hours until the foam has completely dried then brush, working against the pile. Never brush velvet while damp.

bake a Victoria spongecake

This British variant on traditional spongecake is named after the queen who liked to have it with her tea. For the filling, use jam, fresh fruit or buttercream icing. An undecorated cake will keep in an airtight tin for two to three days.

SERVES 6-8

¾ cup butter or block margarine
¾ cup sugar
3 eggs, lightly beaten
1½ cups self-raising flour, sifted
a few drops vanilla extract
a little milk
4-6 tbsp raspberry jam
⅔ cup whipping cream, whipped
2 tbsp icing (confectioner's) sugar

1 Heat the oven to 350°F (180°C). Grease two 8 in. (20 cm) cake pans and line the bases with parchment paper. Beat the butter and sugar until really soft, ideally using a mixer. Gradually beat in the eggs, adding 1 tbsp of flour with each addition. Fold in the remaining flour with the vanilla and enough milk to make a soft batter that will drop from a lifted spoon.

2 Divide between pans, smooth level and bake for 30 minutes or until risen and golden. The spongecake should spring back when lightly pressed in the center. Cool in the tins for a few minutes then turn onto wire racks to cool completely.

3 Spread the jam over the top of one cake and the cream on the underside of the other. Sandwich together then dust the top with sifted icing sugar.

---

liven up food with flavored Vinegars

Vinegars flavored with herbs and spices add an extra dimension to salad dressings and marinades. They are best made with a mild vinegar and will keep for three to six months if stored in scrupulously clean containers in a cool, dark place. Experiment with different flavor combinations as you wish.

YOU WILL NEED **Large glass jar with coated metal lid, cheesecloth, strainer, glass bowl, bottles, plastic funnel, corks or coated metal screw tops**

Tarragon vinegar Makes 2 cups. Pour 2 cups white or cider vinegar into a glass jar. Add a bunch of fresh tarragon, setting aside one or two sprigs for later use. Put on the lid and leave to infuse for four weeks. Strain through cheesecloth into a glass bowl. Put the reserved tarragon sprigs into one or two bottles, pour in the vinegar and seal.

Rosemary vinegar Cover five sprigs of the herb with boiling vinegar, cover and steep for three days before straining and bottling.

Chili vinegar Split two chili peppers in half lengthwise, cover with cold vinegar and steep for four to six weeks before straining and bottling.

---

digitize your Video

The principles for digitizing video are the same as for other "analog" media such as photos, vinyl records and music tapes. You need:

- A device to read or play the analog material (in this instance a VCR or camcorder).
- A physical connection with your computer (an audiovisual cable).
- Some software, such as Windows Movie Maker, to manipulate and replay the digital files.
- Somewhere to store the digitized material. Video files take up a great deal of hard drive space, so it's best to store them on an external hard drive or transfer them to DVD rather than keep them on your computer.

Turn on your computer then connect your VCR or camcorder and turn it on. Your computer will respond by starting up the appropriate software, or by asking you to confirm which software you want to use. Follow the on-screen prompts or click on **Help** to see instructions on how to use your particular software package.

See also CASSETTES, PHOTOS *and* VINYL RECORDS.

V

convert
Vinyl records
to digital

The key requirement for digitizing vinyl records is to have a turntable that you can connect to your computer.

Record player If you have a record player connected to a stereo system, look for two small round sockets labeled "line out." From here run a 3.5 mm stereo plug to two RCA connectors (available from electronics retailers) to the "line in" port on your computer. Or buy a turntable designed specifically for digitizing vinyl records. This comes with its own USB connection.

Software Download some free music-digitizing software such as Audacity.

- Clean your records thoroughly (see opposite) and buy a new stylus.
- Connect your record player to your PC and activate your software.
- Play your records through; in the process the music is converted into digital music files.
- Save your files to CD (*see* CD) or load them onto your MP3 player.

grow Vines outdoors

With the many new varieties now available it's perfectly possible to grow your own grapes outdoors.

Soil and site You'll need free-draining soil that's not deep clay or chalk and a site such as a south or southwest-facing wall or fence that will provide plants with maximum sunlight and protection from spring frosts.

Erect supports Install four strong galvanized horizontal wires 12 in. (30 cm) apart attached to the wall with 8 in. (20 cm) "vine eyes" (for a wall) or eye bolts (for a fence). Tie in a vertical cane support for each plant.

Preparation and planting Dig the soil, incorporating plenty of organic matter. Plant vines about 6 ft (2 m) apart in late autumn or early spring. Fill in with soil mixed with gravel to improve drainage.

YEAR 1, SUMMER Tie the strongest shoot to the support, pinch out others to one or two leaves.

YEAR 1, FALL Cut back to three or four buds.

YEAR 2, SUMMER Train the three strongest shoots to the support wires. Pinch out all other unwanted shoots.

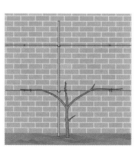

YEAR 2, AUTUMN Tie two good shoots laterally along the bottom wire. Prune the central shoot to three buds.

SUBSEQUENT SPRINGS AND SUMMERS Train the laterals along horizontal wires. Thin out side shoots to 8 in. (20 cm) apart. Feed with a high potash fertilizer as fruit begins to form. Pinch out growing tips above the top wire.

SUBSEQUENT AUTUMNS After harvesting, cut the center shoot back to three buds and tie in new shoots to the bottom wire. Cut fruited stems back to the base.

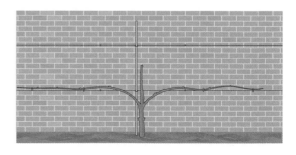

clean Vinyl records

Always clean a vinyl record before you play it; this prolongs the life of the record itself and of the stylus. Neither are easy to replace.

■ Velvet record brushes are the best way to clean an LP. Once commonplace, they are now sold in specialty record shops.
■ If, say, you acquire a rare but grimy record from a garage sale, it's acceptable to wash it with distilled water, but take care not to wet the label.
■ Let the record air dry and then put it in a new, clean inner sleeve, discarding the old one. To prevent warping, store your LPs upright on a shelf.

---

get more Vitamins into your diet

Vitamins nourish the body, help to ward off chronic disease and prevent premature aging. It's all about what you eat—and what you don't.

Vitamins are organic compounds vital to the normal function of the body. The vitamins you need to thrive are the water-soluble B vitamin complex and vitamin C, and the fat-soluble vitamins A, D, E and K. Fat-soluble vitamins are stored in the liver and fatty tissues. Water-soluble vitamins can't be stored; the body uses what it can and excretes the rest. A balanced diet (*see* DIET) usually supplies all the body's needs, but there are measures you can take to boost your supply.

Eat the rainbow Enjoy an abundance of fresh fruit and vegetables across the color spectrum—especially dark-green leafy and orange vegetables and deep-hued berries. Super-fresh homegrown fruit and vegetables are more nutritious than produce that has been packaged, transported and stored.

Raw or cooked? A good intake of raw fruit and vegetables helps to provide nutrients destroyed by cooking, so eat salads and crudités, and choose fruit for dessert. However, studies show that overzealous "raw foodists" can miss out. Tomato products when cooked, for instance, have more available lycopene, a powerful antioxidant. How you cook things can also make a difference—you'll lose fewer nutrients if you steam rather than boil vegetables.

Favor fresh foods "Live" whole, natural foods are richer in vitamins than heavily processed ("dead") ones.

Eat plenty of oily fish for fat-soluble vitamins.

Scrub rather than peel vegetables, or remove as little of the skin as possible. Most peel is edible and rich in vitamins. The nutrients in a potato are mainly concentrated just under the skin. To avoid further vitamin loss, don't slice or cut fruit and vegetables into small pieces or prepare ahead of time.

Steam rather than boil Water-soluble vitamins leach into cooking water. Whether you boil or steam, save the liquid to make soup.

Avoid deep-frying, which is destructive, especially to vitamin E, and don't overcook meat—another sure way to break down vitamins.

know your Vitamins

A balanced diet should provide all the vitamins your body needs (left). Adjust your food intake where you can rather than turning to vitamin supplements.

Vitamin A
Good for: immune system, vision in dim light, skin
Found in: cheese, eggs, oily fish, milk, yogurt

B Vitamins
Essential for: good general health
Found in: a varied, healthy diet
(*see* DIET)

Vitamin C
Good for: general health
Found in: peppers, broccoli, brussels sprouts, sweet potatoes, oranges and other fruit

Vitamin D
Good for: bones and teeth
Found in: mainly formed in the skin on exposure to sunlight, but also in oily fish, eggs, fortified spreads and breakfast cereals

Vitamin E
Good for: protecting cell membranes
Found in: soy, corn and olive oil, nuts and seeds, wheat germ, cereals and cereal products

Vitamin K
Good for: blood clotting, bones
Found in: broccoli, spinach, vegetable oils

make
Vol-au-vents

MAKES 12-14 SMALL VOL-AU-VENT CASES (BOUCHÉES)

1 lb (500 g) puff pastry
all-purpose flour
one beaten egg

1 Heat the oven to 425°F (220°C). Roll out the pastry on a floured surface to ⅟₁₆ in. (3 mm) thick and stamp out 24-28 rounds with a 1-in. (5 cm) diameter pastry cutter. Place half of these on a dampened baking sheet and brush with the beaten egg.

2 Use a 1 in. (2.5 cm) diameter cutter to cut out the centers of the remaining rounds and place them on top of those on the baking sheet, pressing gently to make them stick. Brush with beaten egg. Put the left-over circles onto a baking sheet and brush with beaten egg. Bake rounds and circles for about 15 minutes, until the rounds are well risen and golden. Transfer to a rack, cool, then use a teaspoon to remove any uncooked dough from the centers.

3 Fill as you wish, for example with shrimp in a béchamel sauce; cream cheese with herbs; mushroom, liver or smoked salmon pâté (*see* PÂTÉ); chicken or mayonnaise (*see* MAYONNAISE). Top with the lids.

master the basics of Volleyball

Volleyball is a six-a-side game played over a high net. Two teams use their hands to get a ball over the net, trying to ground it inside the opposition's half of the court. If they are successful in doing this, they gain a point. The team that wins the point then serves, and the game continues until one team reaches 25 points, with at least a two-point lead.

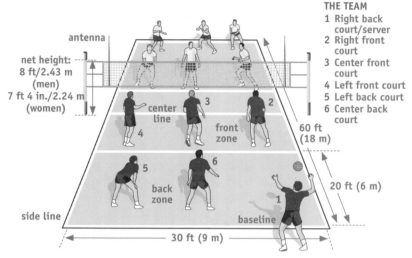

THE TEAM
1 Right back court/server
2 Right front court
3 Center front court
4 Left front court
5 Left back court
6 Center back court

antenna

net height:
8 ft/2.43 m (men)
7 ft 4 in./2.24 m (women)

center line

front zone

60 ft (18 m)

20 ft (6 m)

side line

back zone

baseline

30 ft (9 m)

THE SERVER STANDS behind the baseline, tosses the ball up and strikes it over the net with a flat hand (overhand) or a lightly clenched fist (underhand).

THE RECEIVING TEAM can touch the ball three times before returning it. Catching, carrying and throwing the ball aren't permitted and no player can have two touches in a row. Generally, teams use their three touches to set up the ball to be hit forcefully downward from a position close to the net. This shot—the "spike"—is the key attacking shot in volleyball, and the close "block" is the most important defensive ploy.

WHEN THE RECEIVING TEAM WINS A RALLY, and therefore the right to serve, its players rotate clockwise, so each player plays in every position in the course of a match.

THE DIG Used to take a low ball and divert it upward. Hold your hands together, the arms extended and wrists upward, and meet the ball with the wrists.

THE SET Another technique to send the ball upward to a position where it can be spiked. Played with palms upward, using the fingers to direct the ball with precision.

THE SPIKE Used to hit the ball at speed toward an undefended part of the opponent's court. Jump up close to the net and strike the ball with your clenched fist.

take up Walking

Walking is the most accessible form of exercise, and it's a great way to enjoy town and country.

Planning If possible plan a circular route, chosen to suit your level of fitness. You may want to avoid steep hills or very uneven surfaces. On average, a four to five mile (6.5–8 km) walk on easy terrain will take one-and-a-half to two hours. If you're walking in an unfamiliar area take along a detailed map.

Footwear Wear substantial "walking shoes" that give you good support or, for rough or wet ground, lightweight waterproof walking boots that protect your ankles if you wrench your foot. Wear boots one or two sizes bigger than your regular shoes to allow for a thicker pair of purpose-made walking socks. If possible, try to test boots on a slope before buying to check that your toes don't bang against the end of the boot when coming downhill. Always break in boots in before using them in earnest.

Other equipment Choose warm, loose, breathable clothing such as a fleece, windbreaker or raincoat with pockets large enough for a map, and comfortable pants or shorts. A hat is essential for protection from rain, wind and sun. Layer your clothing. Avoid jeans—they're heavy and slow to dry if you get soaked. In a backpack, pack water and some food if you're going to be out for several hours, plus a small first-aid kit (*see* FIRST-AID KIT) including sunscreen in summer, a map and a cell phone.

How to walk Hold your head high and shoulders back but watch the ground to avoid obstacles. Push off with your back leg and swing your arms for power. To speed up, lengthen your stride rather than taking shorter, quicker steps.

paint a Wall

■ Paint walls before you do the baseboards and other wooden surfaces (but after you have done the ceiling—*see* CEILING).
■ You can apply paint directly to new plaster, but it's best to apply primer first (*see* PAINT). You can paint over old wallpaper, but the results won't be the best. Test an area first to see that the paper doesn't bubble or come away from the wall.
■ When using a roller to apply paint, work from top to bottom in horizontal bands about 20 in. (50 cm) wide. When painting with a brush or a paint pad, work in areas about 20 in. (50 cm) square, and use a combination of diagonal, vertical and horizontal strokes.

make Waffles

Waffles are fun to make but you do need a purpose-made nonstick waffle iron. Serve waffles piping hot with honey, maple or corn syrup and with grilled bacon on the side for a great traditional breakfast.

MAKES ABOUT 12
1½ cups self-rising flour
pinch of salt
3 tbsp sugar
3 eggs, separated
¾ cup plus 1½ tbsp milk
3 tbsp butter, melted
1 tsp vanilla extract
canola oil for greasing

1 Sift the flour and salt into a bowl and stir in the sugar. Make a well in the center and add the egg yolks. Mix thoroughly then beat in the milk and butter alternately to make a batter. Stir in the vanilla extract. (For speed use a food processor to make the batter, then transfer the mixture to a bowl.)

2 Whisk the egg whites until stiff then fold into the batter with a large metal spoon. Grease the waffle iron and heat it as in the manufacturer's instructions. Pour in a little batter to cover about two-thirds of the iron and cook until golden brown—about 3 minutes. The waffle is ready when it stops steaming and the iron opens easily.

prevent and treat
Warts and plantar warts

Warts are benign growths of dead cells in the top layer of the skin caused by a virus, usually papilloma. A wart on the sole of the foot is called a "plantar wart." Because of the weight of the body, they appear quite flat. Almost everyone will develop a wart at some time.

To treat warts Most warts need no treatment. In children, 30-50 percent of warts disappear this way within six months, although some may not go for up to two years.

Seek medical advice if a wart is unsightly, painful or itchy, if there are concerns about it spreading, if you have warts on the genital or rectal area, or if you're over 45.

Try covering the wart with duct tape Leave it covered for six days then remove the tape, soak the wart and rub it with an emery board or pumice. Leave it overnight and cover again in the morning. Continue the six-day cycle for up to two months.

Paint the wart morning and evening with lemon juice, or a few drops of thuja or calendula tincture.

To guard against warts
■ Warts are contagious, so if someone has a wart, avoid contact with it.
■ Don't scratch or pick a wart; this may spread it.
■ Don't share a towel with anyone who has warts, or shoes and socks with anyone who has a plantar wart.
■ Wear flip-flops in communal shower areas and around swimming pools and dry your feet thoroughly.
■ Don't bite your nails (see NAILS); it can encourage warts around them.

dance the Waltz

One-two-three, one-two-three, around you go, light on your feet, gliding across the floor. This may be the simplest of the ballroom dances to learn, but few others match its grace and elegance.

The waltz is a romantic dance in ¾ time characterized by a continuous series of turns (its name comes from the German *walzen* meaning "to revolve"). It can be danced to the classical strains of composers such as Franz Schubert or the Strauss family, or to more modern popular songs such as "Edelweiss" and "Moon River." Either way, it should be performed with fluidity of movement.

The hold The man puts his right hand on the woman's back just below her shoulder blade and clasps her right hand with his left, holding it in a curve with the elbow lifted. She places her left hand on his right shoulder.

The basic step Six steps, counted "one-two-three, one-two-three," make up a basic "box step." The man continues to go forward, alternating the starting leg each time. The steps shown are for the man; the woman's are the mirror image.

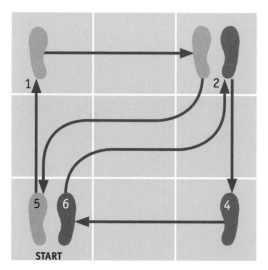

ONE-TWO-THREE The man steps forward with his left foot (1). He steps forward and to the right with his right foot (2). He closes his left foot to his right (3).

ONE-TWO-THREE He steps back with his right foot (4). He steps back and to the left with his left foot(5). He closes his right foot to his left (6).

Try adding some variation The leader dictates this by changing the direction or angle of the turns taken, and the length of each step. He can also add a "rise and fall" movement to the dance, bending his legs slightly at the beginning of each three-step sequence and extending up to his fullest height by the end. This helps to make the movement of the dance appear effortless.

deal with a Wasp sting

Unlike a honey bee, a wasp can sting more than once. Like a bee sting, in rare cases wasp venom can cause a serious allergic reaction (*see* ALLERGIC EMERGENCY). If you experience symptoms other than localized inflammation, swelling and itching, seek medical help. For a simple sting try the following.

- Wash with soap and water.
- Apply antihistamine cream.
- Apply an ice pack to cool the area and reduce swelling.

For additional relief, you can try the following.
- Apply a cotton ball soaked in apple cider vinegar.
- Tape a copper coin over the skin for 15 minutes.
- Press a slice of onion to the sting.

unblock a Washing machine

Always unplug the machine and turn off the water supply before you attempt to clear blockages.

Lint filter This coarse sieve catches bits of fluff, small coins and other objects as water drains from the machine. If it gets blocked, water can remain in the machine and leaks can occur. To check for blockages, open the access hatc, undo the filter cap and pull out the filter assembly. Remove any fluff and other debris, then rinse and refit. It's worth doing this every six months or so as a precaution against future blockages.

Inlet filter If the machine takes a long time to fill, then the inlet filters may be blocked. These filters are inside the screwed inlets to which the hot and cold hoses are attached (some machines only have one cold inlet hose). Pull the machine out from the wall. Unscrew one of the hoses, and put the washer to one side. Use needlenose pliers to remove the filter and its rubber seating. Clean the filter under a running tap and pick out any bits of grit with a pin. Reassemble and replace, then do the same with the other hose.

Outlet hose Check that there's no kink in the hose: if the machine fails to empty, this is often the cause. If not, disconnect the outlet hose from its exit point at the bottom on the back of the machine. You may have to remove a cover, or tip the machine on its side, to gain access to it. Loosen the clip, and remove the hose. Use a length of wire hanger bound in masking tape to fish out any blockage in the pipe. While the hose is off, feel inside the machine. The vanes of the pump should move freely. If not, and you can't free them yourself, call a repair person.

make a Wasp trap

Wasps are beneficial to the environment but unwelcome visitors at a picnic. A trap is easy to make—and they will live to sting another day!

YOU WILL NEED **Plastic bottle (2 qt/L size), sharp scissors or utility knife, jam or molasses or similar sweet bait**

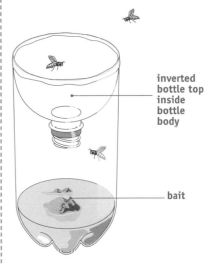

inverted bottle top inside bottle body

bait

1 Cut the top off the bottle at the point where the neck widens right out. Pour a little water into the bottom and add a teaspoon of bait.

2 Invert the bottle top and push it down into the base; make sure it fits snugly. Tape it if necessary.

Wasps will be attracted down this funnel, and once they are in the bottom of the bottle they won't be able to find their way out again. From time to time dispose of them; set them free, away from your home. Do this at night or on a cold day as the wasps will be less active and so less agitated.

Wallpaper
a room
see pages 352-353

W

Wallpaper **a room**

Wallpapering requires a degree of precision, but need not be a difficult job if you equip yourself with the correct tools and are prepared to take your time—don't rush it. Work out how much paper you need, add a bit extra and ensure that the rolls all have the same batch number to be sure that they match perfectly.

YOU WILL NEED Plumb bob, paperhanger's scissors, plastic bucket, paste, wallpaper, paste table, paste brush, smoothing brush, sponge and some clean rags, seam roller, small scissors. Optional: utility knife

ESTIMATING QUANTITIES Measure the height of the walls to work out how many "drops," or lengths of paper, you can get from one roll. Standard rolls are approximately 33 ft (10 m) long. If your paper has a repeating pattern, add the length of one pattern repeat to each drop (this length is usually noted on the packaging) so that the pattern will align.

Measure around the room, including alcoves and chimneys, and divide the total length by the width of the wallpaper; this tells you the total number of drops you'll need.

Calculate how many rolls you require by dividing the total number of drops you need for the room by the number of drops you can get from one roll, rounded up to the nearest whole figure.

PASTING Tie a length of string tautly across the rim of your paste bucket, both to support the brush when not in use, and so that you can remove excess paste from the brush by drawing it across the string.

1 Cut several drops of wallpaper, remembering to allow for any pattern repeat (see above) plus an extra 4 in. (10 cm) for trimming.

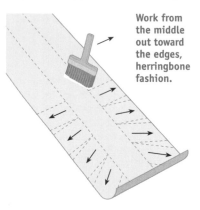

Work from the middle out toward the edges, herringbone fashion.

2 With the paper just overlapping the table edge, apply paste evenly to the back of the paper. Paste from the middle out (above).

3 Fold the ends into the middle, pasted sides together, but don't crease the paper. Number drops before you paste them and hang in that order.

HANGING Begin hanging on the wall next to the window wall (or the wall with the largest window) and work away from the light. This means that any slight overlaps won't cast shadows on the wall.

1 Use the plumb bob to mark a vertical line on the wall at the starting point. This should be at most a paper's width minus ½ in. (15 mm) from one corner of the room.

2 Unfold the top of your first length and align its right edge with the vertical line, allowing 2 in. (5 cm) at the top for trimming. Smooth with the smoothing brush.

3 Smooth down the middle first, then outward toward the edges in a herringbone pattern, working out any bubbles. Unfold the bottom part of the drop, and smooth it down in the same way.

4 Use the back of your scissors to crease the paper where it meets the baseboards and ceiling and trim to length. Butt the next length to the first, matching any pattern and pressing the join with a seam roller.

DECORATIVE EFFECTS You can do more than just cover all four walls with the same paper. Try doing just one "feature" wall in a bold pattern or lavish paper: a large floral design, say, or something pictorial or typographical. For children's rooms you can buy wallpaper murals in a variety of designs. Keep the other walls plain to make a contrast (and to keep the cost down) and choose soft furnishings to coordinate.

Alternatively, use a single drop of patterned paper as a kind of stencilled motif—down the center of a chimney breast, for example, or in the alcoves on either side. Pick a color from the design of the paper and paint the walls to match. Or try hanging a strong stripe pattern horizontally for a strikingly modern effect.

TURNING CORNERS Few corners are a perfect 90 degrees, but you can master the knack of papering them.

At an internal corner, cut the length to ½ in. (15 mm) wider than the furthest distance to the corner. Put it up in the normal way, using the brush to push right into the corner. Measure the offcut, add ½ in. (15 mm) and hang the offcut this distance from the corner on the adjacent wall.

At an external corner, cut paper to wrap 1 in. (2.5 cm) round the corner. No more, or the paper is likely to crease.

After the corner, if the turned-round edge is vertical, butt the next drop of paper to it. If not, you will need to overlap it onto the turned-round edge, matching any pattern as best you can.

WORKING AROUND OBSTACLES
It's not hard to do a tidy job around light switches and fittings.

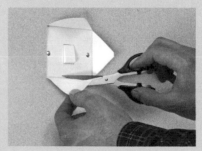

Turn off the power and loosen the screws just enough to tuck some paper underneath. Cut a cross in the paper to the corners of the plate and peel back the flaps. Trim to leave about ⅛ in. (3 mm) of paper and gently push this behind the switch cover using a craft stick, or just smooth the paper into place with the brush. Tighten the screws once the paper has dried, and restore power.

conserve Water

A frugal attitude to water is good for the environment—and it can save you money too.

- If you have a leaky tap, fix it (*see* TAP). One dripping tap can waste more than 1,000 gal (5,000 L) of water a year.
- Take shorter showers and shallower baths. Have a timer in your bathroom and set it when you get in the shower, so you know when it's time to get out. Knock a minute or two off your shower time if you can.
- Attach a rainwater tank to your downpipe (see right).
- Wash your car with a bucket and sponge rather than with a hose.
- Use the half-flush option on your toilet if you have one. If not, place a large plastic bottle of water—with the lid on—inside the tank, well clear of the flush mechanism. With each flush, you'll save as much water as there is in the bottle.
- Turn off the tap while brushing your teeth.
- Rinse dishes in a sink of clean water rather than running them under the tap.
- Don't run your dishwasher or washing machine unless you have a full load.
- Fill the kettle with only as much water as you need.
- Keep a jug of cold water in the fridge, so you don't need to run the tap until the water is cold.
- Water your garden in the evening or early morning, when less of the water will evaporate. If you must use a hose, fit a trigger so that no water spills uselessly on the ground. Don't water your lawn, even if it looks parched; it will turn green and lush again as soon as it rains.

unblock a Waste disposal unit

Minor blockages that slow the rotation of the blades inside a sink's waste disposal unit are easy to clear.

- Take out the drain trap (the little basket in the drain hole), and shake any debris trapped inside into the garbage. Put it back in the drain, and twist it to the closed position.
- Fill the sink with warm water to a depth of 4 in. (10 cm). Add ½ cup of baking soda to the water.
- Turn on the unit, and let it run for a second or two before twisting the drain trap to the open position. Let the soda solution swish through the unit, then run the tap again until you can hear that the unit is spinning freely.

install a Water catchment tank

Rainwater catchment conserves precious water—and rainwater is better for your plants than treated water.

Position your rainwater tank (or barrel) next to a convenient downpipe, and on level ground. Place it on a stand (you must have a stand, so that you can fit a watering can under the tap). There are two ways to divert water from the downpipe into the tank; you can fit a rain diverter, or you can direct the downpipe straight into the top of the tank.

Put the lid on your tank and lock it in place. This is primarily for safety, but it also helps to prevent mosquitoes from laying eggs in the water.

Direct method Saw off the downpipe 8 in. (20 cm) or so above the top of the tank, and use angled downpipe connectors and short, straight sections to drop the pipe through a hole in the lid. Most tanks have holes marked for this purpose; they can be drilled or knocked out.
- With this method, you must also fit an overflow kit, a pipe or tubing that leads from a point high on the side of the tank to drain off excess.

Diverter method This is a hose that leads from the downpipe into a hole marked in the side of the tank. The design of diverters varies—follow the instructions with your kit.
- Measure about 3 in. (8 cm) down from the top of the tank, and cut out a section of the downpipe.
- Insert the diverter, and reattach the downpipe top and bottom.
- With this method you don't need an overflow pipe.

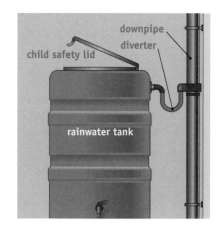

child safety lid

downpipe diverter

rainwater tank

paint a Watercolor scene

A broad horizon and changeable sky provide a perfect backdrop for a simple impressionistic watercolor landscape.

YOU WILL NEED **Sheet of medium-weight art paper, a size 12 round brush, paint in tubes (more convenient than cakes), two big, clear water jars (one for washing the brush, one for mixing colors), palette with mixing wells**

Keep it simple Break down the landscape into broad areas of color, then work with a limited range of colors to create your mixes. Watercolor isn't the medium for fine detail, so simplify any shapes in the scene, such as trees and buildings. Work with dash and spontaneity.

Build up your scene

1 Start with the sky. Mix two washes to match your scene—one brighter, one darker. A blue-based mix and a gray-based one are often effective.

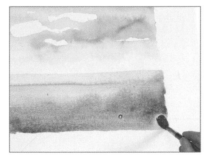

2 Lay a band of the brighter wash across the top of the paper. Then lay the darker wash below, working across and down to the horizon. Don't worry about gaps; they can serve as clouds. Vary the angle of the brush to modulate the color. Lighten the area just above the horizon by laying a wash of clear water.

3 Prepare three mixes of a color for the foreground, one light, one medium and one dark. Paint a band of the lightest across the horizon and work in the medium and then the dark mixes as you make your way down the paper. Allow the colors to flood into each other so that you lose the brush marks.

4 Now add in the details of the scene, using stronger colors and remembering to simplify the shapes. For trees, such as in the scene above, use a darker wash for the base of the foliage and pull the paint down to describe the tree trunks (no need for another color). For crisply defined edges, leave puddles of stronger color to dry.

Water plants
effectively

The plants that need most water are vegetables, container-grown plants and all newly planted annuals, perennials, shrubs and lawns.

Timing In spring and fall, water in the morning to protect from frost damage. In hot weather, water in the early morning or in the evening to reduce evaporation and prevent leaf scorching.

Amount Water well, less often, rather than sprinkling plants daily. This prevents them from becoming stressed and from growing roots too near the surface.

How to water Water as near to the ground as possible. Use a watering can or a hose directed onto individual plants in turn.

For individual plants sink purpose-made watering tubes, or inverted plastic bottles with their bases cut off, next to plants and water into these direct.

Reduce your use of water by collecting rainwater (see opposite). Also, save water used in the kitchen for washing vegetables to water your plants.

✳ golden rules
WATER PLANTS
- **Cut down watering by improving soil with organic matter and adding mulch.**
- **The smaller the plants, the finer the spray should be.**
- **Add water-retaining gel to the soil of container-grown plants.**

remove
Watermarks
from furniture

Watermarks are hard to get out, and no single method works in every instance. The methods given below are for white water stains affecting only the surface of the wood. Black water stains (those that have penetrated the wood's finish) can only be treated by stripping off the finish and bleaching the wood.

If you have a white water stain on a wooden surface, try this method first.

- Gently rub the stain with a cloth dipped in metal polish, car paint cleaner (not wax) or a special ring remover, working with the grain of the wood.
- Buff the stained area with a clean cloth, and apply furniture polish to the whole surface.

If that doesn't work, try one of the following methods. They all do the trick—sometimes.

- Rub on a 50:50 mix of baking soda and plain white toothpaste (never colored toothpaste or gel).
- Apply a thin layer of mayonnaise, and let it sit for an hour.
- Apply petroleum jelly, and leave it for a day.
- Make up a solution of equal parts of vinegar, boiled linseed oil and turpentine. Apply with a soft cloth.
- Apply olive oil using 0000 grade steel wool.

If you balk at trying some of these experiments on beloved or precious items of furniture, then your only option is to have the piece refinished by a professional.

stay on your feet when Waterskiing

There are few more exhilarating experiences than skimming across a body of water behind a speedboat. Once you're up on the skis, it's largely a question of holding on and enjoying the ride.

1 To stay on your feet, you must first get on your feet. Bend your legs until you're almost sitting on the back of your skis and lean back so that the tips of your skis are slightly out of the water. Make sure that the tow rope is fed out between your ski tips.

2 Signal your readiness. The boat will now move forward slowly to take the slack out of the rope. Once the rope has tightened, shout "Go boat!" As the boat slowly accelerates away, stay crouched and keep your weight over the back of the skis as they rise to the surface.

3 Once the skis have broken the surface, slowly push against them to come out of your crouch. Keep your knees bent to absorb any bumps and lean back to counter the pull of the boat. Lean into any turns that the boat makes so that you stay within its wake.

rejuvenate a Waxed jacket

Waxed cotton is a weather-resistant fabric made by weaving cotton yarn into canvas fabric, which is then treated with a mixture of waxes to create a barrier to wind and water while maintaining the cotton's breathability. A waxed jacket, worn frequently, will need reproofing once a year.

- Every time you take off your jacket, immediately remove any dried mud, grit and dirt by sponging, gently hosing or lightly brushing with a soft-bristle brush, and hang it to dry in a well-ventilated space. Don't leave it in direct sunlight.
- The makers of high-quality waxed jackets, such as Barbour, caution against machine washing, tumble drying or dry cleaning. Don't use soaps, detergents, solvents, bleach or starch. When the fabric starts to show shiny or dried-out areas, or when moisture no longer beads and runs off, apply reproofing dressing (available from a sportswear supplier or online) to the affected areas. Ensure the jacket is clean and dry and apply the cream sparingly, in a circular motion, with a lint-free cloth. Wipe off excess and hang to dry overnight.

set up a Webcam

It's easy to install a camera on your computer, and it opens up a new way to communicate with family, friends and colleagues.

- Many laptops and other computers come with a camera already installed. If not, a camera is inexpensive, and a basic model will be adequate for making Skype calls (*see* SKYPE) and for most internet chat purposes.
- Install the driver that was supplied on a CD along with your camera. When prompted, plug your camera into a USB port on your computer. Many webcams also have a built-in microphone, which makes it possible for you to chat with friends and family over the internet.
- It's best to perch your camera on top of your screen if you can. That way the person you're chatting to will have a more-or-less natural view of your face (though it may appear that you're looking at each other's noses).

design a simple Website

Putting together a website is no harder than creating a document in a word-processing program.

Experienced web designers use versatile software such as Front Page or Dreamweaver. If you're a beginner, it's easiest to use a predesigned template and build your website online. Many web companies will allow you to do this for free; take a look at Moonfruit, Google Sites or Mr Site.

Before you start, consider the content of your site. Gather all the text you want to include, plus all the pictures, movies, soundfiles and so forth. Think about the structure and the links. Draw a rough diagram of the various pages, so you have a workable visual hierarchy for your intended site. Keep it simple so that users can easily find their way around the pages.

Go to a free web-design site—in this case Google Sites—and register if you haven't already done so. Choose a template that fits the kind of site you intend to make. You'll find various categories, and a number of differently themed designs within each category.

Choose a name for your project This will be the last part of your site's name, so if it's for a business, use the company name. Click on **Create site**.

You're now ready to begin adapting the template to your own needs Click on **Edit page** and write or cut and paste your text into the boxes that appear. Use the other buttons and links—such as the one saying **"How to change this sidebar"**—to alter the elements of the template so that it conforms to the plan that you have made. Each new page can be slotted into the hierarchy that you sketched out at the beginning.

Use the preview page to check how your site is shaping up. Once you're happy with it, click **Save** and your web pages will go live on the web. You can go back in and change your site at any time.

spot Weather signs

Changes in the weather are caused by rising or falling air pressure—which are visibly reflected in natural phenomena.

cumulonimbus cloud

Clouds are the best clue to incoming weather. Towering cumulonimbus clouds with a dark base are a sure sign of rain. Sometimes you can see the approaching rain at a distance—it appears as a wispy gray smear between the base of the cloud and the horizon. Pendulous blobs hanging from the underside of a cloud—a rare sight—indicate that a severe storm or even a tornado is on the way.

Low-flying swallows are a sign of impending rain. When air pressure is low and air is full of moisture, the insects that they live on aren't carried upward on the air, so the swallows dive to catch them.

Dandelions and tulips close their flowers before rain. So too does the less common scarlet pimpernel. Not for nothing is it also known as the "shepherd's sundial" or the "poor man's weatherglass." If you see its bright red petals closed in the morning, then it's sure to be raining by lunchtime.

determine your ideal
Weight

Your ideal weight depends mainly on how tall you are, but your build also makes a difference.

A simple way to get an idea of your build is to wrap a hand around your wrist. If your thumb overlaps with one of your fingers you have a small frame; if they just touch, you're medium; if they don't touch, you have a large frame. Bear your frame size in mind when using the table below. If you're small-boned you should be toward the lower end of the weight range given for your height. If you're large-framed you should be toward the higher end. Very fit muscular people may weigh more than the stated ranges.

HEIGHT (feet)	MAN WEIGHT (lbs)	WOMAN WEIGHT (lbs)
4'10"	121-146	99-130
4'11"	123-148	100-132
5'	126-150	101-137
5'1"	128-154	104-139
5'2"	130-159	108-143
5'3"	132-163	110-148
5'4"	134-165	112-152
5'5"	137-170	117-154
5'5"	139-174	119-159
5'8"	141-179	121-163
5'9"	143-183	126-165
5'10"	146-187	128-170
5'11"	152-196	132-132
6'	157-201	146-187

control Weeds

Weeding is a regular chore necessary to keep a garden neat and allow your chosen plants to thrive without unwanted competition. Above all, you need to avoid spreading small pieces of the roots of perennial weeds, which quickly sprout into new plants.

Regular hoeing is the best way of removing small weeds, especially annuals. Leave uprooted weeds on the soil surface to dry out, then compost them.

Digging with a trowel or spade is essential for removing the roots of perennial weeds such as bindweed, goutweed and creeping charlie, and for dandelions with long tap roots from which weeds can regrow.

Chemical treatment Kill both shoots and roots of persistent weeds with glyphosate, a systemic weed killer, following the manufacturer's instructions.

Cover up Help to clear areas of perennial weeds by covering them with old carpet or heavy-duty black polyethylene, weighted down and left for a full growing season. *See also* MULCH.

Wet shave your face

The art of shaving is regularly practiced, so with the right materials and technique it can be easily perfected.

- Shave after you shower, or apply a washcloth soaked in hot water before you begin; wet, warm stubble is much easier to remove.
- Apply an even layer of lather to the entire beard area.
- Check your razor; blades grow dull after a few uses, and a blunt razor is more likely to cause nicks and irritation.
- Shave in the direction of growth on your first pass, then across for your second (against the grain gets a closer shave, but can cause razor burn).
- Rinse well with cold water, and apply a moisturizer rather than an alcohol-based aftershave.

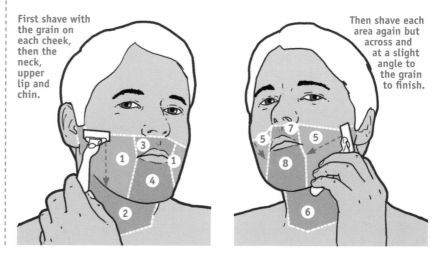

First shave with the grain on each cheek, then the neck, upper lip and chin.

Then shave each area again but across and at a slight angle to the grain to finish.

play Whist

This old British game was once played throughout North America as well. Though rarer these days, there are still plenty of players on both sides of the Atlantic.

Whist is a game for four people who play in pairs to win the highest number of "tricks." Each player cuts the deck of 52 cards (ace ranks high), with the two highest scorers playing the lowest scorers. Partners sit opposite each other.

The deck is cut again and the highest scorer is the first dealer. They then deal the cards one at a time until each player has 13. The last card dealt is shown before going into the dealer's hand and this determines which suit is trumps (the highest scoring).

The dealer turns up the last card dealt to determine which suit is trumps.

The play

■ Players may not comment on their hands, and partners may not signal to each other.
■ The player on the dealer's left starts by laying down any card.
■ Other players must follow suit if they can. If they can't, they can lay down a card from the trump suit or discard a low-scoring card of any suit. The highest of four same-suit cards wins the trick. If trumps are played, the highest trump wins the trick. Even low-ranking trump cards beat cards of a different suit. The winner of each trick starts the next.

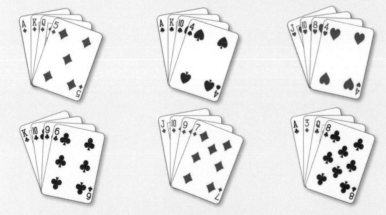

The first five tricks are won by the highest-ranking card in the suit, but, with diamonds as trumps, the ace of clubs in the last trick is beaten by the three of diamonds.

When 13 tricks have been played, the pair who won more tricks scores one point for each trick they won in excess of six. The first partners to score five win. If neither pair has reached five, another hand is dealt. Conventionally, a second deck is waiting, already shuffled.

Whistle
a happy tune

Whistling tunefully, like all musical skills, takes practice. Begin by learning to produce a single note.

■ Form your mouth as if to say "oo."
■ Keeping your mouth in this position, try to make an "ee" sound. This will make you tauten your cheek muscles and force your tongue down in your mouth.
■ Blow a gentle but steady stream of air through your rounded lips.
■ If you don't get a note, try moving the tip of your tongue slightly—you should be able to feel it close to the point where your lower teeth meet your gums.
■ Keep experimenting—eventually you'll find the mouth position that produces a melodious whistle.

golden rule

WHIST WISDOM
■ **When you have four or more trump cards and a similar number in another suit, lead with that second suit. Do the same when you are low on trump cards (two or fewer) and have the same number in another suit.**

Whittle wood

Whittling soft wood with a sharp knife or chisel is a relaxing, satisfying and creative pastime.

Kits are available for beginners. These often contain a selection of knives or blades, and other useful whittling tools, such as palm chisels.

For safety's sake, always wear a carving glove on the hand that holds your work, and use only sharp tools.

■ Draw a centerline on each side of the wood, then "block out"—that is, draw the rough shape of your figure on each surface of your wood, so that you can see from any angle what needs paring away.
■ Work by making small cuts—so that you don't accidentally take off too much, and so as not to strain your hands. Pause at intervals to block out the next stage of your work, then continue whittling.

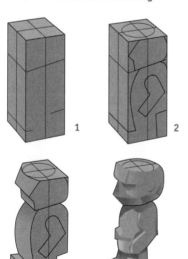

TO MAKE A SMALL MAN draw a centerline on each surface and other guidelines (1). Then draw on the basic body features and the circumference of the head (2). Whittle the wood down to create a block figure (3) then add further detail as you continue to carve (4).

care for a Wig

Synthetic fiber wigs are easier to manage than natural hair varieties, but they need the right care if they are to stay in good condition.

■ When you buy a wig, invest also in the correct accessories—a wig brush and comb, shampoo and conditioner, a proper stand for it, a wig cap and synthetic fiber spray.
■ Don't be tempted to leave your own hair unwashed beneath the wig. Always shampoo your hair before wearing your wig, and wear a nylon wig cap to protect your wig from oils.
■ Brush a wig lightly before washing it, then add a little wig shampoo to a sink of cold (never hot) water. Soak it for a minute until it's wet through then rinse lightly for a further minute. Squeeze the wig out gently—don't wring it. Blot off excess water with a towel. Place the wig back on its stand and wait for it to dry entirely before styling. Condition the wig every few washes.
■ After wearing a wig, brush it through and always store it on its stand to help it to retain its form.
■ Makeup traces around the hairline can be removed by the gentle use of a soft toothbrush with soap and water.

contribute to Wikipedia

To write for Wikipedia, you must first register with the site. You'll find lots of guidance there, but you need to remember some key things.

■ Your article must be on a subject of encyclopedic interest (don't write about your cat, your street or your grandfather).
■ Provide references to reliable sources (gather these before you begin) and write in links to other connected subjects.
■ Your article should be balanced, scholarly and original (there's no point in writing a piece on Elvis Presley; it's already there).
■ Hone your piece in your own "user space" before you move it into the main area. And be flattered, rather than annoyed, if other users add to your entry or edit it. That is how Wikipedia works.

edit a Wikipedia article

You don't have to be a registered user to edit a Wikipedia article. Simply click on an **edit this page** link and make your changes in the box that comes up. Write a brief account of what you've done in the "edit summary" box. If you want to change the meaning of an article or change the facts that it contains, this counts as a "major edit." If you're planning a major edit, consider making your intentions known to other interested editors via a "discussion page." When you incorporate the thoughts and opinions of other users, it's less likely that your changes will be disputed or deleted.

make a Window box

The advantage of making your own window boxes is that you can tailor them exactly to the space you have available. Before being filled, this box could be attached to a wall with strong metal brackets.

YOU WILL NEED **Exterior grade plywood cut to size, drill with spade bit, length of 1 x 1 in. strip of wood, tape measure, pencil, exterior wood glue, screws, screwdriver, clamps, cardboard, saw, wood preservative, paint**

1 Determine the dimensions you require, then buy the plywood for the sides, ends and base cut to size. Use the spade bit to drill holes in the base for drainage.

2 Measure and cut four short lengths of wood for the inside corners and two long ones to support the base. Use the adhesive and screws to attach the corner pieces to the ends. Drill pilot and clearance holes and countersink the clearance holes so that the screw heads lie flush.

3 Fix pieces along the bottom inside edges of the back and front sections. Clamp the back section into position, using cardboard to stop the clamps damaging the wood, and screw the two ends into place. Fix the front into place using the same method.

4 Saw a 1 x 1-in. notch into each corner of the base section and drop it into the box to rest on top of the two long pieces. Treat inside and out with wood preservative, then paint as you wish.

plant and maintain a Window box

Planting Add slow-release fertilizer and water-retaining gel granules to the compost before you plant. For full impact choose simple color schemes such as red geraniums with ivy, or pastel petunias with silver-leaved helichrysum. For north-facing windows choose ferns and impatiens. Plant generously.

Feeding Apply a measure of liquid fertilizer every three or four weeks as plants mature.

Water regularly, as near to plant roots as possible. If you live above other people, or if your box overhangs a sidewalk, put a drip tray under the box so that passersby don't get showered.

protect yourself in a Wildfire

Wildfires can spread incredibly fast, but there are ways to stay safe if you get caught up in one.

Do what you can to reduce the risk to the building where you're staying. Move combustible objects, such as garden furniture and gas canisters, away from the house. Turn off the gas supply. If possible, soak the walls and roof of the house with a hose. Do the same to fences, nearby trees and grass. If the blaze comes close, don't stay to fight the fire.

Protect your home by creating a safety zone about 32 ft (10 m) deep on all sides. Remove old cars, wood piles, felled trees and other debris. Make sure there's enough space for firefighters to protect the rear of your home. Make sure all fences have easily accessible gates. Keep lawns mown short (3 in./7.5 cm or less), as grass cut short won't carry fire. Clear a 10 ft (3 m) space around fuel tanks and fill this space with gravel, rock or short-mown grass.

Be ready to leave quickly Park your car near the exit with windows and vents closed. Carry your keys. Load up the car with drinking water. Plan several escape routes, so that you have options if you encounter a block in the road.

golden rules

MAINTAIN WINDOW BOXES
- **Don't overdo the gel granules —they'll swell too much and push plants out of position.**
- **Replant as soon as plants are past their prime.**

clean Windows
without chemicals

It's inexpensive and effective to clean windows with plain water or a simple homemade solution. Always avoid sunny days for this job—quickly dried glass is more susceptible to streaking.

Plain water Apply water with a sponge, using just enough to prevent drenching the pane, working from side to side. Then wipe down with a squeegee, wad of newspaper, paper towels, chamois or clean, lint-free soft cloth.

Simple cleaner Mix 1½ tbsp white vinegar with 2 cups water and use to fill a spray bottle. Spray on evenly, then buff off with a wad of newspaper, chamois or paper towels.

✶ golden rules
CLEAN WINDOWS
- **Work from the top to the bottom of the pane.**
- **Wipe window corners with a rag before you begin.**
- **Protect indoor windowsills with old towels as you work.**

replace a broken Window pane

Before buying new glass, measure the window opening to the inside of the rabbets (the recesses in which the pane sits). Subtract ⅛ in. (3 mm) from the height and width for an easy fit. Be careful: A wrong-sized pane is useless.

YOU WILL NEED New pane of glass, safety glasses, thick work gloves, hammer, old chisel or hacking knife, pliers, putty, glazing points

1 Wearing goggles and gloves, remove the broken pane, using a hammer if necessary, and dispose carefully of the glass. Then, working on the outside of the window, use an old chisel or hacking knife to dig out fragments of glass and putty from the frame. Pull out any remaining glazing points with pliers.

2 Knead some putty until it's soft, then smooth a thin layer all around the frame. Place the new pane in the frame, and press the edges firmly into the bed of putty.

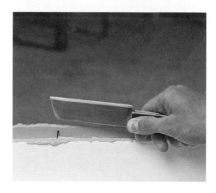

3 Using the back of your hacking knife, tap in new glazing points about 1 in. (2.5 cm) apart to hold the new pane in place. The heads of the points should protrude about ¼ in. (5 mm).

4 Apply more putty to the front of the glass to fill the frame. Use your putty knife as shown right to compact the putty and leave a level surface at 45 degrees to the glass. Draw the knife along the edge of the putty to smooth the putty into a neat bevel. It should cover the heads of the points, and line up with the window frame on the inside edge. Make neat miters at each corner and clean away excess putty from the inside of the window.

paint Windows

Start painting windows early in the day, so that they dry before you close them at night. Protect the glass with masking tape, or use a masking shield.

Casement windows
These should be painted when open, and in the following order.

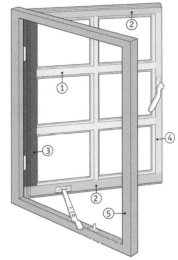

Crossbars and transoms (1), paint horizontal bars first then vertical ones. **Top and bottom rails** (2), including any rabbets that fit around frame. **Hanging stile** (3), the vertical to which the hinges are attached. **Meeting stile** (4), the other vertical, to which the handle is attached. **Window frame** (5). If the inside and outside are painted in different colors or finishes, paint anything visible from inside, when the window is open, in the internal color and vice versa for the outside.

Sash windows
These should be opened so that the bottom window is as high as it will go, and the top window as low as it will go. Paint in the following order, then reverse the sashes and paint the bits of each window that you couldn't reach on the first pass.

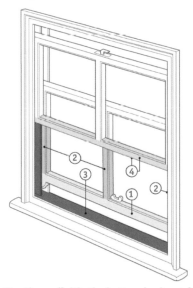
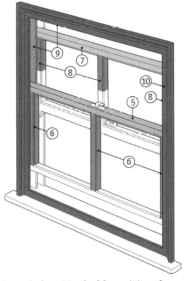

Meeting rail (1), the bottom horizontal of the top window. **Vertical bars** (2) as far as you can reach. **Bottom of the frame** (3), where the inner sash sits when closed, and a very thin coat on the sides or runners. **Bottom horizontal rail of the inner window** (4), including the underside. Swap the position of the sashes at this point, then paint **top horizontal of the inner window** (5) and **vertical bars** (6). **Top horizontal of the outer window** (7), including top edge and **remainder of the vertical bars** (8). Finish with upper inside of **frame and runners** behind the cords (9), and the **frame** (10).

free stuck
Windows

Sash windows can get stuck when the sashes are broken, but a more common reason is that they have been painted shut.

- Run a sharp utility knife down the crack between the window and frame to break the seal of paint.
- Alternatively, apply paint stripper —but only if you're about to repaint, as this will ruin the paint finish on the window.
- Or, insert the tip of a wide-bladed chisel at the bottom of the window from the outside—one sharp downward push might break the paint seal and free the window.

Casement windows can get stuck if they have been painted too often, or when the wood swells in damp or wet weather—a problem that may resolve itself once warmer weather comes. If not, plane the edge of the window that's causing the problem (most likely the bottom edge). Check that the putty around the glass is well covered with paint, as this will help to prevent the wood from swelling.

✷ golden rules
SMOOTH, SMART WINDOWS
- **Metal windows tend to fit more snugly than wooden ones, so you may have to strip them back before you paint, or else they might not close properly.**
- **Sand and clean wooden frames before painting to avoid a buildup of paint, or a poor finish.**

deal with a broken car
Windshield

The windshield on most modern cars isn't prone to shattering. But even a small chip in the driver's sight line can obscure your vision, and will only get worse if you leave it and don't get it repaired.

- If your windshield does shatter while you're driving, don't try to punch out the glass while you're still in motion.
- Slow down and, making use of whatever you can see of the road, find a safe place to stop.
- Stuff rags or newspapers into any vents before firmly and steadily pushing the glass outward onto the hood using a gloved hand, wrench or jack handle.
- If you must drive on, go slowly straight to the nearest garage.

de-ice a frozen
Windshield

- Don't use a credit card to scrape off ice—it might not do the glass much harm, but could render the card useless.
- First, turn on the ignition and put the car's defroster on its highest setting, directed onto the glass.
- Keep a can of deicer and a windshield scraper in your car during winter. Use them to clear the windshields and side windows completely before you set off: it's dangerous to drive with a partially obscured view of the road.
- Never pour hot water on your windshield to melt the ice; it might cause the glass to crack.
See also DRIVE.

learn to Windsurf

Windsurfing is part sailing, part surfing. As a beginner, you should be prepared for some dunkings, but when you first catch the wind and move, you'll discover an altogether exhilarating watersport.

Climbing aboard

1 Stand in waist-high water with your board in front of you and the sail downwind of the board. Climb aboard on your knees and grasp the "uphaul," the line attached to the middle of the mast.

2 Stand up, place one foot on either side of the mast, and start to raise the rig, keeping your back to the wind. Make sure your back is straight and your weight is over the center of the board.

Moving off

1 Find your balance before attempting to move. Let the rig swing freely downwind of you, while keeping hold of the uphaul. Get the feel of the board and make sure you feel comfortable with your position and balance.

2 Hold the boom (the horizontal bar), and pull it across your body as you step back toward the tail of the board. Your front foot should be at the base of the mast. As the wind catches the sail, you'll begin to move off at right angles to the wind. Pull back with your back hand to speed up and relax your pressure to ease off the speed.

match Wine with food

Finding a wine to complement a meal is not very difficult. The basic rule of white wine with fish and white meat and red wine with red meat is a reliable place to start.

Type of wine	Good with
Red wines	
CABERNET SAUVIGNON A grape prominent in Bordeaux and New World wines. Has a distinctive and emphatic taste, with high tannin levels and a flavor of oak that's too strong for delicate foods.	Poultry, roast beef, roast lamb, kidneys, aged hard cheeses
MERLOT The most widely used red wine grape in Bordeaux, now grown around the world. Ripe, smooth and more adaptable than cabernet sauvignon.	Calves' liver, grilled steaks, stews
SYRAH/SHIRAZ Widely used in the Rhône Valley, California, British Columbia, Ontario and Australia. Has flavors of black currant, black pepper and spice.	Steak, roast beef, wild game, meat stews, mushrooms, chili, grilled foods
PINOT NOIR An elegant grape, but challenging to grow and rarely used in blends. Has soft tannins, shades of cherry, strawberry, plum and leaf tea.	Salmon, tuna, venison, duck, baked ham, goose
BARBERA Italy's third-most-planted red grape, also popular in California. Cheap and cheerful, juicy and fruity—perfect with Italian food.	Pizza, tomato and meat pasta, salami
GAMAY French grape used in Beaujolais, but also in parts of Burgundy and North America. Best drunk as a young wine, which is light and summery.	Cold meats, mushrooms. sausages, pâtés
White wines	
CHARDONNAY Originated in Burgundy and used in Chablis. The most widely planted white-wine grape in the world. Dry, rich, honeyed, sometimes oaky, though unoaked wines are available. Pairs well with many foods.	Omelets, fish, chicken, shellfish, mild game, coconut curries
SÉMILLON The major white-wine grape of Bordeaux. Also grown in Chile, Argentina and North America. Strong notes of date or fig. Often blended with Sauvignon. Sweet Sauternes and Barsac are made from overripe Sémillon.	Dry Sémillon: fish, shellfish, pork Sweet Sémillon: blue cheese, aged hard cheese, creamy desserts
SAUVIGNON BLANC Originated in the Loire Valley. Popular around the world. Makes light-to-medium-bodied white that pairs with a ride range of flavors.	Goat's cheese, asparagus, seafood, Thai food
RIESLING Classic grape from the Rhine and Mosel in Germany, Alsace in France and also popular in Australia. Light, aromatic and with a steely acidity; very flexible for pairing with food.	Fish, pork, shellfish, omelet, duck, goose, sushi
PINOT GRIGIO Widely grown in the Venezia and Alto-Adige regions of Italy, and increasingly popular. Crisp and bone dry with an acidic bite, versatile for drinking on its own or with food.	Light and creamy pasta dishes, pork, vegetable ravioli, pâtés

detect and treat
Woodworm

The telltale signs of woodworm attack are the small (⅛ in/3 mm) round holes in the surface made by the adult beetles as they leave. Bare dark holes indicate an old attack; white holes, with small piles of wood dust, indicate recent and possibly ongoing activity that needs to be dealt with immediately to prevent further weakening of the wood.

■ Paint all surfaces of an infected piece of furniture with two coats of a store-bought woodworm killer.

■ Alternatively, inject the holes using a can of woodworm killer with a special nozzle.

■ Furniture beetles won't lay eggs in treated wood, so one application should solve the problem.

⭐ golden rules
KEEPING WINE

■ **If you have wine left over in an open bottle, it should keep for about two days in the fridge. Reseal the bottle with a screw cap or airtight stopper.**
■ **Dessert wines, like sherries and ports, will keep for longer, but taste them to be sure before serving to your guests.**

---

taste Wine like an expert

When a wine waiter brings a bottle to your table you should be shown the label to ensure that it's the wine you ordered. When it's opened and you're offered a little to taste, the point is to check that the wine isn't "off," and that it's as described on the wine list, not to see whether you like it.

■ Take a look at the color. Red wine shouldn't be cloudy or brownish.
■ Smell it first. If it's vinegary that's a sign of oxidation. A musty smell suggests a moldy cork, which will have tainted the wine.
■ If you want to taste the wine, take a small sip and swill it around your mouth to activate all your taste buds. Suck a little air into your mouth as you do this to release all the flavors and aromas.

At a wine tasting there should be a spittoon at hand for you to spit out the samples you taste. Try lots of different wines to get a feel for which sorts you prefer and to learn how to pick out different flavors.

■ The sweetness of the wine is the easiest to detect, and the more it makes your mouth water, the higher its acidity. A balanced acidity is usually the most pleasurable to drink.
■ The drier and earthier the taste of a red wine, the higher its tannin level. Young red wines are low in tannin and good for drinking on their own. Wines high in tannin offer more complex flavors and pair best with food.

---

store and serve Wine

Most white and rosé wines are sold ready for drinking now and don't need storing. Good-quality red wines, except for the lightest, such as Beaujolais, can benefit from careful storage. Even cheaper wines will taste better if you serve them properly and at the right temperature.

To store Ideal conditions for wine storage are darkness and a temperature of around 54°F (12°C). A closet or a garage will be fine, but watch it doesn't freeze in winter.

■ A consistent temperature is more important than coolness. If wine is kept in an area a little cooler or warmer than the ideal, it won't suffer as much as if it's subject to a sudden temperature change.
■ Store bottles in a rack, on their side, so the cork doesn't dry out. Bottles with a screw cap can be stored upright.

To serve Very expensive red wine may benefit from decanting, but most wine is fine served from the bottle. Have a quick taste to make sure the wine is in good condition and at the right temperature.

■ White wine is best served chilled, and red (with rare exceptions) at just below room temperature. An hour or so in the fridge for white wine or three hours at room temperature for red wine should be just right.
■ Open red wine a little ahead of time to let it "breathe."
■ Choose glasses large enough to swill the wine around, since part of the pleasure is to smell it and enjoy the "nose."
■ Keep white wine on ice or otherwise cool while drinking.

set up a Worm compost in your yard

A worm compost bin is an enclosed bin in which worms churn and chew your kitchen waste to produce a rich liquid fertilizer and compost.

Establishing a worm compost bin It will take a couple of months for a worm compost bin to produce fertilizer. Keep feeding it little scraps often.

■ You'll need to buy a starter kit of special tiger worms or red brandlings, as earthworms from the garden are not good composters.

■ Put a wide variety of scraps into your worm compost bin for best results. Try to avoid onion skins and citrus peel, which are too acidic.

■ Worm compost kits usually have several layers. When the bottom tray is full start filling the next—the worms will wriggle up through the perforations.

1 Cover the base of the bottom tray of your bin with cardboard and crumble over a layer of coir or a worm compost bedding block. Mix in a little compost to get the worms started.

2 Add your worms and cover them with a layer of shredded newspaper and a damp sheet of cardboard or hemp matting to keep out the light. Put the lid on and leave it for a month.

3 After a month, start adding your kitchen scraps. Bury meat beneath the surface to avoid attracting pests.

4 The worms will turn the waste into rich garden compost, but also produce an excellent liquid fertilizer, which you should drain from the tap. Dilute this 1:10 parts water and use it to feed your garden plants.

organize your Workstation

A day spent organizing your workspace will pay dividends in helping to maximize your efficiency.

Tidy desk, tidy mind

■ On your desk you should have only the things you need for the task at hand. If there are books, letters and printouts that you have finished with, or don't intend to use today, put them somewhere else.

■ Have a shoebox, tray or file where you keep pending correspondence and move it to a shelf: At least that way, the chaos is contained.

■ Shun desk toys and too many photos—they will clutter your mind as much as your desktop.

■ If possible, don't have your printer on your desk; it takes up far too much useful space.

Filing and organization

■ Use your desk drawers wisely: one for pens, another for paper stationery, another still for personal items, phone chargers and the like.

■ Be organized with filing, creating separate hanging files in drawers for current projects, important paperwork, recently completed jobs and other things that you may need to access at short notice.

■ Move old paperwork into archive boxes until you can dispose of it.

Safe and comfortable working

■ Take care positioning your computer. Don't have your monitor up against a bright window or light, or where glare will dazzle off the screen.

■ Make sure that your chair is supportive and that you're sitting at the right height for your desk. *See also* SIT.

tackle Worms in pets

Even healthy-looking animals can be carrying roundworms and tapeworms. In young pets, worms can cause a pot belly, poor growth and diarrhea. A heavy infestation can even cause a fatal blockage of the intestines. In adult pets, worms can lead to poor coat condition, vomiting and diarrhea. Worms also pose a risk to humans —roundworms in dogs and cats (toxocara), for example, can cause blindness in children, though this is rare. Regular worming is essential to protect pets and people alike. Worms aren't choosy, and will live happily inside you, too.

■ Ask your vet for advice on the most suitable worming treatment to use on a pet.
■ Tapeworms rely on fleas to survive, so regular flea prevention treatment is important. Ask your vet for advice.
■ Note clearly on your calendar when treatments are due.
■ Always observe strict hygiene. Dispose of feces and cat litter every day and always wash your hands afterwards (*see* HANDS). Make sure children do the same and stop them playing with mud. Cover sandpits, too, to avoid cat contamination.

golden rules
GIFT WRAPPING
■ **Work on a firm, flat surface.**
■ **Use double-sided tape fixed between two surfaces of the paper, so that no tape shows on the finished parcel.**
■ **Measure the appropriate amount of paper; too much paper looks untidy.**

Wrap a gift

YOU WILL NEED **Wrapping paper that won't tear, tape measure, scissors, double-sided tape in a dispenser**

Rectangular or square shape
The paper should be wide enough to wrap right round the package, plus 2 in. (5 cm). Its length should be the package length, plus the package depth, plus

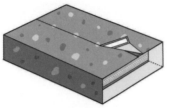

1 Center the package, top down, on the paper and wrap the paper around it. Put tape beneath the top part of the overlap and press it down.

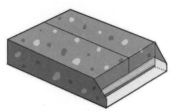

2 Fold the top of the paper over one end, pressing it in at the sides so that the side flaps slant down. Pinch the slants into sharp creases.

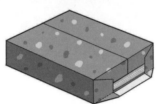

3 Fold the slanted sides inward and press them in firmly at the base so the bottom flap slants in at the sides.

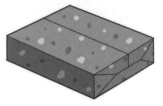

4 Fold the bottom flap of paper up and tape it into place. Repeat for the other end of the package.

Jar or bottle

Cut two squares of pliable paper, such as tissue or foil, with sides as long as twice the height of the jar or bottle plus three times its width. Lay one on the other with their corners alternating. Center the jar or bottle, draw up the paper all round and tie it with a ribbon.

Tubular shape

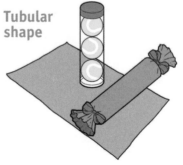

Cut a piece of paper ½ in. (1.5 cm) longer than the tube and wide enough to wrap around the tube, plus 2 in. (5 cm). Use tape to fix the paper in place lengthwise, as for a box (above). At each end tie a ribbon to gather the paper. Spread the gathers evenly.

decorate a pinecone Wreath

Wreaths can be made from almost any plant material but work best with evergreens, buds and berries, or dried seed heads. Some of the foliage and the pinecones can be sprayed gold or silver.

YOU WILL NEED **Thick wire, vine wreath base (from florists' suppliers), evergreen stems such as holly, bay or ivy, shears, thin pliable wire, bunches of rosebuds or berries, pinecones, glue, ribbon, needle and thread. For spraying pinecones beforehand: spray paint, newspaper**

1 Use the thick wire to make a hanger across the back of the wreath base, inserting it between vine stems and winding the ends tightly to secure them. The wire should be short enough to be invisible when the wreath is hung.

2 Strip the leaves from the bases of the evergreen stems and cut to uniform length with shears. Insert them firmly into the wreath so that they overlap and all point the same way. Bind them into place with thin wire until the wreath base is covered.

3 Wrap wire around the trimmed stems of the rosebuds to create small bunches, leaving a tail of wire for pinning to the wreath. Add to the wreath, pushing the wire around the vine stems at the back. Trim off any excess wire with shears.

4 Apply glue to the bases of the pinecones and add at different angles around the wreath. Allow to dry completely. You could also attach the cones using wire. Finally, wind ribbon around the wreath and sew or glue the ends together. Hang up.

prevent
Wrinkles

Wrinkles are inevitable and not all bad (think of laugh lines). Moisturizing can help, but a healthy lifestyle is more important.

■ Eat well (*see* DIET). Have more olive oil, fish, low-fat milk, fruit, vegetables, eggs, nuts and beans. Have less butter, red meat, cakes, pastries, soft drinks, whole milk, margarine, fries and other fried foods.

■ Make sure there are plenty of vitamins in your diet (*see* VITAMINS). Foods rich in vitamin C—such as berries, red peppers and broccoli—can help to maintain skin elasticity.

■ Keep well hydrated by drinking water and not too much alcohol.

■ Cigarettes are ruinous to the complexion as well as to your general health, so try to quit (*see* SMOKING).

■ For "glamorous sun tan" read "solar damage." Use a sunblock. Wear sunglasses in bright light.

■ Don't drink through straws; they can cause wrinkles around the mouth.

■ Sleep on your back so your face isn't constantly crumpled at night. Use soft pillowcases.

■ Avoid frown lines; cultivate a positive state of mind. Don't worry, be happy!

play the
Xylophone

A xylophone is arranged like a piano keyboard (*see* PIANO). You strike the wooden bars with mallets to produce a note. Hold the mallets close to their midpoint, so that they are balanced, and orient them at a slight inward angle. The shorter the bar, the higher the note—hence the xylophone's distinctive wedge shape. Some xylophones have just one row of keys; professional instruments have a second row of bars for sharps and flats (like the black notes on a piano).

■ If you're a beginner, try picking out a tune with one mallet; this will be easy to do if you're familiar with the piano.
■ As you get better, play with a mallet in each hand to create harmonies, and to play phrases more quickly. Really skilled players can wield two mallets in each hand, and so play a maximum of four notes at a time.

master essential Yoga positions

Yoga improves your flexibility, strength and ability to relax. All you need are a yoga mat, clothes that let you move easily and a quiet space.

Practice at least three times a week, but never push yourself further than you can comfortably go. Breathe smoothly through the nostrils, and keep focused. Start with simple postures and always end a session with a few minutes of relaxed breathing, lying on your back. Avoid doing yoga after a meal, and take medical advice before starting if you have any health concerns or are pregnant. Here are some beginner's postures to try. Take between three to ten breaths in each position.

Triangle Stand tall, move your legs comfortably apart and extend your arms out. Point your right foot out, exhale and bend to the right, stretching your right hand toward your ankle and your left toward the ceiling. Look up at your hand and breathe. Hold the pose. Then breathe in and come up. Repeat on the right.

Modified twist Sit with your left leg straight or folded inward (as above). Cross your right foot over to the left side, foot flat. Place your left elbow inside the right knee and reach the hand toward the right ankle. Breathe in, sit up straight, exhale and turn to the right, with the right hand behind you. Repeat on the other side.

Downward dog Start on hands and knees. Tuck your toes under, exhale and raise your hips to form an inverted V. Lower your head, keep your arms and legs straight, with heels down. Push your chest toward your knees as you breathe out to flatten the curve in the upper back. Breathe, hold, then release. Hug your knees and rock from side to side.

Bridge Lie on your back, knees bent, legs hip-width apart, feet forward and arms to your sides. Bring your heels a little closer to the buttocks to make the shins vertical. Inhale and raise the middle of your body. Press arms and feet into the floor to lift yourself higher. Breathe, hold, then release. Hug your knees and rock from side to side.

post a video on YouTube

Posting a short piece of film on YouTube is simple to do—and it's a great way to share life events, opinions and know-how.

Whatever the subject of your video—highlights of your wedding or tips on playing blues guitar, for instance—spend some time making the film as good as you can (*see* FILM). Use the video-editing software on your computer to create something that's both slick and brief. Most YouTube users won't want to watch anything that's longer than a couple of minutes.

■ Before you can upload a finished video clip, you must first register with YouTube. Go to the site and follow the instructions for setting up an account. Once you're registered, you can post videos straight away.
■ Click on **Upload** and then **Upload video**, and specify the file that you want to make public on YouTube; double-click on it to begin the upload.
■ While the film is uploading, give it a title and description along with some keywords, so that your work can be found by people using search engines.

There will be a delay of half an hour or so before your video appears on the site. You'll receive an email notification with a link to its location. Pass the web address on to anyone you think might be interested.

----

learn basic Yo-yo moves

Playing with a yo-yo is addictive, fun and easy to learn. You'll be performing gravity-defying tricks in no time at all.

Basic throw Hold the yo-yo in your palm with the string loop around the middle finger. Curl your arm up beside your ear, palm to the back. Unfurl your arm so that the yo-yo arcs out over your fingertips. When it reaches the end of the string, flip your hand over to pull the yo-yo back up.

Sleeper For your first trick, perform the basic throw with extra speed. The yo-yo should spin ("sleep") at the end of the string until you jerk your hand to wake the yo-yo up and bring it spinning back to your hand.

Walk the dog

1 Throw the sleeper move as described above. As the yo-yo spins on the end of the string touch it lightly to the floor and it will scuttle forward.

2 Flip your hand palm down and give a slight upward jerk. The obedient yo-yo will leap back to your hand. Good doggy!

make perfect
Yorkshire pudding

This traditional English accompaniment to roast beef is popular in some areas of North America, too. The secret to success is piping hot fat and a very hot oven. It can be made as a single dish or as individual popovers, which can cook while the meat rests before carving. With pepper omitted it can be enjoyed as a dessert, topped with maple syrup or poached fruit.

SERVES 4: MAKES 1 LARGE OR 12 INDIVIDUAL PUDDINGS

1 cup all-purpose flour
2 eggs
1¼ cup 1% milk
salt and freshly ground black pepper
2 tbsp canola oil

1 Heat the oven to 425°F (220°C). Sift the flour into a bowl, make a well in the center and add the eggs. Work in the flour, then beat in the milk and seasonings with an electric beater. Alternatively, mix all the ingredients in a food processor.

2 Put the oil into a 12 x 8-in. (28 cm x 18 cm) roasting pan or use it to grease a 12-hole muffin pan. Put your chosen container into the oven, placed on a baking sheet. When the oil is very hot, remove it and pour in the batter mixture. If the fat is at the right temperature, the batter should sizzle as you pour it in. Replace onto the baking sheet. Cook a single pudding for 25-30 minutes, and individual ones for 15-20 minutes, or until crisp and well risen. Serve at once.

make Zabaglione

This rich, impressive Italian dessert is much easier to create than it looks. But it must be made immediately before serving, as it will begin to separate in just five minutes. A key ingredient is Marsala, a fortified Italian wine available in many wine stores.

SERVES 4

4 egg yolks
¼ cup sugar
⅓ cup Marsala
toasted sliced almonds, to garnish
almond biscotti, to serve

1 Put the egg yolks into an ovenproof bowl, add the sugar and briskly whisk together for about a minute. Gradually add the Marsala and whisk in gently.

2 Place the bowl over a pan of simmering water and heat, whisking constantly, for about 10-15 minutes until the mixture is thick and creamy and stands in soft peaks. Spoon into individual glasses and top each with a few almonds. Serve at once accompanied by the almond biscotti.

■ While heating the mixture, don't let the bottom of the bowl touch the simmering water or the eggs may cook too quickly and scramble.

fix a Zipper quickly

Just running the tab up and down may be enough to cure a sticky zipper, but if teeth are broken you may need to replace it. Or try these quick fixes.

Stuck teeth Apply a small amount of lip balm to the teeth and run the zipper up and down. Or try rubbing the teeth with a candle or pencil lead.

Broken pull tab Replace the tab with a paperclip, then bind the clip with thread of a matching or contrasting color.

Slider detached from the bottom teeth Pull the slider to the zipper base, then make a cut into the zipper tape between the teeth about ¼ in. (6 mm) above the slider on the unattached side. Work the teeth into the slider. Pull up the zipper, then use a needle and thread to oversew the two sides of the zipper together just above the cut to form a new stop for the runner.

replace a Zipper

When a zipper breaks on a favorite pair of pants it pays to be able to replace it yourself—but it's essential to make sure that the new and old zippers match exactly in length and as closely as possible in color and weight. This easy technique can be adapted to replace zippers on other garments.

YOU WILL NEED Stitch ripper, small scissors, new zipper, pins, thread, needle. Optional: sewing machine with zipper foot

1 Take out the old zipper, using a stitch ripper to release only the stitches that are holding it in place. Don't undo the waistband stitching but use small scissors to cut off the old zipper at the top.

2 Pin one side of the new zipper to the base of the crotch, then pin into place up to the waistband. Fold the top of the zipper tape under so that the top teeth lie flush with the bottom of the waistband. Tack, then sew into position by hand, using a small neat backstitch (*see* SEWING *and* TACK), or by machine using the zipper foot.

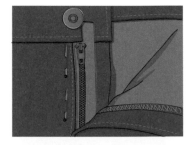

3 Close the zipper, turn the pants inside out, and lay them flat. Pin, then tack, the second side of the zipper into position, again folding under the top of the zipper tape. Backstitch into position by hand, taking care to stitch through only one layer of fabric so that stitches don't show on the outside.

4 On the inside, make a ½-in. (1 cm) row of small, tight overlapping stitches (a bar tack) below the bottom of the new zipper to create a strong hold.

recognize signs of the Zodiac

The complex and arcane system of astrology takes as its starting point 12 signs determined by the position of the sun at the time of birth.

Birth sign	Symbol	Date and type	Characteristics
ARIES *the ram*		March 21-April 19 Cardinal. Element: fire	Impulsive, strong-minded, honest and trusting, dominant, short fuse
TAURUS *the bull*		April 20-May 20 Fixed. Element: earth	Patient, dependable, resolute, practical, loyal, won't budge
GEMINI *the twins*		May 21-June 21 Mutable. Element: air	Versatile, expressive, silver-tongued, changeful, easily bored
CANCER *the crab*		June 22-July 22 Cardinal. Element: water	Tenacious, intuitive, emotional, sensitive, empathetic, traditional, moody
LEO *the lion*		July 23-August 22 Fixed. Element: fire	Lion-hearted, idealistic, dignified, romantic, aspiring, overbearing
VIRGO *the virgin*		August 23-September 22 Mutable. Element: earth	Gentle, hard-working, reliable, sincere, methodical, worrier
LIBRA *the scales*		September 23-October 23 Cardinal. Element: air	Artistic, eloquent, diplomatic, logical, passion for justice, indecisive, fickle
SCORPIO *the scorpion*		October 24-November 21 Fixed. Element: water	Passionate, loyal, resourceful, driven, private, temperamental, doesn't suffer fools gladly
SAGITTARIUS *the archer*		November 22-December 21 Mutable. Element: fire	Friendly, open-handed, open-hearted, confident, honest, fractious, blunt
CAPRICORN *the goat*		December 22-January 19 Cardinal. Element: earth	Earnest, reliable, industrious, cautious, traditional, responsible, bears grudges
AQUARIUS *the water carrier*		January 20-February 18 Fixed. Element: air	Independent, broad-minded, curious, penetrating, progressive, willful
PISCES *the fish*		February 19-March 20 Mutable. Element: water	Sensitive, humane, adaptable, idealistic, good intuition, vulnerable

Each birth sign is governed by a dominant element with symbolic meanings. **Fire** denotes creativity, intuition, a spirit of adventure, the visionary. **Earth** denotes practicality, objectivity, stability—indeed, a sense of being "gounded." **Air** denotes the thinker, with high principles and impartiality, the conceiver of concepts. **Water** denotes a feeling and receptive soul, empathy, understanding and instinct. Additionally, the signs of the zodiac are divided into Cardinal, Fixed and Mutable signs. **Cardinal** signs are characterized by enterprise. **Fixed** signs are characterized by firmness and stability. **Mutable** signs are characterized by adaptability.

INDEX

A

abdominal thrust *see*
  Heimlich maneuver
address labels, creating 6
aerobic exercise 6-7, 171, 206
air travel
  airport check-in 7
  deep vein thrombosis 101
  flight upgrades 136
  jet lag 181
alarm clocks 293
alcohol
  champagne fizz, keeping 63
  champagne, uncorking 63
  cocktails 76-7
  hangovers 159
  hot toddy 172
  parties, quantities for 228
  units 7
  see also wine
allergic reactions
  allergy emergencies 8
  bee sting 26
  hay fever 162
  mosquito bites 209
  wasp stings 351
allergy shots 162
anaphylaxis 8
anchor, dropping 8
animal tracks, identify 9
animal odors 8
animal welfare 286
antacids 164
ants 9
aphids 9
apostrophes 10
appendicitis 10
apples
  apple trees, pruning 147
  toffee apples 333
appliqué 10
aquariums
  emptying 288
  goldfish 150
  setting up 11
architectural styles 12-3
arguments, winning 11
aromatherapy 315
art
  canvas preparation 48
  oil painting 220-1
  portraits 111
  watercolor painting 355
  see also crafts
asparagus 14
asthma attacks 14
astrology 373
astronomy 310-1
athlete's foot 14
attics, insulation 176
avalanche, surviving 14

B

babies
  bathing 19
  childbirth 67
  choking 70
  colic 78
  cradle cap 88
  diaper changing 19
  feeding 19
  fever 126
  looking after 18-9
  routine 18
  sleep time 18
  teething 325
  see also children
baby equipment, sterilizing
  313
backgammon 15
backpacks, packing 15
bad breath 16
badminton 16
bad news, delivering 16
bad weather driving 112-3
ballet 17
balloon animals 17
ball, throwing and catching 17
bandages and slings 20-1, 294
barbecue, lighting 20
baseball 21
basin, blocked 289
basketball 22
bath, resealing 22
bathrooms
  condensation 82
  painting 224
  safety 22
  shower head, descaling 102
batteries
  battery life 23, 179
  iPhones 179
  rechargeable 23
battleships (game) 23
beadwork 23-24
beards, trimming 24
Béarnaise sauce 169
bed bugs 202
bed linen 25, 93
  duvet covers 116
  quilted cover 253
bed-making 25
beef
  beef stock 26
  Bolognese sauce 34
  carving 55
  chilli con carne 68
  cuts 24-5
  goulash 151
  hamburgers 158
  roasting 261
  steak, cooking 309

beer, pouring 26
bee stings 8, 26
bee swarms 26
best before dates 314
bicycles
  maintenance 28-9
  punctures 250-1
bingo 26
birds
  birdhouses 27
  garden pests 146
bites and stings
  bee stings 8, 26
  dog bites 106
  mosquito bites 209
  wasp stings 351
black butter 45
black eyes 42
blackjack 27
bleeding
  first aid 30
  head injuries 163
blindman's buff 31
blinds
  measuring for 30
  roller blind, installing
    30-31
  venetian blinds, cleaning
    344
blinis 31
blisters 31, 45
blockages
  dishwashers 104
  drains 110
  gutters 156
  sinks and basins 289
  toilets 334
  washing machines 351
  waste disposal units 354
blogs 32
blood pressure monitor 32
bloodstains 54, 307
Bloody Mary 77
Bluetooth technology 32, 234
board games
  backgammon 15
  chess 65
  darts 99
  Monopoly 208
  Scrabble 275
body language 33
body mass index (BMI) 33
bonfires 34
bonsai trees 35
books, covering 35, 313
bores, escaping from 36
bottles, cleaning and
    sterilizing 36, 312
bottling 144
boules 36
bowling *see* tenpin bowling
bow tie, tying 36-7
brainstorming 37

bra, measuring up for a 37
brass, cleaning 37
bread
  freezing 143
  making 38-9
  soda bread 297
  stale bread, uses for 39
breakdowns 210
breast examination 39
breastfeeding 78
brickwork
  painting 100
  re-pointing 258
bridge 40-1
broadband speed 40
broken bones 41
broken heart, mending 41
brown butter 45
brownies 42
bruises 41
bulbs
  deadheading 100
  planting 42-3
bullies, dealing with 43
bunions 44
burglar alarms 44
burglars 44
burns and scalds 45
buttons, sewing on 45

C

cacti, growing 46
cakes
  brownies 42
  chocolate cake 69
  decorating 48-9
  freezing 143
  fruitcake 145
  marzipan covering 201
  Victoria spongecake 345
calligraphy 46
calorie cutting 47
camcorders 127
camper, backing up 52
camping
  campfires 47
  campsite, finding 47
  tent, erecting 329
canapés 47, 50, 228
canasta 50
candle making 51
candlewax removal 54
canvas shoes, cleaning 285
car
  accidents 51
  bad weather 112
  cleaning 53
  first-aid kit 130
  games 58-9
  locks, unfreezing 52
  paint scratches 53
  parking in tight spaces 227

Acknowledgments

The publishers would like to thank the following people and organizations for their help and advice:

Sophie Adwick, Wildlife Expert, RSPB; Mark Allen, Scottish Wildfire Forum; Association of British Insurers; Bernice Bass, The British Tenpin Bowling Association; Kate Beddington-Brown, CIFAS – The UK's Fraud Prevention Service; Dave Berriman, National Coaching Officer, English Table Tennis Association; Karen Bessant, Feline Advisory Bureau, International Society of Feline Medicine; The Boarding House, Exeter; British Airways; The British Darts Organization; British Judo Association; British Veterinary Association; Paul Calland, Deputy Station Officer, Morecambe Search and Rescue; Simon Carter, The Scout Association; Liane Cowther, Training Manager, The Horse Trust; Tim Daniels, www.poultrykeeper.com; Mark Diggins, Sportscotland Avalanche Information Service; Dolphin Surf School, Newquay, Cornwall; Patrick Donovan, Chief Executive Officer, British Water Ski & Wakeboard; Nick Eden, Director, Arboricultural Association; Food Standards Agency; Karen Ford, Head of Trading Standards, Milton Keynes Council; Kay Gallagher, The National Bed Federation Ltd; William Gorman, The United Kingdom Tea Council Ltd; Christine Gray, The British Beekeepers Association; Neil Greig, Director of Policy and Research, Peter Rodger, Chief Examiner, and Caroline Homes, Communications Officer, IAM (Institute of Advanced Motorists); Jo Hampson, Smoky Jo's; Roy Henderson, British Association of Skiing Instructors; Phil Holden, Department of Earth Sciences, Open University, Milton Keynes; Keith Horton, Chief Executive, National Ice Skating Association; Pam Horton, British Wheel of Yoga; Alison Howard, Rounders England; Darren Jehan, Bedford Astronomical Society; Lucy Jessop, Architectural Investigator, English Heritage; Kelvin Jones, English Association of Snooker & Billiards; Ryan Jones, England Squash and Racketball; Andrew Kennedy, www.just-fish.co.uk; Elizabeth Larsson, The Croquet Association; Bob Leeds, Football Development Officer, Amateur Football Association; London Luton Airport; Annette Love, Creative Plus Publishing Ltd; Andrew McGrorey, Road Risk Advisory Team, Bedford Borough Council; Faith Mall, Fairtrade; Julian Marczak, President, Association of British Riding Schools; Rosie Mayglothling, Technical Co-ordinator, GB Rowing Team; Pet Owners Association; Pro Coach Cricket Academy, Yorkshire County Cricket Club; Miles Quest, British Hospitality Association; David Radford, www.taichifinder.co.uk; Andrew Reid, High Performance Coach, Swim Ulster; Royal College of Midwives; RYA (Royal Yachting Association); Lauren Sanderson, Amateur Swimming Association; Emma Scott, Professional Affairs Manager, The Textile Institute; Brian Seabright, British Karate Association; Simon Selmon, London Swing Dance Society; Duncan Sivell, Biodiversity Officer, Buglife – The Invertebrate Conservation Trust, Claire Small, Clinical Director, Pure Sports Medicine; David Smith, Performance Coach, Pure Sports Medicine; Karen Sparrow, Optometrist and Education Adviser at the Association of Optometrists (AOP); Richard Stacey-Chapman, Technical Administrator, Volleyball England; Rachelle Stretch, English Amateur Dancesport Association; Dan Thorp, Lawn Tennis Association; Greg Tilbury, PGA Professional, Wavendon Golf Centre; Danielle Waller, Events Manager, SpeedDater Ltd; Sean Wensley, PDSA Senior Veterinary Surgeon, The People's Dispensary for Sick Animals; Chris Whitehead, Chairman, Bristol Pool League; Richard Whitehouse, www.TheGoodGamblingGuide.co.uk; Michelle Whiteman, UK Payments Administration Ltd; Rosie Worrall, Milton Keynes Cats Rescue; Loo Yeo, CID UNESCO, Salsa & Merengue Society; www.hensforhomes.co.uk; www.thetropicaltank.co.uk

Picture credits

T = top; C = center; B = bottom; A = above; L = left; R = right

Front Cover: ShutterStock, Inc, iStockphoto.com; **4 R** ShutterStock, Inc/Oorka; **7** iStockphoto.com/Troels Graugaard; **12 CL** Alamy Images/Robert Harding Picture Library Ltd, **BL** Alamy Images/Ben Ramos, **BR** Alamy Images/bluudaisy; **13** Alamy Images/GFC Collection, **TR** Alamy Images/Images Etc. Ltd, **BR** Alamy Images/Sandra Baker; **14** © RD; **15** ShutterStock, Inc/Anke van Wyk; **18** Getty Images/Gary Houlder; **19 T** Baby Archive, **B** iStockphoto.com; **20** ShutterStock, Inc/Lasse Kristensen; **22** Getty Images/Dorling Kindersley; **26** Getty Images/Tom Grill; **28-29** ShutterStock, Inc/Gravicapa; **30** © RD; **31** Getty Images/Dorling Kindersley; **32** iStockphoto.com/Okea; **33 TL** iStockphoto.com/4x6, **TC** iStockphoto.com/Francisco Romero, **TR** iStockphoto.com/Nicolas Hansen, **BL** iStockphoto.com/Angela Hawkey, **BC** iStockphoto.com/Zone Creative, **BR** Photolibrary.com/Daniel Ehrenworth; **34** Getty Images/Myles New; **40** iStockphoto.com/Olada; **42 T** ShutterStock, Inc/Audi Dela Cruz, **B** © RD; **43** © RD; **47 L** ShutterStock, Inc/bonchan, **C** ShutterStock, Inc/Victor1, **R** iStockphoto.com/Robert Anthony; **48** Photolibrary.com/Michael Powell; **50** iStockphoto.com/Edward O'Neil Photography Inc; **51 TL** Photolibrary.com/Joy Skipper, **TC** Photolibrary.com/Foodfolio, **TR** Photolibrary.com/Eaglemoss Consumer Publications, **CR** © RD, **BR** Photolibrary.com/More Images (Oceania); **52** iStockphoto.com/Brian Jackson; **56** iStockphoto.com/Travellinglight; **57** © RD; **58 T** ShutterStock, Inc/Anat-Oli, **B** Getty Images/National Geographic; **59 TL** ShutterStock, Inc/Aleksandra Duda, **TR** ShutterStock, Inc/Richard Peterson, **C** ShutterStock, Inc/Lantapix, **CB** ShutterStock, Inc/photo-master, **BRA** ShutterStock, Inc/z-art, **B** ShutterStock, Inc/Rocket 400 Studio, **BL** ShutterStock, Inc/Subbotina Anna; **61-62** © RD; **64** ShutterStock, Inc/Creatista; **65 T** ShutterStock, Inc/Carsten Reisinger; **66 & 67 T** © RD, **BL** ShutterStock, Inc/S_Oleg, **BR** ShutterStock, Inc/Ersin Kurtdal; **68 BR** B. Speckart/Shutterstock; **69** Getty Images/Ian O'Leary; **70** © RD; **71** www.garden-collection.com/Marie O'Hara; **72-73** Home Laundering Consultative Council/www.care-labelling.co.uk; **76** iStockphoto.com/Cameron Whitman; **77 TL** iStockphoto.com/okea, **TC** iStockphoto.com/Ergeny Karandaev, **TR** iStockphoto.com/Rebecca Ellis, **BL** iStockphoto.com/Ivan Mateev, **BC** iStockphoto.com/Rebecca Ellis, **BR** iStockphoto.com/Steve Cukrov; **79 L** Corbis/Ocean, **C** Pubilc Domain, **R** ShutterStock, Inc/Chrislofoto; **81** © RD; **82** ShutterStock, Inc/chrisbrignell; **83** © RD; **84** Getty Images/GAP Photos; **85-88** © RD; **89** Getty Images/Anna Williams; **94** Photolibrary.com/David Marsden; **99** ShutterStock, Inc/Tonn; **103** © RD; **105** Getty Images/Andy Crawford; **107** ShutterStock, Inc/homydesign; **108-109** © RD; **112 TL&BL** © RD; **112-113** Alamy Images/Alvey & Towers Picture Library; **113 L** Alamy Images/Mint Photography, **R** Getty Images/Andrew Bret Wallis; **119 L** © RD, **R** ShutterStock, Inc/mates; **126** © RD; **127 T** ShutterStock, Inc/niderlander, **B** ShutterStock, Inc/Dmitriy Shironosov; **128 TR, C&CR** © RD, **BL** Science Photo Library/Mark Sykes; **129** ShutterStock, Inc/Wiktor Bubriak; **132 T** Photolibrary.com/Maximilian Stock Ltd, **B** Dorling Kindersley/Jerry Young; **133** Photolibrary.com/Tony Robins; **134** ShutterStock, Inc/Woodsy; **135-137** © RD; **139** Getty Images/Matthew Ward; **142 L** ShutterStock, Inc/Rey Kamensky; **145** Photolibrary.com/Sian Irvine; **146** www.garden-collection.com/Neil Sutherland; **148 L** Photolibrary.com/Fresh Food Images, **C** Alamy Images/Bon Appetit, **R** Photolibrary.com/Photocuisine; **150** ShutterStock, Inc/Tischenko Irina; **151** © RD; **152** Phil Sheldon Picture Library/Phil Sheldon; **153 T** Golf Picture Library/Matthew Harris, **CL, C&CR** Phil Sheldon Picture Library/Phil Sheldon, **B** Phil Sheldon Picture Library/Hugh Routledge; **154** © RD; **157 T** Getty Images/Dorling Kindersley, **B** www.theassayoffice.co.uk/gem@theassayoffice.co.uk; **160 BL** Getty Images/Wire Image, **BR** Rex Features Ltd/Matt Baron/BEI; **161 TL** Rex Features Ltd/Startraks Photo; **163-164** © RD; **165** Getty Images/Peter Anderson; **168 T** Photolibrary.com/Imagebroker; **169** Getty Images/Ryan McVay; **173** ShutterStock, Inc/Oliver Hoffman; **175-176** © RD; **180 T** Getty Images/Jerry Young, **BL&BR** Dorling Kindersley/Dorling Kindersley; **181** © RD; **182 T** iStockphoto.com/AndersonAnderson, **B** © RD; **185 R** ShutterStock, Inc/Muellek Josef; **187** Photolibrary.com/Photodisc; **190** www.garden-collection.com/Derek St Romaine; **191** www.garden-collection.com/Liz Eddison; **194** Bloomberg via Getty Images; **195** Getty Images/Ivo Noppen; **198** ShutterStock, Inc/Chepko Danil Vitalevich; **200 L** Photolibrary.com/Norman Hollands, **R** Photolibrary.com/Fresh Food Images; **205 T** Photolibrary.com/Monkey Business Images Ltd, **B** Alamy Images/Medical-on-Line; **206** ShutterStock, Inc/Sergey Kamshylin; **210 T** Ruslan Olinchuk/Fotolia, **L** Science Photo Library/Dr. John Brackenbury; **211** www.garden-collection.com/Jonathan Buckley; **213-219** © RD; **220 R** Eaglemoss Publications; **221** Photolibrary.com/Amanda Heywood; **222** ShutterStock, Inc/Ioannis Pantziaras; **223-225** © RD; **226** Photolibrary.com/Fresh Food Images; **228** © RD; **229 L** ShutterStock, Inc/Iwona Grodzka, **229 R & 231** © RD; **232 L** ShutterStock, Inc/barbaradudzinska, **R** ShutterStock, Inc/Subbotina Anna; **233** Getty Images/James Ross; **235** Photolibrary.com/Ingram Publishing; **236** Photolibrary.com/Fresh Food Images; **237** © RD; **238** Photolibrary.com/Fresh Food Images; **240** © RD; **241** ShutterStock, Inc/Monkey Business Images; **242-244** © RD; **245** ShutterStock, Inc/Terrace Studio; **246 L** ShutterStock, Inc/Miguel Andel Salinas Salinas; **248 TC** ShutterStock, Inc/pzAxe, **TR** © RD, **BR** ShutterStock, Inc/ER_09; **249-251** © RD; **252 TR** ShutterStock, Inc/Oorka; **254 L** © RD; **256 TL** Getty Images/Philip Wilkins, **C&BR** © RD; **257** © RD; **258** Alamy Images/David Gee 3; **259** ShutterStock, Inc/Sunnys; **260** Photolibrary.com/Datacraft; **261** Photolibrary.com/Fresh Food Images/Steve Lee; **264 T** www.garden collection.com/Liz Eddison, **L** www.garden-collection.com/Nicola Stocken Tomkins, **BR** www.garden-collection.com/Jonathan Buckley; **265 R** www.garden-collection.com/Liz Eddison, **Inset** © RD; **266 TR** ShutterStock, Inc/Alhovik; **267 C** ShutterStock, Inc/Neda; **269** Getty Images/Annabelle Breakey; **271** Getty Images/Ann Stratton; **272** Photolibrary.com/Tony West; **273** Alamy Images/Philip Bird; **275-280 T** © RD; **282** www.garden-collection.com/Jonathan Buckley, **B** Gap Photos Ltd/Maxine Adcock; **282-283** Gap Photos Ltd/J S Sira; **283** Gap Photos Ltd/Friedrich Strauss; **287-289** © RD; **291** ShutterStock, Inc/Jorg Hackermann; **294 L** www.garden-collection.com/Torie Chugg, **TR** © RD; **296** ShutterStock, Inc/Leodor; **297** Photolibrary.com/Fresh Food Images/Philip Wilkins; **298 & 299 T** © RD, **299 B** Photolibrary.com/Blue Moon Images; **300 T** Photolibrary.com/Fresh Food Images/Huw Jones, **B** © Fotolia; **301** U.P.images/Fotolia; **302-303** Science Photo Library/Dr. P. Marazzi; **305** Dorling Kindersley/Jerry Young; **308** © RD; **310-311** Science Photo Library/Babak Tafreshi; **312** © RD; **313** Photolibrary.com/Fresh Food Images/Martin Brigdate; **314-316 TC, TR, BC & BR** © RD, **BL** ShutterStock, Inc/Wendy Kaveney Photography; **319 L** Getty Images/Brand X/James & James; **324-326 L** © RD; **328 L** Photolibrary.com; **330** Alamy Images; **332-334** © RD; **335** Photolibrary.com/Imagebroker.net/Bodo Schiere; **336-338** © RD; **340** Photolibrary.com/Imagebroker.net/Jochen Jack; **341** © RD; **345** Photolibrary.com/Fresh Food Images/Tim Hill; **348** Photolibrary.com/Fresh Food Images/Philippe Desnerck; **349 L** ShutterStock, Inc/Auremar, **R** Photolibrary.com/Food Collection; **351** © RD; **352 T** www.gapinteriors.com/Clive Nichols, **C** www.gapinteriors.com/Costas Picadas, **BL** © RD, **BR** www.gapinteriors.com/Rachel Smith; **353** © RD; **355** Eaglemoss Publications; **357** ShutterStock, Inc/Sky Light Pictures; **359** ShutterStock, Inc/Francesco Abrignani; **361-362** © RD; **365 T** ShutterStock, Inc/DVARG, **B** iStockphoto.com/eAlisa; **366** SuperStock Ltd./NHPA; **367** www.garden-collection.com/Marie O'Hara; **370** SuperStock Ltd./fstop; **373** ShutterStock, Inc/Cihan Demirok/CIDEPIX

How To Do Just About Anything

Project team

Project Editor Jesse Corbeil
Associate Editor Madeline Coleman
Senior Designer Andrée Payette
Designers Anne Devoe, Chris A. Cant
Proofreader Alison Ramsey
US Managing Editor Lorraine Burton
US Contributing Editor Stephanie Schwartz
Cover Designer George McKeon
Manager, Book Editorial Pamela Johnson
Vice President Editorial Robert Goyette

Writers Jonathan Bastable, Ruth Binney, Rose Shepherd

Illustrators Galia Bernstein/nb illustration, Chris A. Cant/RD, Maurizio De Angelis/Beehive Illustration, Jo Goodberry/nb illustration, Ben Hasler/nb illustration, Scott Jessop/nb illustration, John Ley/a3 studios, Ian Moores Graphics, Sylvie Pinsonneaux/Eye Candy Illustration, Martin Sanders/Beehive Illustration, Glyn Walton/linedesign, Graham White/nb illustration, Darren Whittington/PhosphorArt, John Woodcock, Lee Woodgate/Son of Alan

Authenticators Glynis Barnes-Mellish, Katharine Goddard, David Holloway, Franka Knight, Margaret Maino, Elizabeth Marsh, Sheena Meredith, Patsy North, Cheryl Owen, Tony Rilett, Angelika Romacker, Sara Withers, Rachel Yallop

READER'S DIGEST ASSOCIATION, INC

President & Chief Executive Officer Robert E. Guth
Executive Vice President, RDA and President, North America Dan Lagani
Executive Vice President, RDA and President, Allrecipes.com Lisa Sharples
Executive Vice President, RDA and President, Europe Dawn Zier

Copyright © 2012 by The Reader's Digest Association, Inc.
Copyright © 2012 by Reader's Digest Association (Canada) ULC
Copyright © 2012 by The Reader's Digest Association Far East Ltd.
Philippine Copyright © 2012 by The Reader's Digest Association Far East Ltd.

Library and Archives Canada Cataloguing in Publication

How to do just about anything : solve problems, save money, have fun / the editors at Reader's Digest.

Includes index.
ISBN 978-1-55475-100-6 (hardcover)
ISBN 978-1-60652-414-5 (softcover)

1. Handbooks, vade-mecums, etc.
I. Reader's Digest Association (Canada)

AG105.H853 2012   031.02   C2011-907655-1

We are committed both to the quality of our products and the service we provide to our customers. If you have any comments about the content of this book, write to:

Book Editor, Reader's Digest Association (Canada) ULC, 1100 René-Lévesque Blvd. W., Montreal QC H3B 5H5

or

Book Editor, Reader's Digest Association, Inc.
Adult Trade Publishing
44 South Broadway
White Plains, NY 10601

To order copies of How To Do Just About Anything, visit us at our online store:

In the US: **www.rd.com**
In Canada: **www.readersdigest.ca**

Printed in China

3 5 7 9 10 8 6 4 2 (hardcover)
3 5 7 9 10 8 6 4 2 (paperback)

Note to Readers
The information in this book should not be substituted for, or used to alter, medical therapy without your doctor's advice. For a specific health problem, consult your physician for guidance. The mention of any products, retail businesses, or websites in this book does not imply or constitute an endorsement by the authors or by The Reader's Digest Association, Inc. or by Reader's Digest Association (Canada) ULC.

While the creators of this work have made every effort to ensure safety and accuracy, the publishers cannot be held liable for injuries suffered or losses incurred as a result of following the instructions contained within the book. Readers should study the information carefully and make sure they understand it before undertaking any work. Always observe any warnings. Readers are also recommended to consult qualified professionals for advice.